Providence & Patriotism in Early America 1640-1815

Providence & Patriotism in Early America 1640-1815

John F. Berens

University Press of Virginia
Charlottesville

THE UNIVERSITY PRESS OF VIRGINIA

First published 1978

Library of Congress Cataloging in Publication Data
Berens, John F
Providence and patriotism in early America, 1640–1815.
Bibliography: p.
Includes index.
1. United States—Civilization—To 1783. 2. United States—Civilization—1783–1865. 3. Nationalism—United States—History. 4. Providence and Government of God. I. Title. E162.B45
973 78-5889 ISBN 0-8139-0779-9

Printed in the United States of America

For my mother and father

Contents

Preface

At the very beginning of this study I wish to make clear one point of terminology in the hope of avoiding confusion in the pages that follow. I have chosen to call the cluster of ideas and images which are the subject of this study *providential thought.* I realize that to some readers the rhetoric I will discuss resembles what other scholars have termed *civil millennialism*—the wedding of American destiny and millennial visions. I have deliberately minimized use of the concept of millennial thought (except at two points briefly in chapters 1 and 5) because I think the concept, while relevant, is too restrictive for the subject of my study.

My point of view can perhaps best be illustrated by referring to an insightful passage in Henry F. May's *The Enlightenment in America* ([New York, 1976], p. 251). May there distinguishes among three types of millennial thought in eighteenth-century America. First came what can be labeled *traditional millennialism*, propounded by those citizens ("most Americans") for whom "the millennium remained the period prophesied in the Bible, the return of Christ and his thousand-year reign." Both the *cause* (Divine Providence) and the *end* (the New Jerusalem) were religious. This was the millennialism of Jonathan Edwards and Samuel Davies, of Samuel Hopkins and Timothy Dwight, of John Leland and Jedidiah Morse—indeed, of almost all clerics of all Protestant denominations between 1740 and 1815. Second, May sees a sort of *civil millennialism* (not his phrase) in which the millennium "tended to be vaguely identified with the success of American institutions." This represented the transformation of millennial expectations into general celebrations of the "rising glory of America"; the *cause* was religious (Divine Providence) but the *end* was secular (the American empire for liberty). This was the millennialism of Philip Freneau and Hugh Henry Brackenridge, and of most of the hundreds of Fourth of July orations delivered after 1783. Finally, May traces the rise after 1789 of what he terms *secular millennialism*—expectations of "some future overthrow of all injustice and tyranny on earth, and their replacement by universal brotherhood and peace." This was the millennialism of Tom Paine and Elihu Palmer—but of few other Americans. It was secular millennialism because God was essentially removed from the scheme; both the *cause* (human revolution) and the *end* (the universal republic) were secular. This final millennial strain was professed briefly in the 1790s by extreme defenders of the French Revolution, usually though not absolutely was connected with militant deism, and faded rapidly after 1800.

In the following study I have drawn at times on the ideas and writings of spokesmen for all three of these strains of millennialism. But my subject really approximates chiefly the second type—civil millennialism—and even here the equation is not complete. The concept of Divine Providence—that attribute of God which denoted his active intervention in human affairs to insure the actualization or acceleration of his established world plan—encompassed much more than millennial visions. Thus I have chosen to employ the term *providential thought* to refer to the welter of religious-nationalist ideas articulated in post-1740 America and to talk of millennialism only on those occasions where there was an expressed direct connection between providential rhetoric and the millennium.

Throughout this study I have quoted directly from the sources. Original spelling, italicization, capitalization, and punctuation have been retained (including erroneous or archaic spellings).

This work has gone through several evolutions since its inception. I wish to express my appreciation especially to Robert P. Hay, under whose careful and concerned guidance this work was first pursued. Furthermore, Karel D. Bicha, John D. Krugler, Francis Paul Prucha, S. J., and Michael G. Morrison, S.J., read earlier drafts of the manuscript; in each instance I have profited from their criticisms. I have also benefited greatly from the encouragement and critical assistance of my wife, Ruth D. Roebke-Berens. I alone, of course, am responsible for the conclusions of this study, as well as any errors it may contain.

The staffs of the Rare Book Division and the Newspaper Division of the Library of Congress provided invaluable assistance in my research efforts. I would also like to thank the staffs of the Marquette University Library, the University of Wisconsin-Milwaukee Library, the Library of the State Historical Society of Wisconsin, and the Milwaukee Public Library for assistance in obtaining materials.

Several pages of chapter 1 first appeared in my article "From Puritan to American Providential Thought," *Cithara: Essays in the Judaeo-Christian Tradition* 16 (1977); portions of chapter 3 in "'Good News From a Far Country': A Note on Divine Providence and the Stamp Act Crisis," *Church History* 45 (1976); and sections of chapters 3 and 4 in "'A God of Order and Not of Confusion': The American Loyalists and Divine Providence, 1774–1783," *Historical Magazine of the Protestant Episcopal Church* 47 (1978), published by the Church Historical Society. An earlier version of chapter 5 appeared as "The Sanctification of American Nationalism, 1789–1812: Prelude to Civil Religion in America," *Canadian Review of Studies in Nationalism* 3 (1976). I am grateful to the editors and publishers of these journals for permission to reprint these materials in the present study.

Providence & Patriotism in Early America 1640-1815

Introduction

UNTIL QUITE recently most traditional studies of the intellectual history of eighteenth-century America were organized around the thesis that the term *the American Enlightenment* best conceptualized the era. The composite picture of the American Enlightenment fashioned by scholars was a picture dominated in almost all areas by the concept of secularization. In religion the American Enlightenment supposedly substituted rational, natural religion, or deism, for orthodox Christianity. Likewise, faith in progress and the perfectibility of man, though not absolute, replaced earlier convictions of Original Sin and innate human depravity. In science and the natural realm the American Enlightenment replaced religious with secular analysis while retaining faith in a benevolent if ever-receding First Cause. And in historical composition the American Enlightenment supplanted providential with secular causation. Not all students of the American Enlightenment, to be sure, accepted every one of these conclusions, but the totality of their scholarship formed one broad thesis. That thesis was the secularization of American life, thought, and values in the course of the eighteenth century—"secularization" meaning the de-divinization of the universe, the elimination of the providential world view that had dominated American thought during the seventeenth century.[1]

One of the most significant historiographical developments of the

[1] See Peter Gay, "The Enlightenment," in *The Comparative Approach to American History*, ed. C. Vann Woodward (New York, 1968), pp. 34–46; Max Savelle, *Seeds of Liberty: The Genesis of the American Mind* (New York, 1948), pp. 53, 167; Merle Curti, *The Growth of American Thought*, 3d ed. (New York, 1964), pp. 73, 99; Howard Mumford Jones, *O Strange New World: American Culture, the Formative Years* (New York, 1964), pp. 206, 241–43; Clinton Rossiter, *Seedtime of Liberty: The Origin of the American Tradition of Political Liberty* (New York, 1953), pp. 136–37, 139, 205; Raymond P. Stearns, *Science in the British Colonies of America* (Urbana, Ill., 1970), p. 490; Russel B. Nye, *The Cultural Life of the New Nation, 1776–1830* (New York, 1960), pp. 3–4, 29, 31–33, 43, 61–65, 151–53, 173–75.

last two decades has been a challenge to this thesis. A growing number of scholars have reasserted the continuing relevance of religion and religious rhetoric to Americans before 1815.[2] This present study of providential thought in early America also challenges and balances the earlier theme of secularization. A majority of Americans between the French and Indian War and the War of 1812 manifested more a providential than an enlightened outlook on the events they experienced. There *was* an American Enlightenment, but it was more unlike than like the European Enlightenment. There was no comprehensive enlightened world view in America, at least at the popular level, which supplanted the providential world view that Americans had inherited from the seventeenth century.[3] There was transformation within American providential thought after 1763, but the basic world view of the seventeenth century was not discarded. On the contrary, it continued to serve Americans through and beyond the early national era.[4]

Basically, providential thought was comprised of concepts that were either imparted to early American patriotism by religion or originated elsewhere but were tremendously reinforced by religious images. The most important of these concepts were (1) the motif of America as God's New Israel; (2) the jeremiad tradition; (3) the deification of America's founding fathers; (4) the blending of national and millennial expectations; and (5) providential history and historiography. All of these concepts originated in the New World during the seventeenth century among the Puritans of New England, and chapter 1 attempts to trace the development of these ideas and their nationalization during the Great Awakening.

Chapter 2 discusses this process of the nationalization of Puritan concepts in the context of colonial responses to King George's War

[2] Here see the works (cited later in this study and listed in the bibliography) by such disparate scholars as Catherine Albanese, Bernard Bailyn, Christopher Beam, Carl Bridenbaugh, James Davidson, Nathan Hatch, Alan Heimert, Rhys Isaac, William McLoughlin, Glenn Miller, Perry Miller, Mark Noll, Cushing Strout, and Gordon Wood.

[3] This is the thesis convincingly argued by Henry F. May in his excellent *The Enlightenment in America* (New York, 1976). See especially p. xiv.

[4] See Henry F. May, "The Decline of Providence?" *Studies on Voltaire and the Eighteenth Century* 154 (1976): 1401–16.

and the French and Indian War. The period that began with the first dramatic New World journeys of George Whitefield and ended with the Peace of Paris included significant developments within American providential thought. Between 1740 and 1763 truly national providential concepts and images emerged; ideas that before 1740 had been applied solely to New England came to be applied and accepted in all of America. From the intellectual responses to the last two imperial wars against the French and their Indian allies came a cluster of themes: English America was a bastion of civil and religious freedoms; these freedoms had been achieved through God's design and providence; it was for the maintenance of these blessings that the Lord defended the colonies in times of danger. These interrelated themes in turn were joined to an ever-increasing *intercolonial* conviction that America was the New Israel. The fusion of all these ideas resulted in the first explicit expressions of the conviction that America had been assigned a providential mission somehow connected to the advancement of civil and religious freedom—a full thirteen years before the Declaration of Independence. The national providential concepts forged during the era of the imperial wars served Americans well during the succeeding fifty years of resistance, revolution, and nation-building.

The transformation between 1763 and 1776 of many of the providential themes that had emerged during the decades of the French and Indian wars is the subject of chapter 3. In the Revolutionary era patriotic colonists maintained and expanded the central themes, that God had uniquely blessed the New World as a land of civil and religious freedom and that, as the New Israel, America had a divine mission which concerned the preservation and perpetuation of those freedoms. Building on these tenets, and on the explicit providential language utilized in the 1740s and 1750s, patriots after 1763 made a strikingly easy shift in their perception of the chief threat to the fulfillment of America's mission. Quite simply these Americans, citing the various "conspiratorial" activities of the British ministry, Parliament, and king, argued that Great Britain had replaced France as the power most determined to destroy the colonies' God-given liberties. The colonies were therefore under the command of Divine Providence to resist their parent state, as they had previously resisted Papist France. Providential thought continued to explain best the historical events of the era; as the political and military developments of the great war for the empire had been ordained by Divine Providence for specific ends, so too were the events of the American Revolution. Patriot providential thought in the end cast the coming of the American Revolution as the plan of a benevolent deity and helped prepare and inspire Americans from New Hampshire to Georgia to take up arms to fight the Lord's battles. When the Continental Congress endorsed the Declaration of Independence in July 1776, the basic providential foundations of American patriotism were firmly established.

The activities of Divine Providence in human history, in specific political and military developments and their overriding meaning, constituted the major concern of patriot spokesmen after 1763. Much of the providential thought on these topics, not surprisingly, drew upon themes first articulated during the period of colonial wars. Two such themes were especially dominant. First, the cause of liberty was the cause of God, the overarching theme and aim of Providence in history. Second (and following directly), since America had been singularly exalted in her possession of liberty, her efforts to protect and preserve her rights against the "tyranny" of Britain were in accordance with the divine will. The threats to American liberty might shift, but America's perception of herself as uniquely blessed in her civil and religious institutions remained constant. A caveat to this generalization was filed by the American loyalists, who dissented from the conclusions of patriot providential rhetoric. But loyalist spokesmen nevertheless drew upon many of the same providential symbols and images as the patriots. The American Revolution was an intellectual as well as a military civil war.

Chapter 4 examines how patriots after 1776 fleshed out the many providential themes advanced during the preceding resistance era. The new nation, in the eyes of its citizens, emerged as the Republican Israel, with a glorious future and an equally glorious providential mission. However, other developments distinguished post-1776 from pre-1776 providential thought. During the "Critical Period" between the end of the Revolutionary War and the adoption of the Federal Constitution, providential thought was directed toward domestic partisan ends. Americans found that a broad providential consensus did not preclude ideological conflict within that consensus (as indeed had been foreshadowed by the patriot-loyalist split before 1776). Also, separate but parallel "popular" and "elite" strands of providential thought were enunciated. The Founding Fathers, to a surprising degree, both publicly and privately articulated the same providential images as their more common countrymen. The spokesmen of the American Enlightenment strengthened the legends of America's divine guidance and mission.

The final three chapters deal with providential thought during the early national period (1789–1815). Chapter 5 traces the sanctification of American nationalism during this era. This process stemmed from national uneasiness and apprehension. For Americans the years from the inauguration of George Washington in 1789 through the War of 1812 were troubled ones. Domestic and foreign realities were serious and potentially frightening. At home bitter partisan debate and the possibility of sectional disunion marked the era. The very newness of the United States was also unsettling. Patriots might try to make a virtue of necessity and boast that their nation was a noble experiment unencumbered by the decay of the past, but behind their boasts loomed the possibility of national failure. An experiment by its very nature was something untried, without precedents—and merely wishing it success would not guarantee it. Foreign developments also promoted American uneasiness, and again the situation was paradoxical. Many Americans celebrated the French Revolution as a glorious event, but they also realized that that upheaval threatened America's stability and independence. Europe was at war virtually without respite after 1793; no American could tell at what point the Old World would involve his country in a conflict that would result in national extinction. The early national era was for a significant number of Americans an era of stress, a time of uneasiness.[5]

The role of American nationalism was to overcome or at the least to temper this uneasiness. Nationalism, emphasizing common themes, would negate the divisions of the times and provide Ameri-

[5] This sense of uneasiness below the surface of optimistic bombast has been detected by a number of historians. The best summaries are in Marshall Smelser, "The Federalist Period as an Age of Passion," *American Quarterly* 10 (1958): 391–419, and Paul C. Nagel, *This Sacred Trust: American Nationality, 1798–1898* (New York, 1971), pp. 3–46.

cans with the assurances they craved, supplying them with a distinct identity and hope in troubled times. After 1789 providential thought had one fundamental task—the reinforcement of American nationalism. Public spokesmen employed providential rhetoric and concepts to buttress the main tenets of America's nationalist ideology. Providential thought during the early national period sanctified the nationalist themes of special nation, special destiny, and special mission.

The significance of this sanctification ultimately extended beyond 1815. Because the early national era was greatly influenced by religious values—this was, after all, the period of the second Great Awakening—the presentation of American nationalism in providential language during these years was axiomatic. The practice, though, survived the transition of the United States from a religious to a secular culture in the late nineteenth and early twentieth centuries. Thus well after the demise of providential thought, American patriots professed a national faith in their country's unique importance, destiny, and mission. The sanctification of American nationalism in the years after 1789 was one guarantee that even in secular times American nationalism would constitute a virtual religion.

Essentially there were two major reasons for the continued vitality of providential thought in early national America. In the first place, providential thought mitigated one of the problems the first proponents of American nationalism faced: the lack of "cultural or spiritual elements, generally accepted as a foundation of separate nationhood, which would differentiate" Americans "from other peoples." Providential thought was an important source of union and identity to a people constantly in need of common values. In early national America no less than today "a complex society is held together by certain common assumptions and shared beliefs." After 1789, for a people lacking many traditionally common institutions and customs, faith in the providential destiny of America was one of the most significant shared beliefs. Americans may not have been a particularly consistent church-going people, but their culture was decidedly Trinitarian Protestant. Virtually all citizens could accept the notion of a guardian God and find identity in that acceptance. The blessings of Providence distinguished the United States from other nations, illustrated America's singularness.[6]

The concept of Divine Providence was also an essential basis for national confidence. In Revolutionary and early national America the United States lacked secure, concrete bases for national celebration, and the specter of disunion was always present. History offered little consolation—the classic republics of Greece, Rome, the Netherlands, and Venice had all collapsed through internal divisions. "As yet unable to point to the stupendous material accomplishments" of the post-1865 period—the inventions, the industry, and the military strength that transformed the United States into a world power—patriots after 1789 "resorted" to a providential-sanctified nationalism, seeking and finding there their national purpose and glory. "It was out of the gnawing void resulting from a lack of national self-realization that Americans called on Providence."[7]

Scholars, in analyzing the development of early American nationalism, have described a number of components. They have especially singled out for emphasis the heritage of the colonial past, the impact of the American Revolution and the mythologizing of the Founding Fathers, the secularization of the Puritan vision of the city on a hill, and the rise of an evangelistic Protestantism that depicted America as the greatest field for the work of salvation. Each of these elements contributed to the development of American national consciousness during the Revolutionary and early national eras. And each in turn was strengthened—sanctified—by providential thought after 1789. America's colonial past was sanctified through numerous accounts of Jehovah guiding and sustaining the first white settlers in the New World. The American Revolution became the modern equivalent of the Exodus, a second escape from the "house of bondage" into the "promised land." The Founding Fathers were de-

[6] Hans Kohn, *American Nationalism: An Interpretative Essay* (New York, 1957), p. 18; Martin E. Marty, *Righteous Empire: The Protestant Experience in America* (New York, 1970), p. 148.

[7] Robert P. Hay, "Freedom's Jubilee: One Hundred Years of the Fourth of July, 1776–1876" (Ph.D. diss., University of Kentucky, 1967), pp. 174, 194, 201–2; idem, "Providence and the American Past," *Indiana Magazine of History* 65 (1969): 79–101.

picted as reincarnations of the biblical patriarchs—Washington as Moses was the most popular parallel, but it was not the only one drawn. Providential thought transformed the New Israel's mission from the religious city on a hill of John Winthrop to the political republican experiment of hundreds of post-1789 patriots—yet the new mission, like the old, was ordained and promoted by an omnipotent deity. Providential thought even fashioned the concept of a political millennium, thereby reinforcing both revivalistic evangelism and American exceptionalism. Providential thought was not so much a distinct and separate component of early American patriotism as an important general overview that permeated and shaped—sanctified—the historical, political, and religious aspects of the emerging national consciousness.

In a recent article Paul C. Nagel has cogently discussed the historiography of early American nationalism. His distinctions between scholars are based on their respective conclusions as to whether early American nationalism was supremely confident and optimistic or deeply troubled and self-doubting, even pessimistic.[8] Rather than promoting the centrality of one to the exclusion of the other, historians must recognize that strands of optimism and pessimism coexisted in American patriotism after 1789. Discussing their nation and their national distinctiveness, patriots voiced both self-congratulatory and self-doubtful sentiments. Perhaps the providential thought of the early national era is best seen as a reaction to this ambivalence. Certainly America between 1789 and 1815 experienced many events that seemed to cast doubt on the nation's ability to survive. The rancorous rise of national political parties, the deaths of Washington and other Revolutionary leaders, the sudden emergence and bloody collapse of the French Republic, the Whisky Rebellion, Fries's Rebellion, the turmoil over the Alien and Sedition Acts, the XYZ affair, the Quasi-War, the Kentucky and Virginia resolves, the "Revolution of 1800," the disunionist plottings of embittered New England Federalists, the Burr Conspiracy, the *Chesapeake-Leopard* encounter, the embargo, the War of 1812—such a rapid succession

[8] Nagel, "Historiography and American Nationalism: Some Difficulties," *Canadian Review of Studies in Nationalism* 2 (1975): 225–40.

of disturbing and divisive events strained the national union and undoubtedly challenged the national confidence of Americans.

In such an era providential thought offered much to the citizens of the United States. Repeated references to the providential guidance and providential destiny of America constituted an appeal to the ultimate guarantor of American survival. Ancient Israel had remained God's chosen vessel through turbulent eras; the Republican Israel would do likewise. Ironically, then, the sanctification of American nationalism was an optimistic response to troubling realities. The sanctification of American patriotism after 1789 is evidence, not that the patriots of early national America were supremely confident of their national future, but rather that they were deeply disturbed.

This uneasiness gave rise to another phenomenon, which is the subject of chapter 6—the partisan uses of providential rhetoric during the early national years. The American national political scene after 1789 was dominated by bitter partisan debate. With a vehemence seldom equaled since, American political spokesmen during these years used extreme rhetoric to promote their policies and to attack their opponents. Several factors contributed to a general sense of political uneasiness and urgency after 1789, a sense that found expression in the political rhetoric of the era. In the first place, the years after 1789 were truly critical ones for contemporary leaders and politicians. The United States was a young and untried nation, weak in relation to the powers of the Old World; the United States still lacked many of the traditional bases of a secure national identity. The national government established by the Federal Constitution was precarious, without established traditions or precedents to fall back on. It seemed to many citizens that the new nation might easily take a fatal turn from which there could be no escape.[9]

The political and military chaos of Europe from 1789 through 1815 also reinforced the elements of anticipation and tension in American politics. Then too, despite the extensive religious revivals

[9]Richard Buel, Jr., *Securing the Revolution: Ideology in American Politics, 1789–1815* (Ithaca, N.Y., 1972), pp. 6, 70; John R. Howe, *From the Revolution through the Age of Jackson: Innocence and Empire in the Young Republic* (Englewood Cliffs, N.J., 1973), pp. 3, 73; May, *Enlightenment in America*, pp. 179, 228, 252.

of the era, politics provided for a great many citizens their chief source of entertainment and emotional release. Finally, the concept of legitimate political opposition had not yet crystallized. Both the Federalist and Republican parties, while they held the reins of national power, viewed criticism of their policies as tantamount to treason and saw their political rivals, not as the reflectors, but as the source of opposition.[10]

American providential nationalism did form a patriotic consensus that alleviated some of these tensions. This consensus, however, was unable to diminish partisanship, which rather increased in intensity as the years went by. Within the consensus there was division. This paradoxical situation was understandably disturbing to contemporaries, for, if left unexplained, domestic division might cast doubt on the very unifying tenets Americans needed for their national unity. One way out of this dilemma was to declare that American politics was not *really* divided between two American factions. Rather, one was American and one was un-American, one was national and one was foreign. In this way Americans could admit that partisanship existed and yet deny that that partisanship represented a failure of the American experiment. To this end Federalists and Republicans in turn argued that they were the true representatives of the New Israel and their opponents the tools of a foreign conspiracy. This phenomenon explains why national celebrations like the Fourth of July and days of national fasts and thanksgiving, occasions given over to explications of America's patriotic consensus, were also occasions for fierce partisan rhetoric.[11]

One element in the political rhetoric of the era was the employment of providential concepts for partisan ends. Just as faith in Divine Providence reinforced and sanctified American nationalism, thereby providing comfort and confidence to citizens and legitimizing the American experiment, so also it reinforced and legitimized

[10] David Hackett Fischer, *The Revolution of American Conservatism: The Federalist Party in the Era of Jeffersonian Democracy* (New York, 1965), pp. 182–83; Richard Hofstadter, *The Idea of a Party System: The Rise of Legitimate Opposition in the United States, 1780–1840* (Berkeley and Los Angeles, 1969), pp. ix, x, 2, 86, 90, 123–25.

[11] Buel, *Securing the Revolution*, pp. 138, 167–70; Nagel, *This Sacred Trust*, pp. 28–29; Hay, "Freedom's Jubilee," pp. 30–46.

partisan philosophies. In their efforts to portray themselves as the sole American party (and thus not jeopardize the consensus of the era), both national parties after 1789 attempted to appropriate America's sanctified patriotism for their exclusive use. The traits the two parties shared had much to do with these attempts. Both claimed to be the legitimate heirs of the American Revolution and sought to cast their opponents as its betrayers. Neither party was religiously monolithic, though the Federalists more nearly approximated orthodoxy. Because the two parties were similar in many respects, the partisan employment of providential thought became a means of distinguishing one party from another. The common goals of the rival parties influenced each to turn to American providential thought to differentiate and strengthen their specific political programs.[12]

Providential rhetoric during the War of 1812 is the subject of chapter 7. The War of 1812 saw the continuation (and in one sense the culmination) of both strands of post-1789 American providential thought, the sanctified nationalist and the partisan. By the war's end the former prevailed. The War of 1812 (it seemed) had been won; the union was preserved; Republicanism and America were synonymous; Federalism stood discredited as little short of treason. All these factors contributed after 1815 to an "era of good feelings" in national politics and, at the same time, to the final confirmation of the legends of America's providential guardianship and destiny. Because Republican usage of providential nationalism from 1812 through 1815 seemed to be vindicated by the war's outcome, the sanctified patriotic strain of providential thought stood superior by 1815. For the same reason—the war's apparent confirmation of the reality of the Democrats' claim that they were the sole supporters of America's national consensus—the partisan providential rhetoric of the early national era subsided. It was not to be expected that the utilization of providential images for partisan ends would completely disappear, of course, any more than that political opposition itself would end. When significant political division again surfaced in the 1820s, so did the employment of providential rhetoric for partisan causes. But

[12] James M. Banner, Jr., *To the Hartford Convention: The Federalists and the Origins of Party Politics in Massachusetts, 1789–1815* (New York, 1970), pp. 157n, 163–64, 197–215; Herbert M. Morais, *Deism in Eighteenth Century America* (New York, 1934), pp. 138–45; May, *Enlightenment in America*, p. 257.

there was a significant difference. Since legitimate political opposition—the idea of a two-party system—was increasingly accepted after 1815, political rhetoric had different ends. Such rhetoric was still extreme, but no longer was it necessary for each party to assume exclusive legitimacy. The paradox of division within consensus, so troubling to the spokesmen of early national America, had been resolved.[13]

The War of 1812 expanded and confirmed the sanctified nationalist consensus that patriots had been articulating since the American Revolution. That consensus now included the War of 1812 itself—the "Second War for Independence"—as the latest manifestation of God's care for his Republican Israel. The very survival of the nation confirmed the consensus. Just when it appeared that the fears and anxieties of Americans were unhappily to be borne out, and the United States dealt a mortal blow either by domestic division or foreign invasion, the republic was saved. For the moment, at least, doubts subsided; the Lord had rescued his people. The very nature of the War of 1812—victory and peace coming suddenly after years of frustration, disappointment, and defeat—helped to solidify American patriotism, including its providential underpinnings, into the form it would display through the Civil War.

Between 1740 and 1815 America evolved from colonies to nation. During the 1740s and 1750s the inhabitants of the English seaboard colonies struggled against the French and Indian menace. During the 1760s and 1770s they awakened to a British "conspiracy" to deprive them of their liberties, and from 1775 to 1783 they fought a civil and international war to gain national independence. During the late 1780s they debated the political form their new nation would take. In the 1790s, 1800s, and 1810s they created their own nationalism in the midst of acrimonious political turmoil. From 1812 to 1815 they fought a second war with Great Britain to insure the survival of their republican experiment. In each of these periods, during each of these crises, prominent and common citizens turned to a cluster of providential concepts for, variously, self-assurance, explanation, and union. Throughout the entire period stretching

[13] Hofstadter, *Idea of a Party System*, pp. 212–71; May, *Enlightenment in America*, pp. 313–14.

from the Great Awakening to the Peace of Ghent, American spokesmen depicted their nation as God's New Israel, interpreted their communal mistakes and misfortunes as divine warnings and messages, deified their ancestors, linked their national development with Jehovah's plan for the world, and traced the finger of the Lord through their history. The constant principle, in essence, was that an American was by definition an inhabitant of a nation specially chosen, protected, and guided by Almighty God. This was America's providential thought. The story of the many elements that went into the fashioning of this legend is an important and an impressive one.

I
New England Writ Large

DURING THE seventeenth and early eighteenth centuries, from the establishment of permanent settlements to the Great Awakening, the Puritan inhabitants of the New England colonies in North America viewed their past and present in providential terms. To these men God directed their history, shaped their daily lives, and would guide their future. New Englanders in these years frequently recounted Jehovah's chastisements and visitations, yet never doubted that God was guiding and influencing both their spiritual and secular development. The beliefs that God actively controlled all the natural and human occurrences of the universe and that in particular he was dramatically intervening to reward, chastise, and exalt New England remained constant.

The dominance of these ideas does not mean that New Englanders alone among American colonists believed in the existence and operation of Divine Providence. Such convictions were common to men in all colonies and from all social classes—indeed, most Americans would continue to adhere to these concepts well after the middle of the eighteenth century. New Englanders certainly were not unique in their conviction that Divine Providence ruled their destinies, but among American colonials they insisted most strongly that their Puritan community had a *special* task or mission assigned it by God. Hence New England was under the *special* guidance of the Almighty and could expect *special* manifestations of his approval or anger. The vitality of this pecular set of beliefs—the distinctive articulateness of the Puritans' concept of their providential mission—set the Puritans off from the spokesmen of the middle and southern colonies. In the end the providential themes of New England became special and powerful in American nationalism and American intellectual history because of their cohesiveness—their presentation by so many men so forcefully on so many occasions over so long a period of time. Other peoples have paralleled their development with that of ancient Israel, deified their ancestors, and traced the activities of Divine Providence through their history, but few—certainly no others in America—have done so as consistently or persuasively as the New England Puritans. It is not surprising, then, that the American patriotism which emerged after 1740 was, to a great degree, New England writ large.[1]

The New England Puritans developed or adapted a cluster of providential ideas and traditions that became staple ingredients of American patriotism during the Revolutionary and early national periods. Specifically, these were the paralleling of Israel and New England, the deification of a group of mythical founding fathers, the creation of the jeremiad as a literary form and the jeremiad tradition as a vehicle for expressing communal aspirations, the tentative linking of New England and the commencement of the millennium, and the recounting of the hand of the Lord in the political, social, and military history of New England. Comprehension of the later adaptation or transmutation of these themes by Revolutionary and early national American patriots requires an examination of their Puritan origins.

Some of these practices developed consistently over the seventeenth and early eighteenth centuries; others reflect the particular needs of different Puritan generations. For our purpose, the first generation of Puritan providential thought can be said to have begun with the landing of the Pilgrim Fathers in 1620, extending until about 1670. (Although the Pilgrims and Puritans differed on a number of religious points, they shared a common historical and regional outlook that for convenience can be labeled "Puritan.") The second generation of Puritan providential thought emerged after 1670 and would hold sway among the descendants of John Winthrop and William Bradford until the Great Awakening. While this generational division was not absolute, it is helpful in understanding certain trends within several of the key components of early providential thought.[2]

[1] Sacvan Bercovitch, *The Puritan Origins of the American Self* (New Haven, 1975), pp. 137–38.

[2] Although the generational division has proved a difficult one for scholars to define absolutely, I concur with Emory Elliott, who sees the transition from first- to second-generation Puritanism occurring gradually between the Half-Way Covenant of 1662 and 1670 (*Power and the Pulpit in Puritan New England* [Princeton, N.J., 1975], pp. viii-ix, 55).

The first contribution of Puritan providential thought to American patriotism was the theme of New England as God's New Israel. This derived from the Puritans' emphasis on typology, which has received extensive coverage in recent years.[3] Typology, which dated from the early Christian Fathers, was the practice of allegorically reading the Old Testament. Most of the patriarchs and prophets were seen as precursors, or "types," of Christ, and many of the events in the history of God's ancient covenant people, the Hebrews, were types of the later history of God's Christian church. Thus Moses, Nehemiah, Joseph, and Joshua were read by Puritan divines as types of the Messiah, while the Flood, the Exodus, and the Exile were interpreted as types of the present tribulations and future triumphs of Christ's chosen remnant. Essentially, typology was a feature of the second Puritan generation; although the Puritan fathers paralleled their history with that of ancient Israel, they did not usually undertake the extensive typological examinations of post-1670 Puritans.[4]

Typology, obviously, was essentially religious in nature and intent: to read the Bible as a means of comprehending the fate of the saints. It was this that inspired Urian Oakes's 1673 observation that "this our Common-wealth seems to exhibit to us a specimen, or a little model of the Kingdome of Christ upon Earth." But typology also lent itself to more prosaic comparisons of ancient Israel and New England. The exile of the Jews into the wilderness was a type of the spiritual flight of Protestants from the Catholic Church during the Reformation—but it could also be read as a type of the material Puritan flight from the England of Archbishop Laud after 1630. The very removal of the Puritans from civilized Europe to the "wilderness" of the New World "reminded them of the grand precedent of

[3] My understanding of Puritan typology is derived from the following works: Sacvan Bercovitch, "Typology in Puritan New England," *American Quarterly* 19 (1967): 166–91; Mason I. Lowrance, Jr., "Typology and the New England Way," *Early American Literature* 4 (1969): 15–37; *Early American Literature* 5 (Spring 1970): entire issue; Ursula Bruum, *American Thought and Religious Typology*, trans. John Hooglund (New Brunswick, N.J., 1970); Sacvan Bercovitch, ed., *Typology and Early American Literature* (Amherst, Mass., 1972).

[4] Robert Middlekauff, *The Mathers: Three Generations of Puritan Intellectuals, 1596–1728* (New York, 1971), pp. 106–7.

God's chosen people fleeing from Egyptian oppression" and thus strengthened their convictions of mission and divine election. Typology laid the foundations for Thomas Prince's 1730 observation "that there never was any People on Earth, so parallel in their general History to that of the ancient ISRAELITES as this of NEW-ENGLAND." New England was "Gods Israel." "Behold," exclaimed Cotton Mather in 1690, "you may see an Israel in America, by looking upon this Plantation." "We are the people that do succeed Israel," Thomas Thacher remarked, "We are Jacob." Benjamin Colman made the same point in 1723: "CANAAN *was a good Land, and so is ours*." This repeated parallel was not disheartening, despite the fate of ancient Israel, since the Puritans professed—as Emory Elliott has observed—that an exact "repetition" of the history of the Hebrews "was not inevitable in New England." Instead, New England was both like and greater than ancient Israel; she was truly the *new* Israel. The providential concept of the New-England Israel, derived from the practice of religious typology, was the source of the later celebrations of American Israel that permeated American patriotism during and after the American Revolution.[5]

Like typology, the creation of the legend of the founding fathers was the product of the second generation of Puritan providential thought. After 1660, while many of the first generation were still alive, their descendants fashioned the myth of the golden age of the

[5] Peter Gay, *A Loss of Mastery: Puritan Historians in Colonial America* (Berkeley and Los Angeles, 1966), p. 29; Nathaniel Morton, *New-Englands Memoriall* (Cambridge, Mass., 1669), p. x; Thomas Prince, *The People of New-England Put in Mind of the Righteous Acts of the Lord to Them and their Fathers* (Boston, 1730), p. 21; Jonathan Russell, *A Plea for the Righteousness of God* (Boston, 1704), p. 9; Cotton Mather, *The Serviceable Man* (Boston, 1690), p. 27; Thomas Thacher, *A Fast of God's Chusing* (Boston, 1678), p. 19; Benjamin Colman, *David's Dying Charge to the Rulers and People of Israel* (Boston, 1723), p. 27; Elliott, *Power and the Pulpit*, p. 145; Sacvan Bercovitch, "Horologicals to Chronometricals: The Rhetoric of the Jeremiad," *Literary Monographs, Volume 3*, ed. Eric Rothstein (Madison, Wis., 1970), pp. 47–48; Urian Oakes, *New-England Pleaded with* (Cambridge, Mass., 1673), pp. 19–20, 21, 22–23; Kenneth B. Murdock, *Literature and Theology in Colonial New England* (Cambridge, Mass., 1949), pp. 77, 114, 122–23; Conrad Cherry, ed., *God's New Israel: Religious Interpretations of American Destiny* (Englewood Cliffs, N.J., 1971), p. 27.

fathers.[6] Second-generation Puritans, "committed to a scheme which could not admit of failure, compensated for their thwarted errand" in part by "constructing a legendary past." The ever-present "need to feel a continuity between the past [and] the present" led the spokesmen of the second generation to create "a race of giants in an age of miracles." One aspect of this hagiography was the homogenizing of the founders' motives. Reacting to the controversies growing out of the adoption of the Half-Way Covenant and the collapse of Oliver Cromwell's Commonwealth, second-generation Puritan intellectuals stressed a solely religious motivation for New England's founding. Indeed, on this point they went beyond the Puritan founding fathers themselves. First-generation Puritans had recognized and acknowledged the role that economic and political concerns played in the founding of New England. But to later spokesmen the Puritan colonies had been settled "only" or "meerly" for religion; secular interests had in no way been a factor in the fathers' establishment of the godly community. "Our Fathers came not over into this Wilderness to get the World," Samuel Whitman claimed in 1714. "This was no part of their Errand." The Reverend Thomas Foxcroft typically pointed out that "several repeated Attempts for the Settlement of an English Plantation in the Bay of *Massachusets*, upon *worldly* Views, prov'd abortive," but it had "pleased God to put a visible Distinction upon the Undertakers of this religious settlement, and crown their nobler Enterprize with glorious Success."[7]

Puritan spokesmen strove to surpass each other in their praises of "our Fore-fathers, those men of *Renown*." "Men Eminent in Piety & Virtue," the Puritan fathers "were very much a *chosen* Generation."

[6] Helpful here are Bercovitch, *Puritan Origins*; Elliott, *Power and the Pulpit*; Sacvan Bercovitch, "'Nehemias Americanus': Cotton Mather and the Concept of the Representative American," *Early American Literature* 8 (1974): 220–38; Wesley Frank Craven, *The Legend of the Founding Fathers* (New York, 1956), pp. 5–26.

[7] Bercovitch, "Horologicals to Chronometricals," pp. 41–43, 67; Elliott, *Power and the Pulpit*, p. 13; Bercovitch, *Puritan Origins*, pp. 88, 122; Nicholas Noyes, *New-Englands Duty and Interest* (Boston, 1698), pp. iv-v, 46; John Norton, *An Essay Tending to Promote Reformation* (Boston, 1708), pp. 1–2; Samuel Whitman, *Practical Godliness the Way to Prosperity* (New London, Conn., 1714), pp. 29–30; Colman, *David's Dying Charge*, p. 31; John Webb, *The Duty of a Degenerate People* (Boston, 1734), p. 25; Lawrence C. Sandin, "The Wonderful Works of God: The Idea of Providence in American History, 1620–1800" (M.A. essay, Marquette Uni-

Second-generation spokesmen reinforced William Stoughton's 1668 remark that "God sifted a whole Nation that he might send choice Grain over into this Wilderness." Cotton Mather in his *Magnalia Christi Americana* referred to "that *greatness*, and that *goodness*, which was in the *first grain* that our God brought from *three sifted kingdoms*, into this land, when it was a *land not sown*." John Winthrop, idealized by Cotton Mather as "Nehemias Americanus," had been "pickt out for the worke" of founding New England "by the provident hand of the most high." "The leader of a people in a wilderness had need be a Moses," and lo—there was William Bradford, "an *Instrument*" of the Almighty. The legend of the founding fathers could even be imparted to post-1660 leaders, as in *Pietas in Patriam*, Cotton Mather's 1697 biography of Sir William Phips. Phips, "*The Knight of Honesty*," was "*One Raised by God*!" Like David, Phips ruled wisely and piously over those "whom the Divine Providence . . . gave him the *Ascendant*," always grounding his political and military decisions on "his Hearty Subjection to the *Gospel* of the Lord Jesus Christ."[8]

The deaths of the founders (and of those men after 1660 who approximated the founders) were ominous signs of "Divine Displeasure." "The taking away of the Ancient" was a warning to their sons.[9] Thus the Puritan myth of the founding fathers asserted that

---

versity, 1973), p. 8; Thomas Foxcroft, *Observations Historical and Practical on the Rise and Primitive State of New-England* (Boston, 1730), pp. 15–16.

Elliott, *Power and the Pulpit*, pp. 59–62, notes that initially the device was a creation of the first generation to control the second but that it was later adapted by younger ministers such as Cotton Mather to celebrate the past.

[8] Jonathan Russell, *Plea for the Righteousness*, p. 15; John Rogers, *A Sermon Preached Before His Excellency the Governour* (Boston, 1706), p. 35; Foxcroft, *Observations*, p. 23; W[illiam] Stoughton, *New-Englands True Interest* (Cambridge, Mass., 1670), p. 19; Bercovitch, *Puritan Origins*, pp. 187–205; Edward Johnson, *Johnson's Wonder-Working Providence*, ed. J. Franklin Jameson (New York, 1910), p. 76; Cotton Mather, *Magnalia Christi Americana*, 2 vols. (Hartford, 1853–55), 1:249, 113; Morton, *New-Englands Memoriall*, p. 147; Cotton Mather, *Pietas in Patriam*, ed. Mark Van Doren (New York, 1929), pp. 34–35, 167–68, 55–56.

[9] Increase Mather, *The Day of Trouble is Near* (Cambridge, Mass., 1674), p. 21; Joseph Belcher, *The Singular Happiness of such Heads or Rulers, as Are Able to Choose out their Peoples Way* (Boston, 1701), p. 37; Samuel Dexter, *Our Fathers God, the Hope of Prosperity* (Boston, 1738), p. 29; Cotton Mather, *Pietas in Patriam*, p. 196.

the fathers knew the truth and lived the truth; the duty of their descendants was imitation, not innovation. From this Puritan myth post-1740 American patriots copied similar concepts. Through and beyond 1815 public spokesmen invoked the memory of their ancestors, and God's favor to them, to compel Americans to confront their duty and destiny.

A third contribution of the New England Puritans to American providential nationalism was the jeremiad tradition. Like the legend of the founding fathers, the jeremiad was largely the creation of the Puritan second generation. The jeremiads—election and fast-day sermons preached after 1670—centered on God's displeasure with New England and his manifestations of that displeasure. The intellectual spokesmen of the second generation fashioned a special type of sermon, one designed especially to castigate the people of New England for their sins, warn them of the wrath of God, which falls on the unregenerate, point out the marks of divine anger visible around them, and urge them to repent, reform, and return to the pious ways of their ancestors.[10]

The jeremiad tradition was a two-sided one. At first glance, as Emory Elliott has observed, a literal reading of the jeremiads apparently confirms the traditional view that post-1670 spokesmen displayed "an extraordinary degree of irrational fear and uncertainty" and a "deep sense that they were failing to live up to certain expectations of their parents and their God." The chief failing of New England, the jeremiads insisted again and again, was the abandonment of New England's religious "errand into the wilderness." "God did once plant a Noble vine in *New-England*," Nathaniel Morton lamented, "but it is degenerated into the plant of a strange vine." Increase Mather thundered the same sentiment in 1680: "Men have forgot their Errand into this Wilderness. . . . If the body of the present standing Generation, be compared with what was here forty

[10]For the Puritan jeremiad see Bercovitch, "Horologicals to Chronometricals," pp. 1–124, 187–215; Elliott, *Power and the Pulpit*, pp. 88–135; Perry Miller, *The New England Mind: From Colony to Province* (Cambridge, Mass., 1953), pp. 27–39; Wayne C. Minnick, "The New England Execution Sermons, 1639–1800," *Speech Monographs* 35 (1968): 77–89; David Minter, "The Puritan Jeremiad as a Literary Form," in *The American Puritan Imagination: Essays in Revaluation*, ed. Sacvan Bercovitch (New York, 1974), pp. 45–55, 221–23.

years agoe, What a sad Degeneracy is evident." The jeremiad tradition, as this citation suggests, drew strength from the legend of the founding fathers: as a typical jeremiad in 1725 put it, "We have in a very shameful degree forgotten our Fathers GOD." The original goal had been lost, the fathers' divine mission cast aside: "Our Fathers left the World, for the Enjoyment of Religion in this Wilderness; but [now] the Designs of most are Inverted: Most in these Days are leaving Religion in pursuit of the World."[11]

A multitude of natural and spiritual disasters evidenced the Lord's anger with New England's backsliding. The God of the Puritans, obviously not proscribed by any natural laws, manipulated the physical world to threaten those who had forsaken him. The Puritans were visited with comets, signs from the Lord portending evil days unless they abandoned their pride and worldly sins. Earthquakes were also sent as warnings, all spokesmen agreeing with Cotton Mather that "there is the *Voice of the Lord*, in it, when he *shakes* our Territories." Spectacular fires were further displays of divine anger. Sometimes an epidemic was the form of divine correction; because New Englanders were "a very *degenerate* People," Benjamin Wadsworth grimly noted in 1722, God had "sorely Scourg'd us by Sickness, the *Small Pox*. . . . This *Contagious Sickness* was the *Rod of* GOD, He whip'd us with it, and *whip'd many* (probably above a *Thousand*) of this People to Death by it." Afflictions placed on the land constituted some of the most consistent judgments upon the New England Israel: through repeated bad harvests, blasts, mulcts, mildews, droughts, and frosts, God's errant people were chastised for their sins and commanded to repent and reform. The witches who infested Salem Village in the 1690s were also messengers of divine displeasure.[12]

[11] Elliott, *Power and the Pulpit*, pp. 8, 91; Morton, *New-Englands Memoriall*, pp. 197–98; Increase Mather, *Returning Unto God the Great Concernment of a Covenant People* (Boston, 1680), p. 9; Ebenezer Thayer, *Jerusalem Instructed & Warned* (Boston, 1725), p. 31; Increase Mather, *Day of Trouble*, pp. 23–24; Jeremiah Shepard, *God's Conduct of His Church through the Wilderness* (Boston, 1715), p. 29.

[12] Increase Mather, *Heavens Alarm to the World* (Boston, 1681); Stearns, *Science in the British Colonies*, pp. 154–55; Middlekauff, *The Mathers*, pp. 139–43, 281–95; [Cotton Mather], *The Terror of the Lord* (Boston, 1727), p. 10; Morton, *New-Englands Memoriall*, pp. 162–63; Samuel Cheever, *Wise and Good Civil Rulers to be*

And yet, as both Sacvan Bercovitch and Emory Elliott have clearly demonstrated, the importance of the jeremiads was greater than the sum of these oft-repeated sins and chastisements. For the jeremiads, ironically and paradoxically, served in the end to celebrate the New England experiment rather than condemn it. As Bercovitch has noted in his perceptive analysis of the jeremiad tradition, "The theme of declension" in the jeremiads should not be allowed to obscure "the far more powerful, and distinctive, countertheme of exultation and affirmation." The jeremiads reiterate that God will *not* forsake his people; no matter how far New England has declined (or will decline), God will glorify it. The Puritans after 1670 "acted as if they were damned while presuming they were redeemed." In New England the jeremiad "was a celebration of God's promises." God's chastisements "were a mark of special love and attention." Thus Increase Mather, in the midst of some of the most formidable jeremiads preached in the seventeenth century, could reassure his congregation, "Do not think that God will utterly destroy New England. . . . The Lord hath a great Interest in this Land which he will not easily part with." The Lord "is *our* God still. . . . He is not willing to give up his own Interest here; He waits to be gracious." Cotton Mather was even more emphatic: "Be of a Good Heart, O NEW-ENGLISH *Israel*; Neither will thy God suffer thee to be *Starved* in *thy Wilderness*." In the words of Samuel Torrey, the Almighty "will magnifie *New-England* again before the World. . . . God will glorifie himself before all people in us." These and similar pronouncements within the post-1670 jeremiads have led Emory Elliott accurately to see the era as characterized by "a spirit of optimism." The jeremiad tradition led not to doubt and despair but to "hope and assurance."[13]

Duely Acknowledged by God's People as a Great Favour (Boston, 1726), pp. 41–42; [Cotton Mather], *Duodecennium Luctuosum* (Boston, 1714), p. 14; Benjamin Wadsworth, *True Piety the Best Policy for Times of War* (Boston, 1722), p. 22; Increase Mather, *Day of Trouble*, p. 10; Eliphalet Adams, *A Discourse Occasioned by the late Distressing Storm* (New London, Conn., 1717), pp. 1–13; William Russel, *The Decay of Love to God* (New London, Conn., 1731), p. 39; Prince, *People of New-England*, pp. 31–32; William Billings, *A Warning to God's Covenant People* (New London, Conn., 1733), pp. 21–24; Chadwick Hansen, *Witchcraft at Salem* (New York, 1969), pp. 216–19.

[13] Bercovitch, "Horologicals to Chronometricals," pp. 6, 29–32, 24; Bercovitch, *Puritan Origins*, pp. 53, 55, 115; Sandin, "Wonderful Works," p. 14; Increase

The Puritan jeremiad, then, moved from cataloging the godly community's sins and the Lord's visitations to celebrating the election of the nation and its ultimate glory. This tradition too entered American nationalism after 1740 and was utilized during each of the succeeding periods of crisis—the French and Indian War, the American Revolution, the critical 1790s, the War of 1812. In each instance it served Americans as it had previously served the Puritans.

A fourth area in which the New England Puritans laid the foundations for a later feature of American patriotism was what might be called the "Americanization" of the millennium. First-generation Puritans were deeply inspired by millennial enthusiasm, with both personal and doctrinal ties with the English millenialists of Cromwell's Commonwealth. This enthusiasm receded after about 1650, but throughout the second half of the seventeenth century the Puritans were still reminded that "this is Immanuels Land . . . here the Lord hath caused as it were New Jerusalem to come down from Heaven." Indeed, if the case of Increase Mather is taken as representative, millennial expectations increased rather than decreased during the late seventeenth century. Such visions were strictly religious, of course—centering on the thousand-year reign of the saints and the Second Coming of Christ—but they later proved flexible enough, during the era of the American and French revolutions, to accommodate an essentially secular outlook on the future, the vision of universal peace, brotherhood, and republicanism. America's special role in the millennium was more implicit than explicit in Puritan providential thought, but the notion was present from the beginning.[14]

The genre of providential history comprised the fifth Puritan con-

---

Mather, *An Earnest Exhortation to the Inhabitants of New-England* (Boston, 1676), p. 19; idem, *Returning Unto God*, p. 12; idem, *Day of Trouble*, p. 27; Cotton Mather, *Mirabilia Dei* (Boston, 1719), p. 8; Samuel Torrey, *Mans Extremity, Gods Opportunity* (Boston, 1695), p. 59; Elliott, *Power and the Pulpit*, pp. 173–202 (the quotations are from pp. 179, 201).

[14] James F. Maclear, "New England and the Fifth Monarchy: The Quest for the Millennium in Early American Puritanism," *William and Mary Quarterly*, 3d ser. 32 (1975): 223–60; Johnson, *Wonder-Working Providence*, p. 185; Increase Mather, *Day of Trouble*, p. 26; Sandin, "Wonderful Works," p. 3; Increase Mather, Introduction to Samuel Torrey, *An Exhortation Unto Reformation* (Cambridge, Mass., 1674), p. ii; Middlekauff, *The Mathers*, pp. 189–97; May, *Enlightenment in America*, pp. 153–76.

tribution to a future American patriotism. The great Puritan histories—those of William Bradford, John Winthrop, Edward Johnson, Nathaniel Morton, William Hubbard, and Cotton Mather—and the historical accounts contained in Puritan election, fast, thanksgiving, and anniversary sermons all traced the constant and compelling activities of the Lord as manifested in the political, social, and military affairs of New England.[15] In a sense, this was the Puritan contribution most easily and most completely assimilated into American patriotism after 1740. The sophisticated, and especially the popular, histories of late eighteenth-century and early nineteenth-century America were replete with the activities of Jehovah in behalf of his Republican Israel.

Puritan histories were concerned with two general themes: the successes given to New England by the Lord and the protection afforded the saints by Jehovah. Both could, and did, involve both white- and red-skinned enemies of the Lord's flock. "An observable

[15] William Bradford, *History of Plymouth Plantation, 1620–1647*, ed. Worthington C. Ford, 2 vols. (Boston, 1912); John Winthrop, *History of New England, 1630–1649*, ed. James Kendall Hosmer, 2 vols. (New York, 1908); Johnson, *Wonder-Working Providence*; Morton, *New-Englands Memoriall*; William Hubbard, *The History of the Indian Wars in New England*, ed. Samuel G. Drake, 2 vols. (Roxbury, Mass., 1865); William Hubbard, *A General History of New England* (Boston, 1815); Cotton Mather, *Magnalia Christi Americana*. Helpful secondary accounts include Sacvan Bercovitch, "The Historiography of Johnson's *Wonder-Working Providence*," *Essex Institute Historical Collections* 104 (1968): 138–61; idem, "New England Epic: Cotton Mather's *Magnalia Christi Americana*," *ELH* 33 (1966): 337–50; Ursula Bruum, "Edward Johnson's *Wonder-Working Providence* and the Puritan Conception of History," *Jahrbuch für Amerikastudien* 14 (1969): 140–51; Robert Daly, "William Bradford's Vision of History," *American Literature* 44 (1973): 557–69; Edward J. Gallagher, "An Overview of Edward Johnson's *Wonder-Working Providence*," *Early American Literature* 5 (1971): 30–49; Gay, *Loss of Mastery*, pp. 26–87; Kenneth Alan Hovey, "The Theology of History in *Of Plymouth Plantation* and Its Predecessors," *Early American Literature* 10 (1975): 47–66; Alan B. Howard, "Art and History in Bradford's *Of Plymouth Plantation*," *William and Mary Quarterly*, 3d ser. 28 (1971): 237–66; Kenneth B. Murdock, "Clio in the Wilderness: History and Biography in Puritan New England," *Church History* 24 (1955): 221–38; idem, "William Hubbard and the Providential Interpretation of History," *Proceedings of the American Antiquarian Society* 52 (1943): 15–37; Cecelia Tichi, "The Puritan Historians and Their New Jerusalem," *Early American Literature* 6 (1971): 143–55; Edward K. Trefz, "The Puritans' View of History," *Boston Public Library Quarterly* 9 (1957): 115–36.

hand of God," for instance, was evident in the fate of William Kieft, Dutch governor of New Netherlands, who had constantly harassed the Puritan settlers in Connecticut; on a voyage home to Holland in 1647 his ship ran aground and he drowned. On the other hand, when developments in England threatened the interests of the Puritan colonies, the "Glorious Arm of Divine Conduct" was visible in Protestant successions to the English throne—the Lord elevated William and Mary to power in 1688–89 and then provided the Hanoverian accession of 1714. At home the Almighty was directly behind New England's successful rebellion in the spring of 1689 against the "arbitrary" rule of Sir Edmund Andros. The divine influence was also detected in the defense of New England from the threat of French Canada during Queen Anne's War.[16]

But the most remarkable blessings of God recorded by the Puritans comprised the Almighty's dealings with the American Indians. In 1618, two years before the Pilgrims sailed for the New World, God sent a "great mortality" that decimated the native inhabitants of New England. "By this meanes Christ . . . not onely made room for his people to plant; but also tamed the hard and cruell hearts of the barbarous Indians." Again and again in the course of the seventeenth and early eighteenth centuries the Puritans returned to this incident of the Lord "casting out" the heathen for the benefit of his people. During the early years of settlement, furthermore, when Indian numerical superiority posed a threat to New England's survival, the "Salvages" were restrained by "God striking a dread into their hearts." The Pequot Indians proved intractable (refusing to open up their lands) in 1637, whereupon the Almighty delivered them into the hands of the New England forces in a great slaughter. The result was what one modern ethnohistorian has called the "First Puritan Conquest."[17]

[16] Winthrop, *History of New England*, 2:333; Jeremiah Shepard, *God's Conduct*, p. 22; [Gurdon Saltonstall], *A Sermon Preached Before the General Assembly of the Colony of Connecticut* (Boston, 1697), p. 57; Cotton Mather, *Mirabilia Dei*, pp. 24–25; idem, *The Wonderful Works of God Commemorated* (Boston, 1690), pp. 32–45; [Cotton Mather], *Duodecennium Luctuosum*, pp. 22–24; Sandin, "Wonderful Works," pp. 11–12.

[17] Johnson, *Wonder-Working Providence*, pp. 40–42, 79; Increase Mather, *Heavens Alarm*, p. 9; Jeremiah Shephard, *God's Conduct*, pp. 23, 26; Foxcroft,

A classic example of Puritan providential history was King Philip's (Metacom's) War, of 1675–76, a conflict which, in its depiction by Puritan historians, foreshadowed all the later wars of Revolutionary and early national America.[18] The struggle was, in a real sense, foreordained; Puritan victory was predestined. Since the war was "the Cause of God and his People," it followed that the white soldiers and militiamen were "fighting under the Banner of Gods special Protection." Metacom's War gave reality to the jeremiad tradition. The Indians were "a smart rod and severe scourge" loosed by Jehovah to heighten the Puritans' "calamity." And why was this calamity allowed? "Because of the provoking of his sons and daughters, the Lord hath moved us to anger with a foolish Nation, and moved us to jealousie with those which are not a people." Spiritual pride and worldly-mindedness among New Englanders were the sources of the Almighty's "rebuke." But, although cause for reformation, there was no cause for despair. "God . . . is always wont to remember his People in their low Estate." The "Rage" of Philip and his "barbarous Crew," the Puritans predicted, "shall proceed no further than the Counsel of God had determined." After the Lord had "accomplished his Work upon his People," he would "call his Enemies [the Puritans' Indian foes] to an Account, and punish them for the Pride of their Hearts, and for all their Treachery and Cruelty against his Servants." The Indians would not for long be a "Scourge" to God's people; he would "turn his Hand against them."[19]

Observations, pp. 16–17; Prince, *People of New-England*, p. 25; Dexter, *Our Fathers God*, p. 22; Morton, *New-Englands Memoriall*, p. 23; Cotton Mather, *Magnalia Christi Americana*, 1:54; Bradford, *Plymouth Plantation*, 2:250–52; Francis Jennings, *The Invasion of America: Indians, Colonialism, and the Cant of Conquest* (Chapel Hill, N.C., 1975), pp. 202–27.

[18] For two modern, and quite different, accounts of Metacom's War, see Douglas E. Leach, *Flintlock and Tomahawk: New England in King Philip's War* (New York, 1958), and Jennings, *Invasion of America*, pp. 298–326. Jennings characterizes the war as the "Second Puritan Conquest."

[19] Hubbard, *Indian Wars*, 1:187, 191, 118, 171, 201, 273, 278–79; Peter N. Carroll, *Puritanism and the Wilderness: The Intellectual Significance of the New England Frontier, 1629–1700* (New York, 1969), p. 212; Increase Mather, *Earnest Exhortation*, p. 2; William Hubbard, *The Happiness of a People in the Wisdome of Their Rulers* (Boston, 1676), pp. 49, 54–59; Murdock, *Literature and Theology*, pp. 94–96.

Thus the finger of the Lord must be traced through all the events of 1675–76. When Philip brought his "Conspiracy" out in the open in the spring of 1675, "the special Providence of God" had overruled him, "for when the Beginning of the Troubles first was reported . . . many of the *Indians* were in a kind of Maze, not knowing well what to do." When the New England militiamen mounted their expedition against the Narragansett Indians in the winter of 1675, they were directed by "the good Providence of Almighty God." The invaders did not know which side of the Indian fort to attack, but "he [who] led *Israel* sometime by the Pillar of Fire, and the Cloud of his Presence a right Way through the Wilderness" did "now direct our Forces upon that side of the Fort, where they might only enter." The "Goodness" of the Lord was further the cause of the blessing that during the hard winter of 1675–76 "not one [white] Man was known to dye by any Disease or bodily Distemper." God was also "eminently seen upholding the Spirits of all sorts, Men and Women, so as no Consternation of Mind was seen upon any of them, during the whole Time of the Dispute"—not for the last time did Americans resort to Divine Providence to obscure internal division. Then in 1676 "the righteous Hand of God" at last brought "that Mischief" upon the Indians "which they had without Cause thus long acted against others." Metacom was "driven" to a swamp near his village, "which proved but a Prison to keep him fast, till the Messengers of Death came by Divine Permission to execute Vengeance upon him." Thus New England was rescued by Jehovah from the wiles of this "notorious Traitor."[20]

From Metacom's War the Puritans extracted a confirmation of the principle that "all humane endeavours shall arrive at no other Success, then the Counsel of God hath preordained." It was "manifest" from the events of 1675–76 "that as *the Hearts of all are in the Hands of God, so he turns them as he pleases*, whether to favour his People, or to hate and deal subtilly with his Servants, as seems good to him." But it was quite clear that New England had enjoyed, and would continue to enjoy, much more of the Lord's favor than his hate. Providential history and the jeremiad merged to

[20] Hubbard, *Indian Wars*, 1:59, 93–94, 145, 152–53, 154, 192, 264–65, 272; Jennings, *Invasion of America*, p. 304.

glorify New England even more as the favorite nation of God.[21]

New England providential thought, then, evolved during the seventeenth and early eighteenth centuries into a unified body of concepts: the motif of the New Israel, the golden age of the founding fathers, the jeremiad tradition, millennial expectations, providential history. After 1740 this body of thought was transferred to the rest of the American colonies through the vehicle of the Great Awakening. And this post-1740 "national" providential thought permeated American patriotism through the French and Indian War, the American Revolution, and the War of 1812. Spurred on by the impassioned preaching of George Whitefield, Gilbert Tennent, Jonathan Edwards, Samuel Davies, and other revivalists, the Great Awakening swept through the colonies after 1740. Because the goals of the revivalists, and the expectations which produced these goals, were essentially the same in all regions of America, the Great Awakening gave rise to real intercolonial thought and cooperation. In the end the Great Awakening "not only transcended parochial allegiances but crossed provincial boundaries as well," and so "succeeded in breaking down the local and particular allegiances of Americans." The revivals thus "played an important role in forming a national consciousness" among the peoples of the various colonies, generating "a common interest and a common loyalty."[22] A growing number of historians explicitly point to the Great Awakening as one of the primary foundations of American nationalism.[23]

[21] Hubbard, *Indian Wars*, 1:91, 232, 246, 272.

[22] Alan Heimert, *Religion and the American Mind: From the Great Awakening to the Revolution* (Cambridge, Mass., 1966), pp. 136–40; Winthrop S. Hudson, *Religion in America*, 2d ed. (New York, 1973), p. 76.

[23] See Heimert, *Religion and the American Mind*, pp. viii, 14, 94; Alan Heimert and Perry Miller, eds., *The Great Awakening* (Indianapolis, 1967), p. 563; Peter N. Carroll, ed., *Religion and the Coming of the American Revolution* (Waltham, Mass., 1970), p. xii; Winthrop S. Hudson, ed., *Nationalism and Religion in America: Concepts of National Identity and Mission* (New York, 1970), p. xxiii; Darrett B. Rutman, ed., *The Great Awakening: Event and Exegesis* (New York, 1970), pp. 4–6; Bercovitch, "Horologicals to Chronometricals," p. 81; Cherry, ed., *God's New Israel*, pp. 29–30; Cedric B. Cowing, *The Great Awakening and the American Revolution: Colonial Thought in the Eighteenth Century* (Chicago, 1971), p. 203; William G. McLoughlin, *New England Dissent, 1630–1833: The Baptists and the Separation of Church and State*, 2 vols. (Cambridge, Mass., 1971), 1:xx, 338, 2:776. For a percep-

Whether or not the Awakening was, in the end, as successful as some of its modern students claim, it did serve as a vehicle for the spread of the special themes of New England providential thought to other sections of America. In this sense the revivals were the first steps in the growth of at least the providential strain within American patriotism. Quite obviously, providential thought per se was not limited to New England before the Great Awakening. Americans in all colonies believed in an absolute, intervening deity who controlled and directed all the natural and human developments within the universe. But no colony or section outside New England considered itself to be the New Israel or to have a world-affecting divine mission to perform. Yet by the 1770s these concepts (applied now to all of America) were expressed openly in New York and Pennsylvania, in Virginia and South Carolina, as well as in Massachusetts and Connecticut. Nothing less than a transfer of ideas—the peculiarly sharpened ideas of New England providential thought—had occurred. How did this transfer come about? How did these Puritan themes become American themes? The answer lies in part in the Great Awakening and in the influence of New Englanders on other sections of America in the course of the Awakening.

This influence was sometimes exerted in a general manner—among the pious of America, New England had long been seen as the acknowledged leader in religious concerns. But of greater importance were the activities of its leaders in the propagation of the Great Awakening outside New England. The Puritans, of course, did not alone cause the Awakening or even lead it in the directions it took. But as New England men preached and settled in the middle and southern colonies, they brought with them *specific* providential concepts peculiar to the Puritan commonwealth: the New Israel, the legend of the founding fathers, the jeremiad tradition, the providential historiography of the holy community. In the course of the Awakening they transformed these concepts, applying them not

---

tive critique of this thesis see Nathan O. Hatch, "The Origins of Civil Millennialism in America: New England Clergymen, War with France, and the Revolution," *William and Mary Quarterly*, 3d ser. 31 (1974): 410–12 and idem, *The Sacred Cause of Liberty: Republican Thought and the Millennium in Revolutionary New England* (New Haven, 1977), pp. 25–28.

merely to the godly community of New England but to the godly community throughout America. To be sure, in so doing they did not differ from revivalists born in Pennsylvania or Virginia. The New Englanders' significance lies not so much in their use of this broad concept of divine guidance for the "awakened" as in their spread of refined and special ideas and terminology long since developed in New England and in the intensity with which they propagated these sentiments. Itinerant or transplanted New Englanders served as the agents for the transformation of Puritan into American providential thought.[24]

The Great Awakening succeeded in partially destroying regional boundaries and in giving the "awakened" a sense of intercolonial unity and union. And the New England participation in the Awakening educated men throughout all the colonies to the rhetoric and meaning of a special concept of providential guidance for the New World. The result was a curious, even a paradoxical, situation. Despite the Great Awakening, worldly concerns became the central interests of many Americans. But at the same time the Awakening, through its diffusion of the special providential concepts of New England throughout all of America, provided a unique framework in which to fix and discuss political, military, and social events. As Sacvan Bercovitch has cogently observed, "Early New England rhetoric provided a ready framework for inverting later secular values . . . into the mold of sacred teleology." Thanks to the Awakening, the growth of Enlightenment ideas like the rights of man and eventually national independence could be treated in a religious context, presented as the will of God and the fulfillment of a special American mission ordained by Divine Providence.[25]

The process, to be sure, was slow, and at first largely unarticulated. But the foundations were there, needing only an intercolonial crisis to aid in their crystallization and maturation. The first occasion came in the 1750s, when the French stood as the enemies of the God-given and God-defended liberties of all the American colonies

[24] For the careers of six such New England agents—Jonathan Dickinson, Aaron Burr, James Davenport, Ebenezer Pemberton, Daniel Marshall, and Shubael Stearns—see my "From Puritan to American Providential Thought," *Cithara: Essays in the Judaeo-Christian Tradition* 16 (1977): 59–76.

[25] Bercovitch, *Puritan Origins*, p. 136.

and were so characterized by both supporters and opponents of the Great Awakening. Then after 1763 the imperial crisis with Great Britain precipitated a full national expression of the ideas of divine guidance, divine election, and divine mission—in short, the concept of the American Israel and all that that implied. The "New Englandization" of American thought and culture during the era of the revivals permeated American patriotism and nationalism from the Stamp Act crisis to the Peace of Ghent. In this sense, at least, the Great Awakening had succeeded more than its participants knew.

II
The French and Indian Prelude

THE GREAT AWAKENING transformed the American religious scene; the French and Indian wars of the 1740s and 1750s altered the American imperial scene. That these two exciting and transforming events occurred almost simultaneously had great significance for American patriotism. At the same time that the Great Awakening was providing the *means* for the "New Englandization" of American thought, the imperial wars were providing the opportunities for the *expression* of intercolonial (or protonational) patriotic concepts. Thanks to the New England Puritans, these concepts would include the New Israel motif, the jeremiad tradition, and the other themes of the godly community. Thanks to the Great Awakening and the struggles with the French and their Indian allies, these concepts would be applied to America.

Americans of this era saw a multitude of specific manifestations of Divine Providence. Among the best sources for these concepts are the public sermons and discourses presented to the colonial populace during these years. The majority of such presentations, to be sure, were by ministers, and it would be strange if their efforts did not affirm the existence of Providence. But many of these discourses were delivered on public occasions, and all were presented to lay audiences, hence the views they contain can be assumed to be those of the listeners as well as the speakers. When the ministers of the mid-eighteenth century "spoke to popular emotions"—as they did during the war crises—"they could exert formidable power." Furthermore, lay authors and orators, as well as colonial newspapers, consistently used the same providential images and ideas as the ministers. Far from being an era when clergy and laymen spoke two different languages, the second half of the eighteenth century saw common acceptance by both groups of the existence and operation of Divine Providence in the events around them. Political and military developments were the central concerns of a majority of the colonists, but (as in the seventeenth century) these developments were seen as completing and fulfilling the designs of God—in short, as the ends and intent of a beneficent Providence. The course of history consisted of a progression of secular events, but history itself was never merely secular. Political and military developments occupied the colonial mind, but behind them the hand of God was always discerned.[1]

Americans after 1740, as the New England Puritans had done before them, viewed and interpreted politics and secular concerns within a providential framework. It is not surprising, then, that some of the major themes explored in the public discourses of the era concerned the power and activities of Divine Providence in the secular affairs of men. God ruled and overruled the nations of the earth; "whatever befals states and kingdoms" was to be "attributed to God's over-ruling providence, as the accomplishment of his sovereign pleasure concerning them." The Lord at various times in history selected "Particular Nations and Kingdoms" to be especially under "his Care and providential Rule, and the Civil, Military and Secular, as well as religious and spiritual Interests" of these nations were "either opposed and lost, or established and promoted according to his Permission and Will."[2]

God partially accomplished this by calling to political power those whom he wanted to achieve his ends. "'Tis the great Ruler of the World, that sets up, and pulls down earthly Rulers as he pleases. . . . GOD presides in the Counsels, Courts, and Assemblies of earthly Rulers, to observe, direct, and over-rule their Consultations and Actions." Great men were both the gifts and the agents of a benevolent Providence. In like manner God called forth and used the "Jars and Tumults among Nations" for his own glory and "to bring to pass the wise Designs of his Providence." The Lord, and not earthly forces, was always the ultimate arbiter of wars and battles; the maxim that "Providence always favours an hundred Thousand Men," insisted Boston's Samuel Cooper, was "foolish as well as impious."[3]

[1] May, *Enlightenment in America*, p. 51. See also Hatch, *Sacred Cause of Liberty*, pp. 181–82.

[2] Jonathan Mayhew, *A Discourse Occasioned by the Death of King George II* (Boston, 1761), p. 13; Thomas Balch, *A Sermon Preached to the Ancient and Honourable Artillery Company* (Boston, 1763), p. 15.

[3] Peter Raynolds, *The Kingdom is the Lord's* (New London, Conn., 1757), pp. 20–22; Henry Caner, *God the only unfailing Object of Trust* (Boston, 1751), pp. 5–6;

Americans were frequently reminded, in sermons that were direct continuations of earlier Puritan jeremiads, of God's righteous visitations on peoples and nations for their sins and transgressions. A double effect accrued to this visitational aspect of Divine Providence: evil ways put a nation in misery both because of their own pernicious effects on citizens and because they were affronts to the deity. Elnathan Whitman sounded a familiar theme when he told the rulers of Connecticut that "when Sin & Iniquity abounds among a People, they are in the utmost danger of Destruction and Ruin. Vice & Wickedness in its own Nature tends to ruin and destroy a *People*, but especially it has such a Tendency, as it separates between GOD and them, forfeits the divine *Protection*, and exposes a *People* to the Anger and Displeasure of GOD and his righteous Judgments." Because he was a just God, the Lord had to punish national sins, and because nations existed only in this world, the divine punishments had to be exercised here also. "The Sovereign Ruler of the World" had to "manifest the Holiness of his Nature, and discover the Righteousness of his moral Government, by rendering a wicked and debauched Community, a miserable one." In "the Nature of Things" it could not be otherwise.[4]

If provoked long enough, and if his warnings were slighted or ignored, God would be perfectly justified in utterly destroying a wicked people. The ultimate end of most providential afflictions, however, was not destruction but reformation. Judgments from God were warnings designed to induce a people to abandon sin and cling to the good. After all, as one New Englander pointed out in 1756, "the Father visits the Child with the Rod of Correction, not to drive it away from him, but to subdue its Stubbornness, to make it love, and do its Duty to him; so that he may shew it Favour. The Visitation of Judgments themselves, are designed for our Instruction and Good." If the people would change their ways, the Lord was always eager to

---

James Lockwood, *A Sermon Preached at Weathersfield, July 6, 1763* (New Haven, [1763]), pp. 21–22; Amos Adams, *The Expediency and Utility of War, in the Present State of Things, considered* (Boston, 1759), p. 13; Cooper, *A Sermon Preached Before His Excellency Thomas Pownall* (Boston, [1759]), pp. 34–38.

[4] Whitman, *The Character and Qualifications of good Rulers* (New London, Conn., 1745), pp. 21–22; Noah Hobart, *Civil Government the Foundation of Social Happiness* (New London, Conn., 1751), p. 18.

change their fortunes and prosper them. Thus in the dark days of the French and Indian War, a well-known evangelist pointed out that "A THORO' NATIONAL REFORMATION . . . will do, what Millions of Money and Thousands of Men, with Guns and Swords and all the dreadful Artillery of Death, could not do; it will produce us Peace again."[5] Americans in New England, the middle colonies, and the South all were urged to repent and reform, with the assurance that if they did so the smiles of Providence would once again rest upon them. The Lord was always giving America one more chance; his mercy made him reluctant to abandon his people.[6] The dichotomy of the jeremiad tradition was thus retained after 1740. Spokesmen might chronicle the sins of God's chosen people and the chastisements of the Lord sent for these sins, but the reassurance and optimism of ultimate salvation was always present. Victory in the French and Indian War, of course, would do nothing to dampen this sense of almost inevitable national glory.

These general concepts of the scope and intentions of Divine Providence served as the basis for popular American citations of the specific interventions of Providence during this period of imperial war—the divine activity in human history. Pre-1740 Puritan concepts continued to frame colonial providential thought. Understandably, particular attention was devoted to the regional and intercolonial development of the American colonies. From these investigations emerged ideas and themes that remained strong in American public thought and expression through the American Revolution and well into the nineteenth century. The providential foundation of American patriotism was laid during this era of imperial conflict.

[5] Nathan Bucknam, *The just Expectations of God* (Boston, 1741), pp. 11–12; James Lockwood, *Religion the highest Interest of a civil Community* (New London, Conn., 1754), pp. 48–49; *New-England's Misery* (Boston, 1758), pp. 11–15; Ebenezer Booge, *The Unteachable, forsaken of God* (New Haven, [1756]), p. 9; Samuel Davies, *The Curse of Cowardice* (Woodbridge, N.J., 1759), p. 18.

[6] See John Burt, *Earthquakes, the Effects of God's Wrath* (Newport, R.I., [1755]), pp. 13–17; Samuel Davies, *Religion and Patriotism the Constituents of a Good Soldier* (Philadelphia, 1755), pp. 21–22 (this sermon was preached in Virginia); Gilbert Tennent, *The Happiness of Rewarding the Enemies of our Religion and Liberty* (Philadelphia, 1756), pp. 25–26; Benjamin Throop, *Religion and Loyalty, the Duty and Glory of a People* (New London, Conn., 1758), pp. 25–26.

Basic to the providential history of this era were several common themes. Predating even the colonial wars with the French was the belief that God's purpose in history was the promotion of civil and religious liberty. Liberty was always the divine intent because it was necessary in order for men to live virtuous lives on this earth and ultimately attain salvation. The growth of liberty had been the grand historical theme since the Reformation, and it had been greatly advanced by the discovery and settlement of America. Furthermore, civil and religious liberties were not disjointed blessings; they were inexorably linked and rose or fell together.

The colonial consensus by the 1740s was that God had purposely made America the most free of all the world's peoples. The colonists celebrated and praised their God for the civil and religious freedoms they enjoyed, and they did so in an intercolonial manner. New England's Nathanael Hunn in 1747 might tell his local audience that when he looked out at them "I can but bless God, and congratulate my Country, at the Sight of so many free People, who carry Liberty in their very Faces, whose Countenances shew that they are not galled, & born down by the ignoble Yoke of Tyranny and Oppression; but are contented & happy in Liberty and Plenty." But in tone and imagery his message was no different from Ebenezer Pemberton's remarks to his New York flock: "Blessed be God, he has . . . left us in the full possession of our *civil* and *religious* liberties. Blessed be God, we are not under the government of one of those *insulting* tyrants, who know no law but their own arbitrary wills, who sacrifice their most valuable subjects to gratify their ambition and revenge."[7] Americans were convinced that through the blessings of Divine Providence they enjoyed as great a degree of civil and religious freedom as any people on earth.[8]

This conviction precipitated yet another adaptation of the legend of the founding fathers. In the late seventeenth and early eighteenth centuries the New England descendants of the first-generation Puritan fathers, concerned with a perceived decay of religious piety, had

[7] Hunn, *The Welfare of a Government Considered* (New London, Conn., 1747), pp. 17–18; E[benezer] Pemberton, *A Sermon Delivered at the Presbyterian Church in New-York, July 31. 1746* (New York, 1746), pp. 19–20.

[8] See, e.g., Isaac Stiles, *A Prospect of the City of Jerusalem* (New London, Conn., 1742), p. 33.

discussed the motives for the founding of New England in strictly religious terms. Now, in an era of rising demands for religious pluralism and toleration, another attempt was made by American spokesmen to make the past serve the present. The inhabitants of the colonies now were repeatedly told that they were sprung from ancestors who had come to the New World to protect and nourish their civil and religious freedoms. The sentiments of Samuel Cooper were typical: "Our Progenitors, smitten with a Love of Liberty, and possessed with an uncommon Reverence to the Dictates of Conscience, transplanted themselves into the Wilds of *America*: In this Emigration God was their Guide, and their Defence." In fundamental agreement was New York's William Livingston, who traced the founding of his colony back to those hardy men who, opposed to "arbitrary measures," fled a Spanish-controlled Netherlands and the England of Charles I. From such forefathers the present generation, under God, inherited "the highest relish, for civil and religious LIBERTY." There was widespread acceptance of the claim that the "pious Ancestors" of America had been men "content to dwell in a Desart, if they might here enjoy that Liberty of Conscience, which was unreasonably denied them in their native Country." The fact that these and similar claims were often historically simplistic did not detract one bit from their popularity.[9]

Given these common sentiments of the place of America in the course of providential history, Americans (not surprisingly) viewed the colonial wars of the era as struggles to defend their God-given religious and civil liberties. This theme was expounded again and again in all sections of America, in all types of literature and discourse, and by men of all religious persuasions.[10] Thus during King George's War the French enemy threatened, according to Gilbert Tennent, the "utter ruin" of America's "*Liberties*, civil and religious,

[9] Cooper, *Sermon Before Pownall*, p. 28; [William Livingston], *An Address to His Excellency Sir Charles Hardy* (New York, 1755), pp. v–vi; Andrew Eliot, *An Evil and Adulterous Generation* (Boston, 1753), p. 8.

[10] Heimert, *Religion and the American Mind*, p. 85, says that the supporters of the Great Awakening "saw the imperial war [the French and Indian War of 1754–63] as incidental, even irrelevant, to the central theme of history," but even a cursory reading of the war sermons preached by revivalists refutes this contention. For recent conclusions similar to mine, see Hatch, "Origins of Civil Millennialism," pp. 421–22, and idem, *Sacred Cause of Liberty*, pp. 42–43.

except Almighty *Power* interposes, and infinite *Mercy* prevents."[11] The Almighty (as will soon be seen) did intervene, but when the French menace resurfaced in the 1750s, the new war was presented as the same danger.

During the French and Indian War the expressions of this theme throughout the several regions of America were dramatically similar. In 1758 William Hobby presented to a Massachusetts audience the stakes of the war: "Should we succeed . . . then our Liberty, Property, Life & Religion are continued: Our Privileges & Advantages increased and enlarged. But, should we fail . . . farewell Liberty: Now to be exchanged for slavery! Farewell Property! Nothing hence forwards to be called our own. Farewell Religion; the Sun sets upon the Sanctuary; which is left dark and desolate!" An anonymous Boston poet put into verse the same theme:

> Religion, Liberty's at Stake,
> Your Country and your all;
> Therefore no Hesitation make,
> Go forth both great and small.[12]

A year earlier evangelist Samuel Finley told a Pennsylvania audience that their "*Fathers* purchased this *goodly* HERITAGE for us, at the *Price* of great *Labour*, and much *Blood*; nor thought the *Purchase too dear*, provided they might *entail* it on their *Posterity* for ever. . . . Shall we leave our *Children*, *Slavery* for *Liberty*, *arbitrary Government*, for *Law* and *Equity*, and *Popery*, for the pure *Christian Religion*?" The

[11] Tennent, *A Sermon Preach'd at Philadelphia, January 7. 1747–8* (Philadelphia, 1748), p. 30. Cf. idem, *The Necessity of praising God for Mercies receiv'd* (Philadelphia, [1745]), p. 7.

[12] Hobby, *The Happiness of a People, Having God for their Ally* (Boston, 1758), p. 22; "On the present Expedition," *Boston Evening-Post*, 19 June 1758. For other New England expressions of this theme, see Isaac Morrill, *The Soldier Exhorted to Courage* (Boston, 1755), pp. 21–22; Isaac Stiles, *The Character and Duty of Soldiers Illustrated* (New Haven, 1755), p. 14; Timothy Harrington, *Prevailing Wickedness, and distressing Judgments, ill-boding Symptoms on a stupid People* (Boston, 1756), pp. 28–29; Samuel Webster, *Soldiers, and others, directed and encouraged* (Boston, 1756), p. 16; Throop, *Religion and Loyalty*, p. 24; Sylvanus Conant, *The Art of War, the Gift of God* (Boston, 1759), p. 12; Thaddeus Maccarty, *The Advice of Joab to the Host of Israel* (Boston, 1759), pp. 35–36; Jonathan Mayhew, *Two Discourses Delivered October 9th, 1760* (Boston, 1760), p. 62.

local troops of nearby New Jersey were urged by Abraham Keteltas to "consider that in the present war . . . If the enemy should prevail, then farewell to liberty of conscience, the free enjoyment of our civil and sacred Privileges, and every thing else that is valuable in human life."[13]

In the South the burden of such preaching fell upon the qualified shoulders of Samuel Davies, one of the greatest orators of colonial America. Davies, like his northern compatriots, was more than willing to describe for his listeners the stakes of the French and Indian War: "You are engaged in a Cause of the utmost Importance. . . . to secure the inestimable Blessings of Liberty . . . from the Chains of *French* Slavery . . . to guard your Religion . . . against Ignorance, Superstition, Idolatry, Tyranny over Conscience, Massacre, Fire and Sword . . . to secure the Liberties conveyed to you by your brave Fore-Fathers, and bought with their Blood . . . these are the Blessings you contend for." On other occasions Davies again urged Virginians to keep "Slavery" and "Idolatry" from invading "this Land of Liberty."[14]

Thus from New England to the South public spokesmen urged their countrymen to war with a cluster of interrelated themes: our fathers came to the New World for civil and religious freedom; under Providence they achieved both and handed them down to us; both are today threatened by the French; therefore we must fight to protect and preserve our everything. Then one final theme was added, one again common to all America: the cause we fight for is the cause of God; therefore, if we keep from sin and trust in the Lord, he will

[13] Finley, *The Curse of Meroz* (Philadelphia, 1757), pp. 24, 27; Keteltas, *The Religious Soldier* (New York, 1759), p. 7. For other middle-colony expressions of this theme, see "Sincere Lover of Mankind, and Friend to Pennsylvania," Philadelphia *Pennsylvania Journal*, 12 Sept. 1754; "Philadelphus," ibid., 26 Sept. 1754; Thomas Barton, *Unanimity and Public Spirit* (Philadelphia, 1755), pp. 4, 14; Aaron Burr, *A Discourse Delivered at New-Ark, in New-Jersey, January 1, 1755* (New York, 1755), pp. 40–41; *New-York Mercury*, 13 Jan. 1755; P[hilip] Reading, *The Protestant's Danger, and the Protestant's Duty* (Philadelphia, 1755), p. 6; Aaron Burr, *A Servant of God dismissed from Labour to Rest* (New York, 1757), pp. 21–22; William Smith, *The Christian Soldier's Duty* (Philadelphia, 1757), pp. 29–30, 36.

[14] Davies, *Religion and Patriotism*, pp. 13–14; idem, *Virginia's Danger and Remedy* (Williamsburg, Va., 1756), p. 45; George William Pilcher, *Samuel Davies: Apostle of Dissent in Colonial Virginia* (Knoxville, Tenn., 1971), pp. 158–70.

deliver our enemies into our hands. This theme too was present during King George's War, but, like the others, found its fullest expression in the course of the great war for the empire.[15]

As John Lowell told one of the first groups of New England volunteers in 1755, "You are most certainly engaged in a *good Cause* . . . no other than *the Cause of God*; therefore you may expect his gracious Presence, if you go forth in his Fear, and prosecute it aright." Three years later Joseph Emerson exhorted another body of soldiers in virtually the same language: "the Cause in which you are engaged, is the *Cause of God, the Cause* of Religion, the *Cause* of Liberty. . . . you are to fight . . . for everything near and dear to you, as you are *free* Men, for everything valuable as you are *Christians*."[16] In the middle colonies Gilbert Tennent in 1756 argued that "shedding the Blood of our Enemies in a *lawful War*, is a good work, it is the Lord's work, because enjoin'd and approved of by him," and the next year Samuel Finley, preaching on the dangers of neutrality in the war, insisted that since "the Security of invaluable Rights and Privileges, the Preservation of pure Religion, the Glory of GOD, and the Happiness of Posterity, are all concerned in the [present] *Quarrel*, it is evident that we have a good *Cause*, and are on *the Lord's Side*." As an anonymous New York writer addressed the men of America, "Away to the Field of Battle—Your Country calls—Your cause is just, and God will undoubtedly protect you."[17] In the South, Samuel

[15] For typical expressions of the theme that the cause of King George's War was the cause of God, see Peter Clark, *The Captain of the Lord's Host, Appearing with his Sword Drawn* (Boston, 1741), pp. 43–47, and Jonathan Todd, *The soldier waxing Strong and Valiant through Faith* (New London, Conn., [1747]), p. 39.

[16] Lowell, *The Advantages of God's Presence with his People* (Boston, 1755), p. 18; Emerson, *The Fear of God, an Antidote against the Fear of Man* (Boston, 1758), pp. 19–20. For other typical New England expressions of the theme that the cause of the French and Indian War was the cause of God, see Samuel Checkley, *The Duty of God's People when engaged in War* (Boston, 1755), pp. 28–29; Peter Clark, *Religion is to be minded, under the greatest Perils of Life* (Boston, 1755), p. 22; [Jonathan Ellis], *The Justice of the Present War against the French in America* (Newport, R.I., [1755]), p. 7; Isaac Stiles, *Character and Duty of Soldiers*, p. 15; Samuel Bird, *The Importance of the divine Presence with our Host* (New Haven, 1759), p. 21.

[17] Tennent, *Happiness of Rewarding*, p. 21; Finley, *Curse of Meroz*, p. 26; *N.Y. Mercury*, 11 Aug. 1755. For other typical middle-colony expressions of the theme that the cause of the French and Indian War was the cause of the Lord, see

Davies again stepped to the fore, telling southerners that when they considered "the Justice and Importance" of the war, it was certain that, if they kept from sin, "the Lord of Hosts will espouse it, and render its Guardians successful. . . . The Event . . . is in his Hands, and it is much better there, than if it were in yours."[18] There can have been few colonists who were not exposed to this theme in the course of the French and Indian War.[19]

Yet these same Americans knew that on several occasions during the imperial wars of this era, Anglo-American forces suffered disappointment, frustration, and even destruction. In these instances the righteous armies were defeated and the Lord's enemies triumphed. Why was this so? The answer was obvious, and not long in coming, for at the same time that the preachers and orators told Americans that their cause was just and that God was on their side, they also warned that sin provoked God's wrath and jeopardized their martial efforts. Sinful human deeds could never change the end of providential history, but they could retard the attainment of that end. The course of the colonial wars seemed to offer many illustrations to confirm the fear that colonial transgressions were bringing down the wrath of Jehovah. From New England to the South the jeremiad continued to constitute a basic type of public discourse—and for the same reason that it had been fashioned during the Puritan era. After, no less than before, 1740, the jeremiad tradition was instrumental in enforcing consensus and in promoting a national effort to defeat the enemies of the Lord and his people.[20]

Theodorus Frelinghuysen, *Wars and Rumors of Wars, Heavens Decree over the World* (New York, 1755), p. 39; *N.Y. Mercury*, 18 Aug. 1755; "W.," *Pa. Jour.*, 28 Aug. 1755; William Smith, *Christian Soldier's Duty*, p. 30.

[18] Davies, *Religion and Patriotism*, p. 15.

[19] See also the conclusions of Hatch, "Origins of Civil Millennialism," pp. 422–28, and idem, *Sacred Cause of Liberty*, pp. 44–51.

[20] See, e.g., the following jeremiads (among the many that could be cited): for New England, Clark, *Captain of the Lord's Host*, pp. 39–41; Andrew Eliot, *Evil and Adulterous Generation*, pp. 9–20; Charles Chauncy, *Earthquakes a Token of the righteous Anger of God* (Boston, 1755), pp. 16–22; William Vinal, *A Sermon on the Accursed Thing That hinders Success and Victory in War* (Newport, R.I., 1755), pp. 11–14; Booge, *The Unteachable*, pp. 14–22; Arthur Browne, *The Necessity of Reformation, in Order to Avert Impending Judgments* (Portsmouth, N.H., 1757), pp. 6–10; for the middle colonies, Pemberton, *Sermon*, pp. 16–17; Burr, *Discourse*, pp.

A national sin particularly cited during the French and Indian War, one that by its very nature especially invited divine chastisement, was vain self-confidence and exclusive reliance on human talents. Americans were reminded by Aaron Burr (Jonathan Edwards's son-in-law) that "nothing is more provoking to God, than for a People to cast off their Dependence upon him; overlook *his Hand* in all the signal Dispensations of his Providence, and act as tho' the *Source* of their Safety was wholly *in themselves*. . . . What Madness therefore and Folly, as well as great Wickedness, is it, to put our Confidence in an *Arm of Flesh*?" The Pennsylvania author who assumed the pseudonym "Theotharsus" agreed that "it certainly ill becomes a Christian Nation, such as ours, to express so little a Reverence of, and Dependance upon the Lord of Hosts, and so great a Confidence as we in Fleets and Navies," and concluded that while "Sneering Infidels" might "ridicule" such sentiments, "every reasonable considerate Person will allow them to be just."[21]

With Americans bearing this heavy load of guilt, it was little wonder that the Lord permitted them to be attacked by Papist forces during successive imperial wars. Indeed, King George's War itself was a divine judgment on a sinful nation.[22] When America finally began to reform, God in his infinite mercy stayed his vengeance and peace was restored. But the renewal of open warfare in 1754 demonstrated how quickly the New Israel was wont to worship false gods.

No matter what human factors were involved in the resumption of violence, "however we may resolve the calamitous Events our Nation and Land have experienced, into the Effects of Cowardice, Negli-

24–26; Theodorus Frelinghuysen, *Wars and Rumors of Wars*, pp. 36–38; for the South, J[ohn] Evans, *National Ingratitude Lamented* (Charleston, S.C., 1745), pp. 26–28, and Davies, *Religion and Patriotism*, pp. 18–21. These and other wartime jeremiads challenge Alan Heimert's assertion that "in the course of the [Great] Awakening the themes of the jeremiad all but disappeared from Calvinist sermons" (*Religion and the American Mind*, p. 62).

[21] Burr, *Discourse*, pp. 35–37; "Theotharsus," *Pa. Jour.*, 19 June 1755. Cf. "B.B.," ibid., 12 Jan. 1758.

[22] Clark, *Captain of the Lord's Host*, p. 38; Thomas Prince, *A Sermon Delivered At the South Church in Boston, N.E., August 14, 1746* (Boston, 1746), pp. 35–36.

gence, Stupidity or worse Causes; however we may wonder at the Conduct of Men in important Trusts; yet Religion teaches us to look higher, to esteem these but the Means and Instruments of divine Chastisements." The renewed war was due to "that Disregard of God and Religion—that Sin and Prophaness . . . which are become the too flagrant Characteristics of our Nation and Land in general."[23]

Sin and injustice were to blame for the unfavorable developments of the first years of America's new struggle with her French adversaries. The clearest sign of God's "controversy" with the colonies in the 1750s was Braddock's defeat, a classic example of God punishing a people for their national sins and because they slighted their dependence on him. But Jonathan Mayhew noted in 1755 the utter failure of no less than four Anglo-American expeditions within two years. America's cause, he observed, was just, so in light of "God's fighting against us in his holy providence . . . we have great reason to suspect that we do not stand right with him as a people that is called by his name; but that we have made him our enemy, by fighting and rebelling against him. Who indeed," Mayhew concluded, "can doubt but that this is the case?"[24]

Thus when American spokesmen came to interpret the victories and successes eventually achieved in the imperial wars, they were predisposed to give the glory to Jehovah, the true source of power. For his own glory, for the protection and promotion of liberty, and because Americans still possessed enough virtue to be deemed his people, the Lord intervened and granted the colonies ultimate victory in both struggles. Throughout King George's War, Americans recounted the saving mercies of their divine protector, mercies even more remarkable in view of the continued sins of the colonies. As

[23] Thomas Barnard, *A Sermon Preached to the Ancient and Honourable Artillery Company in Boston, New-England, June 5, 1758* (Boston, 1758), pp. 26–27; Nathaniel Potter, *A Discourse on Jeremiah 8th, 20th* (Boston, 1758), pp. 7–8.

[24] Burr, *Discourse*, pp. 27–28; Checkley, *Duty of God's People*, p. 24; Vinal, *Sermon*, pp. 11, 14–15; Eliphalet Williams, *The Duty of a People, under dark Providences* (New London, Conn., 1756), pp. 39–40; Charles Chauncy, *The Earth delivered from the Curse to which it is, at present, subjected* (Boston, 1756), pp. 23–24; Browne, *Necessity of Reformation*, pp. 10–11; Keteltas, *Religious Soldier*, pp. 14–15; Mayhew, *A Discourse on Rev. XV 3d, 4th* (Boston, 1755), pp. 61–62.

Gilbert Tennent marveled, "A gracious GOD has interposed and unbarr'd his Arm, as in the Days of old, and sent undeserved and almost unexpected Salvations to us, blessed be his Name!"[25]

Without a doubt the greatest favorable manifestation of Divine Providence during King George's War was the Anglo-American capture of the French fortress of Louisburg. After a siege of several months the "Dunkirk of North America," situated on Cape Breton, surrendered to British and American forces on 17 June 1745. American spokesmen immediately celebrated the Lord as the architect of victory. In Boston, Charles Chauncy breathlessly told his congregation, "I scarce know of a Conquest, since the Days of *Joshua* and the *Judges*, wherein the Finger of God is more visible. There has been such a Train of Providences, such a Concurrence of favourable Circumstances, making Way for it, as are truly wonderful." At the same time, in Philadelphia, Chauncy's theological opponent Gilbert Tennent publicly proclaimed, "How admirable . . . is the mercy of God in giving into our Hands this strong Hold of the Enemy of our Religion and Liberties!"[26]

To God alone, and not to any human prowess or skill, was to be attributed the success. It was clear to "*whoever believes that God does at all concern himself with human Affairs*" that "*this whole Business has been determined and directed by him.*"[27] The truth of this conclusion was even more evident upon review of the marvelous coincidences and events that had gone into the capture of Louisburg, events that could only have been coordinated by an all-knowing and all-powerful deity. Among the wondrous acts of Divine Providence detected in the victory, several were of particular interest. The Lord allowed the French brief successes in campaigns against Nova Scotia in order to awaken America to the threat posed by French control of Louisburg. God caused captured English prisoners of war to observe

[25] Tennent, *Sermon*, p. 28.

[26] Chauncy, *Marvellous Things done by the right Hand and holy Arm of God* (Boston, 1745), p. 12; Tennent, *Necessity of praising God*, p. 37. Hatch has also noted the similarity between Old and New Light responses to the capture of Louisburg ("Origins of Civil Millennialism," p. 420n).

[27] *Boston Evening-Post*, 8, 15 July 1745; Jared Eliot, *God's Marvellous Kindness* (New London, Conn., 1745), pp. 21–23; Hull Abbot, *The Duty of God's People to pray for the Peace of Jerusalem* (Boston, 1746), p. 22.

the defenses of Louisburg and then escape with their vital information. He blessed America's harvests so that there would be no lack of supplies for the Anglo-American expedition. He frustrated French attempts to reinforce their fortress. Divine Providence was the cause of so many colonials volunteering for the expedition, and the good health and safe passage the soldiers enjoyed on their voyage to Cape Breton flowed from the same source. The courage of the troops and the complete surprise effected by their landing were also the Lord's doings. Finally, after he had guided his army to the very walls of Louisburg, the Almighty induced the French to surrender without a pitched battle, thereby preventing an undoubtedly great loss of life on both sides.[28] After such a review it was no wonder that Thomas Prince could confidently ask, "Who can in Reason imagine that such a *Multitude* of *various* and *contrary* running *Wheels*, both of *material Causes* and *spontaneous Agents*, shou'd all be made to work together, and in the midst of Thousands of Difficulties and Contingencies, in the happiest Seasons Coincide, to accomplish *this* GREAT EVENT; without a SUPREAM *Contriver*, *Mover* and *Director*?"[29]

No one providential intervention dominated the great war for the empire as the capture of Louisburg did King George's War. But that did not mean that the hand of God was any less discernible in the 1750s and 1760s than in the 1740s—far from it. Public spokesmen now had a multitude of divine mercies to deal with. Providential intervention on the side of America began almost as soon as the war itself. In June 1755 a joint land and sea expedition under the overall direction of British Admiral Edward Boscawen captured several important French forts in Nova Scotia. The skill of the commander was to be praised, but the hand of God and the smiles of Providence were the true cause of victory. On 8 September of that same year the

[28] This review is constructed from the following detailed accounts of the specific activities of Divine Providence in the capture of Louisburg: Chauncy, *Marvellous Things*, pp. 12–19; Jared Eliot, *God's Marvellous Kindness*, pp. 9–21; *Pa. Jour.*, 18 July 1745; Thomas Prince, *Extraordinary Events the Doings of God* (Boston, 1745), pp. 20–32; Gilbert Tennent, *Necessity of praising God*, pp. 37–39; Williamsburg *Virginia Gazette* (Parks), 6–13 June 1745; Samuel Niles, *A Brief and Plain Essay on God's Wonder-working Providence for New-England* (New London, Conn., 1747), pp. 1–34.

[29] Prince, *Extraordinary Events*, p. 32.

gloom caused by Braddock's defeat was partially lifted by the news that an Anglo-American army led by General William Johnson had defeated a major French force at Lake George. This "*signal Victory*; a never-to-be-forgotten-Mercy to the *English* Colonies," was designed to "excite us still to *encourage ourselves* in *the Lord*" and "to hope, notwithstanding the *Ohio-Defeat*, that the God of Armies is yet *for us*, and will *still maintain* our Cause." And maintain it he did: on 25 July 1758 the fortress of Louisburg (which had been returned to the French in 1748) surrendered to an Anglo-American force for the second time in thirteen years. There was universal rejoicing that "British colours once more adorn the walls of Louisbourg. . . . Thus the kind Hand of Providence, has been pleased to assist us in our undertaking, to crown our Endeavours with Success, and make all our Enterprizes terminate to our wishes."[30]

Barely a year later the greatest divine blessing of the French and Indian War was bestowed on the colonies, when a British army under Generals James Wolfe and Jeffrey Amherst captured Quebec, ending forever the French threat to America. After a campaign that saw the advancing Amherst take back the important forts of Ticonderoga and Crown Point, Quebec fell on 18 September 1759.[31] In a typical reaction the publishers of Philadelphia's *Pennsylvania Journal* "*heartily*" congratulated their readers "*on the most remarkable Success which it hath pleas'd Heaven to afford unto his Majesty's Arms*." It was indeed "pleasant to observe the visible Smiles of Providence" in this "successful Undertaking. . . . we stand astonished at the divine Goodness." North and south the theme was the same: "GOD BE PRAISED! QUEBEC IS IN *ENGLISH* HANDS."[32]

When on 8 September 1760, less than a year after the capture of

[30] [Charles Chauncy], *A Letter to a Friend* (Boston, 1755), p. 13; Checkley, *Duty of God's People*, pp. 26–28; Vinal, *Sermon*, pp. 16–17; *Va. Gaz.* (Hunter), 24 Oct. 1755; George Beckwith, *That People A safe, and happy People, who have God for, and among them* (New London, Conn., 1756), pp. 26, 28–29, 60; *Pa. Jour.*, 7 Sept. 1758.

[31] The hand of God was evident here too: see Bird, *Importance of the divine Presence*, p. 12.

[32] *Pa. Jour.*, 25 Oct. 1759; Amos Adams, *Songs of Victory Directed by Human Compassion, and Qualified with Christian Benevolence* (Boston, 1759), p. 25; Charleston *South-Carolina Gazette*, 20–27 Oct. 1759.

Quebec, the king's troops under Amherst occupied Montreal and brought all of Canada under British control, the reactions from American spokesmen were the same as in previous years. This final reduction of Canada, "a Mercy greatly desired," had been achieved "under the Influence and auspicious Smiles of Heaven." Once again the colonists were instructed to offer "*thanks to* HIM, *who has thus subdued our cruel, proud and insulting Enemies under us*!"[33]

Finally, the Lord's influence was evident in the favorable peace terms achieved at the war's end in 1763. The greatest blessing was that the Peace of Paris attained what (so far as Americans were concerned) the war had been fought for, and what Divine Providence had so dramatically intervened for—the promotion of the liberties of America. James Horrocks, an Anglican minister from Virginia, spoke the sentiments of many Americans from all religious persuasions in all regions when he observed that "the first Thing that will naturally present itself to us in our reflecting upon the happy Consequences resulting from the Blessing now given us, is the Security of our Civil Liberty, a Happiness we justly glory in. . . . Oh Liberty! Thou art the Author of every good and perfect Gift, the inexhaustible Fountain, from whence all Blessings flow." Anglo-American success led some spokesmen to hint at the connection between the Protestant triumph and the hastening of the millennium. And victory in the French and Indian War confirmed the cause and the mission of English America. In an observation that both summed up the era of imperial war and pointed directly to 1776, a Boston divine found that "the purpose of the Deity" in delivering America from the French and Indian danger was "to maintain and diffuse among Mankind the blessings of humanity, freedom, and religion," and rhetorically asked if it was not "probable" that "our Nation is now raised to this highth of greatness and dominion, to be the refuge and asylum of Truth and Liberty: by its influence and example to free the western world from Error and Superstition; and to fix on this extensive Continent, what will be its *peculiar* glory, the universal establishment of Civil Freedom and true Religion?" For this reason, then, God had

[33] Jonathan Ingersoll, *A Sermon Preached Before the General Assembly* (New London, Conn., 1761), p. 37; *Boston News-Letter*, 18 Sept. 1760; *Boston Evening-Post*, 22 Sept. 1760.

championed, and would continue to champion, America. A more succinct summation of the basic tenets of American nationalism than this statement would be difficult to find.[34]

Only one element was missing, and it was more than adequately supplied by many other public spokesmen during this era. The conviction that America was the New Israel constituted the final intercolonial theme to emerge from the era of the colonial wars. The Great Awakening was the occasion, and New England men the agents, for the transfer of this central concept of seventeenth-century Puritan ideology to all of America. By the time of the French and Indian War the extent of this transfer was evident. Spokesmen by the 1750s manifested a common intercolonial acceptance of the idea that the settlement of America (not just New England) was comparable to the Exodus. "Were the Children of *Israel* led out of *Egypt*, God Almighty, giving them the Land of the Heathen? So are our Ancestors brought over from Europe to this land." Not only had the same God conducted the two peoples to their respective promised lands, there was furthermore "a very great Analogy and Likeness" between the ways he subsequently prospered them.[35]

The great war for the empire especially illustrated the parallels between the old and new Israels. Because of sin, did not "the Lord speak to us, as he did against *Israel*, by warning Dispensations of his Providence?" The moral conditions of the two peoples were woefully similar. Both had abandoned the Lord to serve mammon; both were notoriously guilty of Sabbath-breaking, profanity, bribery, sedition, and unethical business ventures; both were proud and vain. As a

[34] Samuel Haven, *Joy and Salvation by Christ; his Arm displayed in the Protestant Cause* (Portsmouth, N.H., 1763), p. 34; Lockwood, *Sermon*, p. 18; Horrocks, *Upon the Peace* (Williamsburg, Va., 1763), pp. 6–7; Christopher M. Beam, "Millennialism and American Nationalism, 1740–1800," *Journal of Presbyterian History* 54 (1976): 184–85; James West Davidson, *The Logic of Millennial Thought: Eighteenth-Century New England* (New Haven, 1977), pp. 208–12; East Apthorp, *The Felicity of the Times* (Boston, 1763), p. 19.

[35] Theodorus Frelinghuysen, *A Sermon Preached on Occasion of the Late Treaty* (New York, 1754), p. 9; Ebenezer Devotion, *The Civil Ruler, a Dignify'd Servant of the Lord, but a dying Man* (New London, Conn., 1753), pp. 41–42; Ebenezer Prime, *The Importance of the Divine Presence with the Armies of God's People* (New York, 1759), pp. 3–4; Nathaniel Appleton, *A Sermon Preached October 9* (Boston, 1760), pp. 15–18.

result both nations were visited with the wrath of God, a wrath again strikingly and significantly similar in its actualization. Under divine justice both peoples were "attacked by a potent, a faithless and idolatrous nation, fond of Power . . . perpetually endeavouring to establish a corrupt and superstitious system of Worship, and an arbitrary and despotic scheme of government." The Philistines and Amalekites had served as the rod of God in ancient days; the French and Indians were their modern equivalents.[36]

The national situations of the two Israels, then, were the same—but so was the way to their salvation. As Matthias Harris told the citizens of Lewes, Delaware, in 1757, since "our present situation, in many circumstances, is greatly similar to that of the *Jews* when slaughtered by a cruel and relentless foe, let us act as they did. . . . In their *distress*, they remembered and called upon *that* God, whom, during their prosperity, they had forgotten, or ungratefully neglected; and, as we have imitated them in the *wicked*, so let us follow the commendable part of their conduct." (That Harris, a middle colony Anglican, used such imagery is clear testimony to the ongoing nationalization of concepts derived from the New England Puritans.) If America would reform, the Lord's "Wrath will be appeased, his Judgments removed, his Providence will smile on us, we shall see of his Salvation, and Peace upon our *Israel*—what more can we desire?" When finally the colonists, "like godly *Asa*, cried to the Lord," they were saved.[37]

The French and Indian War was the occasion for the first major presentation and acceptance throughout the colonies of the theme that America was the New Israel which, like Israel of old, was favored by Divine Providence because it had a divine mission to perform. In 1760 David Hall, a Congregationalist minister from Massachusetts, told an audience that "our Colonies, in many re-

[36] Theodorus Frelinghuysen, *Sermon*, p. 10; Harrington, *Prevailing Wickedness*, pp. 19–23; Matthias Harris, *A Sermon, Preached in the Church of St. Peters in Lewes* (Philadelphia, 1757), pp. 9–12; "Philo-Americus," *N.Y. Gaz.*, 26 May 1755; Nathan Stone, *Two Discourses Delivered in Southborough* (Boston, 1761), p. 2; Samuel Haven, *Joy and Salvation by Christ*, p. 28.

[37] Harris, *Sermon*, pp. 35–36; Potter, *Discourse*, pp. 25–26; Samuel Dunbar, *The Presence of God with his People, their only Safety and Happiness* (Boston, 1760), pp. 1–3.

spects, bear a very nigh Resemblance to the Tribes of *Israel*. No people under Heaven . . . have been attended with so many similar Circumstances." Nothing about this claim was really striking; the imagery and the implications of Hall's observation had been prevalent in the Bay Colony for more than a century. But five years earlier Philip Reading, a Pennsylvania Anglican divine, asked a Philadelphia gathering to join with him in imploring God to "bless our Sion, the Vineyard which thine own Right Hand hath planted, and thy good Providence hitherto preserved."[38] In this statement much was striking—and significant. Until the era of the Great Awakening and the colonial wars, the imagery and implications of Reading's words would have been associated neither with the man who uttered them nor the audience which received them. In this similarity of theme and intensity between a New England Calvinist and a non–New England Anglican lies the significance of the providential thought that had emerged by 1763. Perhaps without knowing or intending it, Reading and his fellow public spokesmen at one and the same time looked back to the Puritan fathers of 1630 and forward to the patriots of 1776. The "New Englandization" of the American colonies had been achieved. This intercolonial providential thought would not disappear with the departure of the French, but rather would remain as the fundamental basis of a developing American patriotism.

[38] Hall, *Israel's Triumph* (Boston, 1761), p. 11; Reading, *Protestant's Danger*, p. 28.

III

The God of Liberty or the God of Order?

After 1763 Americans were caught up in a new crisis that inspired additional reliance upon the national providential thought fashioned during the era of the imperial wars. The coming of the American Revolution saw the development of both patriot and loyalist providential rhetoric, each side appealing to a common providential heritage to marshal the support of the American population. By 1776 the patriots had triumphed in this contest of providential ideologies, just as they had triumphed in the political contest over the issue of American independence. Providential themes were an integral part of the patriot response to the constitutional contest with Great Britain. Through the patriot spokesmen of 1763–76 key providential images and concepts were permanently wedded to the creation of the United States. The patriot "God of Liberty" had bested the loyalist "God of Order."

The public literature of the era illustrates both the continuity of themes before and after 1763 and the strong intercolonial support these themes received. The Reverend Gad Hitchcock of Massachusetts, preaching in 1774 on the anniversary of the landing of the Pilgrim Fathers, told his audience that if they took "into consideration the effects produced by oppression in the human mind," they would "find that it has been [God's] design all along, to discountenance oppression in its various forms, and encourage and promote liberty in the world." Hitchcock's colleague Henry Cumings put the case even more strongly one year later: "Slavery tends directly to increase the degeneracy of human nature, and to extinguish every spark of genius: It is the prolific source of ignorance, gross superstition, and savage barbarism: It is the bane of all social virtues, a mortal enemy to the liberal arts and sciences, and to *pure and undefiled religion*. The cause of liberty is therefore the cause of God."[1] Strik-

[1] Hitchcock, *A Sermon Preached at Plymouth December 22d, 1774* (Boston, 1775), pp. 14–15; Cumings, *A Sermon, Preached in Billerica, On the 23d of November, 1775* (Worcester, Mass., [1776]), p. 23. For other New England expres-

ingly similar sentiments were articulated in the middle colonies. In Pennsylvania, William Foster, a Presbyterian minister, rhetorically asked a rural audience, "Is it not agreeable to the divine mind that we should be free, and enjoy the inestimable blessing" of liberty "without the fear of man, which causeth a snare," and answered emphatically, "Certainly it is." Hugh Henry Brackenridge in a patriotic drama agreed that patriots could

take the field,
Sure of success, with this sweet comfort giv'n,
Who fights for FREEDOM,—fights the cause of HEAV'N.

Philip Freneau in "American Liberty, a Poem" (1775) wrote:

Kind watchful power, on whose supreme command
The fate of monarchs, empires, worlds depend,
Grant, in a cause thy wisdom must approve,
Undaunted valour kindled from above. . . .

. . . . .

'Tis done, and see th' omnipotent befriends,
The sword of Gideon, and of God descends.[2]

In the southern colonies too the people were reminded that "LIBERTY" was "Heav'n born." Americans, a South Carolina journal argued, were always justified "by *Reason*, by *Nature*, yea, by *God*

---

sions of this theme, see David S. Rowland, *Divine Providence Illustrated and Improved* (Providence, [1766]), p. 21; "America Solon," *Boston Gazette*, 23 Dec. 1771; "An American," ibid., 2 Nov. 1772; "Humanity," ibid., 9 Nov. 1772; "A Patagonian," ibid., 21 Feb. 1774; "An Address to the Farmers, mechanics, and tradesmen of Rhode-Island," *Newport Mercury*, 11 July 1774, as quoted in Philip Davidson, *Propaganda and the American Revolution, 1763–1783* (Chapel Hill, N.C., 1941), p. 114; Samuel Baldwin, *A Sermon, Preached at Plymouth, December 22, 1775* (Boston, 1776), p. 21; Joseph Perry, *A Sermon, Preached Before the General Assembly* (Hartford, 1775), p. 16; Judah Champion, *Christian and Civil Liberty and Freedom Considered and Recommended* (Hartford, 1776), p. 14.

[2] Foster, *True Fortitude delineated* (Philadelphia, 1776), p. 12; [Hugh Henry Brackenridge], *The Battle of Bunker's-Hill* (Philadelphia, 1776), p. 38; Fred Lewis Pattee, ed., *The Poems of Philip Freneau*, 3 vols. (Princeton, N.J., 1902–7), 1:142–43. For other middle-colony expressions of this theme, see "G.," *New-York Journal*, 24 Sept. 1767; "On Liberty," ibid., 8 Oct. 1767; ibid., 2 May 1771, 1 Oct. 1772; [Alexander Martin], *Liberty. A Poem* (Philadelphia, 1768), p. 12; "A Jersey Farmer," *Pa. Jour.*, 14 June 1775; Robert Ross, *A Sermon, in which the Union of the Colonies is Considered and Recommended* (New York, 1776), p. 24.

himself" in seeking to preserve their "*natural Rights*, and *that Liberty* wherewith God has made us all free."[3] These and similar statements clearly represent extensions of sentiments uttered during the era of the French and Indian wars.

Patriots after 1763 thus began with the conviction that God's plan for human history was the promotion of civil and religious freedom. From this principle they naturally concluded that their own defense of freedom against the encroachments of British "tyranny" was a divine cause. Resistance to British policies, and ultimately the American Revolution and national independence, became the actualization of the will of Divine Providence. Significantly, this belief cut across regional, class, and religious lines. Winthrop S. Hudson correctly concludes that "it was not only the clergy who interpreted the American Revolution as a cause of God in defense of civil and religious freedom. Almost every patriot spoke in these terms."[4]

As one Boston patriot urged his fellow whigs, "Persevere in the glorious Cause in which we are engaged. It is the Cause of our King, our Country, and of God himself." The Reverend Oliver Noble concurred: "The CAUSE of America . . . is the cause of *God*, never did Man struggle in a greater, or more *glorious* CAUSE . . . we *ask*, we *contend*, for nothing more, than what *God* and nature gave us."[5] In Pennsylvania, John Carmichael told a gathering of volunteers that, in its contest with Great Britain, America had on its side not only "all

[3] *S.C. Gaz.*, 30 May, 6 June 1771, 13 June 1774. For other southern expressions of this theme, see "A North-American," ibid., 28 July–4 Aug. 1766; "Philo-Patriae," ibid., 21 Sept. 1769; "Cato's Soliloquy imitated," *Va. Gaz.* (Purdie), 23 May 1766; Norfolk, Va., Sons of Liberty to Richard Bland, ibid., 30 May 1766, and in *Va. Gaz.* (Rind), 30 May 1766; David Griffith, *Passive Obedience Considered* (Williamsburg, Va., [1776]), p. 25.

[4] "A Religious Politician," *Pa. Jour.*, 7 Feb. 1776; "Salus Populi," ibid., 14 Feb. 1776; Hudson, ed., *Nationalism and Religion*, pp. 36–37.

[5] "Hampden," *Boston Gaz.*, 8 Aug. 1774; Noble, *Some Strictures Upon the Sacred Story Recorded in the Book of Esther* (Newburyport, Mass., 1775), pp. 20–21. See also [Stephen Johnson], *Some Important Observations* (Newport, R.I., 1766), pp. 38–39; "Eleutherina," *Boston Gaz.*, 27 Jan. 1772; Samuel Baldwin, *Sermon*, p. 38; Champion, *Christian and Civil Liberty*, pp. 22–23, 28–29. For a private concurrence see Ezra Stiles to Catharine Macaulay, 15 Apr. 1775, as quoted in Pauline Maier, *From Resistance to Revolution: Colonial Radicals and the Development of American Opposition to Britain, 1765–1776* (New York, 1972), pp. 264–65.

the true friends of virtue, of liberty and righteousness," but also "all the angels of heaven," and urged them to take comfort from the certainty that "God will never forsake his side of the question." To many other patriotic inhabitants of Pennsylvania, New York, and New Jersey, it was clear that —in the imagery of Hugh Henry Brackenridge—"We combat in the cause of God."[6] Southerners also rejoiced that "Heaven's high Hosts proclaim our cause their own." As "A Soldier" told the patriots of Virginia at the close of 1775, "We are engaged . . . in the cause of virtue, of liberty, of God. For God's sake then let us play the man."[7] The triple linkage of liberty, America, and Divine Providence, first fashioned by New England Puritans in the seventeenth century and strengthened by anti-French rhetoric in the 1740s and 1750s, was stridently reasserted during (and reinforced by) the coming of the American Revolution.

With God's cause at stake neutrality was out of the question. Failure to come to the defense of American liberty was not only cowardly, patriots asserted, it was positively sinful. As the *New-York Journal* charged, "He who manifests any backwardness in the present glorious struggle for preserving the Liberties of America, betrays the basest ingratitude to Almighty GOD." Pious spokesmen invoked the biblical "Curse of Meroz" against all Americans who refused "to come in to *the help of the Lord, to the help of the Lord against the mighty*." Jeremiah was also enlisted in the noble venture: "Cursed be he that keepeth back his sword from blood in such a cause." Since such a divine cause permitted but one response, the sufferings of loyalists and neutrals, those "secret enemies" to American rights, were readily explainable (at least to whigs). The Lord was clearly

[6] Carmichael, *A Self-Defensive War Lawful* (Lancaster, Pa., [1775]), p. 25; [Brackenridge], *Battle of Bunker's-Hill*, p. 10. See also "A Pennsylvanian," Philadelphia *Pennsylvania Chronicle*, in *N.Y. Jour.*, 19 July 1770; David Jones, *Defensive War in a just Cause Sinless* (Philadelphia, 1775), p. 23; William Foster, *True Fortitude*, pp. 14–15; Alden T. Vaughan, ed., *Chronicles of the American Revolution* (New York, 1965), p. 236.

[7] "The Present Times," *Va. Gaz.* (Dixon and Hunter), 19 Aug. 1775; "A Soldier," ibid., 23 Dec. 1775. See also "Libertas et Natale Solum," *S.C. Gaz.*, *Supplement*, 20 Aug. 1770, and John Rutledge, "Speech to the South Carolina Assembly," 11 Apr. 1776, in Frank Moore, ed., *American Eloquence: A Collection of Speeches and Addresses, by the Most Eminent Orators of America*, 2 vols. (New York, 1867), 1:121.

manifesting "his anger against those who have refused to assist their country against its cruel oppressors."[8]

During this early Revolutionary era patriot spokesmen, imitating earlier Americans, strengthened public opinion by selectively reviewing their colonial history (brief though it was) and discovering there concepts popular in their own day. This reinforcement was to be expected, since "one function of tradition is to provide a focus for the sentiment that binds men together in hours of trial." Seeking such a focus, patriots first went back to the seventeenth-century origins of the New Israel and once again refashioned the legend of the founding fathers. Twin purposes were behind such backward glances: spokesmen sought to reinforce current popular beliefs and thereby inspire continued trust in Divine Providence. These were clearly the aims of the Reverend Amos Adams of Roxbury, Massachusetts, who reminded his flock in 1767, "God, my brethren, *hath called us to liberty*—in a wonderful manner, did he bring our fathers into this land of *liberty*, and now, for more than an *hundred* years, hath he continued us in the full and perfect enjoyment of our . . . liberties—no weapon formed against us hath prospered." Another New England minister later made the same point with even more directness. "The cause in which we are engaged, is the same, for which our worthy ancestors," for the sake of liberty, "encountered all perils and difficulties. And the Almighty manifested his approbation of their cause, by remarkably supporting and prospering their noble exertions. From hence we have reason to hope that he will also graciously appear for us, and espouse our cause."[9]

New Englanders were especially prone to these examinations, since they had decades earlier recast their errand into the wilderness

[8] *N.Y. Jour.*, 14 Dec. 1775; "T. Q.," *Boston Gaz.*, 15 Aug. 1768; William Stearns, *A View of the Controversy subsisting between Great-Britain and the American Colonies* (Watertown, Mass., 1775), p. 32; William Foster, *True Fortitude*, pp. 20–21; Heimert, *Religion and the American Mind*, pp. 334, 406, 503; Samuel West, *A Sermon Preached Before the Honorable Council* (Boston, 1776), in John Wingate Thornton, ed., *The Pulpit of the American Revolution* (Boston, 1860), p. 309.

[9] Michael Kammen, "The Meaning of Colonization in American Revolutionary Thought," *Journal of the History of Ideas* 31 (1970): 337–58; Craven, *Legend of the Founding Fathers*, p. 38; Adams, *Religious Liberty an invaluable Blessing* (Boston, 1768), pp. 48–49; Cumings, *Sermon Preached November 1775*, pp. 17–18.

as the defense of civil and religious freedom.[10] The theme, however, was clearly expressed outside New England. Pennsylvania's Joseph Montgomery, for example, also told Americans that their "forefathers" had "groaned under bondage not inferior to that" of the "Egyptian" until "with invincible courage" they engaged in "the arduous undertaking" of migration to the New World. "The God of Heaven looks down with pleasure, whilst he views the laudible motives—and commands success." Philip Freneau expressed a similar sentiment: "Pitying heav'n the just design surveys, / Sends prosp'-rous gales, and wafts them o'er the seas." Not surprisingly, after reviewing the hand of God in the settlement of America, a Virginia author styling himself "Philo Americanus" told his countrymen, "Continue to be what you hitherto have been, and you may defy men and devils."[11]

With the seventeenth-century libertarian basis of the New Israel firmly established, patriot public spokesmen throughout the colonies turned to it again and again after 1763, citing providential blessings that would reassure and inspire patriots in their current struggle to avert "slavery." As early as 1767 Josiah Quincy, Jr., writing as "Hyperion," concluded that "with the GOD of ARMIES on our side, even the GOD who fought our Father's battles, we fear not the hour of trial; tho' the host of our enemies should cover the field like locusts, and set their Armies in dreadful array against us, yet the sword of the Lord and Gideon shall prevail." Or, as a South Carolinian put it just one year later, "we have a Divine Providence to protect us," and "as it has supported us hitherto," there could be no doubt but that America

[10] Craven, *Legend of the Founding Fathers*, p. 37; Hudson, ed., *Nationalism and Religion*, p. 36. For other typical New England accounts of Divine Providence protecting their seventeenth-century ancestors for the promotion of civil and religious liberty, see Rowland, *Divine Providence Illustrated*, p. 12; "Cincinnatus," *Boston Gaz.*, 11 July 1768; [Silas Downer], *A Discourse, Delivered in Providence, in the Colony of Rhode-Island, Upon the 25th Day of July, 1768* (Providence, 1768), p. 14; Joseph Warren, *An Oration, Delivered March 5th, 1772* (Boston, 1772), pp. 16–17; William Stearns, *View of the Controversy*, pp. 12–13; Joseph Warren, *An Oration; Delivered March Sixth, 1775* (Boston, 1775), pp. 6–7; Champion, *Christian and Civil Liberty*, p. 16.

[11] Montgomery, *A Sermon, Preached at Christiana Bridge and Newcastle, The 20th of July, 1775* (Philadelphia, 1775), pp. 23–24; Pattee, ed., *Poems of Freneau*, 1:144; "Philo Americanus," *Va. Gaz.*, *Supplement* (Purdie and Dixon), 9 Nov. 1769.

"shall have the Continuance of it." Implied in the popular phrase "our fathers trusted in God" was the conviction that, as the Almighty had delivered them, so would he now deliver their sons. Reviewing the hand of God in that previous crusade for liberty (the French and Indian War), patriots found inspiration for their contemporary crusade against British "tyranny" and "infidelity." As the deliverance of America in 1754–63 was not from "the arm of *flesh*, so, may the same Divine protection [now] shield her . . . from the domination of tyranny."[12]

What patriots ultimately derived from this searching of their history is vividly illustrated by the remarks of "An American" in 1774: "My countrymen. . . . I have always observed a remarkable coincidence of Providences in favour of this country, which greatly animates me with the hope that HEAVEN will yet bless us and cause our enemies to flee before us; and I trust that, under the divine blessing, America will grow rich, and great, and happy in [spite of] this oppression which we now feel."[13] The lack of a historical past, as scholars have pointed out, hindered the growth of American nationalism.[14] But the efforts of patriot spokesmen after 1763 to use their past—in particular the legend of the founding fathers and the providential historiography surrounding the fathers and their immediate descendants—in the service of the present suggest that this historical absence was not absolute. Patriots may have had only a century (or less) to work with, but from that century's events they managed to extract a confirmation of their conviction that Divine Providence had singled out America for a glorious mission involving the promotion of liberty. This idea of mission became one of the key ingredients of American patriotism during and then long after the era

[12] "Hyperion," *Boston Gaz.*, 5 Oct. 1767; "A British Carolinian," Charleston *South-Carolina Gazette; and Country Journal*, 11 Oct. 1768; Charles Chauncy, *Trust in God, the Duty of a People in a Day of Trouble* (Boston, 1770), p. 25; Samuel Cooke, *A Sermon Preached at Cambridge, in the Audience of His Honor Thomas Hutchinson* (Boston, 1770), in Thornton, ed., *Pulpit*, p. 173; Samuel Webster, *The Misery and Duty of an oppress'd and enslaved People* (Boston, 1774), p. 31; "R.," *Boston Gaz.*, 26 Feb. 1776; *N.Y. Jour.*, 20 Oct. 1774; *Boston Gaz.*, 27 Jan. 1772.

[13] "An American," *Boston Evening-Post*, 23 May 1774.

[14] Hans Kohn, *The Idea of Nationalism* (New York, 1944), p. 324; Russel B. Nye, *This Almost Chosen People: Essays in the History of American Ideas* (East Lansing, Mich., 1966), pp. 45–46.

of the American Revolution. The American past may not have contained mythical kings or legendary lawgivers upon whom nationalist legends could be founded, but it was made to contain the hand of God—and that hand figured prominently in the crystallization of American providential nationalism during the Revolutionary years.

Yet however often Americans reaffirmed their mission through these historical musings, the road to the achievement of their mission was still long and difficult—and not all the forces working against it came from across the Atlantic. The sins and moral failings of the American people seemed at times to threaten the liberties of the New Israel as seriously as did British policies. The Revolutionary era carried on the jeremiad tradition: sin was seen (at least by pious patriots) as a major cause of political, social, and economic evils. As the Reverend John Joachim Zubly, future member of the Continental Congress and future loyalist, reminded the people of Savannah, Georgia, in 1766, "National sins bring on national calamities."[15] But again, as in earlier decades, this conclusion was always tempered with the belief that in visiting a people (especially a people highly favored in the past) with troubles, God was aiming at reformation, not destruction. "When he visits a people with affliction, or sends his judgments on them, he expects that they search and try their ways and turn [back] to him." When a people took such action, they could be assured that the frowns of Omnipotence would abate and the smiles of Providence return.[16]

The jeremiad tradition, then, was invoked to explain why the colonies in the 1760s and 1770s were threatened with the imminent loss of their God-given freedoms. American sins alone did not cause the British to act as tyrants (tyranny came also from God allowing

[15] J[ohn] J[oachim] Zubly, *The Stamp-Act Repealed*, 2d ed. (Savannah, 1766), p. 17. For similar pronouncements see James Cogswell, *A Sermon, Preached before the General Assembly* (New London, Conn., 1771), pp. 9, 24–25; Nathan Fiske, *The Importance of Righteousness to the Happiness, and the Tendency of Oppression to the Misery of a People* (Boston, 1774), pp. 38–39; Timothy Hilliard, *The duty of a People under the oppression of Man, to seek deliverance from God* (Boston, 1774), p. 16; John Witherspoon, *The Dominion of Providence over the Passions of Men* (Philadelphia, 1776), pp. 18–19.

[16] Moses Parsons, *A Sermon Preached at Cambridge, Before His Excellency Thomas Hutchinson* (Boston, 1772), pp. 29–30. Cf. *Boston Gaz., Supplement (Extraordinary)*, 26 Sept. 1768, and Hilliard, *duty of a People*, pp. 18–19.

Britons to act out their own evil inclinations). But vice and irreligion in the colonies did influence the scope and severity of the contest with the mother country. The constitutional crisis, although allowed especially to permit the fulfillment of America's divine mission, was also sent (in part) to punish the New Israel for her sins. As long as external threats to their liberties existed, patriots could be certain that the Lord was displeased with their moral condition. Thus reformation went hand in hand with self-defense; the jeremiad in the 1760s and 1770s remained strongly relevant to the American mind.[17]

Significantly, these convictions were prominent in all the colonies after 1763. As Jonathan Lee told the General Assembly of Connecticut in the midst of the Stamp Act crisis, "There has been very grievous complaints [among us], of oppression, tyranny, and a corrupt and designing ministry: And of home bred abettors of tyranny. . . . But however just this may be. . . . Who is the moral governor of the world? Is there not a cause [for our misery?] . . . verily it is our iniquities, which have separated us from God, and the smiles of his providence." Later Boston's venerable Charles Chauncy, in the wake of the Boston Massacre, told an audience of Bay Colony whigs, "Our sins are the worst enemies we have. They are . . . the true moral cause of all that we now suffer, or have reason to fear."[18] A Pennsylvania writer in 1772 pointed out to his readers that "our country is the victim of a powerful nation, our *liberty* is tottering and crumbling to nought; and GOD in whom our hopes should center, seems to withdraw his aid. . . . our *debaucheries*, our *luxeries*, our *dress*, and our *decay of business*; examine these I say, and ask ourselves whether these vices are not the consequences of each other, and who punishes the sins of a people but GOD"?[19] And two years later

[17] Perry Miller, "From the Covenant to the Revival," *Nature's Nation* (Cambridge, Mass., 1967), pp. 90–102; Heimert, *Religion and the American Mind*, pp. 423–26.

[18] Lee, *A Sermon, Delivered before the General Assembly* (New London, Conn., 1766), p. 19; Chauncy, *Trust in God*, p. 19. For other typical New England jeremiads see "Christian," *Boston Gaz.*, 4 Nov. 1771; Cogswell, *Sermon*, pp. 35–36; Parsons, *Sermon*, pp. 22–23; Israel Holly, *God brings about his holy and wise Purpose* (Hartford, 1774), pp. 15–16; Gad Hitchcock, *Sermon*, pp. 40–41; Samuel Sherwood, *A Sermon, Containing, Scriptural Instructions to Civil Rulers, and all Free-born Subjects* (New Haven, 1774), pp. 34–38; Samuel Webster, *Misery and Duty*, pp. 27–29.

[19] "Demostenes," *Pa. Jour.*, 11 Nov. 1772. Cf. ibid., 5 Dec. 1771.

William Tennent in like vein lectured a meeting in South Carolina: "While we exclaim against the Instruments of our Calamities . . . we [must not] forget to exclaim against the prevailing Iniquities of our Country, and to consider them as the only Causes which have drawn down the Frowns of Omnipotence upon us."[20] Despite these and similar warnings, however, the sins of America continued so long and so grievously that God in his anger decreed that the contest with Britain be settled only through bloodshed and war. The constitutional crisis would not be peacefully resolved. This fateful development showed the height of the Lord's righteous wrath and ought seriously to be considered and acted upon by all who feared Jehovah and loved their country.[21]

With their frequent resort to this chronicling of their "degeneration," it might at first be expected that patriots would approach resistence and revolution with trepidation, with doubts and fears that perhaps God had or would wholly abandon them for their sins. But the jeremiad tradition, as we have seen, was two-sided, with the anticipation of salvation immediately following—indeed, stemming from—the Lord's chastisements. This was "proved" by the particular events patriots experienced after 1763. Patriots derived the conviction, and even the religious fervor evident in their opposition to Great Britain, from a perception of favorable interventions of Divine Providence in contemporary military and political events. Indeed, they perceived these mercies to such a degree that when war came in 1775, it was seen as another just chastisement of the New Israel—but not one that threatened its destruction. The hand of the Lord displayed in the specific political and military developments leading up to the Revolutionary War proved that God intended America ultimately to prevail.

The first such event to reflect the favoring hand of God (one that

[20] Tennent, *An Address, Occasioned by the Late Invasion of the Liberties of the American Colonies* (Philadelphia, 1774), p. 8. Although published in Philadelphia, this discourse was delivered in Charleston. See also Zubly, *Stamp-Act Repealed*, pp. 17–19, and *Va. Gaz.* (Rind), 1 Sept. 1774.

[21] See Wilmington, N.C., *Cape-Fear Mercury*, 25 Aug. 1775; William Stearns, *View of the Controversy*, p. 28; *An Affectionate Address to the Inhabitants of the British Colonies in America* (Philadelphia, 1776), pp. iii–iv, 50; William Linn, *A Military Discourse, Delivered in Carlisle, March the 17th, 1776* (Philadelphia, 1776), p. 17.

set the pattern for the next ten years) was the Stamp Act crisis of 1765–66.[22] Because of American ingratitude for past mercies, the Lord suffered misguided or malicious British ministers to fashion and pass the Stamp Act, which threatened the colonies with "slavery." But the deity had no intention of allowing the act to achieve its intended purpose; hence when patriots learned in the spring of 1766 of the act's repeal, they knew who had delivered them. "Our FAITH approved, our LIBERTY restor'd, / Our Hearts bend grateful to our Sov'reign Lord." Patriots from Massachusetts to South Carolina were called to thanksgiving "by the voice of divine providence, upon the experience of his kind interposition, in our rescue from the most threatning dangers, and a burden similar to that of the Egyptian task-masters." Through the entire course of patriot resistance—memorials, petitions, economic pressures, the deliberations of the Stamp Act Congress—the activities of God could be traced.[23]

Divine Providence also secured for America "friends" in Britain who helped bring about repeal of the dreaded act. English merchants, members of Parliament, and even George III himself had all been "raised up" and "influenced" by God to listen to America's pleas and rescind the unwise measure. Certainly the greatest of these British allies was William Pitt, hero of the Seven Years' War and leading defender in Parliament of American rights. Pitt had now, according to Jonathan Mayhew, "twice at least been a principal Instrument in the hand of GOD, of saving GREAT BRITAIN and her Colonies from impending ruin." Still, it was necessary to give the final glory not to men but to God. "However earnest and importunate our friends have been, in the court of Great-Britain," Benjamin Throop reminded the citizens of Norwich, Connecticut, "yet if we

[22] For a more extended discussion of the significance of this event, see my " 'Good News From a Far Country': A Note on Divine Providence and the Stamp Act Crisis," *Church History* 45 (1976): 308–15.

[23] Joseph Emerson, *A Thanksgiving Sermon Preach'd at Pepperrell, July 24th. 1766* (Boston, 1766), pp. 10, 15–17; *N.Y. Mercury*, 9 June 1766; *S.C. Gaz.; and Country Jour.*, 29 July 1766; Rowland, *Divine Providence Illustrated*, p. 2; Nathaniel Appleton, *A Thanksgiving Sermon on the Total Repeal of the Stamp-Act* (Boston, 1766), pp. 22–24, 28; Charles Chauncy, *A Discourse on "the good News from a far Country"* (Boston, 1766), in Thornton, ed., *Pulpit*, pp. 140–42; Zubly, *Stamp-Act Repealed*, pp. 6, 20–22.

had not had a friend in the court of heaven, we should never have obtained what we have." Some patriot spokesmen apparently believed that in the (to their minds) worldly years of the later eighteenth century, the danger of attributing too much to human hands was great, and they explicitly warned against such an error in their celebrations of the repeal of the Stamp Act. But if patriots were disposed to ascribe too much to human actions, it was not evident in the observations of 1766.[24]

Temporarily, some patriots gained confidence from the successful resolution of the Stamp Act crisis. Jonathan Mayhew, for instance, told New Englanders that "not improbably" the Lord intended good to come from their "late troubles": the "great shock" that had been given to the liberties of the New World would "end in the confirmation of them." And far to the south Georgians also heard that as a result of their victory over the hated act, the "civil and religious liberties" of the New Israel would, with God's blessing, "be preserved inviolable till time shall be no more."[25] The next years, however, were to prove these sentiments highly overoptimistic. The Stamp Act, patriots soon concluded, was not the only weapon in the arsenal of those dedicated to the destruction of American liberty.

In late June and early July 1767 Parliament passed the Townshend Acts, a series of measures designed to raise money in the colonies by setting new duties on such commodities as glass, paper, and tea. These acts elicited a three-year campaign by patriots to force their repeal. To effect this, merchants and politicians adopted various economic policies, including nonimportation and nonexportation of goods with Britain and the exclusive use of domestic manufactures. The political and economic rationales for these measures

[24] William Patten, *A Discourse Delivered At Hallifax, In the County of Plymouth, July 24th 1766* (Boston, 1766), pp. 20–21; Rowland, *Divine Providence Illustrated*, pp. iii, 15–16, 18, 22; Mayhew, *The Snare Broken* (Boston, 1766), p. iv; Throop, *A Thanksgiving Sermon* (New London, Conn., 1766), pp. 8, 15; "An Ode, Occasioned by the Repeal of the Stamp-Act, and the present Freedom of the Press," *Va. Gaz.*, *Supplement* (Rind), 15 Aug. 1766; Nathaniel Appleton, *Thanksgiving Sermon*, p. 21; Joseph Emerson, *Thanksgiving Sermon*, p. 18; Elisha Fish, *Joy and Gladness* (Providence, 1767), p. 13.

[25] Mayhew, *Snare Broken*, p. 37; Zubly, *Stamp-Act Repealed*, p. 20.

were compelling, but for total acceptance they were also presented to the colonial populace as weapons placed in patriot hands by Divine Providence for the defense of the New Israel's inestimable rights. To ignore the course thus marked out by an "indulgent Providence" would "foolishly" be to "neglect the invitation of Heaven to be happy." The resort to providential thought to bolster even these most secular of tactics is striking indication both of the pervasiveness of providential concepts and of the belief of patriots that the employment of those concepts could only enhance their cause in the eyes of the colonial populace.[26]

Patriot opposition to the Townshend Acts ultimately divided and subsided, but not before it had contributed to the next clear intervention of the Almighty in America's behalf. In 1768, stung by whig activities in Massachusetts, British officials sent three regiments of regular troops to garrison the city of Boston. From this decision eventually came the first significant bloodshed of the resistance era—the Boston Massacre of 5 March 1770. Although a terrible "tragedy" (to patriots), the massacre nevertheless was also seen as a favorable visitation of Providence. For one thing, the massacre portended the eventual defeat of the New Israel's enemies; the blood of the slain martyrs called like the blood of Abel to Almighty God for vengeance and justice. For another, the Lord restrained the passions of the patriotic citizens of Boston, preventing them from wreaking immediate vengeance on the bloody agents of a corrupt ministry. This divine decision was truly great and merciful, for such an attack (although perfectly justifiable in whig eyes) would only have led to even more bloodshed at a time when all the advantages rested with the British. Then too, it clearly was God's overruling influence that caused the authorities (especially Thomas Hutchinson) eventually to realize the dangers of standing armies and remove all the soldiers from Boston proper. In the end the Boston Massacre found its place in the overall providential defense of American liberty. "GOD in *mercy* suffered so early a TRAGEDY and CARNAGE of our brethren . . . that by awakening us out of lethargy, to assert our invaded rights, and unit-

[26] "Atticus, No. II," Annapolis *Maryland Gazette*, 11 May 1769; "A Planter," *S.C. Gaz.*, 1 June 1769; "Brutus," *Va. Gaz.* (Rind), 1 June 1769.

ing us in the general cause before it was too late, he might prevent greater destruction."[27]

Because of this divinely inspired unity, patriots were better prepared when the next crisis came in 1774. Enraged by the Boston Tea Party of 16 December 1773, Parliament between March and June 1774 enacted the series of punitive laws characterized by whigs as the Intolerable Acts. Prominent among them was the Boston Port Act, which shut down entirely all shipping in and out of Boston until that city made restitution for the tea destroyed by Sam Adams and his "Mohawks." Boston refused to comply and appealed to her sister colonies for supplies to avert starvation. The response surprised and gratified even the most confident patriots: food and implements poured into the city from individuals and committees throughout America. For some there could be only one explanation—a "Guardian God," who held "the Hearts of his People in his Hands," was influencing Boston's "distant Brethren" to come to her aid.[28] Most importantly, God used the punishment of Massachusetts to unite the colonies as never before. As "Virginius" told the inhabitants of the Old Dominion, "Wonderful and unaccountable are, my dear fellow citizens, the works and dispensations of Providence! By a strange, but noble species of alchymy, we perceive the greatest possible good resulting from the greatest evil. The Boston port bill, intended by a most *abandoned* ministry to *intimidate* and *divide*, has *joined* together, in an *indissoluble union*, the whole American continent."[29]

When political agitation gave way to armed resistance in April

[27] Samuel Stillman, *A Sermon Preached To the Ancient and Honorable Artillery Company* (Boston, 1770), p. 18n; *Va. Gaz.* (Purdie and Dixon), 19 Apr. 1770; John Lathrop, *Innocent Blood Crying to God from the Streets of Boston* (Boston, 1771), pp. 19–20; Joseph Warren, *1772 Oration*, p. 13; Benjamin Church, *An Oration, Delivered March Fifth, 1773* (Boston, 1773), pp. 19–20; Noble, *Some Strictures*, p. 28.

[28] "G.," *Boston Gaz.*, 11 July 1774. See also William Gordon, *A Discourse Preached December 15th, 1774* (Boston, 1775), in Thornton, ed., *Pulpit*, pp. 221–22; John Lathrop, *A Discourse Preached December 15th 1774* (Boston, 1774), pp. 20–21; Isaac Story, *The Love of Our Country Recommended and Enforced* (Boston, 1775), p. 19; Samuel Adams to Peter T. Curtenius, 9 Jan. 1775, and to Joseph Nye, 21 Feb. 1775, Harry Alonzo Cushing, ed., *The Writings of Samuel Adams*, 4 vols. (New York, 1904–8), 3:166, 181–82.

[29] "Virginius," *Va. Gaz.* (Pinkney), 29 June 1775. See also Hilliard, *duty of a People*, pp. 26–27.

1775, God testified even more dramatically to his commitment to the patriot cause. The British, of course, were believed to be the aggressors at Lexington and Concord; the shot heard round the world had come from a redcoat's gun. It was, therefore, not surprising that "against this horrid injustice the Almighty gave instant judgment: a handful of country militia, badly armed, suddenly collected, and unconnectedly and irregularly brought up to repel the attack, discomfited the regular bands of tyranny; they retreated [to Boston], and [only] night saved them from total slaughter."[30] Significantly, accounts of the Battles of Lexington and Concord presented independently to the citizens of Connecticut, Pennsylvania, and North Carolina all cited the flight of battle-hardened Britons before a handful of enraged patriots as an example of "divine vengeance" and "the interposition of Heaven."[31]

The Battle of Bunker Hill, fought on 17 June 1775, was another manifestation of the divine favor to the patriot cause. In a typical reaction William Linn called on the inhabitants of Carlisle, Pennsylvania, to bless God for the victory on that "ever-memorable action" where "our small army encamped," and "a comparative handful bravely withstood the charge of two thousand of the flower of the British troops." Bunker Hill was an undeniable demonstration that "Providence has . . . favoured the American troops" and clear proof (for those who needed it) that "there is an invisible agent that ruleth in the armies of heaven above, and among the inhabitants of the earth below." Other spokesmen agreed with Hugh Henry Brackenridge that "heaven itself, with snares, and vengeance arm'd," had caused such heavy losses among the attacking British.[32]

In the fall and winter of 1775 the patriots went on the offensive.

[30] William-Henry Drayton, "A Charge to the Grand Jury," 23 Apr. 1776, in Moore, ed., *American Eloquence*, 1:51.

[31] Philadelphia *Dunlap's Pennsylvania Packet*, 1 May 1775, in Frank Moore, ed., *The Diary of the American Revolution: From Newspapers and Original Documents*, 2 vols. (New York, 1860), 1:69; *Cape-Fear Mercury*, 28 July 1775; Champion, *Christian and Civil Liberty*, p. 19.

[32] Linn, *Military Discourse*, pp. 12–13, 16; [Brackenridge], *Battle of Bunker's-Hill*, p. 33. See also *Boston Gaz.*, 25 Sept. 1775; Ezra Sam[p]son, *A Sermon Preached at Roxbury-Camp, Before Col. Cotton's Regiment; On the 20th of July, P.M. 1775* (Watertown, Mass., 1775), p. 20; "Cato," *Va. Gaz.* (Pinkney), 16 Nov. 1775; Champion, *Christian and Civil Liberty*, p. 20.

Two armies invaded Canada to secure that province before it could be reinforced by the British. At first the patriots were successful. One army, commanded by Richard Montgomery, taking the important forts of Crown Point and Ticonderoga on the way, captured Montreal on 13 November 1775, then united with a second unit led by Benedict Arnold, which had traversed the Maine wilderness and stood before the city of Quebec. After failing to take Quebec by storm on 30 December, the combined patriot force laid siege to the city. Surely these favorable (or at least potentially favorable) transactions were the doings of the Lord, indications of his approval of America's righteous cause. But within the next few months the situation was reversed. Decimated by disease and lack of supplies, the patriot army before Quebec was forced to lift its siege on 6 May 1776; in June, Montreal was also abandoned. Yet even in these misfortunes God was instructing America, bringing good out of apparent evil. Two divine lessons were involved: practically, the fate of the Canada expeditions showed the colonies the need for better strategic and military coordination; spiritually, the fate of Montgomery and Arnold illustrated the danger of trusting solely in human resources to the exclusion of God.[33]

While patriot armies were still deep in Canada, one further military operation palpably manifested the hand of Jehovah—the siege of the British army trapped in Boston. After Lexington and Concord, Boston was virtually a British garrison city besieged by 10,000 to 15,000 patriot volunteers. The British position became even more tenuous when George Washington took command of the patriot forces on 3 July 1775. Securing and mounting cannon around the city during the winter of 1775–76, Washington sealed the doom of those inside. Foregoing an attack, the British troops and several hundred loyalists evacuated Boston for Halifax on 17 March 1776, leaving the city to the patriots. Patriot spokesmen enthusiastically saw the departure as yet another signal intervention of Divine Providence and a happy sign that the Lord would surely bless their future

[33] Samuel Baldwin, *Sermon*, p. 35; Nathan Fiske, *Remarkable Providences to be gratefully recollected* (Boston, 1776), p. 29; Thaddeus Maccarty, *Praise to God, a Duty of continual Obligation* (Worcester, Mass., [1776]), p. 22; Ross, *Sermon*, p. 7; Peter Thacher, *An Oration Delivered at Watertown, March 5, 1776* (Watertown, Mass., 1776), p. 11; Champion, *Christian and Civil Liberty*, pp. 20–21.

endeavors. In Hugh Henry Brackenridge's dramatic account Washington, entering Boston with the patriot army, observed, "The hand of Heaven, is visible in this." And this was not a poet's flight of fancy: Washington in fact had "not a doubt" that "this remarkable Interposition of Providence" was for "some wise purpose."[34]

Throughout the entire era of resistance the Almighty also blessed America with three ingredients necessary for success: unity, enthusiasm, and leadership. In promoting union, the hand of God was first evident in the reaction to the Stamp Act, when all classes and sections (it was asserted) were as one in their zeal for "liberty, property, and no stamps." When the contest between Britain and America climaxed after 1774, Divine Providence was again discerned behind colonial solidarity. The "*general union* and *harmony*" that prevailed from north to south was "surely to be ascribed to the Lord, in whose hands are the hearts of the children of men." God was further the author of the remarkable consensus that existed in the First and Second Continental congresses. Delegates from different regions, with disparate backgrounds, persuasions, and personalities, all worked selflessly for the general good of the whole continent. This harmony without question flowed from "the Guardian God of these extended Colonies."[35]

The magnanimity of Providence in thus sponsoring patriot unanimity appeared even more gracious when two special factors were taken into account. First, the British and their loyalist underlings had done everything in their power to divide the colonies. Yet "notwithstanding all the evil machinations of our enemies, to prevent a union of the Colonies, a glorious one" had been constructed, for which it was not "possible to be sufficiently thankful to providence."

[34] Jonas Clarke, *The Fate of Blood-thirsty Oppressors, and God's tender Care of his distressed People* (Boston, 1776), p. 31; Philadelphia *Pennsylvania Evening Post*, 30 Mar. 1776, in Moore, ed., *Diary*, 1:222; Vaughan, ed., *Chronicles*, p. 203; Witherspoon, *Dominion of Providence*, p. 35; [Brackenridge], *Battle of Bunker's-Hill*, p. 46; George Washington to John Augustine Washington, 31 Mar. 1776, John C. Fitzpatrick, ed., *The Writings of George Washington*, 39 vols. (Washington, D.C., 1931–44), 4:477.

[35] Chauncy, *good News*, Thornton, ed., *Pulpit*, p. 128; Mayhew, *Snare Broken*, p. 10; Throop, *Thanksgiving Sermon*, p. 16; Heimert, *Religion and the American Mind*, p. 398; Ross, *Sermon*, p. 27; "A Carolinian, No. VII," *S.C. Gaz.*, 19 Dec. 1774.

Second was the great diversity among the peoples and colonies of America, so pronounced as almost to preclude any discussion of the present grand and glorious union primarily in human terms. As Samuel West marveled,

> I cannot but take notice how wonderfully Providence has smiled upon us by causing the several colonies to unite so firmly together against the tyranny of Great Britain, though differing from each other in their particular interest, forms of government, modes of worship, and particular customs and manners, besides several animosities that had subsisted among them. That, under these circumstances, such a union should take place as we now behold, was a thing that might rather have been wished than hoped for.[36]

Other patriots also stressed the theme that their "union chain" was (in the words of Philip Freneau) "by heaven inspir'd."[37]

It is apparent that in this instance providential thought did not conform to the facts. There was a degree of colonial solidarity, both in Congress and among the general populace, but it was not nearly so strong as patriot spokesmen insisted. Perhaps half of the population stayed neutral or remained loyal to Britain; the Continental congresses were often sharply divided over many vital issues, of which independence was only the most noted. Obviously this theme of a providentially sent unanimity did violence to reality. Why, then, did patriot spokesmen feel compelled to state and restate it? Perhaps they did so in order to shame or pressure those who were neutral into adhering to the patriot cause. Perhaps they feared that to admit anything short of a total commitment would undermine their positions as colonial spokesmen. Then too, admitting a divided America weakened the claim that Americans were a new chosen people inspired to perform a divine mission—indeed, it called into question the entire complex of providential themes that patriot public spokesmen were articulating. As Edward McNall Burns has observed, it is not surprising that "a strongly developed sense of mission should blind a people to numerous realities." In any case, patriots

[36] Samuel Baldwin, *Sermon*, p. 31; West, *Sermon Before the Council*, Thornton, ed., *Pulpit*, p. 303.

[37] Pattee, ed., *Poems of Freneau*, 1:147. See also Ebenezer Baldwin, *The Duty of Rejoicing Under Calamities and Afflictions* (New York, 1776), p. 31; Ross, *Sermon*, pp. 4–5; Drayton, "Charge," Moore, ed., *American Eloquence*, 1:52.

considered the theme of their divinely inspired union and unanimity so vital as to assert it again and again in the face of the contrary.[38]

The hand of Jehovah was also observed in the enthusiasm and energy manifested by the patriots in defense of their rights. When it became clear that the confrontation between Britain and America could be settled only by an appeal to the sword, the Lord "diffused" a "martial spirit" throughout all the colonies. He then saw to it that his people did not lack for qualified leaders. Divine Providence quickly raised up local and national statesmen to proclaim the New Israel's cause and military commanders to promote and defend that cause. Thus was America divinely favored as she moved steadily toward independence and the further implementation of her providential mission.[39]

This wealth of providential blessings and visitations contributed to the crystallization of American nationalism. One of the most important concepts within this developing providential thought was, of course, the depiction of America as God's New Israel. Preachers and orators continued to make extensive use of the New Israel motif throughout the era of the coming of the American Revolution. The explicitness of much of their language is striking, especially when it is recalled that these years comprise a period in American history sometimes characterized as secular and enlightened.[40] In 1768 New

[38] Wallace Brown, *The Good Americans: The Loyalists in the American Revolution* (New York, 1969), pp. 37, 227; Burns, *The American Idea of Mission: Concepts of National Purpose and Destiny* (New Brunswick, N.J., 1957), p. 359.

[39] Gordon, *Discourse*, Thornton, ed., *Pulpit*, pp. 219–20; Ebenezer Baldwin, *Duty of Rejoicing*, pp. 32–33; David Jones, *Defensive War*, p. 24; Story, *Love of Our Country*, pp. 17–18; Samuel Langdon, *Government corrupted by Vice, and recovered by Righteousness* (Watertown, Mass., 1775), in Thornton, ed., *Pulpit*, p. 255; West, *Sermon Before the Council*, ibid., pp. 319–20; Benjamin Rush to Mrs. Rush, 29 May 1776, L. H. Butterfield, ed., *The Letters of Benjamin Rush*, 2 vols. (Princeton, N.J., 1951), 1:99; Maccarty, *Praise to God*, p. 21; Samuel Sherwood, *The Church's Flight into the Wilderness* (New York, 1776), p. iv; Vaughan, ed., *Chronicles*, p. 204.

[40] See, e.g., Curti, *Growth of American Thought*, p. 128, and Jones, *O Strange New World*, p. 341. Even Alan Heimert, who concludes that religion was continually vital to American thought during the eighteenth century, believes that the "period 1765–1775 did see an apparent flagging of American interest in religion and an increasing secular-mindedness in politics," though he holds that "in many respects" this era "represented more an interlude than a thorough transformation of the American mind" (*Religion and the American Mind*, pp. 352–53).

York and Rhode Island newspapers matter-of-factly observed, "Our Country is . . . the American Canaan," while seven years later a Pennsylvania journal labeled internal enemies as the "the chief troubles of our Israel." A New England minister in 1775 lamented with his audience that it was their "unhappy lot to live in the day of the American Israel's trouble." That same year, in a fast-day sermon delivered in Philadelphia before the assembled Continental Congress, the Reverend Jacob Duché described America as "a *Vine-Yard* PLANTED BY THE LORD'S RIGHT HAND" and implored "THE GOD OF HOSTS . . . TO LOOK DOWN FROM HEAVEN AND BEHOLD AND VISIT our American VINE."[41] When newspapers reported the reading of the "Declaration of the Causes of Taking up Arms" (adopted by Congress on 6 July 1775) to the Continental Army, they characterized the Americans as "ISRAELITES," their enemies as "PHILISTINES."[42]

This theme of God's New Israel was reinforced by numerous parallels drawn between America's situation and the Exodus of the Jews from Egypt. This comparison was invoked during each of the major confrontations with Britain after 1763. The Stamp Act, for instance, threatened America with "worse than Egyptian bondage," while its repeal was comparable to the deliverance of the Hebrews from Pharaoh's tyranny. Similar invocations of the Exodus were prompted by the campaign against the Townshend duties and the final crisis following the Boston Tea Party and the Coercive Acts.[43]

[41] *N.Y. Jour.*, 7 Apr. 1768; *Providence Gazette*, 18 Mar. 1768, as quoted in Carl Bridenbaugh, *The Spirit of '76: The Growth of American Patriotism before Independence* (New York, 1975), p. 136; *Pa. Jour.*, 25 Jan. 1775; William Stearns, *View of the Controversy*, p. 10; Duché, *The American Vine* (Philadelphia, 1775), pp. 16, 33. After the Declaration of Independence, Duché became a loyalist, but this action, as Perry Miller has observed, "does not make his *The American Vine* any less a spiritual jeremiad of the sort that most invigorated patriot courage" ("Covenant to Revival," p. 95).

[42] *Pa. Jour.*, 2 Aug. 1775; *Va. Gaz.* (Dixon and Hunter), 12 Aug. 1775.

[43] "Agricola," *Pa. Jour.*, *Supplement*, 23 Jan. 1766; [Stephen Johnson], *Some Important Observations*, pp. 13–21; *N.Y. Gaz.*, 20 Jan. 1766; "A Son of Liberty," *Pa. Jour.*, *Supplement*, 10 Apr. 1766; "Liberty," *Boston Gaz.*, 30 Nov. 1767; "Pro Aris et Focis," ibid., 11 Sept. 1769; "A Carolinian," *S.C. Gaz.*, 27 June 1774; "Common Sense," Philip S. Foner, ed., *The Complete Writings of Thomas Paine*, 2 vols. (New York, 1945), 1:25; John Adams, diary entry, 17 Dec. 1773, and John Adams to Edward Biddle, 12 Dec. 1774, Charles Francis Adams, ed., *The Works of John Adams*, 10 vols. (Boston, 1850–56), 2:324, 9:350.

In paralleling God's old and new Israels, patriot spokesman, like New England Puritans earlier, drew lessons for their own time. Public calamities had been sent to both nations for their sins, so America must reform as had the Lord's first chosen people: "'O Israel! return unto the Lord thy God, for thou has fallen by thine iniquity.'" The history of ancient Israel delineated for patriots the proper action in the face of impending "slavery." Did God, a Virginian asked, "reprove that distinguished people the Israelites, for complaining of the severe treatment of Pharaoh, who *made their lives bitter with hard bondage*? Did he expect that they should pay a blind obedience to all his ordinances? Did he rebuke their murmers, or refuse to hear their Complaints? Surely neither. . . . What a deliverance he wrought for those murmerers and complainers; and what judgment was exercised on their oppressors." The course for America was clear—resist Britain as the Jews had resisted Egypt. "The *example* of GOD'S *ancient* convenant people, when on the brink of ruin," instructed the American people "not to *dispond* or despair" but to commit their "cause to *God*, and stand *Fast*." By 1776 the concept of American Israel had been closely wedded to the political and military defense of the New World's liberty and permanently fixed as a basic tenet of American patriotism.[44]

American nationalism, in the concept of God's New Israel, preceded and even helped create the American nation. As the crisis with Britain reinforced ideas of American uniqueness, it was natural for patriots to speculate more and more on the ultimate reasons why Divine Providence was guiding and supporting America. The absence in America of many of the traditional bases for nationalism also stimulated such development. The colonies lacked many of the permanent historical myths and symbols usually central to the formation of a nationalist ideology. The very absence of these myths and symbols promoted the growth and expression of one common ideological strain that all Americans possessed—providential thought, and particularly its ultimate expression in the notion of the Republican Is-

[44] Samuel Langdon, *Government corrupted*, Thornton, ed., *Pulpit*, p. 249; Griffith, *Passive Obedience Considered*, p. 14; Noble, *Some Strictures*, p. 20. See also Paul A. Varg, "The Advent of Nationalism, 1758–1776," *American Quarterly* 16 (1964): 180–81, who correctly observes that the concept of a New Israel is "not uncommon" to many nationalist ideologies.

rael. Equally important, the forces working against American union before 1776—the religious, social, ethnic, and political differences between and within the thirteen colonies—also led, paradoxically, to the establishment of the providential tenets of an American nationalism before the creation of the American nation itself. Patriots after 1763 were concerned with the defense of their rights. Recognizing that no one colony on its own could stand against Britain, they defined the rights in danger as "American" and called on all colonists to rally to their defense. In their calls they turned (perhaps unconsciously, perhaps not) to a truly intercolonial set of ideas and convictions—the providential thought developed in the era of the Great Awakening and the imperial wars. The expansion after 1763 of the theme of America as God's New Israel was the result. Denied most of the usual past and present foundations of nationalism to refer to in times of crisis, patriot spokesmen in the 1760s and 1770s looked to the future—to the New World's divine mission.

Patriots centered America's mission in the concept of the empire for liberty. As early as 1765 John Adams was convinced "that America was designed by Providence for the Theatre, on which Man was to make his true figure, on which Science, Virtue, Liberty, Happiness and Glory were to exist in Peace."[45] Three years later New York's William Livingston prophesied, "Courage, then Americans! liberty, religion, and [the] sciences are on the wing to these shores: The finger of God points out a mighty empire to your sons. . . . The day dawns in which the foundation of this mighty empire is to be laid. . . . There is no contending with Omnipotence."[46]

The glory of the American empire would rest on its liberties, which would rise to unprecedented heights. A Congregationalist minister saw the thirteen colonies as "the Foundation of a great and mighty Empire . . . to be founded on such Principles of Liberty and

[45] John Adams, diary entry, 30 Dec. 1765, L. H. Butterfield et al., eds., *Diary and Autobiography of John Adams*, 4 vols. (Cambridge, Mass., 1961), 1:282. This was a private observation but one that paralleled other public perceptions of America's destiny: see Bernard Bailyn, *The Ideological Origins of the American Revolution* (Cambridge, Mass., 1967), p. 20.

[46] [William Livingston], *N.Y. Gaz.*, 11 Apr. 1768, as quoted in Bridenbaugh, *Spirit of '76*, p. 137.

Freedom, both civil and religious, as never before took place in the World," and a Pennsylvania Anglican agreed that it was clearly the intent of Divine Providence that "out of the present jarring interests, A NEW AND MORE PERFECT SYSTEM WILL ARISE: which . . . shall perpetuate the liberties of these UNITED COLONIES to the end of time."[47] Hard facts (at least hard to the patriots) were cited in support of these predictions. The distance at which Providence had placed America from Europe showed that God never intended his Republican Israel to be subject to the corruptions of the Old World. Furthermore, the natural and moral resources with which the Lord had blessed America pointed to the same conclusion. There was "no part of this terraqueous globe better fitted and furnished in all the essential articles and advantages, to make a great and flourishing empire; no part of the earth, where learning, religion, and liberty have flourished more for the time." Upon this foundation, with the blessing and guidance of the Creator, the empire for liberty would be constructed.[48]

A much discussed extension of this theme of rising empire was that of America as the asylum of liberty. Like the broader concept of the empire for liberty, the idea that the New World had been ordained by God as a sanctuary for civil and religious freedom (popular even before 1763) was tremendously stimulated by the Revolutionary crisis. Sometimes the image was simply expressed in a general manner: America was the last haven of the goddess of liberty, who had been persecuted and driven from every other shore. On other occasions it was presented in more human terms: in America, "this last Assylum of Liberty," the people of "all other Countries under the Iron Rod, have a Door of Hope open." In either case it was clear after 1763 that patriots bore a divine charge to maintain this open door.

[47] Ebenezer Baldwin, *Duty of Rejoicing*, pp. 38–39; Thomas Coombe, *A Sermon, Preached Before the Congregations of Christ Church and St. Peter's, Philadelphia, on Thursday, July 20, 1775* (Philadelphia, 1775), p. 23. Cf. Samuel Williams, *A Discourse on the Love of our Country* (Salem, Mass., 1775), p. 22; Cumings, *Sermon Preached November 1775*, pp. 9–10; William Smith, *A Sermon On the Present Situation of American Affairs* (Philadelphia, 1775), p. 28.

[48] "Common Sense," Foner, ed., *Complete Writings of Paine*, 1:21; West, *Sermon Before the Council*, Thornton, ed., *Pulpit*, p. 305; Nye, *This Almost Chosen People*, pp. 183–85; Sherwood, *Church's Flight*, p. 17.

"God," they were reminded in imagery strikingly reminiscent of John Winthrop, "has appointed this land of liberty, as a city of refuge to the distressed of all nations."[49]

Finally, discussion began even before 1776 of a divine mission for God's Republican Israel, which had a truly "cosmic" potential.[50] Central was the belief that God's plan for America stretched beyond the securing of an asylum for freedom and even beyond the creation of a great empire for liberty to some manner of general reformation of the entire globe. Out of the preindependence observations, two (one by a famous patriot and one by an obscure preacher) indicate the direction this concept would take. In 1765 John Adams observed, "I always consider the settlement of America with reverence and wonder, as the opening of a grand scheme and design in Providence for the illumination of the ignorant, and the emancipation of the slavish part of mankind all over the earth."[51] Eleven years later Connecticut's Enoch Huntington argued that God had selected America to instruct all other nations in the wisdom of republican politics:

> Providence hath blessed us with the means, and calls upon us, by a virtuous example, to shew and convince the world, that tamely to submit to the arbitrary, lawless, oppressive claims, of kings or courts, when the rights, welfare and happiness of the people is at stake, is so far from being a duty,

[49] Bailyn, *Ideological Origins*, pp. 82–84; Maier, *From Resistance to Revolution*, pp. 265–66; Mayhew, *Snare Broken*, p. 36; "Anglus Americanus," *Pa. Jour.*, 29 June 1774; "Non Quis Sed Quid," *S.C. Gaz.*, 4 July 1774; "Z.," *N.Y. Jour.*, 25 Nov. 1773; *N.Y. Mercury*, 27 Aug. 1764; "A New Liberty Song," *Boston Gaz.*, 15 May 1769; Samuel Williams, *Love of our Country*, pp. 21–22; "A Plain Dealer," *Pa. Jour.*, 13 July 1774.

[50] The phrase is Bernard Bailyn's, in his *Ideological Origins*, p. 32.

[51] John Adams, diary entry, 21 Feb. 1765, Adams, ed., *Works of John Adams*, 1:66. Many scholars have quoted and stressed the significance of Adams's observation: see Kohn, *Idea of Nationalism*, p. 273; Savelle, *Seeds of Liberty*, pp. 555–56; Clinton Rossiter, "The American Mission," *American Scholar* 20 (1951): 21–22; Burns, *American Idea of Mission*, p. 11; Curti, *Growth of American Thought*, p. 74; Bailyn, *Ideological Origins*, p. 140; Ernest Lee Tuveson, *Redeemer Nation: The Idea of America's Millennial Role* (Chicago, 1968), p. 25; Richard B. Morris, *Seven Who Shaped Our Destiny* (New York, 1973), p. 79; Bercovitch, *Puritan Origins*, p. 88; Bridenbaugh, *Spirit of '76*, p. 134; Kenneth Silverman, *A Cultural History of the American Revolution* (New York, 1976), p. 87.

that it is sin, and the contrary is indispensible duty, and every one is called upon to make a resolute, virtuous resistance.[52]

Poets gave the theme its fullest development before Independence. In 1770 in his poem *America* William Livingston rhapsodized,

> O Land supremely blest! to thee is given
> To taste the choicest joys of bounteous heaven;
> Thy rising Glory shall expand its rays,
> And lands and times unknown rehearse thine endless praise.

And in their *Rising Glory of America* Hugh Henry Brackenridge and Philip Freneau rejoiced that "here fair freedom shall forever reign," and prophesied:

> Hail happy land,
> The seat of empire the abode of kings,
> The final stage where time shall introduce
> Renowned characters, and glorious works
> Of high invention and of wond'rous art,
> Which not the ravages of time shall waste
> Till he himself has run his long career.[53]

This theme of America's cosmic mission would receive final development after July 1776, but its expression even before Independence illustrates the continuity within American providential thought.[54]

After all this is said and done, however, there remained one significant group of colonists who dissented from this patriot consensus—the American loyalists. The loyalists did, however, couch their dissent in many of the same terms as their patriot oppo-

[52] Huntington, *The Happy Effects of Union, and the Fatal Tendency of Divisions* (Hartford, 1776), p. 20.

[53] [William Livingston], *America; or, a Poem on the Settlement Of the British Colonies* (New Haven, [1770]), p. 9; [Philip Freneau and Hugh Henry Brackenridge], *A Poem, on the Rising Glory of America* (Philadelphia, 1772), pp. 23, 26–27.

[54] For other typical expressions of the cosmic mission before 1776, see Elisha Fish, *Joy and Gladness*, p. 15; John Tucker, *A Sermon Preached at Cambridge, Before His Excellency Thomas Hutchinson* (Boston, 1771), pp. 42–43; *Cape-Fear Mercury*, 28 July 1775.

nents—including the resort to providential concepts.[55] Thus in 1775, amidst the turmoil and anguish of impending revolution, four American loyalists—two accomplished, two anonymous—reacted to the disturbing turn of events in the American colonies with a strikingly similar image. Driven from his home and now sheltered behind the British redoubts in Boston, Massachusetts, Chief Justice Peter Oliver consoled himself with the observation that "the God of Order may punish a community for a time with their own disorder; but it is incompatible with the rectitude of the Divine Nature, to suffer anarchy to prevail." Harrison Gray, member of His Majesty's Council in the Bay Colony, characterized the activities of the Massachusetts patriots as "of such a malignant atrocious nature, as must expose the wicked perpetrators of it . . . to the vengeance of that Being, who is a God of order and not of Confusion." A loyalist contributor to James Rivington's "impartial" New York newspaper attacked the Association, the patriot economic boycott of Great Britain, warning, "You know the Almighty cannot approve of it, he is a God of order and mercy, and in this association there is neither order nor mercy." And Boston's "X.W." instructed the whigs that "that Cause . . . that calls for the aids of Licentiousness to support it . . . must be a Cause abhorrent to that *Being* who hath declared Himself to be the *God of Order*."[56]

The loyalists began with the belief that the Lord was on *their* side. "The cause which I defend is the cause of God," Jonathan Boucher told his patriot parishioners in 1775. That same year Massachusetts's "Philerine" urged Bay Colony loyalists to "attend seasonably to the calls of reason and [the] dictates of prudence" and thereby "discharge

[55] For a broader discussion of this phenomenon, see my "'A God of Order and Not of Confusion': The American Loyalists and Divine Providence, 1774–1783," *Historical Magazine of the Protestant Episcopal Church* 47 (1978).

[56] Mary Beth Norton, *The British-Americans: The Loyalist Exiles in England, 1774–1789* (Boston, 1972), p. 30; [Harrison Gray], *The Two Congresses Cut Up* (New York, [1775]), p. 4; "A Freeholder of Essex, and *real* Lover of Liberty," *Rivington's New-York Gazetteer*, 5 Jan. 1775; "X. W.," *Massachusetts Gazette: and Boston Weekly News-Letter*, 5 Jan. 1775. Jonathan Boucher also used the phrase "a God of order and not of confusion" in a 1775 sermon: see Rodney K. Miller, "The Political Ideology of the Anglican Clergy," *Historical Magazine of the Protestant Episcopal Church* 45 (1976): 230.

your duty to God."[57] Building on this conviction, loyalist spokesmen insisted that Divine Providence was unmistakably opposed to American independence and a sundering of the British Empire, and clearly supportive of continued Anglo-American union. One tory rejoinder to Tom Paine's *Common Sense* insisted that "*Providence, by its all-wise dispensations, loudly calls on both countries to unite.*" In June 1776 New York jurist William Smith wrote in his diary that "the omniscient Judge of Heaven" would soon decide between the "contending Parties with unerring Rectitude." The verdict of this divine judgment was certain to Smith: the patriots' bid for a "ruinous" separation from England would be frustrated, "for no end . . . is to expect Success by a perfidious & ambitious Violation of that Covenant, under which the Providence of God placed us and our Fathers." Independence was "unrighteous in the Sight of God."[58]

This last claim was basic to loyalist providential thought. The nature of the patriot cause demanded divine opposition; hence, the patriots could not succeed. What the patriots were promoting, the loyalists insisted again and again, was rebellion, and "a rebellion, is an appeal to God in a cause so palpably unjust . . . and so derogatory to God's authority, that . . . it is impossible that it should finally prosper." "Never did a people rebel with so little reason," declared a 1775 contributor to a New York loyalist journal; "therefore our conduct cannot be justified before God! " A common loyalist argument before 1776 was to warn the whigs that if the colonies continued to deny the authority of Parliament, they eventually would (in the words of Jonathan Boucher) "have no appeal but to the God of Battles." And "shall we lift up our Eyes to that God, the Source of Truth and Justice, and implore his Assistance in such a Cause?" Hardly; instead, the patriots would "find, to their cost, that they *fight against God.*" "They who pretend to be such great *Patriots*," a Cambridge, Massachusetts, correspondent bitterly argued in December

[57] Boucher, *A View of the Causes and Consequences of the American Revolution* (London, 1797), p. 456; "Philerine," *Mass. Gaz.: and Boston Weekly News-Letter*, 30 Mar. 1775.

[58] [Charles Inglis], *The True Interest of America Impartially Stated* (Philadelphia, 1776), p. viii; Smith, *Historical Memoirs From 16 March 1763 to 25 July 1778*, ed. William H. W. Sabine, 2 vols. (New York, 1956–58), 1:276–77; L. S. F. Upton, *The Loyal Whig: William Smith of New York and Quebec* (Toronto, 1969), p. 105.

1774, "will be justly chargeable in the sight of GOD, for all the Tumults and Riots that may happen in the *Country*." Thus loyalist spokesmen repeatedly remonstrated that Divine Providence would defeat the wicked goals of the patriots and preserve the British Empire.[59]

Before the Declaration of Independence, Loyalists laced their public and private pronouncements with appeals to Jehovah to restore peace, loyalty, and order to a disturbed and deluded America. Samuel Seabury ended a 1774 pamphlet with the prayer "Save, heavenly Father! O save my country from perdition." Massachusetts lawyer Daniel Leonard, writing as "Massachusettensis," invoked "the God of our forefathers" to "direct" his fellow citizens "in the way that leads to peace and happiness . . . before the evil days come." In the aftermath of Lexington and Concord, New York Assemblyman Isaac Wilkins implored "that God in whose hands are all events speedily restore peace and liberty to my unhappy country," and that same year of 1775 Henry Barry cried, "O righteous God! do thou avert the justice of the empire, and . . . snatch this deluded people from the imminent calamities, danger, ruin, and destruction which await them!" Dr. Peter Oliver, Jr., expressed the same sentiment in a letter to the son of Thomas Hutchinson: "Good God, do thou avert the impending calamity that threatens this former happy land and turn the hearts of these deluded brethren from the power of sin and satan to thy unerring precepts."[60]

Throughout the era of the coming of the American Revolution, loyalists maintained a "trust in God" that the righteous would triumph and the reprobate suffer divine retribution. "Let us hope,"

[59] Boucher, *View*, pp. 422, 579; "A Yeoman of Suffolk County," *Riv. N.Y. Gaz.*, 16 Feb. 1775; [Jonathan Boucher], *A Letter From a Virginian, to the Members of the Congress* ([New York], 1774), p. 27; [John Adams and Daniel Leonard], *Novanglus and Massachusettensis* (Boston, 1819), p. 203; *Mass. Gaz.: and Boston Weekly News-Letter*, 1 Dec. 1774.

[60] Seabury, *Letters of a Westchester Farmer (1774–1775)*, ed. Clarence H. Vance (White Plains, N.Y., 1930), p. 140; [Adams and Leonard], *Novanglus and Massachusettensis*, p. 227; Catherine S. Crary, ed., *The Price of Loyalty: Tory Writings from the Revolutionary Era* (New York, 1973), p. 35; [Henry Barry], *The General, Attacked By a Subaltern* (New York, [1775]), p. 11; Bernard Bailyn, *The Ordeal of Thomas Hutchinson* (Cambridge, Mass., 1974), p. 333.

wrote Jonathan Boucher to a clerical colleague in June 1776, "that He who bringeth Good out of evil, will, in his own good Time, direct to an happy End the present Commotions." But, in the end, the loyalists' pursuit of "the Godlike work of preventing bloodshed in the colonies" was frustrated. Generally denied (especially after 1774) access to the press and pulpit, the warnings and fears of the loyalists were ultimately eclipsed by the decision for American independence.[61]

Before 1776, however, whigs and tories shared a basic providential outlook on human history and a specific providential conceptualization of America's future. Loyalist providential thought, then, is illustrative of—if nothing else—the "Americanness" of the loyalists. Loyalists and patriots differed on a host of specific political, social, and constitutional issues. And they divided dramatically on the question of which side during the Revolutionary contest truly expressed the will of the Lord. But on the basic premise that the hand of God was manifest in the coming of the American Revolution there was no dispute. In retrospect it appears that whichever side had triumphed in the Revolutionary struggle, faith in Divine Providence would have been vindicated. It was the misfortune of the American loyalists that America's protecting Providence proved to be the "God of Liberty" and not the "God of Order."

The Revolutionary years 1763–76 witnessed the crystallization of an American patriotism and providential mission grounded on the key concepts of God's New Israel, empire for liberty, asylum, and world transformation. When the patriots declared America an independent nation in 1776, they did not then have to create an American nationalism. The central providential tenets, at least, of such a nationalism had already been advanced, discussed, and accepted by a majority of Americans throughout the thirteen colonies well before Thomas Jefferson wrote that those colonies "are, and of right ought to be Free and Independent States." Indeed, this nationalism was one of the forces that provided a compelling argument for independence and nationhood. The New Israel, in order to fulfill its divine mission, had to be master of its own destiny (under God's guidance, of

[61] "Letters of Jonathan Boucher," *Maryland Historical Magazine* 9 (1914): 60–61; "Senex," *Riv. N.Y. Gaz.*, 23 Mar. 1775.

course). It was therefore appropriate that the Declaration of Independence concluded with an expression of the new republic's "firm reliance on the protection of Divine Providence."[62] This statement of faith constituted a fitting culmination both to the Declaration of Independence and to the providential thought fashioned during the coming of the American Revolution.

[62] Howard Mumford Jones, *Revolution and Romanticism* (Cambridge, Mass., 1974), p. 156, asserts that the framers of the Declaration, in their references to Providence, had nothing more in mind than the Enlightenment's Great Architect. This was perhaps true for the framers, but we should not therefore ignore the special meanings that Providence carried for the more numerous pious patriots.

IV
From the House of Bondage to the Promised Land

IN SEVERAL ways the era of the Revolutionary War and the Constitution (1776–89) merely continued pre-1776 providential themes. The American Israel motif remained common; the legend of the founding fathers became increasingly (although not exclusively) centered on George Washington; the jeremiad tradition was invoked to inspire commitment and confidence; the hand of God was displayed in the Revolutionary War. In two ways, however, American providential thought was altered (or amplified) during the era of the completion of the American Revolution: the new nation's enlightened elite emerged as major promoters of America's providential ideology, and providential thought interacted with domestic political divisions during the debate over the Federal Constitution. Both developments foreshadowed the disparate roles providential thought would play in the American mind after 1789.

Striking references to God's American Israel were as common after as before the Declaration of Independence. Patriots continued to celebrate "the MIGHTY ACTS of GOD towards this American Israel." Others asked for the continuation of providential blessings on "our Israel," still others for the "American Zion." Parallels between the old and new Israels were extensive, and not limited to New England or to clerics. Anyone reviewing the events of the Revolutionary era would be constrained to conclude, a South Carolinian said in 1789, that the "citizens of the United States, have certainly been the subjects of a divine providential care, not less friendly and beneficent than that which was extended to the antient people of Israel." "No land, that of PALESTINE excepted," declared Timothy Dwight in a 1777 thanksgiving sermon, "hath in the same time experienced more extraordinary interpositions of Providence than this."[1] Patriots

[1] Benjamin Trumbull, *God is to be praised for the Glory of his Majesty, and for his mighty Works* (New Haven, 1784), p. 12; Peter Whitney, *American Independence Vindicated* (Boston, 1777), p. 51; Phillips Payson, *A Memorial of Lexington Battle*

throughout the young republic constructed extensive parallels between the situation of God's first chosen people and the fate of America—comparisons that went to such lengths that one spokesman (perhaps unconsciously but nevertheless significantly) reversed the process and presented the Republican Israel as a model with which to compare the old: "Israel were a free, independent common wealth, planted by God in *Canaan*, in much the same manner that he planted us in *America*."[2]

A favorite manifestation of the New Israel motif continued to be the comparison of the American Revolution to the Exodus. In election sermons, thanksgiving celebrations, and Fourth of July orations, this proved an immensely popular practice.[3] Again and again patriots paired George III and his ministers with Pharaoh and his evil advisers.[4] (To be sure, loyalists under patriot domination ungratefully

---

(Boston, 1782), p. 8; Ezra Stiles, *The United States elevated to Glory and Honor* (New Haven, 1783), in Thornton, ed., *Pulpit*, p. 440; George Duffield, *A Sermon, Preached in the Third Presbyterian Church, in the City of Philadelphia, On Thursday, December 11, 1783* (Philadelphia, 1784), pp. 3, 21–22; Eliphalet Porter, *A Sermon, Delivered to the First Religious Society in Roxbury, December 11, 1783* (Boston, 1784), p. 5; "Senex," *Boston Gaz.*, 6 May 1782; Zebulon Ely, *The death of Moses the Servant of the Lord* (Hartford, 1786), pp. 13, 15; Samuel West, *An Anniversary Sermon, Preached at Plymouth, December 22d, 1777* (Boston, 1778), p. 40; Merle Curti, *The Roots of American Loyalty* (New York, 1946), p. 67; James F. Maclear, "The Republic and the Millennium," in *The Religion of the Republic*, ed. Elwyn A. Smith (Philadelphia, 1971), p. 183; Isaac S. Keith, *The Friendly Influence of Religion and Virtue on the Prosperity of a Nation* (Charleston, S.C., 1789), p. 5; [Timothy Dwight], *A Sermon Preached at Stamford, in Connecticut, upon the General Thanksgiving, December 18th, 1777* (Hartford, 1778), p. 13.

[2] Nathaniel Whitaker, *An Antidote Against Toryism* (Newburyport, Mass., 1777), p. 13.

[3] See, e.g., Phillips Payson, *A Sermon Preached Before the Honorable Council* (Boston, 1778), in Thornton, ed., *Pulpit*, p. 345; John Murray, *Nehemiah, Or the Struggle for Liberty never in vain* (Newburyport, Mass., 1779), pp. 40–41; Robert Smith, *The Obligations of the Confederate States of North America to Praise God* (Philadelphia, 1782), p. 12; Enos Hitchcock, *A Discourse on the Causes of National Prosperity* (Providence, [1786]), pp. 9–10, 22; John Woodhull, *A Sermon, For the Day of Publick Thanksgiving* (Trenton, N.J., 1790), p. 22. This last was preached in December 1789.

[4] See, e.g., *Pa. Jour.*, 18 June 1777; Nicholas Street, *The American States acting over the Part of the Children of Israel in the Wilderness* (New Haven, [1777]), p. 33; *Boston Gaz.*, 23 Feb. 1778; "An American," Newbern *North-Carolina Gazette*, 1 May

complained that they also were "labouring under a tyranny more grievous than Egyptian bondage"—but they were surely "crying in the wilderness.")[5] During the dark days of the Revolutionary War, patriots perceived themselves, like the ancient Hebrews, wandering in a wilderness "of trouble and difficulty; Egyptians pursuing us, to overtake us and reduce us; there is the Red Sea before us . . . a sea of blood." The Jews' possession of the promised land was a type of American independence. As Massachusetts's David Osgood marveled aloud in 1783, "The Egyptian Pharaoh was not more loth to part with his Hebrew slaves, than the British court to give up their once American subjects. By a series of miracles were the Israelites rescued from the house of bondage. And by a series of providential wonders have the Americans emerged from oppression, and risen to liberty and independence." A New Englander put into verse the plan of Jehovah:

> That *Vine* which from Egypt to Canaan I brought,
> With an out-stretch'd, omnipotent arm,
> In AMERICA's soil, from Britannia's bleak isle,
> Shall flourish—and brave ev'ry storm.[6]

Throughout the military struggle for independence patriot spokesmen continued to assert that theirs was "a cause . . . just in the sight of God and man."[7] They repeatedly reassured themselves that

---

1778; Nathan Stone, *The Āgency and Providence of God Acknowledged in the Preservation of the American States* (Hartford, 1780), p. 14; Henry Cumings, *A Sermon Preached at Lexington, On the 19th of April, 1781* (Boston, 1781), pp. 8–10; "Lucullus," Philadelphia *Freeman's Journal*, 5 Mar. 1783; Robert R. Livingston to John Jay, 9 May 1782, Henry P. Johnston, ed., *The Correspondence and Public Papers of John Jay*, 4 vols. (New York, 1890–93), 2:303; Sandin, "Wonderful Works," p. 37.

[5] *Declaration and Address Of His Majesty's Loyal associated Refugees* (New York, 1779), pp. 24–25; "Aristides," New York *Royal Gazette*, 7 Oct. 1778.

[6] Street, *American States acting over*, pp. 7–8; Osgood, *Reflections on the goodness of God in supporting the People of the United States through the late war* (Boston, 1784), p. 20; [Jonathan Mitchel Sewall], *An Oration Delivered at Portsmouth, New-Hampshire, on the Fourth of July, 1788* (Portsmouth, 1788), p. 21.

[7] Simeon Howard, *A Sermon Preached Before the Honorable Council* (Boston, 1780), in Thornton, ed., *Pulpit*, p. 389. For the same theme see "An American," *Md. Gaz.*, 9 Jan. 1777; Josiah Stearns, *Two Sermons, Preached at Epping, in the State of New-Hampshire, January 20th, 1777* (Newburyport, Mass., 1777), p. 38; "Boston," *Boston Gaz.*, 15 June 1778; [Wheeler Case], *Poems, Occasioned by Several Cir-*

God would champion their endeavors because they were championing the rights which the Lord had bestowed upon humanity. As "Montanus" told the Virginia officers in the Continental Army, "The cause . . . in which we are embarked, is just. You are now standing in defense of those inestimable rights which the KING OF HEAVEN has conferred upon all." Joel Barlow in *The Vision of Columbus* also asserted that the American Revolution was "by Heaven approved." The fact that the United States had been forced by British aggression to take up arms further carried with it the promise of divine assistance. And Hugh Henry Brackenridge cited in support of his contention that God would deliver America "the usual course of providence in cases of this nature. If we resolve the history of mankind, we shall scarcely meet with any instance of a young and rising empire given up to be destroyed, by an old and decayed nation." "Although public exultations" during the American Revolution "usually avoided undisguised self-righteousness . . . there was little doubt in any patriot's mind that victory had come because the revolutionary *cause* (freedom) was just."[8]

This conviction, coupled with the memory of the Lord's past blessings upon his New Israel, led patriots throughout America to continue to insist that the cause of America, and specifically the American Revolution, was "the cause of God."[9] Liberty and freedom were both the Creator's intent and the basis of the Revolution. Dwelling on this concept, one enraptured patriot delivered a virtual litany

cumstances and Occurrences (New Haven, 1778), p. 7; "A Friend to Liberty," *Va. Gaz.* (Clarkson and Davis), 30 Oct. 1779; Worthington C. Ford et al., eds., *Journals of the Continental Congress, 1774–1789*, 34 vols. (Washington, D.C., 1904–37), 16:347.

[8]"Montanus," *Va. Gaz.* (Purdie), 30 Aug. 1776; Barlow, *The Vision of Columbus; A Poem in Nine Books* (Hartford, 1787), pp. 167, 180; William Livingston, "Speech to the New Jersey Legislature," 28 Feb. 1777, in Moore, ed., *American Eloquence*, 1:89; Brackenridge, *Six Political Discourses Founded on the Scripture* (Lancaster, Pa., [1778]), p. 40; Cherry, ed., *God's New Israel*, p. 63.

[9]For explicit statements of this conviction, see "An Ode," *Va. Gaz.* (Dixon and Hunter), 24 Aug. 1776; "An American," *Boston Gaz.*, 10 Feb. 1777; Jacob Cushing, *Divine judgments upon tyrants: And compassion to the oppressed* (Boston, 1778), p. 23; Cumings, *Sermon at Lexington*, p. 22; Robert Smith, *Obligations*, p. 33; Richard Walsh, ed., *The Writings of Christopher Gadsden, 1746–1805* (Columbia, S.C., 1966), p. 174.

explaining why God would succor America's cause: "The cause of truth, against error and falshood; the cause of righteousness against iniquity, the cause of the oppressed against the opressor . . . of liberty, against arbitrary power; of benevolence, against barbarity, and of virtue against vice. . . . In short . . . the cause of heaven against hell—of the kind Parent of the universe, against the prince of darkness, and the destroyer of the human race." Again, Hugh Henry Brackenridge spoke for his countrymen: "It is God that crowns our efforts with success. Let the cause in which we are engaged praise God."[10]

After 1776 loyalist spokesmen, on the other hand, continued to argue that *theirs* was Jehovah's cause. New York Anglican minister Charles Inglis informed a newly raised loyalist military regiment in 1777 that "we may humbly and confidently trust that the just Ruler of the Universe favours our Cause—that it hath HIS Approbation who is a God of Order." It was thus little wonder that in 1779 loyalist exiles in Great Britain, addressing George III, called upon "the supreme Disposer of Events, to crown your Majesty's endeavors with a success proportioned to the righteousness of your cause."[11]

The conviction that they were performing the will of God undoubtedly promoted confidence among patriots after 1776. But that confidence did not obscure the jeremiad strain in American providential thought. The belief that "public calamities, though brought upon a people by the hands of wicked and unreasonable men, may always be considered, as divine corrections for prevailing sins" remained a certainty for pious citizens.[12] The righteousness of their cause, Americans were reminded, did not mean that success would

[10] Abraham Keteltas, *God Arising and Pleading His People's Cause* (Newburyport, Mass., 1777), p. 30; Brackenridge, *Six Political Discourses*, p. 58; Whitney, *American Independence Vindicated*, p. 47; "A Round Head," *Boston Gaz.*, 7 July 1777.

[11] Inglis, *The Christian Soldier's Duty Briefly delineated* (New York, [1777]), pp. 17–18; *Royal Gaz.*, 27 Oct. 1779.

[12] Samuel Cooke, *The violent destroyed: And oppressed delivered* (Boston, 1777), p. 17. See also "Meanwell," *Md. Gaz.*, 19 June 1777; *Va Gaz.* (Dixon and Hunter), 17 Jan. 1777; "A Soldier," *Boston Gaz.*, 25 June 1781; William Symmes, *A Sermon, Preached Before His Honor Thomas Cushing* (Boston, 1785), p. 19; Joseph Lathrop, *A Sermon, Preached in the First Parish in West-Springfield, December 14, MDCCLXXXVI* (Springfield, Mass., 1787), p. 12.

necessarily come easy, for "a good cause often suffers, and is sometimes lost, by means of the sin and folly of those, who are engaged in it." This reality weighed especially heavy on the consciences of patriots because they had already received so many divine favors—and God always looked particularly askance at the sins of his chosen people. Continuation of the bloodshed and evil of war, and military setbacks, demonstrated God's controversy with America and demanded reformation. "Nothing obstructs the deliverance of America," declared Timothy Dwight, "but the crimes of its inhabitants; sins, and their authors, are its greatest enemies. If this land be ruined, it will be ruined by its iniquities." Providential and enlightened values merged as clergy and laymen alike castigated America for her sins, called for a return to the simplicity and piety of the past, and viewed the American Revolution as a means to moral regeneration.[13]

During the Revolutionary War the Continental Congress became an exponent of the jeremiad tradition. Congress adopted the Puritan custom of proclaiming annual fast days calling for repentence and reformation to avert the Lord's wrath. These exhortations were not mere propaganda, nor did only clerics or New Englanders have a hand in fashioning them. The proclamations were drafted by laymen, a majority of whom came from middle or southern rather than New England states. Each spring from 1778 through 1782 patriotic Americans were summoned by their national leaders to acknowledge that God in his righteous anger had allowed the war to continue, and to respond with confessions of guilt and professions of reformation. Increase Mather would have had trouble improving on the providential thrust of these Congressional fast proclamations.[14]

[13] Cumings, *Sermon at Lexington*, p. 33; Cyprian Strong, *God's Care of the New-England Colonies* (Hartford, [1777]), pp. 15, 23–24; West, *Anniversary Sermon*, p. 55; Jacob Green, *A Sermon Delivered at Hanover (in New-Jersey) April 22d, 1778* (Chatham, N.J., 1779), pp. 4–5; Cooke, *violent destroyed*, pp. 27–28; Josiah Stearns, *Two Sermons*, p. 33; Street, *American States acting over*, pp. 29–30; [Dwight], *Sermon*, p. 15; Gordon S. Wood, *The Creation of the American Republic, 1776–1787* (Chapel Hill, N.C., 1969), pp. 114–18.

[14] Edward Frank Humphrey, *Nationalism and Religion in America, 1774–1789* (Boston, 1924), pp. 407–39; Hudson, ed., *Nationalism and Religion*, p. 20. For the texts of these fast proclamations see Ford, ed., *Journals of Continental Congress*, 10:229–30, 13:343–44, 16:252–53, 19:284–86, 22:137–38.

Britain too played a role in God's moral government of the universe and in the jeremiad tradition. Patriots were convinced that, in order to punish and correct his people for sin, the Lord frequently allowed their rulers to distress and oppress them.[15] One New Englander found it painfully evident that "the British nation are the rod of God's anger to scourge and chastize us for our sins, as the Assyrian monarch was to God's people of old."[16] However, although Britain was a providential instrument for the punishment of patriot sins, such a role obviously was not the intent of the British ministers who prosecuted the war. They waged war on America to gratify their own ambition and avarice; nothing was further from their minds than doing the will of God. They too were liable to divine punishment, and the justice of America's cause guaranteed that if America reformed she would, with God's assistance, utterly defeat the British. This certainty was reinforced by the unparalleled (to patriots) cruelties of the British armies and their mercenary hirelings, crimes that cried to the Lord for vengeance.[17] For some Patriots these cruelties explained the ultimate defeat of Britain: "She raised up the Rod of oppression against her Children and her Neighbours, and the righteous Hand of Heaven has humbled her in the Dust—she has fallen detested and despised—an Object of Hatred and Contempt."[18] England as the oppressive tyrant acted from human motivations, England as the rod of God from divine direction. The role of the British in the Revolutionary War, like that of the Indians in Metacom's War a

[15] Howard, *Sermon*, Thornton, ed., *Pulpit*, p. 373; Jonas Clarke, *A Sermon Preached Before His Excellency John Hancock* (Boston, [1781]), p. 41; Moses Mather, *A Sermon, Preached in the Audience of the General Assembly* (New London, Conn., 1781), p. 17; Joseph Roby, *A Sermon Delivered at Lynn on the General Fast, May 3, 1781* (Boston, 1781), p. 10.

[16] Street, *American States acting over*, p. 34.

[17] Cooke, *violent destroyed*, p. 11; Cushing, *Divine judgments*, p. 11; Cumings, *Sermon at Lexington*, p. 35; "An American," *N.C. Gaz.*, 24, 31 July 1778; "Appius Claudius," *Boston Gaz.*, 28 Jan. 1782; "Philanthropos," *S.C. Gaz.*, 29 May 1782; Richmond *Virginia Gazette, or, the American Advertiser*, 6 July 1782.

[18] Timothy Matlack, *An Oration, Delivered March 16, 1780* (Philadelphia, 1780), p. 20. Cf. William Gordon, *The Separation of the Jewish Tribes, after the Death of Solomon, accounted for* (Boston, 1777), p. 29, and Jonathan Mason, Jr., *An Oration, Delivered March 6, 1780* (Boston, 1780), p. 19.

century earlier, demonstrated the subordination of human to providential causation in God's moral government of the world.

This same attitude—with the roles reversed, of course—was taken by loyalist spokesmen, who also invoked the jeremiad tradition. "I cannot help observing," remarked one loyalist in 1778, "the misery of the present times, and the deplorable situation both of the American colonies, and the mother country. From whence does it arise? Surely the hand of Providence with its scourge is gone through the land." A year earlier Pennsylvania's Robert Proud articulated the same sentiment when he wrote his brother from Philadelphia (after that city was occupied by the forces of General William Howe) that the American Revolution "with all its Consequences, must be finally left to that over-ruling Hand of Divine Providence, which disposes the Events of Things, and inflicts the Scourge of his Wrath on Mankind, for their Depravity and Revolt from the true Means of their real Interest and Felicity." Usually loyalists did not specifically cite the sins that had so provoked the Lord's anger (Charles Inglis typically simply referred to "Our Transgressions"), although Thomas Bradbury Chandler, Anglican divine from New Jersey, did suggest in 1776 that the "present rebellious disposition of the Colonies" might be "intended by Providence as Punishment" for Britain's failure vigorously to promote Anglicanism in America. The lack of specificity in most loyalist jeremiads, however, is not as surprising as might first appear. There was little need to single out particular or individual transgressions, for all loyalists knew that the sin which had brought down "the vengeance of heaven on a *once happy people*" was the sin of rebellion.[19]

In contrast, a joyful spirit increasingly dominated patriot providential thought after 1776. The jeremiad tradition continued, but the

[19] "Veritas, jun.," *Royal Gaz.*, 26 Aug. 1778; "Letters of Robert Proud," *Pennsylvania Magazine of History and Biography* 34 (1910): 66; Inglis, *Christian Soldier's Duty*, pp. 24–25; idem, *The Duty of Honouring the King* (New York, 1780), p. 32; Wallace Brown, *The King's Friends: The Composition and Motives of the American Loyalist Claimants* (Providence, 1965), p. 121; "A New-York Exile," *Royal Gaz.*, 6 Jan. 1779. For other loyalist uses of the jeremiad, see "Z.," *Rivington's New-York Loyal Gazette*, 8 Nov. 1777, and Wallace Brown, ed., "Viewpoints of a Pennsylvania Loyalist," *Pennsylvania Magazine of History and Biography* 91 (1967): 430.

emphasis was definitely on the second aspect of that tradition—on the Lord's deliverances rather than his displeasures; for every pronouncement on God's wrath there were several panygyrics on God's mercies. The overall thrust of the providential legend was confident, even exuberant. The student of the American mind cannot but be struck by the voluminous instances of providential goodness cited by patriots during the Revolutionary era. To the patriots of the American Enlightenment the hand of God in the events around them could not be ignored. "Whoever attends to the American revolution," insisted Roxbury's Eliphalet Porter in 1783, "in the rise, the progress, and the completion of it, cannot but discern the clear footsteps of that Providence, whose purpose and design no human wisdom or design can defeat."[20] After reviewing the Revolution, one patriot argued that "surely the eye must be blind that cannot see the hand of God in these operations."[21] Not to acknowledge the divine protection provided from 1776 onward was "impious."[22] Pious patriots believed, and insisted, that the actions of Jehovah in the American Revolution demonstrated the deficiency of deism. "*Infidels* themselves," asserted Samuel Spring, "are constrained, *this time* to give credit to the doctrine of God's particular providences: and to repeat this lesson, *Thine O Lord is the victory*."[23] Indeed, some spokesmen claimed that even atheists would have a difficult time persisting in their unbelief after

[20] Porter, *Sermon*, p. 10. For other observations that the hand of God in the Revolution was so manifest that it could not be ignored, see *Md. Gaz.*, 22 Aug. 1776; Ford, ed., *Journals of Continental Congress*, 13:59; Joseph Willard, *A Thanksgiving Sermon Delivered at Boston December 11, 1783* (Boston, 1784), p. 34; Robert Davidson, *An Oration, on the Independence of the United States of America* (Carlisle, Pa., [1787]), p. 13.

[21] Enos Hitchcock, *Discourse*, p. 17.

[22] Ford, ed., *Journals of Continental Congress*, 11:477; David Ramsay, *An Oration on the Advantages of American Independence* (Charleston, S.C., 1778), in Robert L. Brunhouse, ed., *David Ramsay, 1749–1815: Selections from His Writings* (Philadelphia, 1965), p. 189.

[23] Spring, *A Sermon Delivered at the North Congregational Church* (Newburyport, Mass., 1778), p. 22. For the interesting case of Francis Kinloch, a South Carolina deist who was convinced by the American Revolution "that there are certain extensive operations determined upon by providence, which are not to be foreseen, aided, or obviated by human means," see May, *Enlightenment in America*, p. 146.

surveying the wonders wrought by the Lord during the Revolution.[24] The significance of these claims lay not in their refutation of American deists (since there were so few) but rather in their fundamental modification of Enlightenment thought. If the Revolutionary era was predominantly secular and enlightened, one would expect patriots to point to the American Revolution exclusively as proof of the capacity and capabilities of men to alter their own destiny. Patriots did depict the Revolution as a tremendous step in the self-improvement of humanity, but their accounts were usually circumscribed by celebrations of an Old Testament Jehovah.

During the Revolutionary War patriots continued to profess that virtually all Americans from all classes and regions were united in the defense of the rights of man and that this remarkable union had to be ascribed to the Almighty. "To whom but HIM, who turneth the hearts of an whole people as the hearts of one man," Connecticut's James Dana asked, "shall we attribute the union of public bodies? the concurrence and strenuous exertions of all ranks for the common safety?"[25] The disparity among the American people and states was again cited as conclusive evidence that only the Lord could have caused such a glorious union.[26] Seeking to explain this practice, one historian has suggested that during the 1780s public spokesmen ignored all evidence of wartime division in an effort to unite Americans against European criticism and scorn. Another has pointed out that, given the real difficulties and differences that existed among the thirteen states, it is really not so surprising that contemporaries cited Divine Providence as the only rational explanation for what solidarity there was. The American Revolution may not have been a miracle, but the patriots who experienced it could with some justification

[24] Duffield, *Sermon*, p. 1; David Tappan, *A Discourse Delivered At the Third Parish in Newbury, On the First of May, 1783* (Salem, Mass., 1783), p. 8.

[25] Dana, *A Sermon, Preached Before the General Assembly* (Hartford, 1779), pp. 17–18. See also "Philo-Alethias," *Pa. Jour.*, 23 Oct. 1776; West, *Anniversary Sermon*, p. 41; Ramsay, *Oration on the Advantages*, Brunhouse, ed., *Ramsay*, p. 189; Marsh, *Discourse*, p. 8; David Osgood, *Reflections*, pp. 18–19.

[26] Ramsay, *Oration on the Advantages*, Brunhouse, ed., *Ramsay*, p. 189; *Va. Gaz., or, Am. Ad.*, 14 Sept. 1782; Joseph Buckminster, Jr., *A Discourse Delivered in the First Church of Christ at Portsmouth, On Thursday, December 11, 1783* (Portsmouth, N.H., 1784), p. 14.

claim that it approximated one.[27] Whatever its inspiration, this theme continued to receive popular expression throughout the Revolutionary era, with few concessions offered to reality.

After thus promoting union, a guardian God provided statesmen to lead that union and diplomats to promote its interests abroad. Samuel and John Adams, Thomas Jefferson, John Hancock, Benjamin Franklin, John Jay, Henry Laurens, Arthur and Richard Henry Lee, Edmund Pendleton, Patrick Henry, George Clinton, George Wythe, William Livingston, James Bowdoin—these and other distinguished patriots were "raised up" and sustained by Jehovah for the welfare of his Republican Israel. "Through the indulgence of that Providence, which raises up and furnishes such characters, to balance the general depravity of human nature," insisted Massachusetts's Samuel West in still another adaptation of the legend of the fathers, "our own country and times may furnish a list, the lustre of which will not disgrace the worthies of other nations or former ages." In the view of New York's John Rodgers, the Lord further worked his will through the various members of the Continental Congress; "the prudence and firmness of the measures pursued by them, exhibit the fullest evidence of the wisdom of that august body, and the kindness of providence in directing them thereto."[28]

An omniscient Providence also provided for the military needs of America. The Lord diffused a martial spirit throughout the land and furnished enthusiastic warriors for the patriot armies and militias. Following this, America's God gave these soldiers competent and confident military leaders. Conspicuous among these noble generals were Horatio Gates (a "glorious chief" evidently "by Heaven directed") and Nathanael Greene (who had toiled under the protection

[27] Sydney G. Fisher, "The Legendary and Myth-Making Process in Histories of the American Revolution," *Proceedings of the American Philosophical Society* 51 (1912): 55–56; Hudson, ed., *Nationalism and Religion*, pp. xx–xxi.

[28] Israel Evans, *A Discourse, Delivered, On the 18th Day of December, 1777* (Lancaster, Pa., 1778), p. 8; Duffield, *Sermon*, pp. 9–10; Ezra Stiles, *United States elevated*, Thornton, ed., *Pulpit*, pp. 453–54; John Gardiner, *An Oration, Delivered July 4, 1785* (Boston, 1785), p. 36; West, *A Sermon, Preached Before His Excellency James Bowdoin* (Boston, [1786]), p. 11; Rodgers, *The Divine Goodness displayed, in the American Revolution* (New York, 1784), p. 13.

and inspiration of a "gracious Providence" during his defense of the southern states).[29]

But the greatest benefactor sent by Divine Providence was George Washington. In its hunger for national heroes the young republic eventually "deified" Washington, and the process was well underway in the 1770s and 1780s. The legend of the founding fathers was beginning to coalesce around the "father of his country." Again and again during the Revolutionary years patriots north and south insisted that Washington had been "raised up" by God for the mighty tasks of defending the United States and vindicating her rights.[30] In Washington, the Reverend Joseph Buckminster, Jr., asserted, Americans could see "the MAN, whom heaven designed as the principle instrument of accomplishing, one of the greatest revolutions in the nations of the earth." Numerous other patriot spokesmen agreed that the Virginian was the chief "instrument" employed by the Creator for the deliverance of his chosen people.[31] For this end God

[29] Joseph Willard, *The duty of the good and faithful Soldier* (Boston, 1781), pp. 19–20; Eliphalet Porter, *Sermon*, p. 14; Levi Frisbie, *An Oration, Delivered at Ipswich* (Boston, 1783), p. 8; Ezra Stiles, *United States elevated*, Thornton, ed., *Pulpit*, pp. 450–53; Josiah Bridge, *A Sermon Preached Before His Excellency John Hancock* (Boston, 1789), p. 36; "Libertas," *Boston Gaz.*, 8 Dec. 1777; John Rutledge, "Speech to the General Assembly," 18 Jan. 1782, in Moore, ed., *American Eloquence*, 1:122; *Va. Gaz., or, Am. Ad.*, 13 Sept. 1783.

[30] Bernard Mayo, *Myths and Men: Patrick Henry, George Washington, Thomas Jefferson* (Athens, Ga., 1959), pp. 26–27. For explicit statements that Washington had been "raised up," see *N.C. Gaz.*, 31 Oct. 1777; James Dana, *Sermon*, pp. 33–34; Robert Smith, *Obligations*, p. 14; John Marsh, *A Discourse, Delivered at Weathersfield, December 11th, 1783* (Hartford, [1784]), p. 9; Thomas Brockway, *America Saved, or Divine Glory Displayed, in the Late War with Great-Britain* (Hartford, [1784]), p. 17; Davidson, *Oration*, p. 12; Hugh Knox to Alexander Hamilton, 10 Dec. 1777, Harold C. Syrett and Jacob E. Cooke, eds., *The Papers of Alexander Hamilton*, 25 vols. to date (New York, 1961–), 1:366; Samuel Shaw to John Eliot, 12 Apr. 1778, as quoted in William Alfred Bryan, *George Washington in American Literature, 1775–1865* (New York, 1952), p. 26.

[31] Buckminster, *A Discourse, Delivered at Portsmouth, New-Hampshire, November 1st, 1789* (Portsmouth, 1789), p. 6; "The Spectator," *Boston Gaz.*, 27 Jan. 1777; Philadelphia *Pennsylvania Packet*, 24 Dec. 1778, as quoted in Davidson, *Propaganda and the American Revolution*, p. 362; Matlack, *Oration*, p. 9; Tappan, *Discourse*, p. 14; *Md. Gaz.*, 29 Nov. 1781; *Pa. Jour.*, 20 Aug. 1783, 25 Aug. 1787; *Va. Gaz., or, Am. Ad.*, 27 Dec. 1783, 29 Nov. 1786; *Virginia Gazette and Alexandria Advertiser*, 19 Nov. 1789.

"furnished" Washington with "great abilities, and with the most excellent disposition, that he might be a signal blessing to his country." Patriots ought also to thank "all-gracious Heaven" for "preserving the invaluable life" of this "illustrious General."[32]

Comparisons of the famous American commander with various biblical patriarchs promoted both the concept of America as God's New Israel and the providential legend of Washington. In the manner of Cotton Mather and other Puritan biographers, patriot preachers and orators on occasion depicted Washington as "the American NEHEMIAH" or "this American Joshua." Indeed, Washington as Joshua was the thinly disguised parallel portrayed in Timothy Dwight's 1785 epic *The Conquest of Canaan.*[33] But the ultimate parallel was between Washington and the most famous deliverer of God's ancient covenant people. Given the popularity of the New Israel motif and the many comparisons of the American Revolution to the Exodus, it is not surprising that patriots, led by Hugh Henry Brackenridge, quickly discovered that "Moses" was a man "much resembling our general Washington." That Divine Providence, "in the beginning of our contest, seeing our apprehension, for a Moses sent us a Washington, assisted by and aided with many zealous Aarons and valorous Joshuas" was a cause for rejoicing. Patriots needed little urging to follow the advice of a New England poet:

> Let's eye that Providence, adore the hand,
> That rais'd for us a *Moses* in our land.
> O what a blessing to these States! it is our bliss,
> Great WASHINGTON was rais'd for such a day as this.[34]

Popular patriotic accounts of the Revolutionary War frequently consisted of one manifestation after another of the delivering hand of

[32] Samuel Stillman, *An Oration, Delivered July 4th, 1789* (Boston, 1789), p. 21; *Boston Gaz.*, 18 Feb. 1782.

[33] Murray, *Nehemiah*, p. 49; Ezra Stiles, *United States elevated*, Thornton, ed., *Pulpit*, p. 442; Duffield, *Sermon*, p. 18; [Sewall], *Oration*, p. 22; L. Douglass Good, "The Christian Nation in the Mind of Timothy Dwight," *Fides et Historia* 7 (1974): 1–18.

[34] Brackenridge, *Six Political Discourses*, p. 38; Fitzhugh Mackay, *American Liberty Asserted: or British Tyranny Reprobated* (Lancaster, Pa., [1778]), p. 12; [Case], *Poems*, p. 22. Cf. also Tappan, *Discourse*, p. 15, and Symmes, *Sermon*, pp. 7–8.

God.[35] The campaign in and around New York City in the summer and fall of 1776 was the first occasion of divine intervention. Initial British attempts to capture the city were slowed by the elements, clearly under the direction of Heaven. After the British finally landed on Long Island and surprised the raw patriots, Divine Providence provided a route of escape for Washington and his troops. "Survey the plains of Long Island, whither he flew like a guardian angel to protect and bring off his brave troops, surrounded on every side by a host of foes, and with a conduct unparalleled in history secured their retreat across a river of which the enemy's ships were in full possession. Surely Heaven interposed in behalf of America on that day, by permitting such numbers to escape with glory from such a superior force!"[36] Forced to abandon New York and retreat to New Jersey, Washington in December 1776 regrouped, counterattacked, and defeated British and Hessian forces at Trenton and Princeton. Patriots needed little urging to join with William Livingston in offering thanks for this "signal victory" with which it had "pleased the Almighty to crown the American arms."[37]

One of the greatest manifestations of divine assistance was the frustration in 1777 of British attempts to cut the newly independent states in two. Advancing south from Canada toward Albany in the early summer, British General John Burgoyne scored initial victories, seizing Forts Mount Independence and Ticonderoga from the

[35] The providential accounts prepared by patriots of the various campaigns and battles of the Revolution surely qualify the claims of some historians that the Revolutionary era saw the secularization of historical writing in America. They also challenge Daniel Boorstin's assertions (1) that Americans produced few contemporary historical accounts of the Revolution and (2) that "the American was unaccustomed to treating American events as a whole and unused to writing about events taking place outside his own colony" (*The Americans: The National Experience* [New York, 1965], pp. 362–63). Sermons, orations, and newspaper essays from 1776 through 1789 contained many extended historical analyses, most of which unequivocally assigned *American* (and not just local) success to the intervention of Divine Providence.

[36] *Boston Gaz.*, 9 Sept. 1776; *Va. Gaz.* (Dixon and Hunter), 24 Jan. 1777; Portsmouth, N.H., *Freeman's Journal*, 12 Apr. 1777, Moore, ed., *Diary*, 1:381–82.

[37] Livingston, "Speech," Moore, ed., *American Eloquence*, 1:88. Cf. David Avery, *The Lord is to be Praised for the Triumphs of His Power* (Norwich, Conn., 1778), pp. 24–26.

patriots. But this was only an occasion of the Lord bringing good out of evil, for Burgoyne was so elated with these early successes that he abandoned all caution and marched directly into disaster. On 16 August several British and Hessian columns were routed at Bennington by Vermont militia under the direction of the "Great Lord of the heavens, and the God of armies." This triumph, moreover, was only a prelude to an even more glorious event—the surrender of Burgoyne's entire army to General Horatio Gates at Saratoga on 17 October 1777. "A merciful *God*," exclaimed the Reverend Jacob Cushing, "hath crowned *our arms*, with singular success and victory; enabling us to destroy and break up a whole army, under one of the greatest *Generals*, perhaps, that *Britain* can boast of. This is the Lord's doing, and 'tis marvelous in our eyes."[38] The victory was so complete that providential intervention seemed to Noah Smith the only "rational" explanation: "That omnipotent being, who has been pleased to stile himself the GOD of armies, inspired our troops with intrepidity, and directed their charge. . . . Those heroes who were active that day, were the instruments by which our deliverance was effected; but GOD was the author." "We may easily account for the ignominious exit of Burgoyne," asserted Hugh Henry Brackenridge. "It is to be resolved . . . into the providence of God, which he had slighted and despised." In addition, the recognition that through the "unbounded goodness and mercy" of Jehovah, American "FREEDOM and INDEPENDENCE, the never-failing heritage of the brave and virtuous," was guaranteed by Saratoga called for even more "solemn thanksgiving and praise to ALMIGHTY GOD."[39]

Victory seemed even more inevitable when patriots learned that, after Saratoga, France had recognized their independence and entered a formal military alliance with the young republic. Patriots rejoiced that "that GOD who has the hearts of kings in his hands" had

[38] West, *Anniversary Sermon*, pp. 42–43; *Pa. Evening Post*, 4 Sept. 1777, Moore, ed., *Diary*, 1:481; Cushing, *Divine judgments*, p. 26. For other providential interpretations of Saratoga, see Israel Evans, *1777 Discourse*, pp. 11–13; *N.C. Gaz.*, 14 Nov. 1777; Brackenridge, *Six Political Discourses*, pp. 55–57; John Lathrop, *A Discourse, Preached on March the Fifth, 1778* (Boston, 1778), pp. 17–18; Chauncey Whittelsey, *The importance of religion in the civil Ruler* (New Haven, 1778), p. 16.

[39] Smith, *A Speech, Delivered at Bennington* (Hartford, 1779), p. 8; Brackenridge, *Six Political Discourses*, p. 73; *Va. Gaz.* (Purdie), 21 Nov. 1777.

provided "His Most Christian Majesty the King of France" as America's "greatest human friend and supporter."[40] God's mercy was especially appreciated in view of the formidable impediments to such an alliance. America and France had been traditional enemies and were separated by differing customs, habits, and religions—yet when God intended to work some wonder, nothing could stand in his way. As a New York newspaper commented on the alliance in the summer of 1778, "Four years ago, such an event, at so near a day, was not in the view even of imagination: but it is the Almighty who raiseth up; he hath stationed America among the powers of the earth, and clothed her in the robes of sovereignty."[41] And it was not surprising, given the popularity of the Republican Israel motif and biblical allusions to the Revolutionary mind, that some patriot spokesmen discovered yet another type, celebrating "the astonishing magnanimity, generosity, and fidelity of the KING of France, the *Cyrus* of our *Israel*, whose paternal, liberal, effectual aid, afforded to us in our low estate, so remarkably resembles the conduct of that ancient, noble Prince."[42]

In the autumn of 1780 Divine Providence once more came to the assistance of American Israel—the Lord frustrated Benedict Arnold's traitorous conspiracy. Arnold had planned to turn over West Point to the British and betray Washington and his staff into the enemy's hands, but God saw to it that his plots came to nought.[43] "The providential train of circumstances" that attended the detection

[40] Payson, *Memorial*, p. 13. See also *N.C. Gaz.*, 14 Aug. 1778; "Leonidas," *Pa. Jour.*, 29 May 1782; "Philander," *Boston Gaz.*, 28 Apr. 1783; Eliphalet Porter, *Sermon*, pp. 20–21; Oliver Hart, *America's Remembrancer, with Respect to her Blessedness and Duty* (Philadelphia, 1791), pp. 11–12 (preached in Hopewell, N.J., 1789).

[41] Payson, *Memorial*, pp. 13–15; Buckminster, *1783 Discourse*, pp. 12–13; *N.Y. Jour.*, 24 Aug. 1778, Moore, ed., *Diary*, 2:81.

[42] Tappan, *Discourse*, p. 14. For other comparisons of Louis XVI with Cyrus, see Payson, *Sermon*, Thornton, ed., *Pulpit*, p. 347; Murray, *Nehemiah*, p. 50; Clarke, *Sermon Before Hancock*, pp. 47–49.

[43] See the accounts in *Boston Gaz.*, 23 Oct. 1780; *Md. Gaz.*, 6, 13, 20 Oct. 1780; *Pa. Packet*, 3, 10 Oct. 1780, Moore, ed., *Diary*, 2:328, 330–31; *Pa. Jour.*, 4 Oct. 1780; Israel Evans, *A Discourse Delivered Near York in Virginia* (Philadelphia, 1782), p. 28; *The Fall of Lucifer, an Elegiac Poem* (Hartford, 1781), pp. 6, 16; Duffield, *Sermon*, p. 23.

of Arnold's plot, according to the *Pennsylvania Packet*, afforded "the most convincing proofs that the liberties of America are the object of divine protection."[44] A frequent observation was that, of all the providential mercies displayed to that date in the Revolutionary War, this particular one was the most "remarkable" and "wonderful."[45] It was ironic, then, that Arnold, after he fled to British-occupied New York City, published a defense of his treachery in which he claimed that the patriots were warring against the will of God. This arrogance was too much for one Boston journal: "The Traitor *Arnold* had the face to speak of *religion* in his address. . . . He had so totally sold himself to the English, and was so entirely lost to every moral sentiment, as not to perceive that Providence itself had patronized the cause of our independence, by discovering his plots in a manner next to miraculous."[46]

Just one year later God again patronized the cause of his chosen nation by delivering a British army into patriot hands at Yorktown. "The joyous event which the hand of Providence hath produced," one spokesman exulted, "is no less than the Capture of the whole British Army under the command of Lord Cornwallis." The activity of the Almighty was traced through all the facets of the Yorktown campaign. The Lord promoted harmony among the allied American and French armies, kept their moves hidden from the British, provided the French naval victory in Chesapeake Bay that sealed Cornwallis's fate, kept allied losses to a minimum, and led the enemy into errors of judgment from which they could not extricate themselves. Furthermore, Yorktown was a divine judgment against Britain for two special reasons. First, the patriot victory was providential retribution for the cruelties committed by the British armies advancing through the southern states on their way to Yorktown. Second, it constituted a just humbling of British pride. Before his entrapment Cornwallis, like Burgoyne in 1777, had issued haughty proclamations threatening all who did not bow before him. Such sentiments

[44] *Pa. Packet*, 10 Oct. 1780, Moore, ed., *Diary*, 2:323.

[45] See, e.g., Ford, ed., *Journals of Continental Congress*, 18:950–51; *Fall of Lucifer*, p. 14; Peter Powers, *Tyranny and Toryism Exposed* (Westminster, Vt., 1781), p. 16.

[46] Boston *Independent Chronicle*, 8 Dec. 1780, Moore, ed., *Diary*, 2:334.

were offensive to a jealous God, who had quickly humbled both commanders in the dust.[47]

Finally in 1783 peace arrived. Throughout the new nation pious citizens gave thanks to Divine Providence as the giver of freedom and independence. As one American put it, "The long wished for period to the war, is come, and demands our warmest gratitude to Heaven." Particular thanks were due to God that the Peace of 1783 was so favorable to the young republic. Divine patronage included the facts that the United States retained rights to the Newfoundland fisheries and that her new national boundaries included vast tracts of western land not actually controlled by patriot forces at the war's end. Addressing the American Philosophical Society in January 1784, the nationalist poet Francis Hopkinson observed that "by the blessing of Almighty God" the Revolutionary War "hath terminated in . . . a peace highly honourable and advantageous to us." When Americans considered the peace settlement, a clerical cousin of John Adams insisted, they must "take notice of the hand of Providence in accelerating this important event, and establishing it on terms *so honourable* to *America*. Our most sanguine wishes are gratified, and expectations out done!"[48]

When it came to the events of the Revolutionary War, loyalists also attempted to find instances of providential favor—to the arms of Great Britain, of course. Their efforts, however, were strained. After the Battle of Saratoga, for instance, William Smith curiously wrote that "perhaps this event by the unsearchable Wisdom of Heaven may prepare the way for a Reconciliation." James Rivington's *Royal Gazette* did claim in 1778 that "the gracious intervention of divine Providence" had frustrated the French navy's plan to trap a British squadron on the Delaware River and described a British victory over

[47] Nathan Fiske, *An Oration, Delivered at Brookfield, Nov. 14, 1781* (Boston, [1781]), pp. 4, 5–6; Israel Evans, *Discourse Near York*, pp. 31–34; Ford, ed., *Journals of Continental Congress*, 21:1074–76; Robert Smith, *Obligations*, pp. 17–19; Woodhull, *Sermon*, pp. 14–15; *Md. Gaz.*, 25 Oct. 1781; *Pa. Jour.*, 31 Oct. 1781; *N.Y. Jour.*, 12 Nov. 1781, Moore, ed., *Diary*, 2:510; Brockway, *America Saved*, pp. 15–16.

[48] "Consideration," *Boston Gaz.*, 5 May 1783; David Osgood, *Reflections*, pp. 20–21; *The Miscellaneous Essays and Occasional Writings of Francis Hopkinson, Esq.*, 3 vols. (Philadelphia, 1792), 1:360; Zabdiel Adams, *The Evil Designs of Men made Subservient to God for the Public Good* (Boston, 1783), p. 31n.

the Spanish fleet off Cadiz in February 1780 as a "Blessing of Providence." The *Royal Gazette* even claimed in 1781 that "most *providentially* for the good people of America" the "vindictive" leaders of the Continental Congress had spurned conciliatory terms offered them by Britain; the longer the war continued, the worse it would go for the whigs, so that the end result would ultimately be a "union much *more permanent*" than that which had existed before 1776. But compared with the providential accounts of the Revolutionary War penned by patriots, loyalist wartime providential rhetoric was general and sparse.[49]

As if to compensate, loyalist spokesmen constantly attempted to discount patriot references to providential approbation. When a captured patriot commander told New York's loyalist judge Thomas Jones that Divine Providence, during the New York campaign of 1776, had allowed Washington to escape from British General William Howe by putting a mist before Howe's eyes, Jones replied that the rebels were more indebted to opposition members of Parliament than to Providence. In April 1777 William Smith argued with a female patriot who asserted that the Almighty favored the patriot cause, claiming that "the Lord is just and will avenge the Sufferings of his People." "On this Subject," Smith caustically commented, "it is impossible to pour Light in upon her Mind." In an open letter in 1779 to John Jay, then president of the Continental Congress, Charles Inglis insisted that the loyalists "judged it a mockery of the Supreme Being to desire his interposition in behalf of measures which were expressly forbidden in his word, and inconsistent with the spirit of his religion." Such statements may have reinforced the determination of the loyalists to resist the haughty and overbearing rebels, but they were at best a poor substitute for success. No amount of disparagement could ultimately blot out the reality of the patriot victory in 1783.[50]

[49] William Smith, *Historical Memoirs*, 2:240; *Royal Gaz.*, 29 July 1778, 8 Apr. 1780; "Colonus," ibid., 28 Apr. 1781.

[50] William H. Nelson, *The American Tory* (Oxford, 1961), p. 135; William Smith, *Historical Memoirs*, 2:115–16; [Charles Inglis], *The Letters of Papinian* (New York, 1779), p. 67. For similar loyalist pronouncements see Inglis, *Christian Soldier's Duty*, p. 17; *Royal Gaz.*, 13 June 1778, 15 Nov. 1780; "Modestus," ibid., 14 Nov. 1778.

Much of the patriot wartime optimism generated by that victory, however, dissipated rapidly after 1783. America entered a "Critical Period," so named (a century before John Fiske) and so considered by many of its participants. Sin, luxury, and moral failure seemed to jeopardize the Revolutionary achievement; a decline in virtue threatened the peace of the Republican Israel. Enlightened as well as pious Americans believed and lamented that luxury and corruption were rampant as never before. Complaints of poverty and hard times were affronts to a Providence that had blessed America with material benefits unrivaled by any other nation. Providential thought and political ideology joined to attack the deplorable "intestine divisions and animosities" that infected the states in the 1780s; how "provoking" they were to a guardian God who had so recently acted for America's salvation. In his anger at ingratitude and sin the Lord allowed actual violence to break out in Shays's Rebellion. This "insurrection and resistance of lawful authority" was "righteous testimony" of the Almighty's "holy displeasure." The dispersal of the Shaysites, spokesmen warned, was not to be seen as a vindication of national innocence—the Lord instead had stayed his hand and was giving a guilty nation one more chance.[51]

In this atmosphere the Constitutional Convention met in Philadelphia and drew up the Federal Constitution. Presented to the states for consideration in September 1787, the Constitution precipitated a vigorous and often bitter debate before its eventual ratification. An aspect of this constitutional debate was the partisan use of providential imagery. Both Federalist supporters of the Constitution and their Antifederalist opponents appealed to various elements of a common providential thought in their efforts to enact or defeat the Constitution. Yet these were hardly the main elements in the overall campaigns of either group; the vast bulk of the constitutional deliberation was conducted in secular terms and revolved around practical

[51] Wood, *Creation of the American Republic*, pp. 393–94, 413–25; *Md. Gaz.*, 23 Mar. 1786, 24 May 1787; Joseph Lathrop, *Sermon*, p. 20; Joseph Lyman, *A Sermon, Preached Before His Excellency James Bowdoin* (Boston, [1787]), pp. 44, 46–47, 49–50; "Farmer," *Country Journal, and the Poughkeepsie Advertiser*, 11 Apr. 1787; Hatch, *Sacred Cause of Liberty*, pp. 102–18.

political considerations. Appeals to Providence comprised a relatively minor part of the ratification struggle. Such appeals nevertheless do deserve consideration, if not for what was said about the relative merits or demerits of the Constitution then for what these appeals showed about the nature of the American providential consensus after 1783. Partisan usage of the providential legend demonstrated the limitations of that legend; its very breadth and its centrality to American patriotism promoted its employment in all honesty by bitterly opposed groups. Also, the references to Divine Providence in the constitutional debates of 1787–88 presaged the more extensive uses spokesmen would make of providential rhetoric after the rise of national political parties in the 1790s.

Exactly how was Divine Providence employed by the opponents of the Constitution? Antifederalists claimed that there was no need to adopt a new system of government, since America already enjoyed the form that God intended her to have. The Articles of Confederation were "a blessing from heaven," yet Americans were foolishly "impatient to change it, for another."[52] Adoption of the Constitution threatened America's role as the Republican Israel: only "if we STAND STILL," argued one Bay State Antifederalist, will the United States "be like the blessed Canaan, a land flowing with milk and honey."[53] Finally, replacing the Articles with a new Constitution that did not even mention the name of God would be a grievous affront to Heaven. If Americans adopted the proposed system, would it not be righteous "if God, in his anger, should think it proper to punish us for our ignorance, and sins of ingratitude to him, after carrying us through the late war, and giving us liberty." The history of ancient Israel reinforced this point, clearly showing the fate of a nation—even a divinely favored one—that rejected a God-given form of government and demanded another. The Jews had been cursed with

[52] "Candidus," *Ind. Chron.*, 20 Dec. 1787, in Morton Borden, ed., *The Antifederalist Papers* (East Lansing, Mich., 1965), p. 57; "Agrippa," Boston *Massachusetts Gazette*, 14 Jan. 1788; Rebecca Brooks Gruver, ed., *American Nationalism, 1783–1830: A Self-Portrait* (New York, 1970), p. 53.

[53] "John De Witt," Boston *American Herald*, 22 Oct. 1787, in Cecelia M. Kenyon, ed., *The Antifederalists* (Indianapolis, 1966), p. 95.

kings, and America would suffer the same disaster if she embraced the Constitution.[54]

Federalists responded with their own providential rhetoric. "A religious gratitude" to America's "heavenly Benefactor," according to Joel Barlow, a leading Connecticut Wit, dictated that the Revolution be "completed" with a firm national government. It was clear to some Federalists that the delegates at the Philadelphia Convention had labored under the guidance of the divine spirit. As South Carolina's David Ramsay remarked, "Heaven smiled on their deliberations, and inspired their councils . . . hence arose a system, which seems well calculated to make us happy at home and respected abroad." Only through adoption of the Constitution could the United States fulfill its providential destiny. Federalists insisted that ratification of the Constitution would be the actualization of God's will and rejoiced when the process was completed. As the Connecticut Wit and early nationalist poet David Humphreys remarked in a victory oration, "Can we contemplate a whole People, like a nation of Philosophers, discussing and agreeing on a form of government: can we contemplate a work so vast in its import, and so wonderfully effected—not by violence and bloodshed, but by deliberation and consent—without exclaiming . . . in grateful adoration, lo, this is indeed the LORD's doing, and it is marvellous in our eyes!" Finally, Federalists asserted that God's approval of the Constitution was demonstrated by the selection of Washington to head the new government. "It is surely of the Lord," one observed, "that the same worthy character that led our troops, now guides our councils."[55]

The debate over the Constitution was the first occasion for the partisan usage of providential imagery (if one does not include the

[54] "A Farmer and Planter," Baltimore *Maryland Journal*, 1 Apr. 1788, Borden, ed., *Antifederalist Papers*, pp. 71–72; "Agrippa," *Mass. Gaz.*, 20 Jan. 1788; Kenyon, ed., *Antifederalists*, pp. 373–75.

[55] Barlow, *An Oration, Delivered at the North Church in Hartford* (Hartford, [1787]), p. 11; [David Ramsay], *An Oration, Prepared for Delivery before the Inhabitants of Charleston* ([Charleston, S.C.], 1788), p. 3; "Monitor," *Pa. Jour.*, 3 Nov. 1787; Keith, *Friendly Influence of Religion*, p. 6; Cherry, ed., *God's New Israel*, pp. 61, 63–64; Humphreys, *The Miscellaneous Works of Colonel Humphreys* (New York, 1790), p. 339, from an oration given on the 4th of July, 1789; Hart, *America's Remembrancer*, p. 13.

pre-1783 patriot-loyalist debate). Again, the import of this phenomenon should not be overrated; it was a relatively minor aspect of providential thought before 1789. The lesser role of partisan providential rhetoric in this earlier period becomes apparent when contrasted with treatments of America's providential mission articulated after 1776. These were much more unified and spirited than any divisive uses of the providential legend. Whatever their opinion of the Federal Constitution, virtually all Americans agreed on the reality and importance of the Republican Israel's divine task. Tremendously stimulated by the successful Revolution, faith in America's mission reverberated throughout the era.

The theme of America as the great empire for liberty expanded with each succeeding year. Americans north and south were convinced (or sought to convince themselves) that God was offering his Republican Israel a singular chance for national greatness and happiness. What other nation had ever enjoyed the resources and blessings that America did?[56] In America the Lord was "erecting a stage, on which to exhibit the great things of his kingdom"—a stage where "God's greatest works" would be enacted.[57] "A new world," "Americanus" asserted in 1778, "has arisen from the chaos of tyranny and usurpation, the spirit of God has moved upon the face of this western hemisphere, has called forth liberty from amidst confusion and disorder." The United States was destined by Divine Providence to be a great empire where liberty would attain glorious heights.[58] Adoption of the Federal Constitution only made this mission more real (at least to Federalists); the new system of government fulfilled "the designs of Heaven," designs calculated to make Americans "a great and happy people."[59]

[56] See "Z.," *Md. Gaz.*, 15 Aug. 1776; *Pa. Jour.*, 28 Aug. 1776; *Boston Gaz.*, 12 July 1779, 3 Feb. 1783; David Osgood, *Reflections*, p. 31; "Spectator," *Mass. Gaz.*, 26 Aug. 1788.

[57] Brockway, *America Saved*, p. 23. The notion of America as a divine "theater" or "stage" had been "a favorite image" of Cotton Mather (Bercovitch, *Puritan Origins*, p. 129).

[58] "Americanus," *Va. Gaz.* (Dixon and Hunter), 30 Oct. 1778; "The Spectator," *Boston Gaz.*, 3 Feb. 1777; Ramsay, *Oration on the Advantages*, Brunhouse, ed., *Ramsay*, p. 190; Zabdiel Adams, *Evil Designs of Men*, pp. 17, 27; Ezra Stiles, *United States elevated*, Thornton, ed., *Pulpit*, pp. 438–39.

[59] *Country Jour., and Poughkeepsie Ad.*, 15 July 1788.

The successful Revolution also lent further credence to America's providential mission as the asylum of the oppressed. During the war years patriots were reminded that they were fighting so that "our Zion shall become the delight and praise of the whole earth . . . America shall be the place to which the persecuted in other nations shall flee from the tyranny of their oppressors, where they shall find a safe retreat." The successful termination of the Revolutionary War and the achievement of independence simply made this mission more mandatory. As John Gardiner of Boston urged his countrymen, "Let us cheerfully open our arms to the industrious, and to the oppressed of every nation, tongue, and kindred, nor deny to *any*, what THE LORD OF ALL hath made, has given for UNIVERSAL GOOD. As HE hath given *peace*, *liberty*, and *safety*, to us, let us extend the same to ALL."[60] Throughout the Critical Period Americans echoed these sentiments.[61]

The concepts of America as the empire for liberty and the asylum of the oppressed thus received extensive providential reinforcement during the American Revolution. But even more attention was devoted to America's cosmic mission, to the belief that Providence had secured the New Israel's independence in order to effect some manner of global reformation and illumination. This strain of thought was buttressed by another popular image, one strikingly similar to the vision of the first-generation Puritans of New England: America was contending for the rights of all men, so the world was watching America's progress with anxious and hopeful eyes. Patriots insisted that they had been "called in Providence to fight out not the liberties of America only, but the liberties of the world itself." The cause of the United States, "God's own cause," was unquestionably "the grand cause of the whole human race"; hence providential assistance was not surprising. Nor was it surprising that therefore "the eyes of the nations of the earth . . . are upon these States, to see what use they

[60] Nye, *Cultural Life*, pp. 46–47; John C. Rainbolt, "Americans' Initial View of their Revolution's Significance for Other Peoples," *Historian* 35 (1973): 424–26; West, *Anniversary Sermon*, p. 49; Gardiner, *Oration*, p. 36.

[61] See "Philanthropos," *Md. Gaz.*, 6 Mar. 1783; Duffield, *Sermon*, p. 16; Rodgers, *Divine Goodness displayed*, p. 30; *Pa. Jour.*, 2 Nov. 1785; *Va. Gaz., or, Am. Ad.*, 22 Oct. 1785; *Mass. Gaz.*, 11 July 1788.

will make of the great things God has done for us."[62] Americans repeatedly reminded themselves that they must act with wisdom and foresight because the eyes of the world were upon them. And they were correct—perhaps more correct than they knew. Enlightenment spokesmen in Europe supported the American Revolution and viewed the patriot victory as a vindication of their own campaigns for political and religious freedom. American success confirmed for them the validity of faith in reason and man's innate goodness. The providential legend in this instance conformed, rather than did violence, to reality.[63]

In this context Americans insisted that God had supported, and was continuing to support, his Republican Israel in order to effect "world reformation." American survival and success would instruct the world on the civil and religious rights of man. "The great designs of Providence," a southern newspaper editorialized in 1782, "must be accomplished—great indeed. The progress of society will be accelerated by centuries, by this revolution. . . . American ideas of toleration and religious liberty . . . will become the fashionable system of all Europe. . . . 'Light spreads from the day spring in the west, and may it shine more and more until the perfect day.'"[64] Practically, American independence in itself guaranteed that the lot of oppressed peoples all over the world would be ameliorated. Despots now must be less despotic or risk losing their subjects to the new asylum in the West. Thus a significant lessening of cruelty and tyranny—undoubtedly the intent of Providence—would follow the successful Revolution.[65] Patriots were quick to discern such developments. After 1783 they frequently pointed to symptoms of rising liberalism in Britain,

[62] Ezra Stiles, *United States elevated*, Thornton, ed., *Pulpit*, p. 454; Keteltas, *God Arising*, p. 19; Rodgers, *Divine Goodness displayed*, p. 38.

[63] Payson, *Sermon*, Thornton, ed., *Pulpit*, p. 353; Boston *Continental Journal*, 13 July 1780, as quoted in Davidson, *Propaganda and the American Revolution*, p. 369; David Osgood, *Reflections*, p. 31; Peter Gay, *The Enlightenment: The Science of Freedom* (New York, 1969), pp. 555–58; Joyce Appleby, "America as a Model for the Radical French Reformers of 1789," *William and Mary Quarterly*, 3d ser. 28 (1971): 267–86.

[64] *Va. Gaz., or, Am. Ad.*, 11 May 1782.

[65] See Ramsay, *Oration on the Advantages*, Brunhouse, ed., *Ramsay*, p. 188; "Consideration," *Boston Gaz.*, 13 Oct. 1783; Trumbull, *God is to be praised*, p. 22; Barlow, *Oration*, p. 20.

Ireland, France, Spain, and Germany as proof that their providential mission was being fulfilled.[66] The conviction that the Republican Israel's cosmic mission was, under Divine Providence, succeeding grew with each passing year.[67]

The logical culmination and ultimate expression of America's cosmic mission after 1776 lay in the belief that the New Israel had been chosen by God as the "model republic" to demonstrate to the world the validity and superiority of republicanism. As one student of the American mission has concluded, this belief was "an article of collective faith" that can properly be termed "*the* American Mission."[68] Thus "Leonidas" rejoiced that "Heaven seems to intend to make us the link that shall bind the globe together in one common system of interests and benevolence." Thus Joel Barlow in his 1787 epic eulogized America as "the splendid seat by Heaven assign'd / To hear and give the counsels of mankind." In a fitting summation of the Republican Israel's divine cosmic mission, Boston's Samuel Stillman, reflecting that the "republican principles of the American Revolution" were, under the auspices of "Providence," extending their "salutary influence" across the globe, cried out, "May the great work of political reformation go on."[69]

Providential thought during the Revolutionary era was for the most part expressed by common (and today mostly forgotten) preachers, orators, poets, and journalists. In their writings and speeches these patriots articulated a providential legend that modifies the concept of a secular American Enlightenment. But what of the more famous men of the era—the Founding Fathers, the spokesmen of that American Enlightenment? Did they think and speak as their more common countrymen? Or did they rather employ secular, "en-

[66] See the typical accounts in Zabdiel Adams, *Evil Designs of Men*, pp. 24–25; David Osgood, *Reflections*, pp. 29–30; William Pierce, *An Oration, Delivered at Christ-Church, Savannah, on the 4th July, 1788* (Savannah, 1788), pp. 5–6. For the impact of the American Revolution on Western Europe, see Jones, *Revolution and Romanticism*, pp. 216–27, 301–8.

[67] See also the general discussions in Burns, *American Idea of Mission*, pp. 11–14; Nye, *Cultural Life*, pp. 42–48; Cherry, ed., *God's New Israel*, pp. 22–23.

[68] Rossiter, "American Mission," p. 19.

[69] "Leonidas," *Pa. Jour.*, 31 July 1782; Barlow, *Vision of Columbus*, p. 257; Stillman, *Oration*, p. 20.

lightened" concepts and language, to the virtual exclusion of providential imagery? The question is important, for elite rejection of, or abstention from, America's providential consensus would clearly have greatly affected the strength and popularity of that consensus.

Prominent leaders of the American Enlightenment included John Adams, Samuel Adams, John Dickinson, Benjamin Franklin, Alexander Hamilton, Patrick Henry, John Jay, Thomas Jefferson, James Madison, Thomas Paine, Benjamin Rush, George Washington, and James Wilson. These men held diverse personal religious beliefs. Sam Adams and John Jay, for instance, were orthodox, even conservative Christians, while Franklin, Jefferson, and Paine were deists. Washington's personal religious convictions have long been a subject of debate, but the best evidence suggests that he too was a "typical eighteenth-century deist."[70] The religious principles of the remaining Founding Fathers fell somewhere between these two extremes.

Yet despite this religious diversity and despite their reputation as "enlightened" thinkers, the Founding Fathers to an impressive degree accepted, both publicly and privately, many of the tenets of America's providential legend. They accepted first the notion of America as God's Republican Israel. John Dickinson, while a member of Congress, publicly compared the American Revolution to the biblical contest between David and Goliath. In 1776 Franklin and Jefferson presented to the Continental Congress designs for a national seal—Franklin offered as his design Pharaoh drowning in the Red Sea while Moses leads the Israelites to safety, Jefferson the children of Israel guided by pillar and cloud through the wilderness.[71] James Wilson asserted one year later that because the American Revolution was a just contest, "divine Providence" would crown America's "virtuous Struggles" with "abundant Success." Both John

[70] Paul F. Boller, Jr., *George Washington and Religion* (Dallas, 1963).

[71] Ford, ed., *Journals of Continental Congress*, 14:649, 5:689–91; Julian P. Boyd et al., eds., *The Papers of Thomas Jefferson*, 20 vols. to date (Princeton, N.J., 1950–), 1:494–95; John Adams to Abigail Adams, 14 Aug. 1776, Edmund C. Burnett, ed., *Letters of Members of the Continental Congress*, 8 vols. (Washington, D.C., 1921–36), 2:50. As Martin Marty observes, "It is significant that these statesmen—in so many ways uneasy themselves about the Jewish-Christian heritage—drew upon the Bible for symbols which could unite and interpret their peoples' experience" (*Righteous Empire*, p. 24).

Jay and Dickinson insisted that the cause of America was the "cause of God."[72]

Tom Paine publicly professed to believe that "there are such things as national sins, and though the punishment of individuals may be reserved to *another* world, national punishments can only be inflicted in *this*," and asserted that Great Britain was suffering such punishment from a just deity. Jay proclaimed that the American Revolution had occurred in part because patriots "ascribed that to our own prowess which was only to be attributed to the great Guardian of the innocent," and insisted that only national reformation could bring back the smiles of Providence. Both Benjamin Rush and George Washington privately claimed that only "infidels" could ignore the many providential interventions during the course of the Revolution. The Founding Fathers, it seems, were no strangers to the jeremiad tradition.[73]

Nor were they unfamiliar with the providentially reinforced legend of the fathers. Washington and Jay assigned Providence a prominent role in creating and maintaining union during the dark days of the war. Jay and Patrick Henry viewed George Washington as a divine instrument, Henry telling his fellow Virginian that "by the favour of God" he had been kept "unhurt." Washington in turn reinforced his own legendary status by depicting his "humble instrumentality in carrying the designs of Providence into effect."[74]

The Founding Fathers no less than their more common country-

[72] Ford, ed., *Journals of Continental Congress*, 8:404; Jay, "Address of the Convention of the Representatives of the State of New-York to their Constituents," 23 Dec. 1776, Johnston, ed., *Correspondence of Jay*, 1:116; Dickinson to Caesar A. Rodney, 10 June 1779, Burnett, ed., *Letters of Congress*, 4:257.

[73] "The American Crisis II," 13 Jan. 1777, Foner, ed., *Complete Writings of Paine*, 1:66; Jay, "Address of the Convention," Johnston, ed., *Correspondence of Jay*, 1:105, 109–10; Rush to Anthony Wayne, 24 Sept. 1776, Butterfield, ed., *Letters of Rush*, 1:114; Washington to Thomas Nelson, 20 Aug. 1778, Fitzpatrick, ed., *Writings of Washington*, 12:343.

[74] Washington, "Farewell Orders to the Armies of the United States," 2 Nov. 1783, Fitzpatrick, ed., *Writings of Washington*, 27:235; Johnston, ed., *Correspondence of Jay*, 3:296; Henry to Washington, 5 Mar. 1778, William Wirt Henry, *Patrick Henry: Life, Correspondence, and Speeches*, 3 vols. (New York, 1891), 1:548; Jay to Henry Knox, 10 Dec. 1781, and to Washington, 15 Mar. 1786, Johnston, ed., *Correspondence of Jay*, 2:159–60, 3:186; Washington to the Legislature of New Jersey, 6 Dec. 1783, Fitzpatrick, ed., *Writings of Washington*, 27:261.

men discerned the hand of God in each specific military development during the American Revolution. Sam Adams attributed the victory at Saratoga to "the God of Armies, who has vouchsafed in so distinguished a Manner to favor the Cause of America & of Mankind." To Washington also Saratoga was a "Signal Stroke of Providence."[75] Rush and Washington stated that the Lord had raised up France to be America's ally.[76] The frustration of Benedict Arnold's plot was attributed to God by Sam Adams, Paine, Rush, and Washington; as Adams put it, "Arnolds Conspiracy was to have wrought Wonders, but gracious Heaven defeated it."[77] These elite spokesmen were equally united in their judgment on Cornwallis's surrender at Yorktown: Sam Adams judged it a "Divine Blessing," Washington detected "the interposing Hand of Heaven," and Jay and James Madison also gave thanks to the Lord for the victory.[78] When peace came in 1783, Jay acknowledged the Almighty as the author of American independence, and Benjamin Franklin piously commented, "God was pleas'd to put a favourable End to the Contest much sooner than we had reason to expect. His Name be praised."[79]

Those Founding Fathers who favored the Federal Constitution invoked Providence for partisan ends, just as did lesser Federalists.

[75] Samuel Adams to Horatio Gates, 30 Oct. 1777, Cushing, ed., *Writings of Samuel Adams*, 3:414; Washington to John Augustine Washington, 18 Oct. 1777, Fitzpatrick, ed., *Writings of Washington*, 9:399, and cf. pp. 391, 453.

[76] Rush to Abigail Adams, 3 Sept. 1778, and to Nathanael Greene, 15 Apr. 1782, Butterfield, ed., *Letters of Rush*, 1:217, 268; Washington's General Orders, 5 May 1778, and Washington to the duc de Lauzun, 15 Oct. 1783, Fitzpatrick, ed., *Writings of Washington*, 11:354, 27:193.

[77] Samuel Adams to John Adams, 17 Dec. 1780, Cushing, ed., *Writings of Samuel Adams*, 4:232–33; "The Crisis Extraordinary," 4 Oct. 1780, Foner, ed., *Complete Writings of Paine*, 1:185–86; Rush to John Adams, 23 Oct. 1780, Butterfield, ed., *Letters of Rush*, 1:255; Washington to John Laurens, 13 Oct. 1780, Fitzpatrick, ed., *Writings of Washington*, 20:173.

[78] Samuel Adams to William Heath, 21 Nov. 1781, Cushing, ed., *Writings of Samuel Adams*, 4:265; Washington to Thomas McKean, 15 Nov. 1781, Fitzpatrick, ed., *Writings of Washington*, 23:343; Jay to Elbridge Gerry, 9 Jan. 1782, Johnston, ed., *Correspondence of Jay*, 2:168; Madison to Edmund Pendleton, 30 Oct. 1781, Gaillard Hunt, ed., *The Writings of James Madison*, 9 vols. (New York, 1900–1910), 1:158–59.

[79] Jay to Robert Morris, 12 Sept. 1783, Johnston, ed., *Correspondence of Jay*, 3:77; Franklin to Mrs. Jane Mecom, 4 July 1786, Albert Henry Smyth, ed., *The Writings of Benjamin Franklin*, 10 vols. (New York, 1905–7), 9:523.

Rush lamented the activities of Antifederalists but concluded, "All will end well. The last thing that I can believe is that providence has brought us over the Red Sea of the late war [only] to perish in the present wilderness of anarchy and vice." Washington in 1788 traced the "finger of Providence" through the "dark and mysterious events" that induced the states to adopt the Constitution. In the same vein the first president in his inaugural address of 30 April 1789 referred at length to "the benign Parent of the Human Race" who had favored "the American people with opportunities for deliberating in perfect tranquility, and dispositions for deciding with unparalleled unanimity on a form of government for the security of their union and the advancement of their happiness."[80]

Finally, the leaders of the American Enlightenment were equally vocal in their celebrations of America's divine mission. Jay insisted that God had given America a unique chance for national greatness and painted a glowing portrait of the providentially patronized empire for liberty. Franklin prayed that "the Almighty" would "perfect his Work, and establish Freedom in the new World, as an Asylum for those of the Old, who deserve it." The Founding Fathers also subscribed to America's cosmic mission. Franklin, pointing out how the American Revolution would ameliorate the lives of oppressed peoples overseas, termed the Revolution "a glorious task assign'd us by Providence." Rush asserted that "America seems destined by heaven to exhibit to the world the perfection which the mind of man is capable of receiving from the combined operation of liberty, learning, and the gospel upon it." And James Wilson, summing up the Republican Israel's providential nationalism, saw the United States as "subservient to the grand design of Providence with regard to this globe—the multiplication of mankind, their improvement in knowledge, and their advancement in happiness." There is little exaggeration in Conrad Cherry's conclusion that "the American Founding Fathers were as vigorous in their pro-

[80]Rush to Jeremy Belknap, 6 May 1788, Butterfield, ed., *Letters of Rush*, 1:460–61; Washington to Jonathan Trumbull, 20 July 1788, Fitzpatrick, ed., *Writings of Washington*, 30:22 (and cf. additional Washington letters in 1788, pp. 11, 30, 76, 79, 317); James D. Richardson, ed., *A Compilation of the Messages and Papers of the Presidents*, 10 vols. (Washington, D.C., 1907), 1:53–54.

nouncements on America's providential destiny as any clergyman."[81]

To be sure, some qualifications must be placed on certain of the Founding Fathers' references to providential images. Those leaders who were closest to the deistic faith of the European Enlightenment—especially Franklin and Jefferson—did not employ the concept of Divine Providence in the same anthropocentric sense that more common (and more pious) spokesmen did. And John Adams in the 1780s abandoned his earlier conviction of the New World's divine destiny, sadly concluding that there was "no special Providence for Americans."[82] But even with these qualifications the collective views of these spokesmen of the American Enlightenment are significant—they indicate both the limits of that American Enlightenment and the general agreement during the Revolutionary era between leaders and led on the main tenets of America's providential nationalism. Whatever the private religious convictions of the Founding Fathers, their public pronouncements from 1776 through 1789 complemented rather than contradicted popular providential themes.

The era of the Revolutionary War and the Constitution saw two important developments within American providential thought, developments that ultimately were to work at cross purposes. On the one hand, the success of the American Revolution and the establishment of a republican form of government provided the key ingredients for an American providential nationalism. On the other, partisan uses of providential rhetoric during the Critical Period formed a precedent that political parties were quick to imitate. The first trend promoted consensus, the second conflict within an overarching providential framework. Patriots after 1789 were heirs to both legacies. Only time would tell which would prove to be the more momentous.

[81] Jay, "Address of the Convention," and idem, "A Charge to the Grand Jury of Ulster County, New-York," 9 Sept. 1777, Johnston, ed., *Correspondence of Jay*, 1:118–19, 158–65; Franklin to Thomas Viny, 4 May 1779, and to Samuel Cooper, 1 May 1777, Smyth, ed., *Writings of Franklin*, 7:301, 56; Rush to Charles Nisbet, 5 Dec. 1783, Butterfield, ed., *Letters of Rush*, 1:316; Wilson as quoted in May, *Enlightenment in America*, p. 206; Cherry, ed., *God's New Israel*, p. 65.

[82] Norman Hampson, *A Cultural History of the Enlightenment* (New York, 1968), p. 81; Alfred O. Aldridge, *Benjamin Franklin and Nature's God* (Durham, N.C., 1967), pp. 8, 43, 85, 147–48, 202–3; Wood, *Creation of the American Republic*, pp. 569–74.

V

The Sanctification of American Nationalism

PROVIDENTIAL THOUGHT was a necessary, indeed an essential, ingredient of American nationalism from the American Revolution to the Civil War. As one modern student of the phenomenon has observed, "If not *uniquely* American, the idea of a protecting Providence was *characteristic*" of American patriotism during these years; hence "no study of American nationalism can possibly ignore it and remain faithful to the historical fact."[1] The standard studies of American nationalism do not ignore this facet, but none pursues it in depth or traces the evolution from providential thought to "civil religion." Hence it is illuminating to examine closely the providential strain in early American patriotism—to explain why American nationalism was especially permeated by providential rhetoric and symbols during the early national period, and how the unique providential flavor stamped on the key themes of American nationalism during the first years of the republic contributed to the later manifestation of an American civil religion.[2]

American patriotism after 1789, as we shall see, contained many expressions of apparent optimism and assurance. Yet the very plethora of such statements suggests a very real need among Americans for self-assurance and national identity. They were embarked on an "experiment" to determine whether republicanism was a viable form of government. The history of the world's classic republics—Greece, Rome, Venice—offered little assurance; all had been subverted by internal factions or foreign conspiracies. And the events of the 1790s and 1800s seemed to offer even less cause for confidence. The French Republic, produced by the French Revolution, metamorphazed first into the Terror of Robespierre, then into the autocracy of the Directorate, and finally into the imperial despotism

[1] Hay, "Providence and the American Past," p. 80.

[2] Robert N. Bellah, "Civil Religion in America," in *Religion in America*, ed. William G. McLoughlin and Robert N. Bellah (Boston, 1968), pp. 3–23.

over to praise and thanksgiving to Divine Providence for his blessings during the American Revolution. The words of the young Daniel Webster, delivering his first Fourth of July oration at Andover, New Hampshire, in 1800, were typical. Since "the vestiges of heavenly assistance" could be "clearly traced in those events, which mark the annals of our nation," it truly became all patriots "on this day, in consideration of the great things, which the LORD has done for us, to render the tribute of unfeigned thanks to that GOD, who superintends the Universe, and holds aloft the scale, that weighs the destinies of nations."[6] The Fourth of July was explicitly termed "the political Sabbath of freedom."[7] Clear evidence of the sanctification of American nationalism, the Fourth of July became literally the holy day of obligation for American patriots. This concept survived the triumph of a secular American culture as a central component of America's civil religion, so that well after the passing of providential thought the Fourth of July remained for public spokesmen the prescribed time for ritualized pronouncements on the character and consequences of the American experience.[8]

The continuing heritage of the American Revolution thus greatly reinforced the growth of American nationalism, but Americans craved further assurance that they were a uniquely favored people. They therefore shifted their gaze from the past to the present and compared their situation with that of the Old World. These parallels, embellished with providential rhetoric and always favorable to America, provided comfort in an age when war and national disaster were distinct possibilities. By insisting that God was behind their superior position vis-à-vis Europe, Americans assured themselves that their national survival was not ruled by external events over which they exercised little or no control but by an all-powerful Divine Providence. This superiority of course could not be measured in

[6] Webster, *An Oration, Pronounced at Hanover, New-Hampshire, the 4th Day of July, 1800* (Hanover, 1800), p. 8.

[7] Philadelphia *Aurora*, 7 July 1795; Rockne McCarthy, "Civil Religion in Early America," *Fides et Historia* 8 (1975): 31. Cf. *Aurora*, 6 July 1811, and William Hunter, *An Oration; Delivered in Trinity-Church, in Newport, on the fourth of July, 1801* (Newport, R.I., 1801), p. 6: the Fourth of July is the "sabbath of freedom."

[8] Hay, "Freedom's Jubilee"; Howard H. Martin, "The Fourth of July Oration," *Quarterly Journal of Speech* 44 (1958): 393–401.

material terms—the United States obviously was not the economic or military equal of Europe, much less its superior. The significance of the claim lay not in its historical truth or falsehood but in its repeated profession by patriots. The thesis was self-justifying: by telling themselves that the Lord controlled their destiny, Americans in reality were seeking to legitimize their national existence.

Patriots insisted that the "hand of Heaven" had drawn a "line of demarcation" between the United States and the "contaminations" of Europe. Timothy Dwight in his *Greenfield Hill* (1794) urged his countrymen to "Shun the lures / Of Europe," promising that if they did "HEAVEN shall bless thee, with a parent's hand." Clearly, Americans must attribute to Providence the fact that they continued under the smiles of peace while virtually every nation in Europe was racked by the wars stemming from the French Revolution. "Fervent" praise should rise to the "supreme Disposer" for America's "continued exemption from these scenes of devastation and ruin." Until America herself entered those wars in 1812, public spokesmen urged their fellow countrymen, "Let us lift up our eyes and unfold our hearts to heaven, and express our gratitude to that good being, by whose singular blessings the United States are thus most favored and blessed, while the nations of the old world are drenched with blood at the will or the caprice of despotic or ambitious rulers."[9]

Most of the psychological needs of the American people continued to be met by the popular conviction that America was God's Republican Israel. When a Massachusetts minister noted in 1799 that "'OUR AMERICAN ISRAEL' is a term frequently used; and common consent allows it apt and proper," he correctly assessed the mood of many Americans. The image of America as God's New Israel, after 1789 as in previous decades, worked to reassure anxious patriots. Surely the Lord would protect his "American Israelites" as he had the ancient Hebrews.[10] The frequent references after 1789 to the

[9] Hudson, N.Y., *Balance*, 13 Dec. 1803; Dwight, *Greenfield Hill: A Poem in Seven Parts* (New York, 1794), pp. 19–20; David Osgood, *The Wonderful Works of God are to be remembered* (Boston, 1794), p. 15; *Aurora*, 19 May 1804.

[10] Abiel Abbot, *Traits of Resemblance in the People of the United States of America to Ancient Israel* (Haverhill, Mass., 1799), p. 6; "A Citizen," *Poughkeepsie Journal*, 3 July 1793.

American Israel or the American Canaan were more than mere phrases or echoes of earlier Puritan sermons—they were (as always) reminders that America was specially chosen, arguments that her future (despite the disturbing realities of the present day) would be glorious.[11] The many comparisons of the American Revolution with the Exodus (a practice continued from the Revolutionary years) worked to the same ends.[12]

Another key component of America's sanctified nationalism was the deification of George Washington. The legend of the founding fathers came more and more to center on the distinguished Cincinnatus from Mount Vernon. It is not surprising that the providential legend of Washington as the agent of Heaven developed dramatically after 1789. The Washington legend served as a substitute for those common national traits the young republic lacked. In a diversified and divided nation, all Americans could find their identification in Washington. The Virginian did more than symbolize the American experience, he personified it, and thus provided a major degree of union in an era externally characterized by partisanship and discord. The new nation's need for national symbols and its craving for a common father figure overcame even political obstacles, enshrining Washington in a myth of providential guidance and union.[13]

The Washington legend was pervasively expressed through sev-

[11] For typical uses of these phrases see Pilmore, *Blessings of Peace*, p. 6; Spooner, *Discourse*, p. 12; and Eliphalet Nott, *A Discourse Delivered in the Presbyterian Church in Albany, the Fourth of July, A.D. 1801* (Albany, 1801), p. 19. Many more sermons and orations could be cited here.

[12] For typical examples see Elias Boudinot, *An Oration, Delivered at Elizabeth-Town, New Jersey* (Elizabethtown, 1793), pp. 6–7, and Nott, *Discourse*, pp. 5, 9.

[13] The literature on the emergence of a Washington legend is considerable. See Marcus Cunliffe, *George Washington: Man and Monument* (Boston, 1958); Mayo, *Myths and Men*, pp. 37–60; Paul C. Nagel, *One Nation Indivisible: The Union in American Thought, 1776–1861* (New York, 1964), pp. 224–31; Boorstin, *National Experience*, pp. 337–56; Richard W. Van Alstyne, *Genesis of American Nationalism* (Waltham, Mass., 1970), pp. 135–42; Lawrence J. Friedman, *Inventors of the Promised Land* (New York, 1975), pp. 44–78; James H. Smylie, "The President as Republican Prophet and King: Clerical Reflections on the Death of Washington," *Journal of Church and State* 18 (1976): 233–52; Catherine L. Albanese, *Sons of the Fathers: The Civil Religion of the American Revolution* (Philadelphia, 1976), pp. 143–81.

eral popular phrases and images. Many of the Mount Vernon planter's eulogists recalled with approbation a seeming prophecy from Washington's youth. Samuel Davies, the prominent Virginia exponent of the Great Awakening, had speculated after Braddock's defeat in 1755 that Providence had preserved the life of then-Colonel Washington for the future good of his country. How correct this devout divine had been.[14] Americans again and again characterized Washington as a man "raised up by Divine Providence to defend the liberties and vindicate the rights of his country." They loved to portray the Virginian as a leader "designed by divine Providence to be the most conspicuous instrument in the political salvation" of the United States.[15]

Washington's role in the American Revolution figured prominently in his providential legend. By an "impulse more than human" Washington had been selected to command the Revolutionary armies. It was an article of common faith throughout America that Divine Providence had then guided Washington to his victory in the Revolution. "The God of hosts was on our side," exclaimed Virginia's William Wirt, "and Washington—was his apostle." The guiding hand of Jehovah was traced through every aspect of Washington's career as general, lawgiver, and president. A guardian God had endowed the Virginian with the military, legal, and political skills necessary for the sustenance of the Republican Israel. Thus during the American Revolution, Washington had displayed a "spirit and temper critically formed by Providence, for the purpose," for which Americans ought always reverently to thank the "Provident Creator." The Almighty graciously also "preserved" Washington's life until he had finished his labors in behalf of American Israel.[16]

[14] John F. Berens, "'Like a Prophetic Spirit': Samuel Davies, American Eulogists, and the Deification of George Washington," *Quarterly Journal of Speech* 63 (1977): 290–97.

[15] John D. Blair, *A Sermon on the Death of Lieutenant General George Washington* ([Richmond], 1800), p. 8; Samuel Knox, *A Funeral Oration Commemorative of the illustrious Virtues of the late Great and Good General Washington* (Fredericktown, Md., [1800]), p. 2.

[16] Frederick Frelinghuysen, *An Oration on the Death of Gen. George Washington* (New Brunswick, N.J., 1800), p. 6; Wirt, *An Oration Delivered in Richmond on the Fourth of July, 1800* (Richmond, 1800), p. 12; *Charleston Courier*, 3 July 1805, 22 Feb. 1803; Blair, *Sermon*, pp. 16–17.

The popularity of paralleling Washington with religious prototypes suggests how comforting such parallels were—and not just because the device of religious symbolism, stretching back to Cotton Mather, remained a familiar one in early national America. Comparisons between Washington and Old Testament patriarchs were more than literary or oratorical flourishes; they were means to assure the American people that in an age of uncertainty their leaders would be divinely guided to the right decisions. Parallels between Moses, the deliverer of ancient Israel, and Washington, the deliverer of Republican Israel (parallels first drawn during the Revolutionary War) were even more widespread after 1789. The theme of the American Moses was especially prevalent in many of the orations and eulogies delivered in 1799 and 1800, on the occasion of Washington's death, but it was not limited to this one occurrence. Nor was the Washington-as-Moses motif the sole property of any one region of the young republic; patriots from Maine to Georgia utilized the concept.[17]

Even the depiction of Washington as a second Moses was not high enough praise (or strong enough reassurance) for some patriots. The apogee of the providential legend of Washington, and of the general theme of the legend of the founding fathers, was reached in subtle implications that Washington was more than a little akin to Jesus Christ. Although the expressions of this image were never as blatant as many others expressed after 1789, their significance was great. References to Washington as the "savior" of his country or America's "political savior" demonstrate vividly the degree to which providential thought sanctified American nationalism. So too do the explicit characterizations of the "god-like" Washington.[18] In the view of one southern orator, Washington was "a seeming emanation of the divinity, charged with the salvation of his country." A Pennsylvanian, recalling the death of the general, declared, "In that hour the veil of the temple of Liberty was rent in twain." In 1793 a Massachusetts patriot had claimed that Washington was "*Divinely* furnished to

[17] Robert P. Hay, "George Washington: American Moses," *American Quarterly* 21 (1969): 780–91.

[18] Chauncey Lee, *Oration*, p. 8; Boston *Columbian Centinel*, 1, 4, 8 Mar. 1797, 8 Mar. 1800, 3 Mar., 17 July 1811, 18 July 1812; *Aurora*, 23 July 1812; Albany *Balance*, 3 Mar. 1809, 5, 12 Mar. 1811; *Charleston Courier*, 4 Mar. 1811.

preside, / And *justly,* almost deify'd." But in many instances between 1789 and 1812 public spokesmen, finding in the deification of George Washington a major source of comfort and national union, dispensed with the "almost."[19]

The American mission was yet another aspect of American nationalism that continued to be sanctified by providential thought after 1789.[20] The New World was to be a great empire for liberty, an asylum for the oppressed of the globe, and a model for the political emulation of other nations. All three of these components found expression after 1789, but by far the greatest emphasis was awarded the last. Shared by Federalists and Republicans, northerners and southerners, clerics and laymen, the conviction that Divine Providence had raised up republican America to serve as the political model for the modern world, as Israel had served as the religious model for the ancient world, dominated the early national era. Again it is not difficult to discern why. The conviction that America was the providentially ordained model for the world provided reassurance against national failure. America was the wave of the future; instead of America being modeled on the past (which she obviously was not), all the nations of the globe in time would be modeled on the United States. This aspect of America's mission tempered the newness of the experiment and turned the notion of that experiment from a negative to a positive one. The concept, after all, was an ambiguous one—experiments could fail as well as succeed. By insisting that the Lord was behind *theirs*, Americans hedged against the former possibility. Repeatedly relating their providential mission, patriots employed the future as an antidote to the present.[21]

[19] *Charleston Courier*, 25 July 1806; John Ewing Porter, *An Oration, in Commemoration of the American Independence* (Philadelphia, 1804), p. 11; Bunker Gay, *To Sing of Mercy and Judgment* (Greenfield, Mass., 1793), p. 14.

[20] Any student of this aspect of American patriotism owes much to Burns, *American Idea of Mission.* But, when discussing the religious sources of the American mission, Burns tends to rely almost exclusively on the writings and opinions of a few prominent Americans (see, e.g., pp. 11–16), thus obscuring the widespread discussion of mission themes among the general populace. Also, since his book covers the entire span of American history, his remarks on the Revolutionary and early national periods are brief and scattered, and he seems to have missed certain themes (such as the concept of asylum) altogether.

[21] Rossiter, "American Mission," pp. 22–23; Kohn, *American Nationalism*, pp. 150–52.

America as the empire for liberty, "the theatre, where the latter day glory shall be displayed; and the medium through which religion, liberty, and learning," under God, would be "handed round creation," served a vital national need. The theme, of course, emphasized the future: the American empire would grow ever greater, and as such furnished comfort and reassurance against the unpleasantness of the era. No matter how bad things seemed to be—despite partisan wrangling, armed tax resistance, and disunionist schemes—America was "destined by Heaven" as the ultimate "abode of civil and religious freedom." Americans assured themselves that they were approaching rapidly (if they had not already achieved) the summit of national greatness. The great empire for liberty was rising "majestically fair. Founded on a rock, it will remain unshaken by the force of tyrants, undiminished by the flight of time. Long streams of light emanate through its portals, and chace the darkness from distant nations. Its turrets will swell into the heavens, rising above every tempest; and the pillar of divine glory, descending from God, will rest forever on its summit." In *The Columbiad* (1807) Joel Barlow conjured up the same biblical metaphor when he reminded Americans that "Based on its rock of Right your empire lies." In the midst of domestic division it was comforting to reflect—as many citizens did—that Divine Providence had raised up "in this western woody world . . . the GREAT TEMPLE OF LIBERTY." Timothy Dwight articulated the sentiments of all patriots when he depicted the United States: "O happy state! the state, by HEAVEN design'd, / To rein, protect, employ, and bless mankind."[22]

The concept of America as the asylum of the oppressed, however, underwent a significant change after 1789, a change that temporarily diminished its role in America's sanctified nationalist ideology. Whereas the first component of the American mission (the great rising American empire) and the third component (America as re-

[22] Foster, *Sermon*, p. 25; Abraham Redwood Ellery, *An Oration, Delivered July 4th, A.D. 1796, in the Baptist Meeting-House in Newport* (Warren, R.I., 1796), p. 8; Jonathan Maxcy, *An Oration, Delivered in the Baptist Meeting-House in Providence, July 4, A.D. 1795* (Providence, 1795), pp. 19–20; Vernon L. Parrington, ed., *The Connecticut Wits* (New York, 1926), p. 321; Alexander Wilson, *Oration, on the Power and Value of National Liberty* (Philadelphia, 1801), p. 11; Dwight, *Greenfield Hill*, p. 153.

publican model) remained popular because they served to lessen the uncertainties and divisions of the early national era, this second component (America as asylum) suffered because it directly involved those uncertainties and divisions. The asylum image had been highly popular during the decades before 1789, and after that date a significant number of patriots still rhetorically asked, "Where shall man seek an asylum, from the chill hand of penury, and the iron grasp of tyranny? . . . (*blessed be* GOD) *it is*, REALIZED *in* AMERICA—it is REALIZED *by* US!"[23] But an equally significant number of Americans came, through partisan motives, to reject implicitly or explicitly the notion of an American asylum. Seeing that many immigrants adhered to the Republican party, Federalists turned nativist, and in so doing questioned the asylum mission.[24] Jeffersonians continued to reaffirm the divinely ordained asylum principle, but this once unanimously held aspect of America's total providential mission had been sharply bifurcated.[25]

Politics did not affect America's cosmic mission, however. Whatever their other differences, virtually all Americans were as one in proclaiming that their national experience would profoundly affect the destiny of the entire world. The explicitly religious expression of this conviction illustrates how far the process of sanctification had gone, the degree to which the United States was laying the groundwork for its future civil religion. Under Divine Providence, America was to bring about the "emancipation" and "regeneration" of the globe. According to Timothy Dwight, the United States was "by heaven design'd, / Th' example bright, to renovate mankind."[26] The Republican Israel was carrying on the "work of political reformation."[27] "From their birth," the United States "appear to have

[23] Josiah Dunham, *An Oration, for the Fourth of July, 1798* (Hanover, N.H., [1798]), p. 8.

[24] Banner, *To the Hartford Convention*, pp. 89–99; Buel, *Securing the Revolution*, pp. 86, 180.

[25] For its later fortunes see Robert Ernst, "The Asylum of the Oppressed," *South Atlantic Quarterly* 40 (1941): 1–10, and Cecil B. Eby, "America as 'Asylum': A Dual Image," *American Quarterly* 14 (1962): 483–89.

[26] Maxcy, *Oration*, p. 5; Dwight, *Greenfield Hill*, p. 52.

[27] Stillman, *Oration*, p. 20; Joseph Lathrop, *The Happiness of A free Government, and the Means of Preserving it* (Springfield, Mass., 1794), p. 15. Cf. *Enquirer*, 6 June

been *designed* the *political redeemers* of *mankind*! as instruments dropped by the hand of Wisdom to be the safeguard of the whole human race." Americans were (again in the words of Timothy Dwight) the "happy few" whom the Lord had designated "his messengers" to "call mankind to virtue."[28]

This providential rhetoric allowed patriots to depict America as an experiment and a model without succumbing to the uneasy construction which these concepts could have borne. After all, as one patriot solemnly declared, "Liberty descended from Heaven, on the 4th of July, 1776"; therefore America's divine mission was "the promulgation of the Gospel of Liberty." Agreeing with this New Testament image, another public spokesman argued, "It is in America, that the germs of the universal redemption of the human race from domination and oppression have already begun to be developed . . . the voice of Heaven itself seems to call to her sons, go ye forth and disciple all nations, and spread among them the gospel of equality and fraternity." Thus even as patriots exhorted the American people eternally to be vigilant against vice and division so that the "sacred flame" ignited by Divine Providence in the New World did not expire, they hedged the threat by speaking as if the American experiment was virtually predestined to success. By assigning themselves the leading role in the "Lord God omnipotent's" grand scheme "to introduce the days of felicity to man," Americans employed their aspirations to transcend the unpleasant and unsettling realities of the day.[29]

The apogee of the sanctification of America's cosmic mission was the theme that the New Israel's republican experiment would soon usher in a secular political version of the traditionally Christian mil-

---

1807, and *Charleston Courier*, 8 June 1807: "Here shall the great work of political salvation commence."

[28] Dwight, *Greenfield Hill*, p. 27; Thomas Yarrow, *An Oration Delivered at Mount-Pleasant, State of New-York, on the Fourth of July, 1798* (Mount Pleasant, 1798), p. 10.

[29] John Lathrop, Jr., *An Oration, Pronounced July 4, 1796* (Boston, 1796), p. 5; [James] Madison, *Manifestations of the Beneficence of Divine Providence Towards America* (Richmond, 1795), p. 8; Henry Wheaton, *An Oration, Delivered Before the Tammany Society, or Columbian Order* (Providence, [1810]), p. 18; Benjamin Bennett, *An Anniversary Address, Delivered at Middletown-Point Church, on Monday the fifth of July, 1802* (New York, 1802), p. 13.

lennium.[30] How enthralling (and how comforting to the world's first modern republic) it was to hope that "the grand POLITICAL MILLENNIUM is at hand;when tyranny shall be buried in ruins; when all nations shall be united in ONE MIGHTY REPUBLIC!"[31] Inspired equally by the French Revolution and the resultant convulsions that racked Europe and jeopardized America's neutrality, predictions of a fast-approaching political millennium permeated pro-French pronouncements during the last decade of the eighteenth century and even continued into the first years of the nineteenth.[32] When it became painfully clear in the early 1800s that the French Revolution had irrevocably degenerated into the despotism of Napoleon and that republicanism was not *immediately* going to sweep all before it, the concept of a political millennium receded, but its expression is striking evidence of the scope and intensity of the sanctification of the American mission after 1789.

During the Revolutionary era the leading spokesmen of the American Revolution complimented and strengthened America's providential legend by themselves using many of that legend's themes. Now, after 1789, the presidents of the United States—the highest national officials in the land—performed a similar task. George Washington, John Adams, Thomas Jefferson, and James Madison, men whose personal religious views were liberal if not suspiciously unorthodox, reinforced American nationalism by publicly voicing the various components of the young republic's sanc-

[30] Hatch, "Origins of Civil Millennialism," and Tuveson, *Redeemer Nation*, have touched on this relationship, but their discussions fall (respectively) before and after the early national period. Furthermore, the basic emphasis in both studies is on religious millennial thought rather than an explicitly political millennium. Hatch has recently extended his analysis to cover the period 1789–1800 in his *Sacred Cause of Liberty*, pp. 139–75. For discussions of some of the main exponents of millennialism after the Great Awakening, see Beam, "Millennialism and American Nationalism," pp. 182–99, and Davidson, *Logic of Millennial Thought*, pp. 179–297. See also the discussion of how the "Radical Enlightenment" (Paine, Volney, Godwin, Condorcet, and their followers) anticipated a secular millennium in May, *Enlightenment in America*, pp. 153–76.

[31] Blake, *Oration*, p. 18.

[32] See, e.g., Gay, *To Sing*, p. 16; Ellery, *Oration*, pp. 23–24; Chauncey Lee, *Oration*, pp. 15–16; Wilson, *Oration*, pp. 17–18; James Sloan, *An Oration, Delivered at a Meeting of the Democratic Association* (Trenton, N.J., 1802), p. 6.

tified consensus. Acting the role of high priests, these first presidents especially helped to shape the "form and tone" of the nation's subsequent civil religion.[33]

President Washington, for instance, promoted the theme that God had raised America above all other nations, stating that he was "sure there never was a people, who had more reason to acknowledge a divine interposition in their affairs, than those of the United States." Washington further contrasted a happy America with an unhappy Europe and attributed the difference to Divine Providence. Proclaiming 19 February 1795 a day of national thanksgiving, the first president cited America's "exemption hitherto from foreign war" and the "increasing prospect of the continuation of that exemption" as "circumstances which peculiarly mark our situation with indications of the Divine beneficence towards us." In an address to Congress in 1796 the hero of Mount Vernon reaffirmed the Republican Israel's providential mission, asking for the blessings of the "supreme Ruler of the Universe and Sovereign Arbiter of Nations" on the New World's republican "experiment."[34] John Adams, Washington's Federalist successor, promoted the continuing heritage of the American Revolution, citing in his 1797 inaugural address "an over-ruling Providence" as the force that had enabled America to break to pieces the "rod of iron" lifted up by the British in 1776.[35]

Thomas Jefferson, Adams's political rival and successor in the presidential chair, continued the practice of ritually reinforcing American nationalism with providential rhetoric. When war engulfed the Old World in 1803, Jefferson publicly attributed America's favored position to the deity, urging his countrymen to "bow with gratitude to that kind Providence which . . . guarded us from hastily entering into the sanguinary contest and left us only to look on and pity its ravages." As he neared the end of his second term, Jefferson offered a people divided over the embargo his "firm persuasion that Heaven has in store for our beloved country long ages to

[33] Bellah, "Civil Religion," p. 9.

[34] Fitzpatrick, ed., *Writings of Washington*, 32:2; Richardson, ed., *Messages and Papers*, 1:179–80; Fred L. Israel, ed., *The State of the Union Messages of the Presidents, 1790–1966*, 3 vols. (New York, 1966), 1:37.

[35] Richardson, ed., *Messages and Papers*, 1:228.

come of prosperity and happiness." Finally, in a dramatic example of the universality of providential concepts and the sanctification of American patriotism, the deist Sage of Monticello appealed to the image of American Israel. In his second inaugural address Jefferson, adopting the practice of secular typology, publicly implored "the favor of that Being in whose hands we are, who led our fathers, as Israel of old, from their native land and planted them in a country flowing with all the necessities and comforts of life; who has covered our infancy with His providence and our riper years with his wisdom and power."[36]

James Madison also publicly endorsed America's providential consensus. At least before the War of 1812, Madison too contrasted unhappy Europe with happy America, attributing the latter's favored condition to "that Divine Providence whose goodness has been so remarkably extended to this rising nation." And Madison gave presidential sanction to the theme that God would always protect his new chosen people. In his inaugural address of 1809 the Virginia statesman first referred to the intelligence and virtue of the American people, and then concluded, "In these my confidence will under every difficulty be best placed, next to that which we all have been encouraged to feel in the guardianship and guidance of that Almighty Being whose power regulates the destiny of nations, whose blessings have been so conspicuously dispensed to this rising Republic, and to whom we are bound to address our devout gratitude for the past, as well as our fervent supplications and best hopes for the future."[37] The nationalism sanctified by numerous American orators, preachers, and essayists after 1789 was reaffirmed by the highest national officials of the era.

Viewed in its entirety, the sanctification of American nationalism after 1789 was a dramatic process. The composite result can accurately be described as one of the foundations of the nation's future civil religion. What did Americans say about themselves and their country during the early national era? They said that the Fourth of

[36] Ibid., 1:382; Israel, ed., *State of the Union Messages*, 1:72, 99.

[37] Richardson, ed., *Messages and Papers*, 1:468; Israel, ed., *State of the Union Messages*, 1:105.

July was their political sabbath. They said that the American empire was founded on a rock. They spoke of the temple of liberty. They honored Washington as their political savior. They insisted that America would promote world regeneration and world reformation. They rejoiced that they had a call from Divine Providence to preach the republican gospel to all nations. They looked forward to a political millennium. The American providential thought articulated during the early national years clearly foreshadowed the nation's future civil religion.

The American patriotism sanctified after 1789 provided the American people with self-identity. "We have continually experienced the protection of the . . . fostering care of Heaven," a Virginian argued in 1795, "so that within a short period from a *handful*, we have become a *great people*." The blessings of Divine Providence distinguished the United States from other nations, illustrated the Republican Israel's singularness: "God hath not dealt so with any other nation."[38] A sanctified national creed also supplied self-assurance in a turbulent world. Two orators in 1802 spoke directly to this end. "God governs the world," Stanley Griswold told the citizens of Suffield, Connecticut, "and we may place strong confidence in his benignant providence, that he will not forsake a people whom he has led thus far, whom he has distinguished in time past with eminent favors, and for whose prosperity he seems still to be interposing." In neighboring Cheshire, Massachusetts, the inhabitants of that hamlet were reassured by John Leland that "as kind Providence has been so propitious, in appearing in behalf of America, so often, and so wonderfully, we have ground to hope that it will still interpose, again and again."[39]

In recounting their past, eulogizing their heroes, and prophesying their future, American patriots after 1789 turned repeatedly to a

[38] John Bracken, *The duty of giving thanks for National Blessings* (Richmond, 1795), p. 10; Nathan Williams, *Carefully to observe the signatures of Divine Providence, a mark of wisdom* (Hartford, 1793), p. 21; John M'Knight, *The Divine Goodness to the United States of America* (New York, 1795), p. 18; Jacob Larzelere, *A Discourse, on the death of General George Washington* (Mount Holly, N.J., 1800), p. 7.

[39] Griswold, *The Good Land We Live in* (Suffield, Conn., 1802), p. 27; L. F. Greene, ed., *The Writings of the Late Elder John Leland* (New York, 1845), p. 268.

protecting Providence. Providential thought undoubtedly worked to provide at least a measure of self-identity and self-assurance to anxious Americans in the early national years. Both domestic and foreign developments buffeted the United States with blows which, if they did not threaten the very existence of the young republic, nevertheless subjected it to severe strains. At home surrounded by the shrill partisanship of Federalists and Jeffersonians, abroad subjected to the international machinations of both the "shark" of Britain and the "tiger" of France (to adopt Marshall Smelser's analogy), American patriots cultivated their nationalist ideology with feverish attention. At almost every point this ideology was sanctified by providential rhetoric and providential symbols.

VI
Politics and Providence

A MAJOR CAUSE of anxiety in early national America was political uncertainty and partisan rivalry. Although virtually all of the Founding Fathers condemned political parties as factions, as groups inimical to republicanism, parties in fact existed from the early 1790s and were an integral part of the domestic political scene for the remainder of the early national era. The *theory* of American politics, however, did not shift to accommodate the *reality* of American politics. Although parties existed, politicians who were influential members of these parties denied that they *were* members of such organizations. Instead, both Federalists and Republicans clung to the old rhetoric of government and faction, claiming sole political legitimacy and condemning their rivals as domestic demogogues or foreign hirelings.[1] In support of these arguments, spokesmen for both camps attempted to drape their respective causes with the mantle of American patriotism. Since providential thought was such an essential ingredient of early nationalism, Federalist and Jeffersonian spokesmen soon began to employ providential concepts and images for partisan ends.

Partisan borrowings from the young republic's sanctified nationalist consensus after 1789 were illustrative rather than formative—providential thought did not create basic Federalist or Republican policies but was rather utilized to enhance them. Each party used providential rhetoric in similar ways: to advance their own causes and to tear down their opponents; in essence, to identify themselves with America and to exclude their rivals. In many instances both parties used the same language and images, simply applying them to differing sides of an issue. The overriding need to explain the existence of partisan division without calling into ques-

[1] For the efforts of politicians to maintain their basic antiparty position after 1789, see Fischer, *Revolution of American Conservatism*; Buel, *Securing the Revolution*; Hofstadter, *Idea of a Party System*; Daniel Sisson, *The American Revolution of 1800* (New York, 1974).

tion the American consensus lay behind all the partisan providential rhetoric uttered after 1789.

Seeking to equate themselves with the national consensus, Federalists employed providential thought in three major campaigns: to promote Federalism in general and specific Federalist policies in particular; to attack Republicanism in general and specific Republican measures in particular; and to associate Federalism with the major themes of the national providential consensus, especially the image of the American Israel. Federalists first sought to equate their party with America by claiming that Federalism was especially pleasing to God, the political approach destined for the United States by Divine Providence. Hence supporting Federalism was not an option but a divine obligation for Americans, declared an anonymous Boston Federalist in 1807, "a duty you owe to your GOD." Portraying his party as an instrument destined "as if by the kind and gracious interposition of Heaven, to rescue" America "from impending destruction" enabled Massachusetts's Joseph B. Caldwell to equate Federalist policies with America's destiny.[2] Thus Federalist claims that their electoral victories were sent by "an overruling Providence, who has hitherto supported us under every difficulty" were more than mere propaganda; they were arguments that Federalism and American patriotism were synonymous and that a guardian God had testified to their synonymity.[3]

Federalists used the Constitution as a major weapon in their campaign to depict themselves as the only real American element in the new nation. Viewing themselves as the sole legitimate supporters of that document, Federalists lavishly praised it as the ultimate gift of a beneficent Providence. The Constitution, one South Carolinian insisted, was "a beatitude from Heaven. . . . the promulgation of God," and a New Englander agreed that it was "a Constitution framed in Heaven and stamped by the authority of the Almighty Law-Giver

[2] "An Old Whig," *Columbian Centinel*, 28 Mar. 1807; Caldwell, *An Oration, Pronounced on the Thirty-second Anniversary of American Independence* (Worcester, Mass., 1808), p. 20.

[3] *Columbian Centinel*, 28 Jan. 1797. See also ibid., 1 Sept. 1810; Hartford *Connecticut Courant*, in Hudson, N.Y., *Balance*, 2 Oct. 1804; *Charleston Courier*, 15 Sept. 1810.

himself."[4] Reviewing in 1808 "the wisdom and superintendance of that GOD whose kingdom ruleth over all" in the ratification of the Constitution, New England's Enoch Mudge used providential rhetoric to support the exclusive identification of the Federalist party with the American political system.[5]

The same end was served by insisting that only the hand of the Creator had overcome the unholy Antifederalist opposition of 1787–88 (the first manifestation, Federalists maintained, of the nefarious Republican faction).[6] This providential interpretation of the Constitution enabled Federalists to portray their rivals as insidious demagogues ready to profane the holy of holies. As one particularly rabid New York Federalist insisted after seven years of Republican "tyranny," "The constitution of our country is . . . the most perfect, which ever existed. . . . Like the inmost sanctuary, in the Hebrew Temple, it should always be approached with awe and veneration. Never should the rude hands of ignorance be suffered to pollute it by a touch."[7] The providential interpretation of the Constitution thus allowed Federalists to argue that they, as the creators of the national government, were the only legitimate leaders of the Republican Israel.

Federalists next used providential rhetoric to promote the presidency of George Washington. Here of course they had the advantage of building on the founding fathers motif, and in particular on the providential legend of Washington, which figured so prominently in the sanctified national consensus. Since virtually all patriotic Americans agreed in assigning divine direction to Washington's Revolutionary career, Federalists could parade as American nationalists in seeing the same providential guidance behind the controversial deci-

[4] *Charleston Courier*, 18 July 1809; Patricia McCarthy, "Providentialism in America, 1783–1800" (M.A. essay, Marquette University, 1971), p. 11.

[5] Mudge, *An Oration, Pronounced at Orrington, July 4th, 1808* (Boston, 1808), p. 11. Cf. David Osgood, *Wonderful Works of God*, p. 16, and Fraser, *Oration*, p. 20.

[6] For typical Federalist accounts of Providence defeating the Antifederalists of 1787–88, see "A Spectator," *Columbian Centinel*, 20 Jan. 1796; Isaac Parker, *An Oration, Delivered at Castine, July 4th, 1796* (Boston, 1796), pp. 8–9; Nott, *Discourse*, p. 10; Caldwell, *Oration*, p. 19.

[7] Thomas P. Grosvenor, *An Oration, Delivered in Christ-Church, Hudson, on the 4th of July, 1808* ([Hudson, N.Y., 1808]), pp. 11–12.

sions of Washington's administration. Equating Washington with Federalism, and both with the American national consensus, New Hampshire's James Miltimore in 1794 described Washington's presidency as a divine mandate: "The Sovereign of the universe . . . called him to that office." After Washington's death and their own political eclipse, Federalists perpetuated this theme by continuing to link Washington's administration with divine approbation. "The rational, reflecting American people," "A Christian" charged in 1811, "demand sober and serious measures to extricate their country from grievous and heavy embarrassments; and to restore to her . . . the prosperity and plenty which they enjoyed when Heaven smiled upon the Administration of the sainted WASHINGTON!"[8]

In response to despicable Republican charges that only Providence and not the Federalists of Washington's day were responsible for the success of the American experiment, Federalists could cheerfully acknowledge, even in the aftermath of Thomas Jefferson's accession to the presidency:

> Yes—we are indebted to the smiles of a kind Providence, for every blessing. And that smile, which framed our constitution, which placed it under the guardianship of a WASHINGTON . . . was the salvation of our country. Yes—we are contented—nay! proud to acknowledge, that that same God, who led our fathers to fertilize a wilderness; who reared up a WASHINGTON to guide our armies, has also showered floods of prosperity upon the policy of the federal administration.[9]

Federalist journals were thus entirely consistent when they prayed that voters would be directed toward Federalist candidates by "that Being, who panoplied your beloved WASHINGTON in the day of peril."[10] Since Federalism was the only true political expression of the American experiment, it followed that Divine Providence would intervene for its success. Federalist partisan providential rhetoric

[8] Miltimore, *A Discourse Delivered in Newmarket* (Exeter, N.H., 1794), p. 15; "A Christian," *Columbian Centinel*, 27 Feb. 1811.

[9] Thomas P. Grosvenor, *An Oration, Delivered at the Town of Claverack, on the Fourth of July, 1801* (Hudson, N.Y., [1801]), pp. 11–12.

[10] *Columbian Centinel*, 27 Feb. 1805. See also "Arminius," Richmond *Virginia Gazette, and General Advertiser*, 4 Jan. 1799.

both reaffirmed the correctness of the Federalist past and assured the ultimate glory of the Federalist future.

Claims of providential guidance and approval were extended by Federalists to the major policy decisions of Washington's administration, and in every case these providential claims reinforced the Federalist charge that they were the only true American party and their foes the tools of a foreign power. When Federalist clergymen such as Ashbel Green, Abiel Holmes, and David Osgood claimed that Divine Providence had inspired the hero of Mount Vernon to issue the Neutrality Proclamation of 1793, they bolstered the charge that those who criticized the proclamation did so because it preserved the United States from foreign subversion.[11] Washington's handling of the Whisky Rebellion in 1794 was another case in point. Besides using the suppression of the rebellion as an occasion for discrediting the Republican cause in general and the Democratic Societies in particular as foreign-inspired, subversive movements,[12] Federalists interpreted the victory for authority as a divine confirmation of the identification of Federalism with the national government and the nation itself. The frustration of the "hellish" and anti-American designs of the Jacobins, insisted Boston's John Lathrop, Jr., furnished indisputable proof that "American honor and happiness" were "guarded by the wisdom and hand of heaven!"[13] The fight over the Jay Treaty of 1795, an issue that raised political intensity to perhaps its highest pitch since the American Revolution, was viewed in the same manner. Since the treaty was absolutely necessary, Federalists from New England to South Carolina claimed, to maintain Ameri-

[11] See "Marcellus," *Columbian Centinel*, 4 May 1793; Pilmore, *Blessings of Peace*, p. 18; Green, *A Sermon, Delivered in the Second Presbyterian Church in the City of Philadelphia, on the 19th of February, 1795* (Philadelphia, 1795), pp. 27–29; Holmes, *A Sermon, on the Freedom and Happiness of America* (Boston, 1795), p. 14; Osgood, *A Discourse, Delivered February 19, 1795* (Boston, 1795), pp. 19, 29–30.

[12] Marshall Smelser, "The Jacobin Phrenzy: Federalism and the Menace of Liberty, Equality, and Fraternity," *Review of Politics* 13 (1951): 466–70; Buel, *Securing the Revolution*, pp. 127–29.

[13] Lathrop, *An Oration, Written at the Request of the Officers of the Boston Regiment* (Boston, 1795), pp. 15–16. See also "A Citizen," *Columbian Centinel*, 29 Oct. 1794; Bracken, *duty of giving thanks*, pp. 12–16; Alexandria, Va., *Columbian Mirror*, 7 May 1795.

can independence, those who opposed it obviously wanted to subvert that independence. When this anti-American conspiracy against the treaty was finally overcome, all true Americans gave "eternal praises to the God of Peace and Negociation" and to his "servants," the Federalists.[14]

Federalist politicians and preachers thus insisted that Washington had been divinely ordained to fill the presidential chair and sustain the Republican Israel. When Washington retired, God raised up other Federalist leaders to carry on the good work. This partisan providential theme was consistent with the founding fathers providential motif and also with the Federalists' claim that they were the only true Americans; since Federalism was pleasing to God, it followed that he would raise up leaders to advance it. In the 1790s John Adams, Washington's successor and "a man preserved of GOD," was one of the more prominent of these divine instruments.[15] Alexander Hamilton was another. As New York's Federalist minister John Mitchell Mason eulogized in 1804, "That foresight, moderation, and firmness, that comprehension of the public interest, and of the means of promoting it; that zeal, and vigilance, and integrity, which were indispensable" to America's national safety, "the inspiration of God . . . assembled in the soul of HAMILTON." Gouverneur Morris, himself no minor Federalist, felt compelled after reviewing his fellow New Yorker's career to exclaim, "GOD . . . called him suddenly into existence, that he might assist to save a world!"[16] "The guardian angel of freedom" also raised up and preserved other national and local Federalists to carry on his work.[17]

A second broad aim of Federalist providential rhetoric was to

[14] Donald H. Stewart, *The Opposition Press of the Federalist Period* (Albany, 1969), p. 210; "Amen," *Va. Gaz., and Gen. Ad.*, 17 Aug. 1796.

[15] Jacob Fisher, *An Oration, Pronounced at Kennebunk, on the Fourth day of July, 1799* (Portland, Maine, 1799), p. 18. Cf. Frederick Frelinghuysen, *Oration*, pp. 17–18.

[16] J[ohn] M[itchell] Mason, *An Oration, Commemorative of the Late Major-General Alexander Hamilton* (New York, 1804), p. 9; *New-York Evening Post*, 17 July 1804.

[17] "Clarendon," *Columbian Centinel*, 25 Nov. 1797. See also "A Farmer," ibid., 23 Jan. 1799; "Spirit of the Times," ibid., 3 Aug. 1808; *Charleston Courier*, 16 Sept. 1812.

denigrate the Republican opposition. One of the important themes here was the claim that the Republican party was the faction of French deism and infidelity. The charge was partisan and untrue, but events lent it a certain credence. The 1790s and 1800s did see the rise of an organized deism in America that attempted to reach the common man. Deists like Tom Paine and Elihu Palmer tried to turn deism into an organized faith and established newspapers, temples, and regular meetings to propagate their militant principles. Playing on the fact that a small number of prominent American deists were also Republicans, lay and clerical Federalists alike linked infidelity, the French Revolution, and the Republican party in a partisan campaign to discredit and destroy their opposition.[18]

The charge of infidelity was leveled most often against Thomas Jefferson, the alleged leader of the "Frenchified" faction. Again and again Jefferson was charged with secretly professing deism or atheism and harboring hostility to Christianity. These accusations were especially prominent during the presidential campaign of 1800. The influence and the importance of these claims were not equal to their frequency, since Jefferson was narrowly elected in 1800 and overwhelmingly reelected four years later. But as Charles Lerche, an astute student of the political smear in early national America, has concluded, they were the most significant and the most effective of all the partisan charges directed against the Sage of Monticello. Henry F. May agrees: "The charge really hurt."[19]

Continuing their attack, Federalists bolstered their claim to be the sole representatives of America's national character by insisting that

[18] G. Adolf Koch, *Republican Religion: The American Revolution and the Cult of Reason* (New York, 1933), pp. 74–113; Morais, *Deism in Eighteenth Century America*, pp. 19–22; Gary B. Nash, "The American Clergy and the French Revolution," *William and Mary Quarterly*, 3d ser. 22 (1965): 405–6, 408–10; Stewart, *Opposition Press*, pp. 395–97; May, *Enlightenment in America*, pp. 273, 395. As Martin Marty observes, "The threat of infidelity consistently served as a bogey to rally support for the standing order" (*Righteous Empire*, p. 97).

[19] Charles F. O'Brien, "The Religious Issue in the Presidential Campaign of 1800," *Essex Institute Historical Collections* 107 (1971): 82–99; Buel, *Securing the Revolution*, pp. 232–34; Charles O. Lerche, Jr., "Jefferson and the Election of 1800: A Case Study in the Political Smear," *William and Mary Quarterly*, 3d ser. 5 (1948): 472–75; May, *Enlightenment in America*, p. 274.

only Divine Providence stood between their pro-French opponents and America's ruin. While his party still held power, Connecticut's Thomas Day, in the wake of the XYZ revelations, offered "glory to the God of Peace" that the designs of Jefferson and the "*Gallico-Anarchic-Democratic* Farce" he managed had been received only with deserved "contempt."[20] The Jacobin upheaval of 1800 was hard to accept, but Federalists north and south maintained their prior charges by depicting the Democratic takeover as a temporary setback that a protecting Providence would not allow permanently to subvert America's independence.[21] Although their hopes of national resurgence did not materialize, Federalists took comfort from what they considered providential frustrations of Jacobin attempts to deliver America to France. For instance, after 1807 Federalists looked to "an all wise Providence" to save the United States from the Republican-engineered and treacherously inspired economic folly of the embargo,[22] and their prayers were answered, according to Federalist minister David Osgood, of Medfield, Massachusetts, as the "Lord of Heaven and Earth," bringing good out of intended evil, "poured contempt" and failure on the pro-French, anti-American embargo.[23]

Finally, Federalists sought to elevate their partisan causes by linking them to American providential nationalism. In these efforts they drew upon two key concepts: the jeremiad tradition and the secular typology of the New Israel. The jeremiad was popular among Federalists because its themes of corruption and potential destruction

[20] Day, *An Oration, on Party Spirit, Pronounced Before the Connecticut Society of Cincinnati* (Litchfield, Conn., [1798]), p. 23.

[21] See Hudson, N.Y., *Balance*, 6 Mar. 1804; Boston *New-England Palladium*, 1 Jan. 1805; *Charleston Courier*, 29 Jan. 1805; Jonathan H. Lyman, *An Oration, Delivered at Northampton, July 6, 1807* (Northampton, Mass., 1807), p. 5; *Columbian Centinel*, 2 Nov. 1811.

[22] "Brutus," *Columbian Centinel*, 13 Jan. 1808. See also "Curtius," ibid., 23 Jan. 1808; "The People," Albany *Republican Crisis*, 26 Jan. 1808; *Charleston Courier*, 8 Mar. 1808.

[23] Osgood as quoted in *Enquirer*, 12 Oct. 1810. Cf. *Charleston Courier*, 2 June 1810: the embargo and nonintercourse acts, by completely draining the United States Treasury of revenues, prevented James Madison's administration from entering the European war on the side of France and thus constituted "a providential interference of heaven" in America's "behalf."

paralleled their secular political philosophy. Federalist politicians thus appropriated the jeremiad's themes of depravity and redemption and turned them, as James M. Banner has suggested, to "secular, profane, and partisan" ends. The Federalists first used the jeremiad tradition to explain their fall from power and the Republican ascendancy after 1800. This campaign was highly significant, for it enabled the Federalists to deny the legitimacy of the Democratic accession to power. The defeat of Federalism was not the repudiation of its correct principles and policies but a divine chastisement visited on a guilty America. By depicting Republican rule (or more correctly, according to Federalists, misrule) as a divine "punishment, inflicted by God's providence on our folly," the Philadelphia Federalist literary journal *Port Folio* was able to continue to portray the Democratic faction as un-American and illegitimate.[24] Reflecting also the optimistic side of the jeremiad tradition, Federalists were able to hope, indeed anticipate, that God would soon return the United States to Federal glory. It was true, as Jeremiah Perley of Maine, observing the enactment of the Republican embargo in 1807, admitted, that "on evil times we are fallen, and evil men: But let us not despair. What though it be said that the sun of Federalism is set. . . . Heaven forbid. The finger of GOD, which has so often been conspicuous in our deliverance from danger, may yet point out the way that shall conduct us to our peace."[25] In its partisan guise the jeremiad tradition thus enabled the Friends of Order to maintain their claim to sole legitimacy in an era that denied them actual political power.

Federalist uses of the Republican Israel motif were many and var-

[24] Banner, *To the Hartford Convention*, pp. 32–36, 162–63n (and see also the skillful discussion in May, *Enlightenment in America*, pp. 267–68); Philadelphia *Port Folio*, 4 July 1801. For other portrayals of Republican rule as a divine chastisement, see "One Who Revered Washington, and Who Will Support Adams," *Columbian Centinel*, 1 Nov. 1800; "Latitudinarian," ibid., 10 Jan. 1801; "Corregidor," *Charleston Courier*, 1 Dec. 1803; Chauncy Langdon, *An Oration, Delivered in the Town of Poultney, on the Fourth of July, 1804* (Salem, N.Y., 1804), p. 19; Seth Payson, *An Abridgement of Two Discourses, Preached at Rindge, at the Annual Fast, April 11th, 1805* (Keene, N.H., 1805), p. 18.

[25] Perley, *An Anniversary Oration, Delivered Before the Federal Republicans* (Augusta, Maine, 1807), p. 24.

ied, but all worked to reinforce the image of Federalism as the true political expression of the American consensus. Thus in 1798 the Reverend Azel Backus, who would be indicted in 1806 for seditious libel against President Jefferson, compared the followers of Jefferson to those Hebrews who conspired with Absalom against King David.[26] Federalists also portrayed their foes as "Philistines" who threatened the safety of American Israel.[27] But most popular were characterizations of the Democrats as modern Pharaohs oppressing the Israelites. Such parallels served to reinforce the images of the Democrats as alien, anti-American tyrants and the Federalists as the chosen preservers of the American consensus. Their fulminations after 1800 against "homebred Pharaohs" enabled the Federalists, in an era of partisan division, to continue to deny that there was any division in the *American* consensus. After all, how could Pharaoh be a part of that consensus?[28]

On the other side of the coin, Federalists depicted themselves as political Moseses, ready to lead America out of the wilderness of Jacobin tyranny and treason into the promised land of Federal prosperity and peace.[29] In the end, the *Charleston Courier* editorialized in 1805, the guardian God of American Israel would intervene for his cause: "The ear of the Omnipotent heard the blood of ABEL cry against CAIN—The same ear hears, and will heed the voice of the oppressed Federalists crying against the wicked deeds committed against themselves and the country which they saved from British ministerial tyranny."[30] As the righteous defenders of everything that was American against America's and God's foes, the Federalists could always count on the smiles of Divine Providence.

[26] Backus, *Absalom's Conspiracy* (Hartford, 1798). Cf. "Historicus," *N.Y. Evening Post*, 10 Dec. 1801, and "R—d," Albany *Balance*, 12 July 1808.

[27] See, e.g., *N.Y. Evening Post*, 30 Apr. 1804; "A Christian," *Columbian Centinel*, 31 Oct. 1804; Grosvenor, *Oration in Hudson*, p. 21; Hudson, N.Y., *Balance*, 12 July 1808.

[28] *Columbian Centinel*, 26 Nov. 1808. See also "Juvenis," Philadelphia *United States' Gazette*, in *Charleston Courier*, 12 June 1807, and Mudge, *Oration*, p. 13.

[29] See *Columbian Centinel*, 6 July 1791, 30 Mar. 1808; *Charleston Courier*, 20 Aug. 1808, 7 May 1810; James Strong, *An Oration, Delivered Before the Washington Benevolent Society of the County of Columbia* (Hudson, N.Y., 1811), p. 11.

[30] *Charleston Courier*, 31 May 1805.

Federalist uses of providential thought, then, were many—narrow and extreme, simple and sophisticated. The same held true for their Republican rivals. Jeffersonians too turned to America's sanctified national consensus, and, like the Federalists, employed it in three broad campaigns: to promote their own policies, to denigrate their opponents, and to link their partisan cause with a broader providential patriotism. The similarity of approach and language is striking; in many instances all that distinguished Federalist and Republican partisan providential rhetoric were the names of the factions being praised and damned. This similarity, of course, stemmed from the corresponding aim of each party—to claim sole legitimacy for itself and deny the Americanness of the other, thus preventing partisan politics from wrecking America's national consensus. Republicans aimed through providential rhetoric to strengthen the claims that *they* constituted the only true American party and that their opponents were un- or anti-American hirelings of a foreign power.

Because their overall intent was the same as that of the Federalists, Republicans too insisted that their philosophy was particularly pleasing to the Almighty. These claims worked to make Republicanism and American nationalism synonymous. Since the United States was God's chosen nation and since Republicanism was the cause favored by the Lord, Federalism was both un-American and opposed to the will of Jehovah. "The God of Heaven" had "destined better things for America" than Federalist tyranny; "*our beneficent Father*, knows," exlaimed the English-born itinerant Republican preacher Morgan John Rhees in celebration of Thomas Jefferson's inauguration in 1801, "that the highest earthly felicity a people can ask, or HE can give, is a well ordered commonwealth—a regular representative government." After their escape from Federalist oppression all Americans (by definition, Republicans) ought to "prostrate" themselves "in profound adoration" before God that they now "enjoyed the blessings of a free republican government. Of all the blessings of Divine Providence" there was no other which conferred "such true and permanent dignity upon man."[31]

[31] *Aurora*, 21 Mar. 1801; Wheaton, *Oration*, p. 5. For similar expressions see Stephen Thacher, *Oration*, pp. 18–19; *Aurora*, 26 Apr. 1804, 1 Jan., 11 July 1805; C. L. Seeger, *An Oration, Pronounced at Northampton, July 4, 1810*, 2d ed. (Northampton, Mass., 1810), p. 3.

Since Republicanism was the political approach favored by God, it followed that Democrats, like their Federalist foes, could and did point to leaders raised up by God to save America. Federalists had no monopoly on the politicization of the legend of the fathers. Chief among such Republican instruments, not surprisingly, was Thomas Jefferson. In the election of 1800, according to the noted Baptist preacher John Leland, "America's God presided, and seemed to be addressing Americans thus: 'My children. . . . as you are not all instructed in your inalienable rights and the nature of a republican government, I have preserved Jefferson to be a guide and father to you. I have raised him up in righteousness, and will strengthen his hands.'" The "Man of the People," insisted the citizens of Cheshire, Massachusetts, at the beginning of the second year of Jefferson's presidency, had truly been "raised up" by "the Supreme ruler of the Universe" to "defend republicanism and baffle all the arts of Aristocracy."[32] The Monticello deist of course hardly encouraged such sentiments, but his admirers needed no encouragement at all. The fact that these sentiments served to bolster the Republican claim of sole legitimacy only increased their usefulness.

James Madison too, from his service in Congress in the 1790s through his leadership as president after 1809, was an "instrument in the hands of a wise Providence."[33] Not only had the Lord raised up these and other Republican champions to save America, but he also saw to it that the American people achieved that salvation by rewarding the Democrats with national power. Paralleling their Federalist rivals, Republicans also depicted their electoral victories as divine confirmations of the synonymity of America and their partisan cause. The defeat of Federalism and the triumph of Republicanism in 1800, according to Pennsylvania's astute party organizer and clerk of the House of Representatives John Beckley, "was as the decree of

[32] Leland, *A Storke at the Branch. Containing Remarks on Times and Things* (Hartford, 1801), pp. 12–13; *Aurora*, 15 Jan. 1802. For other accounts of Divine Providence "raising up" and preserving Jefferson for the promotion of Republicanism and the defeat of Federalism, see *Aurora*, 21 Mar. 1801, 3 Feb. 1804; Greene, ed., *Writings of Leland*, p. 255; Stonington, Conn., *Patriot*, 5 Feb. 1802; "To Thomas Jefferson," *Enquirer*, 10 Mar. 1809.

[33] *Enquirer*, 7 Feb. 1811. Cf. *Ind. Chron.*, in *Va. Gaz., and Gen. Ad.*, 20 Mar. 1793.

Heaven against the guilty Beltshzzer." As Federal "usurpation and tyranny" hid their "diminished heads" and as "the spirit of liberty" revived throughout America in 1801, Democrats, including Ebenezer Wheelock, nephew of Eleazor Wheelock of Great Awakening fame, rejoiced as "men who feel their dependence on a Sovereign Providence, who under God" were "aiming to promote the good and happiness of mankind."[34]

Jeffersonians further resorted to providential rhetoric to embellish specific programs and decisions, and in these instances a protecting Providence again signified that the Republican party was his chosen vessel for the promotion of America. The Louisiana Purchase of 1803 was a case in point. Since the purchase, Democrats insisted, insured the continued liberty and prosperity of the Republican Israel, it was no wonder that "the train of incident" leading up to the territorial transfer showed that "the mighty plan was teeming in the councils of Eternal Wisdom."[35] The embargo of 1807–9 was another such example. This measure, Republicans argued, was the only means to defend national honor without resort to war. The party faithful were thus loud in their insistence that Providence had clearly marked the embargo as the proper and necessary response to violations of American neutrality and that whoever opposed it warred against God and America.[36]

Democratic spokesmen also used providential concepts to attack their political enemies, whom they defined as the enemies of America. Again the partisan charges, reinforced by providential rhetoric, were a means of denying that partisan conflict represented any division within the American consensus. The Federalists were not true Americans but Anglomen, the corrupt hirelings of the Court of Saint James. Thus it was obvious to one Connecticut Republican essayist that when the Federalists in the 1790s attempted to involve America in a disastrous war with France in order to deliver the New

[34] *Aurora*, 6 Mar. 1801; Ebenezer Wheelock, *An Oration Delivered at Middlebury, Before a large and respectable collection of Republican Citizens* (Bennington, Vt., 1801), p. 11. See also *Aurora*, 7 Jan. 1801, 21 June 1802, and Sloan, *Oration*, p. 3.

[35] Allan B. Magruder, *Political, Commercial and Moral Reflections, on the Late Cession of Louisiana* (Lexington, Ky., 1803), p. 137.

[36] See, e.g., "Pacificus," *Enquirer*, 4, 11 Mar. 1808; "Freedom and Peace, or the Voice of America, a National Song," ibid., 9 Aug. 1808.

Israel back to its former British masters, the "BENEFICENT PROVIDENCE" of the Almighty had defeated their "wicked attempts." After they had been driven from office, Hamilton's henchmen were continually trying to turn the people against their new Republican leaders, but since Republicanism was manifestly the cause supported by Heaven, Democrats such as Boston's "Old South" maintained a justified "trust in God" that these "mischivous designs" would "be baffled, and the United States rise superior to their infernal machinations."[37]

In their third broad area of partisan borrowings from providential thought, Jeffersonians too embraced the image of Republican Israel to bolster narrow political positions. Since their aim again was the aim of the Federalists before them—to present one party as the sole true political expression of the American consensus—the rhetoric they employed had a familiar ring. Did the Anglomen score their Democratic rivals as Philistines? Zealous Republicans responded in kind.[38] Reinforcing their posture as the true guardians of American Israel, Republicans too characterized their liberty-hating foes as modern Pharoahs trying to oppress the Republican Israelites. Was there not further an amazing similarity between the Federalists, who sought to return America to British control, and those Hebrews who murmured against Moses and yearned to return to Egyptian bondage?[39]

Then, taking a positive approach, Republicans such as New Jersey Congressman James Sloan and Connecticut customs official Abraham Bishop compared Jefferson's assumption of the presidency to the Exodus. On the occasion of the celebration of the Louisiana Purchase, major Republican journals hailed Jefferson, "the pacific conqueror," as "more successful" than Moses, "the legislator of the Hebrews," for the former had given his people "the land of promise

[37] "A Friend to Peace, Liberty, and the Constitution," Stonington *Patriot*, 25 Sept. 1801; "Old South," *Ind. Chron.*, in *Aurora*, 14 Oct. 1801.

[38] See, e.g., "Anti-Machiavel," *Aurora*, 24 June 1805, and "The Centinel, No. I," *Enquirer*, 8 Mar. 1810.

[39] "Franklin," Philadelphia *Independent Gazetteer*, in *Aurora*, 19 May 1795; "Try It," *Aurora*, 4 Mar. 1806, 9 Feb. 1807; Nathaniel Howe, *An Oration Pronounced at Paris, Oxford County, Maine, on the Fourth of July, 1805* (Portland, Maine, 1805), p. 6.

without crossing the Red sea." The Republican cause of American freedom, union, and constitutional government ought to be defended as firmly as the ancient Jews had defended the "Ark of the Covenant." Finally, Jeffersonian attempts to free America from her servile and Federalist-inspired dependence on the "flesh pots" of Great Britain approximated, in the eyes of Baltimore editor Hezekiah Niles, the "miracles" wrought by "Providence" for the "deliverance of *Israel*."[40] In depicting themselves as the chosen guides for God's New Israel, Democrats were no less outspoken than their Federalist foes, and the goal was the same in both instances. The rhetoric of secular typology allowed the party employing it to stigmatize its opponents as the enemies of God's divine plan for the United States. In this way partisan division, while highly significant, did not sunder the American national consensus. Political opponents were merely the latest anti-American foes (following Metacom's warriors, the French and their Indian allies of the 1750s, and the British and loyalists of the 1770s) to challenge the attainment of the goals and implications of American nationalism.

Finally, one foreign event—the French Revolution—occasioned a tremendous volume of partisan providential rhetoric. At first, to be sure, Americans almost unanimously viewed the French Revolution with delight. From the first news of the fall of the Bastille until the Reign of Terror, Federalists and Republicans alike praised the French upheaval as a glorious extension of the American Revolution. But ultimately the French Revolution and its promotion of an Anglo-French rivalry exercised an extremely divisive effect on American politics. As one scholar concludes, "Not again until the twentieth century did foreign events create such deep convulsions in American thought nor more sharply divide one American from another."[41] After 1794 Federalists attacked, and Republicans defended, the French Revolution and all its works. In the process both

[40] Sloan, *Oration*, p. 22; Abraham Bishop, *Oration, in Honor of the Election of President Jefferson* ([Hartford], 1804), p. 18; *Aurora*, 14, 19 May 1804; *Enquirer*, 23 May 1804; New Brunswick, N.J., *Brunswick Gazette*, 23 Aug. 1791, as quoted in Stewart, *Opposition Press*, p. 43; James Carson, *An Oration, on the Past and Present State of our Country* (Philadelphia, 1802), p. 16; Baltimore *Niles' Weekly Register*, 21 Nov. 1812.

[41] Banner, *To the Hartford Convention*, p. 17.

parties turned once again to providential rhetoric to bolster their arguments. The partisan usage of providential imagery had its foreign as well as domestic side.

As the major prerequisite for all their subsequent attacks on French principles, Federalists insisted again and again that the American and French revolutions were not the same. There was no basis for comparing two revolutions so dissimilar in their origins, principles, courses, and conduct. The charge was significant, of course, because the providential legend of the American Revolution was central to the American nationalist consensus, which the Federalists (as true Americans) were bound to support. By denying any similarity between the two revolutions, Federalists were able to proclaim on the one hand that God supported America while insisting on the other that the Lord demanded opposition to France. Defenders of the French Revolution were enemies to the American Revolution and America herself.[42]

Federalists first insisted that Divine Providence had pointed out Britain, France's enemy, as America's true foreign friend.[43] The disciples of Washington took great pains to insist that, while the French Revolution was undoubtedly part of God's moral government of the world, there was no evidence that God was on the side of the French. The French Revolution had been allowed by the Creator for some inscrutable end, but it was clearly a case of God bringing a future good out of present evil—and the duty of all true Americans, according to Connecticut's Zechariah Lewis, was "to detest the evil."[44] Federalists were thus highly scornful of the Jacobins, who weakly argued that the French (by virtue of acting a part in God's providen-

[42] For typical Federalist denials that the American and French revolutions were at all similar, see John Lowell, Jr., *An Oration, Pronounced July 4, 1799* (Boston, 1799) and Theodore Dwight, *An Oration, Delivered at New-Haven, on the 7th of July, A.D. 1801* (Hartford, 1801), pp. 19–22.

[43] "A True Whig of 1798," *Md. Gaz.*, 27 Sept. 1798; *Port Folio*, 6 June 1801; *Columbian Centinel*, 13 Aug. 1803; "B.," *N.Y. Evening Post*, 22 Nov. 1805.

[44] Lewis, *An Oration, on the Apparent, and the Real Political Situation of the United States* (New Haven, 1799), p. 23. For a discussion of the changing attitudes in Federalist sermons and orations along these lines, see May, *Enlightenment in America*, pp. 265–67.

tial direction of history) were truly favored of God. Such a conclusion was specious.[45]

A favorite technique was to argue that a guardian God was protecting America from the insidious designs of French predators and their Republican hirelings. This approach, conveniently, both condemned the French Revolution and painted the Democrats as anti-American conspirators. Thus one zealous Federalist asserted that "France has employed her secret agents, her private correspondents, and her jacobin incendiaries, to rouse sedition, and to spread over our land the spirit of disorganization. But by the influence of the genius of freedom, and by the interposition of Heaven, their wicked machinations have all been defeated." The "hand of Providence," according to the Reverend Abiel Abbot, was "signally" manifest in America's "preservation from French liberty and French philosophy" and from the wiles of that "intriguing nation." The Jacobin revolution of 1800 seriously threatened America's independence, but a Federalist journal in Boston took comfort from the fact that "GOD'S GOOD PROVIDENCE" still stood between American freedom and the "yoke of France."[46]

From the 1790s until 1812 Federalists argued that any war with France would be just and hence would receive divine approbation. Surely in such a contest America's enemy would be "the enemy of God," America's cause "the cause of God." In any appeal to arms against France, Americans could "look with confidence for success, to the GOD OF BATTLES." The United States, in the opinion of a South Carolina judge, must "bid defiance to French threats and French troops," and though the United States was "yet but a David in years and strength," the European Goliath would surely fall at her feet, "for

[45] See William Linn, *A Discourse on National Sins: Delivered May 9, 1798* (New York, 1798), p. iv; "Grotius," *Conn. Courant*, 5 Aug. 1799; *Va. Gaz., and Gen. Ad.*, 20 Aug. 1799; "A Dialogue Between a Federalist and a Democrat," Hudson, N.Y., *Balance*, 27 July 1802.

[46] Samuel W. Bridgham, *An Oration, Delivered in the Benevolent Congregational Meeting-House in Providence, on the Fourth of July, A.D. 1798* (Providence, 1798), p. 11; Abbot, *Traits of Resemblance*, p. 22; Boston *Repertory*, in *N.Y. Evening Post*, 18 Sept. 1806.

nothing is impossible to the God of Armies whom we adore."[47] Thanks to the pacific diplomacy of John Adams and the continuing chaos of European events, Federalists were denied the war many of them so avidly anticipated, but had war come they were certain that Divine Providence would vindicate their course of action.

On every point raised by the Federalists in their vilification of the French Revolution, Jeffersonians responded in kind. The cause of the French Revolution—the rights of man—was identical to the cause for which America had contested in her own revolution. Republicans in defending the French Revolution were also defending America's national consensus (just as the Federalists, in denigrating the French cause, were really attacking that consensus). Jeffersonian audiences were repeatedly reminded that "by the hand of God" the United States had been "led on to victory and glory," and that now it was America's "desire and prayer to God" that the French, who were now "engaged in the same honorable cause," might soon experience "the same glorious issue." Republicans were certain that the Lord would prosper the French in their struggle, just as he had America in hers. "Engaged in so righteous a cause as the extirpation of tyranny from off the face of the earth," it was eagerly anticipated that "GOD" would grant the French "success."[48]

These beliefs enabled Republicans consistently to see the hand of an approving deity in the external and internal events of the great French drama. In the heady days of the defeat of the "conspiracy of kings," witnessing the seemingly irresistible spread of French influence across previously enslaved Europe, one New England Democrat celebrated "the late astonishing and glorious successes, with which the divine Providence hath crowned the arms of France, contending for liberty, against the combined legions of royal des-

[47] Elijah Parish, *An Oration Delivered at Byfield July 4, 1799* (Newburyport, Mass., [1799]), p. 17; Charles H. Atherton, *An Oration, Pronounced in the First Parish at Amherst, N.H.* (Amherst, 1798), p. 24; J. F. Grimke, *Charge, Delivered to the Grand Juries of Beaufort and Orangeburgh Districts* (Charleston, S.C., 1798), p. 5.

[48] James Malcomson, *A Sermon, Preached on Monday, the Fourteenth of July, One Thousand Seven Hundred and Ninety-Four, Being the Anniversary of the French Revolution* (Charleston, S.C., 1795), pp. 38–39; *Poughkeepsie Jour.*, 7 Nov. 1792.

potism."[49] As an admiring Jeffersonian journal observed in 1795, "The God of Battles must necessarily be with the French—For nothing short of his Providence, can account for these almost miraculous achievements."[50] Nor did such sentiments cease with the Terror or the Thermidorian Reaction. Well after these unsettling events Republicans still insisted that "our Gallic Brethren, fired by our example, have ventured their single resistance against the most formidable combination of despots, and their unparalleled successes argue a design in Providence that they shall be free, and the cause of liberty universally prevail."[51] Republicans remained as fixed as Federalists in their providential reaction to the French Revolution. Even Napoleon's ever-increasing despotism did not totally destroy the hope that the French Revolution, under Divine Providence, would somehow succeed in extirpating monarchy from the world.

The early national era witnessed two strains of American providential thought. The first sanctified American patriotism and reflected national consensus; the second promoted partisan rivalry and reflected conflict. But the relationship of the two strains was actually more complex. Looking back on the era, we can easily see that political conflict did not have to threaten America's sanctified national consensus. But contemporaries could not and did not accept this thesis. They needed their sanctified nationalism, its common and unifying themes, for self-identity and self-assurance in a turbulent age. If Americans after 1789 had admitted that there was a fundamental split in their national political scene, their nationalism would have been limited at its very inception. And political spokesmen of all persuasions were also heirs to a tradition condemning parties as factions. One way out of this dilemma was to insist that partisan division was not *American* division. For this reason—to admit the reality of partisan conflict and yet insist that all Americans were as

[49] Chandler Robbins, *An Address Delivered at Plymouth, on the 24th day of January, 1793* (Boston, 1793), p. 6. Cf. Philadelphia *National Gazette*, 5 Jan. 1793.

[50] *Ind. Chron.*, in *Greenleaf's New-York Journal*, 11 Apr. 1795.

[51] Joel Foster, *An Oration, Delivered at New-Salem, July 4th, 1797* (Northampton, Mass., 1797), p. 16. See also *Greenleaf's N.Y. Jour.*, 8 Feb. 1797; John M'Knight, *A View of the Present State of the Political and Religious World* (New York, 1802), p. 10; Sloan, *Oration*, pp. 13–14.

one—the rival political parties wielded providential concepts to prove the legitimacy of their cause and the illegitimacy of their opponents'.

As long as the legitimacy of political opposition was denied, as was the case until after the War of 1812, partisan rhetoric would be extreme, insisting that only one party reflected America's national consensus.[52] This goal was shared by both Federalists and Republicans after 1789 and explains their resort to providential imagery in their partisan debates. It is surely paradoxical that divisive language and imagery were employed to limit the significance of internal division. But that is precisely what happened. Historians might later depict the curious simultaneous existence of American political division within an American national consensus, but contemporaries could not and would not admit that these phenomena could coexist. For Americans after 1789 the two strains of providential thought–national and partisan—were not in fundamental conflict but rather in a curious relationship in which each could reinforce the other. Only the political demise of Federalism after the War of 1812 solved the dilemma of the early national era—how to reconcile division within consensus.

[52] For the acceptance of the legitimacy, and even desirability, of political opposition in the years after 1815, see Hofstadter, *Idea of a Party System*, pp. 212–71.

VII
Second Salvation

On 18 June 1812 the United States declared war against Great Britain. From that date until the formal ratification of peace on 17 February 1815, America endured the darkest days it had known since Independence. The fledgling republic struggled militarily and politically, at first to assert itself, then just to survive. During the troubled days of the war the United States was divided as never before. The nation split dramatically over the conflict: Republicans defended the war, its policies, and its purposes, while Federalists virulently condemned the war and all its works. The war witnessed the culmination of Federalist and Republican attempts to deny the legitimacy of their respective political foes. Each party insisted that the other's activities threatened the very survival of the nation. In this period of crisis public spokesmen relied heavily on providential rhetoric to enhance their desires and fears. Providential thought was central to America's disparate responses to the political and military history of the War of 1812.

The Federalists' response to the war was conditioned by their fondness for Great Britain, their loathing of France, and especially the partisan providential rhetoric they had utilized since 1789 to deny the Americanness of the Republican party. As the United States and Britain moved closer to conflict, Federalists were certain that James Madison and his Jacobin henchmen were conspiring to provoke Britain into war, thereby converting the United States into a satellite of Napoleonic France. The Republicans, agents of a foreign and infidel power, were aiming through war to subordinate America to France. Thus, as they perceived their country drifting into war, Federalist spokesmen prayed that "a kind and overruling PROVIDENCE" might "disappoint" America's malevolent rulers. Responding to Democratic charges that "the finger of Heaven pointed to war," one astringent anti-Republican critic replied:

> Yes, the finger of Heaven DOES point to war. It points to war . . . as a flaming beacon warning us of that vortex which we may not approach but with

certain destruction. . . . It announces the wrath to come upon those, who, ungrateful for the bounty of Providence, not satisfied with the peace, liberty, security, and plenty [we have] at home, fly, as it were, into the face of the most high, and tempt his forbearance.

Even after the declaration of war and commencement of hostilities, a South Carolina Federalist journal insisted that "*the Finger of* HEAVEN *points to* PEACE!!!"[1]

Working within the jeremiad tradition, Federalists portrayed the war as a divine chastisement for national sins.[2] This tradition (not surprisingly) was again severely bent to serve partisan ends; the War of 1812 merely accelerated the politicization of this Puritan bequest to American providential thought. To a southern Federalist the war was "the scourge of an avenging God" who was "chastizing" America for "departing from that line of policy" established by the "virtuous WASHINGTON."[3] America's national sins were explicitly equated with the triumph of democracy; by electing irreligious Republicans to office and then acquiescing while those Jacobins enacted cruel and unconstitutional measures, Americans justly merited God's punishment.[4] Again, this partisan providential charge effectively portrayed the Republicans as un-American, illegitimate conspirators—certainly an administration that brought down the wrath of God could not be legitimate.

The claim that a national war was a divine judgment for sin was nothing new in American providential thought, of course; patriots during the American Revolution had said the same. But now some

[1] New York *Commercial Advertiser*, in *Charleston Courier*, 19 June 1811; John Randolph in *Niles' Weekly Reg.*, 13 June 1812; "Ithuriel," *Charleston Courier*, 23 July 1813.

[2] For such portrayals see Samuel Austin, *A Sermon, Preached in Worcester, Massachusetts, on the Occasion of the Special Fast, July 23d, 1812* (Worcester, 1812), pp. 7, 14–17; William Ellery Channing, *A Sermon, Preached in Boston, July 23, 1812* (Boston, 1812), pp. 5–6; Reuben Holcomb, *A Discourse in Two Parts, Delivered at Sterling, Massachusetts, Thursday, July 23, 1812* (Worcester, Mass., 1812), p. 15; Jesse Appleton, *A Sermon, Preached in Boston, at the Annual Election, May 25, 1814* (Boston, 1814), pp. 25–26.

[3] "Ames," *Charleston Courier*, 26 Aug. 1812.

[4] Brown Emerson, *The Equity of God's Dealings with Nations* (Salem, Mass., 1812), pp. 10–14, 20–23; Samuel Worcester, *Courage and Success to the Good* (Salem, Mass., 1812), pp. 17–18.

Americans insisted that a national war was an unjust war. The American people, cried Boston's John Lathrop, must "turn from" this "unrighteous . . . unnecessary and ruinous war, and pray, that he, who ruleth in the heavens, would have mercy" on his errant New Israel.[5] The injustice of the war was compounded by its being an unnatural conflict, aligning the United States with infidel France against Christian Britain—a fact that only reinforced Federalist fears that the real purpose of the war was not to vindicate national honor or liberate impressed sailors but to surrender American independence to Napoleon. Far from seeing opposition to the War of 1812 as treasonous, Federalists (by insisting that the Madison administration was under the thumb of France) defended dissent as the highest expression of American patriotism.[6]

From these convictions—that the current war was a divine judgment, an unjust conflict, and a contest waged against the wrong nation—Federalists concluded that Americans should not anticipate providential intervention. It was a truism to Federalists that the United States could not "hope or expect to receive the Divine Blessing or assistance in a War begun without reasonable provocation—founded on falsehood and misrepresentation;—a War which could, and might, and ought to have been avoided." Far from anticipating providential support, if the nation persisted in prosecuting this "unjust" war, she risked being "plucked up, pulled down, and destroyed" by the hand of Heaven.[7]

The war's unfavorable progress provided Federalists with the proof of this prediction. The military disasters that befell the new nation after June 1812 demonstrated that the war was one "which GOD, in his infinite wisdom and Justice," was rendering "as disgraceful and ruinous in its progress, as it was unprovoked and unjustifiable in its origin." "You are engulfed," Federalists warned the American people, in "a war . . . distinguished by the peculiar FROWNS of

[5] Roger H. Brown, *The Republic in Peril: 1812* (New York, 1964), pp. 165–76; Lathrop, *A Discourse on the Law of Retaliation* (Boston, 1814), pp. 15–16.

[6] See *Charleston Courier*, 28 Aug. 1812, 25 Jan., 6 Nov. 1813; *Columbian Centinel*, 18 Dec. 1813; William Gribbin, *The Churches Militant: The War of 1812 and American Religion* (New Haven, 1973), pp. 16, 40–60.

[7] "An Independent American," *Columbian Centinel*, 14 July 1813; Samuel Austin, *Sermon*, pp. 27–28.

HEAVEN." The "universal disasters and disgrace" attending all the Jacobin attempts to prosecute the conflict conclusively proved "'that the LORD is not on our side.'" Ancient Israel had waged war against the express command of Jehovah and had suffered defeat and humiliation; Republican Israel was following an equally errant path. Such claims were highly selective (they necessitated ignoring any American victories), but Federalists did not hesitate to make them. The war was unjust, and God was discountenancing it.[8]

Federalist spokesmen took a perverse delight in claiming that Jehovah was using the war to punish its authors—and those warmongers were *not* the British. As the American West was racked by Indian uprisings, some Federalists insisted that "this War was first urged by *Kentucky*, *Ohio*, and the inland States, who sent their most vociferous Stentors to declare it; and a righteous Providence is now inflicting on them its direst horrors."[9] Such charges drove home the Federalist point that the Republicans were the true enemies of God's New Israel. The same theme was reinforced in two other ways. First, the Friends of Order increasingly repeated earlier (pre-1812) charges that Madison and his henchmen bore a striking resemblance to Pharoah and his ministers.[10] Second, Federalists contrasted the American Revolution with Mr. Madison's War, discerning providential favor in the former but divine anger in the latter. From 1775 through 1783, a Boston journal charged, Americans had been "engaged in a war" in which they "could confidently look to heaven for a blessing" on their "arms" and "good cause." But now they were embarked on "a war, originating in the basest of selfish motives, totally aggressive in its nature, conducted by folly and profligacy"—and "experiencing the frowns of heaven, in every step."[11] Since the

[8] "An Independent American," *Columbian Centinel*, 31 July 1813; "Massachusetts," ibid., 12 Feb. 1814; "An American," ibid., 30 Dec. 1812; Elijah Parish, *A Discourse, Delivered at Byfield, on the Public Fast, April 7, 1814* (Newburyport, Mass., 1814), p. 23.

[9] *Columbian Centinel*, 17 Feb. 1813. Cf. "Senex," *Conn. Courant*, in *Charleston Courier*, 7 Oct. 1813.

[10] For wartime Federalist depictions of the Republicans as Pharaoh, see Abraham Bodwell, *The Sovereignty of God: A Sermon, Preached in Sandbornton, July 5, 1813* (Concord, N.H., 1813), p. 13; *Columbian Centinel*, 2 Mar., 2 Apr. 1814; Parish, *Discourse*, pp. 4–5, 9.

[11] *Boston Spectator*, 27 Aug. 1814.

current conflict was so dramatically opposed to the spirit of the American Revolution that even Divine Providence witnessed against it, those Democrats who prosecuted the war were enemies to the Revolution and to America itself. The heirs of Hamilton used the providential legend of the American Revolution, a key ingredient of the nation's sanctified consensus, to exclude the Republicans from that consensus and to condemn a war characterized by its proponents as the Second War for Independence.

The Federalists of course were not alone in drawing upon partisan providential rhetoric after 1812. As they struggled to lead America to victory and to maintain the allegiance of the people against the wiles of Federalist "traitors," Republicans resorted to providential imagery in an ever-increasing volume. Their aim was the same after 1812 as before: to depict the Federalist party as a foreign faction and thus assume for themselves the role of sole exponents of America's sanctified nationalism. The grave dangers of the war and the maddening Federalist opposition to it only made the Republicans more determined to achieve that end.

On one point (but one point only) Republicans appeared to agree with their Federalist foes—the War of 1812 could be seen as a divine judgment for national sins. The Federalist party had no monopoly on the jeremiad tradition. Indeed, President Madison himself gave public assent to the theme. Designating 20 August 1812 a day of national fast, the president called on the American people to acknowledge "the transgressions which might justly" have provoked the current "manifestations" of "divine displeasure," and urged his countrymen to solicit God's "merciful forgiveness and his assistance in the great duties of repentance and amendment." Democratic spokesmen quickly followed their president's lead and portrayed the war as evidence of God's anger with the sins of his chosen people.[12]

But only on this basic point did the two parties concur. Whereas Federalists had gone on to argue that the War of 1812 was unjust and incapable of divine approbation, Jeffersonians insisted that they were under a providential command to prosecute the conflict. Democrats

[12] Richardson, ed., *Messages and Papers*, 1:513; John Giles, *Two Discourses, Delivered to the Second Presbyterian Society in Newburyport, August 20, 1812*, 3d ed. (Newburyport, Mass., 1812), pp. 10, 17; "Eugene," *Aurora*, 8 Sept. 1813.

after 1812 emulated the public spokesmen of the Revolutionary epoch, who had depicted the American Revolution as both a divine judgment *and* a holy war favored by Divine Providence. Indeed, even before a declaration of war, some Republicans insisted that any contest with England would be just per se, hence pleasing to God.[13] After June 1812 these claims were pronounced. In a typical expression Richard Rush (son of Revolutionary physician Benjamin Rush) told the United States House of Representatives on the Fourth of July 1812 that, as Americans took up arms, it was their "chief consolation" to know that "before God and before the world, our cause is just." The United States had gone to war in "a cause so sacred, that it enlists on its side all the attributes of Heaven."[14]

Republicans north, south, and west agreed that in waging war with Britain they were carrying out, as Massachusetts's John Stevens put it, "the will of the Lord God of our forefathers." It was certain beyond all doubt that "God approves of the war in which we are now engaged for the defence of our just rights."[15] The issue of impressment, so prominent in the coming of the conflict, loomed large in Republican rhetoric. After all, "man was created in his Maker's own image," and impressment was abhorrent to the deity. The War of 1812 was a just and holy crusade to end this "evil," a crusade "conducted under the assistance and protection of the Most High."[16]

Republicans sought to promote union and confidence by publicly predicting the intervention of Divine Providence in America's behalf. As one pro-war orator told an embattled Democratic gathering in hostile Federalist Massachusetts, "We tremble not for fear of invasion. We have no apprehension that British armies will again ransack our country. It is the determination of the Americans to chastise the nation who tramples on our rights with insufferable insolence. This

[13] See, e.g., *Enquirer*, 3, 10 Dec. 1811.

[14] Rush, *An Oration, delivered by Richard Rush, on the 4th of July, 1812* (Washington, D.C., 1812), p. 20; Baltimore *Patriot*, in *Aurora*, 5 May 1813.

[15] John H. Stevens, *The Duty of Union in a Just War*, 2d ed. (Boston, 1813), pp. 16–17. For similar Republican claims see *Niles' Weekly Reg.*, 29 Aug. 1812; *Aurora*, 4 Nov. 1812, 15 June 1813; Greene, ed., *Writings of Leland*, pp. 374–75; Philip Mathews, *An Oration, Delivered on the 5th July, 1813* (Charleston, S.C., 1813), p. 20; *Enquirer*, 2 Mar., 9 July 1813; Gribbin, *Churches Militant*, p. 8.

[16] Rush, *Oration*, p. 33.

we have, under a sovereign Providence, power to do." A Virginia compatriot agreed: "Confiding in heaven and the justice of our cause . . . we have nothing to fear for the issue of the contest, in which we are engaged." Republicans repeatedly reassured themselves that their "cause was just, and HE who established civil and religious freedom in America will sustain it." As they embarked on the war, Democrats looked to the "God of Battles" to "direct their footsteps to glory and to fame!" The uneven and at times disastrous military history of the war did not diminish such rhetoric; even if the claim of providential intervention often seemed to fly in the face of reality, it was a claim essential to the war's proponents. Faith in divine support allowed Republicans to carry on despite disappointment and defeat; in the end America and America's God would triumph.[17]

After 1812 Republicans continued to depict their Federalist foes not as fellow Americans in honest disagreement with their policies but as foreign lackeys out to destroy American independence. The war years seemed years of extreme danger; hence it is not surprising that Republican providential rhetoric was also extreme. Again the Federalists (and their British masters) were characterized by Democrats as Philistines plotting the destruction of the Republican Israel.[18] Democrats also used the providential legend of the American Revolution to paint their opponents as un-American conspirators and traitors. Emulating the public spokesmen of the Revolutionary War, Republicans invoked the "Curse of Meroz" against those "Tories" who refused to aid the prosecution of the war, or, worse, attempted to frustrate the measures of the national government.[19] Democratic parallels of the American Revolution and the War of 1812, with the attending claim that the smiles of Heaven accorded the former would surely attend the latter also, served the same end. Even before war

[17] Joseph Richardson, *An Oration, Pronounced July 4, 1812, Before the Citizens of the County of Plymouth* (Boston, [1812]), p. 18; *Enquirer*, 6 July 1814; *Niles' Weekly Reg.*, 10 Sept. 1814; *Aurora*, 21 July 1812.

[18] See *Enquirer*, 11 June, 27 Aug. 1814; "Tell," *Aurora*, 9 Sept. 1814; "Ghost of Montgomery," ibid., 27 Sept. 1814.

[19] Joshua Lacy Wilson, *War the Work of the Lord, and the Coward Cursed* (Boston, 1813), pp. 3, 4, 12, 14; Giles, *Two Discourses*, p. 16; "The Old Soldier," *Aurora*, 24 Nov. 1812; Stevens, *Duty of Union*, pp. 3, 4, 21–24; "The Author of the Crisis," *Enquirer*, 1 Mar. 1815; Gribbin, *Churches Militant*, pp. 61, 93, 133.

was an actuality, a New England journal pointedly argued that "God has carried us safely through one war. His hatred of injuries is not less now than then; nor is his arm less omnipotent to save." After June 1812 this theme was repeatedly advanced to enhance courage and enthusiasm and to vindicate Republican prosecution of the war. The patriots of 1812 would imitate the "heroic resistance" of America's Revolutionary demigods, "and like them" would "'come off more than conquerors through Him' who crowned them with victory."[20] During the Revolutionary War, whenever "any misfortune attended WASHINGTON and the *war-men*," America's tories had "clamored lustily against 'the foolish war.'" But the patriots of '76 "were not discouraged. Knowing the justice of their cause, and relying on the favor of the Governor of the Universe, they persevered. . . . Just so will it be now."[21] Through these partisan uses of the providential heritage of the American Revolution, Jeffersonians legitimized the War of 1812 and stigmatized the Federalists as anti-American traitors. Perhaps, the fate of contemporary tories would match that of the Revolutionary era.

Providential rhetoric, then, permeated both Federalist opposition to, and Republican support of, the War of 1812. Partisan providential rhetoric was employed in great detail by both camps to explain and interpret the specific events of the war—land and sea battles, campaigns, victories, and defeats. Both Federalists and Republicans were consistent with their respective general providential interpretation of the war: Federalists depicted an angry Creator punishing a guilty nation embarked on an unjust conflict; Republicans celebrated a guardian God blessing his chosen nation engaged in a holy crusade.

The conquest of Canada was the main American military objective of the War of 1812. The war hawks had depicted Canada as there for

[20] Hartford *American Mercury*, in *Aurora*, 21 Dec. 1811; John Pitman, *An Oration, Pronounced July 4th, 1812, at the Request of the Republicans of the Town of Salem* (Salem, Mass., 1812), p. 7.

[21] Trenton, N.J., *True American*, in *Aurora*, 9 July 1813. For other Republican references to the activities of Providence in the American Revolution (references designed to vindicate the War of 1812), see Giles, *Two Discourses*, p. 10; Richardson, *Oration*, pp. 22–23; *Aurora*, 17 Aug. 1812, 5, 13 Feb. 1813; "A Virginia Farmer," *Enquirer*, 20 Jan. 1814; *Niles' Weekly Reg.*, 9 July 1814; James T. Austin, *An Oration, Pronounced at Lexington, Mass.* (Boston, 1815), p. 21.

the taking, but the initial American effort was a total disaster. General William Hull, commanding a two-thousand-man army at Detroit, confidently crossed into Canada, and Democratic hopes ran high. But Hull was quickly outmaneuvered and defeated, and in August 1812 Detroit itself was captured by the British. It was a severe setback, but Republicans tempered the national humiliation by presenting the loss of Detroit as a potential case of God bringing good out of evil. After all, Hezekiah Niles editorialized, "the ways of Providence" were "inscrutable," with "apparent ills . . . oftentimes real blessings." Perhaps "the strange conduct of general *Hull*" would in the end lead to the "direct road to success."[22]

Total success proved elusive, however. None of the subsequent attempts to conquer Canada succeeded, although American forces did win some victories. This ambiguous military record was reflected in partisan providential rhetoric. Federalists chose to consider the overall failure to take Canada as evidence that Divine Providence frowned on the entire aggressive and unjust contest. There was "something in the events of the war" in which the United States was unhappily engaged "too much like the finger of Heaven, to be mistaken for the vane of chance." In its attacks on Canada, America had been "defeated and disgraced," and thus "most rightly punished, for an unprovoked attack upon the lives and property of an unoffending neighbour." Only "infidels" could ignore this signal manifestation "of Divine interposition." Democrats, on the other hand, insisted that they desired Canada not for selfish ends but to put an end to Indian barbarity and to bring the British aggressors to justice—an object "worthy of an enlightened nation" and one that a "righteous Providence" would "crown with success."[23]

One glorious step toward this end occurred on 10 September 1813, when a squadron commanded by Oliver Hazard Perry defeated a British fleet at the Battle of Lake Erie. Republicans immediately seized on the victory as an example of providential intervention in behalf of America's righteous struggle. The pious Perry himself set the tone by citing "the Almighty" as the source of

[22] *Niles' Weekly Reg.*, 19 Sept. 1812.

[23] *Charleston Courier*, 9 Apr. 1813; "An American Farmer," *Aurora*, 29 June 1813.

his "signal victory." This sentiment, of course, was pleasing to Jeffersonians. "An Aged Citizen" agreed that "it was the power of Providence that gave our Perry the courage, the forethought and the perseverance necessary to the attainment of his glorious victory on the lake. . . . I hope my fellow-citizens see it in this light—that, as our hero said, 'the Almighty has done it'—man being only *his* instrument."[24] Other Democrats, including President Madison, concurred that "the loving kindness of the Almighty" had been displayed on Lake Erie. "Let the Sons of America rejoice, let the Daughters of Columbia be glad, for 'The Lord of hosts is with us; the God of Jacob is our refuge.'"[25]

Jeffersonians insisted that the same divine hand was behind America's successful military efforts against England's Indian allies. Under perfidious British instigation the red warriors had spread havoc and bloodshed across the frontier. Would "the just God of Heaven suffer such barbarity to go unpunished?" Surely not, nor would "their abettors escape the vengeance of a just God."[26] Hence when William Henry Harrison on 5 October 1813 defeated an Anglo-Indian force at the Battle of Thames River and the renowned Tecumseh was slain, Republicans insisted that "Divine Providence" had granted this glorious "success to our arms." The next year, according to "Cato," it similarly "pleased God" to give Andrew Jackson a "signal victory" over the Creek Nation. Thanks to a protecting Providence, the nation's "young and aspiring Eagles" were "rapidly gaining the commanding heights to which Nature and Nature's God seem to beckon them."[27]

The same year, however, also brought the most serious military debacle of the war. In the late summer of 1814 a British expeditionary force penetrated the Chesapeake, defeated a hastily assembled militia army at Bladensburg, and seized and burned Washington. Divine vengeance, Federalists concluded, had clearly fallen on those

[24] *Aurora*, 24 Sept. 1813; "An Aged Citizen," ibid., 21 Oct. 1813.

[25] *Enquirer*, 1 Oct. 1813. See also ibid., 28 Sept. 1813; *Niles' Weekly Reg.*, 25 Sept. 1813; *Aurora*, 4 Oct. 1813, 3 Feb. 1814; Israel, ed., *State of the Union Messages*, 1:123–25; Chillicothe, Ohio, *Weekly Recorder*, 6 Sept. 1814.

[26] "The Old Soldier," *Aurora*, 21 Oct. 1812. Cf. "Agricola," ibid., 11 Mar. 1813.

[27] Ibid., 19 Oct. 1813; "Cato," *Enquirer*, 20 Oct. 1814.

most deserving of it. The spectacle of Madison and his bellicose cohorts fleeing from their burning capital was God's ultimate testimony against the war. As one antiwar spokesman put it, "The indignation of Heaven . . . has now visited our country for placing its confidence in Men who have uniformly set at defiance the common rules of just policy and public morality." Republicans, however, viewed the humiliation as another example of Divine Providence permitting temporary evil in order to produce ultimate good. The burning of Washington had been allowed by a guardian God to rouse national patriotism and union and thus contribute to final victory.[28]

Defenders of the war were not slow in detecting further smiles of the Lord which offset the Washington catastrophe. In the same campaign that witnessed the burning of the capital, a British attack on Baltimore was repulsed. The inhabitants of that city, under "the protection of Providence, to whom all honor and glory should be ascribed," had "done their duty to themselves and their country." The Republican cause was further vindicated on 11 September 1814, when a British invasion force was turned back on New York's Lake Champlain by Thomas Macdonough. "*To the interposition of heaven*," a Vermont newspaper exclaimed, "*be ascribed our glorious victory*." This tremendous success was "an impressive interposition of Divine Providence" and nothing less than a "miraculous . . . deliverance, under God."[29]

Finally, in a fitting conclusion to a just war (just to Republicans, at least), the Lord delivered a veteran English army into Andrew Jackson's hands at the Battle of New Orleans on 8 January 1815. As a Virginia journal concluded after reviewing the particulars of Jackson's stupendous victory, "It were easy to multiply remarks on the importance and value of this unparalleled achievement; but it beggars *all* comment. . . . The God of Battles is surely on our side." News of New Orleans, another Democrat observed, filled "the hearts

[28] "The Spirit of 1775," *Columbian Centinel*, 10 Sept. 1814; *Enquirer*, 27 Aug. 1814; William Sleigh, *A Thanksgiving Sermon, Delivered April 13, 1815, to the Inhabitants of Deering and Hillsborough* (Concord, N.H., 1815), p. 8.

[29] Baltimore *American*, 15 Sept. 1814; Burlington *Vermont Centinel*, 18 Sept. 1814; O[rsamus] C. Merrill, *An Oration, Delivered at the Meeting House in Bennington* (Bennington, Vt., 1815), p. 23.

of good men with reverence to that God who knows the justice of o cause, and who carefully protects us from our enemies."[30]

On land and the inland lakes, Republican claims that Divi Providence favored America's prosecution of the War of 18 seemed (in the main) to be confirmed by events. But the war was al fought on the high seas. There ships of the small American fleet, o several occasions, were surprisingly successful against the renowne British navy. Both Federalist and Republican spokesmen celebrate America's naval victories as providential favors, but each party als enlisted them in disparate partisan arguments. Federalists viewed the nation's success on the oceans as the only favorable manifestation of Providence during the war—and one which damned Republicanism and elevated Federalism in the process. The American navy was the child of Federalism, created and supported by the disciples of Washington in the face of foolish or traitorous Jacobin parsimony. Thus South Carolina Federalist Joshua Toomer, alluding to the Republican Israel's oceanic achievements, invoked the "Sainted Spirit of our Father, our Fellow-Citizen, our Washington," and observed, "Heaven, which has seen fit to chastise the follies and vices of thy children, has, in *its justice* to *thee*, and in *its mercy to us*, by a signal interposition, marked its approbation of the wisdom and purity of thy principles." Republicans too, in reviewing the naval actions of the war, concluded that "hitherto Fortune, or rather . . . *Providence*, has favored us in a signal manner." But Jeffersonians then enlisted these victories in support of their contention that God approved of the just War of 1812. Many unpatriotic Federalists had brazenly claimed that "the finger of Heaven *points against the war*, and whoever voluntarily supports it, *sins against Providence*!" But Democrats threw back at their anti-American, aristocratic foes the retort "In the success of the *navy* how does the finger point!"[31] The wonders of the Lord, on sea as on land, were utilized in partisan debate.

[30] *Enquirer*, 11 Feb. 1815; "The Author of the Crisis," ibid., 1 Mar. 1815. See also *Weekly Rec.*, 2 Feb. 1815; *Aurora*, 10 Feb. 1815; *Niles' Weekly Reg.*, 11 Feb. 1815; *Enquirer*, 15 Feb. 1815; Sleigh, *Thanksgiving Sermon*, p. 10.

[31] Joshua W. Toomer, *An Oration, Delivered in St. Michael's Church, Charleston, South-Carolina; on Monday, the Fourth of July, 1814* (Charleston, 1814), p. 20; Boston *Patriot*, in *Aurora*, 21 June 1813; Salem, Mass., *Essex Register*, in *Aurora*, 18 Feb. 1813.

Besides employing providential rhetoric to interpret events in the New World after 1812, Federalists also applied providential imagery in a more circumspect (but just as real) attack on the war. The Friends of Order employed providential rhetoric to explain the defeat and downfall of Napoleonic France. Through depictions of Divine Providence at work in the overthrow of Napoleon, antiwar spokesmen implicitly attacked the Republican rulers of America as well as the Corsican Anti-Christ. This equation, of course, was entirely consistent in Federalist eyes; after all, the Republicans were really the willing agents of Napoleon. To this end Federalists perceived and celebrated the hand of God manifest in Napoleon's rout in Russia in 1812,[32] his defeat by the Grand Coalition and his exile to Elba in 1814,[33] and his final banishment to Saint Helena following the Hundred Days and Waterloo.[34]

At times the underlying aim of these Federalist accounts—promotion of the argument that God would soon punish the Jacobin rulers of America as he was now punishing France—surfaced in explicit parallels. After claiming that "the Almighty" had granted the Russians victory over Napoleon, one anonymous southern Federalist warned that the pro-French leaders of the United States must now make peace or risk a similar "just retribution" by "Providence." In the summer of 1814, as Napoleon abdicated and the war seemed lost in the New World, another Federalist saw it all as the grand design of God: "Happy Europe—thy crimes are expiated! Unhappy America,

[32] "A Friend to the Rights,—the Regulated Rights of Man," *Columbian Centinel*, 13 Mar. 1813; Bodwell, *Sovereignty of God*, p. 11; "Philopatris," *Charleston Courier*, 26 July 1813; *Speech of Robert G. Harper, Esq. at the Celebration of the Russian Victories* (Baltimore, 1813), pp. 20, 23; Gribbin, *Churches Militant*, pp. 51–55.

[33] Samuel Cary, *A Sermon Preached Before the Ancient and Honorable Artillery Company, in Boston, June 6, 1814* (Boston, 1814), pp. 10–14; Gouverneur Morris, *An Oration, Delivered on Wednesday, June 29, 1814* (New York, 1814), pp. 3, 16, 21; William Ladd, *An Oration, Pronounced at Minot, Maine, on the Fourth Day of July, 1814* (Portland, Maine, 1814), pp. 21–22; Benjamin Whitwell, *An Oration, Pronounced July 4, 1814* (Boston, 1814), p. 14.

[34] James Flint, *A Discourse, Delivered in the Audience of His Excellency Caleb Strong* (Boston, 1815), pp. 4–8, 27; *Weekly Rec.*, 23 Aug. 1815; Gregory T. Bedell, "*Peace on Earth.*" *A Sermon, Delivered in Christ's Church, Hudson, on Christmas Day, December, 1815* (Hudson, N.Y., 1816), pp. 14–15.

having wantonly spurned the best blessings heaven ever showers on nations, courted misery, and sacrificed your own peace, your day of trial is come."[35]

The day of trial indeed came, but America survived to see the arrival of peace in the spring of 1815. At the close of the conflict Federalists and Republicans reacted as they had so often before—both agreed that the peace was a gift of God but then split as to its precise providential meaning. Federalists celebrated the cessation of hostilities as a divine blessing, but used the occasion to condemn once more the unjust and unnecessary war just concluded. Their views were the views of one unshaken Carolinian:

> The Supreme Governor of the Universe, in compassion to a suffering people, hath mercifully interposed and arrested the progress of a war which . . . has cost rivers of precious blood unnecessarily shed; involved the nation in an enormous debt; reduced it to the verge of bankruptcy, and brought distress and embarrassment into every house. . . . Had the unhappy contest . . . continued but a short time longer . . . the U[nited] States would have exhibited a scene of widespread calamity, national and individual. . . . How great then is the gratitude we owe to the "Almighty Disposer of Events," who hath thus mercifully and seasonably interposed to rescue us from the calamities which awaited us.

The disciples of Washington and Hamilton gave thanks "to the God of our fathers" that America was delivered "from the confusion and ruin, which but recently seemed inevitable," and that their nation had survived its "rash plunge . . . into the awful perils of war."[36]

Republicans, celebrating the peace of 1815 as a peace of victory and honor, stressed again the necessity and propriety of the struggle just concluded. As President Madison proclaimed, "The Great Disposer of Events and of the Destiny of Nations," having supported America throughout the course of a war fought to assert "national rights" and enhance "national character," had now granted his Republican Israel "peace and reconciliation." Jeffersonians, "the true friends of their country," were now "as sincere and grateful in celebrating the goodness of God, who restored to them the blessings of

[35] "T.," *Charleston Courier*, 9 Apr. 1813; *Boston Spectator*, 4 June 1814.
[36] "Civis," *Charleston Courier*, 2 Mar. 1815; Flint, *Discourse*, p. 14.

peace," as they had for the past three years been "eager and successful in avenging the insulted rights" of their nation.[37]

The war's outcome vindicated Republican claims. Linking the Battle of New Orleans and the Peace of Ghent, Democrats were able to present America's survival as tantamount to victory—a victory proving that the just War of 1812 had indeed been supported by a guardian God. The Federalists, who had opposed the conflict, stood branded as enemies to God and America. Just as New Orleans and the Federalist blunder of the Hartford Convention led to the political demise of Federalism after 1815, so the apparent vindication of Republican wartime themes resulted in the demise of Federalist partisan providential rhetoric. Democrats in 1815 drove home this point, taunting Federalists with the evidence that the war had been a divine crusade. Addressing the Federalist clergy, who had so vociferously denounced the struggle as unjust and abhorrent to God, one New England Democrat issued an invitation:

> Approach ye Holy Evangelists, whose desks have been polluted with your maledictions against the measure, and the government who adopted it—ye who profanely cursed our armies, while God was blessing them. Approach and behold your confutation, in the victories and glories we have gained. . . . Say ye, was not the Lord God of Hosts with our republican armies, at . . . PLATTSBURGH and NEW-ORLEANS? Did it not "please the Almighty" to give victory on LAKES ERIE and CHAMPLAIN? And did not our OCEAN heroes evince, at various places of the great deep that they were polished shafts from the quiver of the Lord? and dare you persist in your denunciations, and refrain [from] rendering thanksgiving to God for the marvelous deliverances He has vouchsafed our Republic.[38]

Repeatedly the question was scornfully thrown at the Federalists, "Can you close your eyes against the evidence God hath given of his care over this nation in our late contest with old England?"[39] The Federalists were unable, or unwilling, to respond, and the Republi-

[37] Richardson, ed., *Messages and Papers*, 1:561; *Aurora*, 17 Apr. 1815; *Enquirer*, 22 Feb. 1815; Sleigh, *Thanksgiving Sermon*, pp. 3–4.

[38] Merrill, *Oration*, pp. 24–25.

[39] Sleigh, *Thanksgiving Sermon*, p. 16. For other typical taunts see *Niles' Weekly Reg.*, 4 Mar. 1815, and Rutland, Vt., *Rutland Herald*, 23 Aug. 1815, as quoted in Gribbin, *Churches Militant*, p. 134.

can triumph was complete. The combination of Republican providential rhetoric and the outcome of the War of 1812 completed the partisan portrayal of the Federalists as un-American traitors who had desired nothing less that the total defeat of the United States and its recolonization by the British.

The providential thought articulated during the War of 1812 contained a special irony. New England, which had originally contribbuted its special Puritan themes to the nation's providential legend and which had set the providential tone for American responses to the French and Indian War and the American Revolution, had now, in a sense, rejected its offspring. The providential nationalism that was in many ways New England writ large was championed between 1812 and 1815 not by the descendants of the Puritans but by spokesmen from the "barbaric" South and West. New England (Federalist) providential thought during the War of 1812 was local rather than national, shrill rather than serene. Although the situation was not absolute, the large majority of New England public spokesmen after 1812 dissented from the national-providential consensus their fathers had helped to create.

That consensus, however, had long since passed into the mainstream of American thought. The War of 1812 only solidified that consensus. America's providential legend had been strained at several points (the patriot-loyalist split during the American Revolution, the Federalist-Republican rivalry between 1789 and 1815), and it would be strained in the future (the Whig-Democratic split over Manifest Destiny and the Mexican War, the North-South contest that culminated in the Civil War). But the basic ingredients of the providential consensus—the secular typology of God's New Israel, the jeremiad tradition, the legend of the founding fathers, the political millennium to come, the providential interpretation of American history with its "equation of material and spiritual blessings"—had truly been fused by 1815 into an "exuberant national eschatology embodied in the American Dream."[40] The providential thought fashioned by American spokesmen between 1740 and 1815 lay waiting for post-1815 patriots and politicians to use as they saw fit.

[40] Bercovitch, "Horologicals to Chronometricals," p. 75.

Epilogue

Historians of the antebellum American mind have correctly noted the influence of romanticism and evangelism on American nationalism after 1815. To these must be added providential thought, which was equally important to the American self-consciousness after 1815. By the Middle Period, one scholar has recently concluded, "a providential past was a common heritage of all Americans."[1] Both the partisan and the nationalistic strains of American providential thought prevailed in the years following the War of 1812. During the Jacksonian period, for instance, the followers of Old Hickory fashioned a providential legend for their hero and wielded it against their political foes. In his role as a living manifestation of God's guidance of the American republic and the latest example of the legend of the fathers, Jackson served as a "symbol for his age," as a personification of what a significant number of the American people believed about themselves and their country.[2]

The descendants of both Federalists and Republicans adapted earlier providential concepts after 1815, though (as might be expected) these developed along different lines. Former Federalists in particular transformed the jeremiad tradition. Having argued that the War of 1812 was God's just visitation on America for national sins, these spokesmen were left uneasy by the peace of 1815. They were not convinced that America had reformed, and so could not view the peace as a vindication of American virtue, as Jeffersonians did; yet the coming of peace was without question the work of Divine Providence. Federalist descendants were bewildered by God's "seeming decision to reward instead of punish America for its recent actions." Eventually these descendants of the Friends of Order, viewing them-

[1] Welter, *Mind of America*, p. 6.

[2] John William Ward, *Andrew Jackson: Symbol for an Age* (New York, 1955), pp. 101–32. See also the important forthcoming book by Robert P. Hay, *The First Jacksonians: Patriotism as Politics, 1823–1824* (Millwood, N.Y.).

selves "consciously" as "a beleaguered minority," found a way out of their dilemma. The peace of 1815, they concluded, was not a divine blessing at all, but only a temporary abatement of God's wrath. In order to avert the return of that wrath, Americans had to extirpate all sin from their nation. Looking about America in the years after 1815, the heirs of the Federalists discovered specific evils—intemperance, ignorance, and especially slavery—as America's paramount national sins. Only their removal would return America to her national covenant with the Lord. Thus the jeremiad tradition—the insistence that reformation was needed to prevent national disaster—was "transformed" into the reform and abolition movements that flourished from the 1820s to the 1860s.[3]

Post-1815 Democrats transformed America's providential thought during the 1830s and 1840s into the concept of Manifest Destiny. Indeed, as Sacvan Bercovitch has argued, the "secular metamorphosis" of the providential legend that began with the seventeenth-century Puritan fathers appeared "most broadly" in the rhetoric of Manifest Destiny. Thus James Buchanan asserted in 1844 that "Providence" had given to America "a great and important mission" to "spread the blessings of Christian liberty and laws from one end to the other of this immense continent." "The wisdom of an overruling Providence" dictated that Texas, Oregon, and California join the United States. Continental expansion, according to New York Congressman Chesselden Ellis, was but the fulfillment of "an outline drawn by the hand of the Creator himself." Commodore Robert Stockton claimed that the "secret" of American "successes" in the Mexican War was that "the God of armies and Lord of hosts is with us," and argued that the annexation of all of Mexico would be but the completion of America's "duty" to "the providence of God." America's providential mission was thus transformed by the 1840s; the exemplary manifestation of republicanism was to be replaced by the territorial growth of the republic.[4]

[3] William Gribbin, "The Covenant Transformed: The Jeremiad Tradition and the War of 1812," *Church History* 40 (1971): 297–305; idem, *Churches Militant*, pp. 138–44; May, *Enlightenment in America*, pp. 317, 352.

[4] Bercovitch, "Horologicals to Chronometricals," pp. 80–81; Norman A. Graebner, ed., *Manifest Destiny* (Indianapolis, 1968), pp. xxi, liii, 70–71, 210–13, and see also pp. xviii, xxv–vi, xxxix, lvi, 17–18, 157.

The culmination of partisan providential thought after 1815 came during the Civil War era, when northerners claimed that the Lord was justly punishing America for the "sin of slavery" and that only emancipation could return the nation to the smiles of Divine Providence. Ultimately, the victorious North rejoiced that the Civil War had reinforced and purified America's divine, cosmic mission. When the United States finally had been purged of slavery, she was an even more fitting divine vessel for the extirpation of tyranny all over the globe.[5]

More central than these partisan developments, however, was the continuing sanctification of American patriotism by providential thought after 1815. Both the concept of the Republican Israel and faith in America's cosmic mission remained strong from the 1820s through the 1840s; indeed, these themes, mutually reinforcing each other, reached their peak in the American response to the European revolutions of 1848.[6] Though Whigs and Democrats disagreed over the amount of action inherent in America's exemplary mission, both agreed that that mission was ordained by Providence.[7] American presidents continued to act the role of high priests for the nation's evolving civil religion, for the balance of the nineteenth century liberally sprinkling their official pronouncements with references to Divine Providence.[8] The Fourth of July persisted as the occasion for the utterance of volumes of providential rhetoric, rhetoric virtually indistinguishable from that pronounced before 1815.[9] The legend of the Lord's guidance of America was especially strengthened by the popular reaction to two remarkable visitations connected with the

[5] William A. Clebsch, "Christian Interpretations of the Civil War," *Church History* 30 (1961): 212–22; Marty, *Righteous Empire*, pp. 57, 65, 134–35; Cushing Strout, *The New Heavens and New Earth: Political Religion in America* (New York, 1974), pp. 140–204.

[6] John R. Bodo, *The Protestant Clergy and Public Issues, 1812–1848* (Princeton, N.J., 1954), pp. 233, 239–43; Russel B. Nye, *Society and Culture in America, 1830–1860* (New York, 1974), pp. 10–19.

[7] Welter, *Mind of America*, pp. 45–74.

[8] Nagel, *This Sacred Trust*, pp. 78–83, 154–58, 215–18, 272–80.

[9] Hay, "Freedom's Jubilee," pp. 172–202, and idem, "Providence and the American Past," pp. 79–101. For the continuing importance of the Fourth of July oration as a source of popular American attitudes after 1820, see Welter, *Mind of America*, p. 396.

Fourth of July. The simultaneous deaths of John Adams and Thomas Jefferson on 4 July 1826 (the fiftieth anniversary of American independence) and the death of James Monroe exactly five years later, on 4 July 1831, were interpreted by patriots as proof that Divine Providence continued to shape and influence the history and destiny of the United States.[10]

After the Civil War the concept of Divine Providence lost its central place in American patriotism. With the removal of pre-1865 unsettling issues and the addition of more tangible bases upon which to anchor a nationalism, providential thought diminished in importance. By the centennial of American independence the notion of a protecting Providence was no longer central to the American mind. The United States had evolved essentially a secular culture in which religion and religious imagery served chiefly as supporters of nonreligious institutions.[11] After two and a half centuries providential thought had ceased to be a basic ingredient of American thought. The passing of providential thought in the later nineteenth century, however, should not obscure the significance of its prominence in early America.

Providential thought from 1640 to 1815 demonstrated a striking continuity. Many of the themes and concepts professed by Americans in 1763, themes derived from the New England Puritans, were held by their descendants fifty years later. Spokesmen of both generations agreed that the concept of Divine Providence best explained the course of human history; that America was acting a prearranged role in the Lord's moral government of the world; and that America was Jehovah's New Israel, raised up and protected for the performance of some ultimate wonder. Transformation, of course, did occur. The theme of America's providential mission, for instance, evolved from a general notion in the 1760s of the protection and promotion of civil and religious liberty to the specific theme after 1776 of the republican experiment as God's plan for the globe. The providential legend

[10] Robert P. Hay, "The Glorious Departure of the American Patriarchs: Contemporary Reactions to the Deaths of Jefferson and Adams," *Journal of Southern History* 35 (1969): 543–55; idem, "The Meaning of Monroe's Death: The Contemporary Response," *West Virginia History* 30 (1969): 427–35.

[11] Martin E. Marty, *The Modern Schism: Three Paths to the Secular* (New York, 1969), pp. 10, 20, 95–142; idem, *Righteous Empire*, pp. 188–89, 195.

was continually enlarged to include the latest wonder of the Lord—the American Revolution, the Federal Constitution, the French Revolution, the War of 1812. The legend of the fathers expanded to include the heroes of the American Revolution and then focused especially on George Washington. All in all, however, the continuity of providential thought is impressive.

Although the relationship is not an absolute one, it is evident that many public spokesmen in post-1740 America were closer to the mind of the Puritans than the mind of the Enlightenment. The guardian God that these spokesmen acclaimed was not the watchmaker God of the *philosophes*; America's God much more nearly approached the omnipotent, personal, unlimited, interventionist Jehovah of the Old Testament. The activites of the Lord in human history, particularly the history of the Republican Israel, confirmed this. One scholar has accurately concluded that "the belief that America has been providentially chosen for a specific destiny has deep roots in the American past, and it is by no means a belief that has been given up in this secular age." Indeed, the conviction that the United States was God's chosen nation became "so pervasive a motif" that "the word 'belief' does not really capture the dynamic role it has played for the American people."[12] A study of Providence and patriotism in early America confirms and enlarges this conclusion. Providential thought was central to the American mind during the Revolutionary and early national years, not diminishing but flourishing in an age that also witnessed the flowering of the secular American Enlightenment.

The popular mind of post-1740 America is perhaps best seen as a fusion of providential and "enlightened" values. Americans began with the concept of Divine Providence as the director and shaper of history. This theory then reinforced their belief that the end of history was the advancement of liberty, freedom, and self-government. Patriots consistently employed the secular typology of God's New Israel, the jeremiad tradition, the legend of the fathers, and providential historiography to flesh out this belief. The fusion of these elements constitutes the essence of American providential thought in the eighteenth and early nineteenth centuries. If the providential

[12] Cherry, ed., *God's New Israel*, pp. 1, 21.

thought of early America could be compressed into one sentence, that sentence would have to be "Divine Providence is utilizing the United States to achieve universal freedom." If America's providential legend could be reduced to a single image, that image would be the Republican Israel.

It is easy today to underestimate or misunderstand the importance of providential thought to American patriotism. Only clerics now speak of Divine Providence as a theory of historical causation, and even they do so circumspectly. The providential manner of perceiving events is foreign to modern thought and to modern American nationalism. But to early American patriots that manner of perception was both real and comforting. Many Americans expressed faith in a definite hierarchy of causation that assigned Divine Providence the role of the ultimate cause. To these citizens providential thought, more than economic or political theories, best explained the course of American history and the destiny of their nation. Politics and economics as shapers of history were not ignored, but they were decidedly inferior to the hand of God in explaining the true meaning of historical events. Providential thought allowed patriots to fit their national development into a framework dominated by universal foresight, order, and direction. Far from being an inducement to supineness, faith in Divine Providence was a spur to confidence and action. The Americans who made the Revolution, the Constitution, and the new nation were men firmly convinced that they were Heaven's favorites—that they were doing God's republican work in the world.

Bibliography

Index

Bibliography

A Note on Primary Sources

I have tried in this work to discern the elusive "popular" American mind in the era of the American Revolution. The bulk of the sources examined, therefore, are popular—first, sermons and orations delivered on communal or national festivals and anniversaries, and second, newspapers written (or at least read) by ordinary citizens. More than 850 pieces of pamphlet literature and over 45 newspapers were consulted.

New England election sermons from the 1760s, 1770s, and 1780s proved extremely useful. Delivered annually by carefully selected ministers and circulated throughout the countryside as printed pamphlets, these sermons reached a wide audience among the common populace. The election sermons, although delivered by elite spokesmen, were both shapers and reflectors of public opinion. The same holds true for the many fast and thanksgiving sermons delivered during these years. Especially from the 1770s onward, when such sermons were delivered on national fast and thanksgiving days in every state of the union by preachers from all denominations and of all theological shadings, these discourses reflected a national climate of opinion.

After 1776 orations delivered on the Fourth of July constitute perhaps the richest source for the student of the popular American mind, and I have relied heavily on them. These orations were popular in the best and true sense of the word; they were delivered by all types of men—lawyers, doctors, merchants, politicians, farmers, mechanics, students, and soldiers—to both urban and rural audiences in every state of the union. In their totality they accurately reflect popular concepts within American thought.

I have read every surviving sermon and oration delivered on a communal or national occasion in America between 1763 and 1789. After 1789 the number of such publications increased at an ever-expanding rate, so that it seemed no longer mandatory to read every production. Hence the sections of this work dealing with American providential concepts after 1789 are based on a selected number of sermons and orations—selected to reflect as many diverse elements as possible. I have especially attempted to balance these works according to place of delivery and political affiliation. The number of sermons and orations after 1789 read, while not total, is still formidable.

The role of newspapers as reflectors of popular American attitudes, especially after the mid-eighteenth century, is well known. Newspapers therefore comprise the other main source for the present study. Here I have employed an unsophisticated but (I believe) useful sampling approach, concentrating on leading newspapers issued in selected major urban centers. This study is based on the articles and editorials of at least one major newspaper published in five American cities—Boston, New York, Philadelphia, Williamsburg (after 1780, Richmond), and Charleston—for every year between 1740 and 1815. For two reasons, I have also consulted newspapers not published in these five cities. First, there are gaps in the files from these five cities I used, particularly during the Revolutionary War when most of these cities, at least for a time, were occupied by the British. When gaps appeared or files proved incomplete, I have substituted other newspapers from the same region, assuming that they approximate, if not reproduce, the sentiments of the primary newspapers. Secondly, I have balanced newspapers after 1789 according to their political affiliation. Thus major Federalist publications like the Boston *Columbian Centinel* and *Charleston Courier* are paralleled by leading Jeffersonian journals like the Philadelphia *Aurora* and Richmond *Enquirer*.

These works, then—sermons, orations, and newspapers, along with occasional pamphlet essays and the poetry of the era's leading literary figures (Freneau, Brackenridge, Dwight, and Barlow)—have served as the main sources for this study. The works of the Founding Fathers, the "enlightened" elite, have not been ignored, for in a considerable number of instances their views paralleled the many popular providential tenets expressed by more common citizens. But to have relied on the writings of the elite alone, or to have allowed these sources to dictate the course of my examination of American ideas, would have defeated a major intent of the study.

All works printed before 1800 were read from the microprint

edition of *Early American Imprints, 1639–1800*, as prepared by Clifford K. Shipton and the American Antiquarian Society. Works printed after 1800 were consulted from the pamphlet collections in the Library of Congress, Rare Book Division. Newspapers, either in the original or on microfilm, were read at the Library of Congress Newspaper Annex and at various libraries in Milwaukee.

Secondary Sources

I have benefited greatly from the work of numerous historians contained in important secondary works dealing with intellectual trends in pre–1815 America. Rather than citing them all again, I would like simply to note the following studies, which contributed most to my understanding of American thought during the Puritan, Revolutionary, and early national eras. These works are divided into general and thematic accounts.

I. General Works

Ahlstrom, Sydney E. "Religion, Revolution and the Rise of Modern Nationalism: Reflections on the American Experience." *Church History* 44 (1975): 492–504.

Albanese, Catherine L. *Sons of the Fathers: The Civil Religion of the American Revolution*. Philadelphia, 1976.

Bailyn, Bernard. *The Ideological Origins of the American Revolution*. Cambridge, Mass., 1967.

——. "Religion and Revolution: Three Biographical Studies." *Perspectives in American History* 4 (1970): 85–169.

Banner, James M., Jr. *To the Hartford Convention: The Federalists and the Origins of Party Politics in Massachusetts, 1789–1815*. New York, 1970.

Bellah, Robert N. "Civil Religion in America." In *Religion in America*, edited by William G. McLoughlin and Robert N. Bellah, pp. 3–23. Boston, 1968.

Bridenbaugh, Carl. *Mitre and Sceptre: Transatlantic Faiths, Ideas, Personalities, and Politics, 1689–1775*. New York, 1962.

——. *The Spirit of '76: The Growth of American Patriotism before Independence*. New York, 1975.

Brown, Roger H. *The Republic in Peril: 1812*. New York, 1964.

Buel, Richard, Jr. *Securing the Revolution: Ideology in American Politics, 1789–1815*. Ithaca, N.Y., 1972.

Burns, Edward McNall. *The American Idea of Mission: Concepts of National Purpose and Destiny*. New Brunswick, N.J., 1957.

Cowing, Cedric B. *The Great Awakening and the American Revolution: Colonial Thought in the Eighteenth Century*. Chicago, 1971.

Fischer, David Hackett. *The Revolution of American Conservatism: The Federalist Party in the Era of Jeffersonian Democracy*. New York, 1965.

Gribbin, William. *The Churches Militant: The War of 1812 and American Religion*. New Haven, 1973.

Hay, Robert P. "Freedom's Jubilee: One Hundred Years of the Fourth of July, 1776–1876." Ph.D. dissertation, University of Kentucky, 1967.

——. "Providence and the American Past." *Indiana Magazine of History* 65 (1969): 79–101.

Heimert, Alan. *Religion and the American Mind: From the Great Awakening to the Revolution*. Cambridge, Mass., 1966.

Hofstadter, Richard. *The Idea of a Party System: The Rise of Legitimate Opposition in the United States, 1780–1840*. Berkeley and Los Angeles, 1969.

Howe, John R. *From the Revolution through the Age of Jackson: Innocence and Empire in the Young Republic*. Englewood Cliffs, N.J., 1973.

Isaac, Rhys. "Preachers and Patriots: Popular Culture and the Revolution in Virginia." In *The American Revolution: Explorations in the History of American Radicalism*, edited by Alfred F. Young, pp. 125–56. DeKalb, Ill., 1976.

McCarthy, Rockne. "Civil Religion in Early America." *Fides et Historia* 8 (1975): 20–40.

McLoughlin, William G. "The Role of Religion in the Revolution: Liberty of Conscience and Cultural Cohesion in the New Nation." In *Essays on the American Revolution*, edited by Stephen G. Kurtz and James H. Hutson, pp. 197–255. Chapel Hill, N.C., 1973.

Marty, Martin E. *Righteous Empire: The Protestant Experience in America*. New York, 1970.

May, Henry F. "The Decline of Providence?" *Studies on Voltaire and the Eighteenth Century* 154 (1976): 1401–16.

——. *The Enlightenment in America*. New York, 1976.

Middlekauff, Robert. *The Mathers: Three Generations of Puritan Intellectuals, 1596–1728*. New York, 1971.

Miller, Glenn T. "The American Revolution as a Religious Event: An Essay in Political Theology." *Foundations* 19 (1976): 111–20.

Morais, Herbert M. *Deism in Eighteenth Century America*. New York, 1934.

Morgan, Edmund S. "The American Revolution Considered as an Intellectual Movement." In *Paths of American Thought*, edited by Arthur M. Schlesinger, Jr., and Morton White, pp. 11–33. Boston, 1963.

——. "The Puritan Ethic and the American Revolution." *William and Mary Quarterly*, 3d ser. 24 (1967): 3–43.

Murdock, Kenneth B. *Literature and Theology in Colonial New England*. Cambridge, Mass., 1949.

Nagel, Paul C. *This Sacred Trust: American Nationality, 1798–1898*. New York, 1971.

Noll, Mark A. *Christians in the American Revolution*. Grand Rapids, Mich., 1977.

——. "The Church and the American Revolution: Historiographical Pitfalls, Problems, and Progress." *Fides et Historia* 8 (1975): 2–19.

Nye, Russel B. *The Cultural Life of the New Nation, 1776–1830*. New York, 1960.

——. *This Almost Chosen People: Essays in the History of American Ideas*. East Lansing, Mich., 1966.

Rossiter, Clinton. "The American Mission." *American Scholar* 20 (1951): 19–28.

Savelle, Max. "Nationalism and Other Loyalties in the American

Revolution." *American Historical Review* 67 (1962): 901–23.

Spencer, Benjamin T. *The Quest for Nationality: An American Literary Campaign*. Syracuse, N.Y., 1957.

Wood, Gordon S. *The Creation of the American Republic, 1776–1787*. Chapel Hill, N.C., 1969.

II. The New Israel Motif

Bercovitch, Sacvan, ed. *Typology and Early American Literature*. Amherst, Mass., 1972.

——. "Typology in Puritan New England." *American Quarterly* 19 (1967): 166–91.

Bruum, Ursula. *American Thought and Religious Typology*. Translated by John Hooglund. New Brunswick, N.J., 1970.

Cherry, Conrad, ed. *God's New Israel: Religious Interpretations of American Destiny*. Englewood Cliffs, N.J., 1971.

Good, L. Douglass. "The Christian Nation in the Mind of Timothy Dwight." *Fides et Historia* 7 (1974): 1–18.

Hudson, Winthrop S., ed. *Nationalism and Religion in America: Concepts of American Identity and Mission*. New York, 1970.

Lowrance, Mason I., Jr. "Typology and the New England Way." *Early American Literature* 4 (1969): 15–37.

III. The Legend of the Fathers

Bercovitch, Sacvan. "'Nehemias Americanus': Cotton Mather and the Concept of the Representative American." *Early American Literature* 8 (1974): 220–38.

——. *The Puritan Origins of the American Self*. New Haven, 1975.

Boller, Paul F., Jr. *George Washington and Religion*. Dallas, 1963.

Bryan, William Alfred. *George Washington in American Literature, 1775–1865*. New York, 1952.

Craven, Wesley Frank. *The Legend of the Founding Fathers*. New York, 1956.

Cunliffe, Marcus. *George Washington: Man and Monument*. Boston, 1958.

Friedman, Lawrence J. *Inventors of the Promised Land.* New York, 1975.

Hay, Robert P. "George Washington: American Moses." *American Quarterly* 21 (1969): 780–91.

Mayo, Bernard. *Myths and Men: Patrick Henry, George Washington, Thomas Jefferson.* Athens, Ga., 1959.

Smylie, James H. "The President as Republican Prophet and King: Clerical Reflections on the Death of Washington." *Journal of Church and State* 18 (1976): 233–52.

IV. The Jeremiad Tradition

Bercovitch, Sacvan. "Horologicals to Chronometricals: The Rhetoric of the Jeremiad." In *Literary Monographs, Volume 3*, edited by Eric Rothstein, pp. 1–124, 187–215. Madison, Wis., 1970.

Elliott, Emory. *Power and the Pulpit in Puritan New England.* Princeton, N.J., 1975.

Gribbin, William. "The Covenant Transformed: The Jeremiad Tradition and the War of 1812." *Church History* 40 (1971): 297–305.

Kerr, Harry P. "The Election Sermon: Primer for Revolutionaries." *Speech Monographs* 29 (1962): 13–22.

——. "Politics and Religion in Colonial Fast and Thanksgiving Sermons, 1763–1783." *Quarterly Journal of Speech* 46 (1960): 372–82.

Miller, Perry. *Nature's Nation.* Cambridge, Mass., 1967.

——. *The New England Mind: From Colony to Province.* Cambridge, Mass., 1953.

Minnick, Wayne. "The New England Execution Sermons, 1639–1800." *Speech Monographs* 35 (1968): 77–89.

Minter, David. "The Puritan Jeremiad as a Literary Form." In *The American Puritan Imagination: Essays in Revaluation*, edited by Sacvan Bercovitch, pp. 45–55, 221–23. New York, 1974.

Mixon, Harold D. "Boston's Artillery Election Sermons and the American Revolution." *Speech Monographs* 34 (1967): 43–50.

V. Civil Millennialism

Beam, Christopher M. "Millennialism and American Nationalism, 1740–1800." *Journal of Presbyterian History* 54 (1976): 182–99.

Davidson, James West. *The Logic of Millennial Thought: Eighteenth-Century New England.* New Haven, 1977.

Hatch, Nathan O. "The Origins of Civil Millennialism in America: New England Clergymen, War with France, and the Revolution." *William and Mary Quarterly*, 3d ser. 31 (1974): 407–30.

——. *The Sacred Cause of Liberty: Republican Thought and the Millennium in Revolutionary New England.* New Haven, 1977.

Maclear, James F. "New England and the Fifth Monarchy: The Quest for the Millennium in Early American Puritanism." *William and Mary Quarterly*, 3d ser. 32 (1975): 223–60.

——. "The Republic and the Millennium." In *The Religion of the Republic*, edited by Elwyn A. Smith, pp. 183–216. Philadelphia, 1971.

Miller, Glenn T. "'Fashionable to Prophesy': Presbyterians, the Millennium, and the Revolution." *Amerikastudien* 21 (1976): 239–60.

Smith, David E. "Millenarian Scholarship in America." *American Quarterly* 17 (1965): 535–49.

Stein, Stephen J. "An Apocalyptic Rationale for the American Revolution." *Early American Literature* 9 (1975): 211–25.

Strout, Cushing. *The New Heavens and New Earth: Political Religion in America.* New York, 1974.

Tuveson, Ernest Lee. *Redeemer Nation: The Idea of America's Millennial Role.* Chicago, 1968.

VI. Providential Historiography

Buchanan, John G. "Puritan Philosophy of History from Restoration to Revolution." *Essex Institute Historical Collections* 104 (1968): 329–48.

Gay, Peter. *A Loss of Mastery: Puritan Historians in Colonial America.* Berkeley and Los Angeles, 1966.

Murdock, Kenneth B. "Clio in the Wilderness: History and Biography in Puritan New England." *Church History* 24 (1955): 221–38.

Stromberg, Roland N. "History in the Eighteenth Century." *Journal of the History of Ideas* 12 (1951): 295–304.

Tichi, Cecelia. "The Puritan Historians and Their New Jerusalem." *Early American Literature* 6 (1971): 143–55.

Trefz, Edward K. "The Puritans' View of History." *Boston Public Library Quarterly* 9 (1957): 115–36.

Trevor-Roper, Hugh. "The Historical Philosophy of the Enlightenment." *Studies on Voltaire and the Eighteenth Century* 27 (1963): 1667–87.

Index

EXAM CRAM™

CCNA

Second Edition

Michael Valentine

Andrew Whitaker

CCNA Exam Cram, Second Edition

International Standard Book Number: 0-7897-3502-4

Library of Congress Catalog Card Number: 2005904467

Printed in the United States of America

First Printing: November 2005

08 07 06 05 4 3 2 1

Trademarks

All terms mentioned in this book that are known to be trademarks or service marks have been appropriately capitalized. Que Publishing cannot attest to the accuracy of this information. Use of a term in this book should not be regarded as affecting the validity of any trademark or service mark.

Warning and Disclaimer

Every effort has been made to make this book as complete and as accurate as possible, but no warranty or fitness is implied. The information provided is on an "as is" basis. The authors and the publisher shall have neither liability nor responsibility to any person or entity with respect to any loss or damages arising from the information contained in this book or from the use of the CD or programs accompanying it.

Bulk Sales

Que Publishing offers excellent discounts on this book when ordered in quantity for bulk purchases or special sales. For more information, please contact

U.S. Corporate and Government Sales
1-800-382-3419
corpsales@pearsontechgroup.com

For sales outside the U.S., please contact

International Sales
international@pearsoned.com

Publisher
Paul Boger

Executive Editor
Jeff Riley

Acquisitions Editor
Carol Ackerman

Development Editor
Ginny Bess

Managing Editor
Charlotte Clapp

Project Editor
Andy Beaster

Copy Editor
Rhonda Tinch-Mize

Indexer
Chris Barrick

Proofreader
Leslie Joseph

Technical Editors
Ross Brunson
Jeremy Cioara

Publishing Coordinator
Cindy Teeters

Multimedia Developer
Dan Scherf

Interior Designer
Gary Adair

Cover Designer
Anne Jones

Page Layout
Bronkella Publishing

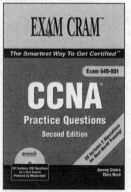

To Dad, who said, "Do not ignore the gift that is in you."

To Mum, who said, "Everybody has something; everywhere has something."

To Ed, who started it all.

To Dave, who set the example.

To Val, for making it bearable.

And most of all, to Liana… for everything.

—Michael Valentine

I dedicate this to the three most important women in my life: Lois, Lucy, and Jennifer (or, as I like to call them, Grandma, Mom, and sweetheart).

And to my students,

I did my best: Now it's your turn.

—Andrew Whitaker

❧

About the Authors

Mike Valentine has been in the IT field for 10 years, focusing on network design and implementation. He currently divides his time between his network consultancy company in Vancouver, British Columbia, and being a senior trainer for The Training Camp, teaching its Cisco programs all over the United States and parts of Europe. Mike teaches CCNA, CCDA, and CCNP and contributes to the development of Cisco courseware and delivery programs. His accessible, humorous, and effective teaching style has demystified Cisco for hundreds of students since he began teaching in 2002. Mike has a Bachelor of Arts degree from the University of British Columbia, and currently holds the MCSE:Security, Net+, Sec+, CCDA, CCNP, and CEH certifications. He has successfully completed the written component on his CCIE and is preparing to take the CCIE lab.

Andrew Whitaker has been working in the IT field for more than 10 years. He currently teaches and develops curriculum for CCNA, CCDA, CCNP, and CEH classes for the Training Camp. He has a Master's degree in Computer Science and currently holds the following certifications: CCSP, CCNP, CCNA, CCDA, CQS-CATM, INFOSEC, MCSE, CNE, A+, Network+, Security+, CEH, and CEI. He has also passed the qualification exam for the CCIE certification and is currently studying for the lab exam.

About the Technical Editors

Jeremy Cioara is a CCIE, MCSE, and CNE. He has focused on network technology for more than a decade. Some of his field work includes network design and consulting at MicroAge, Qwest, and Terminal Processing Systems. Currently, Jeremy is a technical instructor and author on various topics including Cisco IP telephone, routing, and switching. He co-authored CCNA Practice Questions Exam Cram and CCNA Exam Prep for Que Certification.

Ross Brunson holds ten certifications from Linux to Cisco, including the LPIC 1, Linux+, and CCNA. He is currently Senior Advanced Training Engineer with Novell Inc., responsible for custom training for Novell/SUSE's Fortune 100 and Fortune 500 enterprise clients. Prior to Novell, Ross was the Director of Linux and Unix Education for the Training Camp and responsible for establishing the first major LPI boot camp training program in the world.

Acknowledgments

It's an interesting process to trace back events that lead up to where we are now. A few years back, I was a student in a class that was superbly taught by the master, Ed Denzler, and his dangerously competent right hand, Rick Van Luvender. A couple years later, Dave Minutella introduced me to the mysteries of Cisco and showed me what really effective instruction was all about.

Soon after that, Ed and Rick asked me to teach the class they had originally taught me years back. They helped me evolve from a terrified rookie into a somewhat less terrified experienced hand. Ed, Rick, and Dave, you guys know you made me what I am, and I thank you. My respect for you grows with each turn in the road, my friends.

Not long ago, a kindred spirit named Ross Brunson phoned out of a rainy Vancouver sky to ask if I wanted to write a book, and I did. Such serendipitous things happen to me, but not without the good karma of lunatics like Ross. For you, Ross: "I am a Canadian Glider Pilot," and thank you too.

Then came Carol Ackerman, Gin, J.C., Andy, and all the other good people at Que, who took me in—again, as a rookie—and walked me through a thoroughly enjoyable ordeal. I loved every minute of it, and when it was awful, I was just pretending. Let's do it again!

Working with my coauthor and good friend was a privilege—a million thanks, Drew, for commiserating, consulting, and carousing through this gig. What a blast—I'll be your wingman anytime.

But before everyone, there was my Mum and Dad, whose amazing talents and intellect taught me that the greatest ambition to which we can aspire is to fulfill our potential. From them I learned to use my heart, my brain, my hands, and my voice, and if by the end of my life I have achieved half of what they have, I will be very proud. I love you both immensely, and I am fiercely proud of your life's work, both of you. Thank you for giving me such an amazing life.

—Michael Hayes Valentine

What he said…but better.

—Andrew Whitaker

Contents at a Glance

Table of Contents

We Want to Hear from You!

As the reader of this book, *you* are our most important critic and commentator. We value your opinion and want to know what we're doing right, what we could do better, what areas you'd like to see us publish in, and any other words of wisdom you're willing to pass our way.

As an executive editor for Que Publishing, I welcome your comments. You can email or write me directly to let me know what you did or didn't like about this book—as well as what we can do to make our books better.

Please note that I cannot help you with technical problems related to the topic of this book. We do have a User Services group, however, where I will forward specific technical questions related to the book.

When you write, please be sure to include this book's title and author as well as your name, email address, and phone number. I will carefully review your comments and share them with the author and editors who worked on the book.

Email: feedback@quepublishing.com

Mail: Jeff Riley
Executive Editor
Que Publishing
800 East 96th Street
Indianapolis, IN 46240 USA

For more information about this book or another Que Certification title, visit our website at www.examcram.com. Type the ISBN (excluding hyphens) or the title of a book in the Search field to find the page you're looking for.

Introduction

Welcome to *CCNA Exam Cram!* Whether this is your first or your fifteenth *Exam Cram* series book, you'll find information here that will help ensure your success as you pursue knowledge, experience, and certification. This introduction explains Cisco's certification programs in general and talks about how the *Exam Cram* series can help you prepare for Cisco's CCNA Exams, whether you choose the dual- or single-exam path. The materials in this book have been prepared with a very clear focus on testable concepts, configurations, and skills. As much extraneous material as possible, beyond what is needed for background comprehension, has been eliminated so that the book is a distillation of the necessary knowledge to take—and pass—the Cisco CCNA exam(s). The two sample tests with answer keys (Chapters 13–16) at the end of the book should give you a reasonably accurate assessment of your knowledge. We have also included challenge labs to give you the critical hands-on practice you will need to master the simulator questions on the CCNA exam(s). Read the book, understand the material, practice the labs, and you'll stand a very good chance of passing the test.

Exam Cram books help you understand and appreciate the subjects and materials you need to pass Cisco certification exams. *Exam Cram 2* books are aimed strictly at test preparation and review. They do not teach you everything you need to know about a topic. Instead, we present and dissect the topics and key points we've found that you're likely to encounter on a test. We've worked to bring together as much accurate information as possible about the latest CCNA exams.

Nevertheless, to completely prepare yourself for any Cisco test, we recommend that you begin by taking the Self-Assessment that is included in this book, immediately following this introduction. The Self-Assessment tool will help you evaluate your knowledge base against the requirements for a CCNA under both ideal and real circumstances.

Based on what you learn from the Self-Assessment, you might decide to begin your studies with some classroom training, some practice with the Cisco IOS, or some background reading. On the other hand, you might decide to pick up and read one of the many study guides available from Cisco or third-party vendors on certain topics, including the *CCNA Exam Prep* from Que Publishing. We also recommend that you supplement your study program with visits to www.examcram2.com to receive additional practice questions, get advice, and track the CCNA program.

We also strongly recommend that you practice configuring the Cisco devices that you'll be tested on because nothing beats hands-on experience and familiarity when it comes to understanding the questions you're likely to encounter on a certification test. Book learning is essential, but without a doubt, hands-on experience is the best teacher of all! This book includes a CD with a router and switch simulator and lab challenges that you can use to practice your skills.

Taking a Certification Exam

After you've prepared for your exam, you need to register with a testing center. The CCNA exam can be taken in either one or two steps: The single-exam option is the 640-801 exam, and costs $125. The two-exam option requires you to take both the 640-821 INTRO and 640-811 ICND exams, at a cost of $100 each. In the United States and Canada, tests are administered by Prometric and by VUE. Here's how you can contact them:

- **Prometric**—You can sign up for a test through the company's website, at www.prometric.com. Within the United States and Canada, you can register by phone at 800-755-3926. If you live outside this region, you should check the Prometric website for the appropriate phone number.
- **VUE**—You can sign up for a test or get the phone numbers for local testing centers through the Web at www.vue.com/ms.

To sign up for a test, you must possess a valid credit card or contact either Prometric or VUE for mailing instructions to send a check (in the United States). Only when payment is verified or your check has cleared can you actually register for the test.

To schedule an exam, you need to call the number or visit either of the web pages at least one day in advance. To cancel or reschedule an exam, you must call before 7 p.m. Pacific standard time the day before the scheduled test time (or you might be charged, even if you don't show up to take the test). When you want to schedule a test, you should have the following information ready:

- Your name, organization, and mailing address
- Your Cisco test ID
- The name and number of the exam you want to take
- A method of payment (As mentioned previously, a credit card is the most convenient method, but alternative means can be arranged in advance, if necessary.)

After you sign up for a test, you are told when and where the test is scheduled. You should try to arrive at least 15 minutes early. You must supply two forms of identification—one of which must be a photo ID—and sign a nondisclosure agreement to be admitted into the testing room.

All Cisco exams are completely closed book. In fact, you are not permitted to take anything with you into the testing area, but you are given a blank sheet of paper and a pen (or in some cases, an erasable plastic sheet and an erasable pen). We suggest that you immediately write down on that sheet of paper all the information you've memorized for the test. In *Exam Cram 2* books, this information appears on a tear-out sheet inside the front cover of each book. You are given some time to compose yourself, record this information, and take a sample orientation exam before you begin the real thing. We suggest that you take the orientation test before taking your first exam, but because all the certification exams are more or less identical in layout, behavior, and controls, you probably don't need to do this more than once.

When you complete a Cisco certification exam, the software tells you immediately whether you've passed or failed. If you need to retake an exam, you have to schedule a new test with Prometric or VUE and pay another $100 or $125.

If you fail a Cisco test, you must wait five full days before you can take it again. For example, if you failed on Tuesday, you would have to wait until Monday to take it again.

Tracking Your Certification Status

As soon as you pass the Cisco CCNA single exam, or both the INTRO and ICND CCNA test, you are a CCNA. Cisco generates transcripts that indicate which exams you have passed. You can view a copy of your transcript at any time by going to the Cisco website and going to the certifications tracking tool. This tool enables you to print a copy of your current transcript and confirm your certification status.

After you pass the necessary set of exams, you are certified. Official certification is normally granted after three to six weeks, so you shouldn't expect to get your credentials overnight. The package for official certification that arrives includes

- A certificate that is suitable for framing, along with a wallet card.
- A license to use the applicable logo, which means that you can use the logo in advertisements, promotions, and documents, as well as on letterhead, business cards, and so on. Along with the license comes information on how to legally and appropriately use the logos.

Many people believe that the benefits of Cisco certification are among the most powerful in the industry. We're starting to see more job listings that request or require applicants to have CCNA, CCDA, CCNP, and other certifications, and many individuals who complete Cisco certification programs can qualify for increases in pay and/or responsibility. As an official recognition of hard work and broad knowledge, one of the Cisco credentials is a badge of honor in many IT organizations.

How to Prepare for an Exam

Preparing for the CCNA test requires that you obtain and study materials designed to provide comprehensive information about the product and its capabilities that will appear on the specific exam for which you are preparing. The following list of materials can help you study and prepare:

- The official Cisco study guides by Cisco Press.
- Practicing with real equipment or simulators.
- The CCNA Prep Center on Cisco's website, which features articles, sample questions, games and discussions to focus and clarify your studies.
- The exam-preparation advice, practice tests, questions of the day, and discussion groups on the www.examcram.com e-learning and certification destination website.
- **The *Exam Cram* for CCNA**—This book gives you information about the material you need to know to pass the tests. Seriously, this is a great book.
- The *CCNA Exam Prep* book, also from Que publishing, goes into more detail on topics that are summarized in the Exam Cram.

  Together, these two books make a perfect pair.

- **Classroom training**—Cisco training partners and third-party training companies (such The Training Camp) offer classroom training for CCNA. These companies aim to help you prepare to pass the CCNA exam. Although such training can be expensive, most of the individuals lucky enough to partake find this training to be very worthwhile.
- **Other publications**—There's no shortage of materials available about CCNA. The "Need to Know More?" resource sections at the end of each chapter in this book give you an idea of where we think you should look for further discussion.

This set of required and recommended materials represents a good collection of sources and resources about the CCNA exam and related topics. We hope that you'll find that this book belongs in this company.

What This Book Will Not Do

This book will *not* teach you everything you need to know about networking with Cisco devices, or even about a given topic. Nor is this book an introduction to computer technology. If you're new to networking and looking for an initial preparation guide, check out www.quepublishing.com, where you will find a whole section dedicated to Cisco certifications and networking in general. This book will review what you need to know before you take the test, with the fundamental purpose dedicated to reviewing the information needed on the Cisco CCNA exam(s).

This book uses a variety of teaching and memorization techniques to analyze the exam-related topics and to provide you with ways to input, index, and retrieve everything you'll need to know in order to pass the test. Once again, it is *not* a comprehensive treatise on Cisco networking.

What This Book Is Designed To Do

This book is designed to be read as a pointer to the areas of knowledge you will be tested on. In other words, you might want to read the book one time, just to get an insight into how comprehensive your knowledge of networking with Cisco is. The book is also designed to be read shortly before you go for the actual test and to give you a distillation of the entire field of CCNA knowledge in as few pages as possible. We think you can use this book to get a sense of the underlying context of any topic in the chapters—or to skim read for Exam Alerts, bulleted points, summaries, and topic headings.

We've drawn on material from Cisco's own listing of knowledge requirements, from other preparation guides, and from the exams themselves.

We've also drawn from a battery of third-party test-preparation tools and technical websites, as well as from our own experience with Cisco equipment and the exam. Our aim is to walk you through the knowledge you will need—looking over your shoulder, so to speak—and point out those things that are important for the exam (Exam Alerts, practice questions, and so on).

The CCNA exam(s) make a basic assumption that you already have a strong background of experience with the general networking and its terminology. On the other hand, because the CCNA is an introductory-level test, we've tried to demystify the jargon, acronyms, terms, and concepts.

About This Book

If you're preparing for the CCNA exam for the first time, we've structured the topics in this book to build upon one another. Therefore, the topics covered in later chapters might refer to previous discussions in earlier chapters.

We suggest that you read this book from front to back. You won't be wasting your time because nothing we've written is a guess about an unknown exam. We've had to explain certain underlying information on such a regular basis those explanations are included here.

After you've read the book, you can brush up on a certain area by using the Index or the Table of Contents to go straight to the topics and questions you want to reexamine. We've tried to use the headings and subheadings to provide outline information about each given topic. After you've been certified, we think you'll find this book useful as a tightly focused reference and an essential foundation of CCNA knowledge.

Chapter Formats

Each *Exam Cram* chapter follows a regular structure, along with graphical cues about especially important or useful material. The structure of a typical chapter is as follows:

- **Opening hotlists**—Each chapter begins with lists of the terms you'll need to understand and the concepts you'll need to master before you can be fully conversant with the chapter's subject matter. We follow the hotlists with a few introductory paragraphs, setting the stage for the rest of the chapter.

- **Topical coverage**—After the opening hotlists, each chapter covers the topics related to the chapter's subject.

- **Alerts**—Throughout the topical coverage section, we highlight material most likely to appear on the exam by using a special Exam Alert layout that looks like this:

This is what an Exam Alert looks like. An Exam Alert stresses concepts, terms, software, or activities that will most likely appear in one or more certification exam questions. For that reason, we think any information found offset in Exam Alert format is worthy of unusual attentiveness on your part.

Even if material isn't flagged as an Exam Alert, *all* the content in this book is associated in some way with test-related material. What appears in the chapter content is critical knowledge.

- **Notes**—This book is an overall examination of basic Cisco networking. As such, we'll dip into many aspects of .NET application development. Where a body of knowledge is deeper than the scope of the book, we use notes to indicate areas of concern or specialty training, or refer you to other resources.

Cramming for an exam will get you through a test, but it won't make you a competent IT professional. Although you can memorize just the facts you need in order to become certified, your daily work in the field will rapidly put you in water over your head if you don't know the underlying principles of networking with Cisco gear.

- **Tips**—We provide tips that will help you to build a better foundation of knowledge or to focus your attention on an important concept that will reappear later in the book. Tips provide a helpful way to remind you of the context surrounding a particular area of a topic under discussion.

- **Practice questions**—This section presents a short list of test questions related to the specific chapter topic. Each question has a following explanation of both correct and incorrect answers. The practice questions highlight the areas we found to be most important on the exam.

- **Need To Know More?**—Every chapter ends with a section titled "Need To Know More?" This section provides pointers to resources that we found to be helpful in offering further details on the chapter's subject matter. If you find a resource you like in this collection, use it, but don't feel compelled to use all these resources. We use this section to recommend resources that we have used on a regular basis, so none of the recommendations will be a waste of your time or money. These resources might go out of print or be taken down (in the case of websites), so we've tried to reference widely accepted resources.

The bulk of the book follows this chapter structure, but there are a few other elements that we would like to point out:

- **Sample tests**—The sample tests, which appear in Chapters 13 and 15 (with answer keys in Chapters 14 and 16), are very close approximations of the types of questions you are likely to see on the current CCNA exam(s).
- **Answer keys**—These provide the answers to the sample tests, complete with explanations of both the correct responses and the incorrect responses.
- **Glossary**—This is an extensive glossary of important terms used in this book.
- **The Cram Sheet**—This appears as a tearaway sheet, inside the front cover of this *Exam Cram* book. It is a valuable tool that represents a collection of the most difficult-to-remember facts and numbers we think you should memorize before taking the test. Remember, you can dump this information out of your head onto a piece of paper as soon as you enter the testing room. These are usually facts that we've found require brute-force memorization. You only need to remember this information long enough to write it down when you walk into the test room. Be advised that you will be asked to surrender all personal belongings before you enter the exam room itself.

  You might want to look at the Cram Sheet in your car or in the lobby of the testing center just before you walk into the testing center. The Cram Sheet is divided under headings, so you can review the appropriate parts just before each test.
- **The CD**—The CD features an innovative practice test engine powered by MeasureUp, including a full practice exam and two router simulations, giving you the opportunity to assess your readiness for the exam. Cisco simulations validate a person's hands-on skills in addition to knowledge. MeasureUp's Cisco simulations model real-life networking scenarios by requiring the user to perform tasks on simulated Cisco networking devices, measuring troubleshooting and problem-solving skills to address realistic networking problems.

Contacting the Authors

We've tried to create a real-world tool that you can use to prepare for and pass the CCNA certification exams. We're interested in any feedback you would care to share about the book, especially if you have ideas about how we can improve it for future test takers. We'll consider everything you say carefully and will respond to all reasonable suggestions and comments. You can reach us via email at mvalentine@trainingcamp.com and awhitaker@trainingcamp.com.

Let us know if you found this book to be helpful in your preparation efforts. We'd also like to know how you felt about your chances of passing the exam *before* you read the book and then *after* you read the book. Of course, we'd love to hear that you passed the exam—and even if you just want to share your triumph, we'd be happy to hear from you.

Thanks for choosing us as your personal trainers, and enjoy the book. We would wish you luck on the exam, but we know that if you read through all the chapters and work with the product, you won't need luck—you'll pass the test on the strength of real knowledge!

Self-Assessment

This section helps you to determine your readiness for the Cisco Certified Network Associate certification exam. You will be invited to assess your own skills, motivations, education, and experience and see how you compare against the thousands of CCNA candidates we have met.

You can also pre-assess your CCNA readiness by using the accompanying MeasureUp CD in Study Mode.

CCNA in the Real World

The Cisco Certified Network Associate remains one of the most popular certifications in the IT industry. Although Cisco does not publish certification statistics for CCNA, it is safe to say that thousands of new CCNAs are minted each year from all over the world. In the face of a backlash against so-called "paper-only" certification holders, Cisco has worked hard to maintain the credibility of its certifications by making them difficult to achieve, as well as ensuring that the exams test not only their own products and services, but also general networking knowledge. In the last couple of years, Cisco has added router and switch simulators to computer-based tests to test the applied knowledge of candidates, and we can expect this trend to continue. A Cisco certification is still the gold standard for networking professionals.

A candidate who has passed the CCNA has demonstrated three significant capabilities:

- **A mastery of technical knowledge.** With an elevated level of retention and accuracy. The CCNA exam has a pass mark of 849 out of 1,000. Very little room for technical error exists. Successful candidates know their stuff.
- **A demonstrated ability to apply the technical knowledge.** The addition of simulator questions has greatly reduced the possibility that a

candidate can simply memorize all the information and pass the exam. A CCNA is supposed to be able to apply basic router and switch configurations; the simulator questions help prove that the candidate can do so.

- **The ability to perform under pressure.** The CCNA exam(s) require that you proceed at a fairly rapid pace, spending about one minute per question on average. Many candidates find that they have little time left when they finish, and indeed many run out of time altogether—and some fail as a result. Add to this the stress of simply being in an exam environment, the potential of having an employer's performance expectations, personal expectations, and possibly financial or career implications pressuring you as well, and the exam turns into a pressure cooker. All of this is intimidating, and unfortunate for the unprepared. Too bad.

Imagine yourself as an employer looking for a junior networking professional. You want someone who knows their stuff, who can reliably do the actual work of setting up and configuring equipment, and who can do all that under the pressures of time, screaming bosses and customers, and critical deadlines. Enter the successful CCNA candidate.

The Ideal CCNA Candidate

Other than a photographic memory, typing speed that would make Mavis Beacon jealous, and nerves of steel, what makes for the "ideal" CCNA candidate? A combination of skills and experience is the short answer. The successful candidates we have seen—and we have seen thousands from classes that we have taught—had a good mix of the following traits:

Motivation. Why are you taking the CCNA? Here are some of the most common answers to this question that we have seen:

- Because I want to further my career and get a promotion.
- To expand my knowledge; I'm interested in it.
- My job is changing, and the company needs me to get the certification.
- I am unemployed and/or starting a new career.
- The company needs more Cisco-certified people to gain a certain partner status as a reseller.
- We're just burning the training budget for this year.
- I've heard that the computer industry is a good field and that a CCNA guarantees you $85,000 a year.

So what motivates you? Who is paying for the training and exams? What are the implications if you fail? Successful candidates are highly motivated. If you don't care, your chances of passing drop tremendously.

An interest in learning and an ability to learn. Passing a CCNA exam requires taking on board a great deal of new information, much of it obscure and without a referential pattern to make it easier to recall. Candidates who have acquired the skills to do this—and rest assured, these are skills that can be learned—will do better than those who have trouble retaining information. Candidates who simply enjoy learning will find it easier and will do better as a result.

If you have trouble retaining and recalling information quickly and accurately, you will find CCNA certification a difficult thing to achieve. This book is not aimed at teaching you these skills; other books are. In the absence of the ability to learn and retain quickly, patience and persistence are a good substitute. If it takes you a year to pass, you have still passed.

A decent background in IP networking. "Decent" is intentionally vague. We have seen candidates with little experience succeed and candidates with extensive experience fail. Experience is not a guarantee, but it absolutely helps. Many CCNA questions test the basics of networking; many others assume that you know the basics and incorporate the requirement of that knowledge into a more advanced question—the old "question-within-a-question" trick. As a guideline, if you have been involved with business-class networks for about a year, you will probably have absorbed enough knowledge to give you an advantage when it comes to the basics. After a certain point, experience can be a weakness: In the immortal words of Han Solo, "Don't get cocky." If you think that CCNA will be easy because you have 10 years of experience, you are more than likely in for a rude awakening.

Put Yourself to the Test

Now is the time to take a close look at your education, experience, motivation, and abilities. It's worth being honest with yourself; being aware of your weaknesses is as important as being aware of your strengths. Maybe you know someone who can help you with an objective assessment—a friend, a teacher, or an HR person perhaps. Above all, realize that the following questions and comments simply summarize our experience with CCNA candidates. That experience is pretty solid; we have taught CCNA to more than a thousand people. By the same token, though, there is no magic formula; every person is a different story. Your best plan is to be as prepared as you can be in all respects. Now, time to look inward…

Educational Background

While in theory anyone can attempt the CCNA exam, in reality some are better prepared than others. Educational background forms a big part of this preparation. These questions will help to identify education and training that will be of benefit:

1. Have you ever taken any computer science courses at a college level?

   Most college-level IT courses include an element of networking theory. Also, if you are taking this kind of course, you are probably already interested in this topic and will find it easier to master the basics and pick up the advanced stuff. If you have never taken an IT course at this level, you have a steeper learning curve and might be at a disadvantage.

2. Did you attend college and major in a computer-related field?

   If so, you should have most of the basics covered—unless you studied programming; in which case, you might not have covered much in the way of networking. Some colleges actually offer the CCNA as part of the curriculum. Doing a college major in IT is not a prerequisite by any means, but it might be helpful.

3. Have you ever held an IT certification?

   If you have been certified before, you have some idea of what is coming in terms of the depth of knowledge required and the examination process; it also implies at least some involvement in computers and networking.

4. Which certification(s) have you held?

   A previous CCNA will definitely be an asset—but not a guarantee. The CCNA has changed dramatically in the past three years. Previous certification in general networking (perhaps a Net+), or an MCSE, will cover the basics, but not the Cisco-specific information. On the flip side, a certification in Visual Basic or Oracle might not be very helpful for CCNA.

5. Do you currently hold any IT certifications?

   Current information is more relevant—especially in the IT world. Some certifications are more relevant than others, of course, as noted previously.

6. Which certification(s) do you currently hold?

   You might hold other Cisco specialization certs, or current certs from Microsoft, CompTia, or Novell. Again, anything that has tested your networking knowledge will be an asset.

7. Have you ever taken any IT training courses in networking?

   Many people take training courses but do not certify. Any exposure and knowledge gained from these courses will be useful.

8. How much self-study have you done?

   Although it is difficult to do pure self-study and pass the new CCNA, the more you study, the better the chances are that you will retain information. In our experience, it is always more productive to get some training—whether online, with a mentor/tutor, or from a training company—but a significant amount of self-study is always required regardless. The fact that you are holding this book is a very good sign. Read all of it!

9. How long have you been studying for your CCNA?

   This is a tricky equation. The longer you study, the more you are likely to know—but the more you are likely to forget, as well.

10. Is there a formal or informal training plan for you at your workplace?

    Work experience is a great way to gain the knowledge and skills you need for the exam. A training plan can be a good motivator because you might have someone coaching and encouraging you and also because there may be a reward—perhaps a promotion or raise—for completing the program.

Hands-on Experience

It is the rare individual who really understands networks but has never built, broken, and then rebuilt one. For the CCNA exam, a certain amount of hands-on experience is a must. The new simulator questions require you to actually type in router configurations. Ask yourself

1. Does your job allow you to work with Cisco routers and switches on a regular basis?
2. Is there a lab where you can practice? Perhaps at home with borrowed or purchased gear?
3. How long have you been working with Cisco equipment?

At a minimum, you should get a simulator that includes lab exercises for you to practice key skills. If you have access to a lab and equipment you can play with, as you become more advanced, you can build more complicated and realistic test networks.

The major skill areas you need hands-on experience in are

- Basic configuration: IP addresses, passwords
- Dynamic routing protocol configuration
- NAT/PAT (network/port address translation)
- Switching, VLANs, VLAN Trunking Protocol, Trunking
- IP Access Lists

As you think about those areas, picture yourself in front of a Cisco router and assess your level of confidence in being able to quickly and correctly configure it. You should feel no intimidation or uncertainty in being able to tackle these kinds of configurations.

Testing Your Exam Readiness

The CCNA exam will demand a high degree of technical accuracy, applied skill, and the ability to perform under pressure. You can give yourself experience in this environment by practicing on an exam simulator until you are comfortable. You must become technically accurate to about 90–95%, have no difficulty with the simulator tasks, and be able to complete the exam in the appropriate time frame. This can be achieved by repetition, but be careful that you do not simply memorize all the questions in the test pool!

Assessing Your Readiness for the CCNA Exam

There are three "pillars" of success on the CCNA exam: technical excellence, applied skills, and the ability to perform under pressure. Technical excellence is achieved with study, training, and self-testing. Applied skills are learned through practice labs and exams, work experience, and hands-on training and experience. The ability to perform under pressure is gained from situational training such as exam simulators and challenge labs, perhaps with a trainer or mentor. The goal is to increase your confidence level such that you feel as if you *own* the material and want to be challenged to a duel by the exam.

With a combination of educational and work experience, CCNA-specific training, self-study and hands-on practice, you will put yourself in the best position to approach the exam with a high degree of confidence—and pass. Good luck; study hard.

You can also pre-assess your CCNA readiness by using the accompanying MeasureUp CD in Study Mode.

Networking Fundamentals

Terms You'll Need to Understand:

- ✓ Network
- ✓ LAN
- ✓ WAN
- ✓ Mesh
- ✓ Point-to-Point topology
- ✓ Star topology
- ✓ Ring topology
- ✓ Bus topology

Techniques You'll Need to Master:

- ✓ Identifying network technologies
- ✓ Understanding Ethernet

Introduction

A qualified CCNA is expected to have a broad understanding of many different network technologies and a more detailed knowledge of a few specific ones. This chapter introduces the basics of networking and points out some of the concepts that are tested on the CCNA exam(s).

Components and Terms

A *network* is a set of devices, software, and cables that enables the exchange of information between them. *Host devices* are computers, servers, laptops, Personal Digital Assistants (PDAs), or anything a person uses to access the network. *Network devices* are hubs, repeaters, bridges, switches, routers, and firewalls (to name a few). Cables can be copper, fiber-optic, or even wireless radio (which isn't really a cable, but serves the same purpose). The applications used on a network include those that actually enable network connectivity, such as the Transmission Control Protocol/Internet Protocol (TCP/IP) protocol, those that test network links, such as the Internet Control Message Protocol (ICMP), and end-user applications, such as email and File Transfer Protocol (FTP). There are thousands of networkable applications; we are concerned with a small number of them.

Topologies

A topology describes the layout of a network. There are several topologies that you need to know for the exam. These are

- *Point-to-Point*—A point-to-point topology involves two hosts or devices that are directly connected to each other and to nothing else; anything sent by one can only be received by the other. Serial communication is usually point-to-point, but not always.

- *Star*—A star topology is one in which one host or device has multiple connections to other hosts; this is sometimes called hub-and-spoke as well. In a star topology, if a host wants to send to another host, it must send traffic through the hub or central device. Ethernet, if using a hub or a switch and Twisted Pair cabling, is star-wired.

- *Ring*—A ring topology is created when one device is connected to the next one sequentially, with the last device being connected to the first. The actual devices don't necessarily form a circle, but the data moves in a logical circle. FDDI and Token Ring are examples of ring topologies.

- *Bus*—A bus topology uses a single coaxial cable, to which hosts are attached at intervals. The term bus comes from an electrical bus, which is a point from which electrical power can be drawn for multiple connections. Ethernet that uses coaxial cable creates a bus topology.
- *Mesh*—A *full mesh* is a topology with multiple point-to-point connections that connect each location to the others. The advantage is that you can send data directly from any location to any other location instead of having to send it through a central point. There are more options for sending if one of the connections fails. The disadvantages are that it is expensive and complex to implement a full mesh. You can compromise and build a *partial mesh*, which is when only some locations are connected to the other locations.

LAN Technologies

LAN stands for local area network. LANs are short-range, high-speed networks typically found in schools, offices, and, more recently, homes. Over the years, there have been many different types of LANs. Currently, Ethernet is king, and other than wireless technologies, it is the only LAN technology you need to know for the CCNA exam.

Ethernet

Ethernet is the most common LAN technology in use today. Ethernet is a family of implementations, which have evolved into faster and more reliable solutions all based on a common technology.

Ethernet was pioneered by Digital Equipment Corporation, Intel, and Xerox and first published in 1980. The IEEE modified it and gave it the specification 802.3. The way Ethernet works is closely linked to its original connection type: A coaxial cable was used to join all the hosts together. This formed a *segment*. On a single segment, only one host could use the cable at a time; because the wire was coaxial, with one positive conductor and one negative conductor, it created a single electrical circuit. This single circuit could be energized by only one host at a time, or a conflict would result as two hosts tried to talk at once and nothing got through. Much the same thing happens when you and a friend try to send at the same time using walkie-talkies; all that is heard is noise. This conflict is called a *collision*.

CSMA/CD (Carrier Sense Multiple Access with Collision Detection) is the method Ethernet uses to deal with collisions. When a host wants to transmit, it first listens to the wire to see if anyone else is transmitting at that moment.

If it is clear, it can transmit; if not, it will wait for the host that is transmitting to stop. Sometimes, two hosts decide at the same instant that the wire is clear, and collide with each other. When this happens, the hosts that were involved with the collision send a special *jam signal* that advises everyone on that segment of the collision. Then all the hosts wait for a random period of time before they check the wire and try transmitting again. This wait time is tiny—a few millionths of a second—and is determined by the Backoff Algorithm. (The Backoff Algorithm is the mathematical equation a host runs to come up with the random number.) The theory is that if each host waits a different amount of time, the wire should be clear for all of them when they decide to transmit again.

Any Ethernet segment that uses coaxial cable (10-BASE 2, 10-BASE 5) or a hub with twisted-pair cabling is a collision environment.

When a collision occurs

1. A Jam Signal is sent.
2. All hosts briefly stop transmitting.
3. All hosts run the Backoff Algorithm, which decides the random time they will wait before attempting to transmit again.

Collisions have the effect of clogging up a network because they prevent data from being sent. The more hosts you have sharing a wire, and the more data they have to send, the worse it gets. A group of devices that are affected by one another's collisions is called a *collision domain*. As networks grew, it became necessary to break up collision domains so that there were fewer collisions in each one. Devices called *bridges* and *switches* did this; these devices are covered in Chapter 6, "Catalyst Switch Operations and Configuration."

It is possible to eliminate collisions altogether if we can provide separate send and receive circuits; this is more like a telephone (which allows us to speak and hear at the same time) than a walkie-talkie. This requires four conductors—two for each circuit. The use of twisted-pair cabling (not coax), which has at least four conductors (and more likely eight) allows us to create a Full Duplex connection, with simultaneous send and receive circuits. Full Duplex connections eliminate collisions because the host can now send and receive simultaneously.

Modern Ethernet is fast, reliable, and collision free if you set it up right. Speeds of up to 10 gigabits per second are possible with the correct cabling.

Table 1.1 summarizes some of the different Ethernet specifications, characteristics, and cable types. This is not all of them, just an idea of how far Ethernet has come.

Table 1.1 Comparing Ethernet Implementations

IEEE	Cabling	Topology	Speed/Duplex/Media	Maximum Range
802.3	10-BASE 5	Bus	10Mbs Half Duplex Thicknet	500m
802.3	10-BASE 2	Bus	10Mbs Half Duplex Thinnet	185m
802.3	10/100-BASE T	Star	10/100Mbs Half-duplex UTP	100m
802.3u	100-BASE T	Star	100Mbs Half/Full Duplex UTP	100m
802.3u	100-BASE FX	Star	100Mbs Full Duplex Multimode Fiber Optic	400m
802.3ab	1000-BASE T	Star	1000Mbs Full Duplex UTP	100m
802.3z	1000-BASE ZX	Star	1000Mbs Full Duplex Single-Mode Fiber Optic	100km

You should be familiar with the contents of Table 1.1.

WAN Technologies

A wide area network (WAN) serves to interconnect two or more LANs. WAN technology is designed to extend network connectivity to much greater distances than any LAN technology is capable of. Most companies can't afford to build their own WAN, so it is usual to buy WAN service from a service provider. Service providers are in the business of building and selling WAN connectivity; they invest in the equipment, cabling, and training to build transcontinental networks for other businesses to rent. For the CCNA exam, you need to be familiar with four types of WAN connections and the protocols associated with them. WAN connectivity and configuration is covered in detail in Chapter 10, "WAN Introduction." The four WAN connection types are outlined in the following sections.

Dedicated Leased Line Connections

A leased line refers to a connection that is installed and provisioned for the exclusive use of the customer. Essentially, when you order a leased line, you get your very own piece of wire from your location to the service provider's network. This is good because no other customer can affect your line, as can be the case with other WAN services. You have a lot of control over this circuit to do things such as Quality of Service and other traffic management. The downside is that a leased line is expensive and gets a lot more expensive if you need to connect offices that are far apart.

A leased line is typically a point-to-point connection from the head office to a branch office, so if you need to connect to multiple locations, you need multiple leased lines. Multiple leased lines get even more expensive. Leased line circuits typically run the Point-to-Point Protocol (PPP), High-Level Data-Link Control Protocol (HDLC), or possibly Serial Line Internet Protocol (SLIP). (These protocols are covered in detail in Chapter 10.)

Circuit-Switched Connections

A circuit-switched WAN uses the phone company as the service provider, either with analog dialup or digital ISDN connections. With circuit-switching, if you need to connect to the remote LAN, a call is dialed and a circuit is established; the data is sent across the circuit, and the circuit is taken down when it is no longer needed. Circuit-switched WANs usually use PPP, HDLC, or SLIP, and they tend to be really slow—anywhere from 19.2K for analog dialup to 128K for ISDN using a Basic Rate Interface (BRI). They can also get expensive, as most contracts specify a pay-per-usage billing.

Packet-Switched Connections

Packet-switched WAN services allow you to connect to the provider's network in much the same way as a PC connects to a hub: Once connected, your traffic is affected by other customers' and theirs by you. This can be an issue sometimes, but it can be managed. The advantage of this shared-bandwidth technology is that with a single physical connection from your router's serial port (typically), you can establish virtual connections to many other locations around the world. So if you have a lot of branch offices and they are far away from the head office, a packet-switched solution is a good idea. Packet-switched circuits usually use Frame Relay or possibly X.25.

Cell-Switched Connections

Cell switching is similar to packet switching; the difference is that with packet-switched networks, the size of the units of data being sent (called *frames*) is variable. Cell-switched units (cells) are of a constant size. This makes dealing with heavy traffic loads easier and more efficient. Cell-switched solutions such as ATM (Asynchronous Transfer Mode) tend to be big, fast, and robust.

Wireless Networks

There has been a boom recently in the deployment of wireless networks for both LAN and WAN applications. The IEEE 802.11 Wireless Fidelity standard, affectionately know as WiFi, specifies a growing set of standards for short-range, high-speed wireless systems that are good for everything from mobile device connectivity to home media center systems. The advantage is of course the elimination of cables and the freedom of movement; the disadvantages are in range, reliability, and security. Wireless is a good WAN choice for moderate distances (less than 10 miles, for example) with line-of-sight between them—for example, between buildings in a campus. Special antennas are used to make the wireless signal directional and increase the range, often to more than 20 kilometers.

Any of the previous points regarding wireless LANs might appear on the CCNA exam, but at the time of this writing, it is still a very new topic and not heavily tested.

Other Network Technologies

The CCNA exam is chiefly concerned with the previous LAN/WAN systems, but it is interesting to note some of the other directions that networks are headed as well. Following are other types of networks:

- A **MAN**, or metropolitan area network, uses fiber-optic connections to dramatically extend the reach of high-speed LAN technologies. This service is typically only found in urban business centers where large corporations need high bandwidth, hence the metro name.
- A **SAN** is a storage area network. This is a very high-speed, medium-range system that allows a server (or cluster of servers) to access an

external disk storage array as if it were a locally connected hard drive. This opens up huge possibilities for fault-tolerant and centrally-managed data systems, but it's expensive.

- **Content Networks** are developed in response to the huge amount—as well as the kind—of information available on the Internet. Content networks deal with making access to the information faster, as well as logging and controlling access to certain kinds of material.

Sadly, these specialized network types are beyond the scope of CCNA.

Exam Prep Questions

1. Your boss asks you to explain what happens when a collision occurs on an Ethernet segment. Which of the following are accurate? Choose 3.
   - ❑ A. Every device stops transmitting for a short time.
   - ❑ B. When it is safe to transmit again, the devices that collided get priority access to the wire.
   - ❑ C. The collision starts a random backoff algorithm.
   - ❑ D. A jam signal is sent to alert all devices of the collision.
   - ❑ E. Only the devices involved in the collision stop transmitting briefly to clear the wire.
2. How is equal access to the wire managed in a collision-oriented environment such as Ethernet?
   - ❍ A. The hosts are given equal access based on the circulation of a token; hosts can only transmit when they hold the token.
   - ❍ B. Hosts are given prioritized access to the wire based on their MAC address.
   - ❍ C. Hosts are given equal access to the wire by being allowed to transmit at specified time intervals.
   - ❍ D. Hosts signal their desire to transmit by sending a contention alert.
   - ❍ E. Hosts check the wire for activity before attempting to send; if a collision happens, they wait a random time period before attempting to send again.
3. Which of the following are commonly used WAN protocols? Choose 3.
   - ❑ A. WEP
   - ❑ B. WING
   - ❑ C. Frame Relay
   - ❑ D. HDLC
   - ❑ E. AAA
   - ❑ F. PPP
4. Which of the following are IEEE specifications for Gigabit Ethernet? Choose 2.
   - ❑ A. 802.1d
   - ❑ B. 802.11
   - ❑ C. 802.3z
   - ❑ D. 802.1q
   - ❑ E. 802.3ab

5. Which technology is cell-switched?
   - ❍ A. Token Ring
   - ❍ B. FDDI
   - ❍ C. Ethernet
   - ❍ D. Frame Relay
   - ❍ E. ATM
   - ❍ F. PPP
6. Which devices were designed to segment collision domains? Choose 2.
   - ❑ A. Hubs
   - ❑ B. Repeaters
   - ❑ C. MAU
   - ❑ D. Bridge
   - ❑ E. Switch
7. You have just acquired some new office space in a building across the street from your current space, about 350 meters away. You want to arrange for high-speed (10Mbs) network connectivity between them; which of the following choices is a valid connection option?
   - ❍ A. Analog dialup
   - ❍ B. ISDN BRI
   - ❍ C. Ethernet using 100-BASE TX cabling
   - ❍ D. 802.11 Wireless using specialized antennas
8. Which WAN technology is the best choice if you have many remote offices that are in different states, you need always-on connectivity, and you don't have money to burn?
   - ❍ A. Circuit-Switched
   - ❍ B. Leased Line
   - ❍ C. Packet Switched
   - ❍ D. Wireless

Answers to Exam Prep Questions

1. Answers A, C, and D are the correct answers. B is incorrect because there is no method to prioritize access to the wire in Ethernet. Answer E is incorrect because all devices stop transmitting in the event of a collision.

2. Answer is E the correct answer. CSMA/CD is the technology that enables hosts to send if the wire is available and to wait a random time to try again if a collision happens. Answer A is incorrect because it describes Token Ring, not Ethernet. Answers B, C, and D are incorrect because they are fictitious.

3. Answers C, D, and F are correct. The big three WAN protocols are PPP, Frame Relay, and HDLC. There are others, but CCNA does not cover them. Answer A is incorrect because WEP is Wired Equivalent Privacy, a security scheme for wireless networks. Answer B is incorrect because it is fictional. Answer E is incorrect because AAA stands for Authentication, Authorization, and Accounting, a scheme to manage access and activities on networked devices.

4. Answers C and E are correct. 802.3z specifies 1Gb on fiber, and 802.3ab specifies 1Gb on copper. Answers A, B, and D are incorrect; those are the specs for STP, WiFi, and Inter-switch VLAN tagging, respectively.

5. Answer E is correct. ATM is a cell-switched technology. Answers A, B, C, D, and F are incorrect because they use variable-sized frames, not cells.

6. Answers D and E are correct. Bridges and switches segment collision domains. Answers A and B are incorrect because hubs and repeaters have the opposite effect: They make collision domains bigger and more of a problem.

7. Answer D is correct. 802.11 Wireless using specialized antennas is a good choice for this application. Answers A and B are incorrect because analog and ISDN BRI do not provide the required bandwidth. Answer C is incorrect because 100-BASE TX is copper cabling, which has a maximum range of 100 meters. (You might be able to go with Ethernet over fiber-optic cabling, but it is expensive—and it is not one of the offered choices here anyway.)

8. Answer C is the correct answer. Packet-switched networks are a good choice in this context. Answer A is incorrect; circuit-switched connections are a poor choice because they are not usually always on, and they get expensive the longer they are connected. Answer B is incorrect because leased lines have always-on connectivity, but at a prohibitive cost. Answer D is incorrect; wireless does not have the range to cover interstate distances.

Network Models

Terms You'll Need to Understand

- ✓ Access
- ✓ Distribution
- ✓ Core layer
- ✓ Application layer
- ✓ Presentation layer
- ✓ Session layer
- ✓ Transport layer
- ✓ Network layer
- ✓ Data Link layer
- ✓ Physical layer
- ✓ Connection-oriented transmission
- ✓ Connectionless transmission

Concepts and Techniques You'll Need to Master

- ✓ Associating network processes to OSI model layers
- ✓ Associating applications and protocols to their OSI layer
- ✓ Understanding the encapsulation and decapsulation process
- ✓ Understanding inter-host communication
- ✓ Identifying protocols and their port numbers

Introduction

Any complex operation requires a certain degree of structure in order to be understood. When dealing with millions of individuals all designing and building programs, protocols, and equipment that is intended to network together, the use of a theoretical model as a basis for understanding and interoperability is critical. This chapter reviews the Open Standards Interconnect (OSI) model and compares it to the TCP/IP model. Cisco's own three-layer hierarchical model is also mentioned. All of these models are tested, and a strong understanding of the OSI model is necessary for success on the exam as well as useful in the real world.

Cisco Hierarchical Model

Cisco has created a reference model for the functions its equipment performs. The *three-layer hierarchical model* describes the major functional roles in any network and provides a basis for understanding and troubleshooting scalable networks. Figure 2.1 shows a representation of the three-layer model with switches and routers in their typical layers. The following sections describe each layer in more detail.

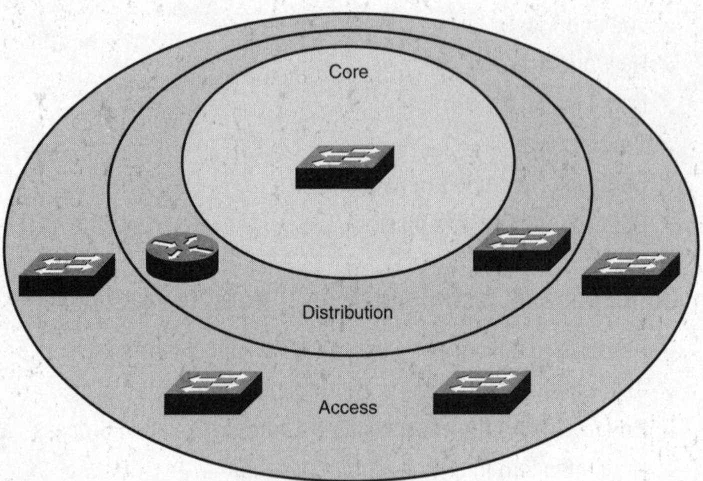

Figure 2.1 The three-layer hierarchical model.

Access Layer

The Access layer is the point that connects end users to the network. This can be achieved by a hub or switch to which PCs are connected, a wireless access point, a remote office connection, a dial-up service, or a VPN tunnel from the Internet into the corporate network.

Distribution Layer

The Distribution layer provides routing, packet filtering, WAN access, and QoS (Quality of Service). The Access Layer devices (usually switches) connect to a router or layer 3 switch so that traffic can be routed to another network. Packet filtering refers to the use of access control lists to identify certain types of traffic and control where it might go—or block it altogether. (We look at ACLs in detail in Chapter 8, "IP Access Lists.")

Traditional WAN access usually involves a specialized interface—perhaps a serial port or ISDN Primary Rate Interface controller. These specialized functions are found on Distribution layer devices such as routers. If our network needs to use QoS features to make it run well, these features are primarily implemented at the Distribution layer.

If our network includes different LAN technologies (Token Ring, Fiber-Distributed Data Interchange, and Ethernet, for example), the translation between these different media types is usually done by a Distribution layer device. Because these devices are typically routers and layer 3 switches, this is also where broadcast domain segmentation happens.

Core Layer

The Core layer is all about speed. Here, we typically find big, fast switches that move the data from the Distribution layer to centralized resources such as mail and database servers, or to other Distribution layer devices, as quickly as possible. The Core does not usually do any routing or packet filtering, but it might do QoS if that is an important part of the network (if using Voice over IP [VoIP], for example).

Advantages of the Three-Layer Model

The exam will focus on the benefits of the Cisco model as well as its particulars. Keep the following points in mind as advantages of Cisco's layered approach to networks:

- Scalability—If we want to add users, it is easy to put an additional Access layer device in place, without having to replace all the Distribution and Core devices at the same time. It is easier to add extended functionality to one layer at a time as needed instead of all at once.
- Cost Savings—An Access Layer device is much cheaper than a Distribution or Core device; also, by upgrading only one layer, we do not have to upgrade all three layers at once, incurring unnecessary costs.
- Easier Troubleshooting—If a component at one layer fails, it will not affect the entire system. It is also easier to find the problem if the failed device affects only one layer.

OSI Model

The International Standards Organization (ISO) defined a seven-layer model to define and standardize networking processes. The *Open Systems Interconnection (OSI)* model facilitates the understanding of the complexities of networking by defining what happens at each step of the process.

You should be clear that the OSI model does not impose rules on network equipment manufacturers or protocol developers; rather, it sets guidelines for functions so that inter-vendor operability is possible and predictable.

Each of the seven layers in the model communicates with the layers above and below, using standardized coding at the beginning of the message that can be interpreted by another device regardless of who made it. So if a vendor decides that they want to build a network device, they have the option of building a completely unique, proprietary system and trying to convince people to buy it; or, they can build a device that works with other devices according to the OSI model.

The seven different layers break up the process of networking, making it easier to understand and to troubleshoot problems. It is possible to test the functionality of each layer in sequence, to determine where the problem is and where to begin repairs.

The seven layers, in order, are as follows:

7. Application
6. Presentation
5. Session
4. Transport
3. Network
2. Data Link
1. Physical

You must know the names of the layers, in order. Start memorizing! You could use a mnemonic; there are several, some of them unprintable, but this one works pretty well:

"**A**ll **P**eople **S**eem **T**o **N**eed **D**ata **P**rocessing."

I don't know if Dave Minutella made that one up, but I'll give him the credit because he taught it to me...

Let's examine what happens at each layer as we send data to another computer.

Layer 7: The Application Layer

If you are using any program or utility that can store, send, or retrieve data over a network, it is a layer 7 application. Layer 7 is sometimes called the user interface layer; for example, when you launch a web browser and type in an address, you are working with a network-aware application and instructing it what to do on the network—that is, go and retrieve this web page. The same thing happens when you save a document to a file server or start a Telnet connection—you create some data that is to be sent over the network to another computer. Some applications or protocols are "hidden" from the user; for example, when you send and receive email, you might use Microsoft Outlook or Eudora or any other mail program you care to name, but the protocols that send and receive your mail are almost always going to be SMTP and POP3.

The Application Layer protocols (and deciphered acronyms) that you should know are as follows:

- **HTTP** (Hypertext Transfer Protocol)—Browses web pages.
- **FTP** (File Transfer Protocol)—Reliably sends/retrieves all file types.
- **SMTP** (Simple Mail Transfer Protocol)—Sends email.

- **POP3** (Post Office Protocol v.3)—Retrieves email.
- **NTP** (Network Time Protocol)—Synchronizes networked device clocks.
- **SNMP** (Simple Network Management Protocol)—Communicates status and allows control of networked devices.
- **TFTP** (Trivial File Transfer Protocol)—Simple, lightweight file transfer.
- **DNS** (Domain Naming System)—Translates a website name (easy for people) to an IP address (easy for computers).
- **DHCP** (Dynamic Host Configuration Protocol)—Assigns IP, mask, and DNS server (plus a bunch of other stuff) to hosts.
- **Telnet**—Provides a remote terminal connection to manage devices to which you are not close enough to use a console cable.

You should be ready to name any of the Application Layer protocols, as well as recognize them either by name or acronym. This gets easier the more experience you have, as they are constantly mentioned in the context of everyday networking.

Layer 6: The Presentation Layer

The Presentation layer is responsible for formatting data so that application-layer protocols (and then the users) can recognize and work with it. If you think about file extensions—such as .doc, .jpg, .txt, .avi, and so on—you realize that each of these file types is formatted for use by a particular type of application. The Presentation layer does this formatting, taking the Application layer data and marking it with the formatting codes so that it can be viewed reliably when accessed later. The Presentation layer can also do some types of encryption, but that is not as common as it used to be since there are better ways to encrypt that are easier on CPU and RAM resources.

Layer 5: The Session Layer

The Session layer deals with initiating and terminating network connections. It provides instructions to connect, authenticate (optionally), and disconnect from a network resource. Common examples are the login part of a Telnet or SQL session (not the actual data movement) and Remote Procedure Call (RPC) functions. The actual movement of the data is handled by the lower layers.

Layer 4: The Transport Layer

The Transport layer is possibly the most important layer for exam study purposes. A lot is going on here, and it is heavily tested.

The Transport layer deals with exactly how two hosts are going to send data. The two main methods are called *connection-oriented* and *connectionless*. Connection-oriented transmission is said to be reliable, and connectionless is *unreliable*. Every network protocol stack will have a protocol that handles each style; in the TCP/IP stack, reliable transmission is done by *TCP*, and unreliable by *UDP*. Now, don't get too wrapped up in the term "unreliable"; this doesn't mean that the data isn't going to get there; it only means that it isn't *guaranteed* to get there.

Think of your options when you are sending a letter: you can pop it in an envelope, throw a stamp on it and put it in the mailbox, and chances are good that it will get where it's supposed to go—but there is no guarantee, and stuff does go missing once in a while. On the other hand, it's cheap.

Your other choice is to use a courier—FedEx's motto used to be, "When it absolutely, positively has to be there overnight." For this level of service, you have to buy a fancy envelope and put a bunch of extra labels on it to track where it is going and where it has been. But, you get a receipt when it is delivered, you are guaranteed delivery, and you can keep track of whether your shipment got to its destination. All of this costs you more—but it is reliable!

This analogy works perfectly when describing the difference between UDP and TCP: UDP is the post office, and TCP is FedEx. Let's look at this more closely, starting with TCP.

Reliable Communication with TCP

The key to reliable communication using TCP is the use of sequence and acknowledgement numbers. These numbers are attached to the various segments of information that are sent between two hosts to identify what order they should be assembled in to re-create the original data, and to keep track of whether any segments went missing along the way. When a host sends a segment of data, it is labeled with a *sequence number* that identifies that segment and where it belongs in the series of segments being sent. When the receiving host gets that segment, it sends an acknowledgement back to the sender with an *acknowledgement number*; the value of this number is the sequence number of the last segment it received, plus one. In effect, the receiver is saying, "I got your last one, now I am ready for the next one."

The first step in establishing a reliable connection between hosts is the *three-way handshake*. This initial signaling allows hosts to exchange their starting sequence numbers and to test that they have reliable communication between them. Figure 2.2 illustrates the three-way handshake in TCP communication.

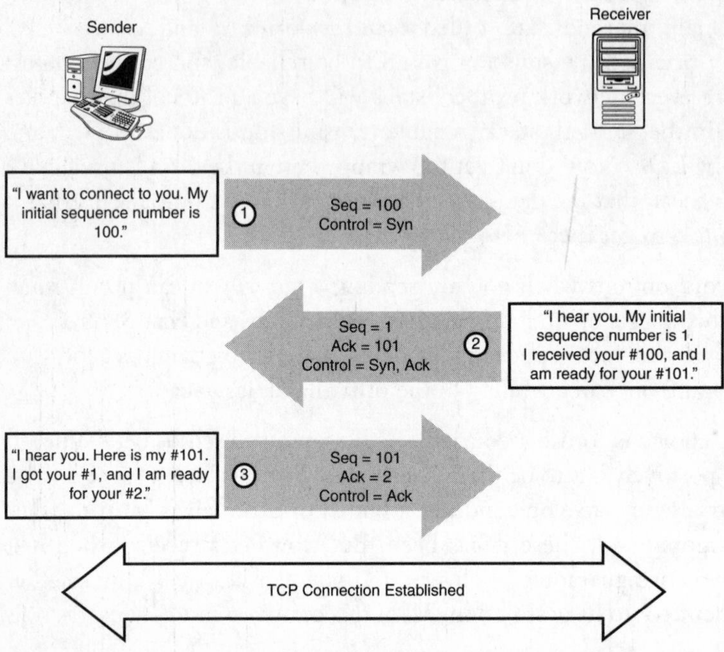

Figure 2.2 The TCP three-way handshake.

From this point, the sender continues to send segments of data. A system known as *PAR (Positive Acknowledgement and Retransmission)* makes sure that all the segments get where they are going. Following are the three main elements of PAR:

1. The sender starts a timer when it sends a segment, and will re-transmit that segment if the timer expires before an acknowledgment is received for that segment.
2. The sender keeps a record of all segments sent and expects an acknowledgement of each one.
3. The receiving device acknowledges the receipt of a segment by sending a segment back to the sender indicating the next sequence number it expects.

If any of the segments of data should go missing—perhaps due to interference, collisions, or a link failure—the sender will not receive an acknowledgement of it and will retransmit it. The sequence number enables the receiver to put all the segments back in the correct order.

Know how the three-way handshake works.

Know the elements of PAR.

Understand that in TCP, reliability is guaranteed by sequence and acknowledgement numbers and the ability to retransmit missing segments.

The TCP Sliding Window

Sometimes a receiver can get very busy—imagine a web server that is getting millions of hits an hour. If it receives more segments than it can handle, it might be forced to drop (discard) some; this is not desirable because the sender(s) would then have to retransmit them; this wastes time and bandwidth and increases delay.

The receiver has a method to tell the sender(s) to slow down the transmission rate. It's called the *Sliding Window*. The window size indicates how many segments can be sent before an acknowledgement will be sent. If it is not busy, the receiver can handle a large number of segments and send a single acknowledgement. If it gets very busy, it can make the window size very small, allowing the sender(s) to send only a few segments before an acknowledgement is sent.

The window size of the sender and receiver is included in the segment header and can change during the lifetime of the conversation. Figure 2.3 shows how the sliding window feature of TCP operates.

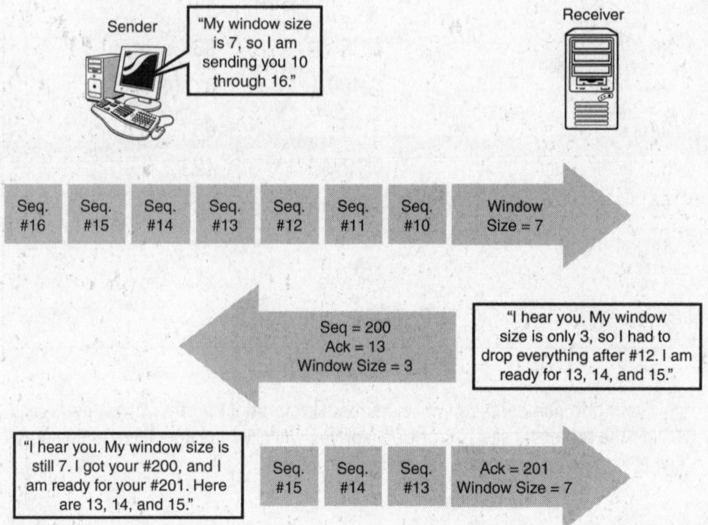

Figure 2.3 The TCP Sliding Window controls how much data is sent before an acknowledgement is needed.

You must understand the definition and advantages of the TCP sliding window.

Port Numbers

Imagine a server that performs a number of functions—for example email, web pages, FTP, and DNS. The server has a single IP address, but can perform all these different functions for all the hosts that want to connect to it. The Transport layer (layer 4) uses port numbers to distinguish between different types of traffic that might be headed for the same IP address.

Port numbers are divided into ranges by the IANA. Following are the current port ranges:

0–1023 Well-Known—for common TCP/IP functions and applications

1024–49151 Registered—for applications built by companies

49152–65535 Dynamic/Private—For dynamic connections or unregistered applications

Port numbers are used by both TCP and UDP protocols. Table 2.1 lists some of the common port numbers you should know for the CCNA exam:

Table 2.1 Common TCP and UDP Port Numbers

TCP		UDP	
FTP	20, 21	DNS	53
Telnet	23	DHCP	67, 68
SMTP	25	TFTP	69
DNS	53	NTP	123
HTTP	80	SNMP	161
POP	110		
NNTP	119		
HTTPS	443		

Know your port numbers! You will either be asked outright for the correct ports (and whether the protocol uses TCP or UDP), or you will need to know them to do something else, perhaps an access-list question.

When a host sends a segment, it specifies the *destination port* that matches the service it wants to connect to. It also includes a *source port* (a random port number from the dynamic range) that acts as a return address for that connection. In this way, a single host can have multiple—possibly hundreds—of connections with the same server, and the server can track each of them because of the different source port numbers for each connection. When the server sends its replies back to the host, the host source ports become the server's destination ports. This system enables the Transport layer to *multiplex* connections—meaning, support multiple connections between the same two hosts.

To understand this better, let's say that Host A wants to start a Telnet session to Server Z. A will send a segment to Z's IP address, with the destination port of 23 and a random source port number (generated by the host operating system) from the dynamic range—let's choose 55440.

When Server Z receives the segment, it looks at the destination port of 23 and realizes that this segment is intended for its Telnet application, so it sends the data (which, in this case, is a request to start a Telnet session) to its Telnet application. When the Telnet application answers, the server sends a reply back to the host. The destination port of this reply is the original source port of the host, and the source port is the originalsegment, it specifies the *destination port* that destination port of the host. Figure 2.4 shows this exchange in action.

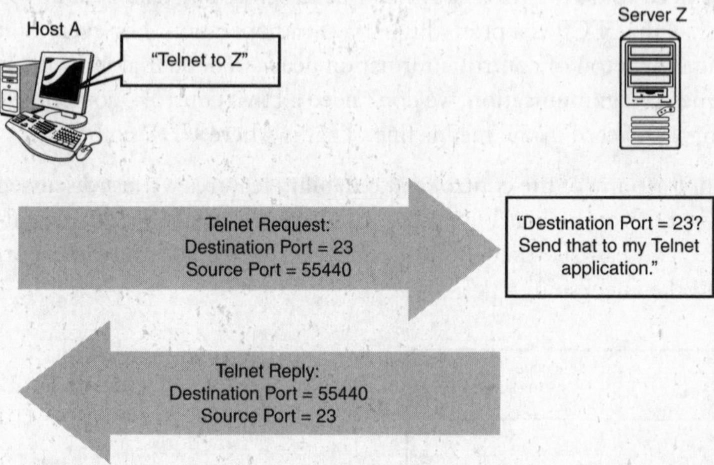

Figure 2.4 Source and destination ports in action.

Using TCP means that we have to include a lot of information with each segment: the sequence number, the acknowledgement number, the source and destination ports, and the window size. All this information is contained in the layer 4 header. A *header* is a label attached to the beginning of the data being sent that contains all the control information; once the header is attached, the data is called a *segment*. Figure 2.5 shows the fields in a TCP header.

Source Port	Destination Port
Sequence Number	
Acknowledgement Number	
Misc. Flags	Window Size
Checksum	Urgent
Options	

Figure 2.5 The TCP header.

Unreliable Communication with UDP

When you look at all the control information that TCP needs to work, and factor in the need to do the three-way handshake before any data is sent, you begin to realize that TCP is a pretty high-overhead operation. For every unit of data being sent, a ton of control information needs to be sent along with it. For some types of communication, we don't need all that control—sometimes, just dropping a postcard in the mail is fine. That is where UDP comes in.

UDP does not use any of the control and reliability features we just discussed in TCP. In fact, if you look at Figure 2.6, which shows what the UDP header looks like, you can see that the only elements in common are the port numbers and the checksum.

Source Port	Destination Port
Length	Checksum

Figure 2.6 The UDP header is a lightweight.

There is no sequencing, no acknowledgements, no window size—and no three-way handshake, either. So you can see that *much* less control information is sent with each segment. With UDP, there is no PAR. You ask for something, and then you get it. If it doesn't work, you have to ask all over again. Most applications, such as a TFTP server for example, will handle any errors and retransmissions—which means that the application itself (up at layer 7) is doing the reliability, *not* layer 4.

The typical UDP connection goes something like this:

Host A: "Hey Server Z, what's the IP address of www.google.com?"

Server Z: "www.google.com is 66.102.7.147."

Or perhaps:

Host B: "Hey Server Z, send me that file using TFTP."

Server Z: "Here's the file."

UDP is good when reliability is not needed—for DNS lookups or TFTP transfers, for example—or when the overhead of TCP would cause more problems than it solves—for example, when doing VoIP. TCP signaling would introduce so much delay that it would degrade the voice quality—plus, by the time any missing voice segment was retransmitted, it would be too late to use it! VoIP uses UDP because it is faster than TCP, and reliability is less important than minimizing delay.

You must be able to identify a TCP header on sight, when compared to a UDP header. Be ready for a twist on the wording such as, "Which provides reliable connections?" So not only do you need to know which header is TCP and which is UDP, but also which one is reliable!

Layer 3: The Network Layer

The Network layer deals with logical addressing—in our CCNA world, that means IP addresses, but it could also mean IPX, AppleTalk, SNA, and a bunch of others. A logical address is one that is assigned to an interface in software—as opposed to one that is burned onto an interface at the factory (as is the case with MAC addresses, as you will see in a minute).

For two IP hosts to communicate, they must be in the same network (Chapter 3, "Concepts in IP Addressing," elaborates on this). If they are in different networks, we need a router to connect the two networks. Finding the way between networks, potentially through hundreds of routers, is called *path determination*. This is the second function of the Network layer. Path determination means routing, and routers are a layer 3 device (so are layer 3 switches, oddly enough).

The last function of the Network layer is to communicate with the layer above (Transport) and the layer below (Data Link). This is achieved by attaching a header to the beginning of the segment that layer 4 built. The addition of this header makes the segment into a *packet* (sometimes called a datagram, but we like packet better). The packet header has a field that indicates the type of segment it is carrying—TCP or UDP, for example—so that the packet can be sent to the correct function at layer 4. Communicating with layer 2 in this case means that an IP packet can be sent to layer 2 to become an Ethernet frame, Frame Relay, Point-to-Point Protocol, or almost any other layer 2 technology. We'll elaborate on this a little later.

One of the big advantages of a logical addressing scheme is that we can make it *hierarchical*. Hierarchical means "organized into a formal or ranked order." Because all the networks are numbered, and we have control over where those networks are set up, it's easy for us to build a really big system: Big networks are broken into smaller and smaller pieces, with the routers closer to the core knowing the big picture and no details, and the routers at the edge knowing their little set of detailed information but nothing about anyone else's. This makes it easier to organize and find all the millions of different networks, using routers. It's roughly equivalent to a postal address. For example, look at the following address:

24 Sussex Drive

Ottawa, Ontario

Canada K1N 9E6

You could probably find it, eventually, because you would know to get to Canada first, and then to the province of Ontario, and then the city of Ottawa (beautiful place). Grab yourself a map, and soon you'll be standing in front of that address—which happens to be the Prime Minister's house, so don't be surprised if the Mounties are curious about you being there.

The alternative to a nicely organized hierarchical system like that is a *flat* topology. In a flat system, there is no efficient way to determine where a single address is, because they are not organized. Imagine if the address were this instead:

30000000

Okay, where is it? We have no idea. Unless we can ask everyone at once if it's their address, we don't really stand a chance of finding it. Flat networks (layer 2) work as long as there are not very many addresses; hierarchical is scalable. Layer 3 is hierarchical, logical addressing that allows us to perform path determination.

You should be familiar with the protocols that exist at layer 3 as well. Table 2.2 lists the ones you need to know, along with a very brief description.

Table 2.2 Layer 3 Protocols	
Protocol	**Description**
IP	IP is the "mother protocol" of TCP/IP, featuring routable 32-bit addressing.
IPX	The equivalent of IP in Novell Netware.
ICMP	Internet Connection Management Protocol. Incorporates Ping and Traceroute, which are layer 3 link testing utilities.
OSPF, IGRP, EIGRP, RIP, ISIS	Dynamic routing protocols that learn about remote networks and the best paths to them from other routers running the same protocol.
ARP, RARP	Address Resolution Protocol (and Reverse ARP). ARP learns what MAC address is associated with a given IP address. Reverse ARP learns an IP address given a MAC address.

You should be familiar with Table 2.2.

Remember that layer 3 is about logical, hierarchical addressing and path determination using that hierarchy—which means routing.

Layer 2: The Data Link Layer

The Data Link layer is responsible for taking the layer 3 packet (regardless of which protocol created it—IP, IPX, and so on) and preparing a frame for the packet to be transmitted on the media. There are, of course, many different layer 2 frame types; in CCNA, we are interested in only the following:

- Ethernet
- Frame Relay
- Point-to-Point Protocol (PPP)
- High-Level Data Link Control protocol (HDLC)
- Cisco Discovery Protocol (CDP)

The type of frame created depends on the type of network service in use; if it is an Ethernet interface, obviously it will be creating Ethernet frames. A router serial port can create several different frame types, including PPP, HDLC, and Frame Relay.

The Data Link layer uses flat addressing—not hierarchical as in layer 3. In Ethernet, the addresses in question are MAC addresses. MAC stands for

Media Access Control. A MAC address is a number assigned by the manufacturer of a NIC, burned in at the factory. For this reason, it is sometimes called a hardware or physical address, again as opposed to the logical addressing at layer 3. A valid MAC address will consist of 12 hexadecimal characters. The first six characters are called the *OUI (Organizationally Unique Identifier)*, and identify the company that made the card. The last six characters are the card serial number. Following are some valid MAC addresses as examples:

00-0F-1F-AE-EE-F0

00-00-0C-01-AA-CD

A MAC address must be unique within a broadcast domain. This is because one of the functions of Ethernet is that a host will broadcast an ARP request to find out the MAC address of a particular IP; if there are two identical MACs in that broadcast domain, there will be serious confusion.

In other layer 2 network types, the addresses are not MACs but serve an equivalent purpose. Frame Relay, for example uses DLCIs (Data Link Connection Identifiers). A dial-up link using regular analog phone or digital ISDN will use the phone number as the layer 2 address of the IP you are trying to reach. Remember that you must always resolve an IP address down to some type of layer 2 address, and there will always be a mechanism to do so.

You must be able to recognize a valid MAC address: 12 valid hex characters.

The first six characters are the OUI or vendor code. All MAC addresses are assigned by the NIC manufacturer and "burned in" at the factory.

MAC addresses are also called hardware or physical addresses.

Layer 2 devices include switches and bridges. These devices read MAC addresses in frames and forward them to the appropriate link. (We'll go into more detail on switching technology in Chapter 6, "Catalyst Switch Operations and Configuration.")

Layer 1: The Physical Layer

The last piece of the OSI puzzle is the actual connection between devices. At some point, you have to transmit your signal onto a wire, an optical fiber, or a wireless medium. The physical layer defines the mechanical, procedural, and electrical standards for accessing the media so that you can transmit your layer 2 frames.

All signaling at layer 1 is digital, which means that we are sending binary bits onto the wire. This can mean energizing a copper cable with electricity, where "electricity on" indicates a binary 1 and "electricity off" indicates a binary 0; or, it can mean blinking a laser down an optical fiber where on = 1 and off = 0. Wireless systems do much the same thing.

By defining standards for the physical layer, we can be assured that if we buy an RJ-45 patch cord (for example), it will fit into and work properly in any interface designed to use it.

Sending Data Between Hosts

You also need to understand the flow of information between two networked hosts. The OSI model describes the framework for this flow. As we move down the layers from Application to Physical, the data is *encapsulated*, which means that headers and trailers are added by each layer. The following section describes the process of creating a piece of data on one host and sending it to another host:

- At layer 7, the user generates some *data*, perhaps an email message or a Word document. This data is passed down to layer 6.
- At layer 6, the *data* is formatted so that the same application on the other host can recognize and use it. The data is passed down to layer 5.
- At layer 5, the request to initiate a session for the transfer of the *data* is started. The data is passed down to layer 4.
- At layer 4, the data is encapsulated as either a TCP or UDP *segment*. The choice depends on what application generated the data. Source and destination port numbers are added, as are sequence and acknowledgement numbers and window size. The segment is passed down to layer 3.
- At layer 3, the segment is encapsulated with a layer 3 header and becomes a *packet*. The packet header contains source and destination IP addresses and a label indicating what layer 4 protocol it is carrying. The packet is passed down to layer 2.
- At layer 2, a header with source and destination MAC addresses is added. This encapsulation creates the *frame*. The trailer at this layer contains an error-checking calculation called the FCS (Frame Check Sequence). The frame header also contains a label indicating which layer 3 protocol it is carrying (IP, IPX, and so on). The frame is sent to the interface for transmission onto the media (layer 1).
- At layer 1, the binary string that represents the frame is transmitted onto the media, whether electrically, optically, or by radio. *Bits* are transmitted across the media to the network interface of the other host.
- When received by the other host, the layer 1 bits are sent up to layer 2.
- At layer 2, the destination MAC is examined to make sure that the frame was intended for this host. The FCS is calculated to check the frame for

errors. If there are errors, the frame is discarded. If there are none, the frame is *decapsulated* and the packet is sent to the correct layer 3 protocol based on the protocol ID in the header.

- At layer 3, the destination IP address is checked to see if it is intended for this host. The packet header is checked to see which layer 4 protocol to send it to. The packet is decapsulated, and the segment is sent up to layer 4.
- At layer 4, the destination port in the segment header is checked and the segment is decapsulated. The data is sent to the correct upper layer application. Depending on the application, it might go directly to layer 7 or through 5 and 6.

This process of encapsulation, transmission, and decapsulation makes data flow in an organized and manageable fashion down the OSI stack on the sender, across the transmission media, and up the OSI stack on the receiving host. It is important to understand that layer 3 on the sender is communicating with layer 3 on the receiver as well by way of the information in the headers.

You must be totally comfortable with visualizing how this process works. You must remember the names of the encapsulations at each layer, in order, backwards and forwards. These are generically called PDUs (Protocol Data Units):

Layer	PDU
Application	Data
Presentation	Data
Session	Data
Transport	Segment
Network	Packet
Data Link	Frame
Physical	Bits

Try a mnemonic: "Did Sally Pack for Bermuda?"

TCP/IP Model

Although the TCP/IP protocol can be fit into the OSI model, it actually uses its own model, which is slightly different. Remember that the OSI model is intended to be a standardized framework, and TCP/IP was originated as a proprietary Department of Defense protocol. It stands to reason that there will be some variances from the official OSI stack. The following section describes these differences.

The TCP/IP model has only four layers:

- Application
- Transport

- Internet
- Network Interface

OSI Layers 5, 6, and 7 have been amalgamated into a single layer called the Application layer. The Application layer features all the same protocols as found in OSI Layer 7: Telnet, FTP, TFTP, SMTP, SNMP, and so on. The Transport layer is equivalent to OSI layer 4. TCP and UDP are located here.

The Internet layer corresponds to OSI layer 3. IP, ARP, and ICMP are the primary protocols here.

Layer 1 and 2 are fused into the Network Interface layer. This is confusing because it is illogical to have a protocol software stack define a physical interface; just remember that the TCP/IP model is a logical framework, and the fact that physical standards are included is necessary because it must connect to the media at some point. The TCP/IP model uses the same definitions for Network Interface standards as the OSI model does for Data Link and Physical layers.

Figure 2.7 directly compares and contrasts the OSI model with the TCP/IP model.

OSI Model	TCP/IP Model
Application	Application
Presentation	
Session	
Transport	Transport
Network	Internet
Data Link	Network Interface
Physical	

Figure 2.7 OSI and TCP/IP models compared.

A great deal of overlap exists between the OSI and TCP/IP models, but you must be clear on the differences and watch for what the exam question is asking about; Cisco is fond of trying to trick you into answering with an OSI answer when it is in fact a TCP/IP model question.

Exam Prep Questions

1. Which protocol will allow you to test connectivity through layer 7?
   - ❍ A. ICMP
   - ❍ B. ARP
   - ❍ C. RIP
   - ❍ D. Telnet
2. Which answer correctly lists the OSI PDUs in order?
   - ❍ A. Data, Packet, Frame, Segment, Bit
   - ❍ B. Bit, Data, Packet, Segment, Frame
   - ❍ C. Data, Segment, Packet, Frame, Bit
   - ❍ D. Bit, Frame, Segment, Packet, Data
3. Which transport layer protocol provides connection-oriented, reliable transport?
   - ❍ A. TFTP
   - ❍ B. UDP
   - ❍ C. Ethernet
   - ❍ D. TCP
   - ❍ E. Secure Shell
4. Which of the following are Application layer protocols? Choose all that apply.
   - ❍ A. Ethernet
   - ❍ B. CDP
   - ❍ C. FTP
   - ❍ D. TFTP
   - ❍ E. Telnet
   - ❍ F. ARP
   - ❍ G. ICMP
   - ❍ H. ATM
5. Match the protocol with its port number:

FTP	80
Telnet	69
TFTP	20, 21
DNS	123
SNMP	25
SMTP	110
NTP	161
POP3	53
HTTP	23

6. Which protocols use TCP? Choose all that apply.
   - ❍ A. DNS
   - ❍ B. SNMP
   - ❍ C. SMTP
   - ❍ D. FTP
   - ❍ E. TFTP
   - ❍ F. POP3
7. Which port numbers are used by well-known protocols that use connectionless transport?
   - ❍ A. 25
   - ❍ B. 53
   - ❍ C. 20
   - ❍ D. 69
   - ❍ E. 161
   - ❍ F. 110
8. Which are elements of PAR? Choose all that apply.
   - ❍ A. Devices that collide must wait to retransmit.
   - ❍ B. The source device starts a timer for each segment and will retransmit that segment if an acknowledgement is not received before the timer expires.
   - ❍ C. Devices will broadcast for the hardware address of the receiver.
   - ❍ D. Source devices keep a record of all segments sent and expect an acknowledgement for each one.
   - ❍ E. The receiving device will drop frames that it cannot buffer.
   - ❍ F. The receiving device will acknowledge receipt of a segment by sending an acknowledgement indicating the next segment it expects.
9. Which layer of the TCP/IP model is responsible for inter-host data movement, using either connection-oriented or connectionless protocols?
   - ❍ A. Network
   - ❍ B. Internet
   - ❍ C. Transport
   - ❍ D. Network Interface
   - ❍ E. Application

10. Which of the following depicts a TCP header?

❍ A.

Source Port	Destination Port
Sequence Number	
Acknowledgement Number	
Misc. Flags	Window Size
Checksum	Urgent
Options	

❍ B.

Source Port	Destination Port
Length	Checksum

Answers to Exam Prep Questions

1. Answer D is the correct answer; Telnet is the only layer 7 protocol listed. All the others only operate at layer 3, so they do not test above layer 3.
2. Answer C is the correct answer. "**D**id **S**ally **P**ack for **B**ermuda?"
3. Answer D is the correct answer. TCP is a transport-layer protocol that uses sequencing, acknowledgements, and retransmission for reliability. Answers A, C, and E are incorrect because TFTP, Ethernet, and Secure Shell are not transport-layer protocols; Answer B is incorrect because UDP does not provide reliability.
4. Answers C, D, and E are correct. Answers A, B, and H are layer 2 protocols; Answers F and G are layer 3 protocols.
5. Answer:

FTP	20, 21
Telnet	23
TFTP	69
DNS	53
SNMP	161
SMTP	25
NTP	123
POP3	110
HTTP	80

6. Answers A, C, D, and F are correct. DNS uses both TCP and UDP; B and E use UDP only.
7. Answers B, D, and E are correct. These ports are used by DNS, TFTP, and SNMP—all of which use unreliable/connectionless UDP transport.
8. Answers B, D, and F are correct; PAR provides reliability by using these three functions. Answer A describes CSMA/CD; Answer C describes ARP; Answer E is a basic hardware function that has nothing to do with the process of PAR although PAR might react to the lost frames by retransmitting them.

9. Answer C is correct; connectionless and connection-oriented protocols are found at layer 4 (Transport). Answer A is incorrect because it is an OSI layer name; Answers B, D, and E are incorrect because those layers do not use connection-oriented or connectionless protocols.

10. Answer A is correct. It depicts a TCP header.

Concepts in IP Addressing

Terms You'll Need to Understand:

- ✓ Binary
- ✓ Hexadecimal
- ✓ Decimal
- ✓ Octet
- ✓ IP address
- ✓ Subnet Mask
- ✓ Subnet
- ✓ Host
- ✓ Increment

Techniques You'll Need to Master:

- ✓ Identifying Address Class and Default Mask
- ✓ Determining Host Requirements
- ✓ Determining Subnet Requirements
- ✓ Determining the Increment

Introduction

The CCNA exam(s) require a near-perfect fluency in subnetting. Success requires speed and accuracy in answering the many questions you will see on this topic. The key to this level of fluency is practice—you must work at your skills until they become second nature.

The following sections discuss binary and hexadecimal numbering systems as compared with the more familiar decimal system. An understanding of binary, in particular, is crucial to success on the test as it is fundamental to computer systems in general, and to topics such as subnetting, access lists, routing, and route summarization in specific.

Binary

Binary is the *language* of digital electronic communication. Binary is another name for Base2 numbering. Our usual numbering system is Base10, in which a single character or column can represent one of 10 values: 0, 1, 2, 3, 4, 5, 6, 7, 8, or 9. The first column indicates how many ones there are in a given value. To represent a value greater than 9, we need another column, which represents how many "tens" there are; if the value we want to represent is greater than 99, we use another column for the "hundreds," and so on. You might notice that each additional column is ten times greater than the preceding one: ones, tens, hundreds, thousands, and so forth—all "Powers of 10": 10^1, 10^2, 10^3, and so on. Base10 is easy because most of us have 10 fingers and have known how to count from an early age.

In binary, or Base2, a single character or column can represent one of only two values: 0 or 1. The next column represents how many "twos" there are; the next column how many "fours," and so on. You'll notice here that the value of each additional column is two times greater than the previous—all "Powers of 2": 2^1, 2^2, 2^3, and so on. This is not a coincidence.

Given that a Base2 or binary column can have only two possible values (0 or 1), this makes it easy to represent a binary value as an electrical value: either off (0) or on (1). Computers use binary because it is easily represented as electrical signals in memory or digital values on storage media. The whole system works because computers are quick at computing arithmetic, and as you'll learn, pretty much all computer operations are really just fast binary math.

Let's take a look at some Base10 (or decimal) to binary conversions. Take the decimal number 176. Those three digits tell us that we have one 100, plus seven 10s, plus six 1s. Table 3.1 illustrates how decimal numbers represent this distribution of values.

Table 3.1 Decimal Values

100,000s	10,000s	1000s	100s	10s	1s
0	0	0	1	7	6

Notice that we have some zeroes in the high-value columns; we can drop those from the beginning if we want to. You will not have to analyze decimal numbers in this way on the exam; we are simply demonstrating how Base10 works so it can be compared to Base2 and Base16 in the same way.

In binary, the columns have different values—the powers of 2. Table 3.2 lists the values of the lowest eight bits in binary.

Table 3.2 Binary Values

128	64	32	16	8	4	2	1

The biggest values in a binary string (the ones at the left) are often called the "high-order" bits because they have the highest value. Similarly, the lowest-value bits at the right are referred to as the "low-order" bits.

You must know the value of each binary bit position! If you have difficulty memorizing them, try starting at 1 and keep doubling as you go to the left.

To represent the decimal number 176 in binary, we need to figure out which columns (or bit positions) are "on" and which are "off." Now, because this is arithmetic, there are a few different ways to do this.

Start with the decimal number you want to convert:

176

Next, look at the values of each binary bit position and decide if you can subtract the highest column value and end up with a value of 0 or more. Ask yourself: "Can I subtract 128 from 176?" In this case, 176-128 = 48.

Yes, you can subtract 128 from 176 and get a positive value, 48. Because we "used" the 128 column, we put a 1 in that column, as shown in Table 3.3.

Table 3.3 Building a Binary String, Part 1

128	64	32	16	8	4	2	1
1							

Now, we try to subtract the next highest column value from the remainder. We get 176 – 128 = 48. We take the 48 and subtract 64 from it.

Notice that you can't do this without getting a negative number; this is not allowed, so we can't use the 64 column. Therefore, we put a 0 in that column, as shown in Table 3.4.

Table 3.4 Building a Binary String, Part 2

128	64	32	16	8	4	2	1
1	0						

Move along and do the math for the rest of the columns: 48 – 32 = 16. We then subtract 16 from 16 and get 0.

Note that when you get to 0, you are finished! So, we used only the 128 column, the 32 column, and the 16 column. Table 3.5 is what we end up with.

Table 3.5 Completed Binary Conversion

128	64	32	16	8	4	2	1
1	0	1	1	0	0	0	0

176 decimal = 10110000 binary.

If you add up 128+32+16, you get 176. That is how you convert from binary to decimal: Simply add up the column values where there is a 1.

You will see several questions on converting from decimal to binary and back, so prepare accordingly.

Hexadecimal

The CCNA exam(s) will ask you a few questions on the conversion of binary to hexadecimal and back, so you need to understand how it works. An understanding of hex is also a useful skill for other areas of networking and computer science.

Binary is Base2; Decimal is Base10; Hexadecimal is Base16. Each column in hex can represent 16 possible values, from 0 through 15. In order to represent a value of 10 through 15 with a single character, hex uses the letters A through F. It is important to understand that the values of 0 through 15 are the possible values of a 4-bit binary number, as shown in Table 3.6.

Table 3.6 Decimal, Binary, and Hex Values Compared

Decimal	Binary	Hex
0	0000	0
1	0001	1
2	0010	2
3	0011	3
4	0100	4
5	0101	5
6	0110	6
7	0111	7
8	1000	8
9	1001	9
10	1010	A
11	1011	B
12	1100	C
13	1101	D
14	1110	E
15	1111	F

You should be able to reproduce Table 3.6 as a quick reference for the exam.

Conversion Between Binary, Hex, and Decimal

The following sections provide an introduction to converting between binary, hex, and decimal. Again, there is more than one mathematical approach to finding the correct answer, but the method shown is simple and reliable.

Decimal to Hexadecimal Conversions

The easiest way to get from decimal to hexadecimal and back is to go through binary. Take the example we used earlier in which we converted 176 decimal to binary:

176 = 10110000

Given that a single hex character represents 4 binary bits, all we need to do is to break the 8-bit string 10110000 into two 4-bit strings like this:

1011 0000

Now, simply match the 4-bit strings to their hex equivalent:

1011 = B

0000 = 0

The answer is simply 10110000 = 0xB0.

The "0x" in front of the answer is an expression that means "the following is in hex." This is needed because if the hex value was 27, we could not distinguish it from 27 decimal.

Hexadecimal to Decimal Conversions

The reverse of the procedure is easier than it seems, too. Given a hex value of 0xC4, all we need to do is to first convert to binary, and then to decimal.

To convert to binary, take the two hex characters and find their binary value:

C = 1100

0100 = 4

Now, make the two 4-bit strings into one 8–bit string:

11000100

Finally, add the bit values of the columns where you have a 1:

128 + 64 + 4 = 196

It is critical to polish your skills in binary. You must be confident and quick in conversions, and the better your understanding of binary, the easier subnetting and other advanced IP topics will be for you. Practice, practice, practice!

IP Address Components

CCNA candidates need to be fluent in their understanding of IP addressing concepts. The following sections detail how IP addresses are organized and analyzed, with a view to answering subnetting questions.

Address Class

Early in the development of IP, the IANA (Internet Assigned Numbers Authority) designated five classes of IP address: A, B, C, D, and E. These classes were identified based on the pattern of high-order bits (the high-value bits at the beginning of the first octet). The result is that certain ranges of networks are grouped into classes in a pattern based on the binary values of those high-order bits, as detailed in Table 3.7:

Table 3.7 Address Class and Range

Class	High-Order Bits	1st Octet Range
A	0	1–126
B	10	128–191
C	110	192–223
D	1110	224–239
E	11110	240–255

You might notice that 127 is missing. This is because at some point the address 127.0.0.1 was reserved for the loopback (sometimes called "localhost") IP—this is the IP of the TCP/IP protocol itself on every host machine.

You absolutely must be able to identify the class of an address just by looking at what number is in the first octet. This is critical to answering subnetting questions.

Default Subnet Mask

Each class of address is associated with a default subnet mask, as shown in Table 3.8. An address using its default mask defines a single IP broadcast domain—all the hosts using that same network number and mask can receive each other's broadcasts and communicate via IP.

Table 3.8 Address Class and Default Masks

Class	Default Mask
A	255.0.0.0
B	255.255.0.0
C	255.255.255.0

One of the rules is that a subnet mask must be a contiguous string of 1s followed by a contiguous string of 0s. There are no exceptions to this rule: A valid mask is always a string of 1s, followed by 0s to fill up the rest of the 32 bits.

Therefore, the only possible valid values in any given octet of a subnet mask are 0, 128, 192, 224, 240, 248, 252, 254, and 255. Any other value is invalid.

You should practice associating the correct default subnet mask with any given IP address; this is another critical skill in subnetting.

The Network Field

Every IP address is composed of a network component and a host component. The subnet mask has a single purpose: to identify which part of an IP address is the network component and which part is the host component. Look at a 32-bit IP address expressed in binary, with the subnet mask written right below it. Figure 3.1 shows an example.

IP Address and Mask: 192.168.0.96 255.255.255.0

Binary IP: 11000000.10101000.00000000.01100000

Binary Mask: 11111111.11111111.11111111.00000000

Network Field (11111111.11111111.11111111) — Host Field (00000000)

Figure 3.1 IP address and mask in binary, showing network and host fields.

Anywhere you see a binary 1 in the subnet mask, it means "the matching bit in the IP address is part of the network component." In this example, the network part of the address is 192.168.0.X, and the last octet (X) will be the host component.

Because there are 24 bits in a row in the mask, we can also use a shortcut for the mask notation of /24. These examples show how a dotted decimal mask can be expressed in slash notation:

192.168.1.66 255.255.255.0 = 192.168.1.66 /24

172.16.0.12 255.255.0.0 = 172.16.0.12 /16

10.1.1.1 255.0.0.0 = 10.1.1.1 /8

This slash notation is sometimes called CIDR (Classless Inter-Domain Routing) notation. For some reason, it's a concept that confuses students, but honestly it's the easiest concept of all: The slash notation is simply the number of 1s in a row in the subnet mask. The real reason to use CIDR notation is simply that it is easier to say and especially to type—and it appears interchangeably with dotted decimal throughout the exam.

Every IP address has a host component and a network component, and the 1s in the mask tell us which bits in the address identify the network component.

The Host Field

If the 1s in the mask identify the network component of an address, the 0s at the end of the mask identify the host component. In the preceding example, the entire last octet is available for the host IP number.

The number of 0s at the end of the mask mathematically define how many hosts can be on any given network or subnet. The 1s in the mask always identify the network component, and the 0s at the end of the mask always identify the host component of any IP address.

Non-default Masks

At this point, you should be able to recognize what class an address belongs to, and what its default mask is supposed to be. Here's the big secret: If a mask is longer than it is supposed to be, that network has been subnetted. So it is clearly another critical skill that you be able to spot those non-default masks.

The Subnet Field

Because we have extended the subnet mask past the default boundary into the bits that were previously host bits, we identify the bits we "stole" from the host part as the subnet field. The subnet field is relevant because those bits mathematically define how many subnets we create. Figure 3.2 uses the same IP address from our previous example, but now we have applied a subnetted mask that is longer than the default. Note that this creates the subnet field.

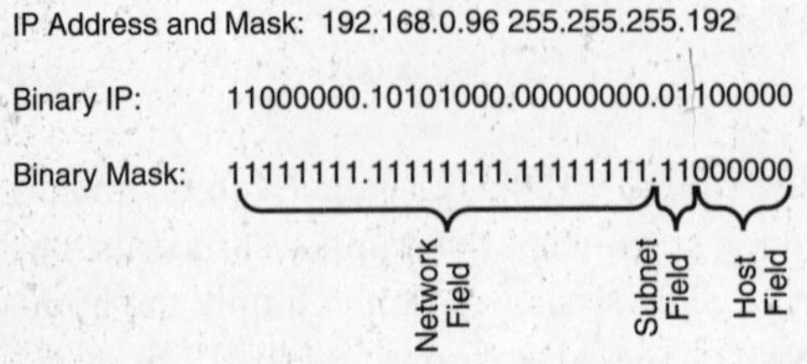

IP Address and Mask: 192.168.0.96 255.255.255.192

Binary IP: 11000000.10101000.00000000.01100000

Binary Mask: 11111111.11111111.11111111.11000000

Network Field | Subnet Field | Host Field

Figure 3.2 IP address and non-default mask in binary illustrating the subnet field.

Figure 3.2 identifies the two extra bits past the default boundary as the subnet field—they used to be in the host field, but we subnetted and stole them to become the subnet field.

Subnetting

Subnetting is not as difficult as it initially seems. Because we are dealing with arithmetic, there is definitely more than one way to do this, but the method shown here has worked well. The following sections work through the process of subnetting. Then, we work on some shortcuts to show how you can subnet quickly because CCNA exam candidates often find that they are pressed for time on the exam.

Address Class and Default Mask

Subnetting happens when we extend the subnet mask past the default boundary for the address we are working with. So it's obvious that we first need to be sure of what the default mask is supposed to be for any given address. Previously, we looked at the IANA designations for IP address classes and the number ranges in the first octet that identify those classes. If you didn't pick up on this before, you should memorize those immediately.

When faced with a subnetting question, the first thing to do is decide what class the address belongs to. Here are some examples:

192.168.1.66

The first octet is between 192 and 223: Class C

Default mask for Class C: 255.255.255.0

188.21.21.3

The first octet is between 128 and 191: Class B

Default mask for Class B: 255.255.0.0

24.64.208.5

The first octet is between 1 and 126: Class A

Default mask for Class A: 255.0.0.0

It's important to grasp that if an address uses the correct default mask for its class, it is not subnetted. This means that regardless of how many hosts the 0s at the end of the mask create, all those hosts are on the same network, all in the same broadcast domain. This has some implications for *classful networks* (ones that use the default mask for the address). Take a Class A for example: A Class A network can have 16,777,214 hosts on it. Almost 17 million PCs on one network would never work—there would be so much traffic from broadcasts alone, never mind regular data traffic, that nothing could get through and the network would collapse under its own size. Even a Class B network has 65,534 possible host IPs. This is still too many. So, either we waste a lot of addresses by not using the whole classful A or B network, or we subnet to make the networks smaller.

This is actually one of the most common reasons we subnet: The default or classful networks are too big, causing issues such as excessive broadcast traffic and wasted IP address space. Subnetting creates multiple smaller subnetworks out of one larger classful network, which allows us to make IP networks the "right" size—big or small—for any given situation.

The Increment

By definition, the process of subnetting creates several smaller classless subnets out of one larger classful one. The spacing between these subnets, or how many IP addresses apart they are, is called the *Increment*. Because we are working with binary numbers, a pattern emerges in which the Increment is always one of those powers of 2 again—another good reason to memorize those numbers.

The Increment is really easy to figure out. It is simply the value of the last bit in the subnet mask. Let's look at some examples. Figure 3.3 shows an IP address and subnet mask in binary.

IP Address and Mask: 192.168.21.1 255.255.255.0

Binary IP: 11000000.10101000.00010101.00000001

Binary Mask: 11111111.11111111.11111111.11000000

Figure 3.3 IP address and default mask in binary.

Note that this is a Class C address, and it uses the correct default mask—so it is not subnetted. This means that there is only one network, so there isn't really an increment to worry about here. It's sufficient at this point to recognize that an address that uses its default mask creates one network (no subnets), so there is no spacing between subnets to consider.

Let's take the same address and subnet it by extending the mask past the default boundary, as shown in Figure 3.4.

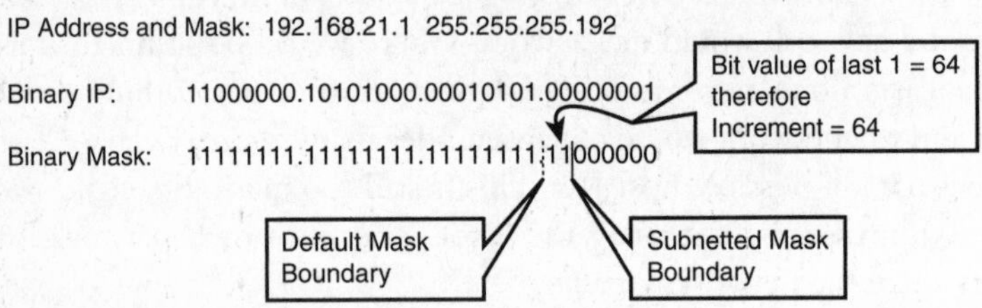

Figure 3.4 IP address and subnetted mask.

The very last bit in the subnet mask in the figure is in the bit position worth 64—so the Increment in this case is 64, which means that the subnets we made are evenly spaced at 64 IP addresses apart.

Think about this for a second. We are doing the subnetting in the fourth octet—that is where the mask changes from 1s to 0s. (The octet where this happens is sometimes referred to as the "Interesting" octet.) The lowest possible value in that fourth octet is 0. If the subnets are 64 IP addresses apart, this means that the first subnet starts at 0, the next one starts at 64, the third at 128, and the fourth at 192—all multiples of the Increment. Note that if we add another 64 to that last 192, we get 256—and that is larger than 255, the largest value that is possible in one octet. So this means we only have room for 4 subnets. Figure 3.5 illustrates this pattern more clearly:

Subnets Created with Increment of 64:

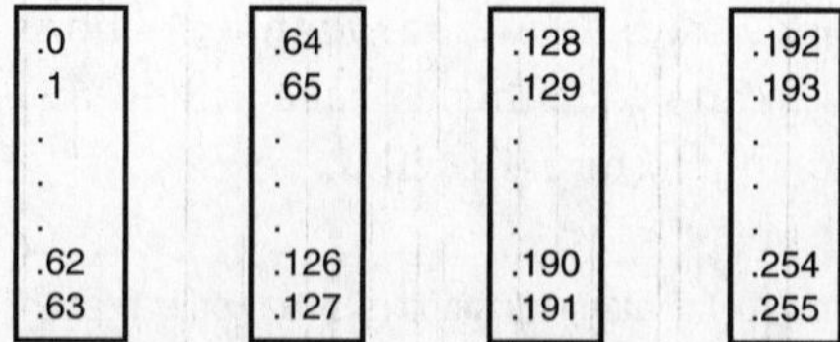

Figure 3.5 Subnets created with Increment of 64.

The multiples of the Increment—0, 64, 128, and 192—are the starting addresses of the subnets we created. The subnets are all 64 addresses long, so we have room to make four subnets before we run out of addresses in the fourth octet.

Figure 3.6 shows our IP and subnet mask—note that the value of the last bit in the mask is 16—and the subnets created with that Increment of 16.

192.168.21.0 255.255.255.240

IP: 11000000.10101000.00010101.00000000
Mask: 11111111.11111111.11111111.11110000

Subnets Created with Increment of 16:

.0	.16	.32	.48	.64	.80	.96	.112	.128	.144	.160	.176	.192	.208	.224	.240
.	.	.	.	.	.	.	.	.	.	.	.	.	.	.	.
.15	.31	.47	.63	.79	.95	.111	.127	.143	.159	.175	.191	.207	.223	.239	.255

Figure 3.6 IP address and subnet mask with Increment of 16.

First of all, you should notice that we are subnetting again—the mask extends past the default boundary. The last 1 in the mask is in the bit position worth 16, so our Increment is 16. The multiples of 16 are 0, 16, 32, 48, 64, 80, 96, 112, 128, 144, 160, 176, 192, 208, 224, and 240. Again, we can't make another subnet because 240 + 16 = 256. Be careful not to start doubling as we did with the binary values; here we are just adding the Increment value each time. It's easy to get confused!

The Increment is really the key to subnetting; if you can determine the Increment, you can see how big your subnets are and how many you have created. Remember, the easy way to find the Increment is to just determine the bit value of the last 1 in the mask.

Number of Hosts

The number of 0s at the end of the mask always defines the number of hosts on any network or subnet. There is a simple mathematical formula that defines how many IP addresses are available to be assigned to hosts.

Hosts is another word for computers, router interfaces, printers, or any other network component that can be assigned an IP address.

Now, no one expects you to be a big fan of algebra, but you need to see and understand the formula.

The number of binary bits you have to use determines the maximum number of different values you can express using those bits. If you have three bits, you can make eight different values—0 through 7, or 000 through 111 in binary. Three bits, and 2^3=8—this is not a coincidence. The binary values you learned earlier—1, 2, 4, 8, 16, 32, 64, 128—are all powers of 2 and define the maximum number of different values you can create if the mask ends in that bit position. So it should come as no surprise that the formula for the number of hosts on any network or subnet is 2^H-2, where H is the number of 0s at the end of the mask.

But why do we subtract 2 in the formula? It's pretty straightforward: Every network or subnet has two reserved addresses that cannot be assigned to a host. The rule is that no host can have the IP address in which all the host bits are set to 0, and no host can have the IP address in which all the host bits are set to 1. These addresses are called the Network ID and the Broadcast ID, respectively. They are the first and last IPs in any network or subnet. We lose those two IP addresses from the group of values that could be assigned to hosts.

Think of a network or subnet as a street with houses on it. Each house has a unique address, and the street has a name. The Network ID is like the street name, and all the houses are hosts on a subnet that is known by its Network ID street name. If two hosts have identical network and subnet fields in their addresses, they are on the same network, and can ping each other and exchange data and all that good stuff. If the network and subnet fields are different, even by one bit, they are on different networks and can't communicate until we put a router between them. The routers act like street intersections; you must get to the right intersection (router) before you can get on to the street you want… but we'll save that for later.

Devices running TCP/IP make a decision about whether a particular IP address is on the network by performing a logical AND operation. The AND is a Boolean function that works like this:

1 AND 1 = 1

1 AND 0 = 0

0 AND 0 = 0

This operation applies to IP networking like this: A host does a logical AND between its own IP and its mask. This determines its Network ID. The host can then do an AND between another IP address and its own mask to determine if that second address is on the same network or some other one.

Let's take the IP address and mask of an imaginary host and display them in binary, as shown in Figure 3.7. The AND operation takes each bit in the address and ANDs it with the corresponding bit in the mask below it; the result is the NetID of the host.

IP Address and Mask: 192.16.20.12 255.255.255.0

Binary IP:	11000000.00010000.00010100.00001100
Binary Mask:	11111111.11111111.11111111.00000000
AND Result:	11000000.00010000.00010100.00000000
	NetID = 192.16.20.0

Figure 3.7 The AND operation determines the NetID.

Now the host knows its own NetID and can compare any other host's address to that to see if the other host has the same NetID. If the two NetIDs are different, traffic has to be sent through a router to get to the other network—and if there is no router, the two hosts can't communicate.

Being able to do the AND operation is a useful skill; a lot of test questions center around the NetID, and being able to find it quickly is a big help.

The Broadcast ID

The *Broadcast ID* is the address of everybody on that network or subnet. Sometimes called a directed broadcast, it is the common address of all hosts on that Network ID. This should not be confused with a full IP broadcast to the address of 255.255.255.255, which hits every IP host that can hear it; the Broadcast ID hits only hosts on a common subnet.

Let's take the previous example of an Increment of 64 and expand on the detail, as shown in Figure 3.8:

Subnets Created with Increment of 64 – NetID and Broadcast ID shown:

.0 N	.64 N	.128 N	.192 N
.1	.65	.129	.193
.	.	.	.
.	.	.	.
.	.	.	.
.62	.126	.190	.254
.63 B	.127 B	.191 B	.255 B

Figure 3.8 Subnets from Increment of 64 with NetID and Broadcast ID shown.

Note that all the multiples of the Increment—the numbers that mark the start of each subnet—have been identified by an "N" for Network ID, and the last IP in every subnet is marked with a "B" for Broadcast ID. This leaves us with 62 IPs left over in each subnet, and any of these (but only these) can be assigned to a host.

This leaves us with a range of IP addresses within every network or subnet that can be assigned to hosts. There is an unofficial convention that the gateway or router for a subnet is assigned the first or the last IP address available, but that is entirely arbitrary.

You need to know exactly what the first and last IP addresses are in any subnet; a lot of questions ask for them, and it's fundamental to understanding what is happening when you subnet.

The first valid IP address is defined as

NetID + 1

In Figure 3.3, the first valid host IPs in each subnet are .1, .65, .129, and .193.

The last valid host is defined as

BroadcastID – 1

In Figure 3.8, the last valid host IPs in each subnet are .62, .126, .190, and .254.

Here are some handy tips to help you keep track of the NetID, first and last hosts, and Broadcast ID:

NetID:	Always Even
First Host:	Always Odd
Last Host:	Always Even
Broadcast ID:	Always Odd

See how the subnetted mask in the previous example has shortened the number of 0s at the end of the mask as compared to the default of 8? We now have only six 0s in the host part, so our formula would be

$2^6 - 2 = 62$

Here's something interesting: It doesn't matter what IP address you use with this mask; that mask will always give you 62 hosts on each subnet. You can pick a Class A address, say 22.1.1.0, and that mask would still make 62 hosts per subnet. The number of 0s at the end of the mask always drives how many hosts are on each subnet, regardless of the address.

So, what happened to all the other host IPs we started with? Remember that subnetting takes a classful A, B, or C network and splits it into several equal-sized pieces. It's just like cutting a pie into pieces; the original amount of pie is still there, but each piece is now separate.

Remember that the number of 0s at the end at the mask always defines how many hosts are on each subnet, regardless of the address in use.

Number of Subnets

Following on with the pie analogy, we know that we slice a classful network into pieces—but how many pieces? There is a simple mathematical relationship to this as well, but it is slightly more complex because of an old rule that we sometimes have to deal with.

The basic formula for the number of subnets is similar to the hosts formula. It is simply 2^S, where S is the number of bits in the subnet field—that means the number of 1s in the mask past the default boundary for that address. If you look at Figure 3.9, you can see how this works.

The default boundary for that Class C address should be at the 24th bit, where the third octet ends and the fourth begins. The subnetted mask extends that by 2 bits into the fourth octet. So, we have stolen 2 bits, and our formula would look like this:

# of subnets = 2^S

S = 2

$2^2 = 4$

IP Address and Mask: 192.168.21.1 255.255.255.192

Binary IP: 11000000.10101000.00010101.00000001

Binary Mask: 11111111.11111111.11111111.11000000

Default Mask Boundary

Subnetted Mask Boundary

Figure 3.9 Subnetted Class C with Increment of 64.

We made 4 subnets, as you saw earlier. To figure out how many bits we stole, we first must know where the default boundary is so that we know where to start counting. This is where knowing the address classes and the correct default masks is critical; if you can't figure this out, you will not be able to answer most subnetting questions correctly, and that would be bad.

Now here's where things get tricky. A rule that some older systems use says that the first and last subnets created are invalid and unusable. The rule is known as the Subnet Zero Rule, and obviously if it is in effect, we lose 2 subnets from the total we create. These two subnets will be referred to from now on as the *zero subnets*. This is confusing and makes things more difficult—but difficult is not something Cisco shies away from on its certification exams. So if you want your CCNA, pay attention to the question and don't complain about how hard it is.

Cisco tests might be difficult and tricky, but they are fair—they will not withhold information you need to answer the question. The test question will always tell you whether the Zero Subnets Rule is in effect; yes, both types of questions are asked.

The Cisco IOS supports the use of the Zero Subnets. The command "ip subnet zero" turns on the ability to use them, so that might be how the question is telling you whether they are in effect. Once you pass your CCNA, you will not likely have to worry about the Zero Subnets Rule again, unless you lose your mind and decide to become a Cisco trainer.

After you determine whether the zero subnets are available, use the following to get the calculation for the number of subnets right:

Zero subnets not available?	Subtract 2 subnets: formula is 2^s-2
Zero subnets available?	Keep all subnets: formula is 2^s

Working with Subnetting Questions

The approach you need to take to any subnetting question is very simple. After you become fluent in subnetting, you can take some shortcuts; but to build a solid understanding, you need to be methodical.

Every subnetting question you ever see will be about one of three things:

- Number of hosts
- Number of subnets
- The Increment

Your task will be to simply figure out what the question is asking for and solve it without getting confused or distracted.

Determining Host Requirements

There are only two scenarios when determining the host requirements: Either you are given a mask and asked how many hosts per subnet this creates, or you are given a requirement for a certain number of hosts and asked to provide the appropriate mask. Either way, the number of 0s at the end of the mask drives how many hosts per subnet there will be; the address to which that mask is applied is irrelevant. Your task is to put the correct number of 0s at the end of the mask such that 2H-2 is greater than or equal to the desired number of hosts, or to determine what the value of 2H-2 actually is. From there, you must choose the correct expression of the mask, either in dotted decimal or CIDR notation.

Determining Subnet Requirements

The scenarios for determining subnet requirements are quite similar to the host questions; either you are told how many subnets you need and asked to provide the appropriate mask, or you are given a mask and asked how many subnets it creates. Note that in both cases (unlike hosts questions), you must know the IP address or at least the class of address you are working with. Creating subnets happens by extending the default mask, so you must know where the mask should end by default—and for that you need to know the class of address. Once you know where to start, simply extend the mask by the correct number of subnet bits such that 2S-2 (or possibly just 2S) gives you the correct number of subnets.

Remember that the zero subnets rule might come into play here; although the majority of questions say that the zero subnets are not valid and therefore the formula should be 2S-2, some questions—and probably more as time goes on—will clearly state that zero subnets are available. Read the question!

Determining Increment-based Requirements

Increment questions are the most challenging and complex subnetting questions, often requiring you to do a lot of legwork before you can get to the answer.

Increment questions often give you two or more IP addresses and masks, and ask you things such as, "Why can't Host A ping Host B?" The answer could be that A and B are on different subnets; to determine this, you need to understand where those subnets begin and end, and that depends on the Increment. Another popular question gives you several IP addresses and masks that are applied to PCs, servers, and routers. The system, as it is described, is not working, and you need to determine what device has been incorrectly configured—perhaps two IPs in different subnets, perhaps a host that is using a NetID or BroadcastID as its address.

The key is to first determine what the Increment is or should be; then, carefully plot out the multiples of the Increment—the Network IDs of all the subnets. Then you can add the Broadcast IDs, which are all one less than the next Network ID. Now you have a framework into which you can literally draw the host IP ranges, without risk of "losing the picture" if you do this all in your head.

All of these skills take practice. Everyone goes through the same process in learning subnetting: For quite a while, you will have no idea what is going on—then suddenly, the light goes on and you "get it." Rest assured that you will get it. It takes longer for some than others, and you do need practice or you will lose the skill.

The Subnetting Chart

So now you should understand concepts and mechanics of subnetting. You can do it and get the right answer almost all of the time, but it takes you a while. This is good—congratulations! If you are not at that point yet, you should practice more before you look at this next section.

What follows is one of many variations of a subnetting chart. This is a good one because it is easy to use under pressure when your brain will behave unpredictably.

You must be able to re-create this chart exactly and correctly before you start your exam. If you make a stupid mistake in creating your chart, you could easily get all of your subnetting questions wrong, and that would probably cause you to fail.

The chart represents the last two octets of a subnet mask, and what effect a 1 or a 0 in the different bit positions will have. It lists the Increment, CIDR notation, the mask in decimal, the number of hosts created, and the number of subnets formed from a Class B and C address. Figure 3.10 shows a completed version.

Increment	128	64	32	16	8	4	2	1	128	64	32	16	8	4	2	1
CIDR:	/17	/18	/19	/20	/21	/22	/23	/24	/25	/26	/27	/28	/29	/30	/31	/32
Mask:	128	192	224	240	248	252	254	255	128	192	224	240	248	252	254	255
Hosts:	32,766	16,382	8190	4094	2046	1022	510	254	126	62	30	14	6	2	-	-
B Subnets:	0	2	6	14	30	62	126	254	510	1024	2046	4094	8190	16,382	-	-
C Subnets:	1	1	1	1	1	1	1	1	0	2	6	14	30	62	-	-

Figure 3.10 The subnetting chart.

Following are steps to recreate the chart:

1. The first row is simply the binary bit position values—the powers of 2. Start at the right with 1, and keep doubling the value as you go left: 1, 2, 4, 8, 16, 32, 64, 128. Repeat for the left side of the chart.
2. The second row is the CIDR notation—the number of 1s in a row in the mask. Our chart starts at the 17th bit, so simply number the second row starting at 17, through 32.
3. The third row is the mask in binary. Add consecutive bit values together from left to right to get the valid mask values of 128, 192, 224, 240, 248, 252, 254, and 255. Or, you can just memorize them…
4. The fourth row is the number of hosts created. Starting at the left, subtract 2 from the first row and enter that value. Do this for the whole fourth octet. When you get to the third octet (the left half of the chart), you will have to change your approach: The value will keep increasing in the same pattern, but subtracting 2 from the top row won't work any more because the top row resets for the third octet. The simplest approach is to keep doubling the top row and subtract 2 from that:

   128x2=256 256x2=512 512x2=1024…

   256-2=254 512-2=510 1024-2=1022…

5. The fifth row is the number of subnets created from a Class B address. Starting at the left side of the chart (the third octet), simply repeat the values from the fourth row. Just remember to start with a single 0 instead of two.

Remember that the Subnet Zero Rule will change your answers and how you use your chart. If the Zero Subnets are allowed, remember to add 2 to each value in the fifth and sixth rows, starting in the third octet for Class B addresses and the fourth octet for Class C addresses.

6. The sixth row of the chart is the number of subnets created from a Class C address. The numbers are exactly the same as in Row 5; just start them in the fourth octet instead. The same caution and tactic about the Zero Subnets applies.

Provided you have built it correctly, your chart is a huge help in answering subnetting questions quickly and accurately. All you need to do is determine what the question is asking for, and then look up that value on your chart. All of the answers you need will be in the same column. Practice building and using the chart until it becomes something you can do without thinking. You will need your brain for other more complicated problems.

Exam Prep Questions

1. Which of the following are alternate representations of the decimal number 227? Choose 2.

   ❍ A. 0x227

   ❍ B. 11100011

   ❍ C. 0x143

   ❍ D. 0xE3

   ❍ E. 11100110

2. Which of the following are alternate representations of 0xB8? Choose two.

   ❍ A. 10110100

   ❍ B. 10111111

   ❍ C. 10111000

   ❍ D. 184

   ❍ E. 0x184

3. You have been asked to create a subnet that supports 16 hosts. What subnet mask should you use?

   ❍ A. 255.255.255.252

   ❍ B. 255.255.255.248

   ❍ C. 255.255.255.240

   ❍ D. 255.255.255.224

4. Given the mask 255.255.254.0, how many hosts per subnet does this create?

   ❍ A. 254

   ❍ B. 256

   ❍ C. 512

   ❍ D. 510

   ❍ E. 2

5. You are a senior network engineer at True North Technologies. Your boss, Mr. Martin, asks you create a subnet with room for 12 IPs for some new managers. Mr. Martin promises that there will never be more than 12 managers, and he asks you to make sure that you conserve IP address space by providing the minimum number of possible host IPs on the subnet. What subnet mask will best meet these requirements?

   ❍ A. 255.255.255.12

   ❍ B. 255.255.255.0

   ❍ C. 255.255.240.0

   ❍ D. 255.255.255.240

   ❍ E. 255.255.255.224

6. Your boss Duncan does not seem to be able to grasp subnetting. He comes out of a management meeting and quietly asks you to help him with a subnetting issue. He needs to divide the Class B address space the company uses into six subnets for the various buildings in the plant, while keeping the subnets as large as possible to allow for future growth. Because the company has not upgraded their Cisco equipment since it was purchased several years ago, none of the routers supports the "ip subnet zero" command. What is the best subnet mask to use in this scenario?

❍ A. 255.255.0.0

❍ B. 255.255.248.0

❍ C. 255.255.224.0

❍ D. 255.255.240.0

❍ E. 255.255.255.224

7. You have purchased several brand-new Cisco routers for your company. Your current address space is 172.16.0.0 /22. Because these new routers support the "ip subnet zero" command, you realize you are about to gain back two subnets that you could not use with the old gear. How many subnets total will be available to you once the upgrades are complete?

❍ A. 4

❍ B. 2

❍ C. 32

❍ D. 62

❍ E. 64

8. Which of the following are true about the following address and mask pair: 10.8.8.0 /24? Choose all that apply.

❍ A. This is a Class B address.

❍ B. This is a Class A address.

❍ C. This is a Class C address.

❍ D. 16 bits were stolen from the host field.

❍ E. 24 bits were stolen from the host field.

❍ F. The default mask for this address is 255.0.0.0.

❍ G. The mask can also be written as 255.255.255.0.

❍ H. The mask creates 65,536 subnets total from the default address space.

❍ I. Each subnet supports 256 valid host IPs.

❍ J. Each subnet supports 254 valid host IPs.

9. Indy and Greg have configured their own Windows XP PCs and connected them with crossover cables. They can't seem to share their downloaded MP3 files, however. Given their configurations, what could be the problem?

   Indy's configuration:

IP:	192.168.0.65
Mask:	255.255.255.192

   Greg's configuration:

IP:	192.168.0.62
Mask:	255.255.255.192

   - O A. Indy is using a Broadcast ID for his IP.
   - O B. Greg is using an invalid mask.
   - O C. Indy's IP is in one of the Zero Subnets.
   - O D. Greg and Indy are using IPs in different subnets.

10. You are given an old router to practice for your CCNA. Your boss Dave has spent a lot of time teaching you subnetting. Now he challenges you to apply your knowledge. He hands you a note that says:

    "Given the subnetted address space of 192.168.1.0 /29, give the E0 interface the first valid IP in the eighth subnet. Give the S0 interface the last valid IP in the twelfth subnet. The Zero Subnets are available. You have 10 minutes. Go."

    Which two of the following are the correct IP and Mask configurations? Choose 2.

    - O A. E0: 192.168.1.1 255.255.255.0
    - O B. E0: 192.168.1.56 255.255.255.248
    - O C. E0: 192.168.1.57 255.255.255.248
    - O D. S0: 192.168.1.254 255.255.255.0
    - O E. S0: 192.168.1.95 255.255.255.248
    - O F. S0: 192.168.1.94 255.255.255.248

Answers to Exam Prep Questions

1. Answers B and D are correct. Answer A in decimal would be 551. Answer C in decimal would be 323. Answer E in decimal is 230.

2. Answers C and D are correct. Answer A in hex is 0xB4. Answer B in hex is 0xBF. Answer E is simply an attempt to trick you—the correct decimal answer is incorrectly expressed as a hex value.

3. Answer D is correct. A will only support 2 hosts; B only 6, and C only 14. Watch out for the minus 2 in the host calculation! Answer C creates 16 hosts on the subnet, but we lose 2—one for the Net ID and one for the Broadcast ID.

4. Answer D is correct. The mask 255.255.254.0 gives us nine 0s at the end of the mask; 2^9-2 = 510. Answer A is checking to see if you missed the 254 in the third octet because you are used to seeing 255. Answer B does the same thing plus tries to catch you on not subtracting 2 from the host calculation. Answer C tries to catch you on not subtracting 2, and Answer E is the Increment of the given mask that you might pick if you were really off track.

5. The correct answer is D. Disregarding for the moment the possibility that Mr. Martin might be wrong, let's look at the requirements. He says make room for 12 managers, and make the subnets as small as possible while doing so. You need to find the mask that has sufficient host IP space without making it bigger than necessary. Answer A is invalid; 12 is not a valid mask value. Remember, a mask is a continuous string of 1s followed by a continuous string of 0s. In answer B, the mask is valid, but it is not correct. This mask has eight 0s at the end, which, when we apply the formula 28 -2 gives us 254 hosts. That makes more than enough room for the 12 managers, but does not meet the "as small as possible" requirement. Answer C has the correct mask value in the wrong octet. That mask gives us eight 0s in the fourth octet, plus another four in the third octet; that would give us 4094 hosts on the subnet. Answer E gives us 30 hosts per subnet, but that only meets half the requirement. This mask does not provide the minimum number of hosts.

6. The correct answer is C. The default mask for a Class B is 255.255.0.0, Answer C extends that mask by three bits, creating 8 subnets (2^3=8). The Zero Subnets are lost because the routers cannot use them, so we are left with six subnets. Answer A is incorrect because it is the default mask for a Class B and not subnetted at all. Answer B and D are incorrect because although they create sufficient subnets, they do not maximize the number of hosts per subnet and so are not the best answer. Answer E uses the correct mask in the wrong octet.

7. Answer E is correct. With "ip subnet zero" enabled, all 64 subnets created by the mask in use become available. Answer A, B, and C are not even close and are simply distracters. Answer D wants to catch you by subtracting the zero subnets.

8. The correct answers are B, D, F, G, H, and J. Answer A and C are incorrect because this is a Class A address. Answer E is incorrect because only 16 bits were stolen. Answer I is incorrect because it does not subtract the two IPs for the NetID and Broadcast ID.

9. Answer D is correct. With that mask, the Increment is 64. Greg is in the first subnet, and Indy is in the second. Without a router between them, their PCs will not be able to communicate above layer 2. Answer A is incorrect; the Broadcast ID for Indy would be .63. Answer B is incorrect; nothing is wrong with the mask. Answer C is incorrect; the Zero Subnets are the first and last created, and Indy is in the second subnet. The question does not mention the Zero Subnets, and in any case Windows XP fully supports them.

10. The correct answers are C and F. This is an Increment question. The Increment here is 8, so you should start by jotting down the multiples of 8 (those are all the NetIDs), and then noting what 1 less than each of the NetIDs is (those are the Broadcast IDs). From there, it is easy to find what the first and last IPs in each subnet are. (Remember that Dave says we can use the Zero Subnets.) Answers A and D are incorrect because they do not use the subnetted address space Dave requested. Answer B is incorrect because it is a NetID. Answer E is incorrect because it is a Broadcast ID.

Working with Cisco Equipment

Terms You'll Need to Understand

- ✓ Interface
- ✓ Line
- ✓ User Exec
- ✓ Privileged Exec
- ✓ Configuration Register
- ✓ ROM
- ✓ RAM
- ✓ NVRAM
- ✓ FLASH

Techniques You'll Need to Master

- ✓ Navigating the Cisco IOS Command Line Interface
- ✓ Assigning IP Addresses
- ✓ Configuring Clock Rate, Bandwidth, Speed, and Duplex
- ✓ Enabling an Interface
- ✓ Troubleshooting Connectivity

Introduction

This chapter introduces you to Cisco equipment. We examine how to connect to it and make initial configurations, as well as how to connect it to other devices to build a network. We review the different types of network connections available, with particular emphasis on those that are tested in the CCNA exams. We also look at where a Cisco device stores the various files it needs to operate, the files needed for the boot process, and the backup and restoration of system files.

Products

The CCNA exam does not test you about product-specific knowledge. That is to say, you are not expected to know what feature cards are available for a 6500 series switch, but you do need to understand the differences between a router and a switch, and you need to understand how their configuration requirements vary.

For our purposes, we use a Catalyst 2950 or 3550 switch and a 1600, 1700, or 2600 series router as example devices. Most of the commands you learn in this chapter also apply to more advanced models.

External Connections

Cisco devices make connections to other devices, and collectively they all create a network. At some point, making a connection means plugging in a cable—even with a wireless system. This section examines some of the various connections found on Cisco routers and switches.

Console

When you first obtain a new Cisco device, it won't be configured. That is to say, it will not do any of the customized functions you might need; it does not have any IP addresses, and it is generally not going to do what you paid for. Now, if you buy a 2950 switch, turn on the power, and plug PCs in to it, it will work to connect those PCs with no further configuration, but you are missing out on all the cool stuff and advanced features. Your new router, on the other hand, will not be capable of doing much for you at all, even if you plug the interfaces in. Routers need basic configuration to function on a network, or they simply consume power and blink at you.

The console port is used for *local management* connections. This means that you must be able to physically reach the console port with a cable that is typically about six feet long. The console port looks exactly like an Ethernet port. It uses the same connector, but it has different wiring and is often (but not always) identified with a pale blue label that says "CONSOLE." If the device is not configured at all—meaning, if it is new or has had a previous configuration erased—the console port is the only way to connect to it and apply configurations. Figure 4.1 shows what a console port looks like.

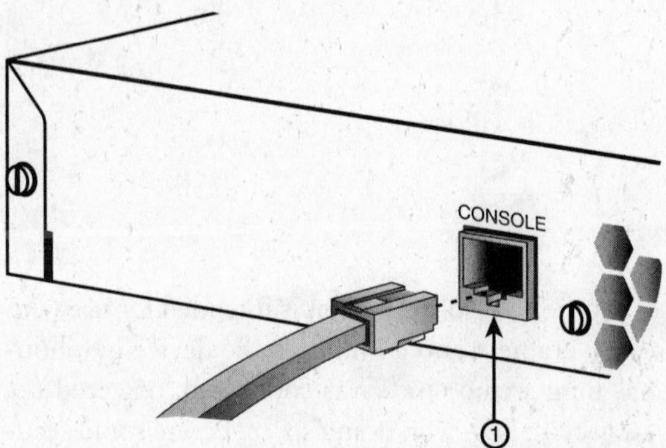

Figure 4.1 The console port (image used with permission from Cisco Systems, Inc.).

Connecting to the console port is done with a special *rollover* cable; a rollover cable has pins 1 through 8 wired to the opposite number, as shown in Figure 4.2.

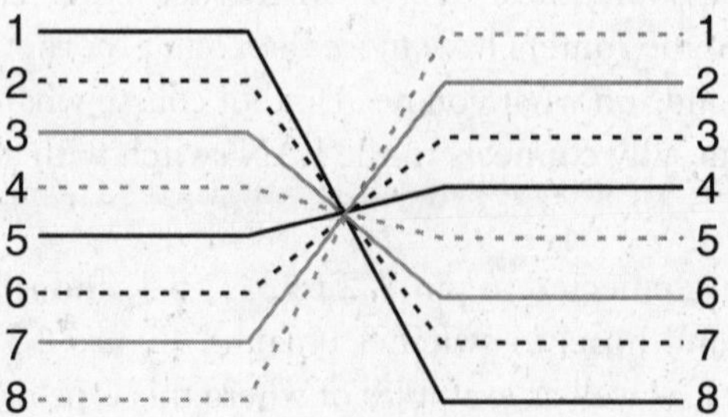

Figure 4.2 Rollover cable pinouts.

One end of the rollover cable has the RJ-45 connector to connect to the console port; the other has either a molded-in 9-pin serial connector, or another RJ-45 and adapters for 9-pin or 15-pin serial connections. Because many new laptops do not have the EIA/TIA 9- or 15-pin serial connections and feature USB ports only, you might need to buy yourself a USB to serial adapter. The serial connection attaches to your workstation's COM port.

Now that you are plugged in, you need to configure a terminal application to communicate with the Cisco device over the rollover cable. You can use Hyperterminal, Procomm, TeraTerm, SecureCRT, or any of a number of others that support character-based terminal emulation. The settings for your terminal session are as follows:

Baud Rate:	9600
Data Bits:	8
Parity:	None
Stop Bits:	1
Flow Control:	None

Your COM port for this connection will vary.

Aux Port

The AUX port is really just another console port that is intended for use with a modem, so you can remotely connect and administer the device by phoning it. This is a great idea as long as the modem is connected, powered up, and plugged in to the phone system; however, doing so can create some security issues, so make sure that you get advice on addressing those before setting this up.

Ethernet Port

An Ethernet port (which might sometimes be a FastEthernet port) is intended to connect to the LAN. Some routers have more than one Ethernet or FastEthernet port; it really depends on what you need and of course what you purchase. The Ethernet port usually connects to the LAN switch with a *straight-through cable*.

A straight-through cable has pin 1 connected to pin 1, 2 to 2, 3 to 3, and so on. It is used to connect routers and hosts to switches or hubs. Figure 4.3 shows the straight-through pinouts, as well as examples of where this type of cable is used.

If you have two or more Ethernet ports, you can connect the others to a high-speed Internet connection such as a cable modem or DSL, or to another, separate LAN.

You must understand how to use rollover, straight-through, and crossover cables, and you must know how to identify them from a diagram of their pinouts.

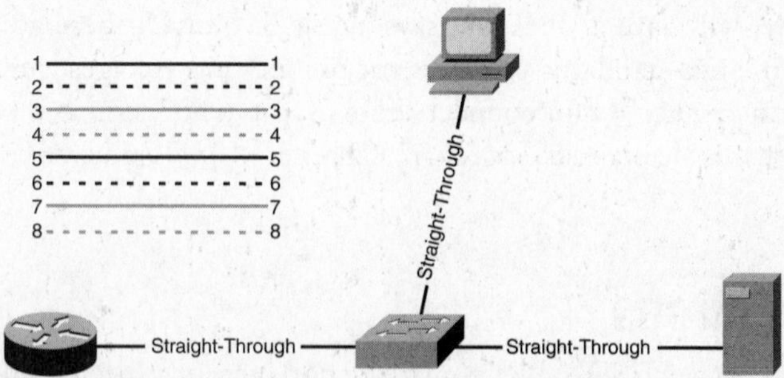

Figure 4.3 Straight-through cable pinouts and applications.

Serial Port

A Cisco serial port is a proprietary design, a 60-pin D-sub. This connector can be configured for almost any kind of serial communication. You simply need a cable that has the Cisco connector on one end and the appropriate type of connector for the service you want to connect to on the other.

Serial ports are almost always used for WAN connections and use one of several different Layer 2 protocols including Frame Relay, PPP, and HDLC. Serial ports can also connect to an ISDN Primary Rate Interface (PRI) service or regular analog telephone service. (For a telephone service, you need a special hardware type called an asynchronous serial port and a modem.)

HDLC is the default encapsulation on a Cisco serial port, and the HDLC protocol here is a Cisco proprietary version of the standardized ISO HDLC that can run multiple Layer 3 protocols, which the ISO version can't do.

You might have one or more serial ports depending on what you need and what you buy.

Know the three WAN encapsulations for a serial port: HDLC, PPP, and Frame Relay. Know that Cisco's HDLC is the default encapsulation for serial ports.

ISDN BRI

A router can have an ISDN BRI port for connection to an ISDN phone system. This allows you to send data, as well as voice, over the digital phone line. You could even send video as long as you're not too ambitious—ISDN BRI bandwidth is only 128k.

The ISDN BRI port will have a label that says either S/T or U; these are important because the two standards use different pinouts and voltages, and you could damage the router if you connect the wrong type of port to the ISDN system. This is explained more in Chapter 10, "Wide Area Networks."

Other Connections

Your router can also have an ISDN PRI controller port; this is a specialized port that allows you to configure your ISDN PRI service with a single module on the router instead of needing external devices. The PRI controller will probably have a label that says "T1 CSU/DSU," with a plug that looks like the RJ-45 connector but is actually an RJ-48.

You can also buy ports for High-Speed Serial communication (perhaps ATM) or even different fiber-optic connections. What you purchase will depend on the services you need to connect to, the model of router you buy, and of course how much money you want to spend.

Connecting and Configuring Cisco Devices

Now that we have examined what our connection options are, we will look at how Cisco devices operate, including the boot sequence, operating system and configuration file location, and basic command line functions.

Device Memory Locations

A Cisco device has four memory types. Each is used for a specific purpose:

- *ROM*, or read-only memory, holds the POST, bootstrap, ROMMON, and RXBoot microcode. The *POST (Power-On Self Test)* is a basic inventory and test of the hardware in the device. The *bootstrap* is responsible for finding an operating system to load. *ROMMON* is a minimal command set that can be used to connect to a TFTP server and restore a missing or corrupted IOS image. *RXBOOT* is a mini-IOS that has a much more familiar command set than ROMMON and more features, so it is easier to use for IOS restoration from TFTP.
- *Flash* memory normally stores the IOS image file. Because flash is simply a file storage area, assuming that you have enough space, you could store other files here as well, perhaps another IOS version, or backups of a configuration. Flash can be either SIMM cards on the mother board,

or PCMCIA cards either externally accessible or inside the case of the router on the motherboard.

- *NVRAM* is Non-Volatile RAM; this means that it will not lose the data stored in it when the power is turned off or fails. The startup-configuration file is stored here.
- *RAM* is similar to RAM on a PC; this very fast memory is where all dynamically learned information is stored, such as routing tables, ARP cache, and buffers.

IOS Startup Process

When you turn on the power, you will see information scrolling down your terminal screen almost immediately. It is a good idea to watch this information, as important messages can be seen here if failures occur during boot.

The IOS startup process is actually more complex than it appears. The basic steps are as follows:

1. Run the POST.
2. Find the IOS.
3. Load the IOS to RAM.
4. Find the configuration.
5. Load the configuration to RAM.

Know the basic steps in the boot process.

Let's look at the process in more detail. The default behavior for a router or switch is as follows:

1. The POST runs.
2. Assuming that there are no critical errors with the POST run, the bootstrap checks the startup-config file in NVRAM for *boot system* commands. These commands might have been entered by the router admin to override the default behavior, perhaps to load a different IOS for test purposes.
3. Assuming that there are no boot system commands, the router loads the first valid IOS image it finds in the flash memory.

4. If there is no usable IOS in flash, the router will begin broadcasting for a TFTP server in the hopes of finding an IOS it can download and use; there are several preconfigured filenames that Cisco has programmed if you want to set up such a system.
5. If no TFTP server can be contacted, or if no valid IOS is found on one, the router will load the RXBOOT mini-IOS. This IOS has a familiar command set, and some of the features of a full IOS. The main purpose of RXBOOT is to allow you to manually connect to a TFTP server to download a valid IOS to flash. The command prompt for RXBOOT looks like this:

   ```
   Router(boot)>
   ```

6. In the unlikely event that RXBOOT fails, the router will load the ROM Monitor (ROMMON). ROMMON can also connect to a TFTP server, but if your router has dropped into ROMMON all by itself, the chances are you have a pretty serious problem. ROMMON command prompts vary with hardware type.
7. Once an IOS is loaded (except for ROMMON), the router looks for the startup-config file in NVRAM. If it is found, it is copied to RAM and renamed running-config.
8. If there is no startup-config file in NVRAM, the router will broadcast for a TFTP server to see if there is a configuration file available for it.
9. If that fails, the router will launch Setup mode.

Note that on most devices, the IOS image is decompressed and copied to RAM to run from there; similarly, the startup-config file is copied from NVRAM and renamed running-config as it is copied into RAM.

Setup Mode

Cisco devices include a feature called Setup mode to help you make a basic initial configuration. Setup mode will run only if there is no configuration file in NVRAM—either because the router is brand-new, or because it has been erased. Setup mode will ask you a series of questions and apply the configuration to the device based on your answers. You can abort Setup mode by typing **CTRL+C** or by saying "**no**" when asked if you want to save the configuration at the end of the interview.

Configuration Register

The configuration register is a four-character hexadecimal value that can be changed to manipulate how the router behaves at bootup. The default value is 0x2102.

The fourth character in the configuration register is known as the Boot Field. Changing the value for this character will have the following effects:

- 0x210**0** = Always boot to ROMMON. There are very few good reasons to do this, except possibly for training or a practical joke.
- 0x210**1** = Always boot to RXBOOT. Again, there are not many reasons to force this.
- 0x2102 through 0x210**F** = Load the first valid IOS in flash; values of 2 through F for the fourth character specify other IOS image files in flash.

Password Recovery

The third character in the configuration register can modify how the router loads the configuration file. The setting of 0x21**4**2 causes the router to ignore the startup-config file in NVRAM (which is where the password is stored) and proceed without a configuration—as if the router were brand-new or had its configuration erased.

This is a useful setting for those times when you do not know the password to enable the router and configure it. Perhaps you forgot the password (we hope not); perhaps the previous admin quit, got fired, or hit by a bus. Either way, we need the password to log in and make changes, so we need to bypass the existing password and change it to something we know. This process is called Password Recovery.

Password Recovery

The Password Recovery process is simple and takes about five minutes depending on how fast your router boots:

1. Connect to the console port, start your terminal application, and power cycle the router. When you see the boot process beginning, hit the Break sequence. (This is usually Ctrl+Break, but it might differ for different terminal applications.) Doing this interrupts the boot process and drops the router into ROMMON.
2. At the ROMMON prompt, enter the command `confreg 0x2142` to set the configuration register to 0x2142.
3. Restart the router by issuing the command `reset`.

4. When the router reloads, the configuration register setting of 0x2142 instructs the router to ignore the startup-config file in NVRAM. You will be asked if you want to go through Setup mode because the router thinks it has no startup-configuration file. Exit from Setup mode.
5. Press Return and enable the router—no password is required because the startup config file was not loaded.
6. Load the configuration manually by entering **`copy startup-config running-config`**.
7. Change the password.
8. Save the new password by entering **`copy running-config startup-config`**.
9. Go to the global config prompt, and change the configuration register back to the default setting with the command **`config-register 0x2102`**. Exit back to the privileged exec prompt.
10. Reboot the router using the **`reload`** command. You will be asked to save your changes; you can do so if you have made additional configuration changes.

That's all there is to it. Don't tell anyone how easy this is.

Know the following:

- What Setup mode is, and how to abort it
- The four configuration register settings described previously and what they do

Command Line Modes

Access to a router or switch command line is referred to as an *Exec session*. There are two levels of access: *user exec* and *privileged exec*. In user exec mode, you have limited access to information and diagnostic commands, and you are not able to make configuration changes to the router. Privileged exec mode gives you the complete command set and full authority to change or erase the configuration.

When you connect to a router using the console port, you see a message like this:

```
Router Con0 is now available.

Press RETURN to get started!
```

Pressing Return takes you to the User Exec Prompt, which looks like this:

```
Router>
```

To go to Privileged Exec mode, you must enter the command **enable**. The prompt will change from > to #, as shown:

```
Router>enable
Router#
```

From this point, you can enter commands to view the status and settings of the router, make some kinds of changes, and erase, back up, or restore the IOS and configuration files.

To make most kinds of changes, however, you must enter the Global Configuration mode. This is done by entering the command configure terminal from the Privileged Exec mode:

```
Router#configure terminal
Router(config)#
```

Notice that the command prompt changes to `Router(config)#`. From this prompt, you can make changes to functions that affect the whole router, or you can enter a more specific configuration mode to work with specialized functions. Some of the possible modes are listed and explained in the following:

```
Router(config)#interface serial 0
Router(config-if)#
```

This is the **Interface configuration mode**. Here you can set IP addresses and subnet masks, change speed, duplex, clock rate and bandwidth, or change the Layer 2 encapsulation of the interface. Changes made here affect only the interface you specified in the interface command.

```
Router(config)#line console 0
Router(config-line)#
```

Line configuration mode allows you to set up line parameters. Lines include the console, AUX, TTY, and VTY connections. The console and aux lines are the local administration connections. TTY lines are synchronous serial connections, usually for analog dialup access with modems. The VTY lines are virtual connections for Telnet access to the router to perform remote administration over an IP network.

```
Router(config)#router rip
Router(config-router)#
```

The *Router configuration mode* is where you set up dynamic routing protocols such as RIP, IGRP, EIGRP, and OSPF. Chapter 9, “Routing,” covers this material in detail.

It is important to understand—and get used to navigating between—the different configuration modes. Some commands only work at a specific configuration mode, and getting used to the IOS quirks is a big part of being prepared for the CCNA exam and being a capable Cisco admin.

Command Shortcuts

Take a look at this command. It backs up the current configuration and saves it so that the router will use it next time it boots up:

```
Router#copy running-config startup-config
```

That's a big hunk of typing. More typing means more time and more errors, so to save time, we can use abbreviations. As long as the abbreviations provide enough information for the IOS to figure out what command you are trying to enter, you can reduce the amount of typing you have to do, saving yourself time:

```
Router#copy run start
```

Or even smaller

```
Router#cop ru st
```

That's a big savings in typing effort.

As you get used to working with the IOS, you will develop your own shortcuts.

The IOS will tell you when you make a mistake, too. There are three error messages:

- Incomplete Command: The IOS needs more command keywords to complete the command. It advises you of the error, and re-types what you entered so that you can complete it. The error looks like this:

  ```
  Router#copy running-config
  % Incomplete Command
  Router#copy running-config
  ```

- Ambiguous Command: The IOS is not sure what command you mean because you abbreviated too much:

  ```
  Router#co ru st
  %Ambiguous command
  ```

➤ Invalid Input: You made a typo or entered a command at the wrong prompt. Notice that the IOS will also show you exactly where the problem happens with a little pointer:

```
Router#cpy run start
         ^
%Invalid input detected at '^' marker
```

Context-Sensitive Help

The IOS has a complete listing of all the commands available. If you get stuck, you can use the question mark `?` to access this help. You can use it in different ways:

On its own, to see a list of all the available command words at a particular prompt

```
Router(config-if)#?
Interface configuration commands:
access-expression   Build a bridge boolean access expression
arp                 Set arp type (arpa, probe, snap) or timeout
backup              Modify dial-backup parameters
bandwidth           Set bandwidth informational parameter
bridge-group        Transparent bridging interface parameters
carrier-delay       Specify delay for interface transitions
cdp                 CDP interface subcommands
cmns                OSI CMNS
custom-queue-list   Assign a custom queue list to an interface
default             Set a command to its defaults
delay               Specify interface throughput delay
description         Interface specific description
exit                Exit from interface configuration mode
fair-queue          Enable Fair Queuing on an Interface
help                Description of the interactive help system
hold-queue          Set hold queue depth
ip                  Interface Internet Protocol config commands
ipx                 Novell/IPX interface subcommands
keepalive           Enable keepalive
llc2                LLC2 Interface Subcommands
load-interval       Specify interval for load calculation for an inter-
face
—More—
```

After a command word, to see the next possible command words

```
Router# copy ?
  running-config
  startup-config
  tftp:
  flash:
```

Don't be afraid to use the help, especially when you are learning. The help commands also function (with limited capabilities) in the router simulator questions on the CCNA exam.

Basic Switch Configuration

A Cisco switch will function perfectly well right out of the box with no configuration required; however, it's a good idea to do a few basic configurations to personalize, secure, and optimize the device.

Setting the Hostname

The default hostname is "Switch," which not only lacks imagination, but also is confusing if you have a lot of them. Changing the hostname is simple:

```
Switch(config)#hostname My2950
My2950(config)#
```

Notice that the hostname actually changed!

Setting a Management IP Address

If you want to Telnet to your switch to manage it remotely, have it participate in an SNMP system, or use the integrated HTTP server for monitoring, your switch needs an IP address and gateway address. These addresses are applied to the VLAN1 interface—unlike a router, a switch has no physical ports that can be assigned IP addresses, so the virtual interface of VLAN1 (the management VLAN) gets the addresses:

```
My2950(config)#interface vlan1
My2950(config-if)#ip address 192.168.1.2 255.255.255.0
My2950(config-if)#exit
My2950(config)#ip default-gateway 192.168.1.1
```

Setting Speed and Duplex on Ethernet Ports

Although the Ethernet interfaces will auto-detect the duplex and speed setting on a 2950, it is usually a good idea to hard-code them when you are sure of what you are connecting to (such as a server, a switch, or router):

```
My2950(config)#interface f0/24
My2950(config-if)#speed 100
My2950(config-if)#duplex full
```

Basic Router Configuration

Routers need a little more configuration than switches to function properly; every interface that you want to use needs an IP address and mask, as well as to be enabled. You will probably need to add static routes or perhaps run a dynamic routing protocol. You need to configure your serial port for connectivity as well.

Serial Port Configuration

As we mentioned before, a Cisco serial port can run several different Layer2 encapsulations—meaning, it can connect to different types of networks. You must be sure that the encapsulation type matches that of the device you are connecting to. In CCNA, we are interested only in three serial encapsulations: HDLC, PPP, and Frame Relay. The command to change the encapsulation is executed at the interface configuration prompt:

```
Router(config)#interface serial 0
Router(config-if)#encapsulation [hdlc ¦ frame-relay ¦ ppp]
```

You might also need to set up the serial speed by configuring a clock rate. Usually this is supplied by the service provider's device, but in training labs we will hook a router directly to another router with a special back-to-back cable. In this situation, one of the devices must be the DCE (Data Communication Equipment), and the DCE sets the clock. Only one device needs the clock rate set.

You can also configure a bandwidth statement on the interface. This one is a little tricky; it looks like we are setting the bandwidth (speed) of the interface, but we really aren't—the clock rate sets the physical speed. What we are doing with the bandwidth command is lying to the routing protocols about the speed of the interface (more on this in Chapter 9). It might have an actual clock speed of 64000 (64K), but we could lie and set the bandwidth to 56K for the purposes of routing information:

```
Router(config-if)#clock rate 64000
Router(config-if)#bandwidth 56
```

Enabling Interfaces

By default, every interface on a router (whether it is brand-new or has been erased) is in a *shutdown* state. This is also known as *administratively down*; while the interface has been perfectly configured with an IP and mask, encapsulation, and whatever else is needed, the admin has decided to effectively turn it off. A shutdown interface doesn't send or receive any data at all, and it causes the other end of a serial link to think it is dead altogether. So when you first configure a new router or one that has had its configuration erased, remember to issue the `no shutdown` command at each interface, or none of the interfaces will work!

```
Router(config-if)#no shutdown
```

Understand that all interfaces are shut down by default until the 'no shut' command is issued.

On a router, every interface is a gateway to another network. For this reason, we do not need to supply a gateway. However, every interface you intend to use will need an IP address and mask. The commands to set an IP are exactly the same as on a switch. Don't forget the `no shutdown` (`no shut` for short):

```
Router(config)#interface s0
Router(config-if)#ip address 10.0.0.1 255.0.0.0
Router(config-if)#no shut
Router(config-if)#interface e0
Router(config-if)#ip address 172.16.0.1 255.255.0.0
Router(config-if)#no shut
```

Securing Routers and Switches

In CCNA Land, security is not an overriding concern. CCNA will not make you a security expert, but you will learn the very basics and how to apply them.

Initially, your router or switch will have no passwords at all; simply pressing Enter will grant you first user, then Privileged Exec access. The Telnet lines are secured by default—they will refuse connections until they are configured with a password.

The minimum security configuration would be to require a password to log in to your devices. Passwords can be applied to the console port, to the VTY lines (controlling Telnet access), and to the Privileged Exec prompt.

The following commands illustrate how to apply basic password security to your router or switch, for the console port (User Exec), VTY lines (for remote administration using Telnet), and Privileged Exec prompt. Lines that begin with an exclamation point are informational remarks and do not configure the device:

```
Router(config)#line con 0
!    The console port is always con 0
Router(config-line)#login
!    Requires a password to access User Exec over the console port
Router(config-line)#password ExamCram2
!    Specifies the password - Note: passwords are case-sensitive.
Router(config)#line vty 0 4
!    There are 5 VTY lines, numbered 0 through 4
```

```
Router(config-line)#login
Router(config-line)#password 23StanleyCups
!
Router(config)#enable password cisco
!    sets the Privileged Exec password to 'cisco'
```

These passwords will all appear in your configuration file in plain text; anyone with access to that file could read them. To encrypt your Privileged Exec password with an MD5 hash, use the `enable secret` command:

```
Router(config)#enable secret squirrel42
```

You can also apply encryption to the other passwords for the console, VTY and TTY lines (but `not` the enable password) using the `service password-encryption` command:

```
Router(config)#service password-encryption
```

Know the password configuration commands cold.

Table 4.1 lists some useful commands to find out information about your router or switch.

Table 4.1 Commands to Retrieve Basic Information

Command	Description
show flash	Lists what files (IOS images, typically) are stored in flash, as well as how much flash memory is used, available, and the total amount.
Show interface	Shows diagnostic information about all interfaces, including whether they are shut down.
Show version	Lists the version of IOS image in use, the actual IOS filename, and the current value of the configuration register.
Show running-config	Shows the current configuration in RAM.
Show startup-config	Shows the configuration that will be loaded the next time the router boots.

Exam Prep Questions

1. Bob types in an excellent initial configuration on his new router, but when he tries to ping the interfaces, they don't answer. What could be wrong?
   - ❍ A. Bob changed the configuration register to suppress pings.
   - ❍ B. Bob needs a new router; this one is clearly defective.
   - ❍ C. The router does not support the IP protocol by default.
   - ❍ D. Bob neglected to issue the `no shut` command at each interface.
2. Given the following:

   c1600-nosy-mz.120-25.bin

   Which of the following is true? Choose 3.
   - ❍ A. This is an IOS image file that does not run on a 2600-series router.
   - ❍ B. This IOS is version 25.
   - ❍ C. This IOS is version 12.0
   - ❍ D. This is not a valid Cisco IOS filename.
   - ❍ E. The `mz` identifies the compression type used.
3. Which two actions will get you out of Setup mode?
   - ❍ A. Typing 'abort setup'
   - ❍ B. Answering 'no' when asked if you want to keep the configuration at the end of Setup mode
   - ❍ C. Waiting until it times out
   - ❍ D. Pressing Ctrl+C
4. What command lists the IOS images stored in flash?
   - ❍ A. show ios
   - ❍ B. list flash
   - ❍ C. show flash
   - ❍ D. show version
5. Jaine sets her configuration register to 0x2142. What is she up to?
   - ❍ A. Changing which IOS image in flash to boot from
   - ❍ B. Forcing the router to boot from RXBOOT
   - ❍ C. Forcing the router to boot from ROMMON
   - ❍ D. Performing a password recovery
6. Which of the following correctly summarizes the boot sequence?
   - ❍ A. Find IOS, Load IOS, POST, Find config, Load config
   - ❍ B. Post, Find IOS, Load IOS, Find config, Load config
   - ❍ C. POST, Find config, Load config, Find IOS, Load IOS
   - ❍ D. ROMMON, RXBOOT, Load IOS, Load config

7. Which of the following applies an encrypted password of `cisco` to the Privileged Exec prompt?
   - ❍ A. enable password cisco
   - ❍ B. enable password cisco encrypted
   - ❍ C. enable cisco secret
   - ❍ D. enable secret cisco
8. What commands apply a password of "Vienna" to all five Telnet connections on a router?
   - ❍ A. line vty 5
login
password Vienna
   - ❍ B. line vty 0 4
login
password vienna
   - ❍ C. interface vty 0 4
login
password Vienna
   - ❍ D. line vty 0 4
login
password Vienna
9. Match the entries in the list on the left with the descriptions on the right:

ROM	Stores compressed IOS images
RAM	Stores startup-config file
FLASH	Stores running config and decompressed IOS
NVRAM	Stores mini-IOS and ROMMON

10. What command must be entered on the DCE device to enable serial communication at a speed of 64 kilobits per second?
    - ❍ A. Router(config)#clock rate 64000
    - ❍ B. Router(config-if)#interface-type dce
    - ❍ C. Router(config-if)#bandwidth 64
    - ❍ D. Router(config-if)#clock rate 64000

Answers to Exam Prep Questions

1. Answer D is correct. Until you issue the no shut command at each interface, the interfaces will effectively be switched off. A is incorrect; you can't use the config register to suppress ping. B may be true, but it is unlikely, so it is not the best choice. C is incorrect because it is false; every IOS supports only IP until you upgrade to one that supports other network protocols as well.
2. Answers A, C, and E are correct. B is wrong; the version is the first number in the fourth name block. D is wrong because c1600-nosy-mz.120-25.bin appears to be a valid IOS name.
3. Answers B and D are correct. Answer A is not a valid command. Answer C is incorrect because Setup mode does not time out.
4. Answer C is correct. Answers A and B, show ios and list flash, are not valid commands; Answer D, the show version command, is incorrect because it lists only the file in use, not all the images in flash.
5. Answer D is correct. 0x2142 is one of the steps in password recovery. Answers A, B, and C (changing which IOS image in flash to boot from, forcing the router to boot from RXBOOT, and forcing the router to boot from ROMMON) are controlled by the config register, but use values other than 0x2142.
6. Answer B is correct. Answers A, C, and D are either out of order or incorrect (D).
7. Answer D is correct. The enable secret cisco applies to an encrypted password cisco. Answer A is incorrect; it is a valid syntax but does not encrypt the password. Answers B and C are not valid syntax.
8. Answer D is correct both in syntax and exact password match. Answer A is incorrect; we must specify a range for the vty lines, 0 through 4. Answer B is incorrect, although it is close to correct; however, the password does not match because it is not capitalized. Answer C is incorrect because it uses interface instead of line.
9. ROM → Stores mini-IOS and ROMMON images

   RAM → Stores running config and decompressed IOS

   FLASH → Stores compressed IOS

   NVRAM → Stores startup-config file
10. Answer D is correct. Answer A is incorrect because it is executed at the wrong command prompt. Answer B is incorrect because it is invalid syntax, and Answer C is incorrect because it sets the bandwidth for routing metrics, not the required DCE clock speed.

Managing Your Router

Terms You'll Need to Understand

- ✓ CDP (Cisco Discover Protocol)
- ✓ ICMP (Internet Control Message Protocol)
- ✓ Telnet

Concepts and Techniques You'll Need to Master

- ✓ Using Telnet
- ✓ IOS Naming Conventions
- ✓ Backing Up and Restoring Your IOS
- ✓ Backing Up and Restoring Your Configuration

Introduction

This chapter deals with managing your Cisco router. It covers IOS naming conventions, backing up and restoring your IOS and configuration, and using the Cisco Discovery Protocol, Telnet, and ICMP.

IOS Naming Conventions

An IOS filename is broken down into four parts:

- Platform
- Feature set
- Run location and compression
- Version

For example, if our IOS name was C2500-D-L.120-9.bin, we could break it down as follows:

- Platform: C2500
- Feature Set: D
- Run Location: L
- IOS Version: 12.0(9)

The feature set identifies the feature contents on the router. Common feature sets include "j" for enterprise, "d" for desktop, and "s" for plus features such as Network Address Translation (NAT), InterSwitch Link (ISL), and Virtual Private Dial-up Networks (VPDN). Although the number of feature sets is too many to list here, Table 5.1 lists the more common ones found on a 2600 platform.

Table 5.1 Feature Sets

Feature Set	Description
I	IP
IS	IP PLUS
J	Enterprise
JS	Enterprise Plus
JK8S	Enterprise Plus with IPSec
D	Desktop

The feature sets are provided as an example only; you do not need to know the feature set codes for the exam. You will need to know, however, what is included in an IOS filename: platform, feature set, compression/run location, and version.

The run location indicates both its execution area and, when applicable, the compression identifiers. Table 5.2 illustrates the common run locations.

Table 5.2 Memory Locations

Code	Location
F	Image runs in flash
M	Image runs in Random Access Memory (RAM)
R	Image runs in Read Only Memory (ROM)
L	Image will be relocated at runtime

The compression identifiers indicate what type of compression is used on the image. Common compression identifiers are shown in Table 5.3.

Table 5.3 Compression Identifiers

Code	Compression
Z	Image is Zip compressed
X	Image is Mzip compressed
W	Image is Stac compressed

For example, image c7200-js-mz is an IOS for the 7200 series router, with enterprise plus software, executed in RAM, and is Mzip compressed.

You can view the IOS files you have stored in flash memory by executing the command `show flash`. This command can be executed from either user exec or privileged exec mode. Following is the output of the `show flash` command on a 1604 router:

```
Router>show flash
PCMCIA flash directory:
File  Length   Name/status
  1   6611048  /c1600-nosy-l.120-25.bin
[6611112 bytes used, 1777496 available, 8388608 total]
8192K bytes of processor board PCMCIA flash (Read ONLY)
```

In this instance, there is only one IOS in flash. Taking the filename, c1600-nosy-l.120-25.bin, you can see that the platform is a 1600 series router with a feature set of 'nosy' (the 1600 designation for IP/IPX/FW Plus) and is relocated at runtime but not compressed. The IOS version is 12.0(25).

Although the `show flash` command will show you all IOS files that you have in flash, it will not show you the IOS that you are currently using if you have more than one IOS. To view the IOS that you are currently using on your router, execute the command `show version`. Like the `show flash` command, the `show version` command may be executed from user exec or privileged exec. Following is the output of the show version command with the relevant portions in bold text.

```
Router>show version
Cisco Internetwork Operating System Software
IOS (tm) 1600 Software (C1600-NOSY-L), Version 12.0(25), RELEASE SOFTWARE
(fc1)
Copyright (c) 1986-2002 by cisco Systems, Inc.
Compiled Tue 31-Dec-02 12:29 by srani
Image text-base: 0x080357F8, data-base: 0x02005000

ROM: System Bootstrap, Version 11.1(10)AA, EARLY DEPLOYMENT RELEASE SOFTWARE
(fc
1)
ROM: 1600 Software (C1600-BOOT-R), Version 11.1(10)AA, EARLY DEPLOYMENT
RELEASE
SOFTWARE (fc1)

Router uptime is 6 minutes
System restarted by power-on
System image file is "flash:/c1600-nosy-l.120-25.bin"
<output omitted for brevity>
```

Know the difference between the **show flash** and the **show version** commands. **show flash** will show all IOS files that you have in flash memory, whereas the **show version** command will show you which IOS file you are currently using.

Back Up and Restore IOS

At some point in your career, you will need to back up, restore, or upgrade your IOS. You can use TFTP, FTP, or RCP to transfer an IOS image to or from a server. TFTP is the most common, so that is covered here. (It is also covered in the CCNA exam.)

TFTP is the trivial file transfer protocol. Unlike FTP, there are no means of authenticating with a username or password or navigating directories. To back up your IOS, you will use the `copy` command from within privileged exec mode. The syntax of this command is copy <from> <to>. Thus, if you want to copy an IOS from your IOS to a TFTP server, the syntax would be `copy tftp flash`. After executing this command, you will be prompted with a number of questions asking for such things as the IOS filename and IP address of the TFTP server. Following is the output of this command. The TFTP server in this example is located at the IP address 172.16.0.254.

```
Router#copy flash tftp

PCMCIA flash directory:
File  Length   Name/status
5148040  /c1600-sy56i-mz.121-20.bin
[5148104 bytes used, 3240504 available, 8388608 total]
Address or name of remote host [255.255.255.255]? 172.16.0.254
Source file name? /c1600-sy56i-mz.121-20.bin
Destination file name [c1600-sy56i-mz.121-20.bin]?
Verifying checksum for 'c1600-sy56i-mz.121-20.bin' (file # 1)...  OK
Copy 'c1600-sy56i-mz.121-20.bin' from Flash to server
as 'c1600-sy56i-mz.121-20.bin'? [yes/no]y
!!!!!!!!!!!!!!!!!!!!!!!!!!!!!!!!!!!!!!!!!!!!!!!!!!!!!!!!!!!!!!!!!!!!!!!!!!!
!!!!!!!!!!!!!!!!!!!!!!!!!!!!!!!!!!!!!!!!!!!!!!!!!!!!!!!!!!!!!!!!!!!!!!!!!!!
!!!!!!!!!!!!!!!!!!!!!!!!!!!!!!!!!!!!!!!!!!!!!!!!!!!!!!!!!!!!!!!!!!!!!!!!!!!
!!!!!!!!!!!!!!!!!!!!!!!!!!!!!!!!!!!!!!!!!!!!!!!!!!!!!!!!!!!!!!!!!!!!!!!!!!!
!!!!!!!!!!!!!!!!!!!!!!!!!!!!!!!!!!!!!!!!!!!!!!!!!!!!!!!!!!!!!!!!!!!!!!!!!!!
!!!!!!!!!!!!!!!!!!!!!!!!!!!!!!!!!!!!!!!!!!!!!!!!!!!!!!!!!!!!!!!!!!!!!!!!!!!
!!!!!!!!!!!!!!!!!!!!!!!!!!!!!!!!!!!!!!!!!!!!!!!!!!!!!!!!!!!!!!!!!!!!!!!!!!!
!!!!!!!!!!!!!!!!!!!!!!!!!!!!!!!!!!!!!!!!!!!!!!!!!!!!!!!!!!!!!!!!!!!!!!!!!!!
!!!!!!!!!!!!!!!!!!!!!!!!!!!!!!!!!!!!!!!!!!!!!!!!!!!!!!!!!!!!!!!!!!!!!!!!!!!
!!!!!!!!!!!!!!!!!!!!!!!!!!!!!!!!!!!!!!!!!!!!!!!!!!!!!!!!!!!!!!!!!!!!!!!!!!!
Upload to server done

Flash device copy took 00:01:24 [hh:mm:ss]
```

To restore or upgrade your IOS from a TFTP server to a router, the syntax would be `copy tftp flash`.

Remember the following troubleshooting steps if you are having difficulties using TFTP:

- Verify that the TFTP server is running.
- Verify cable configurations. You should use a crossover cable between a router and a server or, if you have a switch, use a straight-through cable from the router to the switch and from the switch to the server.
- Verify that your router is on the same subnet as your TFTP server or has a means to route to it somehow (static route or routing protocol).

Backup and Restore Configurations

Backing up and restoring your configuration is no different than it was for your IOS. To save your configuration, you will copy your running-config in RAM to your startup-config in NVRAM by executing the privileged exec command `copy running-config startup-config`. If you want to copy your startup-config file to a TFTP server, you would type `copy startup-config tftp`. If you want to restore your configuration from a TFTP server, you would execute the command `copy tftp running-config`. (You can also elect to copy it to your startup-config.)

If you are using a Linux TFTP server, make sure that you first use the touch command to create a zero-byte file with the name of the IOS image; otherwise, the file will not copy to the TFTP server. Consult the Linux documentation for more information.

Troubleshooting and Remote Management

Having the ability to remotely manage your router is crucial to any network engineer. If you have a wide area network that spans across the world, you do not want to have to fly out to a location every time you have a problem with a router. Three protocols you can use to help you in troubleshooting and remotely manage your routers are

- Telnet
- CDP
- ICMP

Telnet

Telnet operates at the application layer of the OSI model and is used to remotely connect into a router. Configuring Telnet authentication is covered in Chapter 4, "Working With Cisco Equipment." As a review, however, the commands to configure a router to allow Telnet access are as follows (the password 'cisco' is used in this example):

```
Router(config)#enable secret cisco
Router(config)#line vty 0 4
Router(config-line)#login
Router(config-line)#password cisco
```

Remember, you must have an enable password for Telnet access to work. If you do not, you will get the following output when you attempt to access privileged exec mode:

```
Router#telnet 192.168.1.1
Trying 192.168.1.1 ... Open
User Access Verification
Password:
Router>en
% No password set
Router>
```

To close out an active Telnet session, type `exit`.

It is also possible to suspend a Telnet session and resume it later. This is helpful as it keeps you from having to remember the IP address of a router. Instead, you can suspend your Telnet session and resume it later based on its session number, not IP address.

To suspend a Telnet session, press Ctrl+Shift+6, x. (Hold down the Ctrl, Shift, and 6 buttons at the same time. Release them, and then press x.)

To see what sessions you have suspended, execute the `show sessions` command from user exec or privileged exec mode. In the output that follows, there are two Telnet sessions that have been suspended:

```
Router#show sessions
Conn Host                Address             Byte  Idle Conn Name
   1 192.168.1.1         192.168.1.1            0     0 192.168.1.1
*  2 172.16.0.1          172.16.0.1             0     0 172.16.0.1
```

Entries that have an asterisk (*) next to them indicate the last session you were using. There are four methods of resuming a session:

- **Enter key** Pressing the Enter key will take you to the last session you were currently using (as shown by the asterisk in the `show sessions` command).
- **Resume** Typing **`resume`** without specifying a session number will allow you to resume the last session you were using. This is the same as pressing the Enter key.
- **Resume #** Typing resume followed by the session number will resume Telnet for that session. For example, typing **`resume 1`** would resume Telnet for the 192.168.1.1 router.
- **Resume [IP address | hostname]** Instead of giving a Telnet session number, you can also give the IP address or, if you have DNS lookups enabled with a DNS server, you can type in the hostname of the remote router.

Know the commands you use to resume and close a Telnet session (Ctrl+Shift+6, x; show sessions; resume; disconnect). Also, remember that the 'exit' command will close an ***active*** session, whereas the 'disconnect' command will close a ***suspended*** session.

CDP

Sometimes when you Telnet to another router, you might not know what its IP address is. If this is the case, you can use the CDP to discover the layer 3 address of neighboring devices.

CDP is a Cisco proprietary layer 2 (data-link) multicast protocol that is enabled on all Cisco routers and switches. It can be used to discover information about directly connected devices. Although it is a layer 2 protocol, it is not forwarded by Cisco switches. (It is by other vendors, however.)

To view what neighboring Cisco devices you have connected to your router or switch, execute the `show cdp neighbors` command from either user exec or privileged exec mode. Following is an example of this output:

```
Router#show cdp neighbors
Capability Codes: R - Router, T - Trans Bridge, B - Source Route Bridge
                  S - Switch, H - Host, I - IGMP, r - Repeater

Device ID        Local Intrfce     Holdtme    Capability  Platform  Port ID
CoreRouter          Ser 0          144            R       2500      Ser 0
```

Here you see that you are connected to a router named "CoreRouter." You are connected to it out of your local interface serial 0. The holdtime indicates how long it will take to flush this entry out should your router stop hearing CDP frames. CDP sends advertisements every 60 seconds by default and will flush out an entry if it fails to hear a CDP advertisement after 180 seconds. (Timers are manipulated with the `cdp timers` global configuration command.) The capability of this device is 'R,' which stands for router. In fact, from this output you can see that this is a 2500 series router and it is connected to your router out of its serial 0 interface.

Quite a bit of information gets generated from this command, but it did not tell you the IP address of the 2500 nor did it tell you the IOS version running on the 2500. The two commands you can enter through the layer 3 IP address and IOS version are as follows:

- `show cdp neighbors detail`
- `show cdp entry *`

These two commands are functionally equivalent. You can look at a specific device in the `show cdp entry command` or use the wildcard asterisk character to view all entries. Following is the output of the `show cdp neighbors detail` command (the other show command would generate the same output):

```
Router#show cdp neighbors detail
-------------
Device ID: CoreRouter
Entry address(es):
  IP address: 10.0.0.1
Platform: cisco 2500,  Capabilities: Router
Interface: Serial0,  Port ID (outgoing port): Serial0
Holdtime : 171 sec

Version :
Cisco Internetwork Operating System Software
IOS (tm) 2500 Software (C2500-I-L), Version 12.1(20), RELEASE SOFTWARE (fc2)
Copyright (c) 1986-2003 by cisco Systems, Inc.
Compiled Thu 29-May-03 22:00 by kellythw
```

If you need to Telnet into a router but do not know its IP address, use CDP. Remember, only the 'show cdp neighbors detail' and 'show cdp entry *' will show you the IP address and IOS version of neighboring devices.

ICMP

Another useful troubleshooting tool is the ICMP. ICMP is a layer 3 (network) protocol that is used by ping and traceroute. Use the ping command to verify that a host is up. A successful ping uses two primary messages:

- ICMP Type 8 Echo Request
- ICMP Type 0 Echo Reply

If a host is unreachable, you will get an ICMP Type 3 Destination Unreachable message. If a firewall or access-list is blocking ICMP, you will get an ICMP Type 3/Code 13 Destination Unreachable:Administratively Prohibited Message.

Cisco also supports an extended ping feature that is accessible from privileged exec. To access the extended ping feature, enter privileged exec and type **`ping`**. Do not enter an IP address, however; instead, press Enter, and you will be presented with a number of questions. With extended ping, you have the ability to set the size of your ping messages, source interface, number of pings, and timeout settings. Following is the output of the extended ping command. Note that the exclamation mark is an indication of a successful ping:

```
Router#ping
Protocol [ip]:
Target IP address: 10.0.0.1
Repeat count [5]: 1000
Datagram size [100]: 1024
Timeout in seconds [2]:
Extended commands [n]: y
Source address or interface: 172.16.0.1
Type of service [0]:
Set DF bit in IP header? [no]:
Validate reply data? [no]:
Data pattern [0xABCD]:
Loose, Strict, Record, Timestamp, Verbose[none]:
Sweep range of sizes [n]:
Type escape sequence to abort.
Sending 1000, 1024-byte ICMP Echos to 10.0.0.1, timeout is 2 seconds:
!!!!!!!!!!!!!!!!!!!!!!!!!!!!!!!!!!!!!!!!!!!!!!!!!!!!!!!!!!!!!
```

When bringing up a new wide area network circuit, you can do an extended ping and send out 10,000 pings with a size of 1,024 bytes. Watch the results and verify success. If some packets are lost, you know it is not a clean circuit and you should contact your provider.

Traceroute is a technique used when you suspect that a router on the path to an unreachable network is at fault. Traceroute sends out a packet to a destination with a Time To Live (TTL) of 1. If the first hop is not the destination, a destination unreachable message is sent back and the response time in milliseconds is recorded. A second packet is then sent out with a TTL value of 2, and if it is not the destination, an unreachable message is sent back and the response time in milliseconds is recorded. This continues until the destination is reached or until the maximum TTL as defined by the vendor is reached. (Cisco uses 30 as its maximum TTL with traceroute, but this is configurable.)

Traceroute is implemented differently by various vendors. Windows machines use ICMP ping messages, whereas Cisco uses UDP packets sent to port 33434.

Make sure that you know what options are available with extended ping. Also, know why you would use the **traceroute** command.

Exam Prep Questions

1. Which of the following is included in the filename c1600-js-mz.120-9.bin? Select all that apply.
   - ❑ A. Platform
   - ❑ B. Feature set
   - ❑ C. IOS Version
   - ❑ D. Compression Type
2. You are trying to Telnet to a router, but do not know its IP address. What commands can you enter to see the IP address of a neighboring router? Select all that apply.
   - ❑ A. `Show cdp neighbors detail`
   - ❑ B. `Show cdp neighbors`
   - ❑ C. `Show cdp entry *`
   - ❑ D. `Show cdp`
   - ❑ E. `Show cdp entry neighbors`
3. What is the command to back up your IOS to a TFTP server?
   - ❍ A. `copy nvram tftp`
   - ❍ B. `copy tftp nvram`
   - ❍ C. `copy tftp flash`
   - ❍ D. `copy flash tftp`
4. Which of the following commands can you enter to return to the last suspended Telnet session you were using? Assume that the session number is 1. Select all that apply.
   - ❑ A. resume
   - ❑ B. return session
   - ❑ C. return 1
   - ❑ D. resume 1
   - ❑ E. Enter
5. What command will show you the IOS you are currently using on your router?
   - ❍ A. `show nvram`
   - ❍ B. `show flash`
   - ❍ C. `show ios`
   - ❍ D. `show version`
6. What command can you enter to close out a suspended Telnet session?
   - ❍ A. close session
   - ❍ B. disconnect
   - ❍ C. exit
   - ❍ D. quit

7. The 'show cdp neighbors detail' will show you more output than just the 'show cdp neighbors' command. What can you see with the 'show cdp neighbors detail' command that you cannot see with the 'show cdp neighbors' command? Select all that apply.

   ❑ A. IOS version
   ❑ B. Capabilities
   ❑ C. Platform
   ❑ D. Layer 3 address
   ❑ E. Outgoing interface

8. An ICMP ping is composed of which two primary messages? Select two.

   ❑ A. traceroute
   ❑ B. echo reply
   ❑ C. chargen
   ❑ D. echo request
   ❑ E. Ping reply

9. Which of the following commands is used to troubleshoot layer 3 connectivity?

   ❍ A. `telnet`
   ❍ B. `FTP`
   ❍ C. `ping`
   ❍ D. `show cdp neighbors`

10. You suspect that the routing configuration on one of your routers is incorrect because you are unable to reach a remote network. What command can you use to detect which router has a problem routing to a remote network?

   ❍ A. Telnet
   ❍ B. Ping
   ❍ C. Traceroute
   ❍ D. show ip route

Answers to Exam Prep Questions

1. Answers A, B, C, and D are the correct answers. C1600 refers to the platform that the IOS runs on. The 'js' refers to the enterprise plus feature set. The IOS version is 12.0(9) as indicated in the 120-9 section. Finally, the compression and execution area are indicated as 'mz,' which indicates that the image runs from RAM and is Zip compressed.

2. Answers A and C are correct. The commands `show cdp neighbors detail` and `show cdp entry *` are functionally equivalent and would show you the layer 3 IP address of the neighboring router along with platform and IOS version. Answer B is incorrect because this would not give you the IP address of a neighboring router. Answers D and E are incorrect because they're not valid commands.

3. Answer D is the correct answer. This would copy the IOS in flash memory to a TFTP server. Answers A and B are incorrect because the IOS is stored in flash and not NVRAM. Answer C is incorrect because copy tftp flash would upgrade your IOS from a TFTP server rather than copy your IOS to a TFTP server.

4. Answers A, D, and E are correct. Typing **`resume`** and pressing Enter will resume you to the last Telnet session you were in. Typing 'resume 1' will return you to session 1. Pressing the Enter key will also return you to the last session you were using. Answers B and C are incorrect because these are not valid commands.

5. Answer D is the correct answer. The show version command will show you the current IOS you are using. Answer A is incorrect because this is not a valid command. Answer B will show you all the IOS images you have on your router but not the one you are currently using. Answer C is incorrect because this is not a valid command.

6. Answer B is the correct answer. Disconnect will close the last Telnet session you had open. Answer A is incorrect because this is not a valid command. Answer C will close an active Telnet session but not a suspended session, so is therefore incorrect. Answer D will not close out a suspended Telnet session, so it is also incorrect.

7. Answers A and D are correct. The 'show cdp neighbors detail' command will show you both the IOS version and the layer 3 address of a neighboring device. Answers B, C, and E are incorrect because all of these are shown with just the 'show cdp neighbors' command.

8. Answers B and D are correct. ICMP ping messages are composed of echo request (ICMP type 8) and echo reply (ICMP type 0) messages. Answers A, C, and E are wrong because these are not ICMP messages.

9. Answer C is correct. Ping uses ICMP, which operates at the third layer (Network) of the OSI model. Answers A and B are wrong because Telnet and FTP operate at layer 7 (Application). Answer D is wrong because this operates at layer 2 (Data-link).

10. Answer C is the correct answer. Traceroute is used when you try to pinpoint which router has problems getting to a network. Answer A, B, and D are wrong because they do not allow you to detect which router is unable to reach a network.

Catalyst Switch Operations and Configuration

Terms You'll Need to Understand:

✓ Bridge
✓ Switch
✓ Store-and-Forward
✓ Cut-Through
✓ Fragment Free
✓ Duplex
✓ Spanning Tree
✓ Root
✓ Designated
✓ Blocked

Techniques You'll Need to Master:

✓ Differentiating between bridges and switches
✓ Identifying the benefits of bridges and switches
✓ Configuring switch ports
✓ Connecting switches
✓ Identifying the Root switch in a system
✓ Identifying Root, Designated, and Blocked ports in a system

Introduction

This chapter introduces the concepts and modes of Layer 2 Switching and physical-layer connectivity between switches. We also introduce the Spanning Tree Protocol and review some of its enhanced features.

Bridging and Switching

Bridges and switches are devices that segment (break up) collision domains. They are important parts of a network infrastructure, and the concepts presented here are heavily tested on the CCNA exam(s).

Functions of Bridges and Switches

When talking about LANs at the CCNA level, we are almost exclusively interested in Ethernet. You have an idea from Chapter 1, "Networking Fundamentals," of how Ethernet works. This chapter deals with how to make it work at a highly-optimized level by using specialized devices to enhance the simple and adaptable Ethernet technology.

In the early implementations of Ethernet, every device connected to a single wire—Thicknet (10-BASE 5) and Thinnet (10-BASE 2) were the most common physical layer implementations. A little later, hubs were used. All of these technologies did effectively the same thing: connect many different hosts together such that one of them at a time could transmit on the wire. This created a single, often large, collision domain. As you recall from Chapter 1, the bigger the collision domain, the more collisions and the less data that actually gets sent. In these types of implementations, you can lose 50–60% of the bandwidth available just because of collisions. So if we had a 10-BASE T hub, not only did we actually end up with only about 4 or 5Mbs instead of 10Mbs, but also that reduced bandwidth must be shared by all the devices on that segment, instead of each device getting the full 10Mbs. Breaking up (segmenting) collision domains is necessary in order to make them small enough so that devices can reliably transmit data. We can segment using routers, but routers are expensive and difficult to configure; plus, they don't typically have very many ports on them, so we would need a lot of them to segment really effectively.

Bridges were developed to address this issue. A *bridge* isolates one collision domain from another while still connecting them and selectively allowing frames to pass from one to the other. A *switch* is simply a bigger, faster bridge. Every port on a switch or bridge is its own collision domain. The terms bridge and switch can be used interchangeably when discussing their basic operations; we use the term switch because switches are more modern and more common.

A switch must do three things:

- Address Learning
- Frame Forwarding
- Layer 2 Loop Removal

All the descriptions and references in this book are to Transparent Bridging (Switching). By definition, a Transparent Bridge is invisible to the hosts connected through it. Other bridge types (for example, Source-Route, Source-Route Translational) are used in mixed-media networks, including Token Ring and FDDI, that are no longer relevant to the CCNA test.

Address Learning

Address Learning refers to the intelligent capability of switches to remember the source MAC addresses of devices that are connected to its various ports. These addresses are stored in RAM in a table that lists the address and the port on which a frame was last received from that address. This enables a switch to selectively forward the frame out the appropriate port(s), based on the destination MAC address of the frame.

Any time a device that is connected to a switch sends a frame through the switch, the switch records the source MAC address of the frame in a table and associates that address with the port the frame arrived on. Figure 6.1 illustrates a switch that has learned the MAC addresses of the three hosts connected to it, as well as the ports to which they are connected.

Frame Forwarding

After a switch has learned the MAC addresses of the devices connected to it, it can intelligently forward unicast frames to the correct host by comparing the destination MAC of the frame with the addresses in its MAC table; when it finds a match, it then sends the frame out the port associated with that entry. Figure 6.2 illustrates the forwarding decision made by the switch.

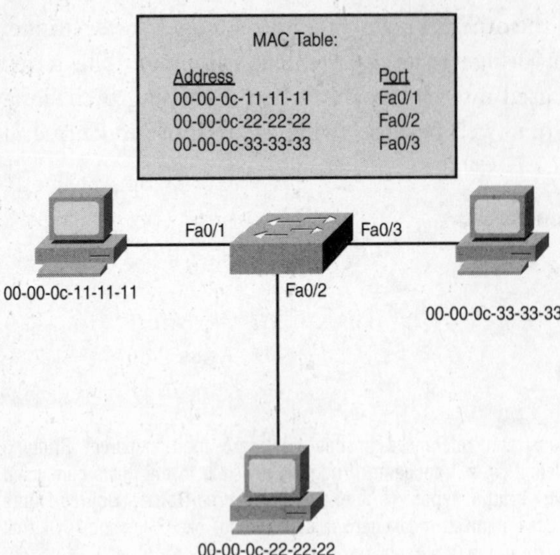

Figure 6.1 A switch with a complete MAC table.

Figure 6.2 The Forward decision.

This is where switches create such a benefit to an Ethernet network: If a switch knows the port to which the destination MAC is connected, the switch will send the frame out that port *and only that port*. This prevents the traffic from being unnecessarily sent to hosts that it is not intended for, significantly improving the efficiency of the network. This is in sharp contrast to the behavior of a hub, which always sends all frames out all ports.

There are some situations in which a switch cannot make its forwarding decision, however. Consider the case in which one of the hosts sends out a broadcast. The MAC address for a broadcast is FF-FF-FF-FF-FF-FF; this is effectively the MAC address of all hosts because every host in a broadcast domain must receive all broadcasts. When the switch receives a broadcast frame inbound on one of its ports, it will check that the source MAC is correctly listed in its MAC table (and update it if necessary) and check the destination MAC of the frame for a match in the table. Because FF-FF-FF-

FF-FF-FF is the MAC of all hosts, the switch must **flood** the frame—it sends it out every port so that the broadcast frame will reach all possible hosts. At this point, the switch is behaving like a hub. This also illustrates why switches (by default) do not segment broadcast domains.

Another scenario in which a switch (by default) is unable to be optimally efficient in the delivery of frames is in the case of a multicast. A *multicast* is a message sent by one host and intended for a specific group of other hosts. This group could be a single host, or a very large number of hosts in different places. The key here is that a single host transmits a stream of data (perhaps a video of a speech or event) to a group of hosts. By default, the switch will treat this the same way as a broadcast, flooding it out all ports to make sure that it reaches all the possible hosts in the group. This is inefficient because the traffic also hits those hosts who do not want the stream. There are several mechanisms and configurations to set it so that only the hosts in the multicast group receive the multicast, but that is well out of the scope of the CCNA exam; the CCNP Building Cisco Multilayer Switched Networks course covers this topic.

Note that the switch will also flood a frame if it does not have an entry in its MAC table for the destination MAC in the frame; although this happens rarely, if the switch doesn't know which specific port to send the frame out, it responds by doing the safest thing and flooding that frame so that it has the best chance of reaching the correct destination. Interestingly, once the destination host responds to that first frame, the switch will enter the missing MAC address into its table and the flood probably won't happen again.

The last situation we should examine is what happens if the sending and receiving hosts are both connected to the same port on the switch. This is most commonly seen when the two hosts are connected to a hub, which is in turn connected to a switch. From the switch's perspective, the two hosts are on the same port. When the sending host transmits a frame, the hub does its thing and floods it out all ports, including the ones connected to the intended receiver and the switch. The receiver simply receives it; the switch checks the source MAC of the frame, updates its MAC table if necessary, and then checks the destination MAC in its table to see which port it should be sent out. When it discovers that the two MACs are associated with the same port, it **filters** the frame: The switch does not transmit the frame out any ports and assumes that the frame will reach its intended recipient without help from the switch. Figure 6.3 illustrates this process.

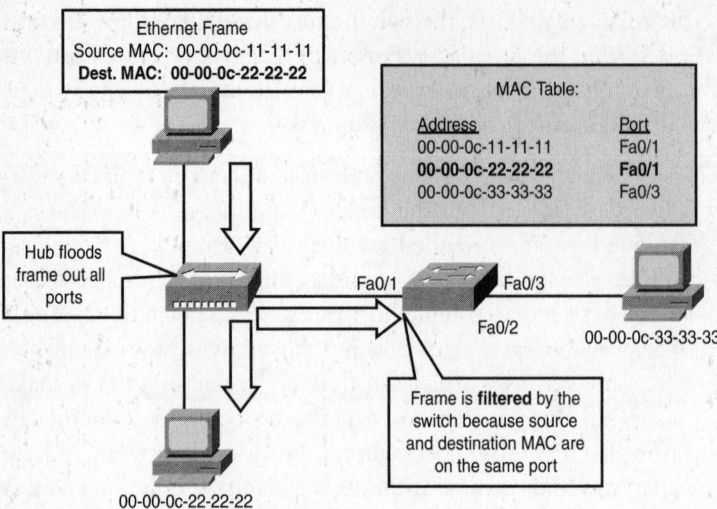

Figure 6.3 The Filter decision illustrated.

You should understand how a switch responds to unicast, broadcast, and multicast frames, and you must know the Filter, Forward, and Flood decision processes. You should also have a clear understanding of the advantages of switches over hubs.

So you have seen how switching gives you a huge efficiency advantage over hubs and coaxial media. Even a low-end switch is preferable to any kind of hub or coax media. You want to be sure that you get the right equipment for the job; different switches run at various speeds, and have diverse limitations on the number of MAC addresses they can support. Although almost any switch is better than any hub, you should take stock of your network, how many hosts, how much and what kind of traffic you expect to support, and choose the switch that best meets your performance and budget requirements.

The Differences Between Switches and Bridges

We have been using the term "switch" interchangeably with "bridge," but there are some significant differences that you need to know about. The key difference is in the technology: Bridges, which are older, do all the work of frame analysis and decision making in software, using the CPU to analyze data stored in RAM. Switches use ASIC (Application-Specific Integrated

Circuit) chips: ASICs are specialized processors designed to do one thing—in this case, switch frames. Depending on the model of switch, the speed difference can be astounding: A bridge typically switches around 50,000 frames per second, whereas a lowly 2950 switch can move an average of 12 million frames per second. (This, of course, depends on the frame size.) A big switch, such as the Catalyst 6500 series, could do 10 times that, depending on the hardware configuration.

Switches also tend to have many more ports than bridges; a bridge by definition has at least two ports, and they didn't get much bigger than 16 ports. Switches can have hundreds of ports, if you buy the appropriate expansion modules.

Other differences include:

- Switches support half- and full-duplex, bridges only half-duplex.
- Switches support different port speeds (10 and 100Mbs, for example), but a bridge's ports must all be the same speed.
- Switches support multiple VLANs and an instance of Spanning Tree for every VLAN (more on this soon).

Table 6.1 summarizes the differences between switches and bridges.

Table 6.1 Switches and Bridges Compared

Comparison	Switches	Bridges
Switching Technology	ASIC (Hardware)	Software
Speed	Fast	Slow
Port Density	High	Low
Duplex	Full and Half	Half Only
VLAN-Aware	Yes	No
Collision Domains	1 per port	1 per port
Broadcast Domains	1 per VLAN	1
STP Instances	1 per VLAN	1

Know the differences between switches and bridges.

Switching Modes

Switches examine the source and destination MAC in a frame to build their MAC table and make their forwarding decision. Exactly how they do that is the topic of this section. There are three switching modes that you need to be aware of: Store-and-Forward, Cut-Through, and Fragment-Free.

Store-and-Forward

Store-and-Forward is the basic mode that bridges and switches use. It is the only mode that bridges can use, but many switches can use one or more of the other modes as well, depending on the model. In Store and Forward switching, the entire frame is buffered (copied into memory) and the CRC (Cyclic Redundancy Check, also known as the FCS or Frame Check Sequence) is run to ensure that the frame is valid and not corrupted.

A CRC is a simple mathematical calculation. A sample of the data (in this case, a frame) is used as the variable in an equation. The product of the equation is included as the CRC at the end of the frame as it is transmitted by the source host. When it is received by the switch, the same equation is run against the same sample of data; if the product value is the same as the value of the CRC in the frame, the frame is assumed to be good. If the value is different, the frame is assumed to be corrupt or damaged, and the frame is dropped. This analysis happens before the forwarding decision is made.

Cut-Through

Cut-Through is the fastest switching mode. The switch analyzes the first six bytes after the preamble of the frame to make its forwarding decision. Those six bytes are the destination MAC address, which, if you think about it, is the minimum amount of information a switch has to look at in order to switch efficiently. After the forwarding decision has been made, the switch can begin to send the frame out the appropriate port(s), even if the rest of the frame is still arriving at the inbound port. The chief advantage of Cut-Through switching is speed; no time is spent running the CRC, and the frame is forwarded as fast as possible. The disadvantage is clearly that bad frames will be switched along with the good; because the CRC/FCS is not being checked, we might be propagating bad frames. This would be a bad thing in a busy network, so some vendors support a mechanism in which the CRCs are still checked but no action is taken until the count of bad CRCs reaches a threshold that causes the switch to change to Store and Forward mode.

Fragment-Free

Fragment-Free mode is a Cisco-proprietary switching method that picks a compromise between the reliability of Store-and-Forward and the speed of Cut-Through. The theory here is that frames which are damaged (usually by collisions) are often shorter than the minimum valid Ethernet frame size of 64 bytes. Fragment-Free buffers the first 64 bytes of each frame, updates the source MAC and port if necessary, reads the destination MAC, and forwards the frame. If the frame is less than 64 bytes, it is discarded. Frames that are smaller than 64 bytes are called *runts*; Fragment-Free switching is sometimes called "runtless" switching for this reason. Because the switch only ever buffers 64 bytes of each frame, Fragment-Free is a faster mode than Store-and-Forward, but there still exists a risk of forwarding bad frames, so the previously described mechanisms to change to Store-and-Forward if excessive bad CRCs are received are often implemented as well.

Know the three switching modes and how they work.

Switch Connections

Switches have the capability of connecting to various types of devices: PCs, servers, routers, hubs, other switches, and so on. Historically, their role was to break up collision domains, which meant plugging hubs in to them. This meant that the switch port had to be able to connect in the same way as the hub—using CSMA/CD, which in turn implies half duplex.

Half duplex means that only one device can use the wire at a time; much like a walkie-talkie set, if one person is transmitting, the other(s) must listen. If others try to transmit at the same time, all you get is a squawk, which is called a collision in network terms. Hubs can only use Half-Duplex communication. Some older NICs (Network Interface Cards), whether for PCs or even for older routers such as the Cisco 2500 series, can only use half duplex as well.

Full duplex is more advanced; in this technology, a device can send and receive at the same time because the send wire is connected directly to the receive wire on both connected devices. This means that we get the full bandwidth of the link (whether 10Mbs, 100Mbs, or 1Gbs) for both transmit and receive, at the same time, for every connected device. If we have a 100Mbs Fast Ethernet connection using full duplex, it can be said that the total available bandwidth is 200Mbs. This doesn't mean 200Mbs up or 200Mbs down, but is the sum of the full 100Mbs up and 100Mbs down for that link; some sales documentation might gloss over this point in an effort to make the switch look better on paper.

Full duplex does give us a major boost in efficiency because it allows for a zero-collision environment: if every device connected to a switch can send and receive at the same time, they cannot collide with each other. The only possible conflict (collision is not the right term here) is within the switch itself, and this problem (should it even happen) is handled by the switch's capability to buffer the frames until the conflict is cleared. Setting up a switch such that every device connected to it is running full duplex (and therefore there are no collisions) is sometimes called *microsegmentation* because every device has been segmented into its own collision domain, in which there are no collisions. You might see a reference to the collision detection circuit being disabled on a switch as soon as full duplex is selected for a switch port. Note that full duplex connections can only be point-to-point, meaning one full duplex device connected to one switch port; half duplex connections are considered multipoint, which makes sense when you consider that a hub might be connected to a half duplex switch port, and there might be several hosts connected to the hub.

Note that not every NIC, whether on a PC or a router, can support full duplex, although it is very rare these days to find a NIC that does not. Most newer NICs have the capability of full duplex, and virtually all switches do as well; furthermore, most NICs and switches can perform an auto-sensing function to determine if the link is full duplex or not and set themselves accordingly.

It is a good practice to set the duplex of certain connections manually to full duplex (or half where necessary), instead of using the Auto function. Connections to other switches, routers, or important servers should be stable and well-known enough to set as full duplex. Doing so avoids potential problems in which the duplex negotiation fails, causing a degradation or loss of connectivity. For connections to hosts, where we don't necessarily have control over the NIC settings, the Auto function is useful.

Duplex Configuration

Setting the appropriate duplex mode is done at the interface configuration prompt. The choices you have are Auto, Full, or Half; the default is Auto, so your switch should work in most cases if you do not make any configuration changes at all. Note that if you manually set duplex to Half or Full, the interface(s) will be locked to that setting and will no longer use the Auto negotiation to dynamically determine the duplex setting of the link(s).

Here is an example of a configuration that sets Interface Fastethernet 0/1 to Full duplex/100Mbs, Interface 0/2 to Half Duplex/10Mbs, and Interface 0/3 to Auto Duplex/Auto speed:

```
2950#config terminal
2950(config)#interface fastethernet 0/1
2950(config-if)#duplex full
2950(config-if)#speed 100
2950(config-if)#interface fastethernet 0/2
2950(config-if)#duplex half
2950(config-if)#speed 10
2950(config-if)#interface fastethernet 0/3
2950(config-if)#duplex auto
2950(config-if)#speed auto
```

STP

Earlier, we mentioned that one of the functions of a switch was Layer 2 Loop removal. This is a critical feature, as without it many switched networks would completely cease to function. Either accidentally or deliberately in the process of creating a redundant network, the problem arises when we create a looped switched path. A *loop* can be defined as two or more switches that are interconnected by two or more physical links.

Switching loops create three major problems:

- Broadcast Storms: Switches must flood broadcasts, so a looped topology will create multiple copies of a single broadcast and perpetually cycle them through the loop.
- MAC table instability: Loops make it appear that a single MAC address is reachable on multiple ports of a switch, and the switch is constantly updating the MAC table.
- Duplicate frames: Because there are multiple paths to a single MAC, it is possible that a frame could be duplicated in order to be flooded out all paths to a single destination MAC.

All of these problems are serious and will bring a network to an effective standstill unless prevented.

Figure 6.4 illustrates a looped configuration and some of the problems it can create:

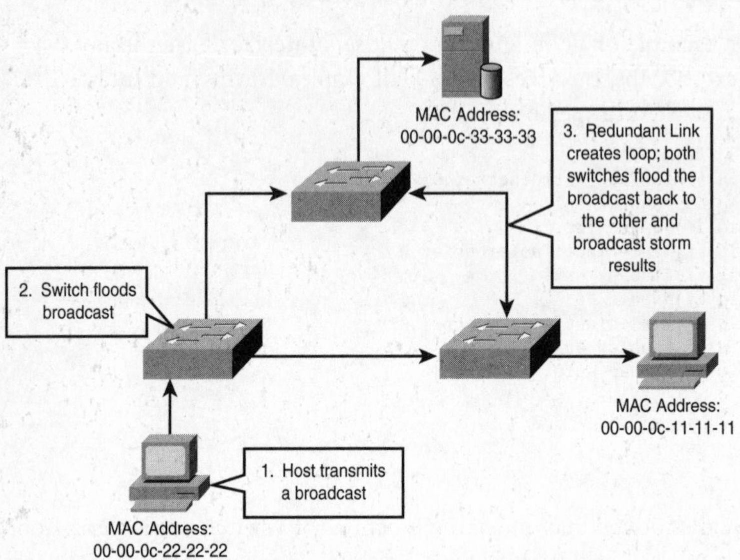
MAC Address:
00-00-0c-33-33-33
3. Redundant Link creates loop; both switches flood the broadcast back to the other and broadcast storm results
2. Switch floods broadcast
MAC Address:
00-00-0c-11-11-11
1. Host transmits a broadcast
MAC Address:
00-00-0c-22-22-22

Figure 6.4 A Layer 2 (Switching) loop.

Other than simple error, the most common reason that loops are created is because we want to build a redundant or fault-tolerant network. By definition, redundancy means that we have a backup, separate path for data to follow in the event the first one fails. The problem is that unless the backup path is physically disabled—perhaps by unplugging it—the path creates a loop and causes the problems mentioned previously. We like redundant systems; we do not like loops and the problems they cause. We need a mechanism that automatically detects and prevents loops so that we can build the fault-tolerant physical links and have them become active only when needed. The mechanism is called the *Spanning Tree Protocol*; STP is a protocol that runs on bridges and switches to find and block redundant looped paths during normal operation. Spanning Tree was originally developed by the Digital Equipment Corporation (DEC), and the idea was adopted and modified by the IEEE to become 802.1d. The two are incompatible, but it is exceedingly rare to find a DEC bridge these days, so the incompatibility is not usually a problem.

EXAM
ALERT
EXAM

STP eliminates Layer 2 loops in switched networks with redundant paths.

Root Election

STP's basic function is to create a loop-free path to a *root bridge*. The root bridge is the bridge or switch that is the root of the Spanning Tree, with the branches being loop-free paths to the other switches in the system. The Root is the switch with the lowest Bridge ID; the ID is determined by a combination of an administrative Priority and the MAC address of the switch. (A switch will usually have a pool of MAC addresses, rather than a single one, that it uses for things like its STP ID.) The Priority is set to 32,768 (8000 hex) by default; if we leave the Priority at the default, whatever switch has the lowest MAC will be the Root. Figure 6.5 illustrates a simple Root selection when all switches are using the default Priority.

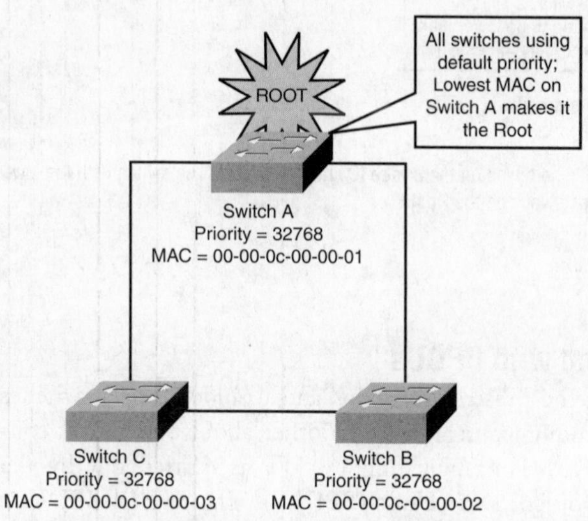

Figure 6.5 Root Bridge Selection with the default Priority.

We cannot change the MAC address of a switch, so what happens if Switch A in the previous example happens to be an old, slow Catalyst 1900? It might get elected the Root because it has a low MAC address, but we really don't want it to be the Root: Usually, we would choose a big, fast switch at the core of the network as the Root. Let's say that Switch C is a hot new switch and we want it to be our Root; how do we override the existing election? The answer is to change the default Priority—remember, the lowest ID wins the election, and the ID is the Priority prepended to the MAC. The ID is one long string, so lowering the Priority makes the ID lower. Thus, if we change the Priority of Switch C to a low value, it will win the election despite the fact that it has a higher MAC than A. Figure 6.6 illustrates this.

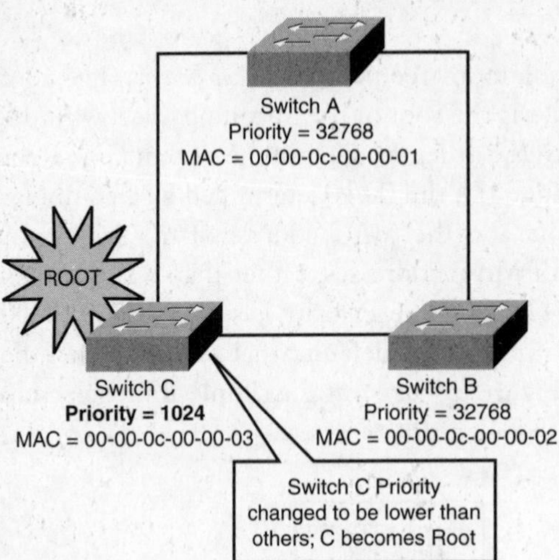

Figure 6.6 Root Election with a modified Priority.

The Root is elected based on the Bridge ID and the Priority. The switch with the lowest Priority will always be the Root.

STP Communication with BPDUs

In order to determine the presence of loops and to block loops, switches must be capable of communicating with each other about the various connections they have. This communication in STP is carried out by the exchange of Bridge Protocol Data Units (BPDUs). The 802.1d BPDU is multicasted every two seconds and includes information the switches need to decide if there are loops, how to fix them, and which switch is the Root. Figure 6.7 shows the fields in an 802.1d BPDU; note the fields for the Bridge ID, the Root ID, and the Root path cost.

Port Types

STP assigns different ports on a switch as different types, depending on where the Root is and where the loops are in the topology. The following sections describe the port types and how they are selected.

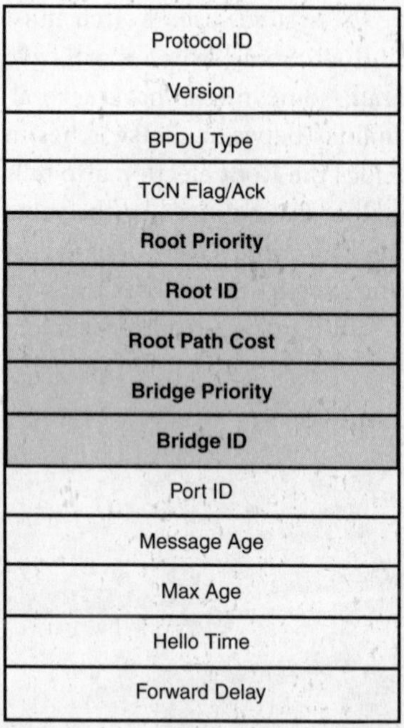

Protocol ID
Version
BPDU Type
TCN Flag/Ack
Root Priority
Root ID
Root Path Cost
Bridge Priority
Bridge ID
Port ID
Message Age
Max Age
Hello Time
Forward Delay

Figure 6.7 Detailed contents of 802.1d BPDU packet.

Root

The Root port on a switch is the one port that has the lowest cost path to the Root switch. Path cost is calculated based on the bandwidth of the links. The IEEE-defined values for STP path cost are listed in Table 6.2; note that there are old and new values. The new values were defined because of the increasingly widespread availability of multi-Gigabit link speeds; previously, a 1Gbs link had the same cost as a 10Gbs link. That made no sense, and would create sub-optimal STP topologies, so the costs were revised.

Table 6.2 STP Path Costs, Old and New

Link Speed	New Cost Value	Old Cost Value
10Gb	2	1
1Gb	4	1
100Mb	19	10
10Mb	100	100

After the switches have elected the Root for the system, each switch must then decide which port it will use to reach the Root. Some switches will have only one port that can reach the Root at all; some might have several, depending on the number and location of uplinks between the switches in the system. The exchange of BPDUs that decides the Root election also tells each switch about the path costs to reach the Root (as indicated by the value of the Root Path Cost field in the BPDU). Each switch adds its own path cost to the path cost received from the neighboring switch and chooses the port with the lowest cost as the Root Port. Figure 6.8 illustrates root port selection in a simple switched network.

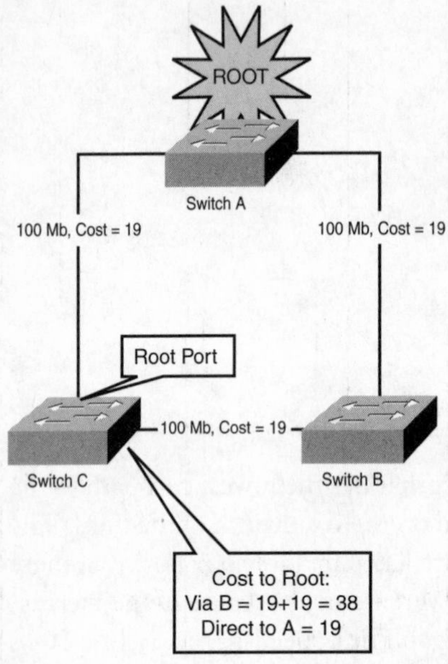

Figure 6.8 The Root port is the one with the lowest Root Path Cost.

Note that the Root itself does not have any Root ports: It does not need to reach the Root; it *is* the Root!

Designated

For each LAN segment, there must be one Designated port. This is the port that will forward traffic to the Root from the LAN segment. The Designated port is the port that has the least cost path to the Root from the LAN segment.

This is often confusing for people to understand. It doesn't come up as often as it used to because shared-media (Thinnet, Thicknet, or hub) environments are not as common as they used to be. With these environments, if you wanted a redundant topology, you could attach two bridges to a single segment. Doing so could cause a loop, so the two bridges would need to establish which one would forward frames and which one would not. The Designated port is the one that will forward frames from the LAN segment to the Root. There is only one Designated port per LAN segment—in other words, only one switch (bridge) will have a Designated port for a LAN segment. Figure 6.9 shows this kind of scenario more clearly.

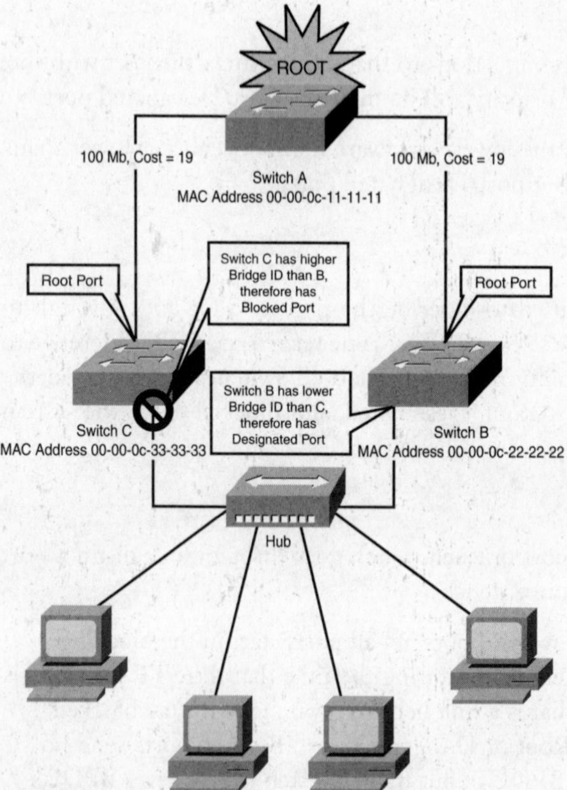

Figure 6.9 The Designated port has the least Root Cost from a LAN segment.

Blocked

A Blocked port is neither the Root port nor the Designated port, but is part of the redundant links between switches. In other words, it lost in the election to choose the active Root or Designated ports, but it might take over one of these roles if the active port failed. A Blocked port is the one that actually stops the loop, so it is just as important as the Root or Designated. A Blocked port does not send any data at all; it only sends BPDUs.

Port Type Selection

The order of criteria a switch goes through when deciding its Root and Designated ports is as follows:

1. The port with the lowest cumulative Root Path Cost will be the Root port/Designated port.
2. If tied between multiple ports, the port that connects to the neighboring switch with the *lowest* Bridge ID becomes the Root port/Designated port.
3. If there are multiple connections to that same switch, the port with the lowest assigned STP priority will be the Root port/Designated port.
4. If tied, the port with the lowest hardware number (Fa0/1 is lower than Fa0/2) will be the Root port/Designated port.

Convergence

Convergence is the term used to describe the process STP goes through to achieve a stable, loop-free network. (The same term is used with reference to routing information stability as well.) When all switches have elected the Root and decided on their Root, Designated, and Blocked ports, the system is said to be converged.

Port States

With 802.1d STP, each port on each switch goes through four distinct port states in the process of convergence:

1. **Blocking**—When a switch boots up, all ports start in the blocking state. This is to prevent loops during the time that the STP topology is converging. A port that is a link between switches will stay blocked unless it becomes a Root or Designated port. Blocked ports send no data at all (not even BPDUs), but they do listen for (receive) BPDUs from other switches. All ports will also go to Blocking mode if a Topology Change Notification BPDU is received. TCNs are issued when a new link is added or removed—the topology of the switched system is altered. When this happens, STP reacts by blocking all ports until loop-free convergence is achieved.

   If a switch dies or a link between switches fails, the other switches connected to it wait for a specific time until they begin the STP convergence process. This interval is called the Max Age Timer, and by default it is 20 seconds. Effectively, it means that a switch will wait until it has missed 10 BPDUs (which are sent every 2 seconds) from a connected switch before it kicks in the STP recalculation.

2. **Listening**—The Listening state enables a Blocked port to begin sending its own BPDUs. By default, the Listening state is 15 seconds.
3. **Learning**—The Learning state is when the switch begins populating its MAC address table. It is not yet forwarding any frames, but it is getting ready to forward by building as complete a MAC table as it can. The Listening state is also 15 seconds by default. The Listening and Learning states together are called the Forward Delay, and you might see their two 15 second timers represented as a single 30-second timer called the Forward Delay Timer.
4. **Forwarding**—The Forwarding state, as its name implies, is when the port starts forwarding frames. This is simply normal operation for a port that is not blocked.

If you take a quick look at these states and their timers, you can see that in 802.1d STP, reaching convergence can take anywhere from 30 to 50 seconds (Forward Delay [15+15]+ MaxAge[20] = 50 seconds). Understand that during this 30 to 50 seconds, no frames are being forwarded at all—no data is being sent anywhere because every port on every switch is either Blocking, Listening, or Learning. This is, of course, very detrimental to the productivity and utility of a network, especially a modern, busy one. A 50-second delay every time a topology change happens is unacceptable, so Cisco (and then the IEEE) created several enhancements to 802.1d STP to speed up the process of convergence. Some of these enhancements are discussed in the following section.

In a converged STP system, all ports are either Blocking or Forwarding. Know the four STP Port States and what exactly the port is doing in each one!

RSTP Enhancements

The Rapid Spanning Tree protocol (RSTP, IEEE 802.1w) has many of its roots in Cisco-created enhancements to ordinary 802.1d STP. The primary goal of these enhancements is to speed up convergence. There are no timers in RSTP; instead, the BPDU becomes much more detailed and informative so that switches can gather more information with greater accuracy. New port states have been defined as shown in Table 6.2.

Table 6.2 RSTP Port States

802.1d STP	802.1w RSTP
Blocking	Discarding
Listening	Discarding
Learning	Learning
Forwarding	Forwarding

Switches wait for only three missing BPDUs before commencing the Spanning-Tree recalculation process. The process of convergence is itself much more rapid because new port types have been defined as well. In addition to the Root and Designated port types in STP, RSTP defines the Alternate and Backup port types. The Alternate port is the port that will become the Root port if the primary Root port fails. The Backup port is the port that will become the Designated if the primary Designated port fails. The BPDUs in RSTP convey information about these port types to neighboring switches. This enhanced communication allows for quicker convergence, without relying on the 30–50 second timers in STP.

Another significant improvement in convergence speed comes from the Rapid Transition to Forwarding features of Edge ports and Link Types. Edge ports are ports that are connected to non–STP-capable devices such as PCs, servers, or routers. These devices will not normally create STP loops, so there is no need for them to block to prevent loops. This function is the same as Cisco's `portfast` command feature.

Another Cisco enhancement deals with port security; this feature set allows you (among several other options) to disable a port if more than one MAC address is detected as being connected to the port. This feature is commonly applied to ports that connect security-sensitive devices such as servers.

The following command syntax restricts access to a single MAC address and shuts the port down if another MAC connects:

```
Switch(config)#interface fa0/21
Switch(config-if)#switchport port-security maximum 1
Switch(config-if)#switchport port-security violation shutdown
```

Link Types refers to a port setting of either full duplex or half duplex. If a port is set for full duplex, RSTP assumes that it is a candidate for rapid transition because there can be only one other device at the end of such a connection. If it is set for half duplex, however, it is conceivable that there could be multiple STP-capable devices on that segment, so by default the RTF functions are disabled. It is possible to override this default.

Exam Prep Questions

1. What is the most common Layer 2 device?
   - ❍ A. Hub
   - ❍ B. Repeater
   - ❍ C. Router
   - ❍ D. Switch
   - ❍ E. Bridge
2. What devices and functions can an administrator use to segment the network, assuming that no VLANs are used? Choose all that apply.
   - ❑ A. Routers to segment broadcast domains
   - ❑ B. Switches to segment broadcast domains
   - ❑ C. Switches to increase the number of collision domains
   - ❑ D. Bridges to segment collision domains
   - ❑ E. Hubs to segment collision domains
   - ❑ F. Bridges to segment broadcast domains
   - ❑ G. Repeaters to segment broadcast domains
3. How many collision and broadcast domains exist on a 12-port switch with default configuration?
   - ❍ A. 2 collision domains, 12 broadcast domains
   - ❍ B. 1 collision domain, 12 broadcast domains
   - ❍ C. 1 collision domain, 1 broadcast domain
   - ❍ D. 12 collision domains, 1 broadcast domain
4. Which of the following are true of switches and bridges? Choose all that apply.
   - ❑ A. Switches have fewer ports and switch in software.
   - ❑ B. Switches have a higher port density and switch using ASIC hardware.
   - ❑ C. Bridges are faster than switches.
   - ❑ D. Switches are faster than bridges.
   - ❑ E. Switches create only one broadcast domain by default.
   - ❑ F. Bridges create only one broadcast domain.
5. Which switching mode sacrifices speed for error-free switching?
   - ❍ A. Segment-Free
   - ❍ B. Store-and-Forward
   - ❍ C. Cut-Throat
   - ❍ D. Fragment-Free
   - ❍ E. Cut-Through

6. What is the function of 802.1d STP?

   ❍ A. Prevents routing loops in redundant topologies
   ❍ B. Prevents Layer 2 loops in networks with redundant switched paths
   ❍ C. Prevents frame forwarding until all IP addresses are known
   ❍ D. Enables the use of multiple routed paths for load-sharing
   ❍ E. Allows the propagation of VLAN information from a central source

7. What defines the root switch in an STP system? Choose 2.

   ❑ A. The switch with the lowest Bridge ID
   ❑ B. The switch with the highest Bridge ID
   ❑ C. The fastest switch
   ❑ D. The switch with the most connections to other switches
   ❑ E. The first switch to send out a BPDU
   ❑ F. The switch with the lowest Priority
   ❑ G. The switch with the highest Priority

8. Which one of the following statements describes a converged STP system?

   ❍ A. All switches are running STP.
   ❍ B. All ports are blocking.
   ❍ C. All ports are forwarding.
   ❍ D. All ports are either blocking or forwarding.

9. Which one of the following is true of the Spanning-Tree Root Path Cost?

   ❍ A. It is the cost of the exit port to the Root.
   ❍ B. It is the bandwidth of the exit port to the Root.
   ❍ C. It is the delay in data transmission to the Root.
   ❍ D. It is the cumulative cost, based on number of hops, to the Root.
   ❍ E. It is the cumulative cost, based on bandwidth, of all links on the path to the Root.

10. Given the diagram, answer the following questions:

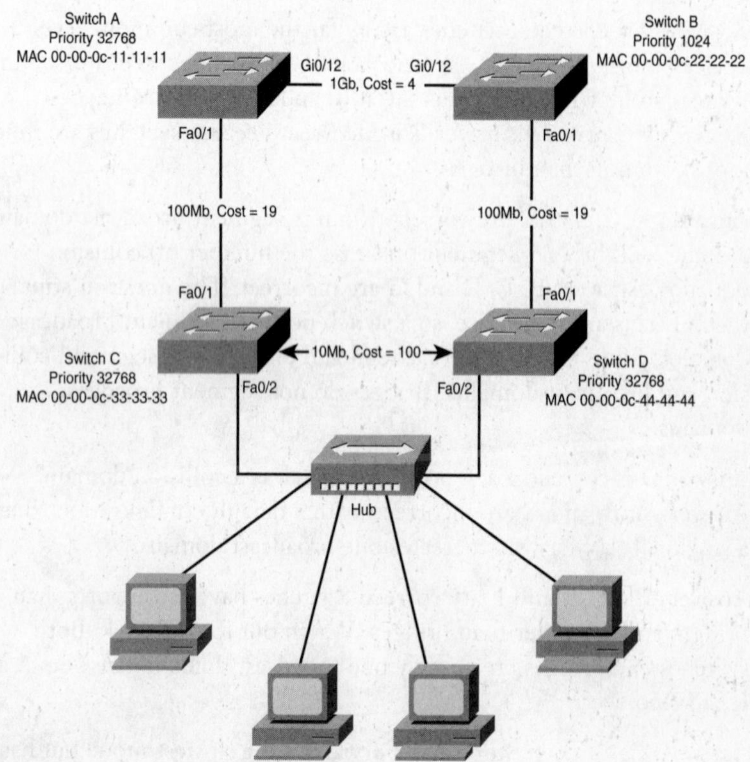

10.1 Which switch will become the Root?

- O A. Switch A
- O B. Switch B
- O C. Switch C
- O D. Switch D

10.2 Which of the following will be the Designated Port for the Ethernet segment between switches C and D?

- O A. Switch C, Fa0/1
- O B. Switch C, Fa0/2
- O C. Switch D, Fa0/1
- O D. Switch D, Fa0/2

Answers to Exam Prep Questions

1. Answer D is correct. Switches are by far the most common Layer 2 device in use. A, B, and C are incorrect because hubs, repeaters, and routers are not Layer 2 devices. (Hubs and repeaters are Layer 1; routers are Layer 3.) Answer E is incorrect because switches are much more common than bridges.

2. Answers A, C, and D are correct. Routers segment broadcast domains; switches and bridges segment (increase the number of) collision domains. Answers B, E, F, and G are incorrect. The question stipulates that VLANs are not in use, so a switch does not segment broadcast domains. Hubs and repeaters extend and enlarge, not segment, collision and broadcast domains. Bridges do not segment broadcast domains.

3. Answer D is correct. Each port on a switch is a collision domain. Answers A, B, and C are incorrect; with a default configuration (that is, a single VLAN), a switch creates one broadcast domain.

4. Answers B, D, E, and F are correct. Switches have more ports than bridges and are faster than bridges. Watch out for the trick: Both switches and bridges create only one broadcast domain. Answers A and C are incorrect.

5. Answer B is correct. Store-and-Forward is the slowest mode but has the advantage of fully error checking every frame for reliability. Answer A, C, D, and E are incorrect. There is no such thing as Segment-Free or Cut-Throat switching. Fragment-Free examines the first 64B of every frame for increased reliability, but is not as fast as Cut-Through.

6. Answer B is correct. STP prevents Layer 2 loops if redundant paths exist. Answers A, C, D, and E are incorrect; STP is not concerned with routing loops, IP addresses, routing in general, or VLAN administration.

7. Answers A and F are correct. The Bridge ID is the Priority prepended to the MAC address of the switch. The switch with the lowest Bridge ID becomes the Root; therefore, the switch with the lowest Priority will always be the Root. Answers B, C, D, E, and G are incorrect; the winning Bridge ID and Priority will be the lowest. The speed of the switch has no bearing on whether it will be the root if left to default settings. The number of connections to other switches has no impact either.

8. Answer D is correct. Convergence in STP means that all ports are either blocked to prevent loops or forwarding to allow data transmission. Answers A, B, and C are incorrect; all switches must run STP or run the risk of loops destabilizing the network.

9. Answer E is correct. The Root Path Cost is the accumulated cost of all the links on the path to the Root. The Cost is calculated based on the bandwidth of the links. Answers A, B, C, and D are incorrect. You must add the STP cost of all the links on the path to the Root; cost has nothing to do with delay or hop count.

10.1 Answer B is correct; Switch B will become the Root because it has the lowest Priority. Remember that even though A has a lower MAC, the Priority overrides this, and the switch with the lowest Priority will be the Root. Answers A, B, and C are incorrect.

10.2 Answer D is correct. Because D has the lower Root Path Cost (at 19) than C (at 23), D will make its port the Designated Port—even though C has a lower Bridge ID. Answer A, B, and C are incorrect; the Designated ports must be connected to the Ethernet segment, and the switch with the lowest Root Path Cost will host the DP. Only if there is a tie for Root Path Cost will Bridge ID become a deciding factor.

VLANs

Terms You'll Need to Understand:

- ✓ VLAN
- ✓ Trunk
- ✓ ISL
- ✓ 802.1Q
- ✓ VTP Server, Client, Transparent
- ✓ VTP Domain
- ✓ Inter-VLAN routing
- ✓ Layer 3 Switching

Techniques You'll Need to Master:

- ✓ Creating and naming VLANs
- ✓ Assigning Switch Ports to VLANs
- ✓ Configuring Trunk links
- ✓ Creating and joining a VTP Domain
- ✓ Troubleshooting VTP and Inter-VLAN routing

Introduction

This chapter introduces the theory, benefits, applications, and implementation of VLANs. Inter-switch connectivity using trunks and the characteristics of different trunking protocols are explained. Finally, Inter-VLAN routing options are described, and troubleshooting tips are reviewed.

VLAN Concepts and Applications

When you plug a bunch of PCs in to a switch and give them all IP addresses in the same network, you create a LAN. A VLAN is a Virtual LAN. The difference is that with VLANs, you still connect all the PCs to a single switch but you make the switch behave as if it were multiple, independent switches. Each VLAN is its own broadcast domain and IP subnet. In this way, you get the ability to use switches to segment broadcast domains, which up to this point was possible only with routers. Figure 7.1 illustrates a simple VLAN configuration:

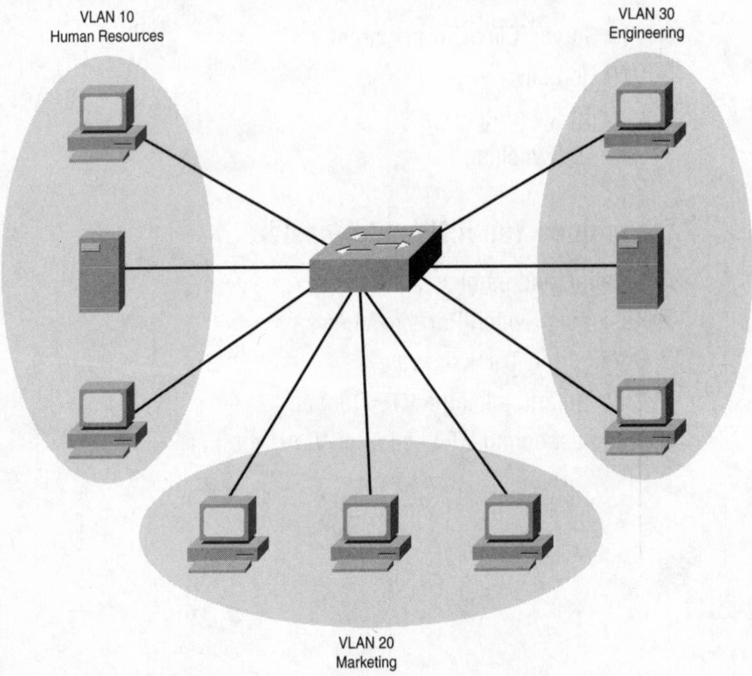

Figure 7.1 VLANs provide a logical segmentation of broadcast domains.

The Definition of a VLAN

A *VLAN* can be defined as a virtual broadcast domain. Instead of segmenting the broadcast domain with routers at Layer 3, you segment using switches at Layer 2. Each VLAN should be associated with its own IP subnet. (No, this is not technically a requirement, but you really want to do it this way!)

VLANs logically divide a switch into multiple, independent switches at Layer 2.

Each VLAN is its own broadcast domain.

Each VLAN should be in its own subnet.

Benefits of VLANs

The advantages of using VLANs are

- VLANs increase the number of broadcast domains while reducing their size; this is the same effect that routers have, but without the need to buy a lot of routers or a big router with a lot of ports, so it's less expensive and easier to administer.
- VLANs provide an additional layer of security: No device in any VLAN can communicate with a device in any other VLAN until you deliberately configure a way for it to do so. An example might be a server in VLAN 10 that holds sensitive employee files for HR; no PCs from other VLANs can access VLAN 10 (or the server in it), unless you specifically configure it to do so.
- VLANs are flexible in terms of how they are used in network equipment: Imagine a building that has LAN cabling and a single switch installed, but four different tenants. You can create four different VLANs, one for each tenant, and no tenant will see or hear from the other tenants on the other VLANs.
- VLANs can span across multiple switches using trunk links. This allows you to create a logical grouping of network users by function instead of location. If you want all the marketing people to be in their own broadcast domain and IP subnet, you can create a VLAN for them on the first switch; then, you can connect another switch using a trunk link, define the same VLAN on that switch, and the marketing users on the second switch are in the same VLAN and can communicate with the marketing users on the first switch, and are isolated from other VLANs on both switches. This capability can be extended across an enterprise

network campus, so that marketing users in the Whitaker Pavilion could in theory be in a VLAN with other marketing users in the Valentine Pavilion.

➤ The ability to trunk VLANs across multiple switches makes adding users, moving users, and changing users' VLAN memberships much easier.

Know the advantages of VLANs:

- ➤ Increase the number of broadcast domains while reducing their size.
- ➤ Provide additional security.
- ➤ Increase the flexibility of network equipment.
- ➤ Allow a logical grouping of users by function, not location.
- ➤ Make user adds, moves, and changes easier.

Figure 7.2 illustrates a multi-switch VLAN system.

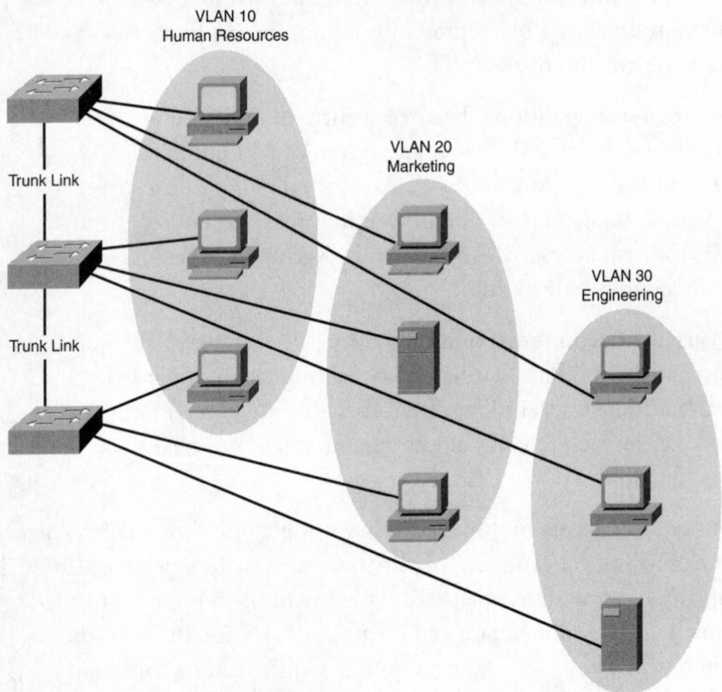

Figure 7.2 VLANs over trunk links allows a logical grouping of users by function.

Implementing VLANs

Implementing VLANs is done in three steps:

1. Create the VLAN.
2. Name the VLAN (this is optional but expected).
3. Assign switch ports to the VLAN.

Know the three steps in VLAN implementation: Create it, name it, and assign ports to it.

The commands to create a VLAN vary depending on the switch model and IOS version; we stick with the Catalyst 2950 using an IOS later than 12.1(9) as our example.

The command to create a VLAN is simply **vlan** [vlan_#]. To name the VLAN, the equally simple command is **name** [vlan_name]. These commands are entered starting at the Global Config prompt.

To create VLAN 10 named HR, VLAN 20 named Marketing, and VLAN 30 named Engineering, the commands look like this:

```
2950#configure terminal
2950(config)#vlan 10
2950(config-vlan)#name HR
2950(config-vlan)#vlan 20
2950(config-vlan)#name Marketing
2950(config-vlan)#vlan 30
2950(config-vlan)#name Engineering
2950(config-vlan)#exit
2950(config)#exit
2950#
```

Note that the Global Config prompt changes to the config-vlan prompt when you create the first VLAN; it is okay to stay in that prompt to continue creating VLANs.

With these commands, you can create all your VLANs at once, or you can go back later and add some more as needed. The VLAN configuration (names and numbers) is not stored in the Running-Config or Startup-Config file in NVRAM; rather, it is stored in Flash memory in a special file called *vlan.dat*. This means that it is possible to erase the Startup-Config file, reload the router, and be confused by the reappearance of VLANs that you thought you just deleted. To delete VLANs, you can do it one at a time using the **no vlan** [vlan_#] command, or to get rid of all of them at once, you can use the command delete flash:vlan.dat, which erases and resets the entire vlan database.

The exact syntax for the **delete flash:vlan.dat** command is critical: no space after **flash** or the colon! If you put a space after **flash**, you will delete the entire flash directory, including your IOS. This is a very bad thing to do, and is actually quite an ordeal to fix.

Cisco switches have a few default VLANs preconfigured; these are intended for the management and essential functionality of Ethernet, Token Ring, and FDDI LANs. VLAN 1, for example, is the management VLAN for Ethernet. All switch ports are in VLAN 1 by default. You cannot change or delete these default VLANs.

Entry-level switches such as the Catalyst 2950 will commonly support up to 64 VLANs defined locally; with the Enterprise IOS, the 2950 can support up to 250. More powerful switches can support up to the maximum of 4,096 VLANs.

VLANs can exist without any ports actually being in them. Adding switch ports to a VLAN is done when you want to put a host into a particular VLAN. Obviously, you need to know which physical ports your hosts are connected to so that you can add the correct port to the correct VLAN; it would be an unpopular move to put a marketing user into the Engineering VLAN; these two groups are mutually hostile.

The commands to add a switch port to a VLAN are executed at the Interface Config prompt—if you think about that, it makes sense because you are putting the port itself into the VLAN. The command is **switchport access vlan** [vlan_#]. What you are saying is "this port shall access VLAN X."

The following example puts ports Fa0/8 into VLAN 10, Fa0/13 into VLAN 20, and Fa0/14 into VLAN 30:

```
2950#config t
2950(config)#interface fa0/8
2950(config-if)#switchport access vlan 10
2950(config-if)#int fa0/13
2950(config-if)#switchport access vlan 20
2950(config-if)#int fa0/14
2950(config-if)#switchport access vlan 30
2950(config-if)#exit
2950(config)#exit
2950#
```

VLAN Membership

The commands in the previous section assign particular ports to a particular VLAN *statically*. (Static VLAN assignment is sometimes called port-based

VLAN membership.) When a user changes ports (moves around the office or campus), you need to repeat the commands at the Router(`config-if)#` prompt for the correct new interface. As you can imagine, if there are a lot of moves, this can become an administrative pain.

There is an alternative called *Dynamic VLAN Membership*. This feature allows you to dynamically assign VLAN membership to switch ports based on the MAC address of the host connecting to the port. You need a little service called the *VLAN Membership Policy Server (VMPS)* that holds a database of all the MAC addresses and the correct VLAN for each one; then you tell the switch ports to do dynamic VLAN assignment. When a host connects to a switch port configured to do Dynamic membership, the switch checks the MAC of the host and asks the VMPS what VLAN that MAC should be in. The switch then changes the VLAN membership of that port dynamically.

This sounds like a wonderful idea, and it can be, but it is difficult to create the VMPS database and to maintain it if your network grows quickly. Imagine having to get and maintain certain knowledge of every MAC address of every host in your network, and then keep the VMPS database updated. Dynamic VLAN membership is a good option if you have a lot of users in a lot of different VLANs moving around to many switch ports, but be ready to wrestle with some administrative issues.

Trunking

For VLANs to span across multiple switches, you obviously need to connect the switches to each other. Although it is possible to simply plug one switch in to another using an Access port just as you would plug in a host or a hub, doing so kills the VLAN-spanning feature and a bunch of other useful stuff too. A switch-to-switch link must be set up as a trunk link in order for the VLAN system to work properly. A trunk link is a special connection; the key difference between an ordinary connection (an Access port) and a Trunk port is that although an Access port is only in one VLAN at a time, a Trunk port has the job of carrying traffic for *all* VLANs from one switch to another. Any time you connect a switch to another switch, you want to make it a trunk.

Some key points about trunks are as follows:

- A trunk can be created only on a Fast Ethernet or Gigabit Ethernet connection; 10Mb Ethernet ports are not fast enough to support the increased traffic from multiple VLANs, so the commands are not available for a regular Ethernet port.

- By default, traffic from all VLANs is allowed on a trunk. You can specify which VLANs are permitted (or not) to cross a particular trunk if you have that requirement, but these functions are beyond the scope of the CCNA exam.
- Switches (whether trunked or not) are always connected with crossover cables, not straight-through cables. In CCNA land, there is no such thing as a "smart port" that will auto-detect a crossed connection and fix it. If two switches are not connected with a crossover cable, there will be no connectivity between them, period.

By default, all VLANs are permitted across a trunk link. Switch-to-Switch trunk links always require the use of a crossover cable, never a straight-through cable.

When creating a trunk, you must choose a trunking protocol. A trunking protocol adds a VLAN identification tag to frames coming into the switch. As those frames are forwarded across the trunk, the VLAN from which the frame originated is identifiable, and the data frame can be distributed to ports in the same VLAN on other switches—and not to different VLANs. This *frame tagging* and *multiplexing* function is what enables VLANs to span multiple switches and still keeps each VLAN as a separate broadcast domain. Figure 7.3 illustrates a simple trunk as it multiplexes frames from two separate VLANs across a single Fast Ethernet Trunk.

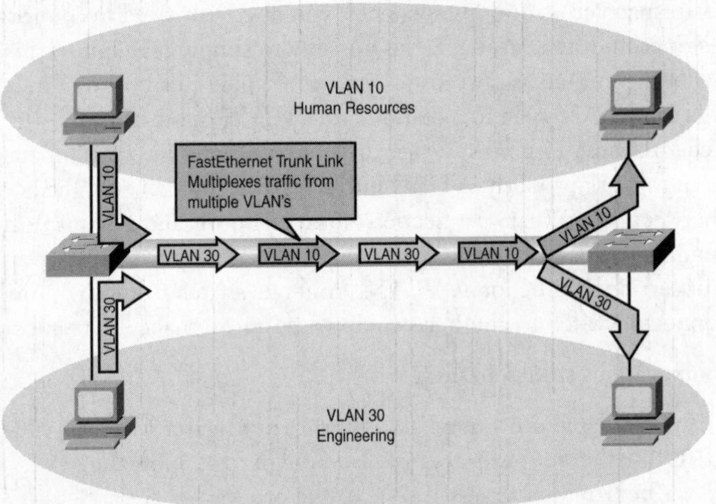

Figure 7.3 Trunks carry traffic from multiple VLANs across a single physical link.

Cisco supports two trunking protocols, ISL and 802.1Q, as described in the next sections.

ISL

The Inter-Switch Link (ISL) protocol is a Cisco-proprietary Layer 2 protocol. ISL operates by re-encapsulating host frames as they are received by the switch port. The ISL encapsulation adds a 26-byte header and a 4-byte trailer to the original host frame. The header includes the VLAN ID (the VLAN number) and several other fields. The trailer is a new CRC to check the integrity of the ISL frame.

There are two significant issues with ISL. The first is that it is Cisco proprietary, meaning that it will work only between two Cisco devices. In a perfect world, of course, everyone would have all Cisco gear, but the reality is a lot of non-Cisco network devices are out there. To complicate matters, Cisco has begun to phase out ISL in favor of 802.1Q; for example, the Cisco 2950 does not support ISL at all, only 802.1Q.

The second issue with ISL is frame size. If a frame is received that is already at the MTU, the addition of the 26-byte header and 4-byte trailer can create frames that are over the Ethernet MTU of 1,518 bytes (with ISL encapsulation, now at 1,548 bytes), which will be dropped as "Giant" frames by devices that do not recognize the ISL encapsulation. Figure 7.4 illustrates an ISL-encapsulated frame.

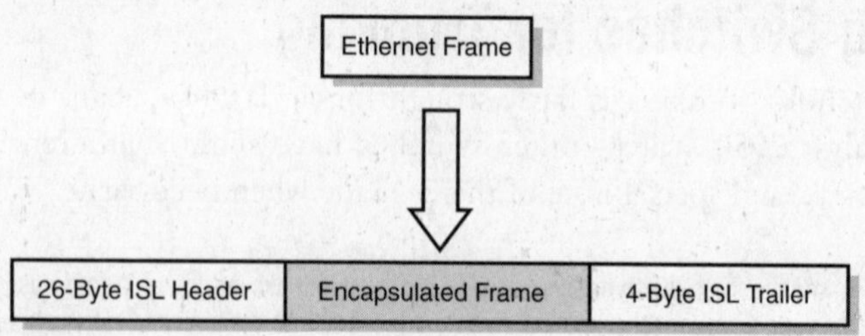

Figure 7.4 ISL Re-encapsulates the original host frame.

802.1Q

The IEEE-standard 802.1Q trunk encapsulation has the advantage of being an industry standard, so inter-vendor operation is much less of a problem. Often referred to as "dot1q" (because geeks like lingo), this protocol does not re-encapsulate the original frame, but instead inserts a 4-byte tag in to the original header. This means that a dot1q frame will be seen as a "baby giant" of 1,522 bytes. Most modern NICs will not reject these frames if they mistakenly receive one. Figure 7.5 shows a dot1q-tagged frame.

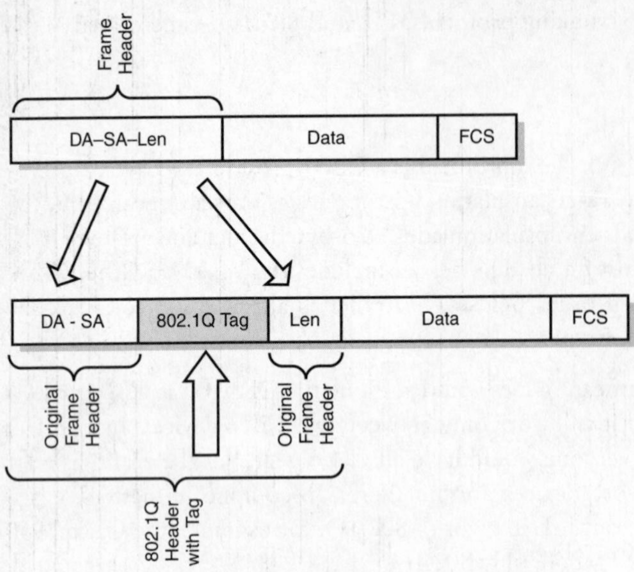

Figure 7.5 802.1Q inserts a 4-byte tag into the existing frame header.

Cisco supports two VLAN frame tagging trunk encapsulations:

- ISL—Cisco proprietary, adds new 26-byte header and 4-byte trailer; Re-encapsulates original frame.
- 802.1Q—IEEE standard, inserts 4-byte tag in to existing header.

Configuring Switches for Trunking

Configuring a switch for trunking is fairly straightforward. Once again, we focus on the Catalyst 2950 switch; other switches have slightly different capabilities and syntax, and special note of this is made when necessary.

Cisco has implemented the Dynamic Trunking Protocol to make setting up trunks easier. DTP can send and/or receive trunk negotiation frames to dynamically establish a trunk link with a connected switch. DTP is not necessary to establish a trunk link, and like many other automatic functions, many administrators would rather not use it and instead manually configure their trunk links. The CCNA exam is not concerned with DTP, but does ask about the five port modes, so an explanation is warranted.

A switch port can be in one of five modes:

- **Off**—In Off mode, the port is an Access port and will not trunk, even if the neighbor switch wants to. This mode is intended for the connection of single hosts or hubs. DTP frames are not sent or acknowledged.

- **On**—In On mode, the port will trunk unconditionally, and trunk connectivity will happen if the neighbor switch port is set to Auto, Desirable, or NoNegotiate. DTP frames are sent but not acted upon if received.
- **NoNegotiate**—Sets the port to trunk unconditionally even if the neighbor switch disagrees. A trunk will form only if the neighbor switch port is set to On, Auto, or Desirable mode. DTP frames are not sent or acknowledged.
- (Dynamic) **Desirable**—This mode actively solicits a trunk connection with the neighbor. DTP frames are sent and responded to if received. A trunk forms if the neighbor is set to On, Desirable, or Auto. If the neighbor is set to NoNegotiate, the trunk will not form because Desirable needs a response from the neighbor, which NoNegotiate will not send.
- (Dynamic) **Auto**—The port trunks only in response to a DTP request to do so. A trunk forms with a neighbor port set to on or desirable. DTP frames are not sent but are acknowledged if received.

Know the five switch port modes: On, Off, Desirable, Auto, and NoNegotiate.

Know the command to set permanent trunking mode:

Switchport mode trunk

To configure a switch port to trunk, we need to set the mode and choose a trunking protocol (assuming that the switch supports more than one to choose from).

The command to set the port mode is **`switchport mode`**, executed at the interface configuration prompt for the port you want to modify. Note that to set NoNegotiate mode, the command is **`switchport nonegotiate`**:

```
2950(config)#int fa0/1
2950(config-if)#switchport mode     access
                                    Trunk
                                    dynamic auto
                                    dynamic desirable
2950(config-if)#switchport nonegotiate
```

To change the trunking protocol, you need to use a different type of switch because the 2950 only supports 802.1Q. We will use a 2900 for our example:

```
2900(config-if)switchport trunk encapsulation [isl ¦ dot1q]
```

Know the syntax to set trunk encapsulation to 802.1Q on a 2900:

switchport trunk encapsulation dot1q

VTP

Now that we have configured our trunk links and built a system of switches to carry our VLAN traffic, we can start creating and naming VLANs and assigning port membership to them. We can do this the hard way, by going to every switch in the system and configuring exactly the same VLAN information on each of them (and doing it again when something changes), or we can do it the easy way by using the VLAN Trunking Protocol (VTP).

VTP is a Layer 2 protocol that takes care of the steps of creating and naming VLANs on all switches in the system. We still have to set port membership to VLANs at each switch, which we can do either statically or using a VMPS.

VTP works by establishing a single switch as being in charge of the VLAN information for a *domain*. In this case, a domain is simply a group of switches that all have the same VTP domain name. This simply puts all the switches into a common administrative group.

VTP Switch Modes

In a VTP domain, there are three types of switches:

- Server mode—This is the one switch that is in charge of the VLAN information for the VTP domain. You may add, delete, and change VLAN information on this switch, and doing so affects the entire VTP domain. This way, we only have to enter our VLAN information once, and the Server mode switch propagates it to all the other switches in the domain.
- Client mode—Client mode switches get VLAN information from the Server. You cannot add, delete, or change VLAN information on a Client mode switch; in fact, the commands to do so are disabled.
- Transparent mode—A Transparent mode switch is doing its own thing; it will not accept any changes to VLAN information from the Server, but it will forward those changes to other switches in the system. You can add, delete, and change VLANs—but those changes only affect the Transparent mode switch and are not sent to other switches in the domain.

VTP Communication

In order for switches to properly communicate with VTP, four elements must be configured. First, you need to have all switches connected by working trunk links. (This, of course, implies crossover cables as well.)

Second, you need a domain name. This name can be anything you like, but make sure that it is unique in a switched system, or you can cause real problems, as you will see. The domain name must be identical on all the switches in the VTP system; this is a common misconfiguration error, and also highly tested. The domain name is case sensitive, too!

Third, you need at least one (and preferably only one) Server mode switch. Yes, you can have more than one, but you don't need or want that.

Fourth, if you want, you can configure a password so that VTP information will not be exchanged if the password does not match on the server and client switch(es). The password is optional, but it must be identical (case sensitive) on all switches in the domain. This is also highly testable!

VTP Pruning

VTP pruning is a way to conserve a little bandwidth on those trunk links. If a client switch has no ports in VLAN 10, and we enable VTP Pruning on the Server mode switch, information about VLAN 10 will not be sent down the trunk to the client mode switch. This way, switches only learn what they need to know.

Configuration

Configuring VTP is done from the global config prompt. The commands are simple:

```
2950(config)#vtp mode [server¦client¦transparent}
2950(config)#vtp domain <vtp_domain_name>
2950(config)#vtp password <vtp_password>
```

Verification and Troubleshooting

The primary command used for verification and troubleshooting VTP is `show vtp status`. The following sample output shows what information can be drawn from this command:

```
2950#show vtp status
VTP Version                     : 2
Configuration Revision          : 0
Maximum VLANs supported locally : 64
```

```
Number of existing VLANs          : 38
VTP Operating Mode                : Server
VTP Domain Name                   : ExamCram2
VTP Pruning Mode                  : Disabled
VTP V2 Mode                       : Disabled
VTP Traps Generation              : Disabled
MD5 digest                        : 0x57 0xCD 0x40 0x65
➥0x63 0x59 0x47 0xBD
Configuration last modified by 10.0.0.1 at 8-13-66 05:30:38
Local updater ID is 10.0.0.1
```

If you compare the outputs of `show vtp status` from two different switches, look for a match between them for the domain name and check that one of them is in Server mode.

The VTP domain name and password must match on all switches in order for VLAN information to be propagated from the Server mode switch.

Inter-Vlan Routing

VLANs define separate broadcast domains and should be separate IP subnets. The only way to get traffic from one VLAN to another is to route between them (Inter-VLAN Routing). We have several choices for how to do this. We could have one router for every VLAN, with an Ethernet port on each connected to a switch port in each VLAN, and then interconnect all the routers; the problem here, of course, is that having so many routers and connections gets expensive and complicated, and latency can be bad.

We could get one big router with a lot of Ethernet ports and could connect one to a port in each VLAN on the switch. This is a little simpler, but still expensive and probably not as fast as it could be unless we really spend the cash.

Our last two choices are to use Router-on-a-Stick (honest, that's what it's called; we wouldn't make something like that up) or Layer 3 switching. The next section details Router-on-a-Stick.

Router-on-a-Stick

This feature takes advantage of trunk links: All VLANs can be transported across a trunk link to be distributed by the neighbor device. Suppose that we built a trunk from a switch to a router? We'd need at least a FastEthernet port on the router, and it would have to support either ISL or 802.1Q. Now all we need to do is build routable interfaces, one for each VLAN.

We do this by using sub-interfaces. A sub-interface is a virtual interface that is spawned from the physical interface, and uses the physical interface for Layer 1 connectivity. A sub-interface can be given an IP address and mask, can be shut down or enabled, can run routing protocols—in fact, there isn't much that a physical interface can do that a sub-interface can't. So if our router has a FastEthernet interface, we can configure it to run 802.1Q, build a subinterface for each VLAN, give those sub-interfaces IP addresses in the appropriate subnets for each VLAN, and let the router route between the VLANs whose traffic is coming up that trunk link. A frame destined for VLAN 30 could come up the trunk link from VLAN 10 to the Router's VLAN 10 sub-interface, get routed to VLAN 30, and leave that same port from the VLAN 30 sub-interface. The hosts in each VLAN will use the sub-interface configured for their VLAN as their default gateway.

The following example configures Router-on-a-Stick for inter-vlan routing between VLANs 10 and 30, using 802.1Q trunking on interface FastEthernet 1/0:

```
Router(config)#int fa0/1
Router(config-if)#no ip address
Router(config-if)#interface fa0/1.1
Router(config-sub-if)#encapsulation dot1q 1 native
!
! Creates sub-interface for Native VLAN 1
! (Required for dot1q functionality)
!
Router(config-sub-if)#int fa0/1.10
Router(config-sub-if)#encap dot1q 10
Router(config-sub-if)#ip address 10.10.10.1  255.255.255.0
!
! Creates sub-interface for VLAN 10 and
! applies IP address in VLAN10's subnet
!
Router(config-sub-if)#int fa0/1.30
Router(config-sub-if)#ip address 10.30.30.1  255.255.255.0
Router(config-sub-if)#encap dot1q.30
!
! Creates sub-interface for VLAN 10 and
! applies IP address in VLAN10's subnet
!
```

Figure 7.6 illustrates a typical Router-on-a-Stick application.

Why is it called Router-on-a-Stick, anyway? Just because the router looks like a lollipop on the end of the trunk "stick." Geeks like to be cute.

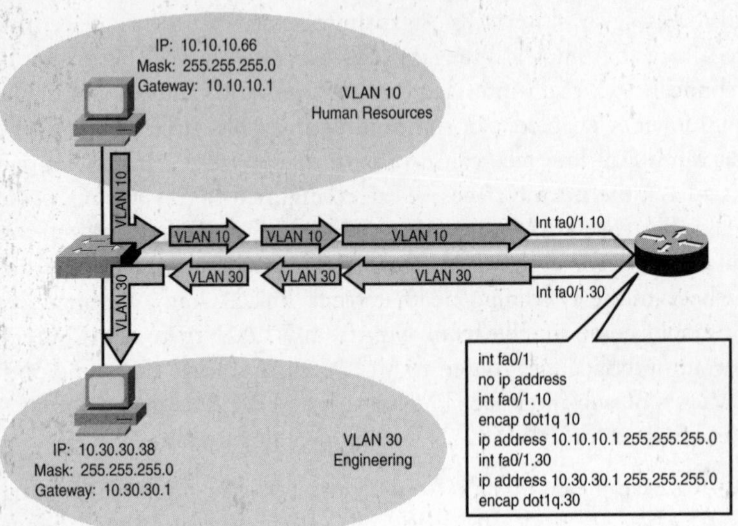

Figure 7.6 Router-on-a-Stick.

L3 Switching

Layer 3 switching is beyond the scope of this exam but deserves mention because it is important and cool.

A Layer 3 switch has the capability to create a virtual routed interface for each VLAN, and route between virtual interfaces for inter-vlan routing. It's similar to Router-on-a-Stick, except that there is no stick, and the router is internal to the switch and extremely fast. If you are routing a lot of inter-vlan traffic, buying and configuring a Layer 3 switch will bring you serious gains in throughput.

Not every switch is Layer 3 capable; the lowly 2950 cannot do it, but a 3550 will. Layer 3 switches are more expensive that Layer 2 switches, but are much more capable.

Exam Prep Questions

1. Which three of the following are steps in the VLAN implementation process?
   - ❑ A. Disable VTP to prevent automatic VLAN creation
   - ❑ B. Create VLANs using unique ID numbers
   - ❑ C. Apply passwords to VLANs to prevent unauthorized changes
   - ❑ D. Optionally name VLANs for easier understanding
   - ❑ E. Assign switch port VLAN membership
   - ❑ F. Convert all switch ports to trunk links to allow hosts to access VLANs
2. Which of the following are advantages of VLANs? Choose all that apply.
   - ❑ A. VLANs eliminate the need for subnets.
   - ❑ B. VLANs offer improved security.
   - ❑ C. Administrative overhead because of adds, moves, and changes is reduced.
   - ❑ D. VLANs encrypt all network traffic for improved security.
   - ❑ E. VLANs allow users to be grouped together by function or department instead of location.
   - ❑ F. VLANs eliminate broadcasts, reducing congestion.
   - ❑ G. VLANs provide virtual broadcast domain segmentation at Layer 2.
   - ❑ H. VLANs increase the number of broadcast domains while reducing their size.
3. Which two of the following are true with respect to trunk links and VLANs? Choose 2.
   - ❑ A. Trunk links enable VLAN traffic to span multiple switches.
   - ❑ B. Trunk links are not possible between switches from different vendors.
   - ❑ C. Trunk links should be given their own subnet to function properly.
   - ❑ D. By default, trunks enable all defined VLANs to traverse the trunk.
4. Which of the following are true with respect to the Layer 3 characteristics of VLANs? Choose 3.
   - ❑ A. All VLANS exist within one subnet.
   - ❑ B. Each VLAN should be associated with its own subnet.
   - ❑ C. VLANs provide Layer 3 broadcast domain segmentation at Layer 2.
   - ❑ D. VLANs provide Layer 2 collision domain separation at Layer 3.
   - ❑ E. In deploying Router-on-a-Stick, hosts should be assigned the IP address of the router sub-interface assigned to the hosts' VLAN as the hosts' default gateway address.

5. Which of the following support the multiplexing of traffic from multiple VLANs across Fast or Gigabit Ethernet links? Choose 2.
   - ❑ A. STP
   - ❑ B. HSRP
   - ❑ C. VTP
   - ❑ D. ISL
   - ❑ E. 802.1d
   - ❑ F. 802.11
   - ❑ G. 802.1Q
6. Which of the following are trunk port modes? Choose all that apply.
   - ❑ A. on
   - ❑ B. idle
   - ❑ C. off
   - ❑ D. blocking
   - ❑ E. auto
   - ❑ F. desirable
   - ❑ G. undesirable
7. Which two commands make a port a trunk and force it to use a multiple-vendor–compatible protocol?
   - ❑ A. Switch(config)#switchport mode trunk
   - ❑ B. Switch(config-if)#switchport mode trunk
   - ❑ C. Switch(config-if)#switchport trunk on
   - ❑ D. Switch(config-if)#switchport trunk compatible-mode
   - ❑ E. Switch(config-if)#switchport trunk encapsulation 802.1q
   - ❑ F. Switch(config-if)#switchport trunk encapsulation dot1q
8. Which of the following are VLAN Trunking Protocol switch modes? Choose all that apply.
   - ❑ A. Domain Controller
   - ❑ B. Server
   - ❑ C. Slave
   - ❑ D. Client
   - ❑ E. Independent
   - ❑ F. Transparent
9. What elements are required in order to create a functioning VTP system between two switches?
   - ❑ A. Matching VTP mode
   - ❑ B. Matching VTP Domain Name
   - ❑ C. Identical VTY password
   - ❑ D. Identical VTP password
   - ❑ E. A functional Access link between them
   - ❑ F. A crossover-cabled trunk link and compatible trunking protocols
   - ❑ G. One switch set to Server, the other to Transparent mode
   - ❑ H. Identical hold-down timers

10. What IOS feature can logically divide a switch into multiple, independent switches at Layer 2 without the use of a SawzAll?

    - ❑ A. STP
    - ❑ B. VLANs
    - ❑ C. GigaStack
    - ❑ D. VTP

Answers to Exam Prep Questions

1. Answers B, D, and E are correct. Create the VLANs, name them, and assign the ports. Answer A is incorrect; VTP does not create VLANs, it updates other switches that you have created. Answer C is incorrect; VLANs do not themselves have passwords, but the VTP system might. Answer F is incorrect; trunk links are only necessary to carry multiple-VLAN traffic between switches or routers. Access ports for hosts are assigned to a single VLAN each, which gives the host access to that VLAN.

2. Answers B, C, E, G, and H are correct; these are all stated advantages of VLANs. Answer A is incorrect; VLANs complement the use of subnets. Answer D is incorrect; VLANs have nothing whatsoever to do with encryption. Answer F is wrong. VLANs do not eliminate broadcasts; they only constrain them.

3. Answers A and D are correct; Trunking protocols label each frame with its originating VLAN number so traffic from multiple VLANs can be multiplexed across a trunk link. By default, traffic from all VLANs is permitted across a trunk. Answer B is incorrect; 802.1Q is a standardized trunking protocol that enables inter-vendor switch links. Answer C is false; trunks are a Layer 2 construct that carry traffic from multiple VLANs and their associated subnets; the trunk itself does not require a subnet of its own to function

4. Answers B, C, and E are correct. A single VLAN should be associated with a single IP subnet; each VLAN is a separate broadcast domain, segmented by the Layer 2 function of the switch, and Router-on-a-Stick configuration creates a virtual gateway (sub-interface) for each VLAN/subnet. Answer A is wrong; each VLAN should have its own subnet. Answer D is wrong; VLANs do not segment collision domains.

5. Answers D and G are correct; these are the two trunking protocols supported by Cisco. Answers A, B, C, E, and F are wrong: STP eliminates Layer 2 loops; HSRP provides redundant gateway functionality; VTP dynamically updates VLAN information; 802.1d is the IEEE specification for STP; and 802.11b is the IEEE specification for Wi-Fi.

6. Answers A, C, E, and F are correct. The on mode, off mode, auto mode, and desirable mode are trunk port modes. Answers B, D, and G are incorrect; these other modes are not associated with trunking.

7. Answers B and F are correct. These two commands make a port a trunk and force it to use multiple-vendor–compatible protocol. Answer A is incorrect; the command must be issued at the config-if prompt. Answers C, D, and E are incorrect because they are invalid commands.
8. Answers B, D, and F are correct. Server, Client, and Transparent are VLAN Trunking Protocol switch modes. Answers A, C, and E are not valid VTP modes.
9. Answers B, D, F, and G are correct. These elements are required to create a functioning VTP system between two switches. Answer A is incorrect; one switch should be the Server for the domain. Answer C is incorrect, VTY is the Telnet lines. Answer E is wrong; we need trunks between switches to make VTP work. Answer H is wrong; hold-down timers are part of a routing protocol, not VTP.
10. Answer B is correct. VLANS have the effect of totally isolating hosts in different VLANs as if they were plugged in to different switches that are not connected. A, C, and D are incorrect; STP prevents Layer 2 loops, GigaStacking uses high-speed connections to make two or more switches appear as one management unit, and VTP dynamically propagates VLAN updates to other connected switches.

IP Access Lists

Terms You'll Need to Understand

- ✓ Standard Access Lists (ACL)
- ✓ Extended ACLs
- ✓ Wildcard Masks

Concepts and Techniques You'll Need to Master

- ✓ Configuring and troubleshooting standard ACLs
- ✓ Configuring and troubleshooting extended ACLs
- ✓ Configuring and troubleshooting named ACLs

Introduction

Access control lists (ACLs) have a lot of uses on Cisco routers. This chapter describes their use as packet filters by which you can filter traffic coming from one network into another. However, keep in mind that an ACL can also be used for the following purposes:

- Classifying and organizing traffic for quality of service—You can use an ACL to categorize and prioritize your traffic with Quality of Service (QoS). QoS is more heavily covered in the Cisco Certified Voice Professional (CCVP) and Cisco Certified Internet Professional (CCIP) tracks, and some in the Cisco Certified Network Professional (CCNP) track.
- Filtering routing updates—ACLs can be used with routing protocols to control what networks are advertised. Routing protocols are discussed further in Chapter 9, "Routing."
- Defining interesting traffic for dial-on-demand routing (DDR)—ACLs can be used to configure what traffic will dial a remote router when using Integrated Services Digital Network (ISDN). ISDN is discussed further in Chapter 10, "Wide Area Networks."
- Network Address Translation (NAT)—ACLs are used to identify inside local addresses when configuring NAT. NAT is discussed in greater detail in Chapter 11, "Advanced IP Concepts."

Although this chapter focuses on using ACLs as packet filters, make sure you do not forget that ACLs are used for a lot more than just packet filtering. The exam will test your knowledge of the various uses of ACLs.

When used as a packet filter, ACLs can be used to filter traffic as it passes through a router. For example, say that Andrew, one of the authors of this book, wanted to block Mike, the other author, from being able to communicate to the web server (see Figure 8.1).

Andrew could go on his router and configure an ACL that would prevent Mike from communicating to the server while allowing all other traffic to pass. ACLs used to filter traffic passing through the router are applied on an interface; when applying the ACL, you must specify if you are filtering traffic coming into (inbound) or leaving (outbound) the interface.

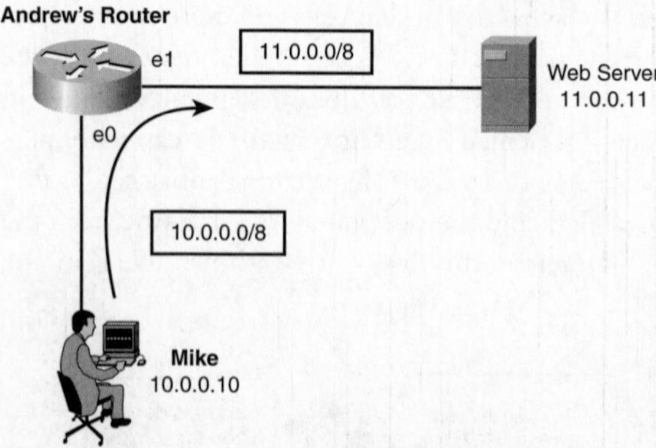

Figure 8.1 ACL example.

Andrew could go on his router and configure an ACL that would prevent Mike from communicating to the server while allowing all other traffic to pass through. ACLs then get applied on an interface in the inbound or outbound direction. When applied inbound, you are filtering traffic as the traffic comes into the incoming interface on the router; when applied in the outbound direction, you are filtering traffic as it leaves the outgoing interface.

In Figure 8.1, the ACL can be applied inbound on Ethernet 0 or outbound on Ethernet 1. This is because Mike's traffic would come inbound on Ethernet 0 and exit on Ethernet 1. If applied inbound on interface Ethernet 1, the ACL would filter the traffic before the router could examine its routing table to determine the outgoing interface; if applied outbound on Ethernet 1, the ACL would filter Mike's traffic after the router looked in its routing table and forwarded the traffic to Ethernet 1. Later in this chapter, you learn some general rules about where you should apply ACLs.

No matter where you apply the ACL, the list will process the packets and check them against your list in the order that you put the statements in. For this reason, you must be careful about the order of the statements. After you have configured your ACL, there is no way to reorder your statements. If Figure 8.1 is our example, and if you wanted to prevent Mike from accessing the web server but allow everyone else on the 10.0.0.0/8 network to access the web server, your ACL would need statements to first deny Mike's computer and then allow everyone else on the network.

Resequence Command

Okay, so a resequence command is available in IOS 12.4, but humor me and pretend that it does not exist; the CCNA test will take the stance that there is no way to reorder your statements.

If the packet is checked against each entry in the ACL and there is no match, the default action is to drop the packet. There is an implicit deny any at the end of the traffic that will drop any packet that does not match an entry in the ACL. Therefore, all traffic is denied except for what you explicitly permit. Figure 8.2 illustrates the logic of an access list that is configured to first deny Mike's computer at 10.0.0.55 and then permit all other traffic from the 10.0.0.0/8 network. (The syntax for this list will be shown later in the chapter.)

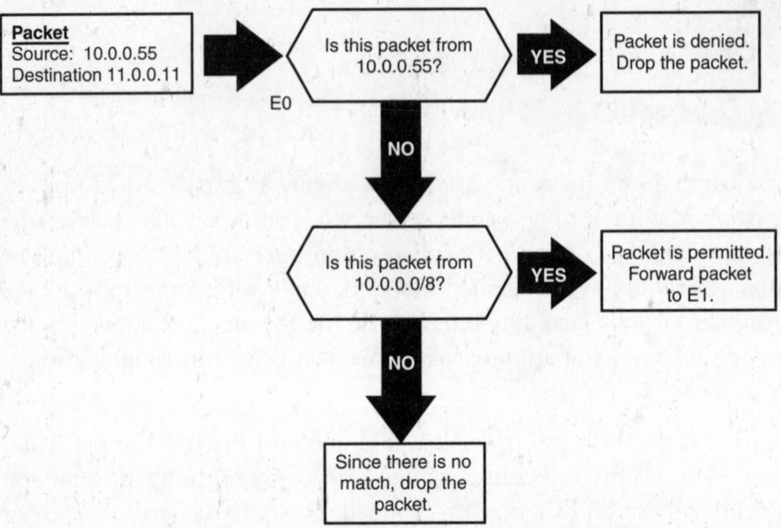

Figure 8.2 ACL logic.

If the order of ACL statements were reversed, and you first permitted the 10.0.0.0/8 network and then denied Mike, Mike would never be denied because the ACL would check Mike's packet and see that he belongs to the 10.0.0.0/8 network and is therefore permitted. The ACL would never get to the deny statement. Figure 8.3 illustrates the logic behind a poorly written ACL that first permitted the 10.0.0.0/8 network and then denied Mike's computer.

Likewise, if your ACL denied Mike's computer but did not permit the rest of the network, any other traffic would be denied because it was not implicitly permitted. You must have at least one permit statement in your ACL. Otherwise, you might as well just shut down the interface because all traffic is dropped.

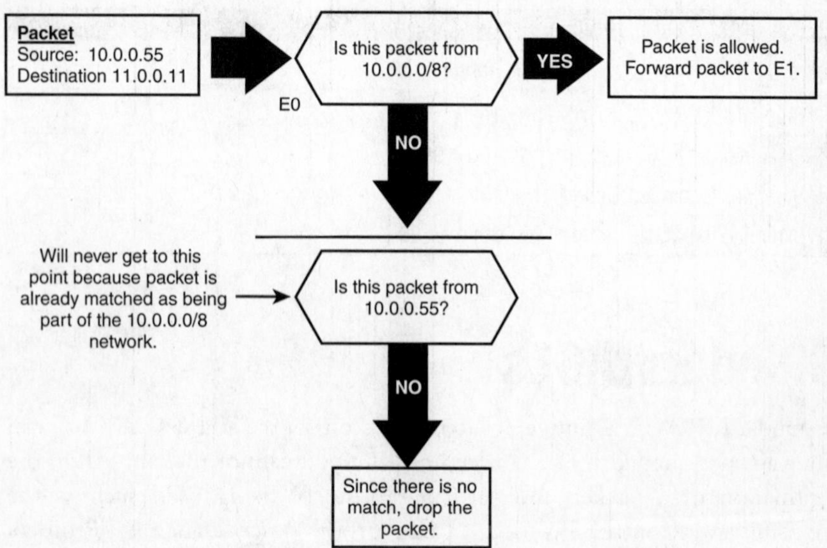

Figure 8.3 ACL logic of a poorly designed access list.

Types of ACLs

The previous examples illustrate the use of IP ACLs. There are many types of ACLs that you can create, including IP, AppleTalk, IPX, MAC addresses, NetBIOS, and other protocols. However, for the CCNA exam, you can breathe a sigh of relief as you only need to be familiar with configuring and troubleshooting IP ACLs.

No matter what type of ACL you use, though, you can have only one ACL per protocol, per interface, per direction. For example, you can have one IP ACL inbound on an interface and another IP ACL outbound on an interface, but you cannot have two inbound IP ACLs on the same interface.

The two types of IP ACLs that you can configure are

- Standard IP ACLs
- Extended IP ACLs

When you create an access list, you will assign it a number. There are predefined ranges for each type of access list. Table 8.1 shows the predefined ranges for IP standard and extended ACLs.

Table 8.1 Access List Ranges	
Type	**Range**
IP Standard	1–99
IP Extended	100–199
IP Standard Expanded Range	1300–1999
IP Extended Expanded Range	2000–2699

Standard ACLs

A standard IP ACL is simple; it filters based on source address only. You can filter a source network or a source host, but you cannot filter based on the destination of a packet, the particular protocol being used such as the Transmission Control Protocol (TCP) or the User Datagram Protocol (UDP), or on the port number. You can permit or deny only source traffic. This is analogous to entering a new country and having customs only check your passport to verify that you (being the source) are allowed to pass through customs.

Extended ACLs

An extended ACL gives you much more power than just a standard ACL. With an extended ACL, you can filter your traffic based on any of the following criteria:

- Source address
- Destination address
- Protocol—TCP, UDP, Internet Control Messaging Protocol (ICMP), and so on
- Source port (if using TCP or UDP)
- Destination port (if protocol is TCP or UDP)
- ICMP message (if protocol is ICMP)

An IP extended access list is analogous to passing through customs, but this time the customs agent verifies not only your identity, but also asks about your destination and the purpose of your stay.

Named ACLs

One of the disadvantages of using IP standard and IP extended ACLs is that you reference them by number, which is not too descriptive of its use. With a named ACL, this is not the case because you can name your ACL with a descriptive name. The ACL named DenyMike is a lot more meaningful than an ACL simply numbered 1. There are both IP standard and IP extended named ACLs.

Another advantage to named ACLs is that they allow you to remove individual lines out of an ACL. With numbered ACLs, you cannot delete individual statements. Instead, you will need to delete your existing access list and recreate the entire list.

Configuring and Implementing

In this next section, you learn how to configure standard, extended, and named ACLs.

Configuring Standard ACLs

Because a standard access list filters only traffic based on source traffic, all you need is the IP address of the host or subnet you want to permit or deny. ACLs are created in global configuration mode and then applied on an interface. The syntax for creating a standard ACL is

```
access-list {1-99 ¦ 1300-1999} {permit ¦ deny} source-address
[wildcard mask]
```

The wildcard mask at the end of the ACL is optional with standard lists and is discussed in the upcoming section "The Wildcard Mask."

As an example, if you wanted to deny Mike's computer at 10.0.0.55 but permit all other hosts on the 10.0.0.0/8 network, you would configure the following ACL:

```
Router(config)#access-list 1 deny 10.0.0.55
Router(config)#access-list 1 permit 10.0.0.0
```

Next, you need to apply the access on an interface. Because you have no way of specifying the destination of your traffic, you should apply the access list as close to the destination as possible. Given Figure 8.1 as our example, interface Ethernet 1 is closest to the destination (the web server). Traffic is leaving this interface heading for the web server, so you should apply this access list outbound on Ethernet 1. The syntax for applying your IP access list on an interface is

```
ip access-group {number ¦ name} {in ¦ out}
```

Because you want to apply this access list outbound on Ethernet 1, the syntax from global configuration would be

```
Router(config)#interface ethernet 1
Router(config-if)#ip access-group 1 out
```

The Wildcard Mask

When you configure your IP standard ACLs, you have the option of using a wildcard mask to better match the hosts and networks you want to filter. Without the use of wildcard masks, the router makes a best guess as to what the mask should be. When using IP extended ACLs, wildcard masks are not optional.

Wildcard masks define how much of an address needs to be looked at in order for there to be a match. For example, in the previous example, you wanted to deny Mike's computer (10.0.0.55) but allow all other hosts on that network (10.0.0.0/8). You want the router to check every bit of the source address as it passes through the router to verify that it matches the complete address 10.0.0.55, so you will need a wildcard mask that tells your router to check every bit. For matching the 10.0.0.0/8 network, however, you need only your router to check the first eight bits because you only need to check the network portion (the 10.0.0.0/8 network) and the source host address will vary.

Wildcard masks use 0s to designate what bits you want to match and 1s to designate those bits that you do not want the router to examine. If you wanted to match the 10.0.0.55 host, you would need a wildcard mask of all 0s to indicate to your router that it needs to check every bit to verify that it matches 10.0.0.55 exactly. This would be a wildcard mask of 0.0.0.0. If you wanted to match the 10.0.0.0/8 network, your wildcard mask would be all 0s in the first octet to match the 10 network and all 1s in the remaining 24 bits to tell your router not to examine the host bits. This wildcard mask, shown in Figure 8.4, would be 0.255.255.255.

If you added the wildcard mask to the syntax you learned earlier, the complete syntax would be

```
Router(config)#access-list 1 deny 10.0.0.55 0.0.0.0
Router(config)#access-list 1 permit 10.0.0.0 0.255.255.255
Router(config)#interface ethernet 1
Router(config-if)#ip access-group 1 out
```

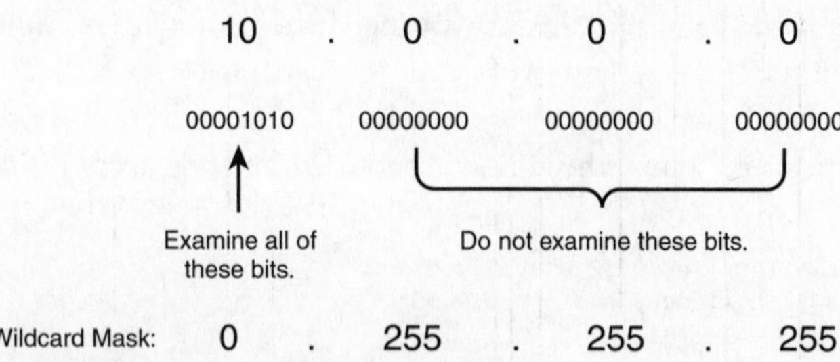

Figure 8.4 Wildcard mask for 10.0.0.0/8.

This example shows matching a class A network. If you wanted instead to match a class B network, the wildcard mask would be 0.0.255.255 to match the first two octets. If you wanted to match a class C network, the wildcard mask would be 0.0.0.255. Notice that the wildcard mask, when used to match a network, is the inverse of the subnet mask. For this reason, the wildcard mask is often called the *inverse mask*.

Now look at what happens when you begin subnetting your networks. Take the 192.168.12.64/28 network for example. This is a subnetted class C network, which falls on the 16-bit boundary in the last octet. You need to match the first three octets entirely and the first four bits of the last octet because they compose the network portion of this address. By writing out the subnetwork and drawing a line at the bit boundary, you can determine how many 0s and 1s you need to make up the wildcard mask. Adding up the 1s in binary gives you the final wildcard mask of 0.0.0.15 to match the 192.168.12.64 subnetwork.

Increments	**128**	**64**	**32**	**16**	**|**	**8**	**4**	**2**	**1**
Subnetwork	0	1	0	0	|	0	0	0	0
Wildcard Mask	0	0	0	0	1	1	1	1	1

If you dislike working with binary and want a shortcut, you can also take the original subnet mask and subtract it from 255.255.255.255. In this example, the subnet mask would be 255.255.255.240 (/28). Subtracting this from 255.255.255.255 gives you the wildcard mask of 0.0.0.15.

Sometimes you do not want to match a network, such as when you want to match a specific host or, on the other extreme, permit or deny every host regardless of their network. There are special wildcard masks and keywords you can use to refer to these unique situations.

To match a specific host such as 10.0.0.55, you need the router to examine every bit. This can be represented with the wildcard mask of 0.0.0.0. Alternatively, you can use the keyword `host` before the host address and not specify any wildcard mask. Thus, the following two commands accomplish the same thing:

```
Router(config)#access-list 1 deny 10.0.0.55 0.0.0.0
Router(config)#access-list 1 deny host 10.0.0.55
```

If you wanted to match all hosts regardless of the network they are on, you can use the designation of an unspecified network (0.0.0.0) with a wildcard mask that does not examine any bits (255.255.255.255). Alternatively, you can use the keyword `any`. The following two commands are functionally equivalent:

```
Router(config)#access-list 1 permit 0.0.0.0 255.255.255.255
Router(config)#access-list 1 permit any
```

Wildcard Masks with Standard ACLs

Although wildcard masks are optional with standard ACLs, you should get in the habit of using them. When you are matching multiple networks with variable length subnet masks (VLSM), Cisco routers will sometimes reorder your statements if you do not specify the exact wildcard mask.

Configuring Extended ACLs

As mentioned earlier, extended ACLs allow you to filter based on the following criteria:

- Source address
- Destination address
- Protocol (IP, TCP, UDP, ICMP, and so on)
- Source port (if TCP or UDP is the protocol)
- Destination port (if TCP or UDP is the protocol)
- ICMP message (if ICMP is the protocol)

The syntax of the command varies slightly if you are filtering for general IP traffic, TCP/UDP ports, or ICMP messages. For just filtering IP traffic, the syntax is

```
access-list access-list-number {deny ¦ permit} ip source source-
wildcard destination destination-wildcard
```

For example, if you wanted to prevent all IP traffic coming from the host 10.0.0.55 to a server with the address of 11.0.0.11 while allowing all other traffic on the 10.0.0.0/8 to access the server, the syntax would be

```
Router(config)#access-list 100 deny ip host 10.0.0.55 host 11.0.0.11
Router(config)#access-list 100 permit ip 10.0.0.0 0.255.255.255
host 11.0.0.11
```

Note the use of the keyword `host` before 10.0.0.55 and 11.0.0.11. This is equivalent to using a wildcard mask of 0.0.0.0.

Because you can specify both the source and destination in the extended ACL, you generally want to apply an IP extended ACL as close to the source as possible so that it is filtered as soon as possible. Using Figure 8.1 as our example, you would apply the access list inbound on interface Ethernet 0 because that is closest to the source of your traffic. The syntax for this would be

```
Router(config)#interface ethernet 0
Router(config-if)#ip access-group 100 in
```

You can also filter based on TCP or UDP port number. The syntax for filtering based on port number is the same but, instead of IP, you specify if the traffic is TCP or UDP and what the port numbers are. You have the option of specifying source port(s) and destination port(s). Remember, if you are filtering traffic going to a destination, you are only going to filter based on the destination port number and not the source port. Because source ports are typically dynamically assigned, it is not as common to specify the source port number. The syntax for an IP extended ACL that filters TCP or UDP ports is

```
access-list access-list-number {deny ¦ permit} {tcp ¦ udp} source
source-wildcard [operator [port-number(s)]] destination
destination-wildcard [operator [port-number(s)].
```

Common operator values are

- **eq**—match any traffic that equals this port number
- **gt**—match any traffic that is greater than this port number
- **lt**—match any traffic that is less than this port number
- **range**—match any traffic within this range of port numbers (requires you to specify a beginning and ending port number)

For the port number, you can either enter the port number or enter the keyword for that protocol. Cisco routers provide keywords for many common protocols such as WWW, FTP, FTP-Data, Telnet, and more.

Using Figure 8.1 again as our example, you can configure an extended ACL to prevent Mike's computer at 10.0.0.55 from sending web traffic to the web server at 11.0.0.11 while allowing everyone else on the 10.0.0.0/8 network web access to the web server. Because this is an IP extended ACL, you will apply it closest to the source as possible, which would be inbound on interface Ethernet 0. The syntax for this ACL would be

```
Router(config)#access-list 100 deny tcp host 10.0.0.55 host
11.0.0.11 eq 80
Router(config)#access-list 100 permit tcp 10.0.0.0 0.255.255.255 host
11.0.0.11 eq 80
Router(config)#interface ethernet 0
Router(config-if)#ip access-group 100 in
```

For ICMP, the syntax is similar, except now you have the option of specifying an ICMP message. The two most common ICMP messages (and the ones to know for the exam) are ECHO and ECHO REPLIES. These messages are used when sending pings to a host. ECHO, sometimes called ECHO REQUESTS, is sent by the sending host, and ECHO REPLIES are sent by the recipient of the ping message to indicate that the host is up. The syntax for an IP extended ACL that filters ICMP is

```
access-list access-list-number {deny ¦ permit} icmp source
source-wildcard destination destination-wildcard [ICMP code ¦
message].
```

Because many computer attacks use ICMP (such as the Ping of Death denial of service attack and Loki ICMP tunneling), it is common for network administrators to block ICMP at their perimeter firewall. ICMP is a helpful tool for troubleshooting, however, so some administrators like to block only ICMP ECHO (ICMP type 8) messages from coming into their networks but still allow ECHO REPLIES (ICMP type 0) in. This configuration allows them to ping outbound and get an ECHO REPLY back, but prevents others from pinging into their network. As an example, if you wanted to block ICMP ECHO messages from the 10.0.0.0/8 network from going to the destination network of 11.0.0.0/8 while allowing all other IP traffic from anywhere to anywhere, the syntax would be

```
Router(config)#access-list 100 deny icmp 10.0.0.0 0.255.255.255
11.0.0.0 0.255.255.255 echo
Router(config)#access-list 100 permit ip any any
Router(config)#interface ethernet 0
Router(config-if)#ip access-group 100 in
```

This ACL blocks all ICMP type 8 echo messages from entering into the 11.0.0.0/8 network while allowing all other traffic. Note that in this example, if there are ICMP pings coming from any other network to the 11.0.0.0/8 network, they would be allowed; only the 10.0.0.0/8 network is prevented from sending pings to the 11.0.0.0/8 network in this example.

Filtering Telnet Access

The ACLs shown so far help you to filter traffic as it passes through the router. In this next example, you will learn how to filter traffic to the router.

Routers are a critical component of any network. If a malicious hacker were to compromise one of your routers, he could reconfigure it to prevent anyone from being able to communicate across your enterprise. Therefore, it is common to use ACLs to control who is allowed Telnet access to your router.

For example, if you wanted to allow only Mike access to Telnet to Andrew's router (see Figure 8.1) but prevent everyone else access, you could create an ACL that allows only Mike's IP address (10.0.0.55). Remember, you do not need to add a statement to block everyone else because all traffic is denied by default unless it is explicitly permitted. Because you are controlling Telnet access to the router and not traffic passing through the router, you need to apply your ACL on the Virtual TeletYpe (VTY) lines and not on an interface. Because VTY lines are inherently Telnet (TCP port 23) traffic, you do not need an extended ACL. Instead, use an IP standard ACL to control what source host(s) are allowed Telnet access to your router. To allow Mike's computer (10.0.0.55) Telnet access but deny everyone else, the syntax would be

```
Router(config)#access-list 1 permit host 10.0.0.55
```

Applying this ACL is different than how you applied ACLs on an interface. When applying an ACL on a VTY line, the syntax is

```
Router(config-line)#ip access-group access-list-number {in | out}
```

Because you are controlling Telnet access to the router, you should apply this ACL inbound on the VTY lines. The complete syntax to create this access list and apply it on all five VTY lines is

```
Router(config)#access-list 1 permit host 10.0.0.55
Router(config)#line vty 0 4
Router(config-line)#access-class 1 in
```

Outbound VTY Access List

ACLs on VTY lines should be applied inbound. When applied outbound, strange things begin to occur. Instead of the ACL specifying who is allowed access to Telnet to a router, the ACL specifies which hosts you are allowed to Telnet to from that router. In other words, the ACL specifies the destination, not the source address. This is a strange oddity that only occurs when applying an access list on a VTY line. For the purposes of the exam, you should remember that ACLs on VTY lines are applied inbound.

Make sure that you feel comfortable with configuring extended ACLs. You should be familiar with filtering IP, TCP, UDP, and ICMP traffic.

Advanced Options

There are a few additional keywords you can add to the end of an ACL to enable advanced options. These are

- `log`
- `log-input`
- `established`

The `log` keyword, when added to the end of an ACL, will log the source address every time a match is made. If you log to buffered memory (enabled with the global configuration command `logging buffered`), you can view these log entries with the command `show logging`. The logging is limited, however, as it logs only the first packet and then logs again in 5-minute intervals. The log option is available for both standard and extended ACLs.

The `log-input` keyword is similar to the `log` keyword, but it also logs the layer 2 address of the source host being matched. In the case of Ethernet networks, this would be the MAC address. In the case of frame-relay, this would be the Data-Link Connection Identifier (DLCI) number. The log-input keyword can only be added to the end of extended ACLs.

The `established` keyword is another advanced feature that will allow traffic through only if it sees that a TCP session is already established. A TCP session is considered established if the three-way handshake is initiated first. This keyword is added only to the end of extended ACLs that are filtering TCP traffic.

You can use TCP established to deny all traffic into your network except for incoming traffic that was first initiated from inside your network. This is commonly used to block all inbound traffic from the Internet into a company's network except for Internet traffic that was first initiated from users inside the company. The following configuration would accomplish this for all TCP based traffic coming in to interface serial 0/0 on the router:

```
access-list 100 permit tcp any any eq established
interface serial 0/0
 ip access-group 100 in
```

Although the access list is using a permit statement, all traffic is denied unless it is first established from the inside network. If the router sees that the three-way TCP handshake is successful, it will then begin to allow traffic through.

Configuring Named ACLs

Up to this point, you have learned how to configure numbered ACLs. This section teaches you how to configure named ACLs.

As mentioned earlier, named ACLs provide the benefit of using descriptive names for your ACLs and the ability to remove individual lines. If you attempt to remove an individual line from a numbered access list, it will delete the entire list; with named ACLs, this is not the case.

The syntax for named ACLs is similar to that of numbered lists. Instead of using a number, you will give it a name. Remember, though, that the number indicates what type of access list you are using (IP, IPX, and so on) and if it is standard or extended. Because you are using a named ACL, you will need to configure your router so that it knows what type of ACL you want to create and if it is to be standard or extended. The syntax for an IP named ACL is as follows:

```
ip access-list {standard | extended} name
```

After entering this global configuration command, you will be presented with the named access control list (NACL) mode where you can enter your permit or deny statements.

For example, to create an extended NACL called DenyMike that blocks the host 10.0.0.55 from sending web traffic (TCP port 80) to the web server at 11.0.0.11 but allows everyone else, the syntax would be

```
Router(config)#ip access-list extended DenyMike
Router(config-ext-nacl)#deny tcp host 10.0.0.55 host 11.0.0.11 eq 80
Router(config-ext-nacl)#permit ip any any
Router(config-ext-nacl)#interface ethernet 0
Router(config-if)#ip access-group DenyMike in
```

Treating Numbered ACLs as Named

Although it is true that you cannot delete individual lines from a numbered ACL, there is a trick around this. If you treat your numbered ACL as a named ACL, you can then delete individual lines. For example, if you had a numbered ACL named 100, you could enter the command 'ip access-list extended 100' and enter named access control list configuration mode for this ACL. Because you are in NACL mode, you can now delete individual lines (even though it is originally a numbered access list). Remember for the test, however, that only named ACLs allow you to delete individual lines in an access list. If you attempt to delete an individual line from a numbered access list, the router will delete the entire list.

Named ACLs provide clarity through descriptive names and ease of configuration because of the ability of deleting individual lines. Although named ACLs might be more attractive for real-world usage, make sure that you feel comfortable with numbered ACLs as well.

Troubleshooting and Verifying ACL Configurations

In an ideal world, nothing would ever go wrong. If you have been working with computers for any length of time, you know that this is not the case. Inevitably, things do go wrong, and you will need to know how to vary and troubleshoot your configuration. There are three commands you should be familiar with when verifying and troubleshooting IP ACLs:

- **Show ACLs**—Shows you what ACLs you have configured on your router
- **show ip ACLs**—Shows you only the IP ACLs you have configured on your router
- **`show ip interface`**—Shows you the direction (inbound/outbound) and placement of an ACL.

The first two commands show only what ACLs you have configured on your router, but they do not show where they have been applied. The third command, `show ip interface`, shows you where the ACL has been applied and in what direction (inbound or outbound). Following is the output of the `show ip interface` command with the relevant portions highlighted:

```
Ethernet0 is up, line protocol is up
  Internet address is 10.0.0.1, subnet mask is 255.0.0.0
  Broadcast address is 255.255.255.255
  Address determined by non-volatile memory
  MTU is 1500 bytes
  Helper address is not set
  Directed broadcast forwarding is enabled
  Multicast groups joined: 224.0.0.1 224.0.0.2
  Outgoing access list is not set
  Inbound  access list is 100
  Proxy ARP is enabled
  Security level is default
  Split horizon is enabled
  ICMP redirects are always sent
  ICMP unreachables are always sent
  ICMP mask replies are never sent
  IP fast switching is enabled
  IP fast switching on the same interface is disabled
  IP SSE switching is disabled
  Router Discovery is disabled
  IP output packet accounting is disabled
```

```
IP access violation accounting is disabled
TCP/IP header compression is disabled
Probe proxy name replies are disabled
```

From this output, you can see that ACL 100 is applied inbound on interface Ethernet 0.

Any time you configure an ACL, you should execute the **show access list** (or show ip ACLs) and **show ip interface** commands to verify the configuration.

Exam Prep Questions

1. Examine Figure 8.5. What will the following ACL do? (Select the best answer.)

```
Houston(config)#access-list 114 deny tcp 172.16.0.0 0.0.255.255
172.31.0.0 0.0.255.255 eq 25
Houston(config)#access-list 114 deny tcp 172.16.0.0 0.0.255.255
172.31.0.0 0.0.255.255 eq 80
Houston(config)#access-list 114 permit tcp 172.16.0.0 0.0.255.255
172.31.0.0 0.0.255.255 eq 25
Houston(config)#access-list 114 permit tcp 172.16.0.0 0.0.255.255
172.31.0.0 0.0.255.255 eq 80
Houston(config)#interface fastethernet0/0
Houston(config-if)#ip access-group 114 in
```

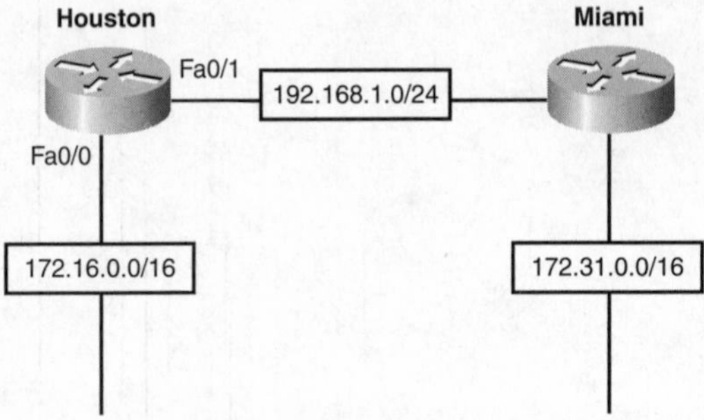

❍ A. Deny SMTP and WWW traffic sourced from Houston's Ethernet network and destined for Miami's Ethernet network.

❍ B. Permit SMTP and WWW traffic sourced from Houston's Ethernet network and destined for Miami's Ethernet network.

❍ C. Nothing. This is an invalid ACL.

❍ D. Deny all traffic.

2. What is true about named ACLs? Select all that apply.

❑ A. Named ACLs allow you to remove individual lines; numbered ACLs do not.

❑ B. The name of the access list must be limited to eight characters or fewer.

❑ C. You must specify if the access list is standard or extended.

❑ D. Named ACLs cannot be used with NAT.

❑ E. You do not need to specify the protocol if you are using a named access list to filter IP traffic.

3. Examine Figure 8.6. Which of the following configurations would allow Telnet access to the Tokyo router for the user named Ross but deny all other Telnet access? Select all that apply.

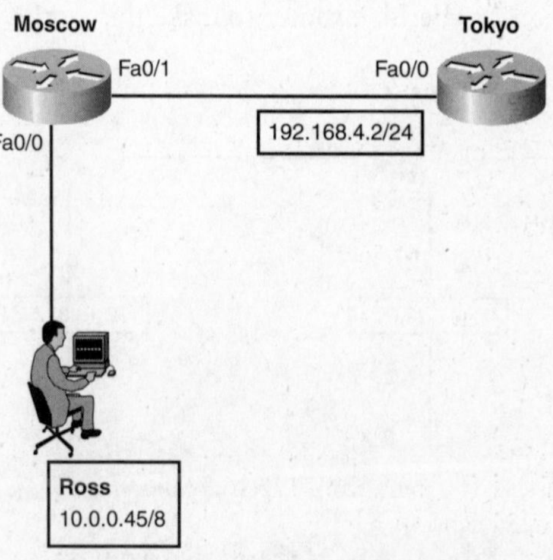

❍ A. Moscow(config)# access-list 100 deny ip any any
Moscow(config)#access-list 100 permit tcp host 10.0.0.45 host 192.168.4.2 eq 23
Moscow(config)#interface fastethernet 0/0
Moscow(config-if)#ip access-group 100 in

❍ B. Moscow(config)#access-list 199 permit tcp host 10.0.0.45 192.168.4.2 0.0.0.0 eq 23
Moscow(config)#interface fastethernet 0/0
Moscow(config-if)#ip access-group 199 in

❍ C. Moscow(config)#access-list 125 permit tcp 10.0.0.45 0.0.0.0 host 192.168.4.2 eq Telnet
Moscow(config)#interface fastethernet0/1
Moscow(config-if)#ip access-group 125 out

❍ D. Tokyo(config)#access-list 173 permit tcp host 10.0.0.45 host 192.168.4.2 eq 23
Tokyo(config)#interface fastethernet0/0
Tokyo(config-if)#ip access-group 173 in

❍ E. Tokyo(config)#access-list 40 permit host 10.0.0.45
Tokyo(config)#line vty 0 4
Tokyo(config-line)#access-class 40 in

❍ F. Tokyo(config)#access-list 87 permit host 10.0.0.45
Tokyo(config)#line vty 0 4
Tokyo(config-line)#access-class 1 in

4. Examine Figure 8.7. Based on the figure, you want to configure an access list that prevents users on the 172.16.32.0/21 and 172.17.32.0/21 networks from sending pings to the 172.18.32.0/21 network. You still, however, want to send pings out from the 172.18.32.0/21 network. What commands would you enter on the Blue router to make this work?

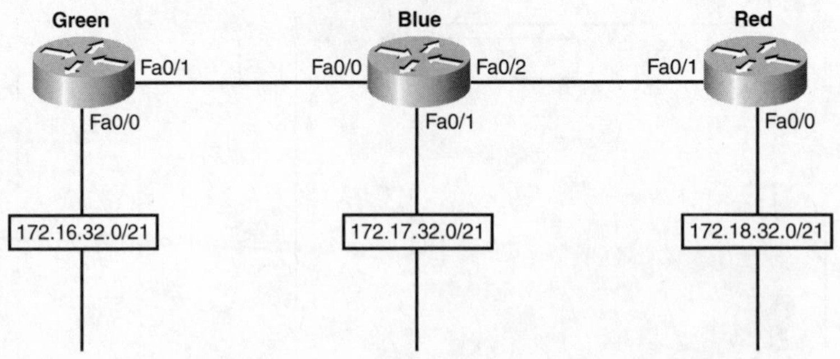

❍ A. Blue(config)#access-list 100 deny icmp 172.16.32.0 0.0.7.255 172.18.32.0.0 0.0.7.255 echo
   Blue(config)#access-list 100 deny icmp 172.17.32.0 0.0.7.255 172.18.32.0 0.0.7.255 echo
   Blue(config)#access-list 100 permit ip any any
   Blue(config)#interface fastethernet 0/2
   Blue(config-if)#ip access-group 100 out

❍ B. Blue(config)#access-list 100 deny icmp 172.16.32.0 0.0.15.255. 172.18.32.0 0.0.15.255 echo
   Blue(config)#access-list 100 deny icmp 172.17.32.0 0.0.15.255 172.18.32.0 0.0.15.255 echo
   Blue(config)#access-list 100 permit ip any any
   Blue(config)#interface fastethernet 0/2
   Blue(config-if)#ip access-group 100 out

❍ C. Blue(config)#access-list 100 deny icmp 172.16.32.0 0.0.7.255 172.18.32.0.0 0.0.7.255 echo
   Blue(config)#access-list 100 deny icmp 172.17.32.0 0.0.7.255 172.18.32.0 0.0.7.255 echo
   Blue(config)#access-list 100 permit ip any any
   Blue(config)#interface fastethernet 0/1
   Blue(config-if)#ip access-group 100 in

❍ D. Blue(config)#access-list 100 deny icmp 172.16.32.0 0.0.15.255. 172.18.32.0 0.0.15.255 echo
   Blue(config)#access-list 100 deny icmp 172.17.32.0 0.0.15.255 172.18.32.0 0.0.15.255 echo
   Blue(config)#access-list 100 permit ip any any
   Blue(config)#interface fastethernet 0/1
   Blue(config-if)#ip access-group 100 in

5. You want to filter FTP access sourced from the 192.168.99.192/27 network yet allow all other traffic to pass. You do not care about the destination. You enter the following command on your router, yet FTP traffic coming from the 192.168.99.192/27 network is still allowed. Why?

```
Router(config)#access-list 100 deny tcp any 192.168.99.192
     0.0.0.31 eq 20
Router(config)#access-list 100 deny tcp any 192.168.99.192
     0.0.0.31 eq 21
Router(config)#access-list 100 permit ip any any
Router(config)#interface serial 0/0
Router(config-if)#ip access-group 100 in
```

❍ A. The port numbers are wrong.
❍ B. FTP uses UDP, not TCP.
❍ C. The source and destination are backward.
❍ D. The permit statement should be first.

Trick!

6. What would be the proper wildcard mask to permit all odd numbered hosts on the 10.48.0.0/12 network?

❍ A. access-list 1 permit 10.48.0.0 0.0.15.255
❍ B. access-list 1 permit 10.48.0.1 0.0.15.254
❍ C. access-list 1 permit 10.48.0.0 0.0.15.1
❍ D. access-list 1 permit 10.48.0.0 0.0.0.254
❍ E. access-list 1 permit 10.48.0.0 0.0.0.255

7. What types of ACLs are processed after the router examines the routing table and sends the packet to the outgoing interface? Select all that apply.

❑ A. IP standard inbound
❑ B. IP extended inbound
❑ C. IP standard outbound
❑ D. IP extended outbound

8. What command can you enter to verify that an access list has been applied on your interface?

❍ A. show ip interface brief
❍ B. show ACLs
❍ C. show ip ACLs
❍ D. show ip interface

9. Where should you apply your ACLs? Select all that apply.

❑ A. Standard ACLs should generally be applied closest to the source.
❑ B. Standard ACLs should generally be applied closest to the destination.
❑ C. Extended ACLs should generally be applied closest to the source.
❑ D. Extended ACLs should generally be applied closest to the destination.

10. What does the following named access list do?

```
Router(config)#ip access-list extended QueACL
Router(config-ext-nacl)#permit tcp any 192.168.15.8 0.0.0.3 eq 119
Router(config-ext-nacl)#interface fastethernet1/3
Router(config-if)#ip access-group QueACL in
```

❍ A. Allows NNTP traffic coming into the Fa1/3 interface to the 192.168.15.8 255.255.255.252 network, but denies everything else.

❍ B. Allows SMTP traffic coming into the Fa1/3 interface to the 192.168.15.8 host, but denies everything else.

❍ C. Allows NNTP traffic coming into the Fa1/3 interface to the 192.168.15.8 host, but denies everything else.

❍ D. Allows SMTP traffic coming into the Fa1/3 interface to the 192.168.15.8/30 network, but denies everything else.

❍ E. Allows all traffic to pass because no deny statement is given.

Answers to Exam Prep Questions

1. Answer D is correct. ACLs are top-down, meaning that they check the packet against your statements in the order that you enter them. In this example, the access list would first deny SMTP and WWW traffic sourced from Houston's Ethernet network and destined for Miami's Ethernet network. Following this, the access list permits SMTP and WWW traffic. However, because this traffic was first denied, the packet will never get permitted. Additionally, because all traffic is denied by default unless explicitly permitted, all other traffic will be denied. Thus, this access list denies all traffic. Answer A, although technically correct, is not the best answer because all traffic is being denied, not just SMTP and WWW traffic. Answer B is incorrect because SMTP and WWW traffic is being denied first. Answer C is incorrect because this is a perfectly acceptable, albeit poorly written, access list.

2. Answers A and C are correct. Answer B is wrong because named ACLs can be longer than eight characters. Answer D is wrong because you can use named ACLs with NAT. Answer E is wrong because you do always need to specify the protocol when using a named access list.

3. Answers B, C, and E are correct. Answer B configures the access list using the host keyword for the 10.0.0.45 host; answer C configures the access list using the host keyword for the 192.168.4.2 host; answer E configures the access list using the host keyword for both the 192.168.4.2 and the 10.0.0.45 host. Answer A is incorrect because the first deny statement would block all traffic, including the Telnet traffic. Answer D is incorrect because this would block Telnet traffic going through the Tokyo router and not traffic going to the Tokyo router. (ACLs applied to an interface are for traffic passing through the router and never for traffic destined to the router.) Answer F is incorrect because the wrong access list is applied on the VTY lines.

4. Answer A is correct. The correct wildcard mask is 0.0.7.255 for all networks. You can apply this access list inbound on Fa0/1 and Fa0/0 or outbound on Fa0/2. Although the general rule is to apply extended ACLs inbound closest to the source, none of the answers did this correctly (making this a tricky question). Answer B is incorrect because the wildcard masks are wrong. Answers C and D are incorrect because they are applied inbound on Fa0/1. The 172.16.32.0/21 network would still have been allowed through. Answer D is additionally wrong because the wrong wildcard mask is used.

5. Answer C is correct. Answer A is wrong because the port numbers are correct. Answer B is wrong because FTP does use TCP. Answer D is wrong because if the permit statement is first, all traffic would be allowed through (ACLs are top-down.)
6. Answer B is correct. All odd numbered hosts would have the one bit turned on in the last octet. Therefore, you need to check all hosts that have the one bit turned on (set to 1). You do not care about the other host bits. The default wildcard mask for a /12 network is 0.0.15.255, but because you want to match only those hosts that have the one bit turned on, you will need a wildcard mask of 0.0.15.254. Answer A is incorrect because this would match both even and odd numbered hosts. Answer C is incorrect because this would match all hosts from 10.48.0.0 through 10.48.255.0. Answers D and E are incorrect because they have the wrong wildcard mask.
7. Answers C and D are correct. Outbound ACLs are processed after the routing table is checked and the outbound interface is chosen. Answers A and B are incorrect because they are both inbound.
8. Answer D is correct. The `command show ip` interface will verify the direction and placement of an access list on an interface. Answer A is incorrect because this shows only brief output that does not include access list information. Answers B and C are incorrect because they do not show where the ACL is applied.
9. Answers B and C are correct. Standard ACLs should generally be applied outbound closest to the destination of the traffic because you have no other way of referencing the destination. Extended ACLs should generally be applied inbound closest to the source because you can specify the destination and you want to filter the traffic as early as possible. Answers A and D are incorrect because the directions are the opposite from what they should be.
10. Answer A is correct. TCP port 119 is used by NNTP, and the wildcard mask 0.0.0.3 matches the 192.168.15.8 255.255.255.252 (/30) subnet. Answers B and D are wrong because this access list permits NNTP, not SMTP. Answer C is wrong because this access list permits traffic to the 192.168.15.8/30 network, not a specific host. Answer E is wrong because no deny statement is necessary; all traffic is implicitly denied, except for what is explicitly permitted.

Routing

Terms You'll Need to Understand

- ✓ Distance Vector
- ✓ Link State
- ✓ Administrative Distance
- ✓ Static routes
- ✓ Default routes
- ✓ Routing Information Protocol (RIP)
- ✓ Interior Gateway Routing Protocol (IGRP)
- ✓ Enhanced Interior Gateway Routing Protocol (EIGRP)
- ✓ Open Shortest Path First (OSPF)

Concepts and Techniques You'll Need to Master

- ✓ Understanding dynamic routing algorithms
- ✓ Understanding the use of Administrative Distances
- ✓ Configuring static routes
- ✓ Configuring RIP
- ✓ Configuring IGRP
- ✓ Configuring EIGRP
- ✓ Configuring OSPF

Introduction

Routing is the process by which a packet gets from one location to another. To route a packet, a router needs to know the destination address and on what interface to send the traffic out (egress interface). When a packet comes into an interface (ingress interface) on a router, it looks up the destination IP address in the packet header and compares it with its routing table. The routing table, which is stored in RAM, tells the router which outgoing, or egress, interface the packet should go out to reach the destination network.

There are three ways to control routing decisions on your router:

- Static routes
- Default routes
- Dynamic routes

Static Routes

Use a static route when you want to manually define the path that the packet will take through your network. Static routes are useful in small networks with rarely changing routes, when you have little bandwidth and do not want the overhead of a dynamic routing protocol, or when you want to manually define all of your routes for security reasons.

Static routes are created in global configuration mode. The syntax for the static route is as follows:

```
ip route <destination network address> [subnet mask]
➥{next-hop-address | interface] [distance]
```

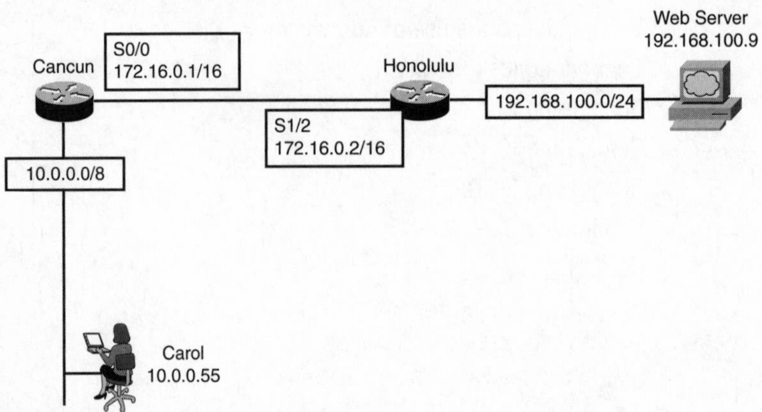

Figure 9.1 Static route example.

For example, in Figure 9.1, Carol is trying to get to a web server on a different network. Her computer will be configured to use the Cancun router as its default gateway, but the Cancun router needs to know how to get to the 192.168.100.0/24 network where the web server resides. Using the Honolulu router as your next hop in the path to the web server, type the following to create a static route on the Cancun router:

```
ip route 192.168.100.0 255.255.255.0 172.16.0.2
```

Instead of routing to the next-hop router, you could also create a default route out of an interface. If you did not know the address of the Honolulu router, you could tell the Cancun router to use interface serial 0/0 to get to the 192.168.100.0 network. The syntax would then be `ip route 192.168.100.0 255.255.255.0 serial 0/0`.

At this point, you have created a route to get to the 192.168.100.0 network attached to the Bermuda router. That will get Carol's data to the web server, but the Bermuda router will also need a route to get traffic back to Carol's network. Using the Cancun router as the next hop, the syntax would be

```
ip route 10.0.0.0 255.0.0.0 172.16.0.1
```

Remember when entering the static route that the destination is a network address, whereas the next-hop address is a specific IP address assigned to another router's interface. As noted previously, you can also create a default route to direct your traffic through a specific interface.

Default Routes

A default route is similar to a static route, but instead of configuring a route to a specific network, you are configuring the router to know where to send traffic for any network not found in its routing table. Default routes are used to establish a gateway of last resort for your router.

There are two ways to create a default route. The first is to use the same command that you used for a static route but use the 0.0.0.0 network as your destination with a subnet mask of 0.0.0.0. For example, to establish a default route to send traffic out serial 0/0 destined for any network not learned through dynamic or static means, type the following:

```
ip route 0.0.0.0 0.0.0.0 serial 0/0
```

If you chose to specify the next-hop IP address of the router, you could type the following instead (assuming a next-hop address of 192.168.1.1):

```
ip route 0.0.0.0 0.0.0.0 192.168.1.1
```

The second method of creating a default route is to use the `ip default-network` command. With this command, any traffic destined for networks not found in the routing table will be sent to the default network. Figure 9.2 illustrates the use of the default network. If Carol is trying to access the Internet, a default route could be configured with the following global configuration command on the Honolulu router:

```
Honolulu(config)#ip default-network 192.168.100.0
```

Note that you do not include the subnet mask in this command. Routing protocols, such as RIP, can propagate this default network to other routers. When Carol attempts to access the Internet, her computer sends traffic to the Cancun router, which is her default gateway. The Cancun router will see a default network of 192.168.100.0, look up this destination in its routing table, and forward her packets to the Honolulu router. The Honolulu router, in turn, will forward the traffic out its interface connected to the 192.168.100.0 network and onto the Internet.

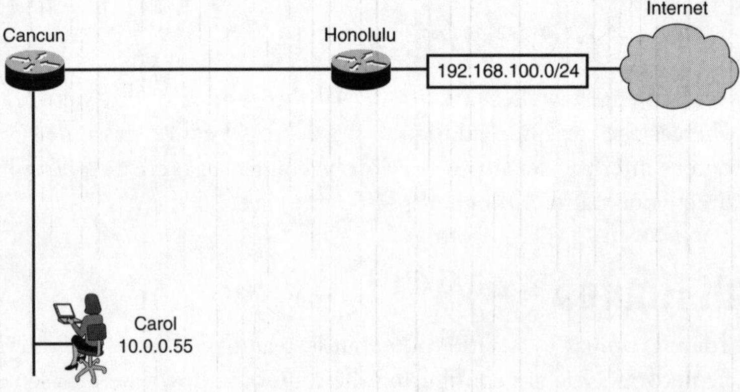

Figure 9.2 Default network example.

Know how to configure a static route, default route, and default network.

Dynamic Routes

Static and default routes are nice, but they are not scalable. If you need a scalable solution, you need to experiment with dynamic routing protocols. For the exam, you need to know the following dynamic routing protocols:

- Routing Information Protocol (RIP)
- Interior Gateway Routing Protocol (IGRP)
- Enhanced Interior Gateway Routing Protocol (EIGRP)
- Open Shortest Path First (OSPF)

Before we get into the details of each of these protocols, you should first understand some of the characteristics of all routing protocol. These characteristics include administrative distances, metrics, distance vector, and link state operations.

Administrative Distance

Administrative distance is the measure of trustworthiness that a router assigns routing protocols. For example, in Figure 9.3, the Jupiter router needs to determine the best route to get to the 10.0.0.0/8 network attached to the Earth router. It has learned of two separate paths; one is learned through EIGRP and the other through OSPF. EIGRP has decided that the best path for a packet destined to the 10.0.0.0/8 network is through Saturn, Mars, and finally Earth. On the other hand, OSPF has determined that the best path is through Pluto and then Earth. The Jupiter router needs to decide which routing protocol it should trust, or prefer, over the other. The one preferred will be the one the router listens to when making decisions on how to route.

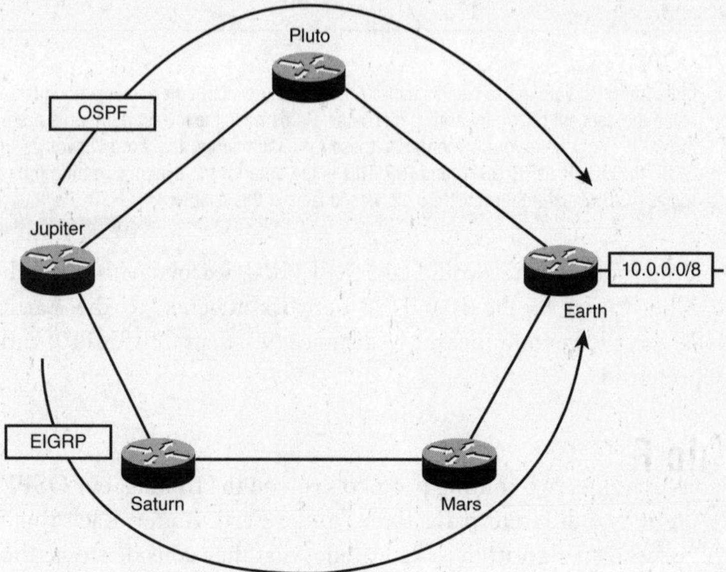

Figure 9.3 Administrative distance decisions.

To determine which routing source is preferred, Cisco has assigned administrative distances to sources of routing information. A router will choose the route that is learned through the source with the lowest administrative distance. Table 9.1 illustrates the default administrative distance value.

It is possible to change the administrative distance of a static route by appending a different administrative distance to the end of the command. For example, the following command assigns the administrative distance of 130 to a static route:

ip route 10.0.0.0 255.0.0.0 serial 0/0 130

Changing the administrative distance of a static route is commonly used when configuring a backup route, called a *floating* static route. If you do not specify an administrative distance at the end of the static route, the default is being used. For the exam, you should be able to look at the syntax of a static route and know what administrative distance is being used.

Table 9.1 Administrative Distances

Routing Source	Administrative Distance
Connected	0
Static	1
EIGRP (internal)	90
IGRP	100
OSPF	110
RIP (version 1 and 2)	120
EIGRP (external)	170

Make sure that you memorize this table. You should know both the values and understand the concept of administrative distances. Remember, the lowest number is preferred. It might help you to memorize these by remembering the word "Eeyore"—EIOR, for EIGRP, IGRP, OSPF, and RIP. This is the order of the dynamic routing protocols. (EIGRP external routes are discussed later in this chapter.)

In Figure 9.3, the Jupiter router would take the EIGRP learned path through Saturn and Mars to get to the 10.0.0.0/8 network attached to the Earth router. EIGRP has a lower administrative distance (90) than OSPF (110) and is therefore preferred.

Metrics

In the previous example, two routing protocols run on the routers, but OSPF and EIGRP chose two different paths to get to the Earth router. Each routing protocol has its own algorithm to determine what they consider to be the best path to a destination network. The main factor in deciding the best path is the routing protocol's *metric*.

A metric is the variable used in the algorithm when making routing decisions. Each routing protocol uses a different type of metric. Table 9.2 illustrates the different metrics used by routing protocols.

Table 9.2 Routing Metrics

Routing Protocol	Metric	Description
RIP	Hop Count	The number of hops, or routers, that a packet has to pass through to reach a destination. The route with the lowest hop count is preferred.
IGRP	Bandwidth, Delay, Reliability, Load, and MTU	Uses the bandwidth and delay of an interface by default, but can be configured to use reliability, load, and MTU.
EIGRP	Bandwidth, Delay, Reliability, Load, and MTU	Same as IGRP, but algorithm produces a 32-bit metric instead of a 24-bit metric.
OSPF	Cost	Cost is defined as 10^8/bandwidth.

Metrics are not the only thing that distinguishes the routing protocols. Routing protocols can be further classified into two categories:

- Distance vector routing protocols
- Link state routing protocols

Distance Vector Routing Protocols

Distance vector routing protocols include RIP and IGRP. EIGRP is a hybrid that contains many of the characteristics of a distance vector protocol. Characteristics of distance vector routing protocols are

- Periodically broadcasts entire routing table out of all interfaces
- Trusts what the other router tells it. (For this reason, distance vector routing is sometimes called "routing by rumor.")

Controlling Routing Loops

Because distance vector routing protocols trust the next router without compiling a topology map of all networks and routers, distance vector protocols run the risk of creating loops in a network.

This is analogous of driving to a location without a map. Instead, you trust what each sign tells you. Trusting the street signs might get you where you want to go, but I've been in some cities where trusting what the signs say will lead you in loops. The same is true with distance vector routing protocols.

Simply trusting what the next router tells it can potentially lead the packets to loop endlessly. These loops could saturate a network and cause systems to crash. This, in turn, makes managers very upset and means that you have to work late into the evening to fix it.

Luckily, distance vector protocols have some mechanisms built in to them to prevent loops. These mechanisms are

- Maximum hop count
- Split-horizon
- Route poisoning
- Poison reverse
- Hold down timers
- Triggered updates

Each router maintains a routing table stored in RAM that lists off each network and the number of hops, or routers, away the network is from itself. All distance vector routing protocols maintain a record of hop count even if they do not use hop count in their routing decisions.

Examine Figure 9.4. Through the use of a dynamic routing protocol, each router will exchange information with the next router. Mars will learn of the networks known by Saturn and Jupiter, and Mars will let Saturn and Jupiter know of the networks that Mars knows about. Table 9.3 shows the networks and associated hop counts for each router.

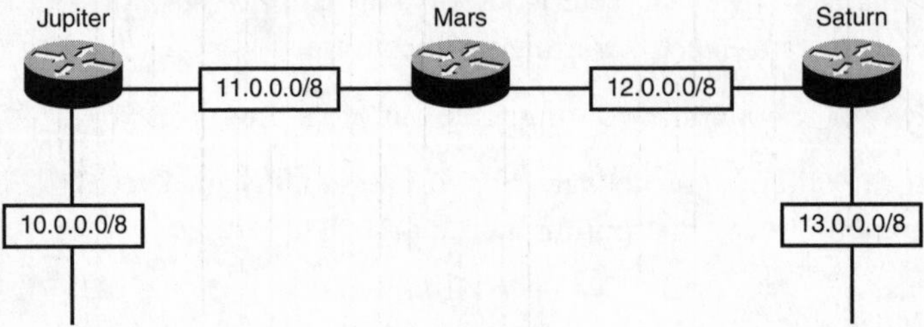

Figure 9.4 Avoiding loops.

Table 9.3 Hop Count

	Network			
	10.0.0.0	**11.0.0.0**	**12.0.0.0**	**13.0.0.0**
Jupiter	**0**	**0**	**1**	**2**
Mars	**1**	**0**	**0**	**1**
Saturn	**2**	**1**	**0**	**0**

Distance vector routing protocols keep track of hop counts because if a route exceeds a maximum hop count limit (determined differently by each routing protocol), the network is considered unreachable. This prevents packets from cycling endlessly across your networks. Table 9.4 shows the maximum hop count for distance vector protocols.

Table 9.4 Maximum Hop Count Values

Routing Protocol	**Maximum Hop Count**
RIP	15
IGRP	Default = 100; maximum = 255
EIGRP	224

Make sure that you know the maximum hop count for all routing protocols. Note that OSPF is not mentioned here. OSPF is a link-state protocol and has an unlimited hop count.

Having a maximum hop count should be enough to prevent loops, but because loops are so dangerous, other methods are used as well. The second method to prevent routing loops is split-horizon. The split-horizon rule states that information about a route should not be sent back in the direction in which it was learned.

Look back at Figure 9.4. The split-horizon rule states that if Saturn tells Mars about the 13.0.0.0/8 network, Mars should not advertise it back to Saturn. If it did, Saturn would be confused and think that it could possibly use Mars to get to the 13.0.0.0 should its interface to that network ever go down. This would cause a packet to loop endlessly as the packet would go to Mars, which would in turn send it back to Saturn. Split-horizon resolves this issue by ensuring that the Mars router never sends information about the 13.0.0.0 network back to the Saturn router that it heard it from.

To make absolutely sure that no loops are created, route poisoning and poison reverse are also implemented. With route poisoning, as soon as a network is thought to be down, it is advertised out with a hop count that is one greater than what is allowed. This would declare the route as being inaccessible. Poison reverse does the same thing but in reverse. The router that hears about a down network, violates split-horizon, and sends back an update with the network being unreachable. Figure 9.5 illustrates how this would look if the routers were running RIP, where the maximum hop count is 15 and a hop count of 16 declares the route inaccessible.

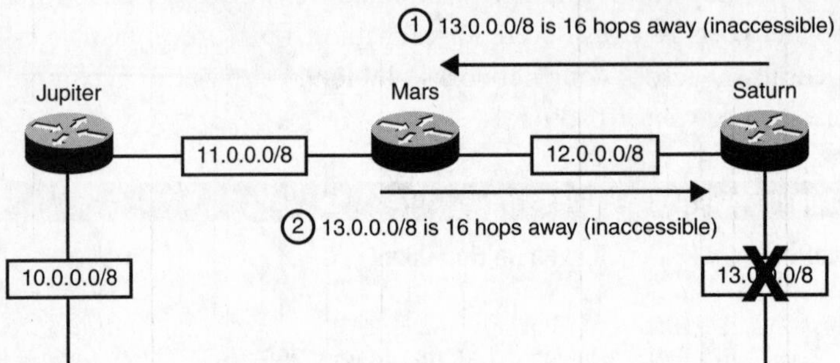

Figure 9.5 Poison reverse and route poisoning.

The next mechanism to prevent loops is holddown timers. When a router receives information that a network is possibly down from a neighbor router, it will not accept any new information from that router for a specified period of time. This is to prevent regular update messages from reinstating a down route. The default hold down timer for RIP is 180 seconds; for IGRP, the holddown timer is 280 seconds.

Link State Routing Protocols

If distance vector routing protocols are like trusting the highway signs when you are on a road trip, link state routing protocols are like having the map in front of you. With link-state routing protocols such as OSPF, your router will know all the networks and the various paths to the networks.

Another protocol that you might see is the Intermediate System-Intermediate System (IS-IS) routing protocol. IS-IS is a link-state protocol like OSPF. Although IS-IS is not a CCNA-level topic, if it should creep into the exam, remember that it is very similar to OSPF. Therefore, IS-IS also supports VLSM, summarization, and supernetting.

The Cisco Hybrid: EIGRP

Extra! Extra! Read all about it! EIGRP solves the world's problems. It's the best of both worlds! You get the best of link state and distance vector routing all built in to one protocol!

Okay, so perhaps that's a little more hype than necessary, but it is not that far from the truth. EIGRP is a Cisco proprietary protocol that combines characteristics of link state and distance vector routing protocols. For example, like a link state routing protocol, it sends out hello messages to discover its neighbors. However, it does not have a built-in hierarchical design like OSPF, thus making it more like a distance vector. You read more about EIGRP later, but for now let's start with a very simple protocol, RIP.

Know the characteristics of distance vector and link state routing protocols and know which of these categories each routing protocol falls into.

RIP

The routing information protocol (RIP) uses the Bellman-Ford algorithm, which simply counts the number of hops, or routers, to a destination network and chooses the path that is the fewest number of hops. Any destination that is more than 15 hops away is considered inaccessible.

Characteristics of RIP

RIP routers exchange information by broadcasting the entire routing table every 30 seconds out all interfaces with RIP enabled. RIP version 2 also sends out updates every 30 seconds but sends out updates using the multicast address of 224.0.0.9 (can be configured to do unicast as well). In addition, version 2 provides the following benefits not available in version 1:

- Routing Authentication
- Classless routing
- Summarization

Implementing RIP

Configuring RIP is straightforward. The four steps to configuring a routing protocol are as follows:

1. Enable the routing protocol.
2. Activate it on interfaces.
3. Advertise directly connected classful networks.
4. Configure optional parameters.

The first step, enable the routing protocol, is done from global configuration mode by typing **`router rip`**. The next two steps, activating RIP on interfaces and advertising networks, is done with a single command, the `network` command.

If you look at Figure 9.6 you see three routers named Larry, Curly, and Moe. For the Moe router, you need to enable RIP and enter the networks you want to advertise. The Moe router has the 192.168.10.0/24 and 192.168.20.0/24 networks directly connected to it. Moe's configuration would be

```
Moe(config)#router rip
Moe(config-router)#network 192.168.10.0
Moe(config-router)#network 192.168.20.0
```

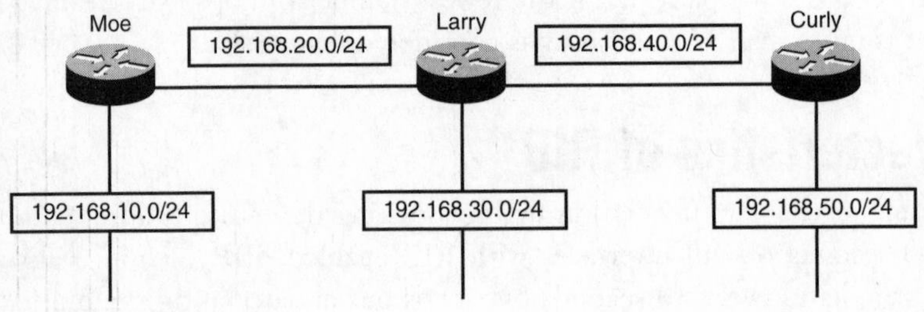

Figure 9.6 RIP example.

Larry has three networks attached to his router. His configuration would be

```
Larry(config)#router rip
Larry(config-router)#network 192.168.20.0
Larry(config-router)#network 192.168.30.0
Larry(config-router)#network 192.168.40.0
```

Finally, we can't forget Curly. Curly's configuration would be

```
Curly(config)#router rip
Curly(config-router)#network 192.168.40.0
Curly(config-router)#network 192.168.50.0
```

When you enter your networks in your RIP configuration, RIP is activated on the interfaces that are assigned those networks. All networks that you listed in your configuration are then sent out all RIP activated interfaces. Thus, the networks that you entered on Curly's router will be sent out to Larry. Larry will take what he learned from Curly, add his own networks, and send them out to Moe. Larry will also learn networks from Moe, add his own networks, and send them out to Curly.

Remember to enter only your directly connected networks. Curly, for example, should not enter 192.168.10.0/24 in his configuration because that network is not directly connected to his router. Also, you should enter classful networks only. This means that even if you are subnetting, you should enter the major class A, B, or C address. In Figure 9.7, our three friends have new networks that are taken from a major class A network. Even though multiple networks are attached to them, enter only the major 10.0.0.0/8 network. Thus, all three routers would have the same configuration:

```
Router(config)#router rip
Router(config-router)#network 10.0.0.0
```

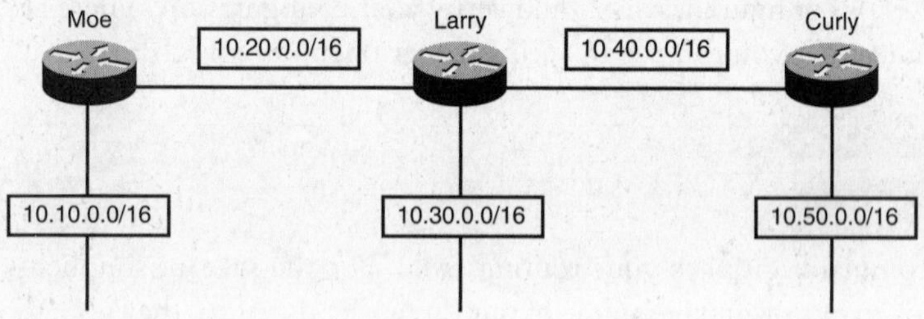

Figure 9.7 RIP example with subnetting.

Finally, you may enter some optional commands. The two optional commands that you should be familiar with for the exam are as follows:

- `version 2`
- `no auto-summary`

Both commands are entered under the RIP routing process. The first command, `version 2`, enables RIP version 2 on your router. RIP version 2 adds the benefits of optional authentication, multicast updates, summarization, and classless routing. Although RIP version 2 does support classless routing, it still automatically summarizes all networks on the default class A, B, and C boundaries. In our previous example in Figure 9.6, RIP version 2 still summarizes the networks at the major 10.0.0.0/8 boundary. (/8 is the default mask for a class A network.) To disable automatic summarization, enter the `no auto-summary` command under the routing process. Using Figure 9.7 again, the complete configuration for Larry's router, assuming that you wanted RIP version 2 with no automatic summarization, is

```
Larry(config)#router rip
Larry(config-router)#network 10.0.0.0
Larry(config-router)#version 2
Larry(config-router)#no auto-summary
```

Note that even though we disabled automatic summarization, we still put the default classful networks in our configuration. RIP is smart enough to go on the interfaces and discover the individual subnetworks and their associated subnet masks.

The three classless routing protocols in this chapter are RIPv2, EIGRP, and OSPF. Remember these three protocols. Also, classless routing, VLSM, summarization, supernetting (another term for summarization), and route aggregation are all related, so if you are asked which routing protocols support these, remember RIPv2, EIGRP, and OSPF.

Verifying and Troubleshooting RIP

Now that RIP is configured, you should verify your configuration. There are two commands that you can use to verify proper operation of RIP:

- `show ip route`
- `show ip protocols`

The first command displays your routing table. For the sake of simplicity, we'll go back to our original example of our three friends before they got creative and started subnetting. Figure 9.8 shows the Larry, Curly, and Moe routers before they subnetted. This time, the names of the interfaces have been included.

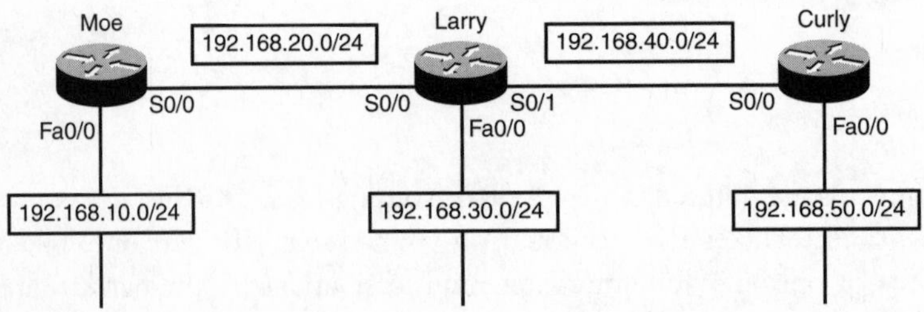

Figure 9.8 RIP example—before subnetting.

After executing the `show ip route` command on Larry's router, you should see the following:

```
Gateway of last resort is not set.
R     192.168.10.0 [120/1] via 192.168.20.1 00:00:08, Serial 0/0
R     192.168.50.0 [120/1] via 192.168.40.2 00:00:16, Serial 0/1
C     192.168.30.0 is directly connected, FastEthernet 0/0
C     192.168.20.0 is directly connected, Serial 0/0
C     192.168.40.0 is directly connected, Serial 0/1
```

You should be comfortable reading the output of this command. Figure 9.9 provides a legend to understand the important elements that make up the output.

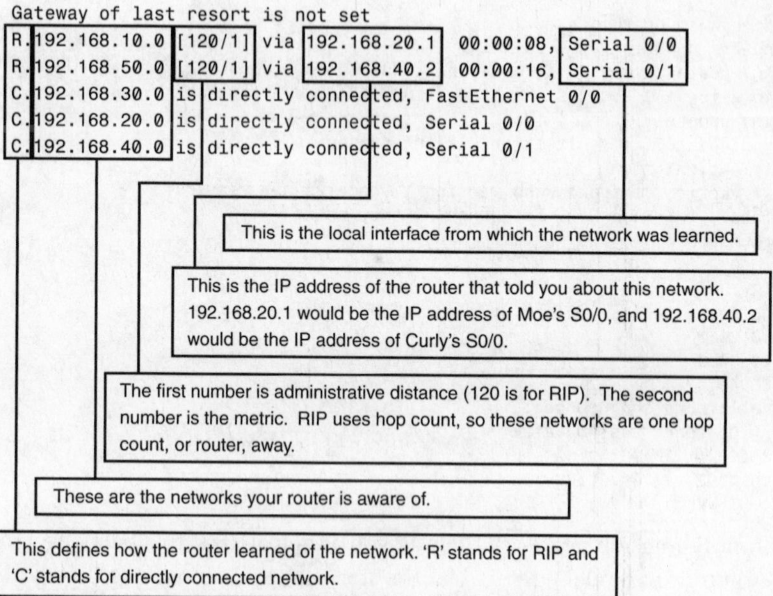

Figure 9.9 Understanding Show IP route.

On Moe's router, the output looks as follows:

```
Gateway of last resort is not set.
R     192.168.30.0 [120/1] via 192.168.20.2 00:00:20, Serial 0/0
R     192.168.40.0 [120/1] via 192.168.20.2 00:00:20, Serial 0/0
R     192.168.50.0 [120/2] via 192.168.20.2 00:00:20, Serial 0/0
C     192.168.10.0 is directly connected, FastEthernet 0/0
C     192.168.20.0 is directly connected, Serial 0/0
```

Notice how the hop count for the 192.168.50.0 network is 2 because that network is two hops away. You must go through the Larry and Curly router to get to this network.

Curly's router has the following output:

```
Gateway of last resort is not set.
R    192.168.10.0 [120/2] via 192.168.40.1 00:00:4, Serial 0/0
R    192.168.20.0 [120/1] via 192.168.40.1 00:00:4, Serial 0/0
R    192.168.30.0 [120/1] via 192.168.40.1 00:00:4, Serial 0/0
C    192.168.50.0 is directly connected, FastEthernet 0/0
C    192.168.40.0 is directly connected, Serial 0/0
```

The second RIP command you should use is the `show ip protocols` command to verify the operation of RIP on your router. Among other things, this command shows you the timers and the networks you are routing. These networks are the same ones you entered under the RIP routing process. Following is the output of this command on the Larry router:

```
Larry# show ip protocols
Routing Protocol is "rip"
Sending updates every 30 seconds, next due in 19 seconds
Invalid after 180 seconds, hold down 180, flushed after 240
Outgoing update filter list for all interfaces is
Incoming update filter list for all interfaces is
Redistribution: rip
Default version control: send version 1, receive any version
Interface        Send Recv Triggered RIP Key-chain
FastEthernet0/0  1    1     2
Serial0/0        1    1     2
Serial0/1        1    1     2
Routing for Networks:
192.168.20.0
192.168.30.0
192.168.40.0
Routing Information Sources:
Gateway Distance Last Update
192.168.20.1 120 00:00:02
192.168.40.2 120 00:00:26
```

Sometimes things do not work the way you anticipated. If this happens, you may want to turn on debugging. Use the `debug ip rip` command to debug the routing process.

You should be very careful when using debug commands. If there is a significant amount of output being generated, it can crash your router. Only turn on debugging if you know it is safe in your environment. If you are not sure, contact Cisco's Technical Assistance Center (TAC) before debugging.

Executing this command on Moe's router generates the following output:

```
Moe#debug ip rip
1. RIP: received v1 update from 192.168.20.2 on Serial0/0
2.        192.168.30.0 in 1 hops
3.        192.168.40.0 in 1 hops
4.        192.168.50.0 in 2 hops
5. RIP: sending v1 update to 255.255.255.255 via Serial0/0
(192.168.20.1)
```

```
6.        network 192.168.10.0, metric 1
7. RIP: sending v1 update to 255.255.255.255 via FastEthernet0/0
(192.168.10.0)
8.       network 192.168.20.0, metric 1
9.       network 192.168.30.0, metric 2
10.       network 192.168.40.0, metric 2
11.       network 192.168.50.0, metric 3
```

For sake of clarity, each line of this output has been numbered.

The metric is added as it leaves the router. By looking at the networks being sent out with a metric of 1, we can glean that this router is configured to route for networks 192.168.20.0 and 192.168.10.0 (lines 6 and 8). You can also look at the interface IP addresses to see what networks are directly connected to the router (lines 5 and 7).

From this output, you can also tell that split-horizon works. The split-horizon rule states that you never advertise a route out of the interface through which it was learned. This router has learned three networks on interface serial 0/0 (lines 2, 3, and 4), but has not advertised out of any of them (line 6).

You need to feel comfortable reading the output of the debug IP RIP command. Remember, it is not useful to send information back in the direction from which it came or to the source from which it came. If the learned route is not returned through the same interface on which it was received, the split horizon rule is in effect.

IGRP

The Interior Gateway Routing Protocol (IGRP) was developed by Cisco in the 1980s as an alternative to RIP. RIP scales up to only 15 hop counts, but IGRP supports up to 255 (with 100 being the default). IGRP has been replaced with Enhanced IGRP and is being removed from the Cisco IOS starting with IOS 12.2(13)T, but we cover IGRP anyway for historical purposes (and because it is still on the exam).

Characteristics of IGRP

IGRP is a distance vector routing protocol that sends out updates every 90 seconds. It has a maximum hop count of 255, but the default is 100. Hop count is used to prevent loops, not as a metric. IGRP uses the bandwidth and delay of an interface for its metric, but can be configured to also factor in the reliability, load, and the maximum transmission unit (MTU) of an interface as well.

Implementing IGRP

The process of configuring IGRP is similar to that of RIP. Follow the same four steps that you did when configuring RIP:

1. Enable the routing protocol.
2. Activate it on interfaces.
3. Advertise directly connected classful networks.
4. Configure optional parameters.

First, enable the routing protocol. This is done with the `router igrp <autonomous system number>` command. The autonomous system number can be any number you prefer between the values of 1 to 65,535, but you must use the same number on all routers if you want them to be able to exchange updates with each other.

The next two steps, activating the routing protocol on the interfaces and advertising your directly connected classful networks, are accomplished using the `network` command just as you did with RIP. For example, if you had the 192.168.10.0/24 and the 192.168.20.0/24 networks connected to your router, your configuration would be

```
Router(config)#router igrp 1
Router(config-router)#network 192.168.10.0
Router(config-router)#network 192.168.20.0
```

As with RIP, make sure that you enter only the directly connected classful networks.

The only optional parameter you should know about for the CCNA exam is the use of the `variance` command. All routing protocols have the capability to load balance traffic across equal cost links, but IGRP and EIGRP has the capability to load balance across unequal cost links. This means that even if the metric were different for two different paths, IGRP and EIGRP could load balance traffic across them in a round-robin fashion. To control the variance allowed between the unequal cost links, use the `variance` command under the routing process. The syntax is `variance <multiplier>`, where the multiplier is the number of times more than the lowest cost link that you want to allow your traffic to load balance traffic across.

For example, if you had a path with a metric of 100 and a path with a metric of 200 and you wanted to load balance your traffic across both paths, you would enter the following command, which would enable your router to load balance across all paths that are two times the lowest cost path:

```
Router(config-router)#variance 2
```

Verifying and Troubleshooting IGRP

Use the same two commands that you used before with RIP to verify IGRP:

- `show ip route`
- `show ip protocols`

There are two debugging commands that you can use for troubleshooting:

- `debug ip igrp events`—This shows the sending and receiving of IGRP packets, along with the number of routes contained in each update.
- `debug ip igrp transactions`—This shows the individual routes being advertised.

EIGRP

EIGRP is a hybrid routing protocol developed by Cisco to replace IGRP. It uses the Diffusing Update Algorithm (DUAL) developed by Dr. J. J. Garcia-Luna-Aceves. Similar to RIP and IGRP, it has a maximum hop count, but its maximum is 224. Unlike RIP and IGRP, however, it does not send out periodic updates. Instead, EIGRP only sends updates when there is a change in the network.

Characteristics of EIGRP

EIGRP uses the same factors as IGRP in building its metric: Bandwidth and Delay of an interface by default, with the option of factoring Reliability, Load, and MTU. The one major difference between EIGRP and IGRP, however, is that EIGRP uses a 32-bit metric and IGRP uses a 24-bit metric. In theory, this allows for more exact calculations in determining the best route, but in practice, this really doesn't make much difference (but is still a good fact to know).

EIGRP maintains three tables as shown in Figure 9.10:

- Neighbor table
- Topology table
- Routing table

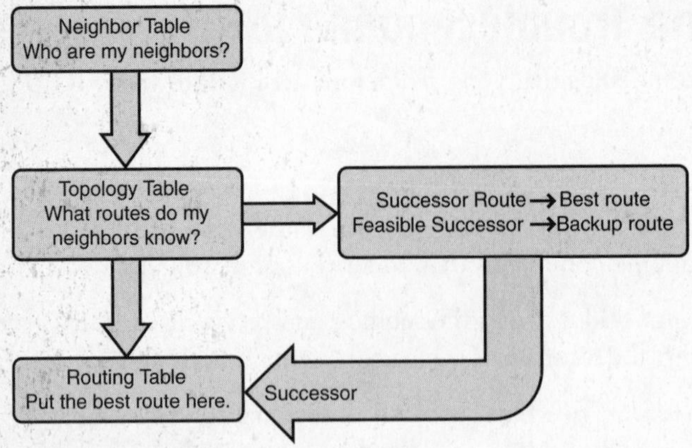

Figure 9.10 EIGRP tables.

EIGRP begins by sending HELLO packets out all active interfaces. The router listens for HELLO packets from other routers. From the HELLO packets, the router learns of neighboring routers, which get listed in the neighbor table. Once the router knows of its neighbors, it begins exchanging routes with its neighbors. These routes go into the topology table, which is similar to a routing table, but no decision has been made yet as to the best route. The DUAL algorithm is run against the topology table, and two routes are determined as a result:

- Successor Route—This is the best route as determined by the DUAL algorithm. This route gets injected into the routing table and is the one used when packets are routed.
- Feasible Successor Route—This is the next best route and is kept in the topology table. It is only used in the event that the primary successor route goes down.

By having a feasible successor route, the router is ready to inject another route into the routing table should the successor ever go down. This makes convergence very rapid with EIGRP.

In addition to being a rapidly converging protocol, EIGRP is the only routing protocol that supports multiple Layer 3 protocols, namely IP, AppleTalk, and IPX. All the other routing protocols mentioned in this chapter only support IP. EIGRP maintains separate tables for each of the three protocols it supports.

Another distinction of EIGRP is its use of two administrative distance values. EIGRP uses administrative distance 90 for routes learned through

EIGRP. Routes can also be redistributed into EIGRP from another routing protocol. When this occurs, redistributed routes get an administrative distance of 170.

Remember the main characteristics of EIGRP:

- Hybrid protocol
- Supports IP, AppleTalk, and IPX
- Uses a 32-bit metric
- Has two administrative distance values, one for internal and one for external (redistributed routes)
- Uses Bandwidth and Delay by default in calculating its metric, but can also factor Reliability, Load, and MTU
- Is backward compatible with IGRP, assuming that the autonomous system number is the same

Implementing EIGRP

Configuring EIGRP is very similar to configuring IGRP. In fact, IGRP and EIGRP can interoperate with each other if you use the same autonomous system number. You'll need to be careful, then, to use a different autonomous system number in your EIGRP process in the event that both IGRP and EIGRP are running in your environment and you do not want them to exchange routes with each other. As with IGRP, the autonomous system number must match on all routers in order for the router to exchange updates.

The following example shows how to configure EIGRP for a router connected to networks 192.168.10.0/24 and 192.168.20.0/24:

```
Router(config)#router eigrp 1
Router(config-router)#network 192.168.10.0
Router(config-router)#network 192.168.20.0
```

Similar to RIP version 2 and OSPF, EIGRP can be a classless routing protocol. By default, it is classful. To enable classless routing, type the following command under the routing process:

```
Router(config-router)#no auto-summary
```

Verifying and Troubleshooting EIGRP

Verification of EIGRP is the same as the other protocols mentioned in this chapter. Use the `show ip protocols` and `show ip route` commands to verify your EIGRP configuration.

OSPF

The Open Shortest Path First protocol was developed by the Internet Engineering Task Force (IETF) in 1988 as a more scalable solution than RIP. It uses the Shortest Path First (SPF) algorithm developed by Edgar Dijkstra. It is a link-state routing protocol, which means that it sends updates only when there is a change in the network, and instead of sending routing updates, it sends link state advertisements (LSAs) instead.

Characteristics

OSPF is a polite protocol. Unlike chatty RIP, which broadcasts out its entire routing table every 30 seconds regardless of whether other routers want to hear it, OSPF takes a more gentleman-like approach to routing. First, OSPF sends out hello messages to neighboring routers to announce itself as an OSPF router and discover who its neighbor routers are. Neighbors have to agree on certain parameters (such as timers and being on a common subnet) before they can become neighbors. Once its neighbor routers are discovered, they begin to exchange link state advertisements, which contain the networks and their associated metrics. After exchanging all routes, the routers send out updates only when there is a change, and they send information only for that affected route, not the entire routing table. Routers take the link state advertisements heard from other routers and place those routes in its link state database (similar to the topology database in EIGRP). Routers then run the SPF algorithm to determine the best route to a destination and place that route in the routing table.

To determine the best path, OSPF uses a metric called cost, which Cisco defines as 10^8/bandwidth. If you had a 100MB link, the cost would be 1 because 100,000,000/100,000,000. Here are some other common costs:

- 10MB: 10
- 1.544MB (T1): 64
- 64k: 1562

These examples are not just included to impress you with the authors' math ability. You should know the formula to determine the cost of a link. Given the bandwidth of an interface, know how to calculate the OSPF cost.

The SPF algorithm places each router as the "root" of a tree and calculates the shortest path from itself to each destination. The shortest path then gets put in to the routing table and is used to route packets to their destination.

Hierarchical Routing

An important concept to grasp with OSPF is that it is a hierarchical protocol. Hierarchical routing protocols break up your autonomous system into multiple areas and summarize routes between areas. If summarized wisely, you can cut down a significant portion of routing updates by only advertising the summarized route.

As the number of networks increases in your domain, the amount of processing required on each router increases. To lower the amount of processing required, you can use route summarization. Route summarization looks for the same sequence of bits used in subnetworks and creates a less-explicit summary route. For example, in Figure 9.11 there are four networks in area 2:

- 172.16.0.0/24
- 172.17.0.0/24
- 172.18.0.0/24
- 172.19.0.0/24

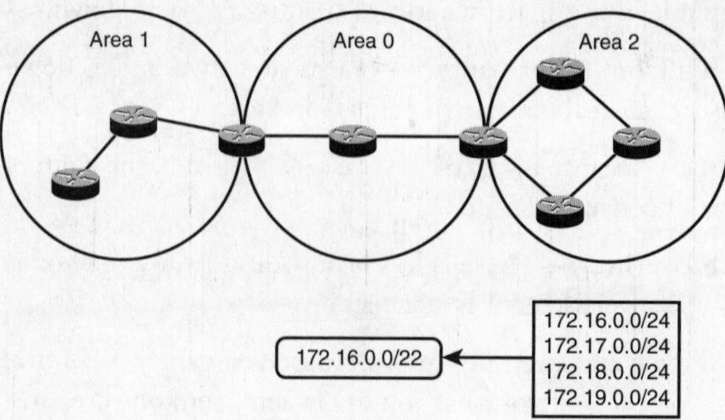

Figure 9.11 OSPF summarization.

The first octet, 172, is the same for all four routes, but the second octet differs. By looking for similar bits, we can create a single summary route:

	128	**64**	**32**	**16**	**8**	**4**	**2**	**1**
16	0	0	0	1	0	0	0	0
17	0	0	0	1	0	0	0	1
18	0	0	0	1	0	0	1	0
19	0	0	0	1	0	0	1	1

The bits are the same up to the 4-bit position. Only the 16-bit position is set to 1, so by ignoring the last two bits (because they change), we are left with 172.16.0.0. The subnet mask has changed, however, because we are no longer working with a /24. Instead, our subnet mask has moved two places to the left because the last two bit positions vary for the four networks. Our resulting summarized route is 172.16.0.0/22 (255.255.252.0). This will be the route that gets injected into area 0 from area 2.

The routers in area 0 and area 1 have to process only the one summarized route instead of four individual routes. There are several benefits to being able to summarize your routes between areas:

- **Less processing on routers**—This is not only because of the single network statement (as opposed to four), but also because of the lack of recalculation should a more specific network (that is, a /24) go down.
- **Instability hidden from other routers**—If a single network goes down in area 2, it will not affect the routers in area 0 and area 1.
- **Fast convergence**—Because fewer routes are sent to area 0, the routers in areas 0 and 1 can converge faster.
- **Less bandwidth overhead**—There is less bandwidth because only one route is sent, so the advertisement is smaller.
- **Greater control over routing updates**—Because you gain control over routing updates, you can control what routes get sent from one area to another.

You might have noticed that both area 2 and area 1 are connected via area 0. Area 0 is the 'backbone' area in OSPF, and all other areas must be connected to it. Routes are then summarized into your backbone area.

Designated and Backup Designated Routers

Summarizing is an excellent way to conserve on your precious bandwidth. On networks that contain more than two routers, OSPF can also conserve bandwidth by electing a designated router for that network that all routers communicate with. Routers exchange information with a designated router instead of each other. This cuts down significantly on the number of advertisements.

The process of using a designated router is somewhat complex, so let's go through it one step at a time. First of all, the designated router (DR) is elected on only two types of networks:

- **Broadcast multi-access**—Ethernet, Token-Ring
- **Nonbroadcast multi-access**—Frame Relay, ATM, X.25

On a point-to-point network with only two routers there is no need for this type of election. As I tell my students, "On point-to-point, there is no point (of having a DR)."

Second, the DR is not the only type of router elected on these types of networks. A backup designated router (BDR) is used in the event that a DR should fail.

The DR and BDR election is as follows:

1. The router with the highest priority becomes the DR. The router with the second highest priority becomes the BDR. Priority is a number between 0 and 255 and is configured on an interface with the command `ip ospf priority <priority_number>`. The default priority is 1, and if the router is set to priority 0, it will never become a DR or BDR.
2. If the case of a tie, such as when every router's priority is left to the default of 1, the tie breaker is the router with the highest router ID.

Every router has an identifier called a router ID (RID) that is used to identify itself in its messages. The router ID is an IP address and is assigned as follows:

1. The router ID can be configured with the `router-id` command under the OSPF routing process. You can choose a valid IP address that you are using on the router or make up a new one.
2. If the `router-id` command is not used, the numerically highest IP address on any loopback interface is chosen as the router ID. A loopback interface is a virtual, software-only interface that never goes down.
3. If you do not have any loopback interfaces configured, the highest IP address on any active physical interface is chosen as the router ID.

See if you can spot the router ID given the following IP addresses on a router:

Serial 0/0: 192.168.100.19

FastEthernet 0/0: 10.0.0.1

Loopback 0: 172.16.201.200

Although the highest IP address is the one configured on the serial interface, there is a loopback interface that takes precedence over any physical interfaces. Therefore, the router ID would be 172.16.201.200.

The **router-id** command is common in the real world, but for the test, make sure that you know the process the router uses to select a router ID if the **router-id** command is not used. It first looks at the highest IP address on any logical (loopback) interface, and if there are no loopback interfaces, it looks at the highest IP address on any active physical interface.

Let's review. On broadcast and non-broadcast multi-access networks, a designated router and backup designated router are elected. The election is done by first choosing the routers with the highest priority value or, if the priorities are same, choosing the routers with the highest router ID. The router ID is chosen by the highest IP address on any loopback interface or, if no loopback interfaces are configured, the highest IP address on any active physical interface. Whew! That's a lot of work, but in the end it will conserve significant amount of bandwidth by minimizing the number of link-state messages.

Now that we have elected a DR and BDR, the next phase is ready to begin. In Figure 9.12, you see five routers. The Mocha router is the DR, and the Latte router is the BDR. Instead of all routers sending link-state advertisements to each other, they only send out messages to the DR and BDR. Messages are sent to the multicast address of 224.0.0.6; both the DR and BDR belong to this multicast group address.

Next, the Mocha router, which is the DR, takes the information it learned from the other routers and sends it back out to all routers, as shown in Figure 9.13. Messages are sent to the AllSPFRouter multicast address of 224.0.0.5; all routers running OSPF are members of this multicast group address.

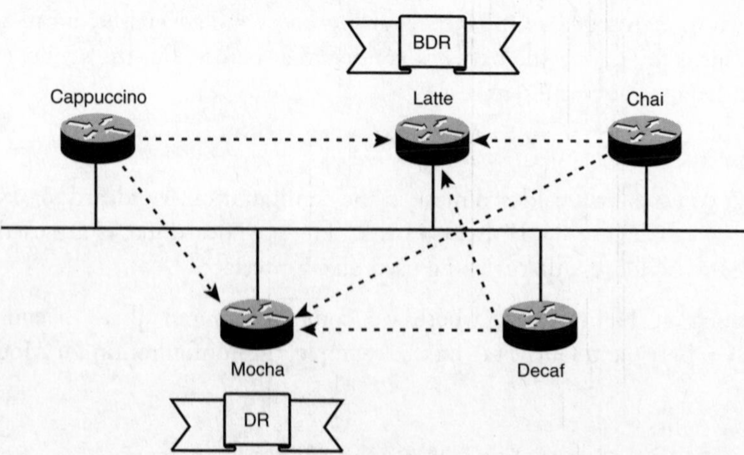

Figure 9.12 OSPF DR/BDR operation.

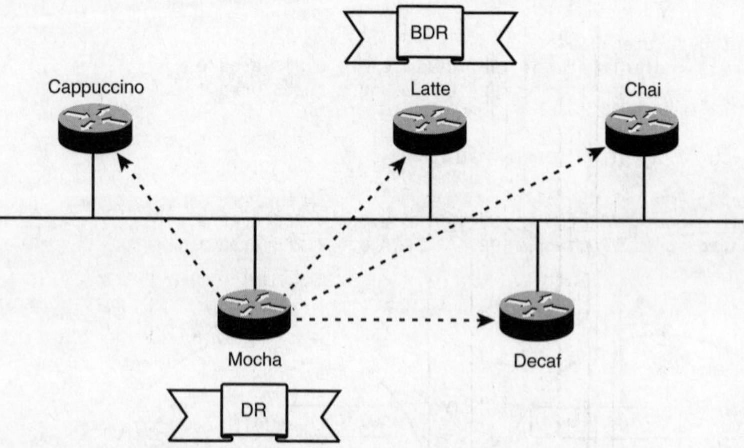

Figure 9.13 DR sends to 224.0.0.6.

Implementing OSPF

Understanding the complexities involved in OSPF is the difficult part; configuring it is fairly straightforward. The process is the same as with the other protocols. First, we enable the routing protocol. This is done with the command router ospf <process-id>. The process ID can be any number you prefer between 1 and 65,535. Note that this is not the same as the autonomous system number found in IGRP and EIGRP. Here, the process ID is local to the router and does not need to match other routers.

The next step is to activate OSPF on your interfaces and advertise your networks. This is done with the network command as before, but the syntax is a little different. Here, the syntax is

```
network <network address> <wild card mask> area <area-id>
```

Note that you specify a wildcard mask in the configuration. Wildcard masks are covered in Chapter 8, "IP Access Lists." Here, wildcard masks are used to match the IP address that is being used on an interface.

Take a look at Figure 9.14, where we come across our three friends again, Moe, Larry, and Curly. Given this example, the configuration for Moe would be

```
Moe(config)#router ospf 1
Moe(config-router)#network 192.168.10.0 0.0.0.255 area 0
Moe(config-router)#network 192.168.20.0 0.0.0.255 area 0
```

Larry's configuration would be

```
Larry(config)#router ospf 1
Larry(config-router)#network 192.168.20.0 0.0.0.255 area 0
Larry(config-router)#network 192.168.40.0 0.0.0.255 area 1
```

Finally, Curly's configuration would be

```
Curly(config)#router ospf 1
Curly(config-router)#network 192.168.40.0 0.0.0.255 area 1
Curly(config-router)#network 192.168.50.0 0.0.0.255 area 1
```

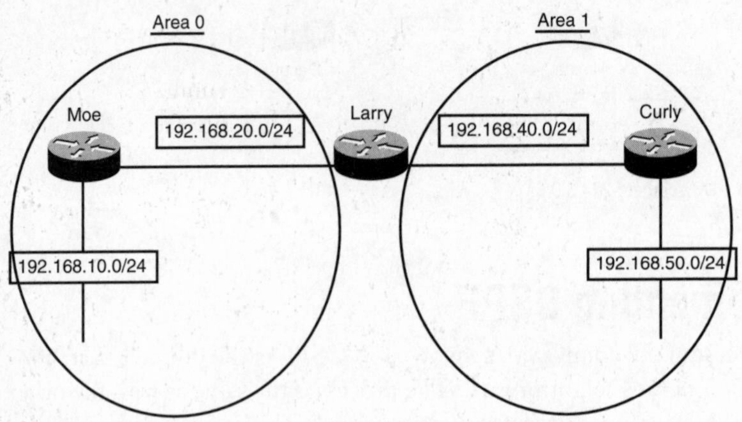

Figure 9.14 OSPF scenario.

The wildcard mask used in these statements is matching the IP address on the interface. Here, we are matching the entire network, of which the IP address is a part. For example, on Curly's router, the command `network 192.168.40.0 0.0.0.255 area 1` tells the router to match all addresses that begin with 192.168.40. The last octet, which has 255 in the wildcard mask, is ignored. The router examines the IP addresses of its directly connected interfaces and activates OSPF on those interfaces that match the statement.

Because you are using wildcard masks to match the IP address on your directly connected interfaces, you could also use the wildcard mask of 0.0.0.0 to match the exact address. Just as with IP access lists in Chapter 8, a wildcard mask of 0.0.0.0 would match a specific address. For example, if Curly had the IP address of 192.168.40.1 on one interface and 192.168.50.1 on another interface, you could configure Curly's router using a wildcard mask of 0.0.0.0:

```
Curly(config)router ospf 1
Curly(config-router)#network 192.168.40.1 0.0.0.0 area 1
Curly(config-router)#network 192.168.50.1 0.0.0.0 area 1
```

Using a wildcard mask that matches the IP address of the interface is equivalent to using a wildcard mask that matches the network where the IP address resides. For the exam, focus on matching the entire network (0.0.0.255 wildcard mask in the previous example); the reasons behind which one you should choose is outside the scope of this book and, for that matter, the exam.

The syntax for OSPF is slightly different from other routing protocols. Make sure that you feel comfortable configuring OSPF. Remember, it uses a process ID, not an autonomous system. Also, OSPF uses wildcard masks and not subnet masks in its configuration.

There are two optional commands that you should be familiar with for the CCNA exam. These commands, configured under the interface, are

- **ip ospf priority** *priority_number*—This is used to change the priority of an interface for the DR/BDR election.
- **ip ospf cost** *cost*—This is used to manually change the cost of an interface.

Verifying and Troubleshooting OSPF

For verification, you can use the `show ip protocols` and `show ip route` as before. Other commands you can use to verify your configuration are

- **show ip ospf interface**—This command displays area ID and DR/BDR information.
- **show ip ospf neighbor**—This command displays neighbor information

You can use the `debug ip ospf events` command to troubleshoot OSPF. This command is helpful to troubleshoot why routers are not forming a neighbor relationship with each other. Similar to EIGRP, OSPF routers form neighbor relationships before exchanging any routing information. Several items must line up, however, in order for a neighbor adjacency to be established:

- Timers must be the same on both routers. OSPF uses hello timers that define how often they send out hello messages and dead timers that define how long after a router stops hearing a hello message does it declare its neighbor as down.
- Interfaces connecting the two routers must be in the same area.
- Password authentication, if being used, must be the same.
- Type of area must be the same. (This last item is outside the scope of the CCNA test, but it is covered on the CCNP BSCI exam.)

Neighbors are formed automatically or can be established through the use of the `neighbor` command done under the routing process. Sometimes the neighbor adjacency does not form, and the `debug ip ospf events` command can help you to troubleshoot what is going wrong. The following debug output shows an example of an adjacency not forming because of two routers having different timers configured:

```
Router#debug ip ospf events
OSPF: hello with invalid timers on interface FastEthernet0/0
hello interval received 10 configured 10
netmask received 255.255.0.0 configured 255.255.0.0
dead interval received 40 configured 60
```

Exam Prep Questions

1. You are working in an environment that is running IP, IPX, and AppleTalk. What routing protocol inherently supports all three of these protocols?
   - O A. RIP version 1
   - O B. RIP version 2
   - O C. OSPF
   - O D. IGRP
   - O E. EIGRP
2. Given the exhibit in Figure 9.15, how would you configure RIP version 1 on the Chicago router?

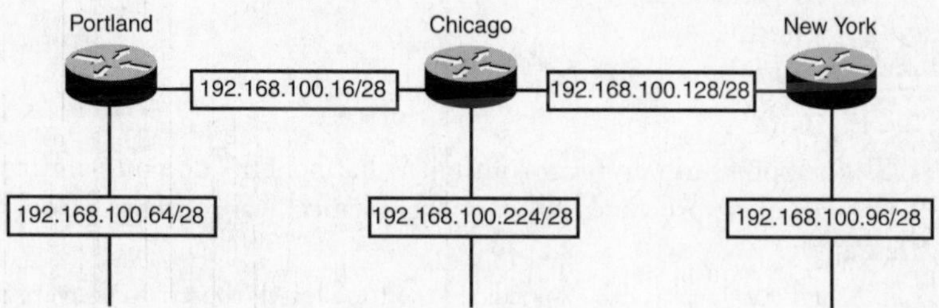

   - O A. Chicago(config)#router rip
     Chicago(config-router)#network 192.168.100.16 255.255.255.240
     Chicago(config-router)#network 192.168.100.224 255.255.255.240
     Chicago(config-router)#network 192.168.100.128 255.255.255.240
   - O B. Chicago(config)#router rip
     Chicago(config-router)#network 192.168.100.0
   - O C. Chicago(config)#router rip
     Chicago(config-router)#network 192.168.100.16
     Chicago(config-router)#network 192.168.100.224
     Chicago(config-router)#network 192.168.100.128
   - O D. Chicago(config-router)#network 192.168.100.0 255.255.255.0
3. How is the router ID chosen in OSPF? Select all that apply.
   - ❑ A. Highest loopback IP address
   - ❑ B. Highest physical IP address if no loopback exists
   - ❑ C. Lowest loopback IP address
   - ❑ D. Lowest physical IP address if no loopback exists

4. Examine the exhibit in Figure 9.16. What routing protocol can you use to accommodate the given addressing scheme? Select all that apply.

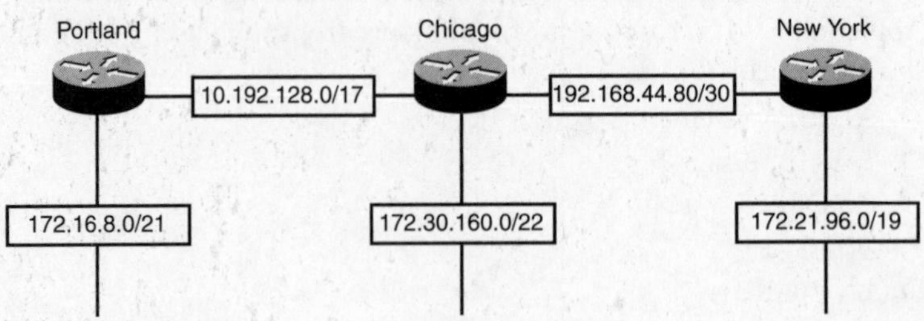

- ❑ A. RIP version 1
- ❑ B. RIP version 2
- ❑ C. EIGRP
- ❑ D. OSPF
- ❑ E. IGRP

5. OSPF supports hierarchical routing. What benefits do you gain from using a routing protocol that supports hierarchical routing? Select all that apply.

- ❑ A. Hierarchical routing speeds up the time for all routers to converge.
- ❑ B. Hierarchical routing requires less configuration.
- ❑ C. Hierarchical routing reduces the amount of routing overhead.
- ❑ D. Hierarchical routing hides network instability from routers in other areas.
- ❑ E. Hierarchical routing requires less design considerations.

6. Given the exhibit shown in Figure 9.17, what path will the Berlin router choose to send a packet to the Paris router?

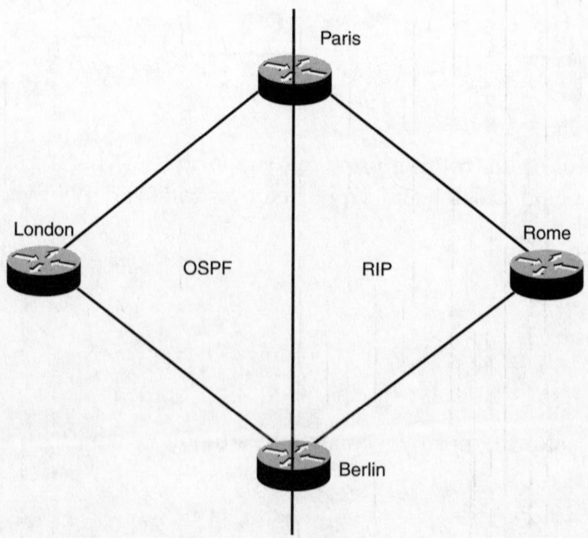

- O A. Berlin will send the packet through the London router to get to Paris.
- O B. Berlin will send the packet through the Rome router to get to Paris.
- O C. Berlin will drop the packet because it does not have a definitive route to Paris.
- O D. Berlin will send the packet to both Rome and London and load balance packets between them.

7. What is the cost of a 128K link in OSPF?

- O A. 1562
- O B. 64
- O C. 781
- O D. 10

8. You have a serial interface with the IP address of 192.168.22.33/30. How would you add this link to area 0 in the OSPF process?

- O A. Router(config-router)#network 192.168.22.32 0.0.0.3 area 0
- O B. Router(config-router)#network 192.168.22.32 255.255.255.252
- O C. Router(config-router)#network 192.168.22.33 0.0.0.3 area 0
- O D. Router(config-router)#network 192.168.22.33 255.255.255.252 area 0

9. Which of the following are methods used by distance vector routing protocols to prevent loops? Select all that apply.
   - ❑ A. Triggered holddowns
   - ❑ B. Triggered updates
   - ❑ C. Split horizon
   - ❑ D. Split updates
   - ❑ E. Holddown timers
10. Which of the following routing protocols supports VLSM and summarization while being scalable and supported by a wide variety of vendors?
    - ❍ A. RIP version 1
    - ❍ B. EIGRP
    - ❍ C. RIP version 2
    - ❍ D. IGRP
    - ❍ E. OSPF
11. Which of the following protocols maintains a topology table?
    - ❍ A. RIP version 1
    - ❍ B. RIP version 2
    - ❍ C. IGRP
    - ❍ D. EIGRP
12. What is required to match in order for EIGRP and IGRP routers to exchange routing information?
    - ❍ A. Autonomous system number
    - ❍ B. Process ID
    - ❍ C. Subnet Mask
    - ❍ D. Router ID

13. Given the exhibit shown in Figure 9.18, what is the correct configuration for the Iceland router?

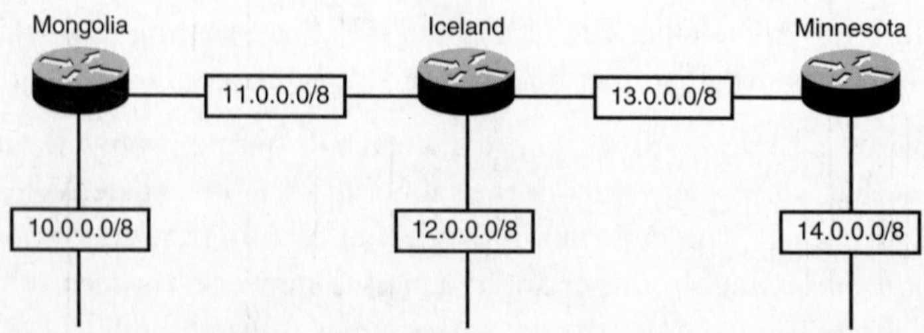

- ❍ A. Iceland(config)#router rip
  Iceland(config-router)#network 10.0.0.0
  Iceland(config-router)#network 11.0.0.0
  Iceland(config-router)#network 12.0.0.0
  Iceland(config-router)#network 13.0.0.0
  Iceland(config-router)#network 14.0.0.0
- ❍ B. Iceland(config)#router rip 100
  Iceland(config-router)#network 11.0.0.0
  Iceland (config-router)#network 12.0.0.0
  Iceland(config-router)#network 13.0.0.0
- ❍ C. Iceland(config)#router rip
  Iceland(config-router)#network 11.0.0.0
  Iceland(config-router)#network 13.0.0.0
- ❍ D. Iceland(config)#router rip
  Iceland(config-router)#network 11.0.0.0
  Iceland(config-router)#network 12.0.0.0
  Iceland(config-router)#network 13.0.0.0

14. What does RIP version 2 add that is not found in RIP version 1? Select all that apply.

- ❑ A. Authentication
- ❑ B. Summarization
- ❑ C. Multicast updates
- ❑ D. VLSM

Answers to Exam Prep Questions

1. Answer E is correct. EIGRP is the only routing protocol that supports IP, IPX, and AppleTalk. RIP, OSPF, and IGRP are routing protocols that only support IP, so therefore answers A, B, C, and D are incorrect.

2. Answer B is correct. RIP version 1 is a classful routing protocol, which means that it does not send out the subnet mask in its update. When configuring RIP, you must put in the default classful networks, even if you are subnetting. In this example, a class C network has been subnetted, but you should enter the network statement using the full class network of 192.168.100.0. Answer A is incorrect because it enters all three networks, and it uses subnet masks. Answer C is incorrect because it enters all three networks. Answer D is incorrect because it enters a subnet mask, which is not used in RIP.

3. Answers A and B are correct. OSPF chooses the highest IP address of any logical loopback interfaces or, if no loopback interfaces are configured, the highest IP address on any physical interface that is active at the moment the OSPF process begins. Answers C and D are incorrect because they imply that the lowest IP address is used, which is not the case with OSPF's router ID.

4. Answers B, C, and D are correct. The addressing scheme is using noncontiguous subnets and therefore requires a routing protocol that supports variable length subnet masks (VLSM). Routing protocols that support VLSM are called classless routing protocols, and RIP version 2, EIGRP, and OSPF are all classless. RIP version 1 and IGRP are classful and only support full length subnet masks.

5. Answers A, C, and D are correct. When you hear the term hierarchical routing, think areas and route summarization. OSPF, which supports hierarchical routing, allows you to summarize networks from one area into another. Instead of routers needing to know about all the individual networks in another area, they only need to know about the summary route. The fewer routes results in faster convergence and less routing overhead and, should a network in an area go down, it will not affect routers in other areas. Answer B is incorrect because OSPF will actually cause additional configuration to be performed. Answer E is incorrect because OSPF typically requires more design than nonhierarchical routing protocols such as RIP in order to ensure an addressing scheme that allows for summarization between areas.

6. Answer A is correct. This question tests on your knowledge of administrative distance. OSPF has an administrative distance of 110, and RIP has an administrative distance of 120. Because OSPF has a lower administrative distance, it is preferred over RIP. Subsequently, the packet will take the path through the OSPF domain to get to Paris. Answer B is incorrect because this path prefers RIP. Answer C is incorrect because the Berlin router does have a route to Paris. Answer D is incorrect because Berlin will not load balance because of the difference in administrative distance between RIP and OSPF.

7. Answer C is correct. Cost is defined as 10^8/bandwidth. Thus, 100,000,000 / 128,000 equals 781. Answer A is incorrect because this is the cost to a 64K link. Answer B is incorrect because this is the cost of a 1.544 T1 link. Answer D is incorrect because this is the cost of a 10MB link.

8. Answer A is correct. The IP address of the interface is 192.168.22.33/30, which is on network 192.168.22.32. Although you could have entered 192.168.22.33 0.0.0.0 area 0, this was not a valid option. Only answer A has the correct network and wildcard mask. This is tricky because it requires you to determine both the network address and the correct OSPF syntax. Answer B uses a subnet mask and not a wildcard mask, so it is incorrect. Answer C is incorrect because it does not list the correct network address. Answer D is also incorrect because it does not list the correct address and because it uses a subnet mask in which a wildcard mask is required.

9. Answers B, C, and E are correct. Triggered updates send out updates whenever there is a change in an effort to speed up convergence. Split horizon tells the router not to send back route information in the direction it received it from. Holddown timers hold on to route information for a period of time to wait for other routers to converge. Answers A and D are incorrect because these do not exist.

10. Answer E is correct. Answer A does not support VLSM or summarization, nor is it scalable. Answer B is incorrect because it is Cisco proprietary and therefore not supported by other vendors. Answer C is incorrect because RIP version 2 is not scalable. Answer D is incorrect because IGRP does not support VLSM or summarization, is not scalable, and is Cisco proprietary.

11. Answer D is correct. EIGRP maintains a neighbor, topology, and routing table. Answers A, B, and C are incorrect; RIP versions 1 and 2 and IGRP do not have topology tables. Instead, they run their algorithm and place the best route directly in the routing table.

12. Answer A is correct. If the autonomous system number is the same between EIGRP and IGRP, routers will automatically exchange routing updates. This makes EIGRP backward compatible with IGRP. Answer B is incorrect because a process ID is used with OSPF and not IGRP or EIGRP. Answer C is incorrect because the subnet masks do not matter with IGRP (it is a classful routing protocol). Answer D is incorrect because router IDs are unique to a particular router and they do not need to match among routers.

13. Answer D is correct. When configuring RIP, remember that you should configure it for all directly connected classful networks only. Answer A is incorrect because it configures more networks than necessary. Answer B is incorrect because no number is added to the end of the router rip command. Answer C is incorrect because it is missing a network.

14. Answers A, B, C, and D are correct. RIP version 2 supports MD5 authentication between routers, summarization, multicast updates to 224.0.0.9 instead of broadcast updates, and variable length subnet masks (VLSM). Remember, if a routing protocol is classless, this means that it supports VLSM and summarization. RIPv2, EIGRP, and OSPF are all classless.

Wide Area Networks

Terms You'll Need to Understand

- ✓ Challenge Handshake Authentication Protocol (CHAP)
- ✓ Password Authentication Protocol (PAP)
- ✓ Permanent Virtual Circuit (PVC)
- ✓ Committed Information Rate (CIR)
- ✓ Local Management Interface (LMI)
- ✓ Network Termination Type 1 (NT1)
- ✓ Network Termination Type 2 (NT2)
- ✓ Terminal Equipment Type 1 (TE1)
- ✓ Terminal Equipment Type 2 (TE2)
- ✓ Backward Explicit Congestion Notification (BECN)
- ✓ Forward Explicit Congestion Notification (FECN)
- ✓ High-Level Data Link Control (HDLC)
- ✓ Point-to-Point Protocol (PPP)

Concepts and Techniques You'll Need to Master

- ✓ Configuring PPP (point-to-point)
- ✓ Configuring Integrated Services Digital Network (ISDN)
- ✓ Configuring Frame-relay

Introduction

There are two major types of networking: local area network (LAN) and wide area network (WAN). This chapter discusses WANs.

A WAN is a network that spans a broad geographical area and includes such technologies as ATM, frame-relay, leased lines, and ISDN. These wide area networking services are leased from providers.

In its simplest definition, wide area networking can be broken down into three categories:

- leased line
- circuit switched
- packet switched

Leased line WAN solutions use synchronous serial interfaces to connect two sites together. This is the easiest to configure and provides the best reliability. However, this is also the most expensive over long distances.

The second option is circuit-switched technologies. These technologies include modems connected to asynchronous interfaces and ISDN technologies. With circuit-switched solutions, you establish a circuit between two sites using a telephone company.

The final option is packet-switched technologies, which also use synchronous serial interfaces similar to leased line solutions, but with these, a virtual circuit is established between two or more sites and your data packets are switched across a service provider's network. The service provider's network is transparent to the customer; you will not be able to see any of your provider's equipment. Packet switched technologies include frame-relay, ATM, and X.25. They are commonly used when leased line solutions become cost prohibitive.

Encapsulation Types

With each WAN solution, there is an encapsulation type. Encapsulations wrap information around your data that is used to transport your data traffic. If you use leased line as your wide area networking choice, you can encapsulate your data inside a High-level Data-Link Control (HDLC) frame, PPP frame, or Serial Line IP (SLIP) frame. For packet-switched networks, you can encapsulate or package your data in X.25 frames, frame-relay, or asynchronous transfer mode (ATM) frames. (ATM and frame-relay actually have multiple encapsulations that you can use.) Finally, in circuit-switched environments, you have HDLC, PPP, or SLIP as you do with leased line, but with circuit-switched solutions, it is more common to use PPP as your choice. This is because of the options available with PPP that are catered to using telephone-based circuit-switched networks. These options include such things as authentication and compression. Table 10.1 illustrates the different encapsulations as they are used by various WAN technologies.

Table 10.1 WAN Encapsulations

	Leased Lines	Circuit-Switched	Packet-Switched
HDLC	X	X	
PPP*	X	X	
SLIP	X	X	
Frame-relay**			X
ATM***			X
X.25			X

* Technically, it is possible to have PPP run over ATM and frame-relay, but it is not necessary to know this for the CCNA exam.

** Frame-relay actually has two types of encapsulations: IETF and Cisco.

***ATM has several types of encapsulations, but it is not necessary to know these for the CCNA exam.

Cisco HDLC

The default encapsulation on a serial interface is HDLC. The original HDLC encapsulation was defined by the International Organization for Standards (ISO), those same folks who developed the OSI model. The ISO version of HDLC had one shortcoming, however; it had no options to support multiple layer 3 routed protocols. As a result, most vendors have created their own form of HDLC. Cisco is no exception as it has its own proprietary form of HDLC to support various layer 3 protocols such as IPX, IP, and AppleTalk. Figure 10.1 illustrates the difference between the ISO and Cisco HDLC frame formats.

Cisco HDLC

Flag	Address	Control	Proprietary Field to support multiple protocols	Data	FCS	Flag

ISO HDLC

Flag	Address	Control	Data	FCS	Flag

Figure 10.1 Cisco and ISO HDLC formats.

Vendors love to test your knowledge of the default settings for their products. Make sure you know that HDLC is the default encapsulation on a serial interface.

PPP

Point-to-point protocol (PPP), defined in RFC 1661, is used to encapsulate network layer protocols over point-to-point links. PPP can be used over asynchronous, synchronous, or ISDN links.

Components

PPP has two sublayers called network control protocol (NCP) and link control protocol (LCP).

NCP is responsible for supporting multiple layer 3 protocols. Each protocol has its own NCP, such as the IPCP for IP communication and IPXCP for IPX communication. Think of NCP as the "packager," as it is responsible for packaging, or encapsulating, your packets into a control protocol that is readable by PPP.

The link control protocol is used for establishing the link and negotiating optional settings. These options include

- **Compression**—You can compress your data to conserve bandwidth across your wide area network. Options for compression are Stacker and Predictor.
- **Callback**—With callback, you dial into a router using a modem or ISDN and then disconnect. The other router then calls you back at a

predefined number. This option is used for centralized billing and security reasons.

- **Multilink**—Multilink allows you to bundle together more than one link to create more bandwidth. (Traffic will load balance across the links.) For example, you can bundle two 64K channels together to get a combined 128K.
- **Authentication**—You can use authentication to verify a router's identity when it is connecting into your router. Options for authentication include CHAP and PAP.

You can think of LCP as the "negotiator" because it is responsible for negotiating these options between two routers.

Know the various options of PPP. Remember CCMA (it sounds similar to CCNA), which stands for compression, callback, multilink, and authentication.

Authentication with PAP and CHAP

There are two types of authentications you can use with PPP:

- Password Authentication Protocol (PAP)
- Challenge Handshake Authentication Protocol (CHAP)

PAP uses a two-way authentication process where the username and password is sent followed by a response message indicating successful or failed authentication. CHAP, however, is much more paranoid about its authentication. It performs a three-way authentication process as shown in Figure 10.2, which takes place not only at the beginning of a connection, but also every two minutes. As if that wasn't paranoid enough, CHAP never sends the password across the link. Instead, an MD5 hash is used to mask the password.

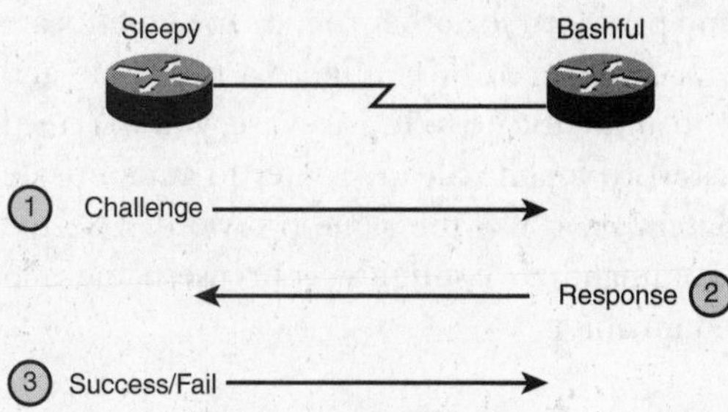

Figure 10.2 CHAP authentication.

Configuration

Configuring authentication is a four step process:

1. Configure your hostname.
2. Configure the username and password list for other routers to authenticate to your router.
3. Enable PPP encapsulation.
4. Enable PAP or CHAP authentication.

The hostname takes on a special significance with PPP as it is used as the username to authenticate to another router. For example, let's say that you had two routers named Sleepy and Bashful, as shown in Figure 10.3. For Sleepy, its hostname is used as the username to authenticate to Bashful. For Bashful, its hostname is used as the username to authenticate to Sleepy. Use the hostname command to configure the hostname on each router:

Sleepy:

```
Router(config)#hostname Sleepy
```

Bashful:

```
Router(config)#hostname Bashful
```

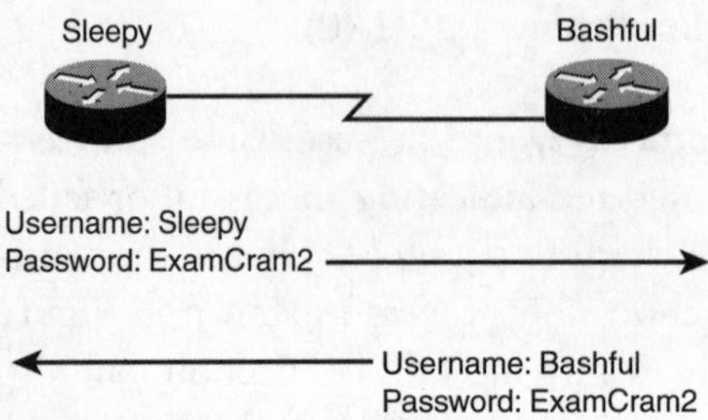

Figure 10.3 PPP configuration example.

Next, configure the username and password for other routers to authenticate to you. For the Sleepy router, you will need to configure a username and password for the Bashful router to authenticate to it. Likewise, you will need to configure a username and password for the Sleepy router to authenticate to the Bashful router. Both routers must use the same password. Use the global configuration `username` command to configure your username and password. The syntax for this command is

```
username name password password
```

For example,

Sleepy:

```
Sleepy(config)#username Bashful password ExamCram2
```

Bashful:

```
Bashful(config)#username Sleepy password ExamCram2
```

The hostnames and passwords are case sensitive. The hostname 'Sleepy' is different from the hostname 'sleepy.' Make sure that you check the case of your letters when configuring PPP authentication.

The third step in configuring PPP is to enable PPP encapsulation on the interface using the `encapsulation` command. For example, to configure PPP encapsulation on the ISDN BRI 0 interface, type the following:

```
Sleepy(config)#interface bri 0
Sleepy(config-if)#encapsulation ppp
```

Finally, you will need to configure your authentication. The interface level command to do this is

```
ppp authentication [chap ¦ chap pap ¦ pap]
```

If you choose the `chap pap` option, it will try CHAP authentication first, and if that fails, it will try PAP. Newer IOS versions (12.3 and 12.4) will also support EAP, MS-Chap, and MS-Chap version 2. Following is the final configuration for the two routers using CHAP authentication:

Sleepy:

```
Router(config)#hostname Sleepy
Sleepy(config)#username Bashful password ExamCram2
Sleepy(config)#interface bri0
Sleepy(config-if)#encapsulation ppp
Sleepy(config-if)#ppp authentication chap
```

Bashful:

```
Router(config)#hostname Bashful
Bashful(config)#username Sleepy password ExamCram2
Bashful(config)#interface bri0
Bashful(config-if)#encapsulation ppp
Bashful(config-if)#ppp authentication chap
```

Verification and Troubleshooting

Verifying and troubleshooting PPP can be done with two commands:

- `show interfaces`
- `debug ppp authentication`

The `show interfaces` command will show you if the line protocol is up or down and the state of LCP. LCP will report in the closed state if it was unable to establish a connection to another router. Following is a sample output from the Sleepy router:

```
Sleepy(config)#show interfaces bri0
BRI0 is up, line protocol is up
Hardware is BRI
  MTU 1500 bytes, BW 64 Kbit, DLY 20000 usec, rely 255/255, load 1/255
  Encapsulation PPP, loopback not set, keepalive not set
 LCP Open
Closed: IPXCP
Listen: CCP
Open: IPCP, CDPCP
<...output omitted...>
```

The `debug ppp authentication` command will show you your authentication as it happens. Following is the output of this command on a router using CHAP authentication:

```
Sleepy#debug ppp authentication
PPP bri0: Send CHAP challenge id=34 to remote
PPP bri0: CHAP challenge from Bashful
PPP bri0: CHAP response received from Bashful
PPP bri0: CHAP response id=34 received from Bashful
PPP bri0: send CHAP success id=34 to remote
```

Frame-Relay

Frame-relay is a scalable WAN solution that is often used as an alternative to leased lines when leased lines prove to be cost prohibitive. With frame-relay, you can have a single serial interface on a router connecting into multiple remote sites through virtual circuits.

Concepts and Terminology

You should be familiar with many terms when working with frame-relay. The following sections introduce you to these terms and their definitions.

Virtual Circuits and Network Design

Your virtual circuits can be either permanent or switched. A permanent virtual circuit (PVC) is always connected and, once up, operates very much like a leased line. A switched virtual circuit (SVC) is more like DDR with ISDN; the circuit is established only when it is needed. Of these two, PVCs are much more common.

DLCI

Circuits are identified by data-link connection identifiers (DLCI). DLCIs are assigned by your provider and are used between your router and the frame-relay provider. In other words, DLCIs are locally significant.

For example, in Figure 10.4, there are three routers named Sleepy, Grumpy, and Bashful. The Sleepy router is connected to a frame-relay provider that provides permanent virtual circuits to both the Bashful and Grumpy routers. DLCI 100 defines the PVC to Bashful, and DLCI 200 defines the PVC to Grumpy. Although it is not shown in the figure, Bashful and Grumpy will likewise have DLCIs to define their PVCs back to Sleepy.

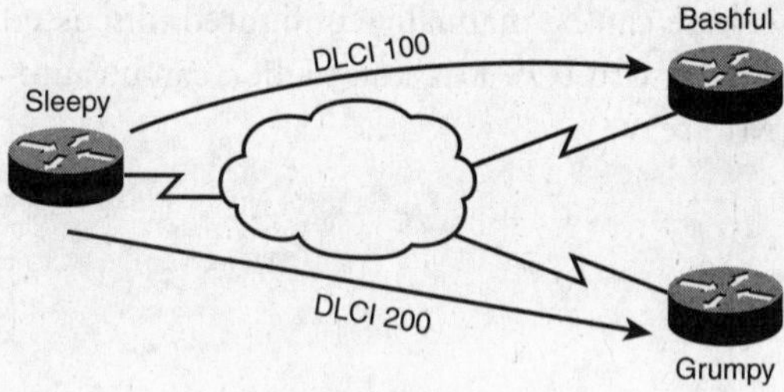

Figure 10.4 Frame-relay PVCs.

As an analogy, DLCIs are like shipping docks. If you work for a shipping company, you might have several ships attached to docks that are each going to a different destination. When you have a package to ship, you just need to take it to the ship headed for the destination. It is the captain's job to know how to reach the destination.

DLCIs are like these docks. They are significant only on your side. You send your packet out the relevant DLCI, and the provider's job is to figure out how to get that frame to its destination.

LMI

Behind-the-scenes is a little helper called the local management interface (LMI) that works as a status enquiry and reporting message. LMI messages are sent between your router and the frame-relay provider's equipment to verify and report on the status of your PVC. The three possible states that your PVC can be in are

- **Active**—Active is good. Active means that everything is up and operational.
- **Inactive**—Inactive is bad. Inactive means that you are connected to your frame-relay provider, but there is a problem with the far-end connection. The problem is most likely between the far-end router and its connection to the frame-relay provider. You should contact your provider to troubleshoot the issue.
- **Deleted**—Deleted is also bad. Deleted means that there is a problem between your router and the frame-relay provider's equipment. You should contact your provider to troubleshoot this issue.

Because of the frequency of LMI messages sent between your router and the frame-relay provider, LMI is also used as a keepalive mechanism. Should your router stop hearing LMI messages it will know that there is a problem with your PVC.

There are three types of LMI. These can be manually configured (discussed later in the configuration section) or, with IOS 11.2 and higher, can be auto-detected. The three types of LMI are

- Cisco
- Ansi
- Q933A

CIR

The committed information rate (CIR) is the guaranteed rate at which you are allowed to pass data for a particular PVC. When ordering a PVC, you will request a local access rate (the bandwidth of the physical connection) and the CIR for a PVC. For example, you may order a T1, which has a local access rate of 1.544Mb, for the Sleepy router and a CIR of 128K for the PVC to Bashful, and a CIR of 512K for Grumpy.

BECN and FECN

Frame-relay is generous with its bandwidth. If there is no congestion on your link, you are allowed to burst above the CIR rate. Any traffic sent above your CIR is marked as being Discard Eligible (DE) and, in the event of congestion, will be dropped.

When congestion does occur, congestion notification messages are sent out to notify both the sending and the receiving routers that congestion has occurred and that they should slow down their transmission rates. A Backward Explicit Congestion Notification (BECN) is sent back to the sender and a Forward Explicit Congestion Notification (FECN) is sent forward to the destination to notify them of congestion.

A BECN message is only sent back to the source when the destination sends a frame back. Because the provider must wait for a message to return in order to set the BECN bit in the frame header, the FECN bit is sent to the destination to request some traffic to be sent back in the reverse direction. Without this, the source might never know that congestion has occurred.

In Figure 10.5, traffic is congested going from the Sleepy router to the Bashful router. A FECN is sent to the Bashful router, and a BECN is sent back to the Sleepy router.

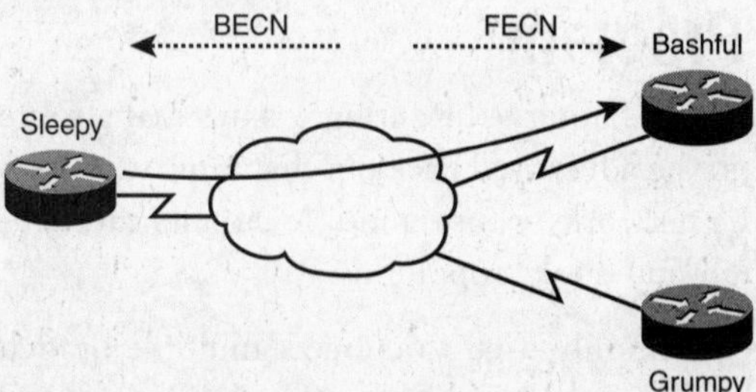

Figure 10.5 Congestion on a Frame-relay network.

Inverse-Arp

Frame-relay needs a mechanism to map layer 3 addresses with layer 2 frame-relay DLCIs. This can be done through a static map command (shown later in the configuration section) or through inverse-arp. Just like Ethernet ARP, inverse-arp is used to map a layer 3 address to a layer 2 address. However, Ethernet ARP maps an IP address to a MAC address and inverse-arp works to map an IP address (or other protocol) to a DLCI.

In Figure 10.6 Sleepy will need a layer 3 to layer 2 map to connect to Bashful, which has IP address 10.0.0.2. Using inverse-arp, Sleepy will automatically create a map telling it to use DLCI 100 to get to IP address 10.0.0.2.

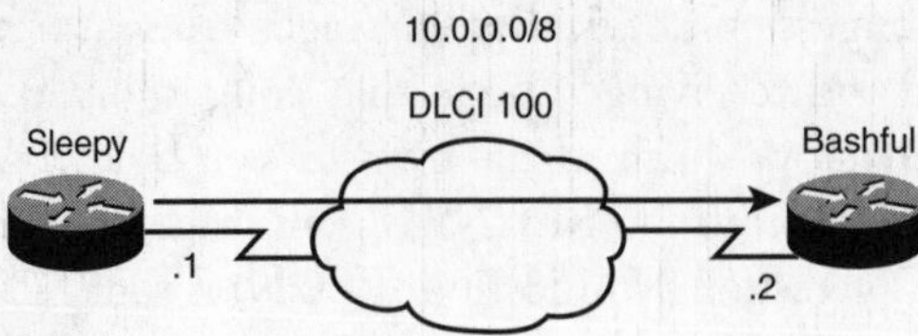

Figure 10.6 Inverse-arp example.

NBMA

Frame-relay is a non-broadcast multi-access (NBMA) medium, which means that broadcast traffic is not allowed to traverse frame-relay traffic. There are ways, however, to circumvent the NBMA nature of frame-relay to allow broadcasts to cross the frame-relay cloud. These are discussed in the configuration section.

The Split Horizon Problem

The split horizon rule (described in Chapter 9, "Routing") states that a route learned on an interface should not be advertised back out that same interface. This poses a problem in NBMA networks where multiple circuits can connect to a single interface in a hub-and-spoke topology.

Hub-and-spoke topologies are commonly used to connect multiple branch offices to a headquarters office. For example, in Figure 10.7, the Bashful and Grumpy routers have circuits to the Sleepy router but not to each other. In this example, Sleepy is operating as the headquarters office. When Grumpy advertises its 13.0.0.0/8 network to the Sleepy router, it is sent into serial 0/0, but the Sleepy router is not allowed to send it back out serial0/0. This causes a problem because serial0/0 is also connected to the Bashful router. As a result, the Bashful router will never know about the 13.0.0.0/8 network.

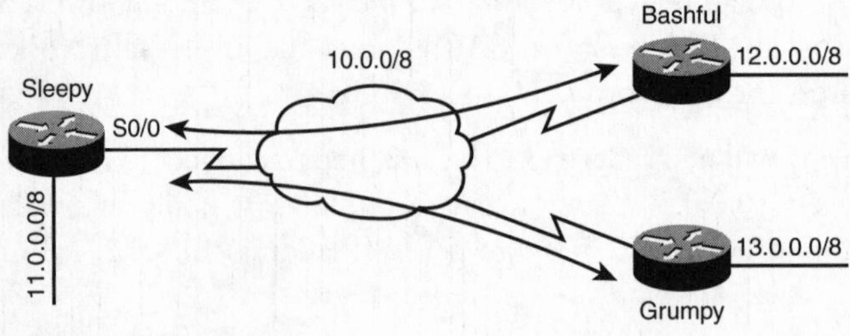

Figure 10.7 Split horizon problem.

You have four options to get around the split-horizon problem:

- Disable split horizon with the `no ip split-horizon` command. If you are not careful, this could create a loop.
- Have a fully meshed topology where every router has a PVC to every other router. This can get expensive.
- Use static routes instead of dynamic routing protocols. This is not a scalable solution.
- Use subinterfaces. This is your best option.

Subinterfaces

A *subinterface* is a subset of an existing physical interface. As far as the router is concerned, the subinterface is a separate interface. By creating subinterfaces, each circuit can be on its own subnet.

There are two types of subinterfaces:

- **point-to-point**—This maps a single IP subnet to a single subinterface and DLCI.
- **multipoint**—This maps multiple DLCIs to a single subnet on a subinterface.

Of these two, only point-to-point subinterfaces address the issue of split horizon. In Figure 10.8, subinterfaces are used on the Sleepy router. Subinterface serial0/0.1 is connected to the Bashful router and subinterface serial0/0.2 is connected to the Grumpy router. Now when Grumpy advertises the 13.0.0.0/8 network to Sleepy, it is sent to the subinterface. Sleepy can forward that information on to the Bashful router because the Bashful router is connected to a different subinterface.

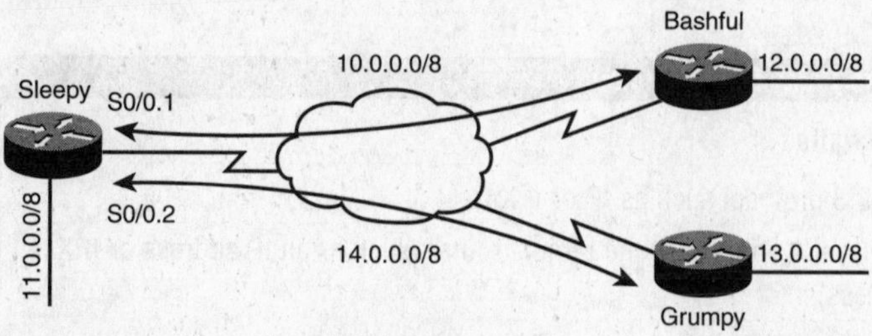

Figure 10.8 Split horizon with subinterfaces.

Configuration

Configuring frame-relay involves the following steps:

- Changing the encapsulation for frame-relay
- Configuring the LMI type (optional for IOS 11.2 or higher)
- Configuring the frame-relay map (optional unless you are using subinterfaces)
- Configuring subinterfaces (optional)
- If using a point-to-point subinterface, configuring your DLCI

To begin, select the frame-relay encapsulation on the interface. There are two types of frame-relay encapsulations: Cisco and IETF. Cisco is the default. The syntax to set your encapsulation is

```
encapsulation frame-relay [ietf]
```

Next, you can configure the LMI type. The three LMI types are Cisco, Ansi, and Q933a. For IOS 11.2 and higher, the LMI type is automatically detected. For earlier IOS versions, enter the following command under the interface:

```
frame-relay lmi-type [cisco ¦ ansi ¦ q933a]
```

The third option, configuring a static frame-relay map, is optional unless you are using subinterfaces. The frame-relay map will map a layer 3 address to a local DLCI. This step is optional because inverse-arp will automatically perform this map for you. The syntax for a frame-relay map is as follows:

```
frame-relay map protocol address dlci [broadcast] [cisco ¦ ietf]
```

Table 10.2 describes each of these parameters.

Table 10.2 Frame-Relay Map Command

Parameter	Description
Protocol	Layer 3 protocol such as IP or IPX.
Address	The layer 3 address of the remote router (such as an IP address or IPX address).
DLCI	Your local DLCI defining your PVC to the remote router.
Broadcast	Optional, this allows for broadcasts and multicasts to traverse your NBMA frame-relay network.
Cisco I IETF	Optional, this allows you to change your frame-relay encapsulation per DLCI.

For example, if you were connected to another router using DLCI 100 and the router had the IP address of 10.0.0.2, your frame-relay map statement would be

```
Router(config-if)#frame-relay map ip 10.0.0.2 100
```

If you want to use a routing protocol across your frame-relay network, you will need to add the keyword `broadcast` to the end of this command. Routing protocols use broadcasts and multicasts by default, and frame-relay does not enable broadcasts and multicasts without the use of the `broadcast` keyword. If you are using inverse-arp to create your maps for you, inverse-arp assumes that you want to use routing protocols and adds the broadcast feature for you.

If you are using a routing protocol in a hub-and-spoke topology, you will probably want to use subinterfaces to avoid the split horizon problem. To configure a subinterface, remove the IP address off the main interface and put it under the subinterface. Configuring a subinterface involves assigning it a number and specifying the type. The following command creates point-to-point subinterface serial0/0.1:

```
Router(config)#interface serial0/0.1 point-to-point
```

To create a multipoint subinterface, enter multipoint instead:

```
Router(config)#interface  serial0/0.1 multipoint
```

After entering one of these commands you will be taken to the subinterface configuration mode where you can enter your IP address:

```
Router(config-subif)#ip address 10.0.0.2 255.0.0.0
```

If you are using a multipoint subinterface, you will need to configure frame-relay maps and you cannot rely on inverse-arp.

If you are using a point-to-point subinterface, you will need to assign a DLCI to the subinterface. This is only for point-to-point subinterfaces; this is not needed on the main interface or on multipoint subinterfaces. To assign a DLCI to a point-to-point subinterface, enter the following command under the subinterface:

```
frame-relay interface-dlci dlci
```

Now let's put the entire configuration together. The following configuration will configure frame-relay for the Sleepy router using a point-to-point subinterface to connect to the Bashful router and a multipoint subinterface to connect to the Grumpy router. (A point-to-point could also have been used, but we'll use multipoint so you can see both methods.) Figure 10.9 shows the topology for the configuration.

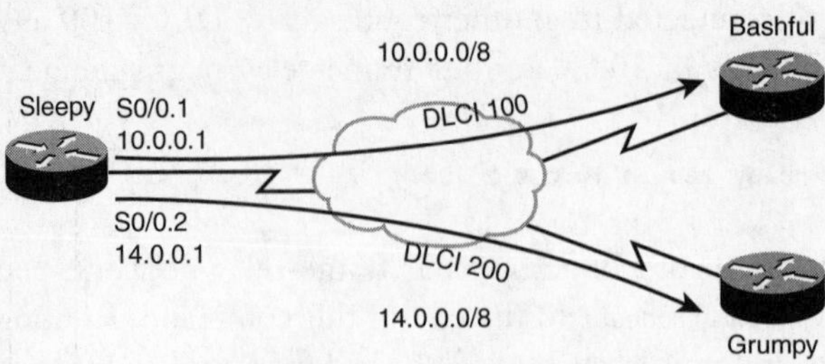

Figure 10.9 Frame-relay configuration.

```
interface serial 0/0
encapsulation frame-relay
!
! Take the IP address off the main interface:
no ip address
!
! Configure the connection to the Bashful router
interface serial 0/0.1 point-to-point
ip address 10.0.0.1 255.0.0.0
frame-relay interface-dlci 100
!
! Configure the connection to the Grumpy router
interface serial 0/0.2 multipoint
ip address 14.0.0.2 255.0.0.0
frame-relay map ip 14.0.0.3 200 broadcast
```

Many engineers like to configure their subinterface number to be the same as the DLCI. For example, if you had a subinterface connected to DLCI 100, your subinterface may be serial 0/0.100.

Verification and Troubleshooting

There are three verification commands and one troubleshooting command you should be familiar with for the exam.

The three commands you can use to verify your configuration are

- `show frame-relay lmi`
- `show frame-relay pvc`
- `show frame-relay map`

Show frame-relay LMI (displayed in the following) will show LMI statistics, including the number of status enquiries sent and received. Because the status enquiries and responses are used as continuous keepalives, these should be incrementing.

```
LMI Statistics for interface Serial1 (Frame Relay DTE) LMI TYPE = ANSI
  Invalid Unnumbered info 0              Invalid Prot Disc 0
  Invalid dummy Call Ref 0               Invalid Msg Type 0
  Invalid Status Message 0               Invalid Lock Shift 0
  Invalid Information ID 0               Invalid Report IE Len 0
  Invalid Report Request 0               Invalid Keep IE Len 0
  Num Status Enq. Sent 140               Num Status msgs Rcvd 139
  Num Update Status Rcvd 0               Num Status Timeouts 0
```

Show frame-relay PVC (displayed in the following) will inform you to the status of your PVC. The status should read ACTIVE. This is also where you will see if your router is receiving BECN and FECN messages.

```
DLCI = 100, DLCI USAGE = LOCAL, PVC STATUS = ACTIVE, INTERFACE = Serial0/0

   input pkts 120          output pkts 70         in bytes 5122
   out bytes 3366          dropped pkts 0         in FECN pkts 0
   in BECN pkts 0          out FECN pkts 0        out BECN pkts 0
   in DE pkts 0            out DE pkts 0
   out bcast pkts 7         out bcast bytes 1366
   pvc create time 1d04h, last time pvc status changed 00:30:32
```

Show frame-relay map (displayed in the following) will show you any static maps configured and maps created by inverse-arp. This command will also show you the status of your PVC.

```
Serial0/0 (up): ip 10.0.0.1 dlci 100(0x64,0x1840), dynamic,
              broadcast,, status defined, active
```

Remember, the three show frame-relay commands and what they do. **Show frame-relay lmi** shows your LMI statistics while **show frame-relay pvc** and **show frame-relay map** will show your PVC status.

For troubleshooting, you can execute the `debug frame-relay lmi` command. This command shows you LMI messages in real-time:

```
Serial 0/0 (out) : StEnq, clock 202121241, myseq 120, mineseen,
119, yourseen 140, DTE up
PVC IE 0x64, length 0x6, dlci 100, status 0, bandwidth 64000
```

ISDN

ISDN is an older technology that is still widely deployed for infrequent low bandwidth transfers or as backup interfaces. If you're like most people, you will find ISDN cumbersome with all the commands and terminology you must learn for the CCNA exam. ISDN stands for Integrated Services Digital Networking, although some would claim jokingly that it stands for "Improvements Subscribers Don't Need" or "It Still Does Nothing." Still, it is on the exam and frequently used in companies for intermittent low bandwidth connections or as a backup to a serial interface.

BRI

ISDN comes in two flavors: Basic Rate Interface (BRI) or Primary Rate Interface (PRI). BRI service is typically used for infrequent low-bandwidth transfers or as backup links, whereas PRI service is typically used for voice communication. A BRI comes with three channels. The first two channels are called Bearer (B) channels that operate at 64K each. These channels are used to pass your video, voice, or data and will use HDLC, PPP, or SLIP encapsulation. The third channel is a Delta (D) channel (sometimes called a Data channel), which operates at 16K. This D channel is used for out-of-band signaling using the Link Access Procedure over D (LAPD) signaling protocol.

The ISDN D channel operates at layers 1 through 3 of the OSI model. ITU has defined the Q.921 standard for layer 2 signaling to connect the ISDN router to the ISDN switch and Q.931 for layer 3 operation between the two ISDN endpoints (such as call setup, release messages, and so on).

Make sure you know that a BRI uses two B channels at 64K each and one D channel at 16K. Remember, the B channel is used to pass data, voice, or video, while all control traffic goes across the D channel using LAPD for out-of-band signaling.

PRI

PRI service varies depending on where you are in the world. The United States, Canada, and Japan all use a PRI service that has 23 B channels and 1 D channel, which all operate at 64K. In the rest of the world, PRI service has 30 B channels and 1 D channel. Extra bits are added for framing to make the total bandwidth of a US/Canada/Japan PRI 1.544MB, whereas the rest of the world uses a PRI of 2.048MB.

Reference Points and Functional Devices

ISDN contains a number of reference points and functional devices. Reference points designate the type of link, and functions define the type of device. Figure 10.10 illustrates the various reference points and functions.

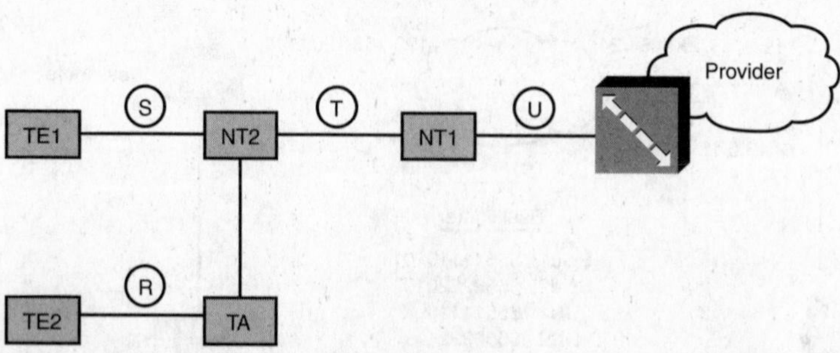

Figure 10.10 Reference points and functional devices.

A TE1 device is a device that is ISDN ready, whereas a TE2 device is not ISDN ready. It makes sense, then, that for a TE2 device to connect to an ISDN network, it must first use a terminal adapter (TA) to make it ISDN ready. As mentioned earlier, an ISDN device can either have an S/T interface or a U interface. If you are using a device with an S/T interface, you will need to use an external NT1. In some countries, you do not have a choice what type of interface you can use. For example, in the United States, you must have a U interface. If you are in England, you must use an S/T interface.

For those readers in the United States, think 'U' for U.S.A. You must have a U interface to connect to your provider.

BRI Configuration

Refer to Figure 10.11 for the following explanation on ISDN configuration.

There are three steps to configuring ISDN BRI service:

- Configure basic connectivity.
- Configure DDR (optional).
- Configure PPP and authentication (optional).

Configuring Basic Connectivity

The first step to configuring basic connectivity is to define the ISDN switch type used by your provider. Your provider will give you this information. Common switch types in the United States include National ISDN, Lucent (AT&T) 5ESS, and DMS-100. The command to set your switch type is

```
isdn switch-type switch-type
```

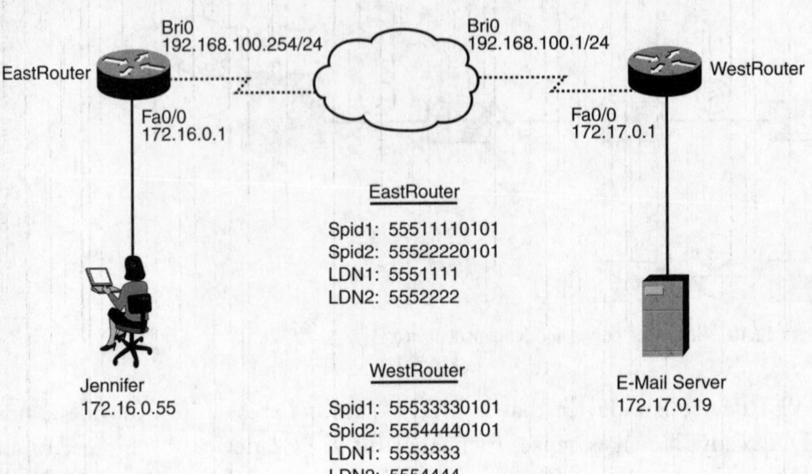

Figure 10.11 ISDN example.

The command can be entered under the BRI interface or in global configuration. If set globally, it will affect all interfaces. If set under the interface, it will only affect that individual interface. For example, to set the ISDN switch type to National ISDN, the Cisco IOS keyword is `basic-ni`:

```
EastRouter(config)#isdn switch-type basic-ni
```

DMS-100 and National ISDN switches require you to also configure service profile identifiers (SPIDs). A SPID is a number provided by your provider that identifies your router to the ISDN switch and is used in provisioning services such as voice or caller ID. You will be assigned one SPID for each B channel. Configure SPIDs under the interface with the following command:

```
isdn spid1 spid-number [local-dial-number]
```

The local dial number (LDN) is your local phone number. For example, to configure the SPIDs on the East router shown in Figure 10.11, type the following:

```
EastRouter(config)#interface bri0
EastRouter(config-if)#isdn spid1 55511110101 5551111
EastRouter(config-if)#isdn spid2 55522220101 5552222
```

Once your switch type and SPIDs are configured, you will need to configure your router with the phone number to dial the remote site. Just as frame-relay needs to map the next hop router to a DLCI, and Ethernet needs to map an IP address to a MAC address, ISDN needs a map as well to correlate the next hop router to a phone number. The interface level command to create this map is as follows:

```
dialer map <protocol> <address> <dial-string>
```

For example, to configure the East router with a dialer map to the West router, the configuration would be

```
EastRouter(config-if)#dialer map ip 192.168.100.1 5553333
```

Configuring DDR

Optionally, you might also configure dial-on-demand routing (DDR). DDR allows you to define what will cause ISDN to place a phone call. For example, given Figure 10.11, the user Jennifer might send an email to the email server at 172.17.0.19. On the East router, you would configure DDR to dial the connection to the West router any time an email attempts to go out the BRI interface. Once the interface is up, however, all traffic is allowed to pass.

Configuring DDR is a three step process:

1. Configure a route to the remote network.
2. Configure what is considered interesting traffic.
3. Configure your idle timeout.

The first step is to configure a route to the remote network. Although it is possible to run routing protocols over an ISDN connection, this is a bad idea; you have a limited amount of bandwidth and do not want the extra overhead of routing protocol traffic. Instead, you will want to use a static route. Here is the static route syntax for the East router:

```
EastRouter(config)#ip route 172.17.0.0 255.255.0.0 192.168.100.1
```

Likewise, the West router will also need a static route so that traffic knows how to get back to Jennifer's network:

```
WestRouter(config)#ip route 172.16.0.0 255.255.0.0
192.168.100.254
```

If you are using routing protocols on your router, you will want to ensure that routing protocol traffic does not traverse your ISDN link. To do this, configure your BRI interfaces to be passive. A passive interface will not send any routing updates out an interface. To configure your BRI interface to be passive, go into your router process and use the `passive-interface` command. For example, if the East router is running RIP, the configuration would be

```
EastRouter(config)#router rip
EastRouter(config-router)#passive-interface bri0
```

Once the route is configured, the next step is to define your interesting traffic. *Interesting traffic* is defined as the type of traffic that is considered important, or interesting, enough to dial the remote site.

You use the `dialer-list` command to define your interesting traffic and the `dialer-group` command to apply it to an interface. To specify any IP traffic as interesting, type the following global configuration command:

```
EastRouter(config)#dialer-list 1 protocol ip permit
```

The number of the list is arbitrary, but it must match the number you specify when applying the list on the interface with the `dialer-group` command:

```
EastRouter(config-if)#dialer-group 1
```

You can also use an access-list if you want to be more specific in defining your interesting traffic. For example, if we wanted only SMTP email traffic from Jennifer's computer to the email server, we could type the following access-list and associate it with a dialer-list:

```
EastRouter(config)#access-list 100 permit tcp host 172.16.0.55
host 172.17.0.19 eq smtp
EastRouter(config)#dialer-list 1 protocol ip list 100
EastRouter(config)#interface bri0
EastRouter(config-if)#dialer-group 1
```

At this point, you have defined what will bring up the line but not what will bring down the connection. To define what will terminate your ISDN call, enter the `dialer idle-timeout` command under the interface. This command lets you set the number of seconds that must transpire with no interesting traffic on the line to bring down the call. Following is the configuration you would enter to set this timer to 30 seconds:

```
EastRouter(config-if)#dialer idle-timeout 30
```

Configuring PPP and Authentication

Configuring PPP and authentication was discussed earlier. The configuration for the East router is as follows:

```
EastRouter(config)#username WestRouter password ExamCram2
EastRouter(config)#interface bri0
EastRouter(config-if)#encapsulation ppp
EastRouter(config-if)#ppp authentication chap
```

There is one additional step you must take, however, when configuring CHAP authentication over ISDN. In the dialer map command, you must enter the hostname of the remote router:

```
EastRouter(config-if)#dialer map ip 192.168.100.1 name WestRouter
5553333
```

Putting It All Together

Here is the final configuration for the East router:

```
!
isdn switch-type basic-ni
dialer-list 1 protocol ip list 100
access-list 100 permit tcp host 172.16.0.55 host 172.17.0.19 eq
smtp
hostname EastRouter
username WestRouter password cisco
!
interface bri0
 ip address 192.168.100.254 255.255.255.0
 encapsulation ppp
 ppp authentication chap
 dialer map ip 192.168.100.1 name WestRouter 5553333
 isdn spid1 55511110101 5551111
 isdn spid2 55522220101 5552222
 dialer idle-timeout 30
 dialer-group 1
!
interface FastEthernet0/0
 ip address 172.16.0.1 255.255.0.0
!
ip route 172.17.0.0 255.255.0.0 192.168.100.1
router rip
 network 172.16.0.0
 network 192.168.100.0
 passive-interface bri0
```

The configuration for the West router is as follows:

```
!
isdn switch-type basic-ni
dialer-list 1 protocol ip permit
hostname WestRouter
username EastRouter password cisco
!
interface bri0
 ip address 192.168.100.1 255.255.255.0
 encapsulation ppp
 ppp authentication chap
 dialer map ip 192.168.100.254 name EastRouter 5551111
 isdn spid1 55533330101 5553333
 isdn spid2 55544440101 5554444
 dialer idle-timeout 30
 dialer-group 1
!
interface FastEthernet0/0
 ip address 172.17.0.1 255.255.0.0
!
ip route 172.16.0.0 255.255.0.0 192.168.100.254
router rip
 network 172.17.0.0
 network 192.168.100.0
 passive-interface bri0
```

Table 10.3 defines the commands used in this section.

Table 10.3 ISDN BRI Commands

Command	Description
Isdn switch-type	Defines the switch-type of your provider.
Isdn spid1, isdn spid2	Used on the interface, this command defines the SPIDs for your two B channels.
Dialer map	Maps the layer 3 address of your neighboring router to its phone number.
Dialer-list	Defines interesting traffic.
Dialer-group	Applies your dialer-list on an interface.
Dialer idle-timeout	Defines how long the router will wait to drop the connection when it stops hearing interesting traffic.

PRI Commands

The steps to configure your PRI are as follows:

1. Configure the switch-type.
2. Configure the timeslots.
3. Configure framing.
4. Configure line encoding.
5. Configure clocking.
6. Configure the D channel.

First, configure the PRI switch type used by your provider:

```
isdn switch-type switch-type
```

Next, configure the timeslots. In the United States, Canada, and Japan, you will configure the T1 controller for 24 timeslots. In the rest of the world, you will configure 30 timeslots on an E1 controller.

```
control {t1 ¦ e1} slot/type
 pri-group timeslots {1-24 ¦ 1-30}
```

Next, configure the framing and line encoding, which define how your data will be transmitted digitally across the wire. T1 controllers typically use super framing (SF) or extended super framing (ESF) with bipolar eight zero substitution (B8ZS) or alternate mark inversion (AMI) line encoding. E1 controllers typically use CRC4 framing and high-density bipolar three zeros

(HDB3) encoding. The commands to configure framing and line encoding are as follows:

```
framing {esf ¦ ef ¦ crc4 ¦ no-crc4 ¦ australia}
linecode {ami ¦ b8zs ¦ hdb3}
```

Next, configure the source of your clocking. The default is to use the clocking provided on the line from a CSU/DSU, but clocking can also be internal or you can loop the clocking from the Rx wire and use it for the Tx wire. The syntax to change your clocking is

```
clocking {line ¦ internal ¦ loop-timed}
```

Finally, configure the D channel as you would with the ISDN BRI. On the D channel, put your IP address and any other optional configuration you want, such as PPP encapsulation. The D channel is timeslot 23 on a T1 and timeslot 15 on an E1. To access timeslot 23 on a T1 connected to your serial0/0 interface, enter the following global configuration command:

```
interface serial0/0:23
```

To access timeslot 15 on an E1 connected to your serial0/0 interface, enter the following global configuration command:

```
interface serial0/0:15
```

Putting this all together, the complete configuration for a PRI on a T1 might look as follows:

```
isdn switch-type primary-ni
interface controller t1 1/0
 pri-group timeslots 1-24
 framing esf
 linecode b8zs
 clocking line
interface serial0/0:23
 ip address 10.0.0.1 255.0.0.0
 encapsulation ppp
```

Exam Prep Questions

1. Frame-relay NBMA networks present problems with split-horizon if the topology is not a full mesh. What could you do to get around issues of split-horizon in frame-relay networks? Select the best answer.

   ❍ A. Enable the command `split-horizon frame-relay` on each serial interface.

   ❍ B. Create subinterfaces and put each DLCI on its own subinterface.

   ❍ C. Disable routing protocols on frame-relay interfaces.

   ❍ D. Create static routes on your spoke routers.

2. What is the name of the ISDN function that has a U reference point and a T reference point?

   ❍ A. NT1

   ❍ B. NT2

   ❍ C. TE1

   ❍ D. TE2

3. Which of the following are components of the LCP phase of PPP? Select all that apply.

   ❑ A. Compression

   ❑ B. Authentication

   ❑ C. QoS

   ❑ D. Multilink

4. What are the three frame-relay LMI types? Select three.

   ❑ A. HDLC

   ❑ B. Cisco

   ❑ C. Q933A

   ❑ D. IETF

   ❑ E. ANSI

5. Given the exhibit, what is the correct syntax for a dialer map on the Lakers router to get to the Bulls router?

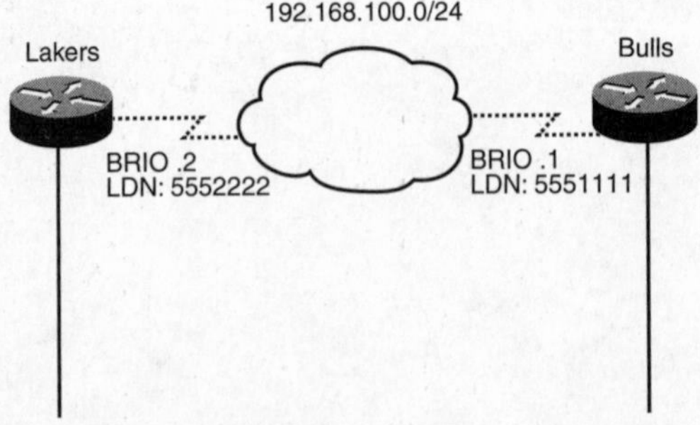

   ❍ A. Dialer map ip 192.168.100.1 5551111

   ❍ B. Dialer map 192.168.100.1 5551111

   ❍ C. Dialer map ip 192.168.100.1 5552222

   ❍ D. Dialer map 192.168.100.1 5552222

6. Examine the two router configurations below. Why is the BRI interface not coming up?

RouterA:

```
hostname RouterA
username Routerb password cisco
dialer-list 1 protocol ip permit
isdn switch-type basic-ni
!
interface bri0/0
 encapsulation ppp
 ppp authentication chap
 ip address 10.0.0.1 255.0.0.0
 dialer map ip 10.0.0.2 5553333
 isdn spid1 55511110101 5551111
 isdn spid2 55522220101 5552222
 dialer idle-timeout 30
 dialer-group 1
!
ip route 172.16.0.0 255.255.0.0 10.0.0.2
```

RouterB:

```
hostname RouterB
username RouterA password cisco
dialer-list 1 protocol ip permit
isdn switch-type basic-ni
!
interface bri0/0
 encapsulation ppp
 ppp authentication chap
 ip address 10.0.0.2 255.0.0.0
 dialer map ip 10.0.0.1 5551111
 isdn spid1 55533330101 5553333
 isdn spid2 55544440101 5554444
 dialer idle-timeout 30
 dialer-group 1
!
ip route 172.17.0.0 255.255.0.0 10.0.0.1
```

❍ A. The static routes are incorrect.

❍ B. Both routers are missing a second dialer map statement.

❍ C. The dialer list statements will not permit any traffic from passing.

❍ D. There is a problem with the PPP CHAP configuration.

7. Given the following configurations, why is the router not routing traffic?

```
router rip
 network 10.0.0.0
 network 11.0.0.0
!
interface fastethernet0/0
 ip address 10.0.0.1 255.0.0.0
!
interface serial0/0
 ip address 11.0.0.1 255.0.0.0
 encapsulation frame-relay
 frame-relay map ip 11.0.0.2 255.0.0.0
```

❍ A. RIP configuration is incorrect.

❍ B. IP addresses are incorrect.

❍ C. The frame-relay map statement is incorrect.

❍ D. Router is missing a static route statement.

8. What command is missing from the following configuration?

```
hostname RouterA
username RouterB password cisco
isdn switch-type basic-ni
dialer-list 1 protocol ip list 101
access-list 101 permit tcp any host 172.16.0.5 eq 25
!
interface bri0/0
 ip address 10.32.0.19 255.248.0.0
 encapsulation ppp
 ppp authentication chap
 dialer idle-timeout 30
 isdn spid1 55511110101 5551111
 isdn spid2 55522220101 5552222
 dialer map ip 10.32.0.20 5553333
!
ip route 172.16.0.0 255.255.0.0 10.32.0.20
```

❍ A. The dialer-group command

❍ B. A second dialer map command

❍ C. Routing protocol configuration

❍ D. A permit any statement in the access-list

9. You have a Cisco router set to the default encapsulation. You connect it to a Juniper router running HDLC encapsulation. Why are the two routers unable to communicate?

❍ A. The default encapsulation on the Cisco router is PPP. You must change it to HDLC.

❍ B. The default encapsulation on the Cisco router is IETF. You must change it to HDLC.

❍ C. Cisco's HDLC implementation is proprietary and is therefore incompatible with other vendor's HDLC implementations.

❍ D. Cisco routers can only connect to other Cisco routers. You must replace the Juniper router with a Cisco router.

10. Assuming no SPIDs or PPP encapsulation, what are the minimum commands to bring up an ISDN line? Select all that apply.
    - ❑ A. Dialer map
    - ❑ B. Dialer list
    - ❑ C. IP address
    - ❑ D. Idle-timeout
    - ❑ E. Switch type
11. What commands can you enter to check the state of your frame-relay PVC? Select all that apply.
    - ❑ A. show frame-relay lmi
    - ❑ B. show frame-relay pvc
    - ❑ C. show frame-relay map
    - ❑ D. show frame-relay status
    - ❑ E. show frame-relay
12. Given the following configuration, why doesn't the ISDN line come up?

```
hostname RouterA
username RouterB password cisco
isdn switch-type basic-ni
dialer-list 2 protocol ip list 110
access-list 110 deny tcp 172.16.0.0 0.0.255.255 172.17.0.0
     0.0.255.255 eq 80
access-list 110 deny tcp 172.16.0.0 0.0.255.255 172.17.0.0
     0.0.255.255 eq 443
access-list 110 deny tcp 172.16.0.0 0.0.255.255 172.17.0.0
     0.0.255.255 eq 25
!
interface bri0/0
 ip address 192.168.55.17 255.255.255.252
 encapsulation ppp
 ppp authentication chap
 isdn spid1 55511110101 5551111
 isdn spid2 55522220101 5552222
 dialer map ip 192.168.55.18 5553333
 dialer-group 2
 dialer idle-timeout 30
!
interface fastethernet0/0
 ip address 172.16.0.1 255.255.0.0
!
router rip
 network 192.168.55.0
 network 172.16.0.0
 passive-interface bri0/0
!
ip route 172.17.0.0 255.255.0.0 192.168.55.18
```

   - ❍ A. You should disable RIP. Routing protocols should not be run on routers with BRI interfaces.
   - ❍ B. The dialer map command is incorrect. It is mapped to a network address and not a valid IP address.
   - ❍ C. The PPP configuration is incorrect. Authentication will fail and will not bring up the line.
   - ❍ D. The dialer list will not allow any traffic to ever bring up a line. This would keep the line down indefinitely.
   - ❍ E. The dialer list is not applied on the interface.

Answers to Exam Prep Questions

1. Answer B is correct. You should create a subinterface for each DLCI. This will require a different subnet on each subinterface, but you resolve split-horizon issues. Answer A is incorrect because there is not a 'split-horizon frame-relay' command. Answers C and D would technically resolve your problem, but they would limit the functionality of your routers. Therefore, answers C and D are not the best answers.

2. Answer A is correct. The NT1 connects the U reference point to the telco and connects the T reference point to the NT2, or, if the NT2 is built into the TE1, the TE1. The NT2 has the S and T reference points, so answer B is wrong. The TE1 has an S reference point, so answer C is wrong. Answer D is wrong because the TE2 has an R reference point connecting it to the TA.

3. Answers A, B, and D are all correct. The LCP phase is responsible for the initial link-setup and negotiating options such as compression, callback, multilink, and authentication. Answer C is incorrect because this not a component of LCP.

4. Answers B, C, and E are correct. Answer A is incorrect because HDLC is a wide area network layer 2 encapsulation, not a frame-relay LMI type. Answer D is incorrect because IETF is a frame-relay encapsulation type, not a frame-relay LMI type.

5. Answer A is correct. The syntax for a dialer map is dialer map <protocol> <address> <dial string>. Dial string can also be called local dial number (ldn) or phone number. Answer B is incorrect because the IP keyword is missing. Answer C is incorrect because it is the wrong LDN. Answer D is incorrect because the IP keyword is missing, and it has the wrong LDN.

6. Answer D is correct. The CHAP configuration on RouterA is using 'Routerb' in the username command, but this should be 'RouterB' (the hostname of RouterB). The username is case sensitive and must match the hostname of the router you are connecting to. If PPP authentication fails, LCP will report a closed state and the link will never be established. Answer A is incorrect because the static routes are correct. Answer B is incorrect because having a single dialer map statement is sufficient. Answer C is incorrect because the dialer list statements will permit all traffic to pass.

7. Answer C is correct. If you were not using routing protocols, the frame-relay map statement would be correct. However, because you are using a router protocol, you must have the broadcast keyword at the end in order for routing protocols to work. Answer A is incorrect because RIP is configured correctly. Answer B is incorrect because the IP addresses are correct. Answer D is incorrect because the router is running RIP and does not need a static route.

8. Answer A is correct. Under the interface should be the command `'dialer-group 1'`. This applies the dialer list created under global configuration. Answer B is incorrect because a single dialer map statement will suffice. Answer C is incorrect because the configuration uses a static route, so routing protocol configuration is not necessary. Answer D is incorrect because the access-list has at least one permit statement.

9. Answer C is correct. Cisco's HDLC contains a proprietary data field that makes it incompatible with other vendor's implementation of HDLC. Answer A and B are incorrect because the default encapsulation is HDLC, not PPP or IETF. Although answer D would make some Cisco salespeople happy, answer D is not the correct answer either. Cisco can communicate with other vendors but not with the default encapsulation.

10. Answers A, C, and E are correct. The three minimal commands are dialer map, ip address, and isdn switch-type. Answer B is incorrect because dialer list is needed only when configuring DDR. Answer D is incorrect because this signifies when to bring down the line when using DDR and is not necessary to bring the line up.

11. Answers B and C are correct. Answer A is incorrect because `show frame-relay lmi` shows your LMI statistics and not your PVC status. Answers D and E are incorrect because these are invalid commands.

12. Answer D is correct. The dialer list, which is used to specify the interesting traffic to bring up a line, is linked to access-list 110. Access-list 110, however, is missing a permit statement and therefore will never bring up the ISDN interface. Answer A is incorrect because you can run RIP on an ISDN router. In this example, a passive interface is configured along with a static route to minimize the overhead on the ISDN interface. Answer B is incorrect because the dialer map is mapped to a valid IP address. Answer C is incorrect because the CHAP configuration is correct. Finally, answer E is incorrect because dialer list 2 is applied on the interface with the command `'dialer-group 2'`.

Advanced IP Concepts

Terms You'll Need to Understand

✓ VLSM
✓ Classful and Classless
✓ Route Summarization
✓ Contiguous
✓ Longest Match
✓ NAT, PAT, and Overload

Techniques You'll Need to Master

✓ Advanced Subnetting
✓ IP Route Table Interpretation
✓ Predicting the Routing Decision
✓ Route Summarization
✓ Configuring NAT and PAT

Introduction

This chapter looks at the relationship between the IP address and subnet mask in more detail, as well as how it can be manipulated for more efficient network functionality. The Network Address Translation/Port Address Translation service is also explained and sample configurations are demonstrated.

VLSM

Variable Length Subnet Masking or VLSM (RFC 1812) can be defined as the capability to apply more than one subnet mask to a given class of addresses throughout a routed system. Although this is common practice in modern networks, there was a time when this was impossible because the routing protocols in use could not support it. RIP and IGRP, as you might recall, do not include the subnet mask of advertised networks in their routing updates; therefore, they cannot publish the existence of more than one mask length. Only classless routing protocols—EIGRP, OSPF, RIPv2, IS-IS, and BGP—include the subnet mask for the networks they advertise in their routing updates and thus publish a level of detail that makes VLSM possible.

The main push for VLSM came from the need to make networks the right size.

Subnetting logically creates the appropriately-sized networks, but without the capability for routing protocols to advertise the existence of both a /26 and a /30 network within the same system. For example, networks were confined to using only /26 masks throughout the system. The use of VLSM has two main advantages that are closely linked:

- It makes network addressing more efficient.
- Provides the capability to perform route summarization (discussed in the next section).

Know the definition of VLSM and its two main advantages.

An illustration of the need for VLSM is shown in Figure 11.1.

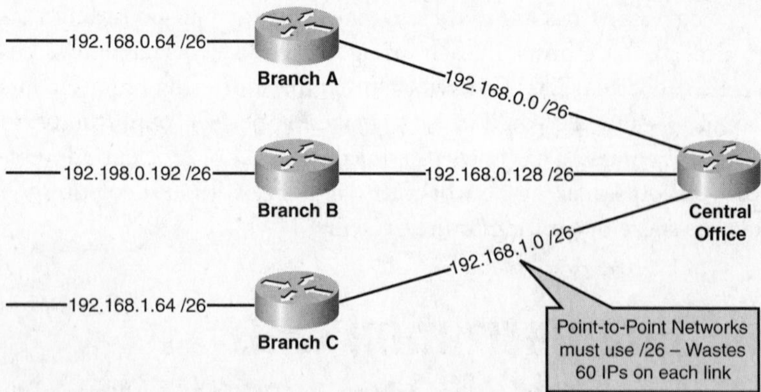

Figure 11.1 Inefficient addressing without VLSM.

The diagram shows several branch offices using subnetted Class C (/26) addresses that provide each branch with 62 possible host IPs. The branches are connected to the central office via point-to-point WAN links. The ideal mask to use for such a link is /30 because it provides only 2 hosts, one for each end of the link. The problem arises when the routing protocols are configured: Prior to VLSM, the /30 networks could not be used because the /26 networks existed in the same system and the classful routing protocols could only advertise one mask per class of address. All networks, including the little /30 links, had to use the same mask of /26. This wastes 60 IP addresses on each WAN link.

With the implementation of VLSM-capable routing protocols, we can deploy a /30 mask on the point-to-point links, and the routing protocols can advertise them as /30s along with the /26s in the branches because the subnet mask for each network is included in the routing updates. Figure 11.2 illustrates the preferred, optimized addressing scheme that takes advantage of VLSM.

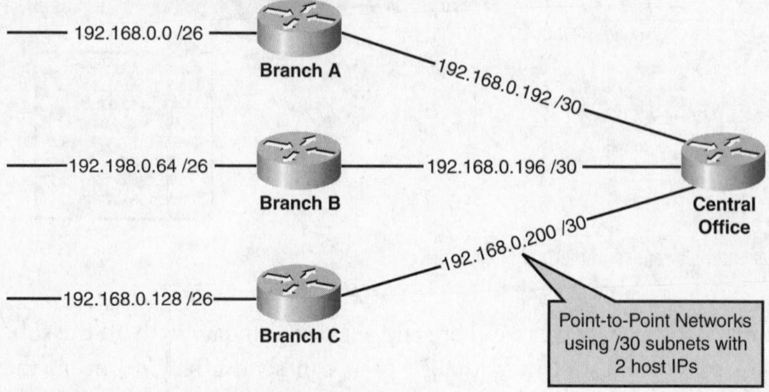

Figure 11.2 Optimized addressing using VLSM.

Note that using VLSM has allowed us to make the point-to-point link networks the ideal size (two hosts on each) using /30 masks. This has allowed us to use a single subnetted Class C network for all the addressing requirements in this scenario—and as you'll see, it makes a perfect opportunity to summarize these routes. This is what is meant by "more efficient addressing"—in other words, making networks the right size without depleting the limited address space or limiting future growth.

Route Summarization

If subnetting is the process of lengthening the mask to create multiple smaller subnets from a single larger network, route summarization can be described as shortening the mask to include several smaller networks into one larger network address. As the network grows large, the number of individual networks listed in the IP route table becomes too big for routers to handle effectively. They get slower, drop packets, and even crash. This, of course, is an undesirable state of affairs. With more than 160,000 routes (at the time of this writing, anyway) known to major Internet routers, some way to reduce the number of entries is not only desirable, but also critical.

In the previous VLSM example, all the subnets for the branches and the WAN links were created from the 192.168.0.0 /24 Class C network. If we take that diagram and put it into context, we can see how route summarization can reduce the number of entries in the route table, as shown in Figure 11.3.

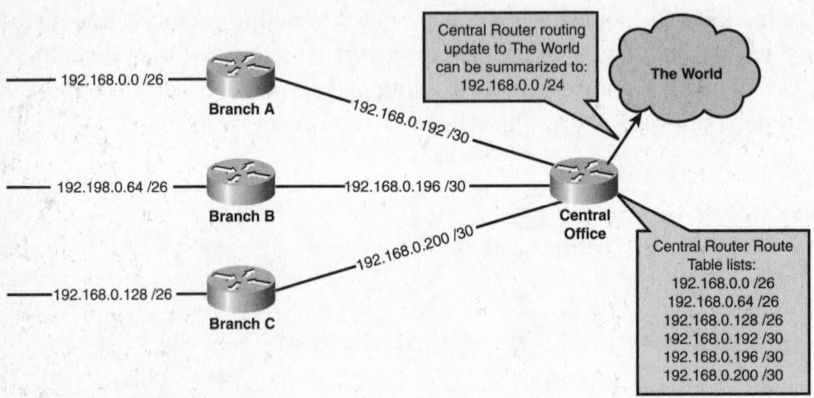

Figure 11.3 Simple route summarization example.

The Central Office router can either send a routing update with all the subnets it knows about listed individually, or it can send a single line in the update that essentially says, "Send anything that starts with 192.168.0 to me." Both methods work; the issue is one of scalability. No router will ever collapse under the load of advertising six subnets, but make it six thousand subnets and it makes a huge difference in performance if you summarize as much as possible.

Route summarization takes a set of contiguous networks or subnets and groups them together using a shorter subnet mask. The advantages of summarization are that it reduces the number of entries in the route table, which reduces load on the router and network overhead, and hides instability in the system behind the summary, which remains valid even if summarized networks are unavailable.

The word "contiguous" sometimes confuses people. It is not a typo of "continuous"; the word means "adjacent or adjoining." For example, when we make subnets using a 16 increment, the first four NetIDs are .0, .16, .32, and .48. Those four subnets are contiguous because they are adjacent to each other. If we take the last four subnets from that same increment, .192, .208, .224, and .240, they are contiguous with each other, but not with the first four—there are a bunch of subnets between the two sets.

Know the definition and advantages of route summarization.

Summarization Guidelines

It is important to follow a few rules and guidelines when summarizing. Serious routing problems will happen otherwise—such as routers advertising networks inaccurately and possibly duplicating other routers' advertisements, sub-optimal or even totally incorrect routing, and severe data loss.

The first rule is to design your networks with summarization in mind, even if you don't need it yet. This means that you will group contiguous subnets together behind the router that will summarize them—you do not want to have some subnets from a summarized group behind some other router. The summary is essentially saying, "I own the networks represented by this summary; send any traffic for them through me." If the network does not exist behind the summarizing router, traffic will be misrouted. Advance planning, including making plenty of room for future growth, will give you a solid, scalable network design that readily lends itself to summarizing. Figure 11.4 shows a badly designed network that will be almost impossible to summarize because the subnets are discontiguous, with individual subnets scattered all over the system.

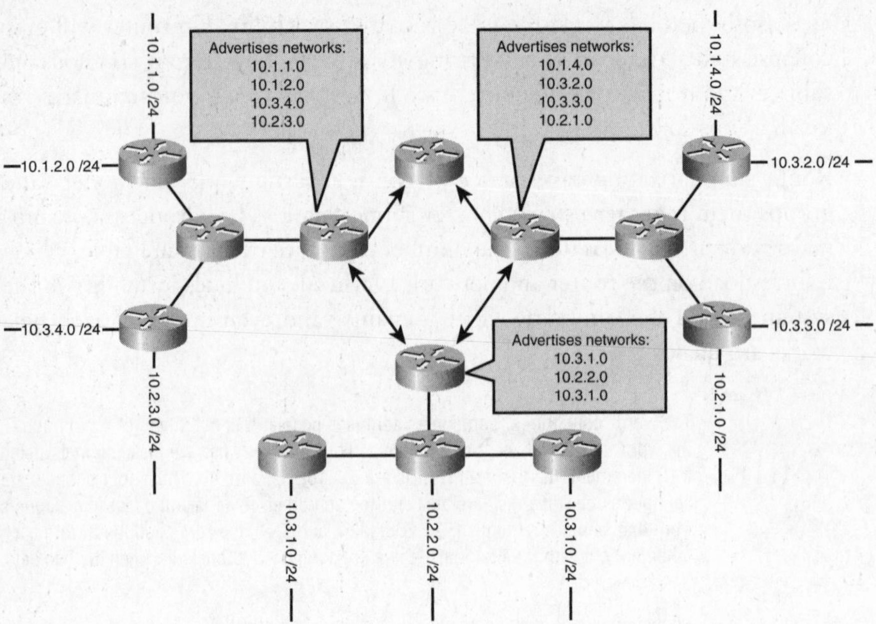

Figure 11.4 Poor planning prevents proper performance.

The second rule is to summarize into the core of your network. The core is where the bigger, faster, busier routers are—like the Central Office router in the previous example. These routers have the job of dealing with high volumes of traffic headed for all different areas of the network, so we do not want to burden them with big, highly detailed route tables. The further you get from the core, the more detail the routers need to get traffic to the correct destination network. It's much like using a map to drive to a friend's house; you don't need a great deal of detail when you are on the highway, but when you get into the residential areas, you need to know very precise information if you have a hope of finding the place.

Figure 11.5 illustrates the same network after your friendly neighborhood Cisco Certified Internetwork Expert has spent the afternoon readdressing the network and configuring summarization. This network will scale beautifully and have minimal performance issues (at least because of route table and routing update overhead).

Following these rules will give you one of the additional benefits of summarization as well: hiding instability in the summarized networks. Let's say that one of the branches is having serious spanning-tree problems because an MCP was allowed to configure a Cisco switch. (This is actually a felony in some states.) That route could be "flapping"—up, down, up, down—as spanning-tree wreaks havoc with your network. The router will be doing its job, sending out updates every time the route flaps. If we were not summarizing, those flapping messages would propagate through the entire corporate system, putting a totally unnecessary and performance-robbing load on the routers. Once you summarize, the summary is stable: It can't flap because it is not a real network. It's just like a spokesperson at a press conference: "The rumors of a fire at the Springfield plant have had no impact on production whatsoever." Meanwhile, the Springfield plant could be a charred hulk. The summary is still valid, and traffic will still be sent to the router connected to the flapping network. This keeps people from asking any more questions about the Springfield fire… however, if someone were to send a shipment to Springfield, it would be hastily redirected to another site (or dropped). All we have done is hide the problem from the rest of the world, so we don't flood the Net with rapid-fire routing updates.

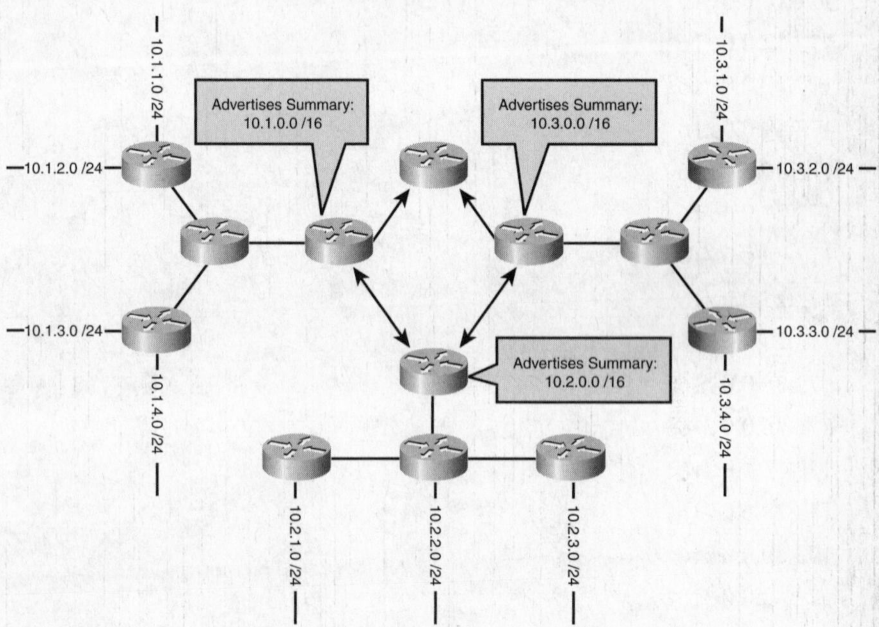

Figure 11.5 Proper planning prevents poor performance.

Determining Summary Addresses

When using classless routing protocols, creating summary addresses is a totally manual process. Classful routing protocols perform automatic summarization, but that is not as fancy as it sounds. They simply treat any subnet as the classful address from which it was created, which works if your networks are built with this in mind; however, in reality that is too simplistic and real networks need more customized summarization. The upshot of all this is that you need to understand how to determine the summary address given a set of networks to be summarized, and you also need to be able to figure out if a particular network is included in a given summary.

Remember that summarization is exactly the opposite of subnetting; in fact, another term for summarization is supernetting. (You might also see it called aggregation.) When we subnet, we lengthen the mask, doubling the number of networks each time we add an extra bit to the mask. Supernetting does the opposite: For each bit we retract or shorten the mask, we combine networks into groups that follow the binary increment numbers.

To illustrate this, let's look at the private Class B address space. These networks are listed as follows:

172.16.0.0 /16

172.17.0.0 /16

172.18.0.0 /16

172.19.0.0 /16

172.20.0.0 /16

172.21.0.0 /16

172.22.0.0 /16

172.23.0.0 /16

172.24.0.0 /16

172.25.0.0 /16

172.26.0.0 /16

172.27.0.0 /16

172.28.0.0 /16

172.29.0.0 /16

172.30.0.0 /16

172.31.0.0 /16

If you look carefully, you will notice that the range of networks is identified in the second octet. The octet where the range is happening is referred to as the interesting octet. This is your first clue where to begin your summarization.

The next step is to figure out what the binary values of the network's range are. The binary values for the interesting octet are shown in Figure 11.6.

16 = 0 0 0 1 0 0 0 0

17 = 0 0 0 1 0 0 0 1

18 = 0 0 0 1 0 0 1 0

19 = 0 0 0 1 0 0 1 1

20 = 0 0 0 1 0 1 0 0

21 = 0 0 0 1 0 1 0 1

22 = 0 0 0 1 0 1 1 0

23 = 0 0 0 1 0 1 1 1

24 = 0 0 0 1 1 0 0 0

25 = 0 0 0 1 1 0 0 1

26 = 0 0 0 1 1 0 1 0

27 = 0 0 0 1 1 0 1 1

28 = 0 0 0 1 1 1 0 0

29 = 0 0 0 1 1 1 0 1

30 = 0 0 0 1 1 1 1 0

31 = 0 0 0 1 1 1 1 1

Figure 11.6 Binary values for Class B private range second octet.

You should see a pattern in the binary values: The first four bits are all the same. The range is actually happening in the last four bits in the second octet; those four bits range from 0000 through 1111; the first four bits are common for all 16 networks in the range.

The next step is to identify those common bits. While you are learning how to do this, it's a good idea to write out the binary for the range and draw a line that represents the boundary between the common bits and the variable bits in the range. Remember, be absolutely sure that your boundary line is in the right place: For all the networks in the range, everything to the left of the line must be identical, and everything to the right will be the ranging values.

The next step is easy. We are about to summarize: All we need to do is to build a subnet mask that puts a 1 under all of the common bits in the range, and a 0 under everything else—Ones to the left of the boundary, and zeroes to the right, as shown in Figure 11.7.

The last step is to actually create the summary statement. A summary is always an IP address plus a mask; the IP is usually a Net ID, and it should be the first network in the range. In our example, the first NetID is 172.16.0.0 so that is the IP we will use. For the mask, the first octet is the same in the whole range, and we have figured out that the first four bits in the second octet are always the same. Remembering that a mask is always a string of 1s followed by a string of 0s, this means that we should mask all eight bits in the first octet and the first four in the second octet, so our mask looks like this:

11111111.11110000.00000000.00000000

That can also be expressed as

255.240.0.0 or /12

So, our summary statement becomes:

172.16.0.0 255.240.0.0

or

172.16.0.0 /12

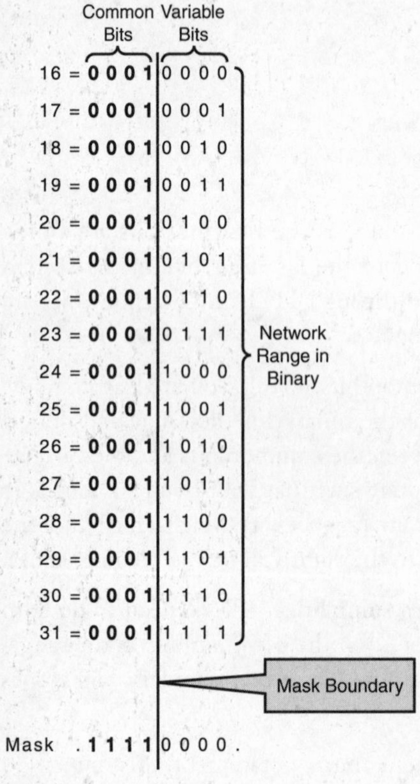

Figure 11.7 Identifying and masking the common bits in a summary.

Reverse engineering this is the same process. You are given a summary statement and asked what networks it includes. The octet in which the mask changes from 1s to 0s is the interesting one, where the range will be defined. Jot down the address and mask in that octet in binary and see what possible values are in the range. Then check the networks to see if those are in the range. Figure 11.8 gives an example.

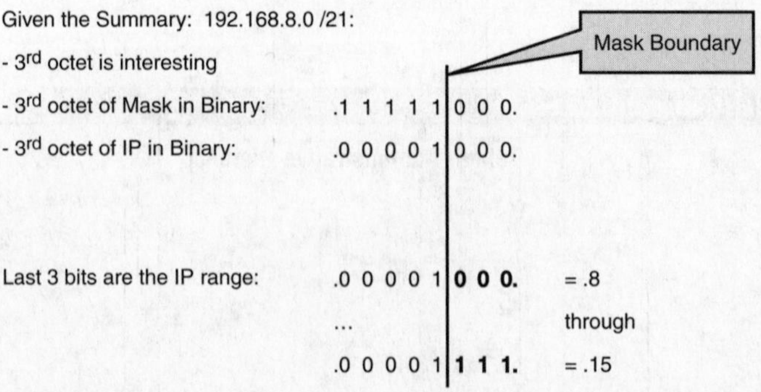

Given the Summary: 192.168.8.0 /21:
- 3rd octet is interesting
Mask Boundary
- 3rd octet of Mask in Binary: .1 1 1 1 1 0 0 0.
- 3rd octet of IP in Binary: .0 0 0 0 1 0 0 0.
Last 3 bits are the IP range: .0 0 0 0 1 0 0 0. = .8
...
through
.0 0 0 0 1 1 1 1. = .15

Therefore, the range of networks is 192.168.8.0 through 192.168.15.0

- Network 192.168.12.0 /24 would be in this range
- Network 192.168.16.0 /24 would not be in this range
- Network 192.168.0.0 /24 would not be in this range

Figure 11.8 Summary address analysis.

The Routing Decision

Routers perform the basic function of switching packets inbound on one interface to another interface outbound. The decision as to which outbound interface to use is based on information stored in the Route Table. The Route Table always stores the best known route to a particular destination network. There are several criteria the router uses to choose which routes are the best, and we now examine four of them.

Administrative Distance

If a router learns of two routes to a given network, say one from RIP and one from OSPF, the routing information source with the lowest administrative distance (AD) will be chosen and used. RIP has an AD of 120, and OSPF has an AD of 110. OSPF, therefore, is more trusted as a source of routing information, and the route learned from OSPF will be installed in the route table.

You should know the ADs of all the routing protocols listed in Table 11.1.

Table 11.1 Administrative Distances

Protocol	Default Administrative Distance
Connected Interface	0
Static Route	1
EIGRP	90
IGRP	100
OSPF	110
IS-IS	115
RIP	120

Valid Next-Hop Address

In all but a few exceptional cases (notably with some static route implementations), the router cannot install a route in the route table unless the next-hop address specified by that route is valid. In other words, if the device to which traffic destined for a particular network must be sent is not available, the route is invalid and will be dropped from the route table.

Best Metric

Given that we might learn more than one route to a given network from any one protocol, the router distinguishes between these routes by comparing the metrics. A *metric* is a measurement of how good a particular route is, expressed as a number. Each routing protocol uses different metrics and different algorithms to calculate them as you saw in Chapter 9, "Routing." The simple rule is: The lower the metric, the better the route. If two routes have equal metrics, more than one route can be used at a time. (The router will load balance using all routes equally.)

Longest Match

The Longest Match rule is the criterion that a router will use to determine the best route given a choice between two or more that are very similar. The longest match refers to the longest prefix length, or the longest matching string of bits in the route as compared to the destination address of the packet being routed.

The concept behind this rule is very simple: The longer the match in the prefix, the more detailed the route is. Let us look at an example to clarify; Figure 11.9 shows a simplified output of the IP Route Table:

```
Simplified IP Route Table:

172.16.8.0 /24 via 192.168.0.1, Ethernet 0
172.16.10.0 /30 via 192.168.0.1, Ethernet 0
172.16.10.64 /26 via 192.168.1.1, Ethernet 1
172.16.10.0 /24 via 192.168.2.1, Ethernet 2
0.0.0.0 /0 via 24.16.5.65, Serial 0
```

Figure 11.9 The longest prefix match is the best route.

Assume that a packet has arrived at the router with a destination IP of 172.16.10.131. The router examines its IP route table and discovers that there are five entries in the route table. The entries are sorted per network according to the length of the mask for that network.

The first entry (172.168.8.0 /24) is compared to the destination IP of the packet. The /24 in the route table entry specifies that the first 24 bits of the prefix should be compared for the longest match. Because the destination IP of the packet is 172.16.10.131, the first 24 bits do not match, and this entry is not a possible route for this packet.

The router repeats the process for the remaining four entries. The second, third, and fourth entries all match for their respective prefix lengths of /28, /26, and /24. The fifth entry is a default route, which by definition matches any address, but with a /0 prefix length.

So now the router must decide which entry is the best route to use for the packet in question. All of the entries are valid, but the one with the longest prefix length match—172.16.10.128 /28—is chosen as the best. The default route is a poor match in this case because there are other, more precise routes with longer prefix matches.

Having made its routing decision, the router switches the packet out the Ethernet 0 interface and begins processing the next packet.

Interpretation of the IP route table is a fundamental and highly testable skill. Make sure that you are fully able to make the correct routing decision given a destination IP and a sample output of **show ip route**.

Network Address Translation

Network Address Translation (known as NAT in network lingo) has become a generic term for several related but different processes. The basic principle involves changing the source IP of a host in the packet header as its traffic crosses the NAT device. We examine the three main implementations of NAT on Cisco routers, along with the applications, advantages, and disadvantages of the NAT service, and finally the configuration commands to implement, verify, and troubleshoot it.

NAT Terminology

A number of unfortunately confusing terms are associated with NAT that in a typically evil plot are usually testable. Figure 11.10 diagrams a typical, simple NAT setup and accurately locates the terms you need to know.

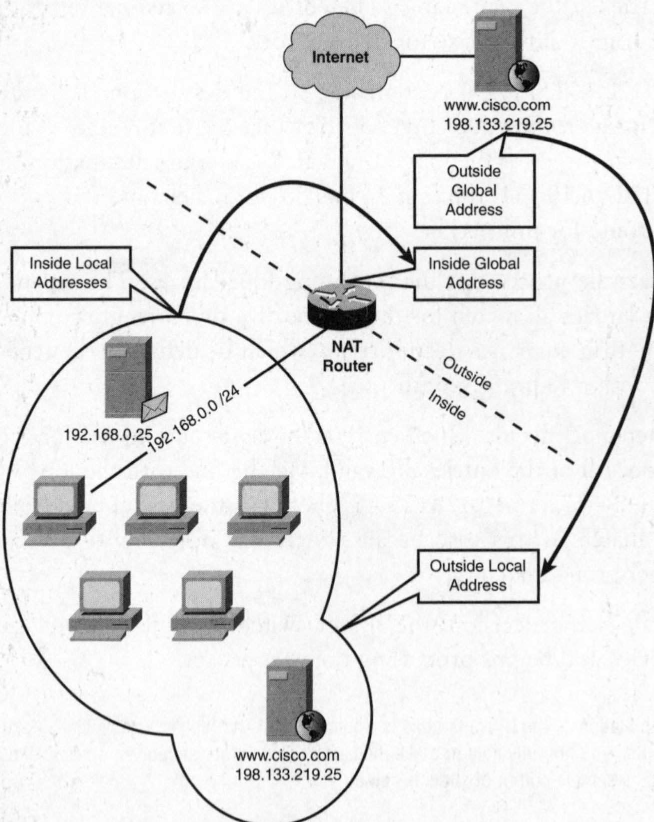

Figure 11.10 NAT terminology put into context.

The terms you need to be familiar with are as follows:

- **Inside**: This refers (typically) to the private side of the network, usually the source of addresses that are being translated.
- **Outside**: This is typically the public side of the network, the address space to which inside hosts are being translated.
- **Inside Local**: These addresses are assigned to inside hosts and are the ones being translated. Inside Local IPs are often RFC 1918 private IPs such as 192.168.*x.x*, 172.16–31.*x.x* and 10.*x.x.x*, but this is by no means a requirement.
- **Inside Global**: These are the addresses to which Inside Locals get translated; often registered IPs obtained from the ISP.
- **Outside Global**: These are typically registered IPs assigned to web servers, mail servers, or any host that is reachable on the public network (Internet, usually) itself.
- **Outside Local**: These are the addresses of Outside Global hosts as they appear on the Inside network; they might or might not have been translated from Outside to Inside, depending on the configuration.

These terms are confusing, and explaining them tends to make things worse.

As a simplification, start with Local and Global: Local addresses are most often the RFC 1918 private ones that we are so familiar with; these will be on the private side of an Internet router. Global addresses are usually real, live, registered IPs, such as www.cisco.com, which at the time of this writing was 198.133.219.25. From this toehold on the terms, you should be able to reconstruct the others—an outside host with a local IP; an inside host with a global IP, and so on.

You must know these terms and where they fit in the NAT system; furthermore, you must be able to apply these terms to the output of some of the NAT verification and troubleshooting commands.

Applications, Advantages, and Disadvantages of NAT

NAT has three main applications:

- If you have more inside hosts than you have outside IP addresses, the NAT service can translate multiple inside hosts to a single outside IP.

The two most common scenarios for this are a typical Internet access router, where all the hosts on the inside are granted Internet access using very few—or even just one—outside IP address, or a modification of that example in which a lot of IPs are available, but not enough for our requirements. In both cases, the problem that NAT solves is the depletion of IP addresses; the fact is that very few registered IPs are available any more, so being able to “reuse” them by NATing many hosts to a few of them is very helpful in extending the lifespan of the Internet address space.

- NAT can be used to solve two related and vexing network issues: The Overlapping Address Space and the Well-Meaning Admin Error. The Overlapping Address Space happens when we connect to another network that uses the same IP address range as we do; typically, this happens when we merge with another company. The problem is that we will have duplicate routes in different locations when the routers start updating each other, leading to instability, misrouting, and general mayhem.

  The Well-Meaning Admin Error (which is better known by a more colorful and unprintable name) happens when the person responsible for the network design either fails to plan for future growth of his network, or simply makes a mistake because of ignorance or arrogance. This most often takes the form of a private network being addressed with public IPs that belong to someone else.

  A real-world example of this occurred when a network consultant for a certain credit union suggested the private address space of 191.168.0.0 /24 for the inside network. This worked fine until Internet connectivity was required; at which time, it was pointed out that the 191.168.0.0 network was a registered Internet range belonging to an insurance firm in the Carolinas. This did cause some issues (for example, when one wanted to ping a domain controller in the head office in Vancouver, the replies came back from a large router somewhere on the East Coast), but the problem was largely hidden by the NAT service, which translated all those inside local IPs (which were incorrectly using outside global addresses) to appropriate outside global addresses.

- NAT can also be used to give a whole cluster of machines (each with different inside local IPs) a single IP address that the clients can use. This is called Load Distribution, and works well for high-volume server clusters such as databases or web servers in which all the clients can use a single virtual IP to reach the service, and that single IP is NATed to all the real IPs of the physical servers.

The advantages of NAT are first and foremost that it conserves the registered IP address space. There is a critical shortage of IPs now, so being able to connect hundreds of hosts to the Internet through a single address is a huge benefit. NAT also provides a certain degree of security because it hides the originating IP address and, if configured properly, prevents bad guys on the Internet from connecting to inside hosts. (The usual caveats here… NAT alone does not provide adequate security, but it can form a part of a secure configuration.) It also helps as a workaround alternative to having to readdress entire networks when address schemes overlap, and makes it easy to change ISP addresses without having to readdress all the inside hosts.

The disadvantages of NAT are primarily that by its very nature, it changes the source IP of traffic, from the actual IP of the host to the Inside Global IP to which it is translated. Some applications do not like this loss of end-to-end IP traceability and stop working. NAT also makes it more difficult when troubleshooting because of that source IP change—and you might be NATed a couple times or more on the journey through the internetwork. Last, the NAT process introduces a certain delay in the transmission of packets as they are rewritten and the translation information is looked up. Spending more money on your NAT box might help speed this up. Call your authorized Cisco VAR, quick!

Know the applications, advantages, and disadvantages of NAT.

Let's look now at the three main NAT implementations.

Static NAT

Static NAT refers to the creation of a one-to-one mapping of an Inside Local IP to an Inside Global IP. Note that this type of NAT does not conserve IP addresses at all because we need one outside IP for every inside IP. Static NAT gives hosts such as mail or web servers access to the Internet even though they are physically on the private network. Perhaps more importantly, it allows us to access that web server from the Internet by creating a static NAT entry from an outside global IP to the server's inside local IP.

Configuring a static NAT entry is easy. The only trick is to make sure that you get NAT working in the right direction: You must be very clear when identifying the Inside interface and the Outside. Figure 11.11 shows a simple network that we use to learn NAT configuration.

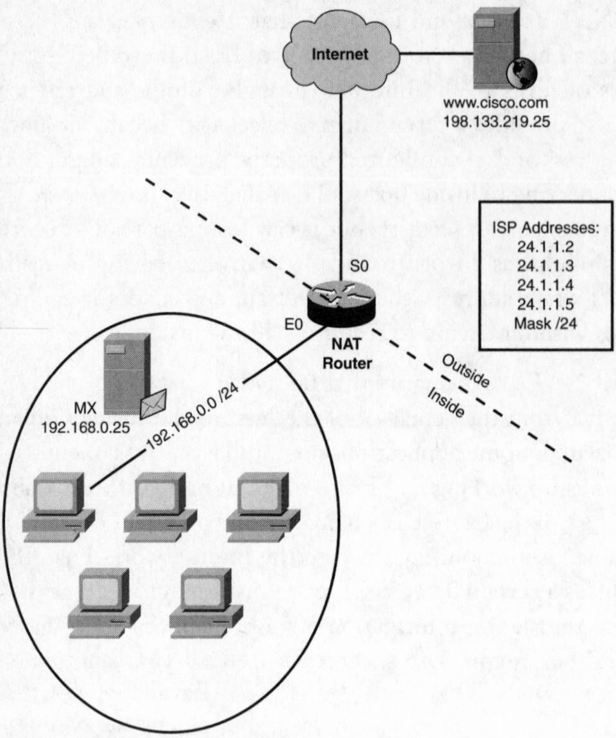

Figure 11.11 Sample NAT network.

Let's create a static NAT entry for the MX (Mail Exchanger) server with the IP of 192.168.0.25. The ISP has told us that we can use a block of IP addresses as shown, from 24.1.1.2 through 24.1.1.6, for our Inside Global addresses. We have decided to use 24.1.1.2 for the Inside Global IP of the MX host.

The global config Static NAT command uses fairly logical syntax:

```
ip nat inside source static <inside local IP> <inside global IP>
```

For our example, the command to enter on the NAT Router would look like this:

```
NAT(config)#ip nat inside source static 192.168.0.25  24.1.1.2
```

Next, we have to identify the Inside and Outside interfaces:

```
NAT(config)#interface e0
NAT(config-if)#ip nat inside
NAT(config-if)#interface s0
NAT(config-if)#ip nat outside
```

And that's all there is to creating a static NAT entry. Remember that static NAT entries use up one outside IP for every inside IP, so they do not conserve the IP address space at all.

Be very familiar with the Static NAT syntax, including the command prompt level at which it is used.

Dynamic NAT

Dynamic NAT enables an inside host to get an outside address when needed; this saves us the trouble of creating multiple static maps, one for each host that wants to use the Internet. Dynamic NAT entries still don't conserve IPs, since we still need one IP for every host that wants to connect to the Internet. Remember that if you have more hosts than outside IPs, some hosts will not get a translation entry and will not be capable of using the Internet. For this reason, it is not used much for Internet connectivity.

One of the interesting concepts introduced with Dynamic NAT is that of the NAT Pool: A *Pool* is a defined group of addresses that are available for translation. Configuring Dynamic NAT involves identifying which hosts are to be translated, and to which addresses they should be translated. Both of these steps can use the `pool` command, but it is more common to use an access list for the inside source and a pool for the outside addresses. The syntax to build a NAT pool looks like this:

```
ip nat pool [pool-name] [first-IP] [last-IP] netmask [mask]
```

The pool name is arbitrary. You can pick something that is meaningful to you. The `first-IP` and `last-IP` are the first and last IPs in the pool range, and the `mask` is the subnet mask of the network those outside IPs are on. Note that you must have the word `netmask` in the syntax! Here's what this command would look like if we used the same network shown in Figure 11.11 and wanted to use the last four IPs in the range that the ISP gave us:

```
NAT(config)#ip nat pool MyPool 24.1.1.3 24.1.1.6 netmask 255.255.255.0
```

Next, we need to identify what hosts get to be translated; we could build another pool to do this, but it is more commonly done with a standard access list:

```
NAT(config)#access-list 1 permit 192.168.0.0 0.0.0.255
```

This list permits any address that starts with 192.168.0.x. Note that in this case, the list is not permitting traffic to or from the hosts; rather, it is identifying those hosts that can be translated.

It is a good idea (a best practices) to specifically deny any hosts that you do not want translated, using your access list. For example, because we already have a static NAT entry for the MX server in our example, we don't want it to get another Dynamic translation, so we would start the access list with the line

NAT(config)#access-list 1 deny host 192.168.0.25

So at this point, we have built the pool of addresses that we will be translating to, we have identified which hosts can be translated (and possibly those that cannot), and all that is left is to configure the NAT process itself:

```
NAT(config)#ip nat inside source list 1 pool MyPool
NAT(config)#interface e0
NAT(config-if)#ip nat inside
NAT(config)#interface s0
NAT(config-if)#ip nat outside
```

The first line tells the router to use List 1 (which we built previously) to identify which hosts can be translated (these are the Inside Source addresses), and then identifies the pool called `MyPool` as the addresses to which the Inside Source Addresses should be translated.

The next lines, as before, tell the router which interface should be Inside and Outside. Remember, if you get these backwards, you will be translating the Internet into your private network... that could be bad.

Note that with a pool of only four addresses, the first four hosts who request a translation will get one (which they keep for 24 hours by default), and any additional hosts who request a translation will not be able to get one. The next section shows how PAT resolves this limitation.

Know the syntax to create a pool of addresses to which hosts can be translated!

PAT

PAT (Port Address Translation, also known as an *extended NAT entry*) leverages the nature of TCP/IP communication by using the source ports of hosts to distinguish them from each other when they are all being translated, possibly to a single outside address.

With PAT, an inside host is given a translation entry that uses not only the host's IP address, but also its source port. Figure 11.12 illustrates the process as three inside hosts are translated to a single outside IP address as they contact different web servers.

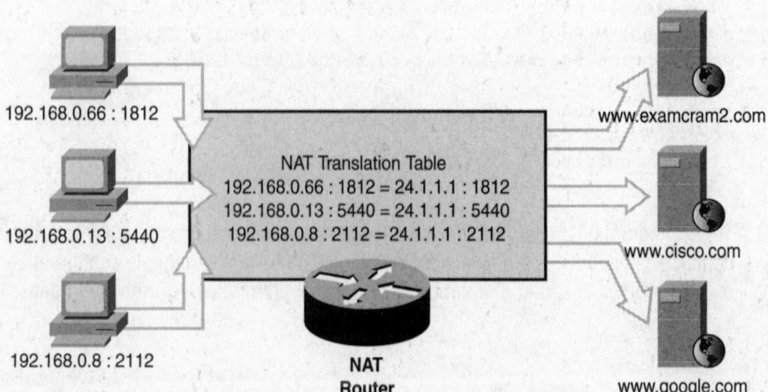

Figure 11.12 The mechanics of PAT.

So you can see now how PAT can hugely extend the registered Internet address space: We could in theory translate thousands of private IPs to a single IP (often, the IP assigned to our Outside interface) using PAT, by extending the Inside Local IP with the randomly-generated source port and mapping that to the Inside Global IP extended by the same port number. With more than 64,000 ports available for this *extended translation entry*, the chances of two hosts randomly choosing the same source port are slim; if it does happen, the conflicting hosts are forced to reset and choose a different port number. We can further reduce the chances of this conflict happening by using a pool for PAT, which makes it very unlikely indeed that two hosts would get the same port *and* Inside Global IP from the pool.

The Cisco term for PAT is *overload* because we are overloading a single Inside Global IP with many Inside Local+Port mappings.

Configuring PAT is very easy; the commands are very similar to Dynamic NAT, with the addition of the keyword `overload` as shown:

```
NAT(config)#access-list 1 permit 192.168.0.0 0.0.0.255
NAT(config)#ip nat inside source list 1 interface serial 0 overload
NAT(config)#interface e0
NAT(config-if)#ip nat inside
NAT(config)#interface s0
NAT(config-if)#ip nat outside
```

Note that we have used the parameters `interface serial 0 overload` at the end of the NAT command; the keyword `overload` turns on PAT, and the `interface serial 0` parameter simply instructs the NAT service to use the existing IP of

Serial 0 as the Inside Global IP for the translation. Here is a sample configuration that ties together a Static NAT entry, creates a pool, and overloads that pool to enable PAT:

```
NAT(config)#access-list 1 deny host 192.168.0.25
NAT(config)#access-list 1 permit 192.168.0.0 0.0.0.255
NAT(config)#ip nat inside source static 192.168.0.25  24.1.1.2
NAT(config)#ip nat pool MyPool 24.1.1.3 24.1.1.6 netmask 255.255.255.0
NAT(config)#ip nat inside source list 1 pool MyPool overload
NAT(config)#interface e0
NAT(config-if)#ip nat inside
NAT(config)#interface s0
NAT(config-if)#ip nat outside
```

This configuration, because it is such a fundamental and important one for Internet-connected networks, is highly tested. You should practice entering this configuration on a real router or router sim until you are totally comfortable with the commands.

Verification and Troubleshooting NAT and PAT

The main command used to verify that your NAT configuration is working is `show ip nat translations`. Figure 11.13 shows a sample output, which could have come from the NAT router in our previous examples.

NAT#show ip nat translations

Pro	Inside Global	Inside Local	Outside Local	Outside Global
tcp	24.1.1.1: 1812	192.168.0.66: 1812	63.240.93.157	63.240.93.157
tcp	24.1.1.1: 5440	192.168.0.13: 5440	198.133.219.25	198.133.219.25
tcp	24.1.1.1: 2112	192.168.0.8: 2112	64.233.187.104	64.233.187.104

Figure 11.13 Sample output from **show ip nat translations**.

Note that all three inside hosts have been translated to the same Inside Global IP (which likely means that we have overloaded the S0 interface). We have proved that the PAT service is functioning because we can see the different port number extensions listed for each host. Note that the Outside Global and Outside Local IPs are the same; this is because we are not translating those IPs back into our inside network. If we were trying to solve the overlapping address space problem, those two IPs would be different for each outside host.

The command `show ip nat statistics` gives us a snapshot of how many translations have been performed, a general overview of how the NAT device is configured, and how much of our pool has been used. Figure 11.14 shows a sample output.

```
NAT#show ip nat statistics
Total translations: 3 (0 static, 0 dynamic, 3 extended)
Outside interfaces: Serial0
Inside interfaces: Ethernet0
Hits: 38 Misses: 3
Expired Translations: 0
Dynamic Mappings:
-- Inside source
access-list 1 pool MyPool refcount 3
Pool MyPool: netmask 255.255.255.0
Start 24.1.1.3 end 24.1.1.6
Type generic, total addresses 4, allocated 3 (75%), misses 0
```

Figure 11.14 Sample output form **show ip nat statistics**.

If you can successfully ping a remote host, chances are good that your NAT / PAT config is at least partially functional.

If you do run into problems, it is possible to clear the NAT translations from the router, using `clear ip nat translation *`. This command clears all dynamic and extended translation entries. To clear a static entry, you must remove the command from your running-config.

Exam Prep Questions

1. Which routing protocols support VLSM? Choose all that apply.

   - ❑ A. RIPv1
   - ❑ B. RIPv2
   - ❑ C. IGRP
   - ❑ D. HSRP
   - ❑ E. EIGRP
   - ❑ F. OSPF
   - ❑ G. BGP

2. What characteristic of VLSM-capable routing protocols enables the use of different subnet masks against a single address class within a system?

   - ❍ A. The capability to configure the protocol on a subnetted interface
   - ❍ B. Compliance with RFC 1918 addressing
   - ❍ C. The use of areas and autonomous systems
   - ❍ D. The inclusion of the subnet mask for each network advertised in routing updates
   - ❍ E. The capability to perform automatic route summarization

3. Which of the following is the best summary statement for the following range of networks?

   192.168.1.0 /24–192.168.15.0 /24

   - ❍ A. 192.168.1.0
   - ❍ B. 192.168.1.0 255.255.240.0
   - ❍ C. 192.168.1.0 0.0.15.0
   - ❍ D. 192.168.1.0 255.255.248.0
   - ❍ E. 192.168.0.0 255.255.240.0

4. Which of the following is the best summary statement for the following range of networks?

   192.168.24.0 /24–192.168.31.0 /24

   - ❍ A. 192.168.24.0 255.255.240.0
   - ❍ B. 192.168.24.0 /28
   - ❍ C. 192.168.24.0 /21
   - ❍ D. 192.168.0.0 /27

5. Which of the following networks are included in the summary 172.16.0.0 /13? Choose all that apply.

   - ❑ A. 172.0.0.0 /16
   - ❑ B. 172.16.0.0 /16
   - ❑ C. 172.24.0.0 /16
   - ❑ D. 172.21.0.0 /16
   - ❑ E. 172.18.0.0 /16

6. What are the advantages of route summarization? Choose three.
   - ❑ A. Ensures job security for network admins because of difficulty of configuration
   - ❑ B. Reduces routing update traffic overhead
   - ❑ C. Reduces the impact of discontiguous subnets
   - ❑ D. Reduces CPU and memory load on routers
   - ❑ E. Identifies flapping interfaces
   - ❑ F. Hides network instability
7. True or false: Route summarization is mandatory.
   - ❍ A. True
   - ❍ B. False
8. Which of the following commands creates a static NAT entry for the host at 192.168.1.80 to the ISP-provided address of 21.21.8.14?
   - ❍ A. ip nat static 192.168.1.80 21.21.8.14
   - ❍ B. ip nat outside 21.21.8.14 inside 192.168.1.80
   - ❍ C. ip nat inside source static 192.168.1.80 21.21.8.14
   - ❍ D. ip nat inside source static 21.21.8.14 192.168.1.80
9. What does the term "overload" mean with respect to Cisco's NAT function?
   - ❍ A. It describes the additional CPU load placed on a router when configured for NAT.
   - ❍ B. It is the command to force the NAT device to use additional addresses from the pool.
   - ❍ C. It describes the default security response to excessive NAT traffic of shutting down the outside interface.
   - ❍ D. It is the command to enable extended NAT entries (PAT) on a Cisco device.
10. Examine the following partial output of show ip route. Which next hop will the router use to send packets to the 172.16.32.0 network?

```
Gateway of last resort is 10.1.1.3
C 192.168.3.0/24 is directly connected, Ethernet1
C 172.16.2.0/24 is directly connected, Serial0
172.16.0.0.0/16 is variably subnetted, 2 subnets, 2 masks
D 172.16.32.0/20 [90/10545152] via 10.1.1.1
D 172.16.32.0/24 [90/314368] via 10.1.1.2
S* 0.0.0.0/0 [1/0] via 10.1.1.3
```

   - ❍ A. The default route
   - ❍ B. 10.1.1.3
   - ❍ C. 10.1.1.1
   - ❍ D. 10.1.1.2

Answers to Exam Prep Questions

1. Answers B,E, F, and G are correct. Answers A and C are wrong; RIPv1 and IGRP do not support VLSM because they do not include the net mask in their updates. Answer D is wrong because HSRP is not a routing protocol.

2. Answer D is correct. Answer A is incorrect because any routing protocol can be configured on a subnetted interface. Answer B is wrong because the RFC 1918 addresses have nothing to do with routing protocol support for VLSM. Answer C refers to the scalability of OSPF—again nothing to do with VLSM. Answer E is characteristic of non-VLSM capable protocols, which automatically summarize to the classful boundary.

3. Answer E is correct. Answers A and C use incorrect syntax; Answer D uses the wrong mask. Answer B looks correct, but it does not use the correct network ID; the range must always start at a binary increment, in this case 0, not 1. Note that the correct summary does include the 192.168.0.0/24 network as well (not just 192.168.1-15.0/24). This is intended to confuse and distract you!

4. Answer C is correct. Answer A uses the wrong mask and supernets more than the specified networks. Answer B subnets instead of summarizes. Answer D uses the wrong address and mask.

5. Answers B, D, and E are correct. The networks in answers A and C are out of the range, which is 16 through 23.

6. Answers B, D, and F are correct. Answer A might have an element of truth, but Cisco does not have much of a sense of humor. Answer C is incorrect because discontiguous subnets are a real problem if you intend to summarize. Answer E is incorrect; route summarization does not identify but rather hides the effects of flapping interfaces.

7. False. Although it might be a good idea in many cases, route summarization is never mandatory (not counting routing protocols that automatically summarize).

8. Answer C is correct; Answer A is missing the `inside source` keyword; Answer B is a fictitious command line; Answer D has the IP addresses reversed.

9. Answer D is correct. Answer A is false; although there is additional overhead on a router running NAT, it is seldom characterized as overloading it. Answer B is false; the router will round-robin through all available pool addresses. Answer C is attractive fiction intended to catch the unaware.

10. Answer D is correct; the longest match rule stipulates that the route with the longest string of bits that match the destination IP prefix of the packet being routed will be the route used. In this case, we have two candidate routes to 172.16.32.0, one with a /20 prefix and the other with a /24 prefix. /24 wins, and the packets will be sent to the next hop of 10.1.1.2 specified by that route.

CCNA Practice Labs

Techniques You Need to Master

- ✓ VLAN creation and naming
- ✓ Assigning switch ports to a VLAN
- ✓ Setting VTP parameters
- ✓ Building trunk links
- ✓ Port Security
- ✓ Assigning IP addresses to a switch and to router interfaces
- ✓ Creating and applying IP access control lists to manage Telnet and ICMP
- ✓ Configuring and troubleshooting static routing
- ✓ Configuring and troubleshooting RIP and OSPF dynamic routing
- ✓ Configuring Static NAT and PAT using a pool of addresses

In this chapter, you are presented with several configuration challenges and scenarios. Your job is to assess the scenario and determine what configurations need to be applied to meet the given requirements or changed to solve a problem. All the skills you practice here are testable; your goal is to finish all the labs in less than 30 minutes.

It is recommended that you have some Cisco equipment to set up and practice on; however, you could use a router simulator instead. Or, simply write your configurations down and compare your answers with the solutions at the end of each lab.

Gear Requirements

As noted earlier, it is best if you can get your hands on the real thing. New Cisco equipment is expensive for the average CCNA candidate, but there are some great deals to be found on eBay or any of the big online auctions. There are even people selling complete CCNA kits, with all the gear and cables you need.

Another option might be to find out if your employer, college, or school has a Cisco lab that you can borrow or rent. A lot of places also rent their Cisco lab equipment so that you can work on labs remotely over the Internet. A quick Google search for "CCNA lab rental" should give you a good start. Shop around!

You could also consider a router simulator. Several products are out there; again, a quick Google search for "Cisco router sim" should get you started in the right direction. Be prepared to spend two or three hundred dollars for a good one. It's a lot of money, but it will be useful for practice and testing configurations even after you have passed CCNA. And, of course, you can always practice for your CCNP. Simulator software has an advantage because it includes all kinds of simulated gear that you might not be able to otherwise obtain, and it's portable, too. You can practice on a laptop whenever and wherever you want.

So what kind of equipment do you need? The labs that follow use two routers and one switch. Here is a breakdown

- 2 routers with 1 serial port and 1 Ethernet port each
- 1 switch (Catalyst 2950 or better)

You will also need the following cables:

- 1 "back-to-back" serial cable (sometimes referred to as DCE-to-DTE)
- 4 straight-through RJ-45 patch cords
- 2 crossover RJ-45 patch cords

It really does not matter what model of router you use, as long as it has the appropriate interfaces and supports a current IOS image—just make sure that you have sufficient RAM and Flash memory to support your chosen IOS. We would suggest at least version 12.2 for the IOS, but any version since 12.0 should work fine. You will need an IOS feature set that includes RIP and OSPF.

CCNA labs do not put any appreciable load on the equipment, so it isn't necessary to buy the newest machine. We have had great success using 1600/2600/3600 series routers and 2950 or 3550 switches. We would strongly recommend against using a Catalyst 1900 switch because although it is still technically part of the CCNA official curriculum, the command set is obsolete and it is not tested any more.

Do NOT perform any of these lab exercises on equipment that is connected to a live/production network. If in doubt, ask your network administrator if what you are about to do is approved.

Lab 1: Switching

- Creating and naming a VLAN
- Assigning switch ports to a VLAN
- Setting VTP parameters
- Building trunk links
- Assigning IP addresses

Scenario

You have been given the task to configure a new switch that your company recently purchased. Your tasks will be as follows:

1. Create and name the following VLANS without entering the VLAN database:
    - VLAN 10, name HR
    - VLAN 20, name Engineering
    - VLAN 30, name Gamers
2. Create the following port associations:
    1. Port fa0/1 in VLAN 10;
    2. Port fa0/2 in VLAN 20;
    3. Port fa0/3 in VLAN 30;
    4. Verify your VLANs and port assignments.
3. Perform the following VTP setup steps:
    1. Set the VTP domain to "ExamCram."
    2. Set the VTP password to "cisco."
    3. Put your switch in Server mode.
    4. Verify your VTP settings.
4. Set interface fa0/12 to permanent trunking mode ("on").
5. Verify your trunk settings.
6. Assign the switch the IP address of 172.16.0.2 /24.
7. Set the switch's default gateway to 172.16.0.1.
8. Set port fa0/18 to allow connection from only one MAC address, and make that port shut down if more than one MAC connects.
9. Set the privileged exec password to "cisco". This password should be encrypted.
10. Secure Telnet access to the switch by applying the password "cisco23" to all five VTY lines. (Your switch may actually have sixteen VTY lines; apply the password to the first five if that is the case.)
11. Secure local console access with the password of "ciscocon."

Lab 2: IP Addressing, Static Routes, and Access Control Lists

- Assigning IP addresses to router interfaces
- Configuring and troubleshooting static routing
- Creating and applying IP access control lists to manage Telnet and ICMP

Scenario

In this lab, you will configure your routers with IP addresses, add static routes, and apply IP access lists to control Telnet and ICMP. Your router might not have a Serial0 interface; you should substitute whichever is the first serial interface on your router.

First, clear the configuration from your switch using the following commands:

- `Switch#erase start`
- `Switch#delete flash:vlan.dat`

You should reboot the switch to completely apply these changes; either power cycle it, or use the privileged exec command `Switch#reload`.

Figure 12.1 shows you how to connect your equipment. You will need to assign a static IP address to your PC(s) as indicated in the diagram. Be sure to connect the DCE end of the serial cable to Router A, or your configurations might not work. Connect the Ethernet ports of both routers to your switch.

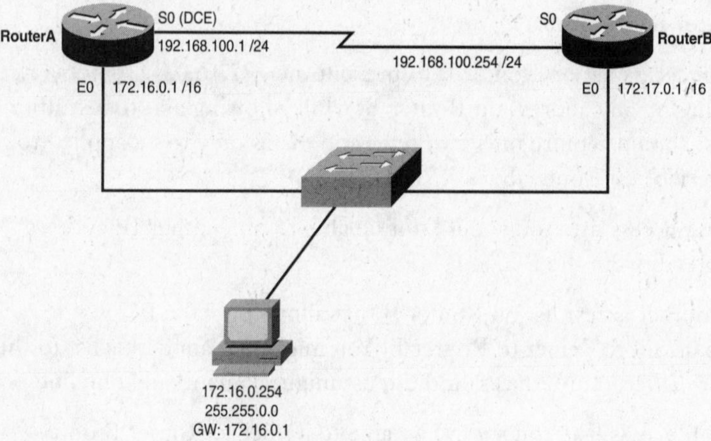

Figure 12.1 Basic network diagram for Labs.

Initially, you will connect your console cable from your PC's COM port to the console port on Router A. You need only one PC to make the labs work, but you can certainly add another if you have one to use.

Tasks

1. Assign Router A the hostname of "RouterA." Set the enable secret and Telnet passwords to "cisco."
2. Assign the following IP addresses to RouterA. Don't forget to enable the interfaces from their default administratively down state.
   - E0—172.16.0.1 /16
   - S0—192.168.100.1 /24
3. Create a static route to the Ethernet network on RouterB.
4. Check the route table on Router A to see if both your connected routes and your new static route have appeared.
5. Connect your console cable to Router B. Assign the following IP addresses to Router B:
   - E0—172.17.0.1 /16
   - S0—192.168.100.254 /24
6. Build a static route for RouterB to the Ethernet network on RouterA.
7. Check the route table on Router B to see if both your connected routes and your new static route have appeared.
8. At this point, you should be able to ping from Router B to the Ethernet port on Router A (172.16.0.1), and from Router A to the Ethernet port on Router B (172.17.0.1).
9. Build an access list on Router B to prevent the 172.16.0.0 /16 network from pinging any address on Router B, while allowing all other traffic. This list should require only two lines and needs only to be applied to one interface on Router B.
10. Test your access list: You should not be able to ping either IP address on Router B from the PC.
11. Build another access list on Router B that allows only the PC (172.16.0.254) to Telnet to Router B. You might not apply this list to the Serial or Ethernet interfaces, and the list might contain only one line.
12. Test your access list: You should be able to Telnet to Router B only from the PC, and not from Router A.

Lab 3: RIP and OSPF

Using the same cabling and IP addressing from the previous lab, in this lab you will configure dynamic routing using RIP and OSPF.

Tasks

1. Remove all static routes and access lists, and then configure RIP on both routers. Be sure to include only directly connected networks in their classful form.
2. Check the route table on RouterB. You should see a RIP route to the 172.16.0.0 network with the IP of the serial port on RouterA as the next hop address.
3. Check the route table on RouterA. You should see a RIP route to the 172.17.0.0 network with the IP of the serial port on RouterB as the nest hop address.
4. Remove RIP from both routers.
5. Configure single-area OSPF, putting all interfaces on both routers into OSPF Area 0.
6. Check the route table on RouterB. You should see an OSPF route to the 172.16.0.0 network with the IP of the serial port on RouterA as the next hop address.
7. Check the route table on RouterA. You should see an OSPF route to the 172.17.0.0 network with the IP of the serial port on RouterB as the next hop address.

Lab 4: NAT

In this lab, you will set up PAT using a pool of addresses. You can leave OSPF running so that your routing will work. The following are the IP addresses in your pool:

192.168.100.2

192.168.100.3

192.168.100.4

192.168.100.5

192.168.100.6

192.168.100.7

Tasks

1. On RouterA, build a standard access-list to define the 172.16.0.0 /16 network as the network that will be NATed.
2. Create the pool of addresses listed previously. Name the pool Campfire. Don't forget that those addresses are on a /24 network.
3. Create the NAT statement, making your access-list the source and the pool Campfire the destination. Don't forget to turn PAT on!
4. Assign the interfaces on RouterA to the correct NAT role (inside and outside).
5. Ping both interfaces on RouterB from the PC.
6. Verify that your PAT configuration is working—make sure that the PC is being translated.

Lab 1 Solution

```
Switch>enable
Switch#configure terminal
Switch(config)#vlan 10
Switch(config-vlan)#name HR
Switch(config-vlan)#vlan 20
Switch(config-vlan)#name Engineering
Switch(config-vlan)#vlan 30
Switch(config-vlan)#name Gamers
Switch(config-vlan)#exit
Switch(config)#interface fa0/1
Switch(config-if)#switchport access vlan 10
Switch(config-if)#interface fa0/2
Switch(config-if)#switchport access vlan 20
Switch(config-if)#interface fa0/3
Switch(config-if)#switchport access vlan 30
Switch(config-if)#exit
Switch(config)#exit
Switch#show vlan brief
<output omitted>
Switch#config t
Switch(config)#vtp domain ExamCram
Switch(config)#vtp password cisco
Switch(config)#vtp server
Switch(config)#exit
Switch#sh vtp status
<output omitted>
Switch#config t
Switch(config)#interface fa0/12
Switch(config-if)#switchport mode trunk
Switch(config)#exit
Switch#show interface fa0/12 trunk
<output omitted>
Switch#config t
```

```
Switch(config-if)#interface vlan 1
Switch(config-if)#ip address 172.16.0.2  255.255.255.0
Switch(config-if)#exit
Switch(config)#ip default-gateway 172.16.0.1
Switch(config)#int fa0/18
Switch(config-if)#switchport port-security maximum 1
Switch(config-if)#switchport port-security violation shutdown
Switch(config-if)#exit
Switch(config)#enable secret cisco
Switch(config)#line vty 0 4
Switch(config-line)#login
Switch(config-line)#password cisco23
Switch(config-line)#line con 0
Switch(config-line)#login
Switch(config-line)#password ciscocon
<ctrl+z>
Switch#copy run start
Switch#exit
```

Lab 2 Solution

```
Router>enable
Router# config t
Router(config)#hostname RouterA
RouterA(config)#enable secret cisco
RouterA(config)#line vty 0 4
RouterA(config-line)#login
RouterA(config-line)#password cisco
RouterA(config-line)#exit
RouterA(config)#interface Ethernet 0
RouterA(config-if)#ip address 172.16.0.1 255.255.0.0
RouterA(config-if)#no shut
RouterA(config-if)#interface serial 0
RouterA(config-if)#ip address 192.168.100.1 255.255.255.0
RouterA(config-if)#no shut
RouterA(config-if)#exit
RouterA(config)#ip route 172.17.0.0 255.255.0.0 192.168.100.254
RouterA(config)#<ctrl-z>
RouterA#show ip route
<output omitted>
(Change to RouterB)
RouterB>enable
RouterB#conf t
RouterB(config)#interface e0
RouterB(config-if)#ip address 172.17.0.1  255.255.0.0
RouterB(config-if)#no shut
RouterB(config-if)#interface s0
RouterB(config-if)#ip address 192.168.100.254  255.255.255.0
RouterB(config-if)#no shut
RouterB(config-if)#exit
RouterB(config)#ip route 172.16.0.0  255.255.0.0  192.168.100.1
RouterB(config)#exit
RouterB#show ip route
<output omitted>
RouterB#ping 172.16.0.1
<output omitted>
RouterB#conf t
RouterB(config)#access-list 101 deny icmp 172.16.0.0  0.0.255.255 any echo
```

```
RouterB(config)#access-list 101 permit ip any any
RouterB(config)#interface s0
RouterB(config-if)#ip access-group 101 in
<ctrl+z>
RouterB#
<change to PC>

C:\WINDOWS\SYSTEM32>ping 192.168.100.254

Pinging 192.168.100.254 with 32 bytes of data:

Reply from 192.168.100.254: Destination net unreachable.
Reply from 192.168.100.254: Destination net unreachable.
Reply from 192.168.100.254: Destination net unreachable.
Reply from 192.168.100.254: Destination net unreachable.

Ping statistics for 192.168.100.254:
    Packets: Sent = 4, Received = 4, Lost = 0 (0% loss),
Approximate round trip times in milli-seconds:
    Minimum = 0ms, Maximum = 0ms, Average = 0ms

C:\WINDOWS\SYSTEM32>ping 172.17.0.1

Pinging 172.17.0.1 with 32 bytes of data:

Reply from 192.168.100.254: Destination net unreachable.
Reply from 192.168.100.254: Destination net unreachable.
Reply from 192.168.100.254: Destination net unreachable.
Reply from 192.168.100.254: Destination net unreachable.

Ping statistics for 172.17.0.1:
    Packets: Sent = 4, Received = 4, Lost = 0 (0% loss),
Approximate round trip times in milli-seconds:
    Minimum = 0ms, Maximum = 0ms, Average = 0ms
<change to RouterB>
RouterB(config)#access-list 1 permit host 172.16.0.254
RouterB(config)#line vty 0 4
RouterB(config-line)#access-class 1 in
<ctrl+z>
RouterB#
<try to Telnet from RouterA; this should fail. Telnet from the PC should
succeed.
```

Lab 3 Solution

```
RouterA#config t
RouterA(config)#no ip route 172.17.0.0 255.255.0.0 192.168.100.254
RouterA(config)#router rip
RouterA(config-router)#network 172.16.0.0
RouterA(config-router)#network 192.168.100.0
<ctrl+z>
RouterA#
<change to RouterB>
RouterB#config t
RouterB(config)#no ip route 172.16.0.0 255.255.0.0 192.168.100.1
RouterB(config)#interface serial 0
RouterB(config-if)#no ip access-group 101 in
RouterB(config-if)#exit
```

```
RouterB(config)#no access-list 101
RouterB(config)#line vty 0 4
RouterB(config-line)#no access-class 1 in
RouterB(config-line)#exit
RouterB(config)#router rip
RouterB(config-router)#network 172.17.0.0
RouterB(config-router)#network 192.168.100.0
<ctrl+z>
RouterB#show ip route
RouterB#sh ip route
Codes: C - connected, S - static, I - IGRP, R - RIP, M - mobile, B - BGP
       D - EIGRP, EX - EIGRP external, O - OSPF, IA - OSPF inter area
       N1 - OSPF NSSA external type 1, N2 - OSPF NSSA external type 2
       E1 - OSPF external type 1, E2 - OSPF external type 2, E - EGP
       i - IS-IS, L1 - IS-IS level-1, L2 - IS-IS level-2, * - candidate
default
       U - per-user static route, o - ODR

Gateway of last resort is not set

R    172.16.0.0/16 [120/1] via 192.168.100.1, 00:00:22, Serial0
C    192.168.100.0/24 is directly connected, Serial0
RouterB#
RouterB#config t
RouterB(config)#no router rip
RouterB(config)#exit
RouterB#
<change to RouterA>
RouterA#config t
RouterA(config)#no router rip
RouterA(config)#router ospf 99
RouterA(config-router)#network 172.16.0.0  0.0.255.255 area 0
RouterA(config-router)#network 192.168.100.0  0.0.0.255 area 0
<ctrl+z>
RouterA#
<change to RouterB>
RouterB#config t
RouterB(config)#no router rip
RouterB(config)#router ospf 10
RouterB(config-router)#network 192.168.100.0  0.0.0.255 area 0
RouterB(config-router)#network 172.17.0.0  0.0.255.255 area 0
<ctrl+z>
RouterB#show ip route
RouterB#sh ip route
Codes: C - connected, S - static, I - IGRP, R - RIP, M - mobile, B - BGP
       D - EIGRP, EX - EIGRP external, O - OSPF, IA - OSPF inter area
       N1 - OSPF NSSA external type 1, N2 - OSPF NSSA external type 2
       E1 - OSPF external type 1, E2 - OSPF external type 2, E - EGP
       i - IS-IS, L1 - IS-IS level-1, L2 - IS-IS level-2, * - candidate
default
       U - per-user static route, o - ODR

Gateway of last resort is not set

C    172.17.0.0/16 is directly connected, Ethernet0
O    172.16.0.0/16 [110/74] via 192.168.100.1, 00:01:49, Serial0
C    192.168.100.0/24 is directly connected, Serial0
RouterB#
<change to RouterA>
RouterA#sh ip route
Codes: C - connected, S - static, I - IGRP, R - RIP, M - mobile, B - BGP
```

```
       D - EIGRP, EX - EIGRP external, O - OSPF, IA - OSPF inter area
       N1 - OSPF NSSA external type 1, N2 - OSPF NSSA external type 2
       E1 - OSPF external type 1, E2 - OSPF external type 2, E - EGP
       i - IS-IS, L1 - IS-IS level-1, L2 - IS-IS level-2, * - candidate
default
       U - per-user static route, o - ODR

Gateway of last resort is not set

O    172.17.0.0/16 [110/74] via 192.168.100.254, 00:00:10, Serial0
C    172.16.0.0/16 is directly connected, Ethernet0
C    192.168.100.0/24 is directly connected, Serial0
RouterA#
```

Lab 4 Solution

```
RouterA#
RouterA#config t
RouterA(config)#access-list 1 permit 172.16.0.0
RouterA(config)#ip nat pool Campfire 192.168.100.2 192.168.100.7 netmask
255.255.0.0
RouterA(config)#ip nat inside source list 1 pool Campfire overload
RouterA(config)#interface s0
RouterA(config-if)#ip nat outside
RouterA(config-if)#interface e0
RouterA(config-if)#ip nat inside
<ctrl+z>
RouterA#
<change to PC>
cmd>ping 172.17.0.0
<output omitted>
<change to RouterA>
RouterA#show ip nat translations
<output omitted>
RouterA#
```

Practice Exam #1

Hints and Pointers

If you are reading this, you likely feel ready to tackle the CCNA exam and need to assess your skills to see if you can spot any weaknesses. As you take this practice exam, the authors recommend the following test taking tips:

- **Read each question twice**—There is a big difference between reading a question that you think reads, "Which of the following are true," but really reads, "Which of the following are **not** true." Be sure to reach each question carefully so that you can fully understand the question.
- **Read the answers starting from the bottom**—When you read the answers from the bottom, you force yourself to carefully read each answer. If you read the answers from the top, you might find yourself quickly selecting an answer that looks vaguely right and skipping over the other answers that might have been a better answer.
- **Time yourself**—The CCNA exam is a 90 minute exam. Time yourself during this practice exam to make sure that you stay within this time limit.
- **If you do not know the answer to a question, make a note of it**—Go back and review any trouble areas later. You should be interested not only in finding the answer to the question, but also in mastering that particular topic in its entirety. If you are unsure about one aspect of a topic, chances are you might be unsure about other areas related to that same topic.

- **Mentally get yourself in the frame of mind to take a test**—To properly assess yourself, take this practice exam as you would take the real exam. This means that you should find yourself a quiet place without any distractions so that you can focus on each question. (Yes, that includes turning off the television.) You can have some scratch paper to write on, but calculators are not allowed on the real exam, so do not use them on the practice exam.
- **Continue taking this practice exam until you get a perfect score**—When you can consistently score high on these practice exams, you are ready to take the real exam.
- **Don't despair**—Should you not do so well on the practice exam, do not worry. It only means that you need to continue studying. Be glad that you are able to spot your weak areas now and not after taking the real exam. Go back through and review your problem areas.

We wish you the best of luck in your pursuit of the coveted CCNA certification.

Practice Exam #1

1. You need to assign an IP address on a router for a new Ethernet network. You need to assign the router to the first IP address on the second useable subnet taken from the major Class C network of 192.168.25.0/24. The subnet must support at least 13 hosts on each subnet, but you must allow for as many subnets as possible. In addition, the router has been configured with the `ip subnet-zero` command. Given these requirements, what address would you assign on the router?

   ❍ A. 192.168.25.14

   ❍ B. 192.168.25.17

   ❍ C. 192.168.25.33

   ❍ D. 192.168.25.49

   ❍ E. 192.168.25.1

2. You have been asked to troubleshoot a NAT configuration for the network shown in the figure. Another engineer has entered the following configuration into the router:

```
access-list 4 permit 172.21.248.0 0.0.1.255
ip nat pool NATPOOL 192.168.191.66 192.168.191.70 netmask
    255.255.255.248
ip nat inside source list 4 pool NATPOOL
!
interface serial 1/0
 ip address 192.168.191.65 255.255.255.248
 ip nat oustide
!
interface fastethernet 0/3
 ip address 172.21.254.1 255.255.254.0
 ip nat inside
!
```

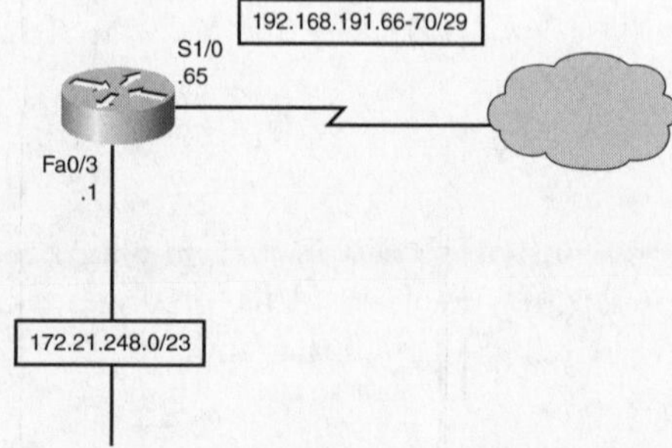

   There is a problem with this configuration: Not all users are able to access the Internet. What is wrong with the configuration that causes this problem?

   ❍ A. The pool configuration is incorrect.

   ❍ B. The `ip nat inside` and `ip nat outside` commands are on the wrong interfaces.

   ❍ C. The keyword `'overload'` is missing.

   ❍ D. The access list is incorrect.

   ❍ E. The IP addresses are incorrect.

3. You need to decide what type of routing solution should be used between RouterB and RouterC. Currently, RouterA, RouterB, and RouterD are all running OSPF, but RouterC and RouterE are running EIGRP. RouterB and RouterC are connected via an ISDN BRI. You want to use a routing solution that will minimize routing overhead on your ISDN BRI WAN link. What routing solution should you use?

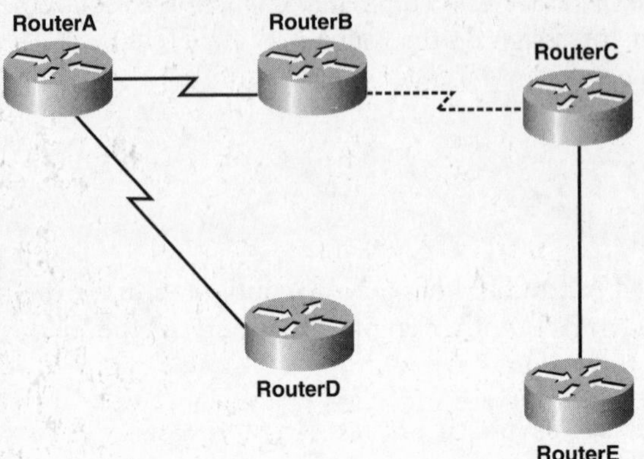

   - ❍ A. OSPF
   - ❍ B. EIGRP
   - ❍ C. RIP
   - ❍ D. Static

4. Which of the following protocols can you use to test network connectivity at the Application layer? Select all that apply.
   - ❑ A. Telnet
   - ❑ B. FTP
   - ❑ C. Ping
   - ❑ D. Traceroute
   - ❑ E. CDP

5. Your manager has asked you to configure a new switch on your network and to use an IEEE standard for trunking. What commands configure this trunk on your new switch? Select all that apply.
   - ❍ A. `switchport access trunk`
   - ❍ B. `switchport mode trunk`
   - ❍ C. `switchport trunk encapsulation dot1q`
   - ❍ D. `switchport trunk encapsulation isl`

6. Which of the following routed protocols does EIGRP support?
   - ❍ A. Appletalk
   - ❍ B. Banyan Vines
   - ❍ C. IPX
   - ❍ D. IP
   - ❍ E. LAT

7. Your boss has asked you to secure your Telnet sessions on your routers. What is the correct configuration to allow only two Telnet sessions to run at a time with an encrypted password of `'Que'`?
   - ❍ A. Configuration #1

     ```
     line vty 0 4
      login
      password Que
     ```
   - ❍ B. Configuration #2

     ```
     line vty 0 2
      password Que
     enable secret Que
     ```
   - ❍ C. Configuration #3

     ```
     line vty 0 1
      login
      password Que
     service password-encryption
     ```
   - ❍ D. Configuration #4

     ```
     line vty 0 1
      login
      enable secret Que
     ```
   - ❍ E. Configuration #5

     ```
     line vty 0 4
      login
      password Que
     service password-encryption
     ```

8. Examine the figure shown. OSPF is running on RouterA, RouterB, RouterC, and RouterD. RIP is running on RouterD and RouterE. Based on the figure, which path will RouterA take to get to RouterD?

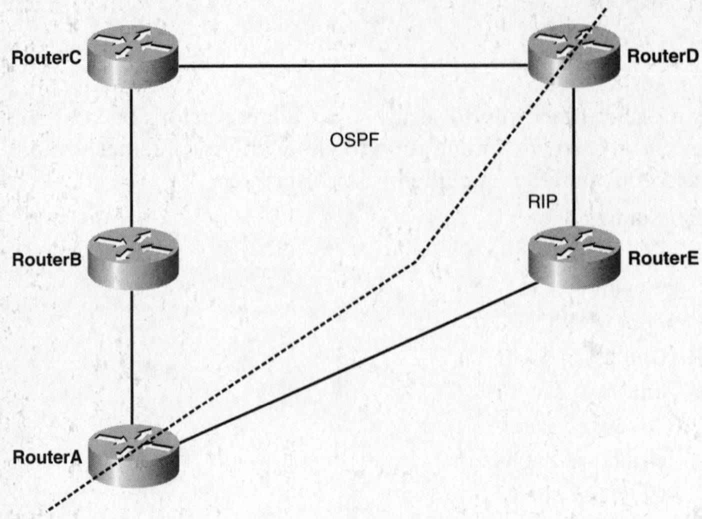

- ❍ A. RouterA will take the path through RouterE.
- ❍ B. RouterA will take the path through RouterB.
- ❍ C. RouterA will load balance across RouterE and RouterB.
- ❍ D. Not enough information is given to answer this question.

9. Which of the following is a valid host IP address? Select all that apply.

- ❑ A. 172.16.17.0/20
- ❑ B. 192.168.4.64/28
- ❑ C. 10.0.145.144/30
- ❑ D. 172.30.15.18/29

10. What would be the correct syntax to create and apply an access list inbound on fastethernet 0/0 that would allow all hosts on the 172.19.40.0/21 network Telnet access to a server with the IP address 10.0.0.55?

   ❍ A. Router(config)#access-list 100 permit udp 172.19.40.0 0.0.7.255 host 10.0.0.55 eq 23
   Router(config)#interface fastethernet0/0
   Router(config-if)#ip access-group 100 in

   ❍ B. Router(config)#access-list 100 permit tcp 172.19.40.0 0.0.15.255 host 10.0.0.55 eq 23
   Router(config)#interface fastethernet0/0
   Router(config-if)#ip access-group 100 in

   ❍ C. Router(config)#access-list 100 permit udp 172.19.40.0 0.0.15.255 host 10.0.0.55 eq 23
   Router(config)#interface fastethernet0/0
   Router(config-if)#ip access-group 100 in

   ❍ D. Router(config)#access-list 100 permit tcp 172.19.40.0 0.0.7.255 host 10.0.0.55 eq 23
   Router(config)#interface fastethernet0/0
   Router(config-if)#ip access-group 100 in

11. You are working on a router that does not have any loopback interfaces. Without the presence of a loopback interface, how do you choose the Router ID in OSPF?

   ❍ A. You must create a loopback interface. Without it, OSPF is not activated.
   ❍ B. It is the highest IP address among all physical interfaces that are active when OSPF is started.
   ❍ C. It is the highest IP address among all physical interfaces regardless if they are active when OSPF first starts.
   ❍ D. It is the lowest IP address among all physical interfaces.

12. Your boss asks you to implement a wide area network solution that is good for voice, video, and data. She requires that you also choose a solution that uses out-of-band signaling. What solution do you recommend?

   ❍ A. ISDN
   ❍ B. ATM
   ❍ C. Frame relay
   ❍ D. Leased lines
   ❍ E. SMDS

13. Which of the following information is included with the `show cdp neighbors detail` command? Select all that apply.

   ❑ A. Device name
   ❑ B. Platform
   ❑ C. Capabilities
   ❑ D. IOS version
   ❑ E. IP address

14. You try to create a VLAN that is automatically propagated out to all other switches. The switch allows you to create the VLAN, but it is not propagated to other switches. You execute the `show vtp status` command (shown below). What is wrong?

```
Switch> show vtp status
VTP Version                      : 2
Configuration Revision           : 0
Maximum VLANs supported locally: 250
Number of existing VLANs         : 15
VTP Operating Mode               : Transparent
VTP Domain Name                  :
VTP Pruning Mode                 : Disabled
VTP V2 Mode                      : Disabled
VTP Traps Generation             : Disabled
MD5 digest                       : 0xBF 0x84 0x94 0x33 0xFC 0xAF 0xB5
0x70
Configuration last modified by 0.0.0.0 at 0-0-00 00:00:00
```

- ❍ A. No domain name is assigned. You must first assign a domain name before any VLAN information is sent out to other switches.
- ❍ B. The VTP version number is wrong.
- ❍ C. You must first enable VTP pruning.
- ❍ D. You must change the VTP mode to Server before any VLAN information is sent out to other switches.

15. How many broadcast domains are there in the figure shown?

- ❍ A. One
- ❍ B. Two
- ❍ C. Three
- ❍ D. Four
- ❍ E. Five

16. Examine the figure shown. Your computer has the IP address 172.16.64.201/22, and you try to access a website on the web server with the IP address 172.16.129.48/22. Unfortunately, you are unable to access the site. Below are the partial configurations on RouterA and RouterB:

RouterA

```
interface fastethernet3/1
 ip address 172.16.64.1 255.255.252.0
interface bri0/0
 ip address 172.16.22.190 255.255.255.252.0
ip route 172.16.128.0 255.255.252.0 172.16.24.185
```

RouterB

```
interface fastethernet0/0
 ip address 172.16.128.1 255.255.252.0
interface bri0/0
 ip address 172.16.24.185 255.255.252.0
ip route 172.16.64.0 255.255.252.0 172.16.22.190
```

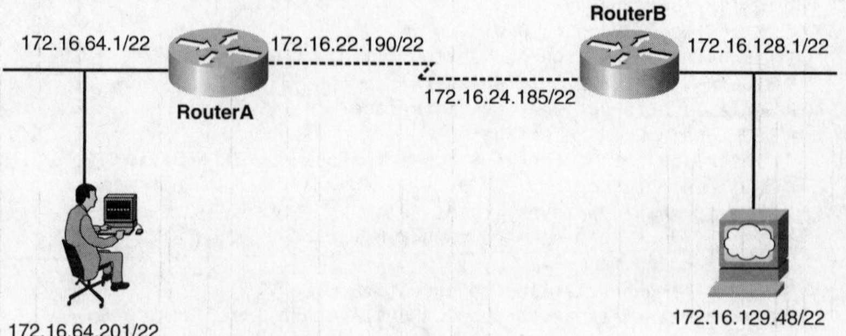

Why are you unable to access the website?.

- ❍ A. The static route is incorrect on RouterA.
- ❍ B. The bri0/0 on RouterA is on a network different from bri0/0 on RouterB.
- ❍ C. The server is on a network different from fastethernet0/0 on RouterB.
- ❍ D. The static route on RouterB is incorrect.
- ❍ E. Your computer uses an invalid IP address.

17. You are responsible for a large wide area network. An engineer at a branch office informs you that he loses his configuration every time he reboots his router. You ask him to send you the output of show version (shown below). Based on this output, what causes his problem?

```
Cisco Internetwork Operating System Software
IOS (tm) 1600 Software (C1600-NOSY-L), Version 12.0(25),
   RELEASE SOFTWARE (fc1)
Copyright (c) 1986-2002 by Cisco Systems, Inc.
Compiled Tue 31-Dec-02 12:29 by srani
Image text-base: 0x0200544C, data-base: 0x025DDA44
ROM: System Bootstrap, Version 11.1(12)XA, EARLY DEPLOYMENT
   RELEASE SOFTWARE (fc1)
ROM: 1600 Software (C1600-RBOOT-R), Version 11.1(12)XA,
   EARLY DEPLOYMENT RELEASE
 SOFTWARE (fc1)
Router uptime is 5 hours, 32 minutes
System restarted by reload
System image file is "flash:c1600-nosy-l.120-25.bin"
cisco 1604 (68360) processor (revision D) with 18432K/6144K bytes of
memory.
Processor board ID 14223432, with hardware revision 00000000
Bridging software.
X.25 software, Version 3.0.0.
Basic Rate ISDN software, Version 1.1.
1 Ethernet/IEEE 802.3 interface(s)
1 Serial(sync/async) network interface(s)
1 ISDN Basic Rate interface(s)
 U interface with external S bus interface for ISDN Basic
   Rate interface.
System/IO memory with parity disabled
8192K bytes of DRAM onboard 16384K bytes of DRAM on SIMM
System running from RAM
7K bytes of non-volatile configuration memory.
16384K bytes of processor board PCMCIA flash (Read/Write)
Configuration register is 0x2142
```

- ❍ A. There is not enough memory to run the IOS.
- ❍ B. The IOS is Early Deployment Release software, which should never run on production equipment.
- ❍ C. The flash is too small to load the IOS.
- ❍ D. The configuration register is wrong.

18. Examine the figure. You are running EIGRP on all routers, but you are unable to route to all networks in the diagram. You have narrowed the problem down to RouterB. Below is the EIGRP configuration for RouterB:

```
RouterB(config)#router eigrp 1
RouterB(config-router)#network 192.168.206.16
RouterB(config-router)#network 192.168.0.96
RouterB(config-router)#network 192.168.0.64
```

What is wrong with this configuration that causes this problem?

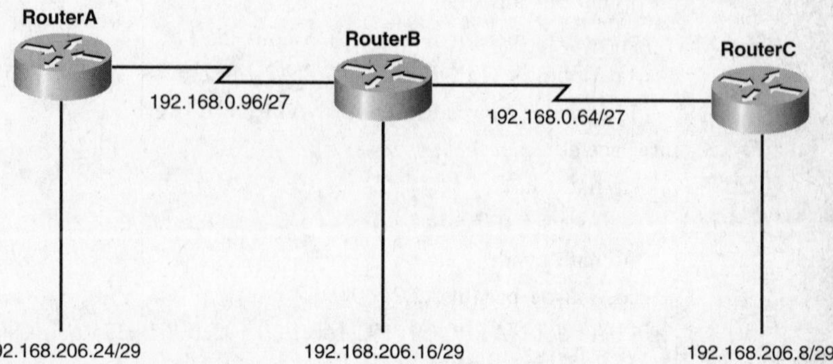

- ❍ A. It is missing the no auto-summary command.
- ❍ B. The network statements are wrong.
- ❍ C. The mask is missing.
- ❍ D. It is missing the auto-summary command.
- ❍ E. The maximum-paths command is missing.

19. At what layer of the OSI model is the frame check sequence?

- ❍ A. Application
- ❍ B. Transport
- ❍ C. Network
- ❍ D. Physical
- ❍ E. Data-link

20. You have the public range of 2.2.2.0/25 from your ISP. You want to subnet this further to create a public address pool of six addresses that you are going to use to NAT your inside local addresses. Which of the following configurations allow you to NAT your inside local addresses of 192.168.14.0/24 to a pool of six addresses taken from the 2.2.2.0/25 subnet?

❍ A.
```
interface ethernet0
 ip nat inside
interface serial0
 ip nat outside
access-list 1 permit 192.168.14.0 0.0.0.255
ip nat pool NATPOOL 2.2.2.9 2.2.2.14 netmask 255.255.255.248
ip nat inside source list 1 pool NATPOOL overload
```

❍ B.
```
interface ethernet 0
 ip nat inside
interface serial 0
 ip nat outside
access-list 1 permit 2.2.2.8 0.0.0.7
ip nat pool NATPOOL 192.168.14.0 192.168.14.255 netmask
255.255.255.0
ip nat inside source list 1 pool NATPOOL overload
```

❍ C.
```
interface ethernet 0
 ip nat inside
interface serial 0
 ip nat outside
access-list 1 permit 192.168.14.0 0.0.0.255
ip nat pool NATPOOL 2.2.2.9 2.2.2.15 netmask 255.255.255.240
ip nat inside source list 1 pool NATPOOL overload
```

❍ D.
```
interface ethernet 0
 ip nat inside
interface serial 0
 ip nat outside
access-list 1 permit 2.2.2.0 0.0.0.255
ip nat pool NATPOOL 192.168.14.1 192.168.14.254 netmask
255.255.255.0
ip nat inside source list 1 pool NATPOOL overload
```

21. Examine the figure. You are running frame-relay between two routers. When you check the status of the interface on RouterA, it shows that the interface is up, but the line protocol is down. What is wrong?

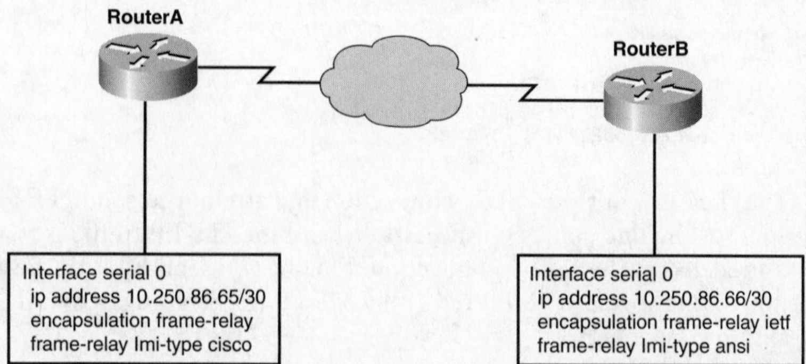
RouterA
RouterB
Interface serial 0
ip address 10.250.86.65/30
encapsulation frame-relay
frame-relay lmi-type cisco
Interface serial 0
ip address 10.250.86.66/30
encapsulation frame-relay ietf
frame-relay lmi-type ansi

- ❍ A. The LMI types do not match.
- ❍ B. The encapsulation types do not match.
- ❍ C. The configuration is incomplete.
- ❍ D. The routers are on different subnets.

22. Ping and Traceroute operate at what layer of the OSI model?

- ❍ A. Network
- ❍ B. Transport
- ❍ C. Application
- ❍ D. Session
- ❍ E. Data-link

23. The output of the `show ip route` command is shown below. A packet is sent destined for the 192.168.5.0/24 network. What happens? Select all that apply.

```
Router#show ip route
CODES: C - CONNECTED, S - STATIC, I - IGRP, R - RIP, M - MOBILE, B - BGP
       D - EIGRP, EX - EIGRP EXTERNAL, O - OSPF, IA - OSPF INTER AREA
       N1 - OSPF NSSA EXTERNAL TYPE 1, N2 - OSPF NSSA EXTERNAL TYPE 2
       E1 - OSPF EXTERNAL TYPE 1, E2 - OSPF EXTERNAL TYPE 2, E - EGP
       I - IS-IS, L1 - IS-IS LEVEL-1, L2 - IS-IS LEVEL-2, * - CANDIDATE
          DEFAULT
       U - PER-USER STATIC ROUTE, O - ODR
GATEWAY OF LAST RESORT IS NOT SET
D       172.16.0.0 [90/2195456] VIA 10.16.10.1,  00:09:45, SERIAL0
D       172.31.1.0 [90/2681856] VIA 192.168.10.5 00:01:55, SERIAL1
C       10.0.0.0 IS DIRECTLY CONNECTED, SERIAL0
C       192.168.10.0 IS DIRECTLY CONNECTED, SERIAL1
```

- ❑ A. The packet is sent out interface Serial 1.
- ❑ B. The packet is sent out interface Serial 0.
- ❑ C. The packet is dropped.
- ❑ D. The packet load balances across interfaces Serial 0 and Serial 1.
- ❑ E. An ICMP Destination Unreachable message is sent back to the source.

24. You type the following configuration into a router:

```
access-list 100 permit tcp any any eq www
dialer-list 1 protocol ip list 100
isdn switch-type basic-ni
interface bri0
 ip address 10.0.0.1 255.0.0.0
 dialer-group 1
 dialer map ip 10.0.0.2 5551111
 isdn spid1 55511110101 5551111
 isdn spid2 55522220101 5552222
```

You then test out the ISDN connection and attempt to send HTTP traffic. The line comes up successfully, and the HTTP traffic is transmitted across the ISDN connection. Finally, you send FTP traffic and notice that it is also permitted. Why is FTP traffic going across the ISDN connection?

❍ A. The access-list is configured incorrectly.
❍ B. The dialer-list is not applied correctly.
❍ C. The dialer-list command specifies only what traffic will bring up the ISDN connection, not what traffic is allowed across after the connection is up.
❍ D. FTP traffic is a subset of HTTP, so it is therefore allowed across the ISDN connection.

25. In OSPF, what is the cost of a T1?

❍ A. 1,544
❍ B. 10
❍ C. 100
❍ D. 64

26. What is a common subnet mask on point-to-point wide area network links that would allow only two valid IP addresses?

❍ A. 255.255.255.224
❍ B. 255.255.255.240
❍ C. 255.255.255.248
❍ D. 255.255.255.252
❍ E. 255.255.255.255

27. Which of the following commands configures a default gateway address on a switch?

❍ A. Switch#ip default-gateway 10.0.0.1 255.0.0.0
❍ B. Switch(config)#ip default-gateway 10.0.0.1 255.0.0.0
❍ C. Switch(config)#ip default-gateway 10.0.0.1
❍ D. Switch(config-router)#ip default-gateway 10.0.0.1

28. What is the maximum hop count for EIGRP?
    - ❍ A. 255
    - ❍ B. 224
    - ❍ C. 15
    - ❍ D. 1
    - ❍ E. Unlimited
29. What is happening in the spanning-tree learning state?
    - ❍ A. Port is transitioning to forward state.
    - ❍ B. Port is preventing loops.
    - ❍ C. Port is forwarding data.
    - ❍ D. Port is populating the MAC table.
30. What type of cable would you use between a router and a switch?
    - ❍ A. Rollover cable
    - ❍ B. Null modem cable
    - ❍ C. Crossover cable
    - ❍ D. Straight-through cable
31. You type the following configuration into a router. When you execute the `show ip route` command, however, you do not notice any new routes. What is wrong with the configuration that causes this problem?

```
router rip
 network 10.0.0.0
 network 172.19.0.0
 version 2
interface serial 0/0
 ip address 10.0.0.1 255.0.0.0
 frame-relay map ip 10.0.0.2 100
 frame-relay interface-dlci 100
 no frame-relay inverse-arp
interface ethernet 0/0
 ip address 172.19.0.1 255.255.0.0
```

    - ❍ A. The frame-relay map command is missing the broadcast keyword.
    - ❍ B. RIP should be running version 1, not version 2.
    - ❍ C. Inverse-arp should be enabled.
    - ❍ D. RIP is not activated on the interfaces.
32. What is used in factoring the routing metric used by IGRP and EIGRP? Select all that apply.
    - ❑ A. Bandwidth
    - ❑ B. Hop count
    - ❑ C. Delay
    - ❑ D. Cost

33. CHAP can be described as what type of authentication?
   - ❍ A. One-way handshake
   - ❍ B. Two-way handshake
   - ❍ C. Three-way handshake
   - ❍ D. Four-way handshake

34. What does the following access control list do?

```
Router(config)#ip access-list extended QueACL
Router(config-ext-nacl)#permit tcp 172.30.31.192 0.0.0.15 10.0.4.0
          0.0.3.255 eq 110
Router(config-ext-nacl)#permit tcp 172.30.31.192 0.0.0.15 10.0.4.0
          0.0.3.255 eq 25
Router(config-ext-nacl)#interface fastethernet0/0
Router(config-if)#ip access-group QueACL in
```

   - ❍ A. Allows NTP and SNMP from the 172.30.31.192/28 network to the 10.0.4.0/22 network
   - ❍ B. Allows SMTP and POP from the 172.30.31.192/29 network to the 10.0.4.0/21 network
   - ❍ C. Allows SMTP and POP from the 172.30.31.192/28 network to the 10.0.4.0/22 network
   - ❍ D. Allows SNMP and POP from the 172.30.31.192/28 network to the 10.0.4.0/21 network

35. You enter the following configuration into a router, but when you go to test it, you are unable to initiate the ISDN call. What is wrong?

```
router rip
 network 10.0.0.0
 network 192.168.200.0
 version 2
 no auto-summary
 passive-interface default
 no passive-interface eth0
interface ethernet0
 ip address 10.0.0.1 255.0.0.0
interface bri0
 ip address 192.168.200.93 255.255.255.252
 encapsulation ppp
 ppp authentication chap
 dialer map ip 192.168.200.94 name RouterB 5553333
 isdn spid1 55511110101 5551111
 isdn spid2 55522220101 5552222
 dialer-group 40
 dialer idle-timeout 30
isdn switch-type basic-ni
ip route 192.168.200.96 255.255.255.224 192.168.200.94
dialer-list 4 protocol ip permit
hostname RouterA
username RouterB password QUE
```

   - ❍ A. The dialer-group is applied incorrectly.
   - ❍ B. The RIP configuration is incorrect.
   - ❍ C. The PPP authentication is configured incorrectly.
   - ❍ D. The dialer map is configured incorrectly.
   - ❍ E. The configuration is incomplete.

36. Routing occurs at what layer of the TCP/IP model?
   - ❍ A. Internet
   - ❍ B. Network
   - ❍ C. Application
   - ❍ D. Transport
37. Where is the feasible successor route stored in EIGRP?
   - ❍ A. Neighbor table
   - ❍ B. Route table
   - ❍ C. Adjacency table
   - ❍ D. Topology table
   - ❍ E. Link state database
38. Which of the following addresses are on the same network as the host with an IP address of 192.168.6.81/29? Select all that apply.
   - ❑ A. 192.168.6.79
   - ❑ B. 192.168.6.89
   - ❑ C. 192.168.6.85
   - ❑ D. 192.168.6.82
39. On what type of networks would you elect a DR? Select all that apply.
   - ❑ A. Broadcast multi-access
   - ❑ B. NBMA
   - ❑ C. Point-to-point
   - ❑ D. Point-to-multipoint
   - ❑ E. Point-to-multipoint non-broadcast
40. What type of cable would you plug into a T1 interface with a built-in CSU/DSU?
   - ❍ A. Serial
   - ❍ B. Rollover
   - ❍ C. UTP
   - ❍ D. Coax
   - ❍ E. Fiber
41. What is the default configuration register value?
   - ❍ A. 0x2142
   - ❍ B. 0x2100
   - ❍ C. 0x2101
   - ❍ D. 0x2102

42. In the following configuration, what does the number 2 represent?

```
Router eigrp 2
 network 192.168.100.0
 network 172.16.0.0
```

- ❍ A. Process ID
- ❍ B. Autonomous system number
- ❍ C. The number of networks
- ❍ D. The router ID

43. Which of the following commands would correctly configure Telnet access for three VTY lines and encrypt both the enable and Telnet passwords?

- ❍ A. enable password que
  service password-encryption
  line vty 0 2
   login
   password que
- ❍ B. enable secret que
  service password-encryption
  line vty 0 3
   login
   password que
- ❍ C. enable secret que
  service password-encryption
  line vty 0 2
   login
   password que
- ❍ D. enable secret que
  service password-encryption
  line vty 0 4
   login
   password que

44. Which of the following are mechanisms that distance vector routing protocols use to prevent loops? Select all that apply.

- ❑ A. Split horizon
- ❑ B. Poison reverse
- ❑ C. Spanning-tree
- ❑ D. Dijkstra algorithm
- ❑ E. Hold-down timers

45. You have a class B network that you want to subnet to create at least 1,000 networks with as many hosts as possible on each subnet. What subnet mask should you use?

- ❍ A. 255.255.255.224
- ❍ B. 255.255.252.0
- ❍ C. 255.255.255.192
- ❍ D. 255.255.254
- ❍ E. 255.255.255.128

46. Examine the figure. You want to configure an access list that would permit everyone on the 172.16.0.0/16 network to access resources on the 172.18.0.0/16 network but deny everyone else. You configure the following `access-list`:

```
access-list 1 permit 172.16.0.0 0.0.255.255
```

On what router and in what direction should you apply this access list?

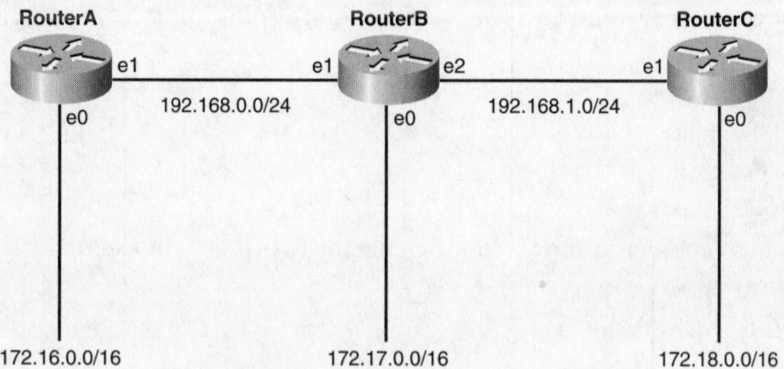

- ❍ A. Apply it inbound on RouterA's Ethernet 0 interface
- ❍ B. Apply it outbound on RouterA's Ethernet 1 interface
- ❍ C. Apply it inbound on RouterB's Ethernet 1 interface
- ❍ D. Apply it inbound on RouterC's Ethernet 1 interface
- ❍ E. Apply it outbound on RouterC's Ethernet 0 interface

47. What is the broadcast address for the 172.19.48.0/21 network?

- ❍ A. 172.19.55.255
- ❍ B. 172.19.48.255
- ❍ C. 172.19.63.255
- ❍ D. 172.19.51.255
- ❍ E. 172.19.64.255

48. What is the benefit to having a hierarchical design with OSPF? Select all that apply.

- ❑ A. Smaller routing tables mean less overhead.
- ❑ B. If a network in an area goes down, it will not affect the summarized route in other areas.
- ❑ C. Convergence is faster.
- ❑ D. Less configuration on the area border routers.
- ❑ E. Feasible successors are chosen faster.

49. In spanning-tree, how long does it take a port to go from the blocking state to the forwarding state?

- ❍ A. 10 seconds
- ❍ B. 20 seconds
- ❍ C. 30 seconds
- ❍ D. 40 seconds
- ❍ E. 50 seconds

50. What device would you use to create more collision domains on your network?

- ❍ A. Router
- ❍ B. Hub
- ❍ C. Switch
- ❍ D. Repeater

51. Which command shows you the current IOS that is in use on a router?

- ❍ A. Show version
- ❍ B. Show flash
- ❍ C. Show IOS
- ❍ D. Show running-config

52. Examine the figure. RIP is configured between RouterA, RouterB, and RouterC; however, you are unable to ping the 172.20.0.0/16 network from RouterA. The configurations of the routers are as follows:

RouterA

```
router rip
 network 172.16.0.0
 network 172.17.0.0
```

RouterB

```
router rip
 network 172.18.0.0
 network 172.19.0.0
```

RouterC

```
router rip
 network 172.19.0.0
 network 172.20.0.0
```

What is wrong with the configuration that causes this problem?

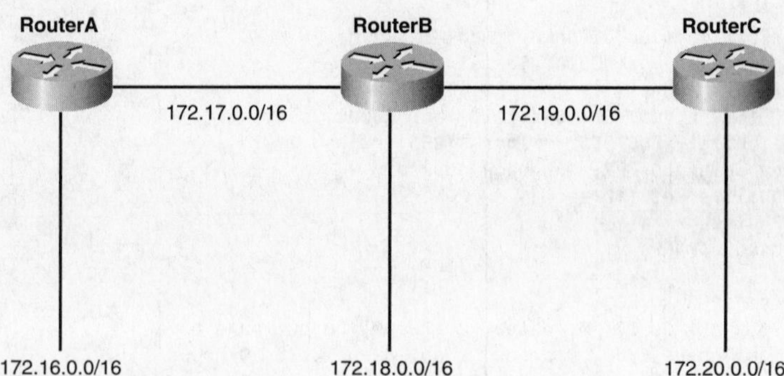

❍ A. The command `'version 2'` is missing on all three routers.
❍ B. A default route is missing.
❍ C. The configuration on RouterB is incomplete.
❍ D. There is not enough information to answer this question.
❍ E. The interface connected to the 172.18.0.0/16 is shut down.

53. Below is the output of the show interface serial 0 command that has been executed on two routers. Both routers are connected to each other on the serial interfaces through a leased line; however, you are unable to ping across the serial interface. What is wrong?

RouterA

```
Serial 0 is up, line protocol is down
Hardware is MCI Serial
Internet address is 192.168.15.170, subnet mask is 255.255.255.0
MTU 1500 bytes, BW 1544 Kbit, DLY 20000 usec, rely 255/255, load 1/255
Encapsulation HDLC, loopback not set, keepalive set (10 sec)
Last input 0:00:08, output 0:00:00, output hang never
Output queue 0/40, 0 drops; input queue 0/75, 0 drops
Five minute input rate 0 bits/sec, 0 packets/sec
Five minute output rate 0 bits/sec, 0 packets/sec
8192 packets input, 141256 bytes, 0 no buffer
Received 5125 broadcasts, 0 runts, 0 giants
4 input errors, 0 CRC, 0 frame, 0 overrun, 0 ignored, 3 abort
1 carrier transitions 21351 packets output, 1531572 bytes,
0 underruns 0 output errors, 0 collisions, 2 interface resets, 0
restarts
```

RouterB

```
Serial0/0 is up, line protocol is down
Hardware is PowerQUICC Serial
Internet address is 192.168.15.170/24
MTU 1500 bytes, BW 1544 Kbit, DLY 20000 usec,
reliability 255/255, txload 1/255, rxload 1/255
Encapsulation PPP, loopback not set
Keepalive set (10 sec)
LCP Closed
Closed: IPXCP
Listen: CCP
Open: IPCP, CDPCP
Last input 00:00:00, output 00:00:00, output hang never
Output queue 0/40, 0 drops; input queue 0/75, 0 drops
Five minute input rate 0 bits/sec, 0 packets/sec
Five minute output rate 0 bits/sec, 0 packets/sec
2251 packets input, 13515 bytes, 0 no buffer
Received 61367 broadcasts, 0 runts, 0 giants
8 input errors, 0 CRC, 0 frame, 0 overrun, 0 ignored, 2 abort
2 carrier transitions 23515 packets output, 89234 bytes,
0 underruns 0 output errors, 0 collisions, 2 interface resets, 0
restarts
```

❍ A. The encapsulations do not match.

❍ B. There is a problem with the cable on RouterA.

❍ C. The provider's router is misconfigured.

❍ D. There is a problem with the cable on RouterB.

❍ E. There is a clocking problem on RouterA.

54. What is wrong with the following OSPF configuration that causes this problem?

```
Router ospf 65535
 network 192.168.0.4 255.255.255.252 area 0
 network 192.168.0.8 255.255.255.248 area 1
interface fastethernet 0/0
 ip address 192.168.0.9 255.255.255.248
interface serial 0/0
ip address 192.168.0.5 255.255.255.252
```

❍ A. The IP addresses and the network statements under the router configuration do not match.

❍ B. The process ID number is too high.

❍ C. The wrong masks are used under the OSPF process.

❍ D. The areas are not the same for the two networks.

55. Given the following output, how were the hosts learned on the router?

```
Router# show hosts
Default domain is Que
Name/address lookup uses domain service
Name servers are 255.255.255.255
Host                 Flag            Age    Type            Address(es)
RouterA        (perm, OK)  0         IP             192.168.100.1
RouterB        (perm, OK)  0    IP            192.168.200.1
```

❍ A. Through a DNS server

❍ B. Through the IP host command

❍ C. Through the DNS dynamic-discovery command

❍ D. Through a routing protocol

❍ E. Through ARP

56. On what type of device would you typically configure the clock rate?

❍ A. Router.

❍ B. Switch.

❍ C. CSU/DSU.

❍ D. This is configured on the provider's router.

57. CDP is found at what layer of the OSI model?

❍ A. Datalink

❍ B. Network

❍ C. Transport

❍ D. Session

❍ E. Application

58. Which of the following are valid modes used to switch frames? Select all that apply.

❑ A. Store-and-Forward

❑ B. Cut-Through

❑ C. Cut-Free

❑ D. Fragment-Free

❑ E. Store-and-Fragment

59. What would cause an OSPF adjacency not to form between two routers? Select all that apply.
   - O A. Routers are using incompatible IOS versions.
   - O B. The interfaces connecting the two routers are on different subnets.
   - O C. Routers are using different OSPF passwords.
   - O D. The interfaces connecting the two routers are in different areas.
   - O E. The process ID numbers do not match between the two routers.
60. Where is `startup-config` kept on a router?
   - O A. RAM
   - O B. NVRAM
   - O C. ROM
   - O D. Flash

Answer Key to Practice Test #1

1. B
2. E
3. D
4. A,B
5. B,C
6. A,C,D
7. C
8. B
9. A,D
10. D
11. B
12. A
13. A,B,C,D,E
14. D
15. B
16. B
17. D
18. A
19. E
20. A
21. B
22. A
23. C,E
24. C
25. D
26. D
27. C
28. B
29. D
30. D
31. A
32. A,C
33. C
34. C
35. A
36. A
37. D
38. C,D
39. A,B
40. C
41. D
42. B
43. C
44. A,B,E
45. C
46. E
47. A
48. A,B,C
49. E
50. C
51. A
52. C
53. A
54. C
55. B
56. C
57. A
58. A,B,D
59. B,C,D
60. B

Question 1

Answer B is the correct answer. A /28 network would give you 14 hosts on each network. The network increment of a /28 network is 16. Because the `ip subnet-zero` command is on the router, you can use the zero subnet, making the second subnet 192.168.25.16 and the first useable IP address 192.168.25.17. Answers A, C, D, and E are incorrect because each of these addresses is on a different subnet.

Question 2

Answer E is the correct answer. According to the diagram, the network attached to the FastEthernet0/3 interface is 172.21.248.0/23, although the configuration shows that FastEthernet 0/3 is configured for 172.21.254.1/23, which is on a different subnet. Answer A is incorrect because there is nothing incorrect with the pool configuration. Answer B is incorrect because the `ip nat outside` and `ip nat inside` commands are on the correct interfaces. Answer C is incorrect because the scenario does not ask you to overload your pool of addresses. Answer D is incorrect because there is nothing incorrect with the access list configuration.

Question 3

Answer D is the correct answer. On ISDN BRI interfaces, you have two B channels operating at 64Kbs each. With only 64Kbs per channel, you do not have a lot of bandwidth with which to work. Therefore, you should use every precaution you can to minimize any network overhead on your ISDN interfaces. Because static routes do not send out any routing updates, you should use static routes with ISDN BRI interfaces to minimize overhead. Answers A, B, and C are all incorrect because they do send out routing updates (LSAs in the case of OSPF) and therefore do not conserve your routing overhead.

Question 4

Answers A and B are the correct answers. Both Telnet and FTP operate at the Application layer of the OSI model. Answers C and D are incorrect because Ping and Traceroute use ICMP; ICMP operates at the Network layer of the OSI model. Answer E is incorrect because CDP operates at the Datalink layer.

Question 5

Answers B and C are the correct answers. The IEEE standard for trunking is 802.1q. Use the `switchport mode trunk` and `switchport trunk encapsulation dot1q` commands to configure an 802.1q trunk between two switches. Answer A is incorrect because this is an invalid command. Answer D is incorrect because this would configure Inter-switch link trunking, which is a Cisco proprietary method of trunking and not an IEEE standard.

Question 6

Answers A, C, and D are the correct answers. EIGRP supports AppleTalk, IP, and IPX. Answers B and E are incorrect because EIGRP does not support Banyan Vines or LAT.

Question 7

Answer C is the correct answer. You want to configure two Telnet sessions. Because Cisco begins its numbering with 0, you would configure lines 0 through 1. The commands to configure Telnet authentication are login and password. The service password-encryption global configuration command is used to encrypt all unencrypted passwords on your router. Only answer C has the correct configuration. Answer A is incorrect because it configures all five Telnet lines and not just the first two. Answer A is also incorrect because it is not encrypting your passwords. Answer B is incorrect because it configures the first three Telnet lines and not just the first two. Answer D is incorrect because it does not have the proper configuration for Telnet authentication. Finally, answer E is incorrect because it configures all five configuration lines and not just the first two.

Question 8

Answer B is the correct answer. RouterA is learning of the networks attached to RouterD via OSPF and RIP. When a router is learning of networks through more than one routing source, it chooses the best path based on whichever source has the lowest administrative distance. RouterA is learning the path through OSPF from RouterB and through RIP from RouterE. OSPF has an administrative distance of 110, and RIP has an administrative distance of 120. Because RIP's administrative distance is higher than OSPF's administrative distance, the path through RouterB is preferred. Answer A is incorrect because OSPF has a lower administrative distance than RIP. Answer C is incorrect because RouterA will choose RouterB based on administrative distance. Answer D is incorrect because enough information is given to answer this question.

Question 9

Answers A and D are the correct answers. Answers B and C are incorrect because these are network addresses and therefore cannot be configured on hosts.

Question 10

Answer D is the correct answer. Answers A and C are incorrect because Telnet uses TCP and not UDP. Answer B is incorrect because the wildcard mask for the 172.19.40.0/21 network is incorrect.

Question 11

Answer B is the correct answer. OSPF will first choose the highest IP address on any loopback interface for its router ID. If no loopback interfaces are configured, the highest IP address on any active physical interface is chosen. Answer A is incorrect because you do not loopback interfaces to run OSPF. Answer C is incorrect because the interfaces must be active (up) when OSPF is initialized in order for OSPF to consider using them as the router ID. Answer D is incorrect because the highest IP address is chosen, not the lowest.

Question 12

Answer A is the correct answer. ISDN is good for voice, video, and data and has a separate channel (D) for out-of-band signaling. Although some of the other answers might be good for voice, video, and data, none provide out-of-band signaling like ISDN.

Question 13

Answers A, B, C, D, and E are the correct answers. You can view all of these with the `show cdp neighbors detail` command. Note that the `show cdp entry *` command is equivalent.

Question 14

Answer D is the correct answer. Only VTP Server mode allows you to make VLAN changes that propagate out to other switches. Currently, the switch operates in VTP Transparent mode, so any changes are local to the switch. Answers A, B, and C are incorrect because domain name, version numbers, and VTP pruning are irrelevant to passing VLAN information between switches.

Question 15

Answer B is the correct answer. Routers break up your broadcast domains. There is one router in this diagram with two interfaces. Each interface is in its own broadcast domain, so there are two broadcast domains in this diagram.

Question 16

Answer B is the correct answer. Interface BRI0/0 on RouterA is on the 172.16.20.0/22 network, but interface BRI0/0 on RouterB is on the 172.16.24.0/22 network. Answers A and D are incorrect because there is nothing incorrect with the static routes. Answer C is incorrect because the server and the router's interface are on the 172.16.128.0/22 network. Finally, answer E is incorrect because the IP address 172.16.64.201/22 is a completely valid IP address.

Question 17

Answer D is the correct answer. The configuration register, shown in the very last line of the output, is 0x2142. This setting causes the router to bypass the startup-configuration every time the router boots. Bypassing the configuration makes it appear as if the configuration is lost (although it is still present in a NVRAM). To load the configuration, you should set the configuration register to 0x2102 (done with the `config-register 0x2102 global configuration` command). Answers A, B, and C are incorrect because they all pertain to IOS issues, but the problem is not with the IOS; the problem is with the configuration being lost.

Question 18

Answer A is the correct answer. EIGRP is classful by default, which means that it automatically summarizes your subnetworks at the /8, /16, and /24 bit boundaries. The `no auto-summary` command, entered within the EIGRP configuration mode, causes EIGRP to become classless and sends out the subnet mask in updates. Answer B is incorrect because there is nothing incorrect with the network statements. Answer C is incorrect because the mask is not necessary. (As a side note, EIGRP can use wildcard masks like OSPF, but they are not required.) Answer D is incorrect because you want to disable auto-summary, not turn it on. Finally, answer E is incorrect because the maximum-paths command modifies load-balancing parameters, which is irrelevant to the problem.

Question 19

Answer E is the correct answer. The frame check sequence (FCS) is a checksum added to the end of Ethernet frames. (Ethernet operates at the datalink layer.) Answers A, B, C, and D, are therefore incorrect.

Question 20

Answer A is the correct answer. Only answer A has the correct configuration that allows for a pool of six addresses. Answers B and D are incorrect because the access-lists are referencing the inside global addresses instead of the inside local addresses and the pools are referencing inside local addresses instead of inside global addresses. Answer C is incorrect because the pool allows for seven addresses and not six.

Question 21

Answer B is the correct answer. Although the LMI types do not have to match, the encapsulation types do. One router uses IETF encapsulation, and the other uses the default (Cisco). Answer A is incorrect because the routers can run different LMI types. (LMI runs only from the router to the frame-relay provider and can therefore be different on both sides of the frame-relay virtual circuit.) Answer C is incorrect because the configuration is complete. Answer D is incorrect because the routers are both on the same 10.250.86.64/30 subnet.

Question 22

Answer A is the correct answer. Ping and Traceroute use ICMP, which operates at the network layer.

Question 23

Answers C and E are the correct answers. The 192.168.5.0/24 network is not in the routing table, and a default route was not set up (as evidenced by the statement `GATEWAY OF LAST RESORT IS NOT SET`). Therefore, you can say goodbye to any packet destined for the 192.168.5.0/24 network. The router drops the packet and sends back an ICMP type 3 Destination Unreachable (DU) message to the source of the packet. Because the routing table does not have this entry, answers A, B, and D are incorrect.

Question 24

Answer C is the correct answer. The dialer list in the configuration references access list 100. Access list 100 causes any HTTP traffic to bring up the ISDN connection. However, this access list is not used as a packet filter, so after the ISDN line is up, all traffic (including non-HTTP traffic) is allowed across the link. Answers A and B are incorrect because the configuration is configured correctly. Answer D is incorrect because FTP is not a subset of HTTP.

Question 25

Answer D is the correct answer. Cisco defines OSPF cost as 10^8/bandwidth. If you take 100,000,000 (10^8) and divide it by the 1,544,000 (a T1), you get 64.766. Because remainders are not factored into the metric, you are left with 64. For the test, you should know the common metrics such as 1 for a 100Mb connection, 10 for a 10Mb connection, 64 for a T1 connection, and 1,562 for a 64Kbs connection. Answer A is incorrect because this is the bandwidth of a T1 and not the cost. Answer B is incorrect because this is the cost for a 10Mb link. Answer C is incorrect because this would be the cost for a 1Mb link.

Question 26

Answer D is the correct answer. A /30, or 255.255.255.252, mask is common on point-to-point wide area network links because this mask allows for two addresses. Because you need only two addresses on point-to-point links, this mask is ideal because it gives you just enough addresses to assign IP addresses to both routers while saving on your overall IP address space.

Question 27

Answer C is the correct answer. Only answer C has the correct configuration to assign a default gateway. Answers A and D are incorrect because the command should be entered from global configuration mode. Answer B is incorrect because you do not enter the subnet mask with this command.

Question 28

Answer B is the correct answer. Although the default maximum is 100, the absolute maximum hop count for EIGRP is 224. Answer A is incorrect because 255 is the absolute maximum hop count for IGRP, not EIGRP. Answer C is incorrect because this is the maximum hop count for RIP. Answer D is incorrect because this is the TTL used for routing updates, not the maximum hop count. (Having a TTL of 1 means that the routing updates will be sent only to the next router; the next router will then have to generate a new routing update and send it out to pass it on.) Answer E is incorrect because EIGRP does have a maximum hop count; OSPF is the routing protocol with an unlimited hop count.

Question 29

Answer D is the correct answer. The spanning-tree states are blocking, listening, learning, and forwarding. In the learning state, the port is populating the MAC table so that when it moves to forwarding state, it is capable of making intelligent decisions as to where it should send frames. Otherwise, without the learning state, when the port becomes active, it would flood frames out all ports until it learns MAC addresses. Answer A is incorrect because this describes the listening state and not the learning state. Answer B is incorrect because this describes the blocking state. Finally, answer C is incorrect because this describes the forwarding state.

Question 30

Answer D is the correct answer. You would use a straight-through cable between a router and switch. The switch is then responsible for crossing over the transmit and receive communication path. Answer A is incorrect because a rollover cable is used to connect to a console port. Answer B is incorrect because a null modem cable is used between two asynchronous serial ports. Answer C is incorrect because a crossover cable would be used between two switches or between two routers, but not between a router and a switch.

Question 31

Answer A is the correct answer. Without the broadcast keyword, broadcast and multicast-based routing updates are not sent across the link. Answer B is incorrect because the RIP version is irrelevant to get RIP to work across frame-relay. Answer C is incorrect because inverse-arp has nothing to do with getting your routing updates across a frame-relay network. Finally, answer D is incorrect because RIP is activated on the interfaces. When you enter the network statements under the RIP configuration mode, it automatically enables RIP on the interfaces where those networks reside.

Question 32

Answers A and C are the correct answers. IGRP and EIGRP can also factor in reliability, load, and MTU. Answer B is incorrect because this is the metric used by RIP. Answer D is incorrect because this is the metric used by OSPF and IS-IS.

Question 33

Answer C is the correct answer. CHAP is a three-way handshake authentication protocol. One router sends a challenge, the second router sends an MD5 hash of the password, and the first router sends a success or fail response (therefore, three messages).

Question 34

Answer C is the correct answer. The access list is permitting TCP port 110 and 25, which POP and SMTP use. Answer A is incorrect because NTP (UDP 123) or SNMP (UDP ports 160 and 161) do not use these ports. Answer B is incorrect because the masks are incorrect. Answer D is incorrect because SNMP traffic is not referenced in the access list; only POP and SMTP are.

Question 35

Answer A is the correct answer. The dialer list is 4, but it is applied as number 40. Answers B, C, and D are incorrect because there is nothing incorrect with the remaining configuration. Answer E is incorrect because the configuration is complete.

Question 36

Answer A is the correct answer. Routing occurs at the Internet layer of the TCP/IP model. Answer B is incorrect because the Network layer is on the OSI model, not the TCP/IP model. Answers C and D are incorrect because these are different layers.

Question 37

Answer D is the correct answer. The feasible successor is stored in the topology table. Should the successor route go down in the routing table, the feasible successor would take over and the DUAL algorithm would work to elect a new feasible successor. Answer A is incorrect because this is where you would find neighbor information and not the feasible successor. Answer B is incorrect because this is where you would find the successor. Answers C and E are incorrect because these tables are used with OSPF, not EIGRP.

Question 38

Answers C and D are the correct answers. The IP address is on the 192.168.6.80/29 network. A /29 network uses an increment of 8, so the next network is 192.168.6.88. Therefore, your range is 192.168.6.80–192.168.6.87 but, because you cannot use the first or last address of each subnet (they are the network and broadcast addresses), your range of valid host addresses are 192.168.6.81–192.168.6.86. Only answers C and D have IP addresses in this range.

Question 39

Answers A and B are the correct answers. DR elections are used with OSPF routing. These elections occur only on broadcast multi-access and non-broadcast multi-access (NBMA) networks.

Question 40

Answer C is the correct answer. If the router has a built-in CSU/DSU, you use a standard straight-through RJ-45 UTP connector coming from the wall jack to the router. While you may also use a RJ-48 STP connector, this was not one of the answers. If the CSU/DSU were external, you would have a straight-through cable from the wall jack to the CSU/DSU and then a serial cable from the CSU/DSU to the router. Because the question mentions a built-in CSU/DSU, you use a UTP cable.

Question 41

Answer D is the correct answer. This is the default configuration register value. Answer A is incorrect because this value is used when performing password recovery on a router. Answer B is incorrect because 0x2100 boots your router into ROM Monitor mode. Answer C is incorrect because 0x2101 boots your router into RxBoot mode in ROM.

Question 42

Answer B is the correct answer. EIGRP and IGRP both require autonomous system numbers. This can be any number you want between 1 and 65,535, but all routers must share this same number for routing updates to pass between them. Answer A is incorrect because process IDs are used in OSPF, not EIGRP. Answer C is incorrect because the number is the AS number, not the number of networks. Answer D is incorrect because the router ID is chosen automatically and is not specified with the `router eigrp` command. Answer D is also incorrect because, although there are router IDs with EIGRP, at the CCNA level the router IDs take on only significance with OSPF.

Question 43

Answer C is the correct answer. You need the `enable secret` and `service password-encryption` commands to encrypt your passwords. Because the question asks to configure only three Telnet lines, you configure lines 0–2. Therefore, answer C is correct. Answer A is incorrect because the enable password is not encrypted. Answer B is incorrect because the command line vty 0 3 encrypts four Telnet sessions and not two (which the question asks). Finally, answer D is incorrect because it configures all five Telnet sessions.

Question 44

Answers A, B, and E are the correct answers. Reverse poisoning and triggered updates are other options used to prevent loops in switched networks. Answer C is incorrect because spanning-tree is used to prevent loops in switched networks, not routed networks. Answer D is incorrect because the Dijkstra algorithm is used with OSPF, which is a link-state routing protocol, not distance-vector.

Question 45

Answer C is the correct answer. The subnet mask 255.255.255.192 is borrowing 10 bits from a class B network. The formula to determine your networks (assuming that you cannot use subnet-zero) is 2^n-2. Borrowing 10 bits gives you 1,022 networks (2^{10}-2=1022). Answer A is incorrect because the

255.255.255.224 mask gives you 2,046 networks and 30 hosts. Although this meets the requirement of providing at least 1,000 networks, it does not provide as many host addresses as the 255.255.255.192 mask. (It provides 62 host addresses on each network.) Answer B is incorrect because it only gives you 62 networks. Answer D is incorrect because it only gives you 126 networks. Finally, answer E is incorrect because it only gives you 510 networks.

Question 46

Answer E is the correct answer. A standard access list has been configured, and the general rule is that standard access lists should be applied as close to the destination as possible. The Ethernet 0 interface on RouterC is the interface closest to the destination. Therefore, answer E is correct, and the other answers, which apply it on other routers or on the wrong interface, are incorrect.

Question 47

Answer A is the correct answer. A /21 subnet has a network increment of 8 in the third octet. The next network, then, is 172.19.56.0. One less than the next network is 172.19.55.255 (answer A). Answer B is incorrect because this is a valid host address on the same network. Answer C is incorrect because this is a broadcast address on the 172.19.56.0 network. Answer D is incorrect because this a valid host address on the same network. Finally, answer E is incorrect because this is a valid host address on the 172.19.64.0 network.

Question 48

Answers A, B, and C are the correct answers. Having a hierarchical design makes it easy to supernet (summarize your networks). This question really tests to see if you understand the benefit of summarizing your networks. Summarizing your networks results in less overhead, which, subsequently, equate to smaller routing tables (answer A). If a particular subnet goes down, it does not affect the summarized route in other areas (answer B). Also, having fewer routes means that the routers have less to process, which results in faster convergence (answer C). Answer D is incorrect because summarization actually involves more configuration on a router, not less. Answer E is incorrect because feasible successors are used with EIGRP, not OSPF.

Question 49

Answer E is the correct answer. The blocking state takes 20 seconds, and the listening and learning states take 15 seconds each for a total of 50 seconds.

Question 50

Answer C is the correct answer. Switches (and bridges) are used to create more collision domains because each segment on a switch or bridge is its own collision domain. Answer A is incorrect because a router is used to create more broadcast domains, not collision domains. Answer B is incorrect because a hub actually creates more congestion on a network and not fewer collision domains. Answer D is incorrect because a repeater amplifies only a signal and does not create more collision domains.

Question 51

Answer A is the correct answer. Show version displays the name of the current IOS version in use on a router. Answer B is incorrect because this shows you the name of all IOS images on a router but not the one currently in use. Answer C is incorrect because this is an invalid command. Finally, answer D is incorrect because this command shows you the current configuration in NVRAM and not the current IOS version.

Question 52

Answer C is the correct answer. RouterB is missing the 172.17.0.0/16 network. Answer A is incorrect because the RIP version 2 is not necessary to make this scenario work. Answer B is incorrect because a default route is unnecessary. Answer D is incorrect because you do have enough information to answer this problem. Finally, although the interface connected to 172.18.0.0/16 does need to be up for you to communicate across the network, nothing in the scenario indicates that the interface is down. In addition, the better answer is C because, even if the interface is not shut down, it cannot work unless the 172.17.0.0/16 network is added under the RIP process on RouterB.

Question 53

Answer A is the correct answer. RouterA uses HDLC encapsulation, and RouterB is using PPP encapsulation. Answers B and D are incorrect because nothing in the output indicates that there is a problem with the cabling. Answer C is incorrect because nothing in the output reveals information about how the provider is configured. Finally, answer E is incorrect because the problem is with the encapsulations, not clocking. However, clocking problems can cause the line protocol to not function, although the output indicates that the problem is with encapsulations and not clocking.

Question 54

Answer C is the correct answer. OSPF uses wildcard masks and not subnet masks. The correct OSPF configuration is

```
Router OSPF 65545
 network 192.168.0.4 0.0.0.3 area 0
 network 192.168.0.8 0.0.0.7 area 1
```

Answer A is incorrect because the IP addresses on the interfaces are on the same networks referenced under the OSPF routing process configuration. Answer B is incorrect because the number of the process ID is irrelevant. Answer D is incorrect because the areas do not have to be same number.

Question 55

Answer B is the correct answer. The output shows the flag `perm`, which means that they were permanently learned through the IP host global configuration command. Answer A is incorrect because the flag `temp` would show if they were learned through a DNS server. Answer C is incorrect because there is no such thing as a DNS dynamic-discovery command. Answer D is incorrect because routing protocols have nothing to do with learning hostname to IP address mappings. Answer E is incorrect because DNS or static mappings are used to map IP address to hostnames, not ARP. ARP is used to map IP addresses to MAC addresses.

Question 56

Answer C is the correct answer. The clock rate is typically configured on the CSU/DSU in production networks. Often, the CSU/DSU comes built into the router, but even if it is built into the router, the CSU/DSU still provides the clocking and not the router. Although it is true that you can configure clocking on a router with the clock rate interface command, this is done on lab environments and not on production networks. The question asks for the typical configuration, not for unique lab environments. Therefore, answer C is correct and answer A is incorrect. Answers B and D are incorrect because clocking is not configured on switching or on the provider's network. Although it is possible to provide clocking from the provider, this is not the typical configuration. For the CCNA exam, remember that clocking is done at the CSU/DSU.

Question 57

Answer A is the correct answer. CDP uses multicasts frames at the Datalink layer of the OSI model. All other answers reference other OSI layers and are therefore incorrect.

Question 58

Answers A, B, and D are the correct answers. Answers C and E are not valid switching modes.

Question 59

Answers B, C, and D are the correct answers. In addition to these answers, the interfaces connecting the two routers must be configured to use the same timers and stub configuration (stub areas are covered more heavily on the CCNP exams and not at the CCNA level). Answer A is incorrect because the two routers can run different IOS versions. Answer E is incorrect because the process ID is locally significant to each router and does not have to match the process ID on other routers.

Question 60

Answer B is the correct answer. Answer A is incorrect because this is where the running-config is kept. Answer C is incorrect because this is where the bootstrap code, ROM Monitor mode, and RxBoot are found. Answer D is incorrect because this is where the IOS images are stored.

Practice Exam #2

1. Which of the following are valid host addresses on the same subnet as the 192.168.14.69/28 host? [Select all that apply.]
   - ❍ A. 192.168.14.63
   - ❍ B. 192.168.14.65
   - ❍ C. 192.168.14.81
   - ❍ D. 192.168.14.64
   - ❍ E. 192.168.14.78

2. Your co-worker calls you and informs you that VTP is not working between two switches. What advice can you give your co-worker to troubleshoot VTP? [Select all that apply.]
   - ❍ A. Make sure that a trunk is configured between the two switches.
   - ❍ B. Make sure that both switches are in the same VTP domain.
   - ❍ C. Make sure that both switches are operating in the same VTP mode.
   - ❍ D. Make sure that both switches are using the same VTP password.
   - ❍ E. Make sure that both switches are using the same hostname.

3. When configuring frame-relay subinterfaces, what configuration steps should you take for the main interface? [Select all that apply.]
   - ❍ A. Configure the DLCI on the main interface.
   - ❍ B. Configure the IP address on the main interface.
   - ❍ C. Take the IP address off the main interface.
   - ❍ D. Configure the frame-relay encapsulation on the main interface.
   - ❍ E. Take the frame-relay encapsulation off the main interface.

4. What statement is true for a named access list that is not true for a numbered access list?
   - ❍ A. You can only do a standard named access list; you can not do an extended named access list.
   - ❍ B. You can delete individual lines in a named access list; you cannot delete individual lines in a numbered access list.
   - ❍ C. You can only apply named access lists on VTY lines; you cannot apply them on an interface.
   - ❍ D. You can only do IP named access lists; you cannot do IPX named access lists.

5. Which switching mode would you use if you were concerned about error-free transport?
   - ❍ A. Cut-Through
   - ❍ B. Fragment-Free
   - ❍ C. Store-and-Forward
   - ❍ D. Fragment-Forward

6. Which key sequence would you use to cause your cursor to go to the beginning of a typed command?
   - ❍ A. Ctrl-A
   - ❍ B. Ctrl-Z
   - ❍ C. Ctrl-N
   - ❍ D. Ctrl-P

7. Examine the output below. Based on this output, which of the following are true statements?

```
RIP: received update from 10.0.0.1 on Serial 0
     172.16.0.0 in 1 hops
     172.17.0.0 in 2 hops
     172.18.0.0 in 3 hops
RIP: Sending update to 255.255.255.255 via Serial 0 (10.0.0.2)
     subnet 192.168.0.0, metric 1
RIP: Sending update to 255.255.255.255 via Ethernet 0 (192.168.0.1)
     subnet 10.0.0.0, metric 1
     subnet 172.16.0.0, metric 2
     subnet 172.17.0.0, metric 3
     subnet 172.18.0.0, metric 4
```

   - ❍ A. Split-horizon is not working.
   - ❍ B. The router is running RIP version 2.
   - ❍ C. The router is on the 172.16.0.0 network.
   - ❍ D. Split-horizon is working.
   - ❍ E. You will not be able to ping a host with the address of 172.18.15.9.

8. You have just created a configuration in your favorite text editor with some basic commands that you want to put on a new router (see configuration below). You copy your template and paste it into the new router. When you go to telnet into the router, you get a message saying that your computer could not open a connection to the host. What is wrong?

```
! Configuration for new router
hostname NewRouter
enable password letmein
service password-encryption
interface Ethernet 0
 ip address 192.168.125.97 255.255.255.240
interface serial 0
 description ***WAN Link to Cincinati***
 encapsulation frame-relay
 ip address 192.168.125.113 255.255.255.252
line vty 0 4
 login
 password letmein
 logging synchronous
```

- ❍ A. The encapsulation is wrong on the serial interface.
- ❍ B. The telnet configuration is incomplete.
- ❍ C. The Ethernet interface is missing the `no shut` command.
- ❍ D. The `login` and `password` commands are entered in the wrong order.
- ❍ E. The router is missing a console password.

9. Which of the following commands shows you if a router is acting as the designated router for one of its interfaces?

- ❍ A. `show ip ospf database`
- ❍ B. `show ip ospf interface`
- ❍ C. `show ip ospf`
- ❍ D. `show ip ospf summary-address`

10. Which of the following correctly matches the names of the protocol data units (PDUs) with their respective layers?

7. Application	A. Data
6. Presentation	B. Bits
5. Session	C. Frames
4. Transport	D. Segments
3. Network	E. Packets
2. Data-Link	
1. Physical	

- ❍ A. 7-A, 6-A, 5-A, 4-D, 3-E, 2-C, 1-B
- ❍ B. 7-A, 6-A, 5-A, 4-E, 3-D, 2-C, 1-B
- ❍ C. 7-A, 6-A, 5-A, 4-C, 3-E, 2-D, 1-B
- ❍ D. 7-A, 6-A, 5-A, 4-D, 3-C, 2-E, 1-B

11. Where will a router boot to if the configuration register is set to 0x2101?
    - ❍ A. RAM
    - ❍ B. FLASH
    - ❍ C. ROM
    - ❍ D. NVRAM

12. The following configuration is applied on your router, but you are unable to initiate the ISDN connection. What is wrong?

```
isdn switch-type basic-ni
hostname RouterA
dialer-list 10 protocol ip list 10
access-list 10 deny host 192.168.14.4
access-list 10 permit 192.168.14.4 0.0.0.0
username RouterB password Que
ip route 172.16.0.0 255.255.0.0 10.0.0.2
interface bri0/0
 ip address 10.0.0.1 255.0.0.0
 dialer-group 10
 dialer idle-timeout 15
 dialer map ip 10.0.0.2 name RouterB 5553333
 isdn spid1 55511110101 5551111
 isdn spid2 55522220101 5552222
```

    - ❍ A. The dialer map configuration is wrong.
    - ❍ B. The `dialer load-threshold` command is missing.
    - ❍ C. The static route is wrong.
    - ❍ D. The access list is not permitting any traffic.
    - ❍ E. The dialer idle-timeout is too small.

13. What commands would you use to see the layer 3 information of a neighboring Cisco device? [Select all that apply.]
    - ❍ A. `show cdp neighbors`
    - ❍ B. `show cdp neighbors detail`
    - ❍ C. `show cdp entry *`
    - ❍ D. `show cdp traffic`

14. You just connected three switches together via trunk links. Based on the following output, which switch will be the root bridge?

```
Floor1#show spanning-tree
Spanning tree 1 is executing the IEEE compatible Spanning Tree protocol
 Bridge Identifier has priority 32768, address 0002.fd29.c602
 Configured hello time 2, max age 20, forward delay 15
Floor2#show spanning-tree
Spanning tree 1 is executing the IEEE compatible Spanning Tree protocol
 Bridge Identifier has priority 16384, address 0002.fd29.c604
 Configured hello time 2, max age 20, forward delay 15
Floor3#show spanning-tree
Spanning tree 1 is executing the IEEE compatible Spanning Tree protocol
 Bridge Identifier has priority 32768, address 0002.fd29.c601
 Configured hello time 2, max age 20, forward delay 15
```

❍ A. The Floor1 switch.

❍ B. The Floor2 switch.

❍ C. The Floor3 switch.

❍ D. There is not enough information to answer this question.

15. Which of the following are valid frame-relay encapsulations? [Select all that apply.]

❍ A. Cisco

❍ B. Ansi

❍ C. Q933A

❍ D. IETF

16. You need to subnet a class C network to allow for at least eight subnets with as many hosts as possible on each subnet. The command `ip subnet-zero` is applied on your router. What subnet mask would meet this requirement?

❍ A. 255.255.255.128

❍ B. 255.255.255.192

❍ C. 255.255.255.224

❍ D. 255.255.255.240

❍ E. 255.255.255.248

17. What is the maximum hop count for OSPF?

❍ A. 15

❍ B. 224

❍ C. 255

❍ D. Unlimited

18. What is true about the User Datagram Protocol (UDP)? [Select all that apply.]

❍ A. UDP performs a three-way handshake before transferring data.

❍ B. UDP uses less bandwidth than TCP.

❍ C. UDP provides reliable delivery.

❍ D. UDP is a connectionless protocol.

19. If the IOS is not found in flash memory when the router boots up, where will the router go to find an IOS image?
   - ❍ A. The router will attempt to find a TFTP server.
   - ❍ B. The router will attempt to load an IOS from RAM.
   - ❍ C. The router will load the mini-IOS in ROM.
   - ❍ D. The router will boot into ROM Monitor mode.

20. Which of the following is not a step you would take when configuring VLANs on a switch?
   - ❍ A. Create the VLAN
   - ❍ B. Name the VLAN
   - ❍ C. Assign a password to the VLAN
   - ❍ D. Associate the VLAN with an interface

21. Examine the figure below. A user sitting at HostA is sending a packet of data to HostB. When the packet returns, what will be the destination MAC address when the packet is coming from HostB and going

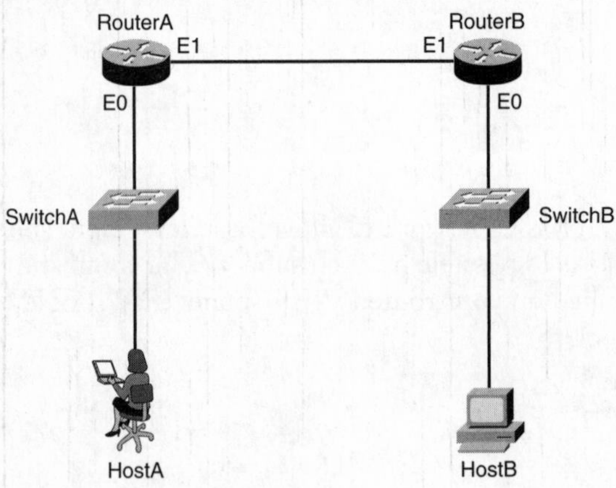

to RouterB?
   - ❍ A. RouterA's E0 MAC address
   - ❍ B. HostA's MAC address
   - ❍ C. RouterB's E0 MAC address
   - ❍ D. SwitchB's MAC address

22. Which of the following are examples of private IP addresses? [Select all that apply.]
   - ❍ A. 172.31.14.0
   - ❍ B. 172.33.0.10
   - ❍ C. 192.186.0.8
   - ❍ D. 10.5.0.0

23. Which of the following describes the difference between a switch and a bridge?

❍ A. A bridge is typically faster than a switch.

❍ B. A switch is faster than a bridge.

❍ C. A bridge is a layer 1 device, and a switch is a layer 2 device.

❍ D. A switch is a layer 1 device, and a bridge is a layer 2 device.

24. Which of the following is the correct configuration that would allow telnet access from the 10.0.0.5 host to your router?

❍ A.

```
access-list 100 permit tcp host 10.0.0.5 any eq telnet
        line vty 0 4
            access-class 100 in
```

❍ B.

```
access-list 1 permit host 10.0.0.5
        line vty 0 4
            ip access-group 1 in
```

❍ C.

```
access-list 1 permit host 10.0.0.5
        line vty 0 4
            access-class 1 in
```

❍ D.

```
access-list 100 permit tcp host 10.0.0.5 any eq telnet
        line vty 0 4
            access-class 100 out
```

25. You want your router to be a DR on its Ethernet segment. All the other routers on the segment are set to the default priority value. Which of the following commands would configure your router to win the DR election?

❍ A. `router ospf <process-id>`

`ip ospf priority 255`

❍ B. `router ospf <process-id>`

`ospf priority 255`

❍ C. `interface Ethernet 0`

`ip ospf priority 255`

❍ D. `interface Ethernet 0`

`ospf priority 255`

26. You execute the `show ip interface brief` command on a router and see that an interface is administratively down. What could you do to bring the interface to the up state?

❍ A. Execute the `no shutdown` command on the interface

❍ B. Reset the cable on the interface

❍ C. Execute the `interface up` command on the interface

❍ D. Enter the `clock rate` command on the interface

27. Examine the figure. HostA is unable to communicate with HostB. What is wrong?

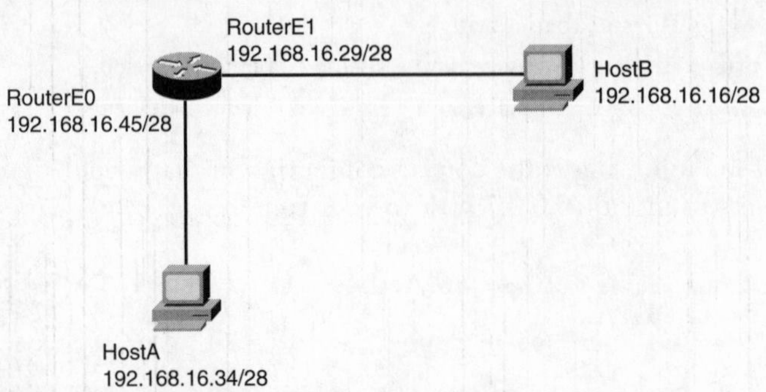

❍ A. HostA has an invalid IP address.
❍ B. HostB has an invalid IP address.
❍ C. The router's E0 interface has an invalid IP address.
❍ D. The router's E1 interface has an invalid IP address.

28. Which of the following routing protocols support VLSM? [Select all that apply.]

❍ A. RIPv1
❍ B. RIPv2
❍ C. IGRP
❍ D. EIGRP
❍ E. OSPF

29. Which of the following commands would you use to display an administrative message when a person connects to a router?

❍ A. `banner message`
❍ B. `banner motd`
❍ C. `banner`
❍ D. `banner display`

30. What are the types of frame-tagging used on trunks to carry VLAN traffic? [Select all that apply.]

❍ A. STP
❍ B. ISL
❍ C. 802.1d
❍ D. 802.1q
❍ E. VTP

31. At what layer of the OSI model would you find windowing and sequence numbers?
   - ❍ A. Application
   - ❍ B. Data-Link
   - ❍ C. Network
   - ❍ D. Physical
   - ❍ E. Transport

32. What is the name of the signaling protocol that operates on the ISDN D channel?
   - ❍ A. PPP
   - ❍ B. HDLC
   - ❍ C. LAPD
   - ❍ D. LAPB
   - ❍ E. SLIP

33. Examine the figure. How many collision domains are there in this network?

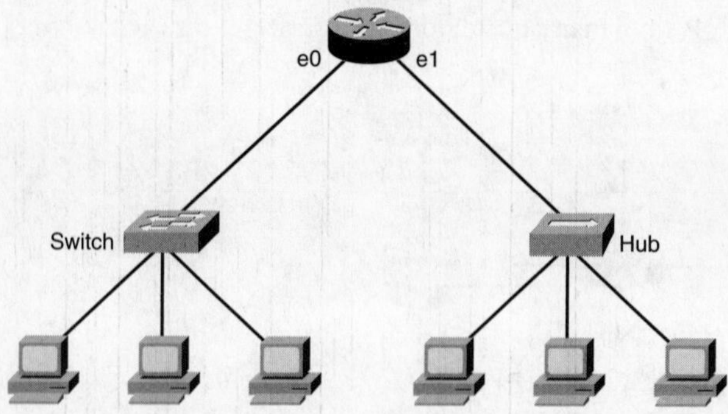

   - ❍ A. One
   - ❍ B. Three
   - ❍ C. Five
   - ❍ D. Seven
   - ❍ E. Nine

34. What is the binary number 10010011 in decimal notation?
   - ❍ A. 144
   - ❍ B. 146
   - ❍ C. 147
   - ❍ D. 139
   - ❍ E. 140

35. Examine the figure. This network is small with only 15 hosts on an Ethernet segment and a single connection out to the Internet. What routing protocol would you recommend between RouterA and the ISP router?

- A. A default route on RouterA and a static route on the ISP router
- B. BGP on RouterA and a static route on the ISP router
- C. RIP on both RouterA and the ISP router
- D. A static route on both RouterA and the ISP router
- E. A default route on both RouterA and the ISP router

36. Examine the figure. You are a consultant for this network. The network is running RIPv1 and, despite your best efforts, the company refuses to convert to RIPv2. The company has been given a class C address, which it wants to subnet to allow for one useable subnet on each network segment. Assuming RIPv1, how many host addresses can it get on each subnet?

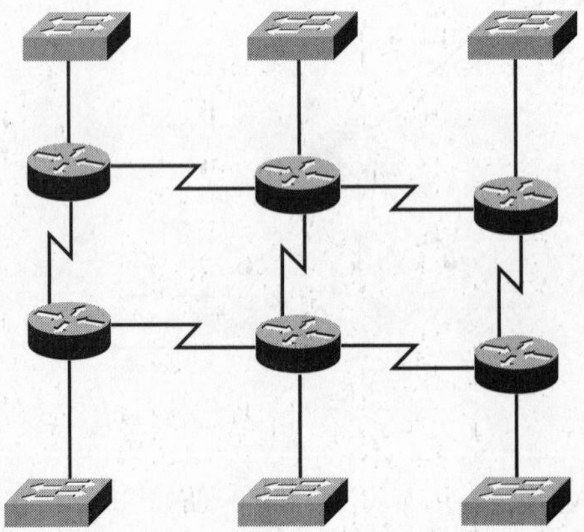

- A. You cannot subnet with RIPv1
- B. 6
- C. 30
- D. 14
- E. 2

37. The following access-list would permit which of the following host addresses? [Select all that apply.]

```
access-list 19 permit 172.17.80.0 0.0.15.255
```

- ❍ A. 172.17.95.12
- ❍ B. 172.17.96.100
- ❍ C. 172.17.84.0
- ❍ D. 172.17.99.2
- ❍ E. 172.17.97.4

38. Which of the following are examples of wide area network encapsulations? [Select all that apply.]

- ❍ A. CHAP
- ❍ B. PPP
- ❍ C. ISDN
- ❍ D. HDLC
- ❍ E. Frame-relay

39. Examine the figure. The company in the diagram has just implemented EIGRP, but routing does not appear to be working. What could be missing from the configuration to prevent EIGRP from working?

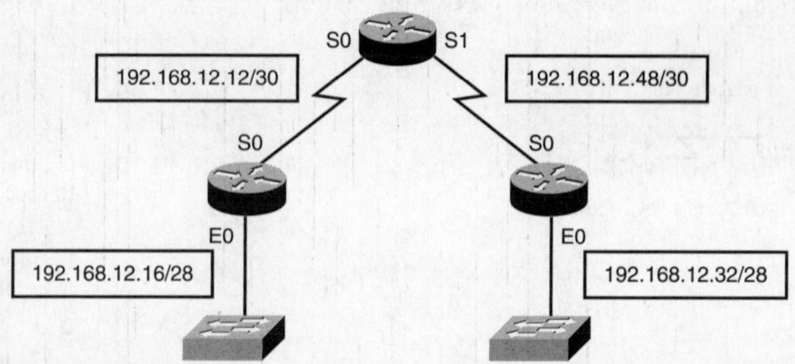

- ❍ A. Nothing is missing; EIGRP supports full-length subnet masks (FLSM) only.
- ❍ B. The `no auto-summary` command is missing on all routers.
- ❍ C. The subnet masks are missing from the configuration.
- ❍ D. The `auto-summary` command is missing on all routers.
- ❍ E. The `version 2` command is missing on all routers.

40. You are running RIP on a router but you are unable to receive any routing updates across your frame-relay network. Given the configuration output below, what is wrong?

```
interface fastethernet0/0
 ip address 10.16.0.1 255.240.0.0
interface serial0/0
 ip address 192.168.44.133 255.255.255.252
 encapsulation frame-relay
 no frame-relay inverse-arp
 frame-relay map ip 192.168.44.134 100
 frame-relay interface-dlci 100
router rip
 version 2
 network 10.0.0.0
 network 192.168.44.0
```

❍ A. The `frame-relay map` command is incomplete.

❍ B. The RIP configuration does not specify the correct networks.

❍ C. Inverse-arp needs to be enabled.

❍ D. RIP will not work across frame-relay as it is a non-broadcast multi-access medium, and RIP requires broadcast communication.

❍ E. The serial interface is on a different subnet than the IP address specified in the `frame-relay map` command.

41. You have just downloaded an IOS called c7200-j-mz. What information is included in this filename? [Select all that apply.]

❍ A. Platform

❍ B. Feature set

❍ C. Compression type

❍ D. Interface types

❍ E. Memory requirements

42. Examine the figure below. Assuming you are running both EIGRP and RIP, what path would RtrA take to get to RtrE?

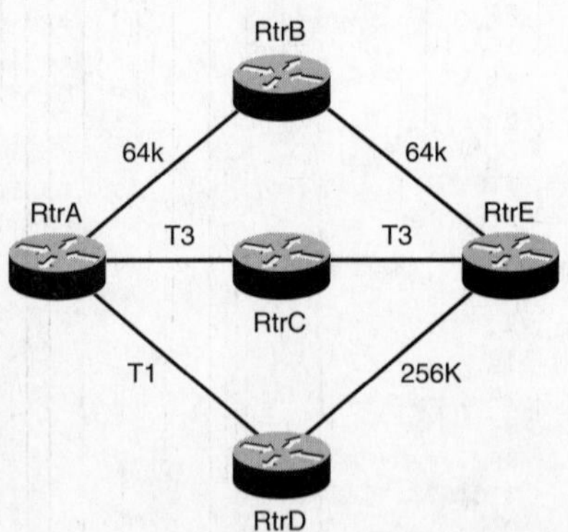

❍ A. It will take the path through RtrB.

❍ B. It will take the path through RtrC.

❍ C. It will take the path through RtrD.

❍ D. It will load balance across all three routers.

43. Examine the figure below. Given the diagram and the following configuration, why is NAT not working?

```
Interface serial 0
 ip address 200.100.50.25 255.255.255.252
Interface ethernet 0
 ip address 10.1.0.1 255.255.0.0
Interface ethernet 1
 ip address 10.2.0.1 255.255.0.0
Interface ethernet 2
 ip address 10.3.0.1 255.255.0.0
Access-list 1 permit 10.1.0.0 0.0.255.255
Access-list 1 permit 10.2.0.0 0.0.255.255
Access-list 1 permit 10.3.0.0 0.0.255.255
Ip nat inside source list 1 interface serial 0
  overload
```

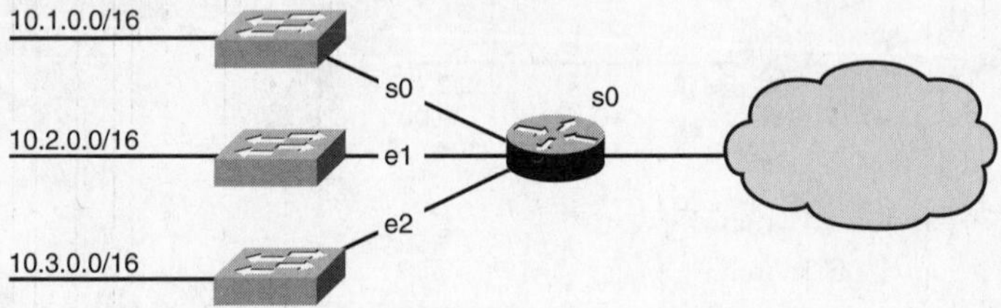

❍ A. It is using the wrong access-list.

❍ B. The `ip nat inside` and `ip nat outside` commands are missing.

❍ C. The IP addresses are incorrect.

❍ D. The `ip nat pool` command is missing.

44. Given the following output of two switches, why is VLAN information not being sent between them?

```
Switch1#show vtp status
VTP version                          2
Configuration revision               10
Maximum VLANs supported locally      68
Number of existing VLANs             8
VTP Operational Mode                 Server
VTP Domain Name                      TTC1532
VTP Pruning Mode                     Disabled
<output omitted>
Switch2#show vtp status
VTP version                          2
Configuration revision               10
Maximum VLANs supported locally      68
Number of existing VLANs             8
VTP Operational Mode                 Server
VTP Domain Name                      TTC1523
VTP Pruning Mode                     Disabled
<output omitted>
```

- ❍ A. The VTP operational mode is incorrect.
- ❍ B. The switches are running the wrong VTP version for Ethernet LANs.
- ❍ C. VTP pruning is disabled.
- ❍ D. The VTP domain names are incorrect.

45. Examine the figure below. All ports are running FastEthernet. The default STP priority is being used. Which port would go into blocking mode?

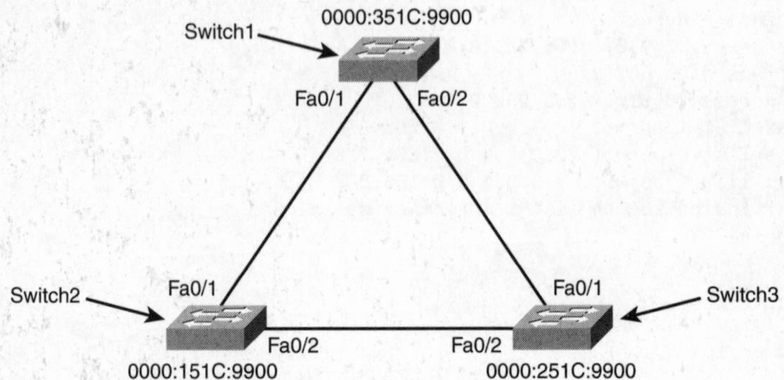

- ❍ A. Fa1/0 on Switch2
- ❍ B. Fa0/1 on Switch3
- ❍ C. Fa0/2 on Switch1
- ❍ D. Fa0/1 on Switch1

46. Examine the figure. Based on this diagram, which ports are access ports? [Select all that apply.]

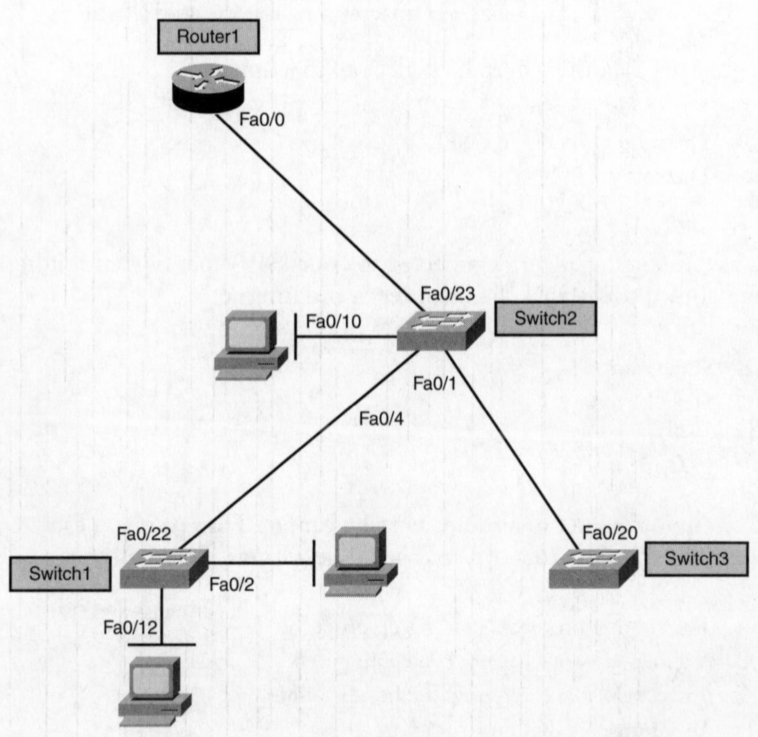

- ❍ A. Switch1:Fa0/2
- ❍ B. Switch2:Fa0/1
- ❍ C. Switch1:Fa0/12
- ❍ D. Switch2:Fa0/10
- ❍ E. Router1:Fa0/0
- ❍ F. Switch3:Fa0/20

47. What is `inverse arp` used for?

- ❍ A. `Inverse arp` maps a MAC address to an IP address.
- ❍ B. `Inverse arp` maps a DLCI address to an IP address.
- ❍ C. `Inverse arp` maps a dialer string to an IP address.
- ❍ D. `Inverse arp` maps a Router address to an IP address.

48. Entering the `show ip route` command on a router shows the following output:

```
O    172.16.0.0/16 [110/1562] via 192.168.1.1, 00:41:09, Serial0
```

What is true about this output? [Select all that apply.]

❍ A. The router is running EIGRP.
❍ B. The router is running OSPF.
❍ C. The cost is 1562.
❍ D. The hop count is 1562.

49. You have a single network connected to your ISP. What type of routing would allow the internal clients to reach the Internet?

❍ A. RIP
❍ B. Static route
❍ C. Default route
❍ D. OSPF
❍ E. EIGRP

50. You attempt to telnet to a router but you cannot. However, you can successfully ping the router. What could be wrong? [Select all that apply.]

❍ A. The routing protocol is not set up properly.
❍ B. A telnet password has not been configured.
❍ C. An access-list is configured on the VTY lines.
❍ D. An interface is shut down.

51. Which of the following are valid unicast addresses? [Select all that apply.]

❍ A. 192.168.14.5/30
❍ B. 192.168.14.40/30
❍ C. 192.168.14.123/30
❍ D. 192.168.14.13/30

52. If you send a packet to a network that a router does not have in its routing table and no default route is established, what will the router do with your packet? [Select all that apply.]

❍ A. It will send an ICMP destination unreachable message back to the source of the packet.
❍ B. It will drop the packet.
❍ C. It will send the packet back to the source.
❍ D. It will send an ICMP administratively prohibited message back to the source.

53. Which of the following shows the correct mode to perform an extended ping?
    - O A. Router>
    - O B. Router#
    - O C. Router(config)#
    - O D. Router(config-if)#

54. Which of the following are examples of application layer protocols? [Select all that apply.]
    - O A. HTTP
    - O B. Telnet
    - O C. DHCP
    - O D. ARP
    - O E. SMTP

55. What are the components that make up a Bridge ID? [Select all that apply.]
    - O A. IP address
    - O B. MAC address
    - O C. Priority number
    - O D. Platform number

56. What command would show you a list of cached and permanent host entries on your router?
    - O A. `show dns entries`
    - O B. `show dns`
    - O C. `show host entries`
    - O D. `show hosts`

57. Which routing protocols use bandwidth and delay in their metric? [Select all that apply.]
    - O A. OSPF
    - O B. RIPv1
    - O C. IGRP
    - O D. EIGRP
    - O E. RIPv2

58. You want to map the IP address of 10.0.0.5 to the phone number 5551111 while using CHAP authentication. The remote router is called QueRouter. What command would successfully create this dialer map?
    - O A. `Router(config-if)#dialer-map ip 10.0.0.5 name QueRouter 5551111`
    - O B. `Router(config)#dialer map ip 10.0.0.5 name QueRouter 5551111`
    - O C. `Router(config-if)#dialer map ip 5551111 name QueRouter 10.0.0.5`
    - O D. `Router(config)#dialer map ip 5551111 name QueRouter 10.0.0.5`
    - O E. `Router(config-if)#dialer map ip 10.0.0.5 name QueRouter 5551111`

59. In EIGRP, where would you find the feasible successor route?

- ❍ A. Neighbor table
- ❍ B. Topology table
- ❍ C. Route table
- ❍ D. Adjacency table

60. Which of the following commands would correctly configure a default gateway on a switch?

- ❍ A. `Switch(config-if)#ip default-gateway 10.0.0.1`
- ❍ B. `Switch(config)#default gateway 10.0.0.1`
- ❍ C. `Switch(config-route)#default gateway 10.0.0.1`
- ❍ D. `Switch(config)#ip default-gateway 10.0.0.1`

Answer Key to Practice Test #2

1. B, E
2. A, B, D
3. C, D
4. B
5. C
6. A
7. D
8. C
9. B
10. A
11. C
12. D
13. B, C
14. B
15. A, D
16. C
17. D
18. B, D
19. A
20. C
21. C
22. A, D
23. B
24. C
25. C
26. A
27. B
28. B, D, E
29. B
30. B, D
31. E
32. C
33. C
34. C
35. A
36. D
37. A, C
38. B, D, E
39. B
40. A
41. A, B, C
42. B
43. B
44. D
45. C
46. A, C, D
47. B
48. B, C
49. C
50. B, C
51. A, D
52. A, D
53. B
54. A, B, C, E
55. B, C
56. D
57. C, D
58. E
59. B
60. D

Question 1

Answers B and E are the correct answers. The 192.168.14.69 host is on the 192.168.14.64/28 network with an increment of 16 with 14 valid host addresses on each subnet. The range of valid host addresses for this network is 192.168.14.65 through 192.168.14.78. Answers B and E both fall within this range. Answer A is incorrect because this is a broadcast address. Answer C is incorrect because this address is on a different network. Answer D is incorrect because this is a network address.

Question 2

Answers A, B, and D are the correct answers. You need a trunk configured between the two switches for VTP to work. Both switches need to be in the same VTP domain and have the same VTP password. Answer C is incorrect because the modes can differ. Answer E is incorrect because the hostname is irrelevant.

Question 3

Answers C and D are the correct answers. When configuring subinterfaces, you should configure the encapsulation on the main interface but take the IP address off of it and place it under the subinterface. Answer A is incorrect because the DLCI should go under the subinterface and not on the main interface. Answer B is incorrect because the IP address should go under the subinterface. Answer E is incorrect because the frame-relay encapsulation goes on the main interface and not the subinterface.

Question 4

Answer B is the correct answer. Named access lists allow you to delete individual lines; numbered do not. If you attempt to delete an individual line out of a numbered access list, the entire list will be removed. Answer A is incorrect because you can do both an IP extended and an IP standard named access list. Answer C is incorrect because named access lists can be used for more than just VTY line access control. Answer D is incorrect because you can do named access lists for other protocols—such as IPX—as well.

Question 5

Answer C is the correct answer. Store-and-forward checks the frame check sequence at the end of the frame to verify that the entire frame is correct. Answer A is incorrect because cut-through checks only the destination MAC address. Answer B is incorrect because fragment-free checks the first 64 bytes of each frame. Answer D is incorrect because there is no such thing as fragment-forward.

Question 6

Answer A is the correct answer. Ctrl+A takes you to the beginning of the line. Answer B is incorrect because Ctrl+Z exits your configuration mode and takes you to the root of the privileged exec mode. Answer C is incorrect because Ctrl+N retrieves the next command from your command history buffer. Answer D is incorrect because Ctrl+P retrieves the previous command from your command history buffer.

Question 7

Answer D is the correct answer. Split-horizon is working (which makes answer A incorrect) because the routes received on Serial 0 are not sent back out Serial 0. Answer B is incorrect because version 1 is being used, not version 2. Answer C is incorrect because the router is on the 10.0.0.0 and 192.168.0.0 network and not the 172.16.0.0 network. Finally, answer E is incorrect because you can ping the host 172.18.15.9 because it is only three hops away.

Question 8

Answer C is the correct answer. The default state of an interface is shut down. Unless the no shut command is entered, the interface remains down and you are unable to ping it. Answer A is incorrect because nothing in the scenario or configuration indicates that there is a problem with the encapsulation. Answer B is incorrect because the telnet configuration is complete. Answer D is incorrect because the order of the commands under the VTY lines does not matter. Finally, answer E is incorrect because a console password is not necessary to telnet into a router.

Question 9

Answer B is the correct answer. `show ip ospf interface` shows you if you are a DR, BDR, or DROTHER (not a DR or BDR). Answer A is incorrect because the show ip ospf database command shows you the OSPF LSA database, but not if you are the DR. Answer C is incorrect because the `show ip ospf` command shows you general information about the OSPF process, but not about the DR decisions. Answer D is incorrect because the `show ip ospf summary-address` shows you networks that have been summarized, but not the DR or BDR routers.

Question 10

Answer A is the correct answer. Application, Presentation, and Session layers all relate to Data. The Transport layer relates to segments. The Network layer relates to packets (also called datagrams). The Data-Link layer relates to frames. Finally, the Physical layer relates to bits. The other answers are wrong because the orders of the PDUs are incorrect.

Question 11

Answer C is the correct answer. If the configuration register is 0x2101, the router boots to RxBoot in ROM. Answers A and D are incorrect because the router cannot boot from RAM or NVRAM. Answer B is incorrect because 0x2102 is the configuration register to boot to flash.

Question 12

Answer D is the correct answer. The access list is first denying a host, and then later permitting it. However, access lists are top-down, which means that the host will only be denied. Because there are no other permit statements in the access list, no traffic will be designated as interesting traffic to bring up the ISDN connection. Therefore, answer D is correct. Answers A and C are incorrect because the dialer map and static route are correct. Answer B is incorrect because the `dialer load-threshold` command is not necessary. Answer E is incorrect because the `dialer idle-timeout` value is irrelevant.

Question 13

Answers B and C are the correct answers. Both commands will show you the IP address (layer 3 information) of neighboring devices. Below is sample output of these commands with the layer three (network layer) information highlighted.

```
--------------
Device ID: Router
Entry address(es):
  IP address: 192.168.100.254
Platform: cisco 1604,  Capabilities: Router
Interface: Serial0,  Port ID (outgoing port): Serial0
Holdtime : 128 sec
<…output omitted for brevity...>
```

Answer A is incorrect because this command is limited and does not give you the IP address. Answer D is incorrect because this command shows only CDP statistics, not IP addresses.

Question 14

Answer B is the correct answer. The Floor2 switch has the lowest priority (16384) so is therefore the root bridge. The Floor1 and Floor3 switch (answers A and C) have higher priorities, so therefore they are not the root bridge. Answer D is incorrect because enough information is included in the question to answer it.

Question 15

Answers A and D are the correct answers. This question depends on your ability to memorize facts; you either know this, or you don't. Answers B and C are incorrect because these are LMI types and not frame-relay encapsulations.

Question 16

Answer C is the correct answer. The subnet mask 255.255.255.224 with the `ip subnet-zero` command allows for 8 subnets and 30 hosts on each subnet. Answer A is incorrect because it allows only for 2 subnets. Answer B is incorrect because this allows only for 4 subnets. Answers D and E are incorrect because you can get more subnets out of a mask of 255.255.255.224 than you can with masks of 255.255.255.240 (/28) or 255.255.255.248 (/29).

Question 17

Answer D is the correct answer. OSPF has an unlimited hop count. Answer A is incorrect because this is the hop count for RIP. Answer B is incorrect because this is the maximum hop count for EIGRP. Answer C is incorrect because this is the maximum hop count for IGRP.

Question 18

Answers B and D are the correct answers. UDP uses less bandwidth and is a connection-less protocol. Answers A and C are incorrect because these describe TCP.

Question 19

Answer A is the correct answer. If the router is unable to find an IOS in Flash memory, it resorts to searching for a TFTP server to download an IOS. Answer B is incorrect because a router never attempts to load an IOS from RAM. Answer C is incorrect because the router only attempts to load RxBoot (the mini-IOS) after failing its TFTP request. Finally, answer D is incorrect because the router does not attempt to go to ROM Monitor mode unless all other options have failed.

Question 20

Answer C is the correct answer. There is no way to assign a password to a VLAN. Answers A, B, and D are all incorrect because these are steps you would take to create a VLAN.

Question 21

Answer C is the correct answer. When the packet is returning on the remote segment, it will have the source MAC address of HostB and the destination MAC address of RouterB. Answers A, B, and D are incorrect because they do not return on any of these choices.

Question 22

Answer is A and D. Answer A is a private Class B address, whereas answer D is a private Class A address. Answers B and C are incorrect because they are public addresses.

Question 23

Answer B is the correct answer. A switch uses ASIC chips and is therefore faster than a bridge (making answer A incorrect). Answers C and D are incorrect because bridges and switches are both layer 2 devices.

Question 24

Answer C is the correct answer. This is the only answer with the correct configuration. Answers A and D are incorrect because these are extended access lists, which is not necessary on VTY lines. Answer B is incorrect because the wrong command is used to apply the access list on the VTY lines.

Question 25

Answer C is the correct answer. OSPF priority is changed on an interface with the `ip ospf priority` command. Answers A and B are incorrect because the commands are done on an interface and not under the OSPF router configuration mode. Answer D is incorrect because the wrong command is used under the interface.

Question 26

Answer A is the correct answer. To enable an interface from the administratively down state, you must execute the `no shutdown` command. Answer B is incorrect because nothing is wrong with the cable. Answer C is incorrect because there is no such thing as the `interface up` command. Answer D is incorrect because the `clock rate` command is not necessary to take an interface out of the administratively down state.

Question 27

Answer B is the correct answer. HostB has a network address and not a valid host address. Answers A, C, and D are incorrect because these are all valid IP addresses.

Question 28

Answers B, D, and E are the correct answers. Variable length subnet masks (VLSM) are supported by EIGRP, RIPv2, and OSPF. RIPv1 and IGRP (answers A and C) only support full length subnet masks (FLSM).

Question 29

Answer B is the correct answer. `banner motd` is used to create a banner. Answers A, C, and D are incorrect because these are all bogus commands.

Question 30

Answers B and D are the correct answers. Answers A and C are incorrect because they refer to the spanning-tree protocol and not frame-tagging. Answer E is incorrect because this refers to the VLAN Trunking Protocol.

Question 31

Answer E is the correct answer. Windowing and sequence numbers are components of TCP, which is found at the Transport layer. TCP is not found at the other layers, so answers A, B, C, and D are incorrect.

Question 32

Answer C is the correct answer. LAPD is the name of the signaling protocol used on ISDN D channels. Answers A, B, and E are incorrect because these are found on the ISDN B channels. Answer D is incorrect because this is used with X.25.

Question 33

Answer C is the correct answer. There are four collision domains on the left out of the router's ethernet 0 interface (one collision domain for each segment coming out of the switch), and there is one collision domain on the right out of the router's ethernet 1 interface. Because there are only five collision domains in all, answers A, B, D, and E are all incorrect.

Question 34

Answer is C is the correct answer. This question just tests your ability to do binary. The 128, 32, 2, and 1 bits are all turned to 1. 128+32+2+1=147. Therefore, only answer C is correct, and the others are incorrect.

Question 35

Answer A is the correct answer. You need a default router on RouterA to allow the users to access the Internet. The ISP, however, would suffice with a simple static route because there is only one network attached to RouterA. Answers B, C, D, and E are incorrect because these solutions would not meet the objective.

Question 36

Answer D is the correct answer. You have 13 subnets, so you need a /28 subnet mask, which would allow for 13 hosts. Because the company is running RIPv1, you must use the same subnet mask on all links.

Question 37

Answers A and C are the correct answer. This access list permits all hosts on the 172.17.80.0/20 network. The range of valid IP addresses would be 172.17.80.1 through 172.17.95.254. Only answer A and C fall within this range.

Question 38

Answers B, D, and E are the correct answers. Answers A and C are incorrect because these are not valid wide area network encapsulations.

Question 39

Answer B is the correct answer. The `no auto-summary` command is needed because you are using variable length subnet masks. Without the `no auto-summary` command, VLSM is not allowed. Answer A is incorrect because EIGRP does support VLSM. Answer C is incorrect because the subnet masks are not necessary to make this work. Answer D is incorrect because you need the `no auto-summary` command. (The `auto-summary` command is already there.) Answer E is incorrect because this is a RIP command, not an EIGRP command.

Question 40

Answer A is the correct answer. The `frame-relay map` command is missing the keyword broadcast at the end, which is necessary to support the use of broadcast and multicast based routing protocols. Answer B is incorrect because the RIP configuration does specify the correct networks. Answer C is incorrect because `inverse-arp` is irrelevant to making this work. Answer D is incorrect because RIP will work across NBMA networks when you have the broadcast keyword added to the end of the `frame-relay map` command. Answer E is incorrect because the IP addresses are correct.

Question 41

Answers A, B, and C are the correct answers. The platform code is `c7200`, the feature set code is `'j'`, and the compression type code is `'mz'`. Answers D and E are incorrect because these are not included in the IOS filename.

Question 42

Answer B is the correct answer. Assuming that you are running both EIGRP and RIP, the router will take the path that EIGRP chooses (lower administrative distance). Because EIGRP looks at bandwidth as one component of its composite metric, EIGRP would take the path through RtrC. This is the only path it would take; therefore, answers A, C, and D are incorrect.

Question 43

Answer B is the correct answer. The `ip nat inside` and `ip nat outside` commands are missing from the interfaces. Answer A is incorrect because the access list configuration is correct. Answer C is incorrect because the IP addresses are correct. Answer D is incorrect because the configuration is performing NAT overload and does not need a pool.

Question 44

Answer D is the correct answer. The two switches are using different VTP domain names. Answer A is incorrect because the modes are fine. Answer B is incorrect because nothing is wrong with the VTP version. Answer C is incorrect because VTP pruning does not need to be enabled to make VTP operational.

Question 45

Answer C is the correct answer. The root bridge would be the Switch2. Interface Fa0/1 on Switch1 and Fa0/2 on Switch3 would both be root ports and go into forwarding mode. For Fa0/2 on Switch1 and Fa0/1 on Switch3, the tie breaker would be the bridge ID. Since Switch1 has a higher MAC address and the default priority is being used, Switch1 would place Fa0/2 in blocking mode and Fa0/1 on Switch3 would go into forwarding mode. Only Fa0/2 on Switch1 would be in blocking mode, so answers A, B, and D are incorrect.

Question 46

Answers A, C, and D are the correct answers. Access ports are those ports connected to access devices such as computers. Answers B, E, and F are incorrect because these are trunk ports that are connecting switches and routers together.

Question 47

Answer B is the correct answer. Inverse arp maps a frame-relay data link connection identifier (DLCI) to the next hop IP address. Answers A, C, and D are incorrect because these are not the correct definition of inverse arp.

Question 48

Answers B and C are the correct answers. The 'O' in the output, along with the administrative distance of 110, indicates that this entry was learned via OSPF. The cost is included next to the administrative distance (1562). Answer A is incorrect because the router is running OSPF and not EIGRP. Answer D is incorrect because OSPF uses cost as its metric and not hop count.

Question 49

Answer C is the correct answer. If you only have a single network, a default route would be sufficient. Answers A, D, and E are incorrect because they are not necessary if you only have a single network.

Question 50

Answers B and C are the correct answers. If telnet has not been properly configured or an access list is blocking you, telnet will not work. Answers A and D are incorrect because the question states that you are able to ping the router (which you would not be able to do if answers A and D were correct).

Question 51

Answers A and D are the correct answers. Answer B is incorrect because this is a network address, and answer C is incorrect because this is a broadcast address.

Question 52

Answers A and B are the correct answers. The router will drop the packet back and send an ICMP destination unreachable message back to the source. Answer C is incorrect because the router will drop the packet, not send it back. Answer D is incorrect because administratively prohibited messages are only sent if the packet was denied because of a filter such as an access list.

Question 53

Answer B is the correct answer. You need to be at the root of privilege exec to perform an extended ping. Answers A, C, and D are incorrect because you cannot perform an extended ping from these modes.

Question 54

Answers A, B, C, and E are the correct answers. Answer D is incorrect because this is a network layer protocol.

Question 55

Answers B and C are the correct answers. The bridge ID is composed of a configurable priority plus the base MAC address. Answers A and D are incorrect because these are not used in calculating the bridge ID.

Question 56

Answer D is the correct answer. Answers A, B, and C are incorrect because these are all invalid commands.

Question 57

Answers C and D are the correct answers. Answer A is incorrect because OSPF uses cost. Answers B and E are incorrect because RIP uses hop count.

Question 58

Answer E is the correct answer. Answer A is incorrect because there is no hyphen between dialer and map. Answer B is incorrect because the command is entered from global configuration mode and the correct command is performed in interface configuration mode. Answers C and D are incorrect because they use the wrong syntax for the command.

Question 59

Answer B is the correct answer. The feasible successor is the backup route and is found in the topology table. Answers A and C are incorrect because the feasible successor route is not found in the neighbor or route table. Answer D is also incorrect because the feasible successor is not found in the adjacency table and because the adjacency table is used with OSPF and not EIGRP.

Question 60

Answer D is the correct answer. Answer A, although the correct syntax, is not entered from global configuration mode. Answers B and C are incorrect because they are the wrong syntax.

CD Contents and Installation Instructions

The CD features an innovative practice test engine powered by MeasureUp, including additional questions plus two router simulations, giving you yet another effective tool to assess your readiness for the exam. Cisco simulations validate a person's hands-on skills in addition to knowledge. MeasureUp's Cisco simulations model real-life networking scenarios by requiring the user to perform tasks on simulated Cisco networking devices. MeasureUp's simulations measure troubleshooting and problem-solving skills to address realistic networking problems. The CD also includes a helpful "Need to Know More?" appendix that will break down by chapter extra resources you can visit if some of the topics in this book are still unclear to you.

Multiple Test Modes

MeasureUp practice tests are available in Study, Certification, Custom, Adaptive, Missed Question, and Non-Duplicate question modes.

Study Mode

Tests administered in Study Mode allow you to request the correct answer(s) and explanation for each question during the test. These tests are not timed. You can modify the testing environment *during* the test by clicking the Options button.

Certification Mode

Tests administered in Certification Mode closely simulate the actual testing environment you will encounter when taking a certification exam. These tests do not allow you to request the answer(s) or explanation for each question until after the exam.

Custom Mode

Custom Mode allows you to specify your preferred testing environment. Use this mode to specify the objectives you want to include in your test, the timer length, and other test properties. You can also modify the testing environment *during* the test by clicking the Options button.

Adaptive Mode

Tests administered in Adaptive Mode closely simulate the actual testing environment you will encounter when taking an adaptive exam. After answering a question, you are not allowed to go back; you are only allowed to move forward during the exam.

Missed Question Mode

Missed Question Mode allows you to take a test containing only the questions you missed previously.

Non-Duplicate Mode

Non-Duplicate Mode allows you to take a test containing only questions not displayed previously.

Question Types

The practice question types simulate the real exam experience.

Random Questions and Order of Answers

This feature helps you learn the material without memorizing questions and answers. Each time you take a practice test, the questions and answers appear in a different randomized order.

Detailed Explanations of Correct and Incorrect Answers

You'll receive automatic feedback on all correct and incorrect answers. The detailed answer explanations are a superb learning tool in their own right.

Attention to Exam Objectives

MeasureUp practice tests are designed to appropriately balance the questions over each technical area covered by a specific exam.

Installing the CD

The minimum system requirements for the CD-ROM are as listed here:

- Windows 95, 98, ME, NT4, 2000, or XP
- 7MB disk space for testing engine
- An average of 1MB disk space for each test

If you need technical support, please contact MeasureUp at 678-356-5050 or email support@measureup.com. Additionally, you'll find Frequently Asked Questions (FAQs) at www.measureup.com.

To install the CD-ROM, follow these instructions:

1. Close all applications before beginning this installation.
2. Insert the CD into your CD-ROM drive. If the setup starts automatically, go to step 6. If the setup does not start automatically, continue with step 3.

3. From the Start menu, select Run.
4. Click Browse to locate the MeasureUp CD. In the Browse dialog box, from the Look In drop-down list, select the CD-ROM drive.
5. In the Browse dialog box, double-click on `Setup.exe`. In the Run dialog box, click OK to begin the installation.
6. On the Welcome Screen, click Next.
7. To agree to the Software License Agreement, click Yes.
8. On the Choose Destination Location screen, click Next to install the software to `C:\Program Files\MeasureUp Practice Tests\Launch`.

If you cannot locate MeasureUp Practice Tests through the Start menu, see the section later in this appendix titled "Creating a Shortcut to the MeasureUp Practice Tests."

9. On the Setup Type screen, select Individual Typical Setup. Click Next to continue.
10. On the Select Features screen, click the check box next to the test(s) you purchased. After you have checked your test(s), click Next.
11. On the Enter Text screen, type the password provided in this receipt, and click Next. Follow this step for any additional tests.
12. On the Select Program Folder screen, verify that the Program Folder is set to MeasureUp Practice Tests, and click Next.
13. After the installation is complete, verify that Yes, I Want to Restart My Computer Now is selected. If you select No, I Will Restart My Computer Later, you will not be able to use the program until you restart your computer.
14. Click Finish.
15. After restarting your computer, choose Start, Programs, MeasureUp Practice Tests, Launch.
16. On the MeasureUp welcome screen, click Create User Profile.
17. In the User Profile dialog box, complete the mandatory fields and click Create Profile.
18. Select the practice test you want to access, and click Start Test.

Creating a Shortcut to the MeasureUp Practice Tests

To create a shortcut to the MeasureUp Practice Tests, follow these steps:

1. Right-click on your desktop.
2. From the shortcut menu select New, Shortcut.
3. Browse to `C:\Program Files\MeasureUp Practice Tests` and select the `MeasureUpCertification.exe` or `Localware.exe` file.
4. Click OK.
5. Click Next.
6. Rename the shortcut MeasureUp.
7. Click Finish.

After you have completed step 7, use the MeasureUp shortcut on your desktop to access the MeasureUp products you ordered.

Technical Support

If you encounter problems with the MeasureUp test engine on the CD-ROM, you can contact MeasureUp at 678-356-5050 or email support@measureup.com. Technical support hours are from 8 a.m. to 5 p.m. EST Monday through Friday. Additionally, you'll find Frequently Asked Questions (FAQs) at www.measureup.com.

If you'd like to purchase additional MeasureUp products, telephone 678-356-5050 or 800-649-1MUP (1687), or visit www.measureup.com.

Need to Know More?

CCNA Exam Prep 2 (Exam 640-801)

ISBN: 0-7897-3519-9

Our good friend and mentor Dave Minutella, along with his coauthors Heather Stevenson and Jeremy Cioara, have just produced the companion volume to this book. The *CCNA Exam Prep 2* covers all the CCNA material in much greater detail and in a superbly accessible writing style. If you like our book, you'll like theirs, too.

www.cisco.com/go/prepcenter

Cisco recently launched the CCNA Prep Center. To access the site, you will need to create a user ID. Once you are logged in, there is a wide variety of articles, practice tests, practice simulators, and games to work with.

CCNA Self-Study: Introduction to Cisco Networking Technologies (INTRO)

ISBN 1-58705-161-3

Cisco Press produces the authoritative study and exam prep guides for CCNA. These books cover the full CCNA curriculum in exhaustive detail; for this reason, they are less testfocused than this book and contain material that will not be tested.

CCNA Self-Study: Interconnecting Cisco Network Devices (ICND)

ISBN 1-58705-142-7

CCNA INTRO Exam Certification Guide

ISBN 1-58720-094-5

CCNA ICND Exam Certification Guide

ISBN 1-58720-083-X

CCNA Command Quick Reference (Cisco Networking Academy Program)

ISBN: 1587131595

www.examcram2.com

www.cramsession.com

Que Publishing and Que Certification have a wealth of resources for CCNA (and dozens of other) certifications.

www.ieee.org

The IEEE is the standards authority for networking. For information on any 802.x standard, they are the original source.

www.iana.org/assignments/port-numbers

For the definitive—and exhaustive—list of port numbers, visit this website.

www.cisco.com/warp/public/473/spanning_tree1.swf

Cisco has created a simple and effective Flash presentation on the Spanning-Tree Protocol. It's a bit dated in that it uses bridges instead of switches, but the theory is well presented.

Cisco IOS Access Lists

ISBN 1-56592-385-5

O'Reilly has published Jeff Sedayao's excellent and definitive work on Cisco Access Lists for years now. If your job involves using ACLs, you want this book on your shelf. It's the one with the donkey on it.

www.cisco.com/univercd/home/home.htm

Cisco's UniverCD website hosts documentation on almost every facet of its complete product range. Most of this is highly advanced, but a quick search for any CCNA topic will give you more information than you need, direct from the source.

Glossary

access list
Rules applied to a router that will determine traffic patterns for data.

administrative distance
A value that ranges from 0 through 255, which determines the priority of a source's routing information.

advanced distance vector protocol
A routing protocol that combines the strengths of the distance vector and link state routing protocols. Cisco Enhanced Interior Gateway Routing Protocol (EIGRP) is considered an advanced distance vector protocol.

Application layer
The highest layer of the OSI model (Layer 7). It is closest to the end user and selects appropriate network services to support end-user applications such as email and FTP.

ARP (Address Resolution Protocol)
A protocol used to map a known logical address to an unknown physical address. A device performs an ARP broadcast to identify the physical address of a destination device. This physical address is then stored in cache memory for later transmissions.

AS (autonomous system)
A group of networks under common administration that share a routing strategy.

ATM (Asynchronous Transfer Mode)
A dedicated-connection switching technology that organizes digital data into units and transmits them over a physical medium using digital signal technology.

attenuation
A term that refers to the reduction in strength of a signal. Attenuation occurs with any type of signal, whether digital or analog. Sometimes referred to as *signal loss*.

bandwidth
The available capacity of a network link over a physical medium.

BECN (Backward Explicit Congestion Notification)
A dedicated-connection switching technology that organizes digital data into 53-byte cell units and transmits them over a physical medium using digital signal technology.

BGP (Border Gateway Protocol)
An exterior routing protocol that exchanges route information between autonomous systems.

boot field
The lowest four binary digits of a configuration register. The value of the boot field determines the order in which a router searches for Cisco IOS software.

BPDU (Bridge Protocol Data Unit)
Data messages that are exchanged across the switches within an extended LAN that uses a spanning tree protocol topology.

BRI (Basic Rate Interface)
An ISDN interface that contains two B channels and one D channel for circuit-switched communication for data, voice, and video.

bridge
A device used to segment a LAN into multiple physical segments. A bridge uses a forwarding table to determine which frames need to be forwarded to specific segments. Bridges isolate local traffic to the originating physical segment, but forward all non-local and broadcast traffic.

broadcast
A data frame that's sent to every node on a local segment.

carrier detect signal
A signal received on a router interface that indicates whether the Physical layer connectivity is operating properly.

CDP (Cisco Discovery Protocol)
A Cisco proprietary protocol that operates at the Data Link layer. CDP enables network administrators to view a summary protocol and address information about other directly connected Cisco routers (and some Cisco switches).

channel
A single communications path on a system. In some situations, channels can be multiplexed over a single connection.

CHAP (Challenge Handshake Authentication Protocol)
An authentication protocol for the Point-to-Point Protocol (PPP) that uses a three-way, encrypted handshake to force a remote host to identify itself to a local host.

checksum
A field that performs calculations to ensure the integrity of data.

CIDR (Classless Interdomain Routing)
Implemented to resolve the rapid depletion of IP address space on the Internet and to minimize the number of routes on the Internet. CIDR provides a more efficient method of allocating IP address space by removing the concept of classes in IP addressing. CIDR enables routes to be summarized on powers-of-two boundaries; therefore, it reduces multiple routes into a single prefix.

CIR (Committed Information Rate)
The rate at which a Frame Relay link transmits data, averaged over time. CIR is measured in bits per second. This is the committed rate that the service provider guarantees for a Frame Relay connection.

classful addressing
Categorizes IP addresses into ranges that are used to create a hierarchy in the IP addressing scheme. The most common classes are A, B, and C, which can be identified by looking at the first three binary digits of an IP address.

classless addressing
Classless addressing does not categorize addresses into classes and is designed to deal with wasted address space.

CO (central office)
The local telephone company office where all local loops in an area connect.

configuration register
A numeric value (typically displayed in hexadecimal form) used to specify certain actions on a router.

congestion
A situation that occurs during data transfer if one or more computers generate network traffic faster than it can be transmitted through the network.

console
A terminal attached directly to the router for configuring and monitoring the router.

convergence
The process by which all routers within an internetwork route information and eventually agree on optimal routes through the internetwork.

counting to infinity
A routing problem in which the distance metric for a destination network is continually increased because the internetwork has not fully converged.

CPE (customer premise equipment)
Terminating equipment such as telephones and modems supplied by the service provider, installed at the customer site, and connected to the network.

CRC (cyclic redundancy check)

An error-checking mechanism by which the receiving node calculates a value based on the data it receives and compares it with the value stored within the frame from the sending node.

CSMA/CD (Carrier Sense Multiple Access/Collision Detection)

A physical specification used by Ethernet to provide contention-based frame transmission. CSMA/CD specifies that a sending device must share physical transmission media and listen to determine whether a collision occurs after transmitting. In simple terms, this means that an Ethernet card has a built-in capability to detect a potential packet collision on the internetwork.

cut-through switching

A method of forwarding frames based on the first six bytes contained in the frame. Cut-through switching provides higher throughput than store-and-forward switching because it requires only six bytes of data to make the forwarding decision. Cut-through switching does not provide error checking like its counterpart store-and-forward switching.

DCE (data communications equipment)

The device at the network end of a user-to-network connection that provides a physical connection to the network, forwards traffic, and provides a clocking signal used to synchronize data transmission between the DCE and DTE devices.

DDR (dial-on-demand routing)

The technique by which a router can begin and end a circuit-switched connection over ISDN or telephone lines to meet network traffic demands.

de-encapsulation

The process by which a destination peer layer removes and reads the control information sent by the source peer layer in another network host.

default mask

A binary or decimal representation of the number of bits used to identify an IP network. The class of the IP address defines the default mask. A default mask is represented by four octets of binary digits. The mask can also be presented in dotted decimal notation.

default route

A network route (that usually points to another router) established to receive and attempt to process all packets for which no route appears in the route table.

delay
The amount of time necessary to move a packet through the internetwork from source to destination.

demarc
The point of demarcation is between the carrier's equipment and the customer premise equipment (CPE).

discard eligibility bit
A bit that can be set to indicate that a frame can be dropped if congestion occurs within the Frame Relay network.

distance vector protocol
An interior routing protocol that relies on distance and vector or direction to choose optimal paths. A distance vector protocol requires each router to send all or a large part of its route table to its neighboring routers periodically.

DLCI (data link connection identifier)
A value that specifies a permanent virtual circuit (PVC) or switched virtual circuit (SVC) in a Frame Relay network.

DNS (domain name system)
A system used to translate fully qualified hostnames or computer names into IP addresses, and vice versa.

domain
See *AS (autonomous system)*.

dotted decimal notation
A method of representing binary IP addresses in a decimal format. Dotted decimal notation represents the four octets of an IP address in four decimal values separated by decimal points.

DTE (data terminal equipment)
The device at the user end of the user-to-network connection that connects to a data network through a data communications equipment (DCE) device.

dynamic route
A network route that adjusts automatically to changes within the internetwork.

EGP (Exterior Gateway Protocol)
A routing protocol that conveys information between autonomous systems; it is widely used within the Internet. The Border Gateway Protocol (BGP) is an example of an exterior routing protocol.

EIGRP (Enhanced Interior Gateway Routing Protocol)
A Cisco proprietary routing protocol that includes features of both distance vector and link state routing protocols. EIGRP is considered an advanced distance vector protocol.

encapsulation

Generally speaking, encapsulation is the process of wrapping data in a particular protocol header. In the context of the OSI model, encapsulation is the process by which a source peer layer includes header and trailer control information with a Protocol Data Unit (PDU) destined for its peer layer in another network host. The information encapsulated instructs the destination peer layer how to process the information.

EXEC

The user interface for executing Cisco router commands.

FCS (frame check sequence)

Extra characters added to a frame for error control purposes. FCS is the result of a cyclic redundancy check (CRC).

FECN (Forward Explicit Congestion Notification)

A Frame Relay message that notifies the receiving device that there is congestion in the network. An FECN bit is sent in the same direction in which the frame was traveling, toward its destination.

Flash

Router memory that stores the Cisco IOS image and associated microcode. Flash is erasable, reprogrammable ROM that retains its content when the router is powered down or restarted.

flat routing protocol

A routing environment in which all routers are considered peers and can communicate with any other router in the network as directly as possible. A flat routing protocol functions well in simple and predictable network environments.

flow control

A mechanism that throttles back data transmission to ensure that a sending system does not overwhelm the receiving system with data.

Frame Relay

A switched Data Link layer protocol that supports multiple virtual circuits using High-level Data Link Control (HDLC) encapsulation between connected devices.

frame tagging

A method of tagging a frame with a unique user-defined virtual local area network (VLAN). The process of tagging frames allows VLANs to span multiple switches.

FTP (File Transfer Protocol)

A protocol used to copy a file from one host to another host, regardless of the physical hardware or operating system of each device. FTP identifies a client and server during the file-transfer process. In addition, it provides a guaranteed transfer by using the services of the Transmission Control Protocol (TCP).

full duplex

The physical transmission process on a network device by which one pair of wires transmits data while another pair of wires receives data. Full-duplex transmission is achieved by eliminating the possibility of collisions on an Ethernet segment, thereby eliminating the need for a device to sense collisions.

function

A term that refers to the different devices within ISDN. For example, a terminal equipment type 1 function is a device that has ISDN capabilities, whereas a terminal equipment type 2 function is a device that does not have ISDN capabilities. A terminal equipment type 2 function needs a terminal adapter function, which would be an ISDN capable adapter such as a router with an ISDN interface.

global configuration mode

A router mode that enables simple router configuration commands—such as router names, banners, and passwords—to be executed. Global configuration commands affect the whole router rather than a single interface or component.

half duplex

The physical transmission process whereby one pair of wires is used to transmit information and the other pair of wires is used to receive information or to sense collisions on the physical media. Half-duplex transmission is required on Ethernet segments with multiple devices.

handshake

The process of one system making a request to another system before a connection is established. Handshakes occur during the establishment of a connection between two systems, and they address matters such as synchronization and connection parameters.

HDLC (High-level Data Link Control)

A bit-oriented, synchronous Data Link layer protocol that specifies data encapsulation methods on serial links.

Header

Control information placed before the data during the encapsulation process.

hierarchical routing protocol

A routing environment that relies on several routers to compose a backbone. Most traffic from non-backbone routers traverses the backbone routers (or at least travels to the backbone) to reach another non-backbone router. This is accomplished by breaking a network into a hierarchy of networks, where each level is responsible for its own routing.

hold-down
The state into which a route is placed so that routers will not advertise or accept updates for that route until a timer expires.

hop count
The number of routers a packet passes through on its way to the destination network.

hostname
A logical name given to a router.

HSSI (High-Speed Serial Interface)
A physical standard designed for serial connections that require high data transmission rates. The HSSI standard allows for high-speed communication that runs at speeds up to 52Mbps.

ICMP (Internet Control Message Protocol)
A protocol that communicates error messages and controls messages between devices. Thirteen different types of ICMP messages are defined. ICMP enables devices to check the status of other devices, to query the current time, and to perform other functions such as `ping` and `traceroute`.

IEEE (Institute of Electrical and Electronics Engineers)
An organization whose primary function is to define standards for networks LANs.

IGRP (Interior Gateway Routing Protocol)
A Cisco proprietary distance vector routing protocol that uses bandwidth and delay for its metric.

initial configuration dialog
The dialog used to configure a router the first time it is booted or when no configuration file exists. The initial configuration dialog is an optional tool used to simplify the configuration process.

inside global
The term to describe your inside addresses after they have been translated with network address translation (NAT). Inside global addresses are registered addresses that represent your inside hosts to your outside networks.

inside local
The addresses on the inside of your network before they are translated with network address translation (NAT).

integrated routing
A technique in which a router that is routing multiple routed protocols shares resources. Rather than using several routing protocols to support multiple routed protocols, a network administrator can use a single routing protocol to support multiple routed protocols. The Enhanced Interior Gateway Routing Protocol (EIGRP) is an example of a routing protocol that supports integrated routing.

interdomain router

A router that uses an exterior routing protocol, such as the Border Gateway Protocol (BGP), to exchange route information between autonomous systems.

interfaces

Router components that provide the network connections in which data packets move in and out of the router. Depending on the model of router, interfaces exist either on the motherboard or on separate, modular interface cards.

interior routing protocol

A routing protocol that exchanges information within an autonomous system. Routing Information Protocol (RIP), Interior Gateway Routing Protocol (IGRP), and Open Shortest Path First (OSPF) are examples of interior routing protocols.

intradomain router

A router that uses an interior routing protocol, such as the Interior Gateway Routing Protocol (IGRP), to convey route information within an autonomous system.

IP (Internet Protocol)

One of the many protocols maintained in the TCP/IP suite of protocols. IP is the transport mechanism for Transmission Control Protocol (TCP), User Datagram Protocol (UDP), and Internet Control Message Protocol (ICMP) data. It also provides the logical addressing necessary for complex routing activity.

IP extended access list

An access list that provides a way of filtering IP traffic on a router interface based on the source and destination IP address or port, IP precedence field, TOS field, ICMP-type, ICMP-code, ICMP-message, IGMP-type, and TCP-established connections.

IP standard access list

An access list that provides a way of filtering IP traffic on a router interface based on the source IP address or address range.

ISDN (Integrated Services Digital Network)

A communications protocol offered by telephone companies that permits telephone networks to carry data, voice, and other traffic.

ISL (interswitch link)

A protocol used to enable virtual local area networks (VLANs) to span multiple switches. ISL is used between switches to communicate common VLANs between devices.

keepalive frames

Protocol Data Units (PDUs) transmitted at the Data Link layer that indicate whether the proper frame type is configured.

LAN protocols

Protocols that identify layer 2 protocols used for the transmission of data within a local area network (LAN). The three most popular LAN protocols used today are Ethernet, token ring, and Fiber Distributed Data Interface (FDDI).

LCP (Link Control Protocol)

A protocol that configures, tests, maintains, and terminates Point-to-Point Protocol (PPP) connections.

link state packet

A broadcast packet that contains the status of a router's links or network interfaces.

link state protocol

An interior routing protocol in which each router sends only the state of its own network links across the network, but sends this information to every router within its autonomous system or area. This process enables routers to learn and maintain full knowledge of the network's exact topology and how it is interconnected. Link state protocols use a "shortest path first" algorithm.

LLC (Logical Link Control) sublayer

A sublayer of the Data Link layer. The LLC sublayer provides the software functions of the Data Link layer.

LMI (Local Management Interface)

A set of enhancements to the Frame Relay protocol specifications used to manage complex networks. Some key Frame Relay LMI extensions include global addressing, virtual circuit status messages, and multicasting.

load

An indication of how busy a network resource is. CPU utilization and packets processed per second are two indicators of load.

local loop

The line from the customer's premises to the telephone company's central office (CO).

logical addressing

Network layer addressing is most commonly referred to as *logical addressing* (versus the physical addressing of the Data Link layer). A logical address consists of two parts: the network and the node. Routers use the network part of the logical address to determine the best path to the network of a remote device. The node part of the logical address is used to identify the specific node to forward the packet on the destination network.

logical ANDing

A process of comparing two sets of binary numbers to result in one value representing an IP address network. Logical ANDing is used to compare an IP address against its subnet mask to yield the IP subnet on which the IP address resides. ANDing is also used to determine whether a packet has a local or remote destination.

MAC (Media Access Control) address

A physical address used to define a device uniquely.

MAC (Media Access Control) layer
A sublayer of the Data Link layer that provides the hardware functions of the Data Link layer.

metric
The relative cost of sending packets to a destination network over a specific network route. Examples of metrics include bandwidth, delay, and reliability.

MIB (management information database)
A database that maintains statistics on certain data items. The Simple Network Management Protocol (SNMP) uses MIBs to query information about devices.

multicasting
A process of using one IP address to represent a group of IP addresses. Multicasting is used to send messages to a subset of IP addresses in a network or networks.

multipath routing protocol
A routing protocol that load balances over multiple optimal paths to a destination network when the costs of the paths are equal.

multiplexing
A method of flow control used by the Transport layer in which application conversations are combined over a single channel by interleaving packets from different segments and transmitting them.

NAT (Network Address Translation) Overload
The process of translating your multiple, internal IP addresses to a single registered IP address on the outside of your network.

NBMA (nonbroadcast multiaccess)
A multiaccess network that either does not support broadcasts or for which sending broadcasts is not feasible.

NCP (network control protocol)
A collection of protocols that establishes and configures different Network layer protocols for use over a Point-to-Point Protocol (PPP) connection.

NetBIOS (Network Basic Input/Output System)
A common Session layer interface specification from IBM and Microsoft that enables applications to request lower-level network services.

NIC (network interface card)
A board that provides network communication capabilities to and from a network host.

NOS (network operating system)
A term used to describe distributed file systems that support file sharing, printing, database access, and other similar applications.

NVRAM (nonvolatile random access memory)
A memory area of the router that stores permanent information, such as the router's backup configuration file. The contents of NVRAM are retained when the router is powered down or restarted.

OSI (Open Systems Interconnection) model
A layered networking framework developed by the International Organization for Standardization. The OSI model describes seven layers that correspond to specific networking functions.

OSPF (Open Shortest Path First)
A hierarchical link state routing protocol that was developed as a successor to the Routing Information Protocol (RIP).

packet switching
A process by which a router moves a packet from one interface to another.

PAP (Password Authentication Protocol)
An authentication protocol for the Point-to-Point Protocol (PPP) that uses a two-way, unencrypted handshake to enable a remote host to identify itself to a local host.

parallelization
A method of flow control used by the Transport layer in which multiple channels are combined to increase the effective bandwidth for the upper layers; synonymous with *multilink*.

path length
The sum of the costs of each link traversed up to the destination network. Some routing protocols refer to path length as *hop count*.

PDU (Protocol Data Unit)
A unit of measure that refers to data that is transmitted between two peer layers within different network devices. Segments, packets, and frames are examples of PDUs.

peer-to-peer communication
A form of communication that occurs between the same layers of two different network hosts.

ping
A tool for testing IP connectivity between two devices. Ping is used to send multiple IP packets between a sending and a receiving device. The destination device responds with an Internet Control Message Protocol (ICMP) packet to notify the source device of its existence.

POP (point of presence)
A physical location where a carrier has installed equipment to interconnect with a local exchange carrier.

PPP (Point-to-Point Protocol)
A standard protocol that enables router-to-router and host-to-network connectivity over synchronous and asynchronous circuits such as telephone lines.

Presentation layer
Layer 6 of the OSI model. The Presentation layer is concerned with how data is represented to the Application layer.

PRI (Primary Rate Interface)
An ISDN interface that contains 23 B channels and 1 D channel for circuit-switched communication for data, voice, and video. In North America and Japan, a PRI contains 23 B channels and 1 D channel. In Europe, it contains 30 B channels and 1 D channel.

privileged mode
An extensive administrative and management mode on a Cisco router. This router mode permits testing, debugging, and commands to modify the router's configuration.

protocol
A formal description of a set of rules and conventions that defines how devices on a network must exchange information.

PSTN (public switched telephone network)
The circuit-switching facilities maintained for voice analog communication.

PVC (permanent virtual circuit)
A virtual circuit that is permanently established and ready for use.

RAM (random access memory)
A memory area of a router that serves as a working storage area. RAM contains data such as route tables, various types of caches and buffers, as well as input and output queues and the router's active configuration file. The contents of RAM are lost when the router is powered down or restarted.

RARP (Reverse Address Resolution Protocol)
This protocol provides mapping that is exactly opposite to the Address Resolution Protocol (ARP). RARP maps a known physical address to a logical address. Diskless machines that do not have a configured IP address when started typically use RARP. RARP requires the existence of a server that maintains physical-to-logical address mappings.

reference point
Identifies the logical interfaces between functions within ISDN.

reliability
A metric that allows the network administrator to assign arbitrarily a numeric value to indicate a reliability factor for a link. The reliability metric is a method used to capture an administrator's experience with a given network link.

RIP (Routing Information Protocol)
A widely used distance vector routing protocol that uses hop count as its metric.

ROM (read-only memory)
An area of router memory that contains a version of the Cisco IOS image—usually an older version with minimal functionality. ROM also stores the bootstrap program and power-on diagnostic programs.

ROM monitor mode
A mode on a Cisco router that allows basic functions such as changing the configuration register value or uploading an IOS via xmodem.

route aggregation
The process of combining multiple IP address networks into one superset of IP address networks. Route aggregation is implemented to reduce the number of route table entries required to forward IP packets accurately in an internetwork.

route poisoning
A routing technique by which a router immediately marks a network as unreachable as soon as it detects that the network is down. The router broadcasts the update throughout the network and maintains this poisoned route in its route table for a specified period of time.

route table
An area of a router's memory that stores the network topology information used to determine optimal routes. Route tables contain information such as destination network, next hop, and associated metrics.

routed protocol
A protocol that provides the information required for the routing protocol to determine the topology of the internetwork and the best path to a destination. The routed protocol provides this information in the form of a logical address and other fields within a packet. The information contained in the packet enables the router to direct user traffic. The most common routed protocols include Internet Protocol (IP) and Internetwork Packet Exchange (IPX).

router ID
The router identifier used with OSPF. The router ID is selected as the highest IP address among all loopback interfaces. If loopback interfaces are not configured, the router ID is the highest IP address of any active physical interface at the moment that OSPF is initialized.

router modes
Modes that enable the execution of specific router commands and functions. User, privileged, and setup are examples of router modes that allow you to perform certain tasks.

routing algorithms
Well-defined rules that aid routers in the collection of route information and the determination of the optimal path.

routing loop
An event in which two or more routers have not yet converged and are propagating their inaccurate route tables. In addition, they are probably still switching packets based on their inaccurate route tables.

routing protocols
Routing protocols use algorithms to generate a list of paths to a particular destination and the cost associated with each path. Routers use routing protocols to communicate among each other the best route to use to reach a particular destination.

RS-232
A physical standard used to identify cabling types for serial data transmission for speeds of 19.2Kbps or less. RS-232 connects two devices communicating over a serial link with either a 25-pin (DB-25) or 9-pin (DB-9) serial interface. RS-232 is now known as *EIA/TIA-232*.

running configuration file
The current configuration file that is active on a router.

RXBoot
A router-maintenance mode that enables router recovery functions when the IOS file in Flash has been erased or is corrupt.

Session layer
As layer 5 of the OSI model, the Session layer establishes, manages, and terminates sessions between applications on different network devices.

setup mode
The router mode triggered on startup if no configuration file resides in nonvolatile random access memory (NVRAM).

shortest path first
See *link state protocol.*

sliding windows
A method by which TCP dynamically sets the window size during a connection, enabling either device involved in the communication to slow down the sending data rate based on the other device's capacity.

SMTP (Simple Mail Transfer Protocol)
A protocol used to pass mail messages between devices, SMTP uses Transmission Control Protocol (TCP) connections to pass the email between hosts.

socket
The combination of the sending and destination Transmission Control Protocol (TCP) port numbers and the sending and destination Internet Protocol (IP) addresses defines a socket. Therefore, a socket can be used to define any User Datagram Protocol (UDP) or TCP connection uniquely.

Spanning Tree Protocol
A protocol used to eliminate all circular routes in a bridged or switched environment while maintaining redundancy. Circular routes are not desirable in layer 2 networks because of the forwarding mechanism employed at this layer.

split horizon
A routing mechanism that prevents a router from sending information that it received about a network back to its neighbor that originally sent the information. This mechanism is useful in preventing routing loops.

SPX (Sequenced Packet Exchange)
The layer 4 protocol used within NetWare to ensure reliable, connection-oriented services.

startup configuration file
The backup configuration file on a router.

static route
A network route that is manually entered into the route table. Static routes function well in simple and predictable network environments.

store-and-forward switching
A method of forwarding frames by copying an entire frame into the buffer of a switch and making a forwarding decision. Store-and-forward switching does not achieve the same throughput as its counterpart, cut-through switching, because it copies the entire frame into the buffer instead of copying only the first six bytes. Store-and-forward switching, however, provides error checking that is not provided by cut-through switching.

subinterface
One of possibly many virtual interfaces on a single physical interface.

subnetting
A process of splitting a classful range of IP addresses into multiple IP networks to allow more flexibility in IP addressing schemes. Subnetting overcomes the limitation of address classes and allows network administrators the flexibility to assign multiple networks with one class of IP addresses.

switch
Provides increased port density and forwarding capabilities as compared to bridges. The increased port densities of switches enable LANs to be microsegmented, thereby increasing the amount of bandwidth delivered to each device.

TCP (Transmission Control Protocol)
One of the many protocols maintained in the TCP/IP suite of protocols. TCP provides a connection-oriented and reliable service to the applications that use it.

TCP three-way handshake
A process by which TCP connections send acknowledgments between each other when setting up a TCP connection.

TCP windowing
A method of increasing or reducing the number of acknowledgments required between data transmissions. This enables devices to throttle the rate at which data is transmitted.

Telnet
A standard protocol that provides a virtual terminal. Telnet enables a network administrator to connect to a router remotely.

TFTP (Trivial File Transfer Protocol)
A protocol used to copy files from one device to another. TFTP is a stripped-down version of FTP.

traceroute
An IP service that allows a user to utilize the services of the User Datagram Protocol (UDP) and the Internet Control Message Protocol (ICMP) to identify the number of hops between sending and receiving devices and the paths taken from the sending to the receiving device. Traceroute also provides the IP address and DNS name of each hop. Typically, traceroute is used to troubleshoot IP connectivity between two devices.

trailer
Control information placed after the data during the encapsulation process. See *encapsulation* for more detail.

Transport layer
As layer 4 of the OSI model, it is concerned with segmenting upper-layer applications, establishing end-to-end connectivity through the network, sending segments from one host to another, and ensuring the reliable transport of data.

trunk
A switch port that connects to another switch to enable virtual local area networks (VLANs) to span multiple switches.

tunnel
A tunnel takes packets or frames from one protocol and places them inside frames from another network system. See *encapsulation*.

UDP (User Datagram Protocol)
One of the many protocols maintained in the TCP/IP suite of protocols, UDP is a Layer 4, best-effort delivery protocol and, therefore, maintains connectionless network services.

user mode
A display-only mode on a Cisco router. Only limited information about the router can be viewed within this router mode; no configuration changes are permitted.

V.35
A physical standard used to identify cabling types for serial data transmission for speeds up to 4Mbps. The V.35 standard was created by the International Telecommunication Union-Telecommunication (ITU-T) standardization sector.

virtual connection
A logical connection between two devices created through the use of acknowledgments.

VLAN (virtual local area network)

A technique of assigning devices to specific LANs based on the port to which they attach on a switch rather than the physical location. VLANs extend the flexibility of LANs by allowing devices to be assigned to specific LANs on a port-by-port basis versus a device basis.

VLSM (variable-length subnet masking)

VLSM provides more flexibility in assigning IP address space. (A common problem with routing protocols is the necessity of all devices in a given routing protocol domain to use the same subnet mask.) Routing protocols that support VLSM allow administrators to assign IP networks with different subnet masks. This increased flexibility saves IP address space because administrators can assign IP networks based on the number of hosts on each network.

VTP (VLAN Trunking Protocol)

A protocol for configuring and administering VLANS on Cisco network devices. With VTP, an administrator can make configuration changes centrally on a single Catalyst series switch and have those changes automatically communicated to all the other switches in the network.

WANs (wide area networks)

WANs use data communications equipment (DCE) to connect multiple LANs. Examples of WAN protocols include, but are not limited to, Frame Relay, Point-to-Point Protocol (PPP), High-level Data Link Control (HDLC), and Integrated Services Digital Network (ISDN).

well-known ports

A set of ports between 1 and 1,023 that are reserved for specific TCP/IP protocols and services.

Index

Numbers

A

B

C

D

E

F

G - H

I

J - K - L

M

N

O

P

Q - R

S

U - V

W - Z